ECONOMIC ORIGINS OF DICTATORSHIP AND DEMOCRACY

This book develops a framework for analyzing the creation and consolidation of democracy. Different social groups prefer different political institutions because of the way they allocate political power and resources. Thus, democracy is preferred by the majority of citizens but opposed by elites. Dictatorship, nevertheless, is not stable when citizens can threaten social disorder and revolution. In response, when the costs of repression are sufficiently high and promises of concessions are not credible, elites may be forced to create democracy. By democratizing, elites credibily transfer political power to the citizens, ensuring social stability. Democracy consolidates when elites do not have a strong incentive to overthrow it. These processes depend on (1) the strength of civil society, (2) the structure of political institutions, (3) the nature of political and economic crises, (4) the level of economic inequality, (5) the structure of the economy, and (6) the form and extent of globalization.

Daron Acemoglu is Charles P. Kindleberger Professor of Applied Economics in the Department of Economics at the Massachusetts Institute of Technology and a member of the Economic Growth Program of the Canadian Institute for Advanced Research. He is also affiliated with the National Bureau of Economic Research, Center for Economic Performance, and Centre for Economic Policy Research and is a Fellow of the European Economic Association. Professor Acemoglu previously taught at the London School of Economics. He received the award for best paper published in the *Economic Journal* in 1996 for his paper "Consumer Confidence and Rational Expectations: Are Agents' Beliefs Consistent with the Theory?", the inaugural T. W. Shultz Prize at the University of Chicago in 2004, and the inaugural Sherwin Rosen Award for outstanding contribution to labor economics in 2004. Professor Acemoglu is editor of the eminent journal *Review of Economics and Statistics* and associate editor of the *Journal of Economic Growth.* He is the recipient of the 2005 John Bates Clark Medal from the American Economic Association, awarded to the most outstanding economist working in the United States under age 40.

James A. Robinson is Professor of Government at Harvard University. He previously taught at the University of California, Berkeley, the University of Southern California, and the University of Melbourne. He is a member of the Economic Growth Program of the Canadian Institute for Advanced Research and affiliated with the Centre for Economic Policy Research. A 2002 Carnegie Scholar and a 1999–2000 Hoover Institution Fellow, his research has been published in leading journals such as the *Quarterly Journal of Economics, American Economic Review, American Political Science Review,* and *Journal of Economic Literature.* Professor Robinson is on the editorial board of *World Politics.* Together with Professors Daron Acemoglu and Simon Johnson, Professor Robinson is coauthor of the forthcoming book, *The Institutional Roots of Prosperity.*

Economic Origins of Dictatorship and Democracy

DARON ACEMOGLU

JAMES A. ROBINSON

CAMBRIDGE
UNIVERSITY PRESS

CAMBRIDGE
UNIVERSITY PRESS

32 Avenue of the Americas, New York NY 10013-2473, USA

Cambridge University Press is part of the University of Cambridge.

It furthers the University's mission by disseminating knowledge in the pursuit of education, learning and research at the highest international levels of excellence.

www.cambridge.org
Information on this title: www.cambridge.org/9780521671422

First published 2006
Reprinted 2006 (twice), 2007 (twice)
First paperback edition 2009
8th printing 2012

A catalogue record for this publication is available from the British Library

Library of Congress Cataloguing in Publication data

Acemoglu, Daron.
Economic origins of dictatorship and democracy / Daron Acemoglu, James A. Robinson.
p. cm.
Includes bibliographical references and index.
ISBN-13: 978-0-521-85526-6 (hardback)
ISBN-10: 0-521-85526-8 (hardback)
1. Democracy – Economic aspects. 2. Democratization. 3. Equality.
4. Political culture. 5. Dictatorship. 6. Comparative government.
I. Robinson, James A., 1960– II. Title.
JC423.A248 2005
321.8 – dc22 2005011262

ISBN 978-0-521-85526-6 Hardback
ISBN 978-0-521-67142-2 Paperback

To the memory of my parents, Kevork and Irma, who invested so much in me. To my love, Asu, who has been my inspiration and companion throughout.

Daron Acemoglu

To the memory of my mother, from whom I inherited my passion for books and my indignation at the injustices of this life. To the memory of my father, from whom I inherited my fascination for science and my curiosity about this extraordinary world.

James A. Robinson

Contents

PART TWO. MODELING POLITICS

PART THREE. THE CREATION AND CONSOLIDATION OF DEMOCRACY

PART SIX. APPENDIX

Preface

A fundamental question in political science and political economy is which factors determine the institutions of collective decision making (i.e., the "political institutions"). In tackling this question, a natural initial distinction is between democratic and nondemocratic institutions. Why is it that some countries are democracies, where there are regular and free elections and politicians are accountable to citizens, whereas other countries are not?

There are a number of salient empirical patterns and puzzles relevant to answering this question. For instance, while the United States moved very early toward universal white male suffrage, which was attained by the early 1820s by northern and western states and by the late 1840s for all states in the Union, such a pattern was not universal in the Americas. Elsewhere, republican institutions with regular elections were the norm after countries gained independence from colonial powers such as Spain and Portugal, but suffrage restrictions and electoral corruption were much more important. The first Latin American countries to implement effective, relatively noncorrupt universal male suffrage were Argentina and Uruguay in 1912 and 1919, respectively, but others, such as El Salvador and Paraguay, did not do so until the 1990s – almost a century and a half after the United States.

Not only is there great variation in the timing of democratization, there also are significant qualitative differences in the form that political development took. Democracy was created, at least for white males, with relatively little conflict in the United States and some Latin America countries, such as Costa Rica. In other places, however, democracy was often strenuously opposed and political elites instead engaged in mass repression to avoid having to share political power. In some cases, such as El Salvador, repression was ultimately abandoned and elites conceded democracy. In others, such as Cuba and Nicaragua, elites fought to the bitter end and were swept away by revolutions.

Once created, democracy does not necessarily consolidate. Although the United States experienced a gradual movement toward democracy with no reverses, a pattern shared by many Western European countries such as Britain and Sweden, democracy in other countries fell to coups. Argentina is perhaps the most extreme example of this: the political regime switched backwards and forwards between democracy and nondemocracy throughout most of the twentieth century.

What determines whether a country is a democracy? Which factors can explain the patterns of democratization we observe? Why did the United States attain universal male suffrage more than a century before many Latin American countries? Why, once created, did democracy persist and consolidate in some countries, such as Britain, Sweden, and the United States, and collapse in others, such as Argentina, Brazil, and Chile?

In this book, we propose a framework for analyzing the creation and consolidation of democracy that we use to provide tentative answers to some of these questions.

The framework has the following three fundamental building blocks:

1. Our approach is "economic-based" in the sense that we stress individual economic incentives as determining political attitudes, and we assume people behave strategically in the sense of game theory.
2. We emphasize the fundamental importance of conflict. Different groups, sometimes social classes, have opposing interests over political outcomes, and these translate into opposing interests over the form of political institutions, which determine the political outcomes.
3. Political institutions play a central role in solving problems of commitment by affecting the future distribution of *de jure* political power.

To starkly illustrate our framework, consider a society in which there are two groups: an elite and the citizens. Nondemocracy is rule by the elite; democracy is rule by the more numerous groups who constitute the majority – in this case, the citizens. In nondemocracy, the elite get the policies it wants; in democracy, the citizens have more power to get what they want. Because the elite loses under democracy, it naturally has an incentive to oppose or subvert it; yet, most democracies arise when they are created by the elite.

Why does a nondemocratic elite ever democratize? Since democracy will bring a shift of power in favor of the citizens, why would the elite ever create such a set of institutions? We argue that this only occurs because the disenfranchised citizens can threaten the elite and force it to make concessions. These threats can take the form of strikes, demonstrations, riots, and – in the limit – a revolution. Because these actions impose costs on the elite, it will try to prevent them. It can do so by making concessions, by using repression to stop social unrest and revolution, or by giving away its political power and democratizing. Nevertheless, repression is often sufficiently costly that it is not an attractive option for elites. Concessions may take several forms – particularly policies that are preferred by the citizens, such as asset or income redistribution – and are likely to be less costly for the elite than conceding democracy.

The key to the emergence of democracy is the observation that because policy concessions keep political power in the hands of the elite, there is no guarantee that it will not renege on its promises. Imagine that there is a relatively transitory situation in which it is advantageous for the citizens to contest power. Such a situation may arise because of wars or shocks to the economy, such as a harvest failure, a collapse in the terms of trade, or a depression. If repression is too costly, the elite would like to buy off the citizens with promises of policy concessions – for example, income redistribution. However, by its very nature, the window of opportunity for contesting power is transitory and will disappear in the future, and it will be relatively easy for the elite to renege on any promises it makes. Anticipating this, the citizens may be unsatisfied with the offer of policy concessions under unchanged political institutions and may choose to revolt.

In our framework, the key problem is that the politically powerful cannot necessarily commit to future policy decisions unless they reduce their political power. Democracy then arises as a credible commitment to pro-citizen policies (e.g., high taxation) by transferring political power between groups (from the elite to the citizens). Democratization is more of a credible commitment than mere promises because it is associated with a set of institutions and greater involvement by the citizens and is therefore more difficult to reverse. The elite must democratize – create a credible commitment to future majoritarian policies – if it wishes to avoid more radical outcomes.

The logic underlying coups against democracy is similar to that underlying democratizations. In democracy, minority groups (e.g., various types of elites) may have an incentive to mount a coup and create a set of more preferable institutions. Yet, if there is a coup threat, why cannot democracy be defended by offering concessions? Democrats will certainly try to do this, but the issue of credibility is again central. If the threat of a coup is transitory, then promises to make policies less pro-majority may not be credible. The only way to credibly change policies is to change the distribution of political power, and this can only be achieved by institutional change – a coup or, more generally, transition to a less democratic regime.

The main contribution of our book is to offer a unified framework for understanding the creation and consolidation of democracy. This framework, in particular, highlights why a change in political institutions is fundamentally different from policy concessions within the context of a nondemocratic regime. An important by-product of this framework is a relatively rich set of implications about the circumstances under which democracy arises and persists. Our framework emphasizes that democracy is more likely to be created:

- when there is sufficient social unrest in a nondemocratic regime that cannot be defused by limited concessions and promises of pro-citizen policies. Whether or not this is so, in turn, depends on the living conditions of the citizens in nondemocracy, the strength of civil society, the nature of the collective-action problem facing the citizens in a nondemocracy, and the details of nondemocratic political institutions that determine what types of promises by the elite could be credible; and

- when the costs of democracy anticipated by the elite are limited, so that it is not tempted to use repression to deal with the discontent of the citizens under the nondemocratic regime. These costs may be high when inequality is high, when the assets of the elite can be taxed or redistributed easily, when the elite has a lot to lose from a change in economic institutions, and when it is not possible to manipulate the form of the nascent democratic institutions to limit the extent to which democracy is inimical to the interests of the elite.

Similarly, these factors also influence whether, once created, democracy is likely to survive. For example, greater inequality, greater importance of land and other easily taxable assets in the portfolio of the elite, and the absence of democratic institutions that can avoid extreme populist policies are more likely to destabilize democracy.

Beyond these comparative static results, our hope is that the framework we present here is both sufficiently rich and tractable that others can use parts of it to address new questions and generate other comparative statics related to democracy and other political institutions.

The topics we address in this book are at the heart of political science, particularly comparative politics, and of political economy. Nevertheless, the questions we ask are rarely addressed using the type of formal models that we use in this book. We believe that there is a huge payoff to developing the types of analyses that we propose in this book and, to that end, we have tried to make the exposition both simple and readable, as well as accessible to scholars and graduate students in political science. To make the book as self-contained as possible, in Chapter 4 we added an introductory treatment of the approaches to modeling democratic politics that we use in the analysis. Although the analysis is of most direct interest and generally accessible to political scientists, we hope that there is a lot of material useful for advanced undergraduates, graduate students, and academics in economics interested in political economy. In fact, one of the authors has taught parts of this book in a graduate-level economics course.

The main prerequisite for following the entire content of the book is a knowledge of basic ideas from complete information game theory at the level of Gibbons (1992). Nevertheless, we have designed the first two chapters to be a generally comprehensible and nonmathematical exposition of the questions we address and the answers we propose.

In writing this book, we incurred many debts. During the eight-year period that we worked on these topics, we gave many seminars on our research from Singapore to Mauritius, from Oslo to Buenos Aires and Bogotá. Many scholars made suggestions and gave us invaluable ideas and leads, and we apologize for not being able to remember all of them. However, we would like to mention several scholars whose unflagging enthusiasm for this research greatly encouraged us at an early stage: Ruth Collier, Peter Lindert, Karl Ove Moene, Kenneth Sokoloff, and Michael Wallerstein. Particular mention should go to Robert Powell, not only for his enthusiasm and encouragement but also for the intellectual support he has shown us over the years. We would particularly like to thank James Alt for organizing a four-day "meet the authors" conference at the Center for Basic Research in the Social Sciences at Harvard in January 2003. The conference not only forced us to produce a draft, it also gave us invaluable feedback and new energy and ideas. Robert Bates suggested that we change the word *political* to *economic* in the title of the book, and he also suggested the format for Chapter 1. Grigore Pop-Eleches suggested the use of diagrams to convey the main comparative statics of the book and also provided many detailed comments.

In addition to the ideas and comments of these people, we received many useful suggestions from the other participants, including Scott Ashworth, Ernesto Calvo, Alberto Diaz-Cayeros, David Epstein, John Huber, Michael Hiscox, Torben Iverson, Sharyn O'Halloran, Jonathan Rodden, Kenneth Shepsle, and Andrea Vindigni. We also received useful feedback and suggestions from students at Berkeley and the University of the Andes in Bogotá, including Taylor Boas, Mauricio Benitez-Iturbe, Thad Dunning, Leopoldo Fergusson, Maiah Jakowski, Sebastián Mazzuca, and Pablo Querubín. Several friends and students also read large portions of the manuscript and gave us invaluable comments and feedback: Alexandre Debs, Thad Dunning, Scott Gehlbach, Tarek Hassan, Ruben Höpfer, Michael Spagat, Juan Fernando Vargas, Tianxi Wang, and Pierre Yared. We would also like to thank Timothy Besley, Joan Esteban, Dominic Lieven, Debraj Ray, Stergios Skaperdas, and Ragnar Torvik for their comments. We are grateful to Ernesto Calvo for providing the historical data on income distribution in Argentina that appears in Chapter 3 and to Peter Lindert for his help with the British data on inequality. Alexandre Debs, Leopoldo Fergusson, Pablo Querubín, and Pierre Yared also provided invaluable research assistance.

1 Paths of Political Development

To understand why some countries are democracies whereas others are not, it is useful to distinguish between different characteristic paths that political institutions take over time. Only some of these paths end in democracy, at least at this moment in time. These stylized paths help us to orient ourselves among the complexities of real-world comparisons, and they illustrate the main mechanisms that we believe link the economic and political structure of a society to political institutions.

There are four main paths of political development. First, there is a path that leads from nondemocracy gradually but inexorably to democracy. Once created, democracy is never threatened, and it endures and consolidates. Britain is the best example of such a path of political development. Second, there is a path that leads to democracy but where democracy, once created, quickly collapses. Following this, the forces that led to the initial democratization reassert themselves, but then democracy collapses again and the cycle repeats itself. This path – where democracy, once created, remains unconsolidated – is best exemplified by the Argentinian experience during the twentieth century. Logically, a third path is one in which a country remains nondemocratic or democratization is much delayed. Because there are important variations in the origins of such a path, it is useful to split nondemocratic paths into two. In the first path, democracy is never created because society is relatively egalitarian and prosperous, which makes the nondemocratic political status quo stable. The system is not challenged because people are sufficiently satisfied under the existing political institutions. Singapore is the society whose political dynamics we characterize in this way. In the second of these nondemocratic paths, the opposite situation arises. Society is highly unequal and exploitative, which makes the prospect of democracy so threatening to political elites that they use all means possible, including violence and repression, to avoid it. South Africa, before the collapse of the apartheid regime, is our canonical example of such a path.

In this chapter, we illustrate these four paths and the mechanisms that lead a society to be on one or the other by examining the political history of the four countries. We discuss the dynamics of political development in all cases, exploring why they ended in consolidated democracy in Britain, unconsolidated democracy in Argentina, and persistent nondemocracy – albeit of different forms – in Singapore and South Africa. Our discussion highlights many of the factors that subsequent analysis will show to be crucial in determining why a society moves onto one path rather than another.

1. Britain

The origins of democracy in Britain lie with the creation of regular Parliaments that were a forum for the aristocracy to negotiate taxes and discuss policies with the king. It was only after the Glorious Revolution of 1688 that Parliaments met regularly, and they did so with a very restrictive franchise. The membership of Parliament at this stage was inherited from feudal notions about the existence of different "estates" in society. These orders were the clergy and the aristocracy, who sat in the House of Lords by right, and the commons, who sat in the House of Commons. Members of the Commons were, in principle, subject to elections, although from the eighteenth century through the middle of the nineteenth century, most elections were unopposed so that no voting actually took place (Lang 1999, p. 12). Candidates tended to be proposed by the leading landowners or aristocrats and, because there was no secret ballot and voting was open and readily observed, most voters did not dare go against their wishes (Namier 1961, p. 83; Jennings 1961, p. 81).

Nevertheless, the constitutional changes that took place following the Civil War of 1642–51 and Glorious Revolution of 1688 led to a dramatic change in political and economic institutions that had important implications for the future of democracy (North and Thomas 1973; North and Weingast 1989; O'Brien 1993; Acemoglu, Johnson, and Robinson 2005). These changes emerged out of conflict between the Stuart monarchs intent on maintaining and expanding their absolutist powers and a Parliament intent on reigning them in. Parliament won. The outcome was a restructuring of political institutions that severely limited the monarchy's powers and correspondingly increased those of Parliament. The change in political institutions led to much greater security of property rights because people no longer feared predation by the state. In particular, it placed power into the hands of a Parliament in which was represented merchants and landowners oriented toward sale for the market. By the late eighteenth century, sustained economic growth had begun in Britain.

The first important move toward democracy in Britain was the First Reform Act of 1832. This act removed many of the worst inequities under the old electoral system, in particular the "rotten boroughs" where several members of Parliament were elected by very few voters. The 1832 reform also established the right to vote based uniformly on the basis of property and income.

The First Reform Act was passed in the context of rising popular discontent at the existing political status quo in Britain. Lang (1999, p. 26) notes

> Fear of revolution, seen as a particular risk given the growth of the new industrial areas, grew rather than diminished in the years after Waterloo, and Lord Liverpool's government (1821–1827) resorted to a policy of strict repression.

By the early nineteenth century, the Industrial Revolution was well underway, and the decade prior to 1832 saw continual rioting and popular unrest. Notable were the Luddite Riots of 1811–16, the Spa Fields Riots of 1816, the Peterloo Massacre in 1819, and the Swing Riots of 1830 (see Darvall 1934 and Stevenson 1979 for overviews). Another catalyst for the reforms was the July revolution of 1830 in Paris. The consensus among historians is that the motive for the 1832 reform was to avoid social disturbances. Lang (1999, p. 36) concludes that

> the level of unrest reinforced the case for immediate reform now, rather than later: it was simply too dangerous to delay any longer. Just as Wellington and Peel had granted emancipation to avoid a rising in Ireland, so the Whigs... should grant reform as the lesser of two evils.

The 1832 Reform Act increased the total electorate from 492,700 to 806,000, which represented about 14.5 percent of the adult male population. Yet, the majority of British people could not vote, and the aristocracy and large landowners had considerable scope for patronage because 123 constituencies contained fewer than one thousand voters. There is also evidence of continued corruption and intimidation of voters until the Ballot Act of 1872 and the Corrupt and Illegal Practices Act of 1883. The Reform Act, therefore, did not create mass democracy but rather was designed as a strategic concession. Unsurprisingly, the issue of parliamentary reform was still very much alive after 1832, and it was taken up centrally by the Chartist movement.

Momentum for reform finally came to a head in 1867, largely due to a juxtaposition of factors. Among these was a sharp business-cycle downturn that caused significant economic hardship and increased the threat of violence. Also significant was the founding of the National Reform Union in 1864 and the Reform League in 1865, and the Hyde Park Riots of July 1866 provided the most immediate catalyst. Searle (1993, p. 225) argues that

> Reform agitation in the country clearly did much to persuade the Derby ministry that a Reform Bill, any Reform Bill, should be placed on the statute book with a minimum of delay.

This interpretation is supported by many other historians (e.g., Trevelyan 1937; Harrison 1965).

The Second Reform Act was passed in 1867; the total electorate expanded from 1.36 million to 2.48 million, and working class voters became the majority in all urban constituencies. The electorate was doubled again by the Third Reform Act of 1884, which extended the same voting regulations that already existed in the boroughs (urban constituencies) to the counties (rural constituencies). The Redistribution Act of 1885 removed many remaining inequalities in the distribution of seats and, from this point on, Britain only had single-member electoral constituencies (previously, many constituencies had elected two members – the two candidates who gained the most votes). After 1884, about 60 percent of adult males were enfranchised. Once again, social disorder appears to have been an important factor behind the 1884 act (e.g., Hayes 1982; Lang 1999, p. 114).

Following the Great War, the Representation of the People Act of 1918 gave the vote to all adult males over the age of twenty-one and women over the age of thirty who were ratepayers or married to ratepayers. Finally, all women received the vote on the same terms as men in 1928. The measures of 1918 were negotiated during the war and may reflect to some extent a quid pro quo between the government and the working classes who were needed to fight and produce munitions. Garrard (2002, p. 69) nevertheless notes that

> most assumed that, if the system was to survive and "contentment and stability prevail," universal citizenship could not be denied to men, perceived to have suffered so much and to have noticed Russia's Revolution.

Overall, the picture that emerges from British political history is clear. Beginning in 1832, when Britain was governed by the relatively rich, primarily rural aristocracy, strategic concessions were made during an eighty-six-year period to adult men. These concessions were aimed at incorporating the previously disenfranchised into politics because the alternative was seen to be social unrest, chaos, and possibly revolution. The concessions were gradual because, in 1832, social peace could be purchased by buying off the middle classes. Moreover, the effect of the concessions was diluted by the specific details of political institutions, particularly the continuing unrepresentative nature of the House of Lords. Although challenged during the 1832 reforms, the House of Lords provided an important bulwark for the wealthy against the potential of radical reforms emanating from a democratized House of Commons. This was so at least until just before the First World War, when the showdown with Herbert Asquith's Liberal government over the introduction of elements of a welfare state led to substantial limitations of the power of the Lords. After 1832, as the working classes reorganized through the Chartist movement and later the trade unions, further concessions had to be made. The Great War and the fallout from it sealed the final offer of full democracy. Although the pressure of the disenfranchised was more influential in some reforms than others, and other factors undoubtedly played a role, the threat of social disorder was the driving force behind the creation of democracy in Britain.

The emergence of democracy in Britain and its subsequent consolidation took place in a society that had long shed nearly all the remnants of medieval organization and that had successfully resisted the threat of absolutism. They also took place in the context of rapid industrialization, urbanization, expansion of the factory system, rising inequality, and – in the period after the Repeal of the Corn Laws – rapid globalization of the economy.

2. Argentina

The beginnings of the modern Argentine Republic were in 1810 when it declared its independence. Following this period, the country was immersed in a chaotic series of civil wars and internal conflict over the structure of power and political institutions. The chaos finally abated in the 1860s. In 1853, a new constitution was written and, in 1862, Bartolomé Mitre was elected the first president of the unified republic. Mitre set about creating a state in the facilitating context of the first of a series of agricultural export booms that would sustain the Argentine economy until 1930. He created a national bureaucracy, taxation system, and legal system, and this period saw the foundation of electoral politics. However,

> The electoral law of 1853, which purported to allow popular participation in the political process, from the beginning proved itself a sham. Elections were invariably ritualistic parodies, staged-managed by lackeys of the powerful, with only a minute fraction of the electorate participating. (Rock 1987, p. 129)

After Mitre, Domingo Sarmiento became president and around him formed a party, the Partido Autonomista Nacional (PAN). Successive PAN presidents maintained power until 1916 by manipulating elections. However, they did so in the context of rising social discontent. After 1889, there was an effective opposition in the Unión Cívica, which in July 1890 launched a revolt against the government. After 1891, the Unión Cívica Radical (Radicals), under the leadership of Hipólito Yrigoyen, launched revolts in 1893 and 1905. However, despite the continuation of regimes based on the control and coercion of the electorate,

> Argentine elites were becoming aware of the unfolding similarities between Western European societies and their own, with the growing cities and the emergence of new social classes. Democracy's attractiveness lay in its promise of protecting political stability, for if political exclusion were maintained . . . the nation risked a repetition of the upheavals of the early 1890's. (Rock 1987, pp. 184–5)

In 1910, Roque Sáenz Peña, one of the leading advocates of political reform, became president. As Rock (1987, p. 188) put it:

> Radicals, socialists, and indirectly the anarchists helped fuel the movement for reform during the early years of the century. Progressives amongst the elite feared the growing popular support for the Radicals, wondering where their next revolt would come from.

The so-called Sáenz Peña Law was passed in 1912 when the secret ballot was introduced and fraudulent electoral practices outlawed. Universal male suffrage, originally introduced in the 1853 Constitution, finally became a reality. Smith

(1978, p. 10) argues that reform "was a calculated maneuver to salvage the prevailing system. Concerned with labor unrest and the apparent threat of violence."

Following these reforms, Yrigoyen was elected president in 1916.

> The reforms also brought surprises. Sáenz Peña and his supporters had espoused electoral reform in the belief that the old oligarchic factions would adapt to the new conditions and unite into a strong conservative party that would enjoy large popular support . . . instead, the conservatives repeatedly failed in their efforts at unity. (Rock 1987, p. 190)

As a consequence, the Radical party began to dominate Argentine politics, posing a severe threat to traditional interests. In 1916, Conservatives won 42 percent of the vote but by 1928 they had slipped to 25 percent. Smith (1978, p. 21) notes "this situation contrasts sharply with that in Sweden and Britain . . . where traditional elites continued to dominate systems after the extension of suffrage." Consequently, "by 1930 Yrigoyenists had a substantial delegation in the upper chamber and they threatened to gain a full majority in the upcoming elections" (Smith, 1978, p. 12). Thus, "the political system came to represent an autonomous threat to the socioeconomic system . . . Understandably enough, in view of their initial expectations, Conservatives came to see democracy as dysfunctional" (Smith 1978, p. 15; see also Potter 1981).

In September 1930, Yrigoyen was deposed by a military coup, followed in 1931 by a fraudulent election. "The election of 1931 restored power to the same broad complexion of groups that had controlled it before 1916 – the pampas' exporting interests and the lesser landowners of the provinces" (Rock 1987, p. 217). During the remainder of the 1930s, Conservatives continually used electoral fraud to maintain power, although by 1940 they were trying to reincorporate the Radicals to some extent. This sequence of Conservative administrations was ended by a military coup in 1943.

After the coup in 1943, a series of military men assumed the presidency; however, the main feature of this period was the rise to power of Juan Domingo Perón, first as a member of the military junta and then as the elected president after 1946. Perón had moved the military regime onto a more radical and pro-labor path and organized a political machine around the state control of the labor movement. During his first presidency, Perón engineered a huge increase in wages and social benefits for the working classes. His policies were aimed at redistributing away from the rural sector toward the urban sector. Part of these policies included an aggressive pro-industrial policy of protection and import substitution (O'Donnell 1978, p. 147). Perón was reelected in 1951, albeit in an election tainted by corruption and the repression of the opposition, and he was subsequently removed from power by a coup in 1955. Between 1958 and 1966, civilian governments highly restricted by the military returned, only to be swept away by another coup in 1966 (see O'Donnell 1973; for the seminal analysis).

In 1966, General Juan Carlos Onganía became president, but his regime was quickly opposed by substantial social mobilization (Rock 1987, p. 349). Cavarozzi (1986, p. 36) notes the significance of "the popular insurrection of 1969... [which] fused together blue and white collar workers, students and the urban poor." This revolt against the dictatorship was followed by more, particularly in 1971, and coincided with the emergence of several armed groups and guerillas dedicated to the overthrow of the regime.

Democracy was re-created in 1973 when Perón returned from exile and was elected president in the first truly democratic election since his first election in 1946. However, democratization unleashed the same distributional conflicts that it had before and "As in 1946, the kernels of his program were income redistribution in favor of labor, the expansion of employment, and renewed social reform" (Rock 1987, p. 361). In 1976, the Perónist government, led by Perón's third wife Isabel after his death in 1974, fell to a coup under the leadership of General Jorge Videla. "Once in power, the Army embarked on the conquest of any lingering resistance to a revolution in government whose aim was the total dismantlement of the Perónist state" (Rock 1987, p. 366). The regime that lasted until the Falklands (Malvinas) War of 1982–3 was the most repressive in Argentine history. Some ten thousands people "disappeared" and many thousands more were imprisoned without trial, tortured, and forced into exile. General Roberto Viola succeeded Videla in 1981 but was forced from office the same year by General Leopoldo Galtieri.

As the military became more and more beleaguered and popular protests against them rose, they launched the ill-fated invasion of the Falkland (Malvinas) Islands. Galtieri resigned when the Argentine forces surrendered in June 1982 and, the following year, democratic elections led to the election of Radical president Raúl Alfonsin. Argentina was a democracy again and it has stayed one with Alfonsin being followed by Carlos Menem in 1990, Fernando de la Rúa in 2000, and – after a bewildering succession of temporary presidents during the economic crisis of 2001–2 – by Néstor Kirchner in 2003.

The political history of Argentina therefore reveals an extraordinary pattern where democracy was created in 1912, undermined in 1930, re-created in 1946, undermined in 1955, fully re-created in 1973, undermined in 1976, and finally reestablished in 1983. In between were various shades of nondemocratic governments ranging from restricted democracies to full military regimes. The political history of Argentina is one of incessant instability and conflict. Economic development, changes in the class structure, and rapidly widening inequality, which occurred as a result of the export boom from the 1880s, coincided with pressure on the traditional political elite to open the system. But, the nature of Argentine society meant that democracy was not stable. Traditional interests were too threatened by the rise to power of the Radicals and continuously worked to undermine democracy. The economic changes of the 1930s only exacerbated this conflict. The workers became stronger and more militant as they found a leader in Perón, and the distributional conflicts then became embedded in the pro-Perón, anti-Perón struggle. Dictatorial regimes collapsed because of social protests, and democracies collapsed because the radical, populist, and often unsustainable policies they adopted induced military coups.

3. Singapore

Sir Stamford Raffles acquired the island of Singapore from its local Malay ruler for the British East India Company in 1819 (Turnbull 1989; Huff 1994; Milne and Mauzy 1990; 2002). At that time, the island, comprising 622 square miles and lying just 176 kilometer north of the equator, was sparsely populated with just a few hundred inhabitants. It soon became an important trading port for the East India Company and expanded rapidly as a commercial center and entrepôt. This role continued even after the collapse of the East India Company (Singapore became a Crown Colony in 1867 as part of the Straits Settlement) and expanded with the British colonization of the Malayan peninsular after the 1870s and the development of an export economy in Malaya based on commodities such as tin and rubber.

After the Second World War and a traumatic occupation by the Japanese, a political awakening occurred in Singapore as in many other British colonies as they began to anticipate independence. The first elections for a legislative council were held in 1948 under a very restricted franchise in which a majority of the council was still appointed by the British Governor. The late 1940s and early 1950s were characterized by labor unrest, strikes, and demonstrations. In 1955, they forced the British to introduce a new constitution proposed by the Rendel Commission, in which a majority of seats of the legislative council were to be elected and the leader of the majority party would become chief minister. However, the 1955 elections were followed by more riots and social unrest, constitutional negotiations were reopened, and new elections were planned for 1959 with Singapore granted almost complete internal self-rule. The franchise was universal suffrage, and the People's Action Party (PAP) under Lee Kuan Yew won forty-three of the fifty-one seats in the 1959 election.

From the beginning, the PAP aggressively promoted industrialization. One of its strategies was taming the trade-union movement and creating a pliant labor force to attract multinational companies. In 1959, it began to reduce the power of unions, which was finally achieved in 1967 and 1968 when all unions were brought under government control. This was accomplished by the creation of a government body, the National Trade Union Congress, and strikes were made illegal. At the same time, Lee Kuan Yew and the leaders of the PAP distanced themselves from the more radical elements of the party. As a result, in 1961 the party split with thirteen parliamentary members resigning to form a new party, the Barisan Sosialis (BS). Despite this setback, the PAP bounced back and, even before independence, began to show its skill at political maneuver:

> The PAP then strengthened its grip on power, harassing the BS and the trade unions. Most dramatically, prior to elections in 1963, the PAP used the police special branch to mount a sweep called Operation Cold Store, obliterating the BS's top level leadership. (Case 2002, p. 86)

As a result, in the 1963 elections the PAP took thirty-seven out of fifty-one seats, with the BS winning thirteen.

In this initial phase, the PAP saw integration with Malaya as part of its strategy of economic development because it would guarantee a large market for Singaporean firms. In 1963, Malaya, Singapore, Sabah, and Sarawak merged to form the Federation of Malaysia. However, in 1965, Singapore was expelled as a result of tensions between Malay and Chinese politicians (e.g., Lee Kuan Yew had campaigned in Kuala Lumpur in the 1964 Malaysian general elections, to the outrage of Malaysian politicians).

After the creation of the republic in 1965, the PAP began to harass its political opponents. As a consequence, all the BS members resigned their parliamentary seats and boycotted the 1968 elections. In these circumstances, the PAP won all fifty-eight seats, although fifty-one were uncontested. The PAP also won every seat in 1972, 1976, and 1980 against an assortment of opposition parties with the BS contesting elections again after 1972. Finally, a 1981 by-election resulted in the first opposition member since 1968. A second opposition member was elected in 1984 and by 1991 there were four. However, the opposition only ran candidates in a minority of seats; the PAP was consequently always guaranteed a majority in the Parliament. In 1997, the PAP won eighty-two of the eighty-three seats. In the 2001 elections, the PAP won eighty-one seats. To avoid a real opposition appearing in this period and to appease desires for some sort of alternative representation, the PAP introduced nonconstituency Members of Parliament who were allocated to those opposition losers who received the most votes. By 2001, there were nine of these members of the legislature. In 1990, Lee Kuan Yew retired as Prime Minister and was replaced by Goh Chok Tong, who was succeeded in 2004 by Lee's son, Lee Hsien Loong.

Throughout this period, the PAP extended its control over society, particularly through its control of the media. Case (2002, p. 89) demonstrates that "political activism in Singapore risks blacklisting, shunning, lawsuits, tax investigations, lost business opportunities, and detention without trial." To maintain its power, the PAP also engages in extensive gerrymandering to avoid losing any seats. Although the initial electoral system was based on British-style single-member districts, there is now a mix of these and multimember districts (called group representation constituencies). Rodan (1997, p. 178) notes that "single constituencies in which opposition parties came within striking distance of defeating PAP candidates in the last election have disappeared, usually subsumed under group representation constituencies comprising sitting PAP candidates."

When it comes to election time, the PAP also engages in blatant threats to the electorate to influence their votes. Rodan (1998, p. 179) notes that in 1997, the electorate

> ... were given a stark choice: return government candidates and benefit from a range of expensive new public programs, or have this withheld or delayed in retaliation for electing PAP opponents.... Threats by Goh concerning the multimillion dollar housing upgrading program caused special concern. Given that around 86% of Singaporeans live in government built flats, the electorate is highly vulnerable to such intimidation. The announcement of a new system of vote counting enabling the government to ascertain voting preferences down to precinct levels of 5,000 voters reinforced the threat.

Given its size and colonial history, Singapore lacks an aristocracy – landed or otherwise – which has been important for Singaporean politics. It has an urbanization rate of 100 percent, and the ethnic composition of its population is approximately 75 percent Chinese, 15 percent Malay, and 8 percent from the Indian subcontinent. Prior to independence, Singapore also lacked large capitalists or business interests and, since independence, the largest capitalists involved in Singapore are foreigners, who are seemingly promoted by the PAP at the expense of indigenous business interests. Founded by English-educated professionals and middle-class people, the PAP recruits its politicians from the professions and the civil service, not through party members. Indeed, the party exists mostly as an electoral machine; otherwise, it works through the government rather than through some independent grassroots organization. Lee Kuan Yew said in 1984, "I make no apologies that the PAP is the Government and the Government is the PAP" (quoted in Milne and Mauzy 1990, p. 85).

Overall, we see that Singapore moved to democracy and independence as its citizens protested against British colonial rule, but the PAP rapidly established one-party rule after 1963. Since then, the economy has boomed, inequality has been low, and the PAP has maintained power through relatively benign means, fostering popularity through extensive social welfare programs as well as engaging in threats and coercion. Although there has been imprisonment and harassment, there have been no "disappearances" and there is apparently little opposition to PAP rule and little pressure for political change.

4. South Africa

The European presence in South Africa began in 1652 when the Dutch East India Company founded a colony in Table Bay. Its aim was to grow food and provisions for its ships sailing around the Cape of Good Hope from Europe to Asia. The Dutch settlements gradually expanded at the expense of the indigenous Khoikhoi but only extended about 100 miles inland by the end of the eighteenth century. The strategic position of the Cape Colony meant that it became an important prize in geopolitical competition. During the Napoleonic Wars, it was seized by the British first in 1795 and then again – this time conclusively – in 1806, and the colony was amalgamated into the British Empire.

The British, like the Dutch East India Company, initially had no designs on the interior and were more concerned with the safety of the shipping routes to India and Asia. However, the colonial policies of the British alienated many of the Dutch settlers, who became known as Boers or Afrikaners. In response, the Boers moved inland en masse, founding the Orange Free State in 1854 and the Transvaal in 1860.

The British government had formalized the political institutions of the Cape Colony in 1853 when it introduced a bicameral parliament that could legislate on domestic matters, although subject to a veto from London. The executive branch of government consisted of officials appointed by the colonial office. The franchise for the legislature did not specifically disenfranchise people based on racial origins but, instead, adopted the British system of property and income restrictions (Thompson 1995, p. 65).

The political balance between the British Empire and the Boer Republics was altered by the discovery of diamonds in Kimberley and gold on the Witwatersrand in the 1870s. The labor relations in these areas quickly exhibited a pattern that would subsequently become known as "apartheid," with blacks being unable to dig for diamonds, forced to carry passes to impede labor mobility, banned from desirable occupations that became reserved for whites, and forced to live in segregated communities and camps. The British annexed the diamond fields in 1871, the Transvaal in 1877, and, in 1879, finally vanquished the powerful Zulu Kingdom. However, the Transvaal successfully rebelled in 1881 and it was only after the South African War of 1899–1902 that the British government conquered all of the Boer Republics. The British moved the colonies toward a union and, in 1910, the Cape Colony, Natal, Orange Free State, and Transvaal were joined to form the Union of South Africa.

That first government, run by Louis Botha and Jan Smuts, gradually began to reinforce many of the vast inequalities in South African society, a process that culminated in the creation of full-blown apartheid with the election of the National Party (NP) under D. F. Malan in 1948. For example, in 1913, the Natives Land Act stopped Africans from purchasing land outside of "native areas," which were reserves set aside for Africans, consisting in 1939 of about 12 percent of the land area (Africans represented 70 percent of the population in this period; see Thompson 1995, Table 1, p. 278).

At the same time, the first organized black political consciousness began to emerge with the founding of the African National Congress (ANC) in 1912. At first, it was a modest movement organized by middle-class Africans but, following the Second World War, the ANC became radicalized because of the failure to liberalize the system. In 1943, the ANC adopted a statement called *Africans' Claims in South Africa*, demanding for the first time universal adult suffrage.

The application of apartheid after 1948 reached its apogee during the prime-ministership of Hendrik Verwoerd between 1958 and 1966. The government attempted to move all Africans into eight (then ten) homelands, and only Africans whose labor was needed in the white economy could be present in "European areas." They had to carry "passes," proving that they were legally outside of the tribal areas.

The apartheid regime was sustained by massive infringements on political and civil rights. The government established tight control over the media and had a monopoly on radio and television. The police were given vast powers to arrest people without trial and hold them indefinitely in solitary confinement. Under the Public Safety Act of 1953, the government could declare a state of emergency and rule by proclamation.

Throughout the 1950s, the ANC continually contested in the streets and in the law courts the policies of the NP. In one such demonstration in Sharpeville in 1960, a riot exploded and police fired into the crowd, killing eighty-three people. After this incident, the government moved to finally eradicate the ANC and, in 1964, Nelson Mandela and other top leaders were imprisoned on Robben Island. Despite losing much of their leadership to South African prisons or exile, the ANC continued to be the focus of opposition to the regime. The NP pressed ahead with its goal of creating independent homelands (or bantustans), where all Africans would be citizens. In 1976, the Transkei and Bophuthatswana were declared independent nations by the government (although they were never recognized by any other national government or international agency).

In 1976, a riot in Soweto, a large African township just outside Johannesburg, ended in 575 deaths (Thompson 1995, pp. 212–13). Soweto marked a turning point. In the 1960s, the apartheid government had managed to crush the ANC leadership, but

> after the Soweto uprising, a protest culture pervaded the black population of South Africa. Students and workers, children and adults, men and women, the educated and the uneducated became involved in efforts to liberate the country from apartheid. (Thompson 1995, p. 228)

The apartheid government had no choice but to make some concessions. It immediately announced the cessation of the creation of homelands; however, as soon as the turmoil subsided, the government reneged and two more homelands were created in the early 1980s. More significant, the government moved to legalize African trade unions and in 1984 introduced a new constitution in which both Indians and Coloureds had their own legislatures. The whites remained in a solid majority in the legislature. After P. W. Botha was elected president, he had only one Indian and one Coloured in his cabinet, neither with a specific portfolio. After 1984, the government also removed job reservations, which stopped Africans from undertaking specific occupations.

Nevertheless, the basic philosophy or structure of apartheid was unaltered. These concessions were, therefore, not sufficient to prevent the strikes, riots, and social unrest that became more widespread. For instance, in 1985, 879 people were killed in political violence, and there were 390 strikes involving 240,000 workers. The African trade unions, whose legitimization had been a concession after Soweto, were in the forefront of antistate activities. In June 1986, the Botha government responded to these events by declaring a state of emergency and sending the army into the townships to restore order.

The situation got worse for the apartheid regime in October 1986 when the United State imposed sanctions. From the mid-1980s onward, sensing the infeasibility of continuing with the same set of institutions, many members of the South African white elite started to make overtures to the ANC and black leaders. The industrial chaos caused by the strikes was severely damaging to profits and, from the late 1970s onward, there was sustained capital outflow from South Africa (Wood 2000, Figure 6.3, p. 154). Prominent white businessmen met with the ANC in London and other places, and Mandela himself was moved from Robben Island and had many discussions with different members of the Botha government.

> As Mandela recognized, if there was to be peaceful transition, a way would have to be found to reconcile the ANC demand for majority rule with "the insistence of whites on structural guarantees that majority rule will not mean domination of the white minority by the blacks." (Thompson 1995, p. 244)

In February 1989, L. W. de Klerk took over from P. W. Botha as the head of the NP and was elected president in September.

> De Klerk . . . understood that domestic and foreign pressures were undermining the racial order. De Klerk concluded that the best hope for his people was to negotiate a settlement from a position of strength, while his government was still the dominant force in the country. (Thompson 1995, p. 244)

At the beginning of 1990, he lifted the ban on the ANC and released Mandela from prison. Intense negotiations started over the nature of the transition from the apartheid era and what sort of society would follow it. Constitutional negotiations began in December 1991 with the NP proposing a series of measures to weaken the threat of black majority rule.

> South Africa was to become a confederation of states with vast and irremovable powers. Its central executive was to be a coalition of every party that won a substantial number of seats in an election, the chairmanship was to rotate among party leaders, and all decisions were to be made by consensus or special majorities. (Thompson 1995, p. 248)

Such stipulations were unacceptable to the ANC and in June 1992 the negotiations broke down. In September, they were restarted and, by February 1993, there was an agreed-upon timetable for transitions to the April 1994 election.

An interim constitution was agreed upon with the first new Parliament elected in 1994, charged with devising a permanent constitution. The interim constitution incorporated thirty-four basic principles and dictated that no subsequent amendment would be valid if it contradicted them; whether it did so was to be determined by a constitutional court appointed by President Mandela. Other amendments required a two-thirds majority of both Houses of Parliament. The main concession to the NP was that there had to be compulsory power-sharing in the cabinet, with any party that won at least twenty seats in the national assembly getting representation in the cabinet in proportion to its seats. The ANC received 62.7 percent of the vote in the 1994 election.

From its roots, like many colonial societies, South Africa was a society of great inequalities, both economic and political. In the twentieth century, this inheritance led to a highly undemocratic polity in which only whites were enfranchised. After the Second World War, Africans began to successfully mobilize against this political status quo, and they were able to exert increasing pressure, rendering the existing apartheid regime infeasible and threatening mass revolt. Attempts by the regime to make concessions, although leaving the system basically unaltered, failed to achieve this objective, and the apartheid regime maintained power through the use of extensive repression and violence. In 1994, the regime was forced to democratize rather than risk potentially far worse alternatives.

5. The Agenda

We see four very different paths of political development in these narratives. Britain exemplifies the path to consolidated democracy, without any significant reversals in the process. Argentina illustrates the possibility of a transition to an unconsolidated democracy, which then reverts back to nondemocracy, with the process potentially repeating itself multiple times. Singapore is an example of a society in which a nondemocratic regime can survive a long time with relatively minor concessions but also without significant repression. South Africa before the collapse of apartheid exemplifies a nondemocratic regime that survives by using repression. We now propose a framework to understand these various paths and develop predictions for when we expect to see one path versus another.

2 Our Argument

Why did Britain, Argentina, Singapore, and South Africa follow different political paths? More generally, why are some countries democratic whereas others are ruled by dictatorships or other nondemocratic regimes? Why do many nondemocracies transition into democracy? What determines when and how this transition takes place? And, relatedly, why do some democracies, once created, become consolidated and endure whereas others, like many of those in Latin America, fall prey to coups and revert back to dictatorship?

These are central questions for political science, political economy, and social science more generally, but there are neither widely shared answers nor an accepted framework to tackle them. The aims of this book are to develop a framework for analyzing these questions, provide some tentative answers, and outline future areas for research. As part of our investigation, we first provide an analysis of the role of various political institutions in shaping policies and social choices, emphasizing how politics differs in democratic and nondemocratic regimes. To do so, we model the attitudes of various individuals and groups toward different policies and, therefore, toward the political institutions leading to these policies.

To facilitate the initial exposition of our ideas, it is useful to conceive of society as consisting of two groups – the elites and the citizens – in which the latter are more numerous. Our framework emphasizes that social choices are inherently conflictual. For example, if the elites are the relatively rich individuals – for short, the rich – they will be opposed to redistributive taxation; whereas the citizens, who will be relatively poor – for short, the poor – will be in favor of taxation that would redistribute resources to them. More generally, policies or social choices that benefit the elites will be different from those that benefit the citizens. This conflict over social choices and policies is a central theme of our approach.

Who is the majority and who is the elite? This depends to some extent on context and the complex way in which political identities form in different societies. In many cases, it is useful to think of the elite as being the relatively rich in society, as was the case in nineteenth-century Britain and Argentina. However, this is not always the case; for instance, in South Africa, the elites were the whites and, in many African countries, the elites are associated with a particular ethnic group. In other societies, such as Argentina during some periods, the elite is the military.

It may not be a coincidence that in many situations the elite and the rich coincide. In some cases, those who are initially rich may use their resources to attain power, perhaps by bribing the military or other politicians. In other circumstances, power may be attained by people who are not initially rich. Nevertheless, once attained, political power can be used to acquire income and wealth so that those with power naturally tend to become rich. In either case, there is a close association between the elite and the rich.

Our theory of which societies will transit from dictatorship to democracy and under what circumstances democracy will be consolidated is related to the conflict between the elite and the citizens over politics. These groups have opposing preferences over different political institutions, democracy and dictatorship, which they recognize lead to different social choices. However, we also emphasize that political institutions do not simply determine the extent of redistribution or who benefits from policies today, they also play the role of regulating the future allocation of political power. In democracy, the citizens have more power both today and in the future than they would in nondemocratic regimes because they participate in the political process.

The framework we develop is formal, so our exposition emphasizes both the concepts that we believe are essential in thinking about democracy as well as how those concepts and issues can be formally modeled using game theory.

1. Democracy versus Nondemocracy

At the outset, we have to be clear about the precise questions that we tackle and the basic building blocks of our approach. In building models of social phenomena, an often-useful principle is the so-called Occam's razor. The principal, popularized by the fourteenth-century English philosopher William of Occam, is that one should not increase the number of entities required to explain a given phenomenon beyond what is necessary. In other words, one should strive for a high degree of parsimony in formulating answers to complex questions. Given the complexity of the issues with which we are dealing, we frequently make use of this principle in this book not only to simplify the answers to complex questions but, perhaps even more daringly, to also simplify the questions. In fact, in an attempt to focus our basic questions, we use Occam's razor rather brutally and heroically. We abstract from many interesting details and also leave some equally important questions out of our investigation. Our hope is that this gambit pays off by providing us with relatively sharp answers to some interesting questions. Of course, the reader is the judge of whether our strategy ultimately pays off.

Our first choice is about the classification of different regimes. Many societies are today governed by democratic regimes, but no two democracies are exactly alike and most exhibit a number of marked institutional differences. Consider, for instance, the contrast between the French presidential system and the British parliamentary system, or that between the majoritarian electoral institutions as used in the United States and the system of proportional representation used in much of continental Europe. Despite these differences, there are some important commonalities. In a democracy, the majority of the population is allowed to vote and express their preferences about policies, and the government is supposed to represent the preferences of the whole population – or, using a common description, "democracy is the government by the people for the people." In contrast, many other countries are still ruled by dictators and nondemocratic regimes.[1] There are even more stark differences between some of these nondemocratic regimes than the differences between democracies. For example, reflect on the contrast between the rule of the Chinese Communist Party since 1948 and that of General Pinochet in Chile between 1973 and 1989. When we turn to other nondemocratic regimes, such as the limited constitutional regimes in Europe in the nineteenth century, the differences are even more marked.

Nevertheless, these nondemocratic regimes share one common element: instead of representing the wishes of the population at large, they represent the preferences of a subgroup of the population: the "elite." In China, it is mainly the wishes of the Communist Party that matter. In Chile, most decisions were made by a military junta; it was their preferences, and perhaps the preferences of certain affluent segments of the society supporting the dictatorship, that counted. In Britain before the First Reform Act of 1832, less than 10 percent of the adult population – the very rich and aristocratic segments – was allowed to vote, and policies naturally catered to their demands.

From this, it is clear that democracies generally approximate a situation of *political equality* relative to nondemocracies that, in turn, represent the preferences of a much smaller subset of society and thus correspond more to a situation of *political inequality*. Our focus is to understand the social and economic forces pushing some societies toward regimes with greater political equality versus those encouraging the development of more nondemocratic systems. In our models, except in Chapter 8, we work with a dichotomous distinction between democracy and nondemocracy. Nevertheless, in deciding how democratic actual regimes are and in empirical work, it is more useful to think of various shades of democracy. For example, none of the nineteenth-century reform acts in Britain introduced universal adult suffrage, but they were all movements in the direction of increased democracy. We want to understand these movements; to do so, we begin by simply considering a move from nondemocracy to full democracy (universal adult suffrage). Our definition is "Schumpetarian" (Schumpeter 1942) in the sense that we emphasize that a country is democratic if a certain political process takes place – if certain key institutions, such as free and fair elections and free entry into

[1] In the text, despite the title of our book, we prefer to use the term *nondemocracy* to alternatives, such as *dictatorship* or *authoritarian regime*, because it has fewer specific connotations than any of the other terms.

politics, are in place. To the extent that democracy is associated with particular outcomes, it will be because they stem from its institutional features.

Our approach means that we are not simply interested in when universal adult suffrage was introduced but rather in understanding all movements in the direction of increased democracy. For example, in Argentina, universal male suffrage was introduced by the constitution of 1853, but electoral corruption was so endemic that democracy was not a reality until after the political reforms under President Sáenz Peña in 1912. In this case, we consider 1912 to be a key movement toward democracy. In the case of Britain, the reforms of 1867 greatly extended voting rights, but universal male suffrage was not conceded until 1919. However, electoral corruption was eliminated and secret voting was introduced in 1872. In this case, we see 1867 as representing an important step toward political equality in Britain.

We have less to say on the extension of suffrage to women. In almost all European countries, voting rights were first given to adult men and subsequently extended to women. This reflected the then-accepted gender roles; when the roles began to change as women entered the workforce, women also obtained voting rights. It is likely, therefore, that the mechanisms that we propose better describe the creation of male suffrage than the extension of voting rights to women.

Our dichotomous distinction between democracy and nondemocracy makes sense and is useful only to the extent that there are some important elements central to our theory and common to all democracies but generally not shared by nondemocracies. This is indeed the case. We argue that democracy, which is generally a situation of political equality, looks after the interests of the majority more than nondemocracy, which is generally dominated by an elite and is more likely to look after its interests. Stated simply and extremely, nondemocracy is generally a regime for the elite and the privileged; comparatively, democracy is a regime more beneficial to the majority of the populace, resulting in policies relatively more favorable to the majority.

We claim that nondemocracy represents political inequality relative to democracy. In democracy, everybody has a vote and, at least potentially, can participate in one way or another in the political process. In nondemocracy, an elite, a junta, an oligarchy, or – in the extreme case – just one person, the dictator, is making the decisions. Hence, the contrast in terms of political equality makes sense. This, of course, does not mean that democracy corresponds to some ideal of political equality. In many successful democracies, there is one-person-one-vote, but this is far from perfect political equality. The voices of some citizens are louder, and those with economic resources might influence policies through nonvoting channels, such as lobbying, bribery, or other types of persuasion. Throughout the book, when we discuss political equality in democracy, it is always a *relative* statement.

Overall, the outlines of our basic approach are taking shape. We think of regimes falling into one of two broad categories: democracy and nondemocracy.

Democracy is thought of as a situation of political equality and characterized by its relatively more pro-majority policies. Often pro-majority policies coincide with pro-poor policies, especially a greater tendency to redistribute income away from the rich toward the poor. In contrast, nondemocracy gives a greater say to an elite and generally opts for policies that are less majoritarian than in a democracy.

2. Building Blocks of Our Approach

We have now determined the basic focus of our investigation: to understand why some societies are democratic, why some societies switch from nondemocracy to democracy, and why some democracies revert back to dictatorships. We have already mentioned some of the building blocks of our approach; it is now time to develop them more systematically.

The first overarching building block for our approach is that it is economic.[2] By this term, we do not mean that individuals always act rationally according to some simple postulates. Nor do we mean that there are only individuals, and no social groups, in society. Instead, we mean that individuals have well-defined preferences over outcomes or the consequences of their actions; for example, they prefer more income to less and they may prefer peace, security, fairness, and many other things. Sometimes masses of individuals have interests in common or even act collectively. However what matters is that individuals *do* have well-defined preferences that they understand. They evaluate various different options, including democracy versus nondemocracy, according to their assessments of their (economic and social) consequences. In such situations, the economic approach suggests that people often behave strategically and that their behavior should be modeled as a game. Game theory is the study of situations with multiple decision makers, interacting strategically. The basic tenet of game theory is that individuals choose between various strategies according to their consequences. Our economic focus and the presence of important interactions between various political actors render all the situations analyzed herein essentially "game theoretic." We, therefore, make heavy use of game theory in modeling preferences over different regimes and transitions between these regimes.

To see the implications of these assumptions, consider a group of individuals for whom democracy and nondemocracy have the same consequences in all spheres, except that democracy generates more income for them; they naturally prefer more income to less. Therefore, we expect these individuals to prefer democracy to nondemocracy. At some level, this postulate is very weak; but, at another level, we are buying a lot with our economic focus. Most important, we are getting a license to focus on the consequences of the regimes, and preferences over regimes are derived from their consequences. Such an approach is consistent with many

[2] In political science, such an approach is often called "rational choice."

historical accounts of the motivations of different actors. For example, in 1839, the Chartist J. R. Stephens argued:

> The question of universal suffrage . . . is a knife and fork question, a bread and cheese question . . . by universal suffrage I mean to say that every working man in the land has a right to a good coat on his back, a good hat on his head, a good roof for the shelter of his household, a good dinner upon his table. (quoted in Briggs 1959, p. 34)

The alternative would have been simply to assume that one group dislikes democracy whereas another group likes democracy – for example, because of certain ideological preferences or biases (Diamond 1999). Indeed, Diamond (1992, p. 455) argues that

> democracy becomes truly stable only when people come to value it widely not solely for its economic and social performance but intrinsically for its political attributes.

We are not denying that such ideological preferences exist, but we believe that individuals' and groups' preferences over regimes derived from the economic and social consequences of these regimes are more important. Later in the book, we discuss how introducing ideological preferences affects our results, and the general message is that – as long as these do not become the overriding factors – they do not affect our conclusions.

Our second building block is that politics is inherently conflictual. Most policy choices create distributional conflict; one policy benefits one group whereas another benefits different individuals. This is a situation of *political conflict* – conflict over the policies that society should adopt. These groups – for example, the rich and the poor – have conflicting preferences over policies, and every policy choice creates *winners* and *losers*. For instance, with high taxes, the rich are the losers and the poor are the winners, whereas when low taxes are adopted, the roles are reversed. In the absence of such conflict, aggregating the preferences of individuals to arrive at social preferences would be easy; we would simply have to choose the policy that makes everybody better off. Much of political philosophy exists because we do not live in such a simple world, and situations of conflict are ubiquitous. Every time society (or the government) makes a decision or adopts a policy, it is implicitly siding with one group, implicitly resolving the underlying political conflict in one way or another, and implicitly or explicitly creating winners and losers.

Although the economic approach emphasizes individual preferences and motivations, many individuals often have the same interests and sometimes make the same decisions. Moreover, groups of individuals may be able to act collectively if there are no collective-action problems or if they can solve any that exist. If this is the case, then we can usefully discuss conflict and who is in conflict with whom in terms of groups of individuals. These groups may be social classes, somewhat similar to Marxist accounts of history and politics, or they may be urban agents, ethnic or religious groups, or the military. Our focus on social groups as key political actors is motivated by our sense that the most important forces in political conflict and change are groups of individuals.

Leaving aside issues of political philosophy related to how a just or fair society should reconcile these conflicting preferences, how does society resolve political conflict in practice? Let us make this question somewhat more concrete: suppose there are two policies, one favoring the citizens and the other favoring the elites. Which one will the society adopt? Because there is no way of making both groups happy simultaneously, the policy choice has to favor one group or the other. We can think that which group is favored is determined by which group has *political power*. In other words, political power is the capacity of a group to obtain its favorite policies against the resistance of other groups. Because there are always conflicting interests, we are always in the realm of political conflict. And, because we are always in the realm of political conflict, we are always under the shadow of political power. The more political power a group has, the more it will benefit from government policies and actions.

What is political power? Where does it come from? In thinking of the answers to these questions, it is useful to distinguish between two different types of political power: *de jure political power* and *de facto political power*. Imagine Thomas Hobbes's (1996) state of nature, where there is no law and man is indistinguishable from beast. Hobbes considered such a situation to argue that this type of anarchy was highly undesirable, and the state, as a leviathan, was necessary to monopolize force and enforce rules among citizens. But, how are allocations determined in Hobbes's state of nature? If there is a fruit that can be consumed by one of two individuals, which one will get to eat it? The answer is clear: because there is no law, whoever is more powerful, whoever has more brute force, will get to eat the fruit. The same type of brute force matters in the political arena as well. A particular group will have considerable political power when it has armies and guns to kill other groups when policies do not go its way. Therefore, the first source of political power is simply what a group can do to other groups and the society at large by using force. We refer to this as de facto political power. Yet, and fortunately so, this is not the only type of political power. Today, key decisions in the United Kingdom are made by the Labour Party, not because it can use brute force or because it has acquired de facto power through some other means but rather because political power has been allocated to it by the political system (i.e., it was voted into office in the last general election). As a result, among policies with conflicting consequences, the Labour Party can choose those that are more beneficial to its constituency or to its leaders. We call this type of political power, allocated by political institutions, de jure political power. Actual political power is a combination of de jure and de facto political power, and which component matters more depends on various factors – a topic that we discuss later.

Finally, we refer to the social and political arrangements that allocate de jure political power as *political institutions*. For example, an electoral rule that gives the right to decide fiscal policies to the party that obtains 51 percent of the vote is a particular political institution. For our purposes, the most important political institutions are those that determine which individuals take part in the political decision-making process (i.e., democracy versus nondemocracy). Therefore, a major role of democracy is its ability to allocate de jure political power. In democracy, the majority has relatively more de jure political power than it does in nondemocracy. That democracies look after the interests of the majority of citizens more than nondemocracies is simply a consequence, then, of the greater de jure political power of the majority in democracy than in nondemocracy.

3. Toward Our Basic Story

Armed with the first two basic building blocks of our approach, we can now start discussing preferences over different regimes. Typically, there is political conflict between the elites and the citizens, and democracies look after the interests of the citizens more than nondemocracies. It is, therefore, natural to think that the citizens have a stronger preference for democracy than the elites. So, if there is going to be conflict about which types of political institutions a society should have, the majority of citizens will be on the side of democracy and the elites will be on the side of nondemocracy. This is a good starting point.

We could add more empirical content to this structure by assuming that the elites were the relatively rich and the majority the relatively poor. Indeed, in many instances, the transition from nondemocracy to democracy was accompanied by significant conflict between poorer elements of society, who were hitherto excluded and wanted to be included in the political decision-making process, and the rich elite, who wanted to exclude them. This was most clearly the case in nineteenth-century Europe, particularly Britain, as we saw in Chapter 1, when initially the middle classes and subsequently the working classes demanded voting rights. Their demands were first opposed by the rich elite, who then had to concede and include them in the political system.

In line with this account of political developments in nineteenth-century Europe, Aminzade (1993, p. 35) describes the arrival of universal male suffrage to French politics as follows:

> French workers, mainly artisans, constituted the revolutionary force that put the Republican party in power in February 1848 . . . and working class pressure from the streets of Paris forced liberal Republican leaders . . . to reluctantly concede universal male suffrage.

Perhaps, more tellingly, the key players in the process of democratization saw it as a fight between the rich and the poor. Viscount Cranborne, a leading nineteenth-century British Conservative, described the reform struggle as

> . . . a battle not of parties, but of classes and a portion of the great political struggle of our century – the struggle between property . . . and mere numbers. (quoted in Smith, 1966, pp. 27–8)

The conflict between the poorer and richer factions of society was also a defining characteristic of most instances of the introduction of universal suffrage in Latin America in the first half of the twentieth century – including the experiences in Argentina in 1912, as we saw in Chapter 1, but also in Uruguay in 1919, in Colombia in 1936, and in Venezuela in 1945. The arrival of democracy in South Africa and Zimbabwe similarly followed a conflict between the rich whites and poor blacks.

This discussion, therefore, highlights how the majority of citizens want democratic institutions because they benefit from them and, therefore, will strive to obtain them. Given our definition of political power, we can say that the citizens are more likely to secure a transition to democracy when they have more de facto political power. Thus, we have already constructed a simple theory of democratization: the citizens want democracy and the elites want nondemocracy, and the balance of political power between the two groups determines whether the society transits from nondemocracy to democracy (and perhaps also whether democracy, once created, becomes consolidated or reverts back to nondemocracy later).

This could be viewed as a simplified version of our theory of democratization. But, in fact, it is so simplified that some of the essential features of our theory are absent. Most important, the role that democracy or, more generally, political institutions play is trivialized.

The theory says that democracy leads to social choices more favored by the majority of citizens; hence, the citizens prefer democracy to nondemocracy, and democracy results when the citizens have sufficient political power. However, if the citizens have sufficient political power, why don't they use this power to simply obtain the social choices and policies that they prefer rather than first fight for democracy and then wait for it to deliver those policies to them? Is democracy simply a not-so-necessary intermediate step here? One could argue so.

This is only a feature of the simple story we have told so far, and it is a characteristic of neither real-world political institutions nor of our theory. In practice, political institutions play a much more fundamental role than being a simple intermediating variable: they regulate the future allocation of political power between various social groups. They play this role because we do not live in a static world like the one described in the previous narrative but rather in a dynamic world, where individuals care not only about policies today but also about policies tomorrow. We can capture this important role of political institutions and obtain a more satisfactory understanding of democracy and democratization by incorporating these dynamic strategic elements, which is what our theory of democratization attempts to do.

4. Our Theory of Democratization

Consider the simplest dynamic world we can imagine: there is a "today" and a "tomorrow," and the elites and the citizens care about policies both today and tomorrow. There is nothing that prevents society from adopting a different policy tomorrow from the one it chose today. Thus, it is not sufficient for the citizens to ensure policies they prefer today; they would also like similar policies to be adopted tomorrow. Suppose we are in a nondemocratic society, which generally looks after the interests of the elites. Citizens have de facto political power today, so they can obtain the policies they like, but they are unsure whether they will have the same political power tomorrow. Given that we are in a nondemocratic society, tomorrow the elites may become more powerful and assertive and the citizens may no longer have the same political power. Can they ensure the implementation of the policies they like both today and tomorrow?

This is where political institutions may be important relative to the static world described previously. Institutions, by their nature, are *durable* – that is, the institutions of today are likely to persist until tomorrow. A democratic society is not only one where there is one-person-one-vote today but also one that is expected to remain democratic at least in the near future. This durability was already implicit in our definition of political institutions as a means of allocating political power: they regulate the *future* allocation of political power. For example, democracy means that tomorrow there will be a vote to determine policies or to decide which party will rule and the whole population will participate. Nondemocracy means that much of the population will be excluded from collective decision-making processes.

Imagine now that the citizens do not simply use their de facto political power today to obtain the policies they like now, but they also use their political power to change the political system from nondemocracy to democracy. If they do so, they will have effectively increased their de jure political power in the future. Instead of nondemocracy, we are now in a democratic regime where there will be voting by all. With their increased political power, the citizens are therefore more likely to secure the policies they like tomorrow as well.

We have now moved toward a richer theory of democratization: transition to democracy – or, more generally, a change in political institutions – emerges as a way of regulating the future allocation of political power. The citizens demand and perhaps obtain democracy so that they can have more political say and political power tomorrow. Returning to the beliefs of the Chartist J. R. Stephens (quoted in Briggs 1959), we can now see that he was correct in demanding universal suffrage as a means of securing the "right to a good coat . . . a good hat . . . a good roof . . . [and] a good dinner" for working men rather than directly demanding the coat, the roof, and the dinner. Those would have been only for today, whereas universal suffrage could secure them in the future as well.

Notice an important implicit element in the story: *the transitory nature of de facto political power*. The citizens are presumed to have political power today but uncertain about whether they will have similar power tomorrow. The balance between the elites and the citizens or, more generally, between various social groups is not permanent, is not set in stone, is not the same today as it will be tomorrow; it is transitory. This is reasonable in the dynamic and uncertain world in which we live. It will be even more compelling when we think of the sources of political power for the disenfranchised citizens in nondemocracy. First, let us try to understand why the transitory nature of political power matters. Suppose that the citizens have the same political power tomorrow as they have today. Why should they need political institutions to help them? If their political power is sufficient to obtain the policies they like (even to obtain the institutions they like) today, then it will be so in the future as well, and there will be no need to change the underlying political institutions. It is precisely the transitory nature of political power – that the citizens have it today and may not have it tomorrow – that creates a demand for change in political institutions. The citizens would like to lock in the political power they have today by changing political institutions – specifically, by introducing democracy and greater representation for themselves – because without the institutional changes, their power today is unlikely to persist.

So why do the citizens have political power in nondemocracy? The answer is that they have de facto rather than de jure political power. In nondemocracy, the elites monopolize de jure political power but not necessarily de facto political power. The citizens are excluded from the political system in nondemocracy, but they are nonetheless the majority and they can sometimes challenge the system, create significant social unrest and turbulence, or even pose a serious revolutionary threat. What is there to stop the majority of the population overwhelming the elite, which constitutes a minority, and taking control of society and its wealth, even if the elites have access to better guns and hired soldiers? After all, the citizens successfully occupied Paris during the Paris Commune, overthrew the existing regime in the 1917 Russian Revolution, destroyed the dictatorship of Somoza in Nicaragua in 1979, and in many other instances created significant turbulence and real attempts at revolution. However, a real threat from the citizens requires the juxtaposition of many unlikely factors: the masses need to solve the collective-action problem necessary to organize themselves,[3] they need to find the momentum to turn their organization into an effective force against the regime, and the elites – who are controlling the state apparatus – should be unable to use the military to effectively suppress the uprising. It is, therefore, reasonable that such a challenge against the system would only be transitory: in nondemocracy, if the citizens have political power today, they most likely will not have it tomorrow.

Imagine now that there is an effective revolutionary threat from the citizens against nondemocracy. They have the political power today to get what they want and even to overthrow the system. They can use their political power to obtain "the coat, the roof, and the dinner," but why not use it to obtain more, the same things not only for today but also in the future? This is what they will get if they can force a change in political institutions. Society will make a transition to democracy and, from then on, policies will be determined by one-person-one-vote, and the

[3] That is, individuals should be convinced to take part in revolutionary activity despite the individual costs and the collective benefits to them as a group.

citizens will have more political power, enabling them to obtain the policies they desire and the resulting coat, roof, and dinner.

In practice, however, changes in political institutions do not simply happen because the citizens demand them. Transitions to democracy typically take place when the elite controlling the existing regime extend voting rights. Why would they do so? After all, the transfer of political power to the majority typically leads to social choices that the elite doesn't like – for instance, higher taxes and greater redistribution away from it in the future, precisely the outcomes it would like to prevent. Faced with the threat of a revolution, wouldn't the elite like to try other types of concessions, even giving the citizens the policies they want, rather than give away its power? To answer this question, let us return to the period of effective revolutionary threat. Imagine that the citizens can overthrow the system and are willing to do so if they do not get some concessions, some policies that favor them and increase their incomes and welfare.

The first option for the elite is to give them what they want today: redistribute income and more generally adopt policies favorable to the majority. But, suppose that concessions today are not sufficient to dissuade the citizens from revolution. What can the elite do to prevent an imminent and, for itself, extremely costly revolution? Well, it can promise the same policies tomorrow. Not only a coat, a roof, and a dinner today but also tomorrow. Yet, these promises may not be *credible*. Changing policy in the direction preferred by the citizens is not in the immediate interest of the elite. Today, it is doing so to prevent a revolution. Tomorrow, the threat of revolution may be gone, so why should it do so again? Why should it keep its promises? No reason and, in fact, it is unlikely to do so. Hence, its promises are not necessarily credible. Noncredible promises are worth little and, unconvinced by these promises, the citizens would carry out a revolution. If it wants to save its skin, the elite has to make a credible promise to set policies that the majority prefer; in particular, it must make a credible commitment to future pro-majority policies. A credible promise means that the policy decision should not be the elite's but rather placed in the hands of groups that actually prefer such policies. Or, in other words, it has to transfer political power to the citizens. A credible promise, therefore, means that it has to change the future allocation of political power. That is precisely what a transition to democracy does: it shifts future political power away from the elite to the citizens, thereby creating *a credible commitment to future pro-majority policies.* The role that political institutions play in allocating power and leading to relatively credible commitments is the third key building block of our approach.

Why, if a revolution is attractive to the citizens, does the creation of democracy stop it? This is plausibly because revolution is costly. In revolutions, much of the wealth of a society may be destroyed, which is costly for the citizens as well as the elite. It is these costs that allow concessions or democratization by the elite to avoid revolution. In reality, it will not always be the case that democracy is sufficiently pro-majority that it avoids revolution. For example, the citizens may anticipate that, even with universal suffrage, the elite will be able to manipulate or corrupt political parties or maybe it will be able to use its control of the economy to limit the types of policies that democracy can implement. In such circumstances, anticipating that democracy will deliver few tangible rewards, the citizens may revolt. However, to limit the scope of our analysis, we normally restrict our attention to situations where the creation of democracy avoids revolution. Historically, this seems to have been typical, and it means that we do not delve deeply into theories of revolution or into the modeling of post-revolutionary societies.

We now have our basic theory of democratization in place. In nondemocracy, the elites have de jure political power and, if they are unconstrained, they will generally choose the policies that they most prefer; for example, they may choose low taxes and no redistribution to the poor. However, nondemocracy is sometimes challenged by the citizens who may pose a revolutionary threat – when they temporarily have de facto political power. Crucially, such political power is transitory; they have it today and are unlikely to have it tomorrow. They can use this power to undertake a revolution and change the system to their benefit, creating massive losses to the elites but also significant collateral damage and social losses. The elites would like to prevent this outcome, and they can do so by making a credible commitment to future pro-majority policies. However, promises of such policies within the existing political system are often noncredible. To make them credible, they need to transfer formal political power to the majority, which is what democratization achieves.

This story of democratization as a commitment to future pro-majority policies by the elites in the face of a revolutionary threat and, perhaps more important, as a commitment made credible by changing the future distribution of political power is consistent with much historical evidence. As illustrated by the British, Argentinian, and South African political histories discussed in Chapter 1, most transitions to democracy, both in nineteenth- and twentieth-century Europe and twentieth-century Latin America, took place amid significant social turmoil and revolutionary threats. In addition, the creation of democratic societies in most former European colonies in the 1950s and 1960s was the result of pressure by the disenfranchised and relatively poor colonials against the colonizing power. Such threats of turmoil and social disorder similarly accompanied the recent spate of democratizations in Africa (Bratton and van der Walle 1997) and Eastern Europe (Bunce 2003). To quote a classic European example, in presenting his electoral reform to the British Parliament in 1831, Prime Minister Earl Grey was well aware that this was a measure necessary to prevent a likely revolution. He argued:

> There is no-one more decided against annual parliaments, universal suffrage and the ballot, than I am. My object is not to favour, but to put an end to such hopes and projects . . . The principle of my reform is, to prevent the necessity of revolution . . . reforming to preserve and not to overthrow. (quoted in Evans 1996, p. 223).

Lang's (1999, pp. 38–9) conclusion mirrors Grey's:

> The Whigs were aware of the support among working people for the bill.... However, they were also quite determined not to allow the working classes to hold any sort of dominant position in the new electoral system. Passing the bill therefore saved the country from risings and rebellion; the content of the bill saved the country from the "evils "of democracy. Needless to say, disappointment among the working classes was likely to be intense once they realized how little they had gained from the bill, but by then they would have lost their middle class allies, won over to the system by the bill, and would be powerless to do anything about it.

The same considerations were also determining factors for the later reforms. For example,

> as with the First Reform Act, the *threat* of violence has been seen as a significant factor in forcing the pace [of the 1867 Reform Act]; history... was repeating itself. (Lee 1994, p. 142).

Similarly, the threat of revolution was the driving force behind democratization in the French, German, and Swedish cases. For example, Tilton (1974, pp. 567–8) describes the process leading to the introduction of universal male suffrage in Sweden as follows:

> neither [of the first two reform acts] passed without strong popular pressure; in 1866 crowds thronged around the chamber while the final vote was taken, and the 1909 reform was stimulated by a broad suffrage movement [and] a demonstration strike... Swedish democracy had triumphed without a revolution – but not without the *threat* of a revolution. (italics in original)

The threat of revolution and social unrest played an equally important role in the establishment of voting rights for the populace in Latin America. We saw in Chapter 1 how in Argentina, universal male suffrage was effectively institutionalized in 1912 by President Roque Sáenz Peña when the secret ballot was introduced and fraudulent electoral practices outlawed. The movement toward a full democracy was driven by the social unrest created by the Radical Party and the rapid radicalization of urban workers. In Colombia, the creation of universal suffrage during the administration of Liberal President Alfonso López Pumarejo in 1936 was similarly inspired; leading Colombianist historian David Bushnell (1993, p. 185) describes it as follows:

> López... was a wealthy man... yet he was well aware that Colombia could not go on indefinitely ignoring the needs and problems of what he once described as "that vast and miserable class that does not read, that does not write, that does not dress, that does not wear shoes, that barely eats, that remains... on the margin of [national life]." In his opinion such neglect was not only wrong but also dangerous, because the masses would sooner or later demand a larger share of the amenities of life.

Similarly, the reinstatement of democracy in Venezuela in 1958 was a response to intense uprisings and unrest. In describing the situation, Kolb (1974, p. 175) wrote:

> ...in dramatic intensity and popular violence, the events on January 21 and 22 in Caracas...was a true popular revolution of Venezuelan citizens...armed with rocks, clubs, home-made grenades, and Molotov Cocktails, against a ferocious and well-trained Police force.

The evidence is, therefore, consistent with the notion that most moves toward democracy happen in the face of significant social conflict and possible threat of revolution. Democracy is usually not given by the elite because its values have changed. It is demanded by the disenfranchised as a way to obtain political power and thus secure a larger share of the economic benefits of the system.

Why does the creation of democracy act as a commitment when we know that democracy often collapses once created? This is because although coups sometimes occur, it is costly to overthrow democracy, and institutions, once created, have a tendency to persist. This is mostly because people make specific investments in them. For instance, once democracy has been created, political parties form and many organizations, such as trade unions, arise to take advantage of the new political circumstances. The investments of all these organizations will be lost if democracy is overthrown, giving citizens an incentive to struggle to maintain democracy. Moreover, once democracy has been created, the majority may have greater control over the military than they had under a nondemocratic regime, which changes the underlying balance of de facto power.

Finally, the trade-off for the elite, facing the threat of revolution by the citizens, is not simply between policy concessions and democratization. A further alternative would be to use force and repression. For example, the white South African regime rejected calls for democracy and kept itself in power for decades by using the military to repress demonstrations and opposition. Similarly, Argentine military regimes of the 1960s and 1970s killed thousands of people to avoid reintroducing democracy; this has been the pattern in many other Latin American countries including Guatemala and El Salvador. In Asia, nondemocratic regimes in China and Burma have used force to block demands for democracy. This was also true in Eastern European countries during the dominance of the Soviet Union – for example, in Hungary in 1956 and Czechoslovakia in 1968. It is clear why repression is attractive for elites because it allows them to maintain power without having to make any concessions to the disenfranchised. Nevertheless, repression is both costly and risky for elites. It leads to loss of life and destruction of assets and wealth, and – depending on the international climate of opinion – it may lead to sanctions and international isolation, as happened in South Africa during the 1980s. Moreover, repression may fail, which could cause a revolution – the worst possible outcome for the elites. These considerations imply that only in certain circumstances will repression be attractive. When we incorporate this into the analysis, we see that democracy arises when concessions are not credible and repression is not attractive because it is too costly.

5. Democratic Consolidation

A theory of democratization is not sufficient to understand why some countries are democratic whereas some others are ruled by dictatorships. Many countries become democratic but eventually revert back to a nondemocratic regime as a result of a military coup. This has been an especially common pattern in Latin America. As we saw in Chapter 1, Argentina is a striking example of the instabilities of Latin American democracy. Similarly, the path to democracy has been marred by switches to dictatorships in Brazil, Chile, Guatemala, Peru, Venezuela, and Uruguay. Why has democracy been so hard to consolidate in much of Latin America?

To answer this question, we need to develop a theory of coups or, alternatively, a theory of democratic consolidation. What is a consolidated democracy? A democracy is consolidated if the set of institutions that characterize it endure through time. Our theory of democratic consolidation and coups builds on the different attitudes of the elites and the citizens toward democracy. Once again, the citizens are more pro-democratic than the elites (because democracy is more pro-citizen than nondemocracy). Consequently, when there is a situation with the military on the side of the elite and sufficient turbulence to allow a military takeover, the elites might support or sponsor a coup to change the balance of power in society.

The reason that the elites might want to change political institutions, from democracy to nondemocracy, is similar to the reason that the citizens want democratization. What the elites care about is changing policies in their favor, and political turbulence and the alignment between their interests and those of the military might give them the opportunity to do so. However, there is the issue of the transitory nature of de facto political power. They will have this opportunity today but not necessarily tomorrow. Any promise by the citizens to limit the extent to which policy is pro-majority in the future is not credible within the context of democratic politics. Tomorrow, the threat of a coup may be gone and democratic politics will again cater to the needs of the majority, therefore choosing the policies it prefers without worrying about the elite undermining its power via a coup. However, this is precisely what made democracy so costly for the elite in the first place. To change future policies in a credible way, the elites need political power. A coup is their way of increasing their de jure political power so they can pursue the policies they like. In other words, a coup enables the elites to turn their transitory de facto political power into more enduring de jure political power by changing political institutions.

A related reason that a coup may arise is that, in the midst of political and social turbulence, the military and the elite segments of society may be, perhaps rightly, worried about the future sustainability of democracy and even of the capitalist system and want to preempt a potential move farther toward the left or even a revolution.

6. Determinants of Democracy

Now that we have a theory of democratization, we can ask which factors make the emergence and consolidation of democracy more likely. We have so far explained how our theory can account for transitions from nondemocracy to democracy and possibly back again to nondemocracy. However, just as important are *the comparative statics* of the equilibrium, meaning how the equilibrium changes when some underlying factors change. These comparative statics enable us to explain why some countries transition to democracy whereas others do not, and why some countries remain democracies whereas democracy collapses in other countries. These comparative statics can then guide empirical and historical work in understanding the incidence of democracy.

6.1 Civil Society

6.1.1 Democratization

Our framework implies that a relatively effective threat of revolution from the citizens is important for democratization. When the citizens are not well organized, the system will not be challenged and transition to democracy will be delayed indefinitely. Similarly, when civil society is relatively developed and the majority is organized, repression may be more difficult. Therefore, some degree of development in civil society is also necessary for democratization. We take such development as given in this book and it plausibly represents the outcomes of long-run historical processes (e.g., Putnam 1993).

6.1.2 Consolidation

The strength and nature of civil society is as important for the consolidation of democracy as it is for its creation in the first place. Not only is a well-organized civil society necessary to push for democracy, it is also necessary to protect it. When civil society is better organized, coups are easier to resist, more costly to undertake, and less likely to succeed. Hence, democracy is more likely to be consolidated.

6.2 Shocks and Crises

6.2.1 Democratization

In our theory, democratizations occur because of the transitory nature of de facto political power. In some situations, the collective-action problem is easier to solve, opponents to the regime are easier to coordinate, and revolutions are easier and less costly to carry out. These are typically times of crises – for example, harvest failures, economic depressions, international financial or debt crises, and even wars. Such crises and macroeconomic shocks are intrinsically transitory and lead to short-term fluctuations in de facto political power. Our theory, therefore, predicts that democratizations are more likely to arise in a situation of economic or political crisis. A clear example is the democratization in Argentina after the Falklands (Malvinas) War in 1983.

6.2.2 Consolidation

Just as opponents of dictatorship can gain temporary de facto power when there are political or economic crises, so can opponents of democracy. Our analysis suggests that, as with democratizations, coups are more likely to arise in situations of crisis. An illustrative example is the coup against Allende in Chile in 1973, which came during the first big rise in oil prices and a large economic depression.

6.3 Sources of Income and Composition of Wealth

6.3.1 Democratization

Another important determinant of the trade-off between democracy and repression is the source of income for the elites. In some societies, the elites are heavily invested in land, whereas in others, the elites are those with investments in physical and human capital. There are likely to be three major differences in the attitudes of landowners and (physical and human) capital owners toward democracy and nondemocracy. First, land is easier to tax than physical and human capital. Therefore, landowners have more to fear from democracy than nondemocracy, which makes them more averse to democracy. Second, social and political turbulence may be more damaging to physical and human capital owners who have to rely on cooperation in the workplace and in the trading process, which makes landowners more willing to use force to preserve the regime they prefer. Third, different sets of economic institutions are feasible in a predominantly agrarian economy, which influence the relative intensity of elites' and citizens' preferences over different regimes. For instance, labor-repressive institutions, such as slavery, are relatively more efficient with agricultural technology than in industry (Eltis 2000). This implies that democracy is worse for elites because the changes in collective choices that it brings undermine their preferred set of economic institutions. All three considerations imply that democratization is more likely in a more industrialized society where the elite own significant physical and human capital than a more agricultural society where the elites are mainly invested in land. Stated differently, democracy is more likely when the elites are industrialists rather than landowners.

Although the nature of revolutions is not the focus of this book, these ideas also have interesting implications for the incidence of revolutions. For example, they can help account for why most revolutions – for example, in Russia, Mexico,

China, Vietnam, Bolivia, and Nicaragua – take place in primarily agrarian societies. We suggest that this is because landed elites favor repression rather than concessions and, when repression fails, revolutions take place. In more urbanized and industrialized societies, where the elites are invested in capital, concessions are favored and revolutions are observed less often.

6.3.2 Consolidation

The source of income for the elites also impacts the decision of whether to mount a coup. If the elites are heavily invested in land, then coups may tend to be less costly. More important, democracy is relatively worse for such individuals given that land can be taxed at higher rates than capital, and also that economic institutions under democracy are further from those preferred by the elites. In contrast, when the elites' wealth is mostly in the form of physical and human capital, coups are more expensive for them and democracy is less threatening. As a result, democracy is less likely to consolidate when the elites are landowners than when they are capitalists.

6.4 Political Institutions

6.4.1 Democratization

Our framework also suggests that the nature of democratic political institutions may be crucial for explaining why some societies democratize but others do not. In particular, when the elites can use repression to avoid democratizing, they do so because they anticipate that democracy will be harmful for their interests. So far, our characterization of democracy as the rule of the majority has been overly stylized in order to communicate the main elements of our analysis. In reality, one person's vote may be worth more than another's and, in particular, the elites may be able to exercise more or less influence over what happens in a democracy – even though their influence is relatively less than it is in a dictatorship.

One way they can do this is through the design of democratic institutions. In his 1913 book, *An Economic Interpretation of the U.S. Constitution*, Beard argued that the constitution was written by rich property holders with an eye to maintaining the worth of their assets (including, one should add, their slaves) in the face of likely radical democratic pressures.[4] Beard argued that

> inasmuch as the primary object of a government, beyond the mere repression of physical violence, is the making of the rules that determine the property relations of society, the dominant classes whose rights are thus to be determined must perforce obtain from the government such rules as are consonant with the larger interests necessary to the continuance of their economic processes, or they must themselves control the organs of government. In a stable despotism the former takes place; under

[4] Although many details of Beard's arguments are now contested, the general thrust of his argument is accepted by many scholars. For instance, Wood (1969, p. 626) notes in his seminal book that the constitution "was intrinsically an aristocratic document designed to check the democratic tendencies of the period." See McGuire (1988) for partially supporting statistical evidence.

> any other system of government, where political power is shared by any portion of the population, the methods and nature of this control become the problem of prime importance – in fact, the fundamental problem in constitutional law. The social structure by which one type of legislation is secured and another prevented – is a secondary or derivative feature arising from the nature of the economic groups seeking positive action and negative restraint. (1913, p. 13)

Even the notion of representative democracy, as opposed to participatory or direct democracy, can be seen as an attempt to dilute populist pressures and undermine the power of the majority (as argued by Manin 1997).

Clearly, then, democratic political institutions can be structured to limit the power of the majority. A more recent example is the constitution written during the dictatorship of General Pinochet in Chile, which attempted to minimize the threat of socialism in Chile by engaging in systematic gerrymandering and the underrepresentation of urban areas, and which otherwise attempted to cement the veto of the military over democratic decision making (Londregan 2000; Siavelis 2000).

Another example, discussed in Chapter 1, is the way that the South African constitution was written in an attempt to protect the interests of whites under democracy.

If a nondemocratic regime or elite can design or manipulate the institutions of democracy so as to guarantee that radical majoritarian policies will not be adopted, then democracy becomes less threatening to the interests of the elites. Less threatened, the elites are more willing to create democracy in the first place. For instance, when democracy is less threatening, it will be less attractive to use repression to avoid it. Thus, Pinochet's constitution, according to our framework, facilitated democratization in Chile. It may even be the case that, as in South Africa, the majority of citizens are themselves willing to restrict their policy options to facilitate a transition to democracy. As we discuss in Chapter 6, the ANC realized that it had to make concessions to the whites about the structure of democratic institutions. For the ANC, this was better than carrying on with the fight against the apartheid regime. By giving the elite credible guarantees, a process of democratization is facilitated that might otherwise not take place.

6.4.2 Consolidation

Just as the structure of democratic institutions influences democratization in the first place, so it helps to determine whether democracy consolidates. In particular, institutions that place limits on pro-majoritarian policies in democracy are likely to help consolidation. In fact, the elites may be quite influential in democracy because they control a strong upper house, like the Prussian Junkers in nineteenth-century Germany, or the British aristocracy in the House of Lords, or because they control the party system. Knowing that in democracy they will be able to insure against the most excessively majoritarian policies, the elites will be less willing to undertake action against democracy.

An interesting example in this context is the links between the elite and both traditional ruling parties in Colombia. Throughout the twentieth century, the Liberal and Conservative Parties managed successfully to avoid the entry of left-wing parties by manipulating electoral institutions, particularly the form of proportional representation. Without a left-wing party, highly redistributive political agendas did not emerge in Colombia. Interestingly, Colombia has one of the most consolidated democracies in Latin America, although there are often complaints that the system does not represent the interests of the majority.

Another example of the connection between political institutions and democratic consolidation is the claim that presidential democracies may be more unstable than parliamentary democracies and more prone to coups (Linz 1978, 1994). This idea makes sense in our framework because, whereas in a legislature checks and balances and lobbying may allow the elites to block radical policy proposals, a directly elected president is more likely to represent the preferences of the majority in society and, therefore, to be more populist. Hence, presidential systems may be more threatening to the interests of the elites and thus induce more coups.

Paradoxically, then, this perspective might also help explain why the consolidation of democracy in Chile may have run smoothly after the systematic gerrymandering that General Pinochet arranged in the electoral rules. This manipulation underrepresented urban areas at the expense of more conservative rural areas, thus reducing the political power of the left. The consequence was a less redistributive but more stable democracy. Turkey and Thailand provide other examples in which constitutions written or commissioned by the military may have helped democratic consolidation. Haggard and Kaufman (1995, p. 110) note:

> Ironically, the greater security for the armed forces during the initial years of the transition probably *reduced* the threat to civilian authority in Chile, Turkey, and Korea.

However, whereas increasing the power of the elites in democracy may promote democracy, giving the elites too much power will undermine it. In our framework, democracy arises from conflict between elites and disenfranchised majorities who are prepared to accept democracy rather than something more radical because it gives them more political power than nondemocracy. If the elites have too much power in democracy, democracy will do little to improve the welfare of the majority. In this case, democracy is not a solution to social conflict, and the result will either be revolution or an elite that keeps itself in power through repression.

6.5 The Role of Inter-Group Inequality

6.5.1 Democratization

Our framework makes predictions about the effect of *inter-group inequality* – inequality between groups – on the creation and consolidation of democracy. For convenience, we outline these using the word *inequality* to refer to inter-group inequality. However, these predictions about inter-group inequality may not translate into statements about standard measures of inequality and income distribution (e.g., the labor share or the Gini coefficient). This is particularly true when political conflict is not rich versus poor but rather along other lines, perhaps between ethnic or religious groups.

Everything else being equal, greater inter-group inequality makes revolution more attractive for the citizens: with revolution, they get a chance to share the entire income of the economy (minus what is destroyed in revolution), whereas in nondemocracy, they obtain only a small fraction of these resources. Because an effective threat of revolution is the spark that ignites the democratization process, greater inter-group inequality should be associated with a greater likelihood of democratization.

There is also another reason why inter-group inequality might contribute to democratization. Recall that democratization occurs as a credible commitment to future redistribution, when the promise of redistribution is not sufficient to stave off the threat of revolution. The stronger the threat of revolution, the more likely it is that this promise will be insufficient and that the elite will be forced to create democracy. Because greater inter-group inequality contributes to the strength of the threat of revolution, it makes democratization more likely via this channel as well.

This discussion of the role of inter-group inequality is one-sided, however. It highlights how greater inequality increases the threat of revolution and thus the demand for democracy by the citizens. However, inter-group inequality may also affect the aversion that the elites have to democracy. To see why consider a standard model of redistributive taxation as in Meltzer and Richard (1981). Note that as the gap between the elites and the citizens rises (i.e., as inter-group inequality increases), the burden placed on the elites, even *at a constant tax rate*, rises. This is because with greater inequality, a larger share of total tax revenues will be raised from the elites, who now command a greater fraction of the resources in the economy. Therefore, greater inter-group inequality typically increases the burden of democracy on the elites, even if the tax rate remains constant or changes little. Moreover, many approaches suggest that greater inter-group inequality should increase the tax rate, contributing to this effect. If this is so, there would be another reason for greater inequality to increase the burden of democracy on the elites. With greater inequality, the benefits from redistribution increase, inducing the citizens to prefer higher levels of taxation.[5] Overall, therefore, it seems compelling that the costs of redistributive taxation and democratic politics to the elites and, hence, their aversion to democracy should be generally higher for the elites in a society where the difference in incomes between the elites and the citizens is greater.

[5] As discussed in Chapter 4, there are theoretical and empirical arguments for why the relationship between inequality and redistribution may be more complex (e.g., greater inequality may enable the elites to lobby more effectively against redistribution in democracy). Nevertheless, it is generally the case that with greater inter-group inequality, democracy imposes a greater burden on the elites than nondemocracy does.

How does this affect the relationship between inter-group inequality and transition to democracy? The most important implication is that as inequality increases and democracy becomes more costly for the elites, repression becomes more attractive. Therefore, greater inter-group inequality may also discourage democratization.

Putting these two pieces of the story together, we find that there is a nonmonotonic (i.e., inverted U-shaped) relationship between inter-group inequality and the likelihood of transition to democracy. In the most equal societies, revolution and social unrest are not sufficiently attractive for the citizens; either there are no challenges to nondemocratic systems or any challenges can be met by temporary measures, such as some limited redistribution. In other words, in these fairly equal societies, the citizens are already benefiting from the productive resources of the economy or even perhaps from the growth process, so they do not make further strong demands. This may be the reason why democracy arrived late in a number of equal and rapidly growing economies, such as South Korea and Taiwan, and has yet to fully arrive in Singapore. In stark contrast, in the most unequal societies (e.g., South Africa prior to 1994), the citizens have great reason to be unhappy and often try to rise up against the authority of nondemocracy. Now, however, the elites have a lot to lose from abandoning the system that looks after their own interests and transitioning into one that will place a greater redistributive burden on them. Thus, instead of democracy, a highly unequal society is likely to result in a repressive nondemocracy – or, sometimes when repression is not enough, perhaps even experience a revolution. This mechanism can also explain the persistence of nondemocratic regimes in the highly unequal countries of Latin America, such as El Salvador and Paraguay. This account, then, suggests that democracy has the best chance to emerge in societies with middle levels of inequality. Here, the citizens are not totally satisfied with the existing system, and the elites are not so averse to democracy that they resort to repression to prevent it. This is the situation we find in Britain and Argentina in the late nineteenth and early twentieth centuries.

6.5.2 Consolidation

Inequality also critically influences the propensity of a democracy to consolidate. Because the main threat against democracy comes from its redistributive nature, the greater redistribution away from the elites the more likely they are to find it in their interest to mount a coup against it. Therefore, greater inequality is likely to destabilize democracy because, as observed previously, the burden of democracy on the elites is increasing in the income gap between them and the citizens.

This comparative static result with respect to inequality offers a potential explanation for why democracy may have been more difficult to consolidate in Latin America than in Western Europe. Latin American societies are considerably more unequal and, therefore, suffer more from distributional conflict between the elites and the citizens. Our framework predicts that in highly unequal societies, democratic policies should be highly redistributive but then abruptly come to an end with a coup that reverts back to much less redistributive policies. This pattern is reminiscent of the oscillations of many Latin American countries between the highly redistributive but unsustainable populist policies of short-lived democracies and the fiscally more conservative approach of subsequent nondemocratic regimes. Tellingly, Kaufman and Stallings (1991, p. 27) also emphasize a close connection between unconsolidated democracy and populist redistribution:

> ... established democracies (Venezuela, Colombia and Costa Rica in our study) were also associated with orthodox macro policies.... It was the transitional democracies (Peru, Argentina and Brazil) that followed populist policies.

Combining the effects of inequality on democratization and coups, we can see that equal societies never democratize in the first place. This helps to account for Singapore's path of political development. Higher but still relatively low levels of inter-group inequality lead societies to democratize and, once created, democracy is consolidated because it is not so costly for the elites that a coup is desirable. This may capture Britain's path of political development. Even higher levels of inequality still lead to democratization, but democracy does not consolidate because coups are attractive. As a result, the outcome is unconsolidated democracy, which is the path that Argentina followed in the twentieth century. Finally, at the highest levels of inequality, democracy is so threatening for the elites that they use repression to avoid it, a situation that characterized South Africa until 1994.[6]

6.6 The Middle Class

6.6.1 Democratization

Perhaps the most famous treatise on the origins of democracy is Moore's (1966) *Social Origins of Dictatorship and Democracy*. Our work owes a natural intellectual debt to Moore, especially because we paraphrased his title. In our theory, the major factor that distinguishes democracy from nondemocracy is the greater political equality of democracies; so far, we have only distinguished between two groups: the elites and the citizens. This was mainly for simplification (again, an application of Occam's razor). Nevertheless, in many circumstances, a third group between the elite and the great mass of citizens may be of significance. In general, this group could be identified in different ways but, following the emphasis of many scholars, it is useful to think of this group as the middle class forming a distinct political actor. When the middle class is brought into our framework, we obtain a range of interesting results, some of them vindicating the emphasis that Moore and other scholars placed on the middle class.

The first role that the middle class can play in the emergence of democracy is as the driver of the process. Recall that in our framework, democracy emerges in

[6] These are all, of course, statements where "other things are held equal." Inter-group inequality is not the only thing that determines whether a society democratizes or a democracy consolidates.

response to a serious revolutionary threat or significant social unrest. The middle class can be the driver in this process by playing a key role in the revolutionary movement or by fueling and maintaining it. Almost all revolutionary movements were led by middle-class actors and, more important, a number of the major challenges to the existing regime; for example, the uprisings that helped induce the First Reform Act in Britain or those during the Paris Commune in France or the revolts of the Radical Party in Argentina were largely middle-class movements (see O'Donnell and Schmitter 1986, pp. 50–2, on the crucial role of the middle class in contemporary democratizations). Therefore, the middle class – by virtue of its more comfortable economic situation and the greater education of its members – can be a critical catalyst in the process toward democracy. This might also explain why many of the early moves toward democracy in Europe were only partial. If the middle class is the key actor, it may be sufficient for the elites to co-opt the middle class rather than concede a comprehensive democracy to all those who are excluded from the political system. The resulting picture resembles the gradual move toward democracy experienced in much of Western Europe: first, the middle classes are included in the political process and then the franchise is extended to the mass of citizens.

Perhaps the more important role of the middle class is that of a *buffer* in the conflict between the elites and the citizens. Recall that when the elites expect democracy to adopt policies highly unfavorable to them, they prefer repression to democratization. The presence of a large and relatively affluent middle class ensures that they play an important role in democratic politics and, because they are more prosperous than the citizens, they will typically support policies much closer to those that the elites prefer. Therefore, by limiting the amount of policy change induced by democracy, a large and affluent middle class may act like a buffer between the elites and the citizens in democracy. It does this by simultaneously making democratization more attractive for the elites than repression and changing policy enough that the citizens are content not to revolt.

The role of the middle class in the transition to democracy might help us understand the contrast between the political histories of Costa Rica and Colombia on the one hand and Guatemala, El Salvador, and Nicaragua on the other. Despite many similarities in their colonial histories and economic structures, these five countries have had very different political trajectories (Paige 1997; Nugent and Robinson 2002). Costa Rica and Colombia have become stable albeit restricted democracies since the middle of the nineteenth century and successfully made the transition to effective universal suffrage in 1948 and 1936, respectively. Guatemala, El Salvador, and Nicaragua, on the other hand, were dominated by dictators in the nineteenth century and initial moves toward democracy – for example, in El Salvador in the late 1920s and in Guatemala between 1945 and 1954 – were snuffed out by coups and repression. These three societies made the transition to democracy very late. One important difference among these countries is that there is a relatively large and affluent middle class, especially smallholder coffee producers, in Costa Rica and Colombia but not in the other three. Perhaps as a consequence, democratic politics, once installed, has been much more conflict-ridden in Guatemala, El Salvador, and Nicaragua than in Costa Rica and Colombia.

6.6.2 Consolidation

The middle class may play an important role in consolidating democracy by limiting redistribution. A society with a large and affluent middle class will engage only in limited redistribution away from the elites toward the citizens and, therefore, provide a much smaller threat to the interests of the elites. This might be useful in understanding why many Western European and some Latin American societies, like Costa Rica and Colombia, with comparatively large middle classes have also had relatively stable democracies, whereas El Salvador and Guatemala, which lack such a middle-class buffer, have had difficulty consolidating democracy.

6.7 Globalization

There is no doubt that there are stronger economic links between nations today than forty years ago. Countries are more closely linked internationally today, with economic organizations such as the European Union, NAFTA, Mercosur, and Asean; there are much larger volumes of goods and services being traded, and much larger cross-border financial transactions. Do these major economic and political changes have implications for the circumstances under which democracy will arise and consolidate?

6.7.1 Democratization

Globalization might contribute to democratization in a number of distinct ways. First, international financial integration means that capital owners, the elites, can more easily take their money out of a given country. This makes it more difficult to tax the elites and reduces the extent to which democracy can pursue populist and highly majoritarian policies. International financial integration, therefore, makes the elites feel more secure about democratic politics and discourages them from using repression to prevent a transition from nondemocracy to democracy.

Second, international trade affects factor prices and, via this channel, modifies redistributive politics. Countries differ in their factor endowments, and the relative abundance of factors of production determines patterns of specialization and the impact of trade on relative prices. One implication of increased international trade is an increase in the rewards to the relatively abundant factor in each country. In the case of less developed nations – which are typically those still in nondemocracy today and, therefore, the main candidates for democratization – this means an increase in the rewards to labor. Intuitively, before the advent of significant trade flows, less developed countries had an excess of labor and a shortage of capital, depressing the rewards to labor and increasing those to capital. Trade opening will pull these rewards toward those prevailing in the rest of the world, thus increasing the rewards to labor and potentially reducing the return to capital. Trade opening will, therefore, reduce the gap between the incomes of labor and capital, thus changing the extent of inequality between capital owners and labor owners.

The specific implications of our framework depend on three things: (1) the nature of relative factor abundance; (2) the nature of political identities; and (3) where a country is on the inverted U-shaped relationship between inter-group inequality and democratization. Imagine that nondemocratic countries are labor abundant, political conflict is between rich capital-owning elites and poor labor-owning citizens, and inequality is sufficiently high that the elites use repression to stay in power. In this case, increased trade integration will reduce the extent of inequality between the elites and the citizens and will make democracy less redistributive. Because democracy will then be less threatening to the elites, they will be less inclined to use repression to avoid democracy. In such circumstances, globalization promotes democracy. Nevertheless, our framework does not imply that the impact of globalization on factor prices always promotes democracy. Let's continue to postulate that conflict is between the rich and the poor and that we are on the part of the inverted U-shaped relationship where the rich use repression to stay in power. Now consider Latin American countries such as Argentina, Brazil, and Uruguay in the late nineteenth century. In these countries, the elites owned a lot of land and they were also land abundant. As predicted by the theory of international trade, pre–First World War globalization led to large increases in returns to land (O'Rourke and Williamson 1999). In our framework, this increases inter-group inequality and makes the elites less likely to democratize. It also increases the proportion of elite wealth invested in land, another factor that we suggest makes democracy more threatening to the elites. By the converse of these arguments, in this case, globalization would impede democratization (as long as we are on the part of the inverted U-shaped relationship where inequality discourages democratization, as assumed previously).

Third, increased international trade also means that disruption of economic activity may become more costly for many less developed nations that are now integrated into the world economy and, therefore, repression may now be much more costly for the elites, again favoring democracy.

Finally, increased political integration and the end of the Cold War (if not hijacked by the war against terrorism) might imply that countries that repress their citizens can perhaps expect stronger sanctions and reactions from the democratic world. This effectively increases the costs of repression, promoting democracy. This might be especially important because a number of nondemocratic regimes in the Cold War Era, such as Mobutu's disastrous dictatorship in Zaire, were kept alive by the explicit or implicit support of the international community.

6.7.2 Consolidation

Just as globalization can induce democratization, so it can aid democratic consolidation. Indeed, all of the mechanisms listed that link increased globalization to democratization also imply that coups will be less likely. This is either because coups become more costly in a more integrated world or because globalization implies that democracy is less threatening to the elites.

7. Political Identities and the Nature of Conflict

Most of the comparative static results discussed so far do not depend on the identity of the elite; they apply even in societies where the nature of political conflict is not along class lines. In South Africa, race may be more salient, although race and socioeconomic class overlap to a large extent. In Rwanda, it may be more plausible to think of groups forming along the lines of ethnicity: Hutu or Tutsi. In Mauritius, political conflict has been between people of East Indian descent and a heterogeneous coalition of others, some of whom are rich (i.e., the white sugar planters and Chinese business elites) and some very poor (i.e., mostly the descendents of African slaves). In the latter case, there is no simple overlap between ethnicity or race and class (Bowman 1991).

As long as one accepts the premise that the interests of individuals are partly about economic outcomes, our basic analysis remains unaltered. Consider our ideas about political institutions. Here, we showed that if political institutions were such as to limit the type of policies that could occur in democracy, they tended to induce consolidated democracy. This result applies even in Mauritius. If institutions limit democracies, then they limit what the East Indian majority can do to the Creole minority. Hence, they reduce the incentive of a Creole dictatorship to repress democracy and, once democracy has been created, they make coups less attractive – exactly as in our previous analysis.

Next, consider the ideas we developed about the connection between the composition of the wealth of the elite and democratization or coups. These ideas apply immediately in this case. Even when politics is East Indian against Creole, as the economy develops and capital becomes more important than land, repression and coups become more costly and (pro–East Indian) democracy becomes less redistributive. As in our baseline analysis, this tends to create a consolidated democracy, even in Mauritius. Interestingly, Mauritius has been a consolidated democracy since independence, and this process of consolidation has taken place in the context of the radically declining importance of land, the rapid development of industry, and the expansion in the importance of human capital.

The nature of political identities may undoubtedly influence the form of collective choice under democracy, which ties our analysis to several important traditions in political science. For example, contrast a society where political identities and cleavages are on the basis of class with one where there are many cross-cutting cleavages or race, ethnicity, religion, or region. The pluralist model of democracy is one in which society is indeed divided into many different groups. A standard claim about a pluralistically based society is that it generates less income redistribution and smaller welfare states because the many different cleavages stop a broad coalition in favor of redistribution emerging. In consequence, for instance, pluralistic societies do not have strong socialist parties (Lipset and Marks 2000). If this is the case, then our theory suggests that such societies would be more likely to have consolidated democracy because elites would have little to fear from majority rule. This helps explain the longevity and stability of democracy in the United States, often thought to be the epitome of a pluralistic society.

8. Democracy in a Picture

The previous discussion illustrates the various empirical implications of our theory for the circumstances under which a society becomes and stays a democracy. To fix ideas, it is useful to use simple pictures to illustrate the circumstances under which different regimes arise. To map our comparative statics about inter-group inequality into the data, we do this in the context in which the elites are the rich and the citizens are the poor. Recall the four "paths" of political development that we sketched in Chapter 1. The first, the British path, was one of fully consolidated democracy. The second, the Argentine path, was that of unconsolidated democracy. The third path, that of Singapore, was persistent nondemocracy in which the political status quo can be sustained without serious repression. The fourth path, that of South Africa, was persistent nondemocracy with repression. The comparative statics of our theory allow us to depict these different outcomes in a picture.

In essence, the different political outcomes occur because these societies differ fundamentally in their underlying economic structures, and it is this that motivates the title of our book. In addition, we also emphasize differences in political institutions, to some extent historically determined, to some extent consciously chosen with the nature of the regime in mind. To keep the pictures simple, we assume that conditions are such that a revolution never occurs in equilibrium, and we also abstract from the use of concessions (e.g., they are always insufficiently credible to stop revolt) so that if revolution is a threat, a nondemocratic regime must choose between repression or conceding democracy.

Consider Figure 2.1, which captures the predictions of our theory for democratization. On the horizontal axis, we plot inequality, with moves from left to right corresponding to greater inequality. The origin represents a completely equal society. On the vertical axis, we plot the historically determined costs of repression that are exogenous, such as the extent to which repression destroys assets in society. We have divided the resulting square into different regions that represent how different structures lead to different paths of political development. When

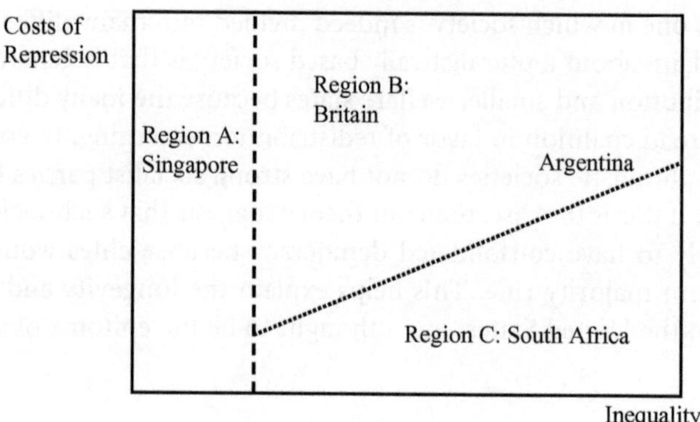

Figure 2.1. Democratization.

inequality is sufficiently low, the cost of repressing or mounting coups is irrelevant because the poor are sufficiently content under the political status quo not to rock the boat. This corresponds to Region A, where there is nondemocracy that remains unchallenged, and in it we place Singapore. In Region B, inequality is higher and revolution becomes a threat. However, the cost of repression is sufficiently high that democracy is created. In this region, we place both Britain and Argentina. Finally, in Region C, inequality is so high that revolution is a threat to nondemocracy but the cost of repression is sufficiently low that democracy can be avoided. This is the case of South Africa until 1994. The cost of repression in South Africa might have been lower because the disenfranchised groups were black Africans and Coloureds, and exclusion and repression were justified by an explicitly racial philosophy.

To study the consolidation of democracy, we must turn to Figure 2.2. Here, there are just two regions separated by an upward-sloping curve. When the cost of a coup is zero, the rich are always willing to undertake a coup. However, as the cost of a

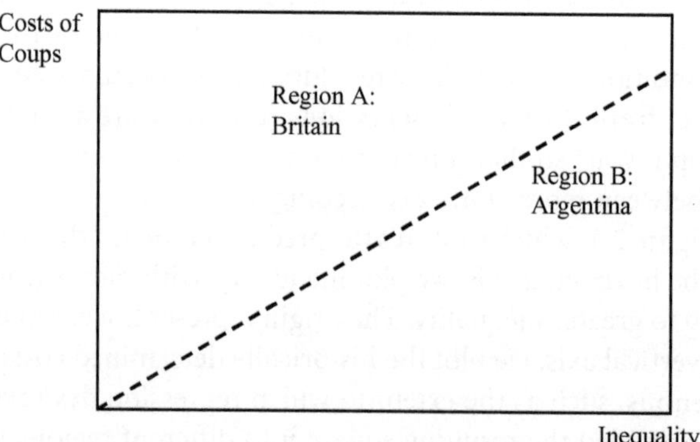

Figure 2.2. Democratic Consolidation.

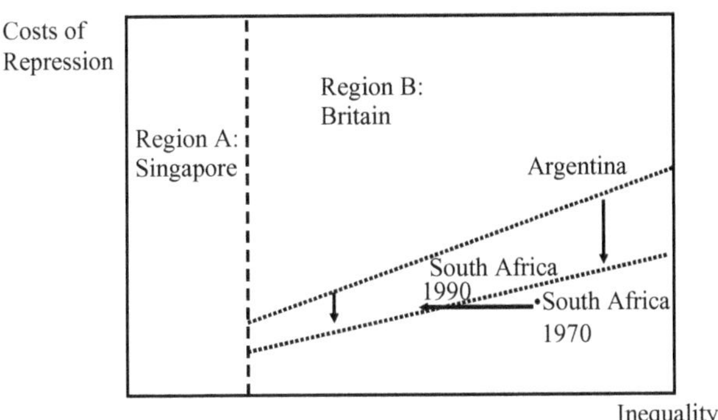

Figure 2.3. Democratization in South Africa.

coup rises, inequality must be sufficiently high (i.e., democracy must be sufficiently costly to the rich) for it to be worthwhile. Figure 2.3 has just two regions. We have placed Britain in Region A. Once created, democracy will consolidate if it is not too redistributive and if coups are sufficiently costly. However, when inequality is very high, the costs of a coup may be sufficiently low that it is attractive. This is the case in Region B, where democracy is unconsolidated; here, we have placed Argentina. Singapore is, of course, not in this picture because it has yet to make the transition to democracy.

These simple pictures also allow us to trace out the paths of political development of different countries. For example, we look at the history and future of democracy in South Africa in Figure 2.3. Why did South Africa finally move so belatedly to a democratic regime? The arrows in Figure 2.3 capture part of the story. From the mid-1970s onward, inequality fell in South Africa, making democracy less threatening for the white elite. At the same time, the industrial sector rose at the expense of the agricultural sector, and human and physical capital became more important. In terms of the picture, this means that at a given level of inequality, the elites are less willing to repress. This moves the boundary between Region C and Region B downward. Changes in the global environment, particularly globalization, also have the effect of moving the same boundary downward, implying that for fixed levels of inequality, the cost of repression had to be lower to justify the persistence of dictatorship. Thus, some time between 1970 and 1994, South Africa moved out of Region C into Region B, and democracy was created.

What does the future hold for South Africa? To see this, we must turn to Figure 2.4, which asks whether democracy will consolidate after apartheid. Because inequality is still very high, one might conjecture that South Africa would be in Region B and, therefore, an unconsolidated democracy. Nevertheless, the impact of development of the South African economy, increasing importance of physical and human capital, and increased globalization has the effect of moving the boundaries between Regions A and B down. Now, for a given cost of a

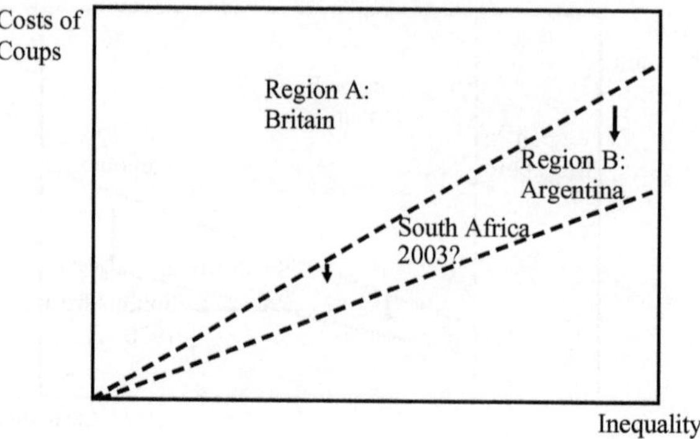

Figure 2.4. Democratic Consolidation in South Africa?

coup, inequality must be higher to justify mounting a coup against democracy. Moreover, as discussed in Chapter 1, the structure of political institutions after apartheid was designed specifically to protect the interests of the whites, a factor that again moves this line down. Thus, although one cannot be certain of the future (witness the evolution of democracy in Zimbabwe since 1980), one might hope that South Africa had transitioned into Region A rather than Region B.

Prediction in the case of Singapore seems much easier. Figures 2.1 and 2.2 suggest that if and when Singapore becomes a democracy, it is very likely to consolidate.

9. Overview of the Book

The remainder of our book develops the arguments outlined in this chapter. The remainder of this part continues to lay the scene. In Chapter 3, we survey the empirical evidence about cross-country patterns of democracy. We show that richer countries are more likely to be democratic, more educated countries are more likely to be democratic, and more unequal countries are generally less democratic. We emphasize the basic correlations in the data and do not take a strong view on causal relationships. Chapter 3 also discusses the large literature in political science and sociology on the creation and consolidation of democracy, and we explain how our research contributes to this work.

Part 2 surveys existing models of collective decision making in democracies and nondemocracies. In Chapter 4, we focus on democracies and provide a simple analysis of basic issues in the study of collective choice, electoral politics, and competition, which is useful in later parts of the book. We also introduce some basic models of two-group distributional conflict, paying special attention to the relationship between inequality and redistribution, the implications of different political identities, and the factors that determine the distribution of power in democracy. In Chapter 4, we also propose a reduced-form model of the distribution of power in a democracy. The appendix at the end of the book develops a series of models that provide microfoundations for this reduced form. In Chapter 5, we analyze nondemocracy with particular attention to the collective-action problem and the issue of commitment.

Part 3 provides our approach to democratization. In Chapter 6, we introduce our basic model of democratization. This chapter formalizes many of the issues already mentioned in this introductory chapter, giving us ways to think about the role of political power and the role of political institutions in allocating future political power. It illustrates how democratization creates a credible commitment to future redistribution by transferring political power to the majority in society. It also shows how democratization may be a response by the elite in the face of a credible threat of revolution by the majority. We see the possibility of an inverted U-shaped relationship between inter-group inequality and democracy in this chapter. Chapter 7 then develops our basic model of coups against democracy and studies the circumstances under which democracy, once created, consolidates.

Part 4 discusses a number of important extensions to this basic framework and some applications. In Chapter 8, we analyze how the presence of a large and affluent middle class affects the balance of the distributional conflict between the elites and the citizens in ways that can help create and consolidate democracy. Chapter 9 introduces factor endowments and markets to endogenize the distribution of income and discusses the impact of the structure of the economy on the creation and consolidation of democracy. In this chapter, we also conjecture about mechanisms that might account for political development – that is, the question of why and whether countries transition to democracy as they become richer, and the potential reasons for the relationship between income and democracy. Chapter 10 extends our model to allow for international trade and mobility of factors of production among countries and studies how globalization alters and adds to the results we have derived until this point.

Part 5 discusses the future of democracy and concludes the book.

3 What Do We Know about Democracy?

In this chapter, we provide an overview of previous research on democracy. We depict some of the most salient "stylized facts" about democracy that have been emphasized and much debated in the literature. Because a reevaluation of the existing empirical evidence is not our main focus, we present these patterns diagrammatically without using formal econometric techniques. Although these patterns may not correspond to causal relationships, they are still informative about the correlates of democracy in the data, thus potentially informative about the type of models we should develop. In the final two sections we discuss the existing approaches to democracy and explain how our approach differs from and contributes to the existing literature.

1. Measuring Democracy

The first challenge facing a quantitative analysis of the patterns of democracy is to develop reliable and informative measures. There has been much controversy over this issue in political science, mostly because there is disagreement about what actually constitutes a democracy. Many scholars, however, accept the definition proposed by Schumpeter (1942), who argued that democracy was

> . . . the institutional arrangement for arriving at political decisions in which individuals acquire the power to decide by means of a competitive struggle for the people's vote. (p. 250)

In practice, then, democracy is associated with a particular set of institutions, such as free and fair elections, the accountability of politicians to the electorate, and free entry into politics. Even accepting a Schumpeterian definition, countries differ as to the extent to which any of the institutional conditions are satisfied. This suggests to most scholars the need to make a finer distinction than simply between a democracy and a nondemocracy.

Our first and main measure of democracy is the Freedom House political rights index, which has been used by many other scholars in quantitative work on democracy (e.g., Barro 1997, 1999). This index ranges from 1 to 7, with 7 representing the least political freedom and 1 the most freedom. A country gets a score of 1 if political rights come closest to the ideals suggested by a checklist of questions, beginning with whether there are free and fair elections, whether those who are elected rule, whether there are competitive parties or other political groupings, whether the opposition plays an important role and has actual power, and whether minority groups have reasonable self-government or can participate in the government through informal consensus. The main checklist includes three questions on the electoral process, four questions on the extent of political pluralism and participation, and three questions on the functioning of government. For each checklist question, 0 to 4 points are added, depending on the comparative rights and liberties present (0 represents the least, 4 represents the most). These scores are totaled and used to determine where a country resides on the 1 to 7 scale.[1] Following Barro (1999), we supplement this index with the related variable from Bollen (1990, 2001) for 1960 and 1965, and we transform both indexes so that they lie between 0 and 1, with 1 corresponding to the most democratic set of institutions.

The Freedom House index, even when augmented with Bollen's data, enables us to look only at the postwar era. The Polity IV dataset, on the other hand, provides information for all countries since independence starting in 1800. To look at pre-1960 events and to check on our main measure, therefore we also look at the other widely used measure of democracy: the composite Polity index, which is the difference between the Polity's democracy and autocracy indexes.[2] The Polity democracy index ranges from 0 to 10 and is derived from coding the competitiveness of political participation, the openness and competitiveness of executive recruitment, and the constraints on the chief executive. For instance, constraints on the executive is coded on a 7-point scale running from "unlimited authority" where "there are no regular limitations on the executive's actions (as distinct from irregular actions such as the threat or actuality of coups and assassinations)," to "executive parity or subordination" where "accountability groups have effective authority equal to or greater than the executive in most areas of activity." A country would receive the lowest score for constraint on the executive if "constitutional restrictions on executive action are ignored" or "there is no legislative assembly or there is one but it is called or dismissed at the executive's pleasure." A country would receive the highest score, on the other hand, if "a legislature, ruling party or council of nobles initiates much or most important legislation" or "the executive is chosen by the accountability group and is dependent on its continued support to remain in office." The Polity autocracy index also ranges from 0 to 10 and is constructed in a similar way to the democracy score based on scoring countries

[1] See Freedom House (2004) and http://www.freedomhouse.org/research/freeworld/2003/methodology.htm.

[2] See Marshall and Jaggers (2004) and http://www.cidcm.umd.edu/inscr/polity/.

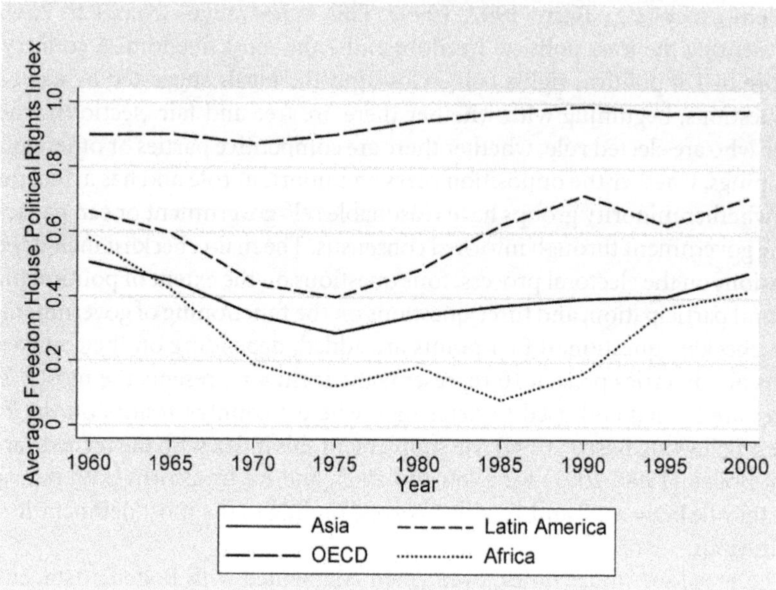

Figure 3.1. Evolution of Democracy 1960–2000.

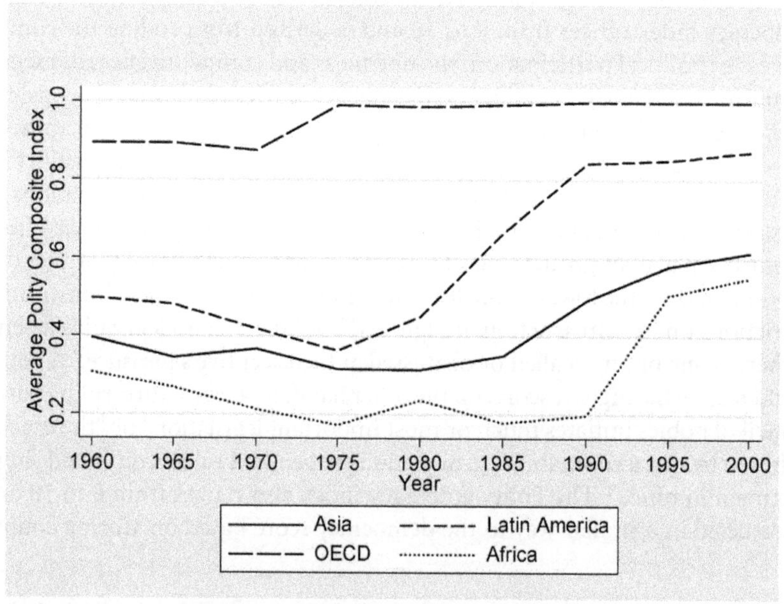

Figure 3.2. Evolution of Democracy 1960–2000.

according to the competitiveness of political participation, the regulation of participation, the openness and competitiveness of executive recruitment, and the constraints on the chief executive. To facilitate comparison with the Freedom House score, we also normalize the composite Polity index to lie between 0 and 1.

Both of these measures enable us to distinguish between different shades of democracy. An alternative empirical approach has been defended and used by Przeworski and his coauthors (Przeworski, Alvarez, Cheibub, and Limongi 2000, Chapter 1), who argue that a simple dichotomy between democracy and nondemocracy is the most useful empirical definition. In addition to the dichotomous classification, these authors add other provisos to the definition of a democracy, most important that a country cannot be democratic unless a political party has been observed to lose power. Hence, according to Przeworski et al. (2000), Botswana has never been a democracy because, even though all agree that elections are free and fair, that there is free entry into politics, and that the government is accountable to the people, the Botswana Democratic Party has won every election since independence in 1966. Japan would not have been a democracy for most of the post–Second World War period until the Liberal Democratic Party lost power, and South Africa today is not counted as a democracy because the ANC has formed the government since the end of apartheid.

Although there is a lively debate among political-science scholars about the virtues of continuous versus dichotomous measures, none of the patterns discussed here depend on this choice. Our preference is for more fine grained measures, although dichotomous measures also have advantages. For example, they enable a clearer discussion of transitions from and to democracy; in the following section, we use the dichotomous measures developed by Przeworski et al. (2000) and augmented by Boix and Rosato (2001) to discuss transitions to and from democracy.

2. Patterns of Democracy

Figures 3.1, 3.2 and 3.3 plot the values of the normalized Freedom House, Polity scores, and the augmented Przeworski et al. (2000) index, respectively, for our basic 1960–2000 sample. These figures show that Organization for Economic Cooperation and Development (OECD) countries entered the period almost fully democratic and stayed there. In contrast, democracy declined in other parts of the world, particularly in Latin America and Africa, although from the mid-1970s onward, we can detect what Huntington (1991) calls the "third wave" of democratization. Figure 3.4 uses the Polity data back to 1840 for all the countries that were independent during this period. This picture vividly displays the onward march of democracy in the OECD in the period leading up to the First World War and shows evidence of the "first and second waves of democracy," the first before the First World War and the second after the Second World War.

Figures 3.5 and 3.6 show the most famous correlation about democracy, first investigated by Lipset (1959): rich countries tend to be more democratic.

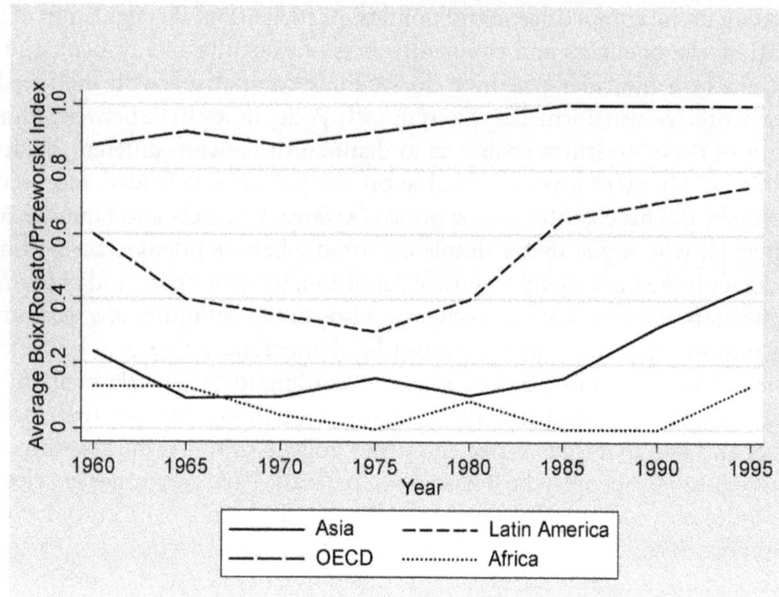

Figure 3.3. Evolution of Democracy 1960–1995.

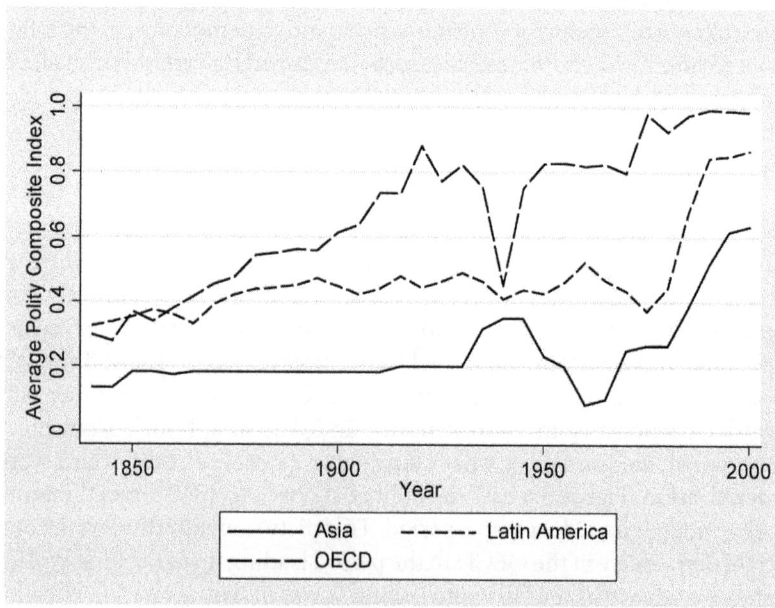

Figure 3.4. Evolution of Democracy 1840–2000.

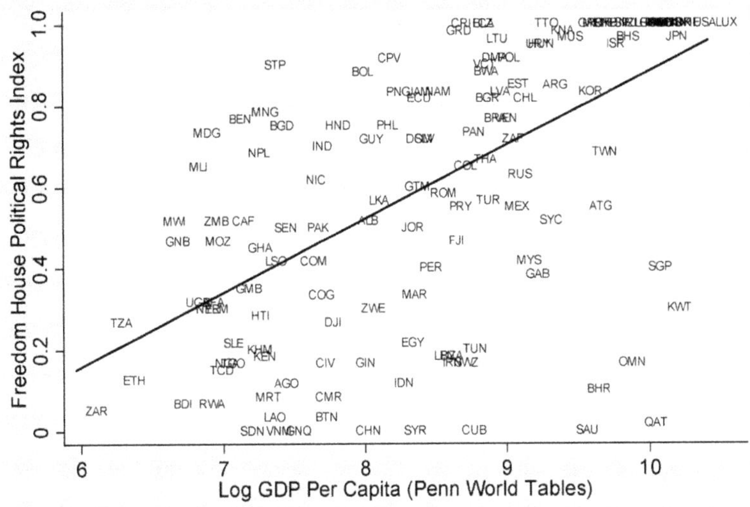

Figure 3.5. Democracy and Income 1990s.

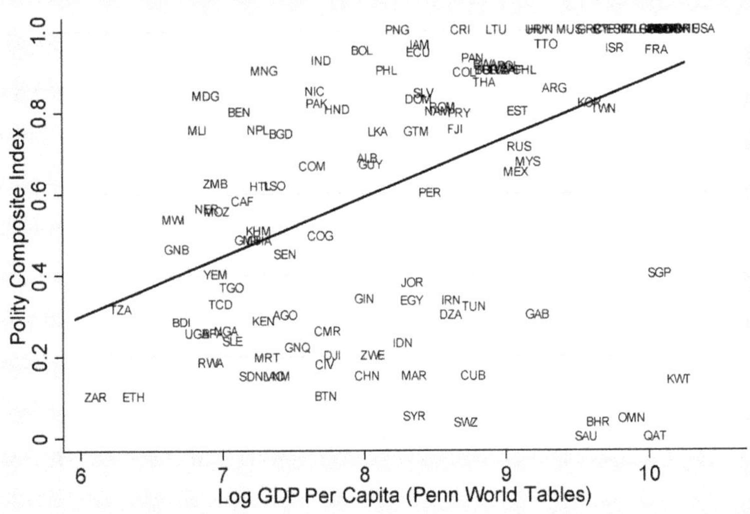

Figure 3.6. Democracy and Income 1990s.

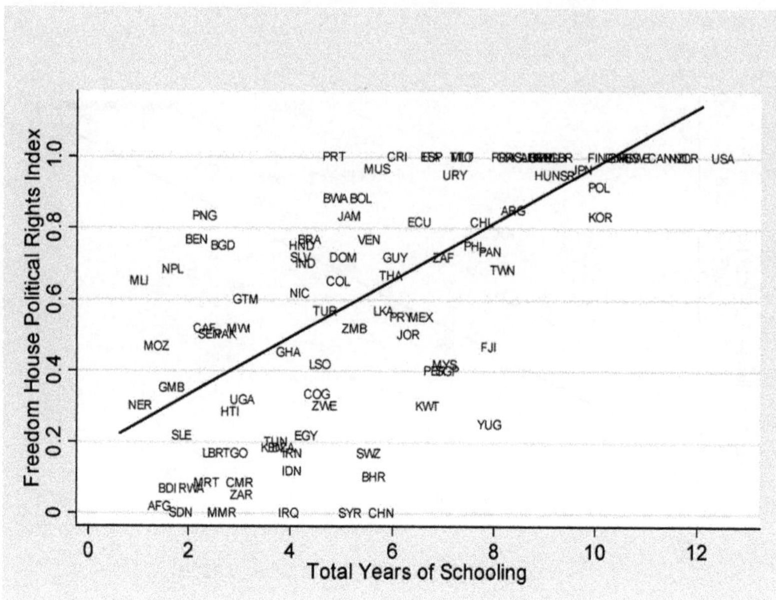

Figure 3.7. Democracy and Education 1990s.

Figure 3.5 shows this by plotting the average Freedom House index during the 1990s versus the average log gross domestic product (GDP) (income) per capita during the 1990s (in purchasing-power party terms, calculated from the latest version of the Summers–Heston data set; Heston, Summers, and Atten 2002). Figure 3.6 does the same using the average Polity score during the 1990s. Both figures show a strong positive relationship between income and democracy. The richer countries, such as the United States, Canada, Australia, New Zealand, and those in the European Union, are all democratic, whereas the poor countries in sub-Saharan Africa, South Asia, and Central America are less democratic.

Figures 3.7 and 3.8 show another well-known correlation: more educated countries (i.e., those with higher levels of average years of schooling as reported in the data set by Barro and Lee 2000) also tend to be more democratic.

Both of these patterns have been influential in the thinking of scholars working on democracy. In particular, the positive association between income and democracy (and, to a lesser extent, between education and democracy) has been the cornerstone of the famous modernization theory advocated by Lipset (1959) and many others since. Building on the insights of the modernization theory, many scholars today believe that democracy is only possible in sufficiently educated and rich societies. Furthermore, a common view both in the literature and the popular press is that an increase in economic prosperity and the level of education will naturally bring a process of democratization. Although influential, these views suffer from a lack of a well-articulated theory explaining when and how democracies

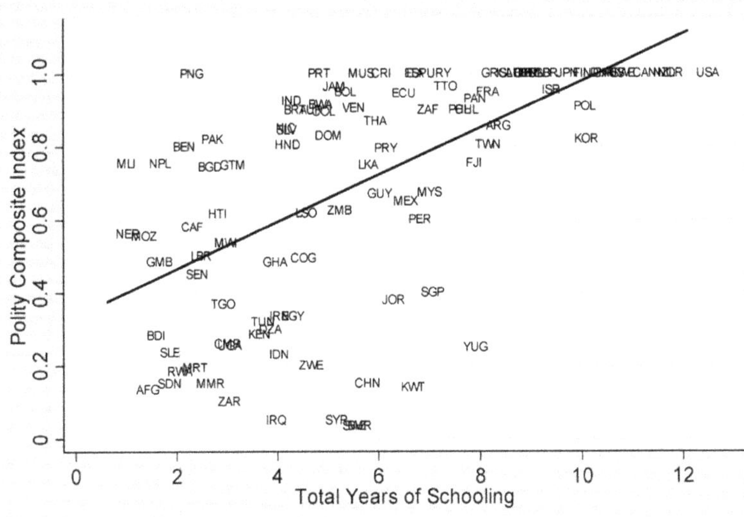

Figure 3.8. Democracy and Education 1990s.

emerge and consolidate. The purpose of this book is to develop such a theory and use it to understand, among other things, the potential links between economic prosperity and democracy.

Another pattern in the data is emphasized by Przeworski et al. (2000). These authors argue and document that the positive association between income and democracy is largely driven by the tendency of rich countries to remain democratic, whereas poor countries have a greater tendency to experience decline in their democracy score (i.e., suffer coups and other actions against democracy). Figures 3.9 and 3.10 illustrate this tendency using the Przeworski et al. (2000) data. Figure 3.9 is a histogram of the fraction of countries of different income levels that start as nondemocracy and transition to democracy. The sample includes countries that were nondemocratic in 1965, 1970, 1975, 1980, 1985, and 1990, and measures democratizations in each case during the next five years. Countries are placed in income quintiles constructed according to the average world income distribution between 1965 and 1990. This figure shows that countries in the top two quintiles have a greater tendency to transition to democracy; however, there is no monotonic relationship between income and the fraction of nondemocracies that transition to democracy. Figure 3.10 is constructed analogously but for transitions from democracy to nondemocracy, rather than the reverse. There is a more striking relationship between transitions and income quintiles. Although countries at the bottom two quintiles face a high likelihood of transitioning into nondemocracy in any five-year period, this probability is much lower for those in the third quintile,

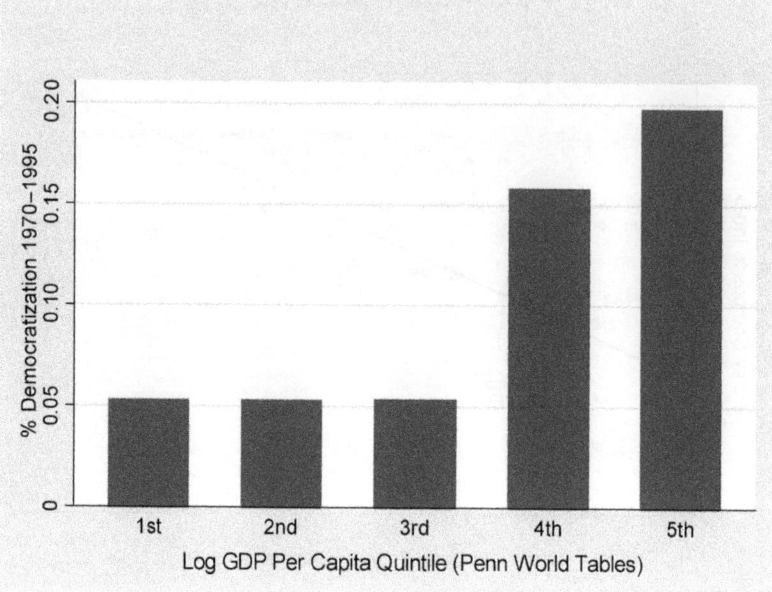

Figure 3.9. Transitions to Democracy and Income 1970–1995.

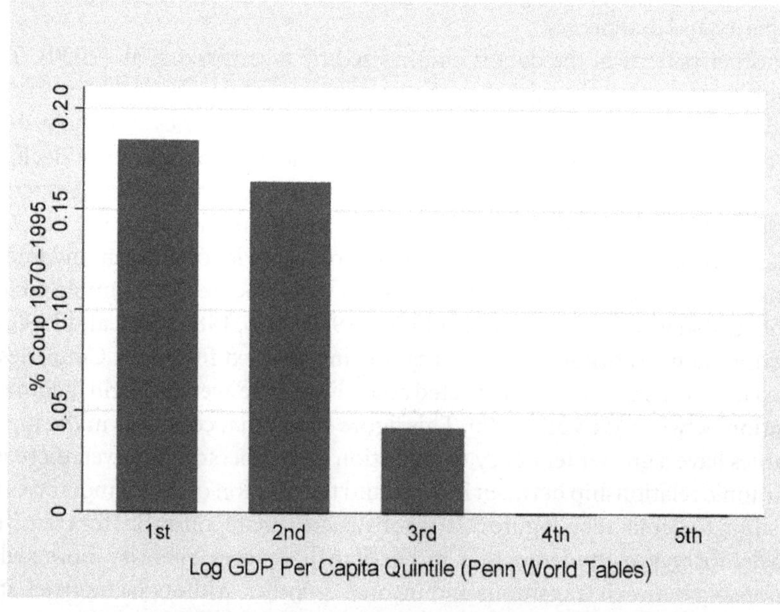

Figure 3.10. Transitions to Nondemocracy and Income 1970–1995.

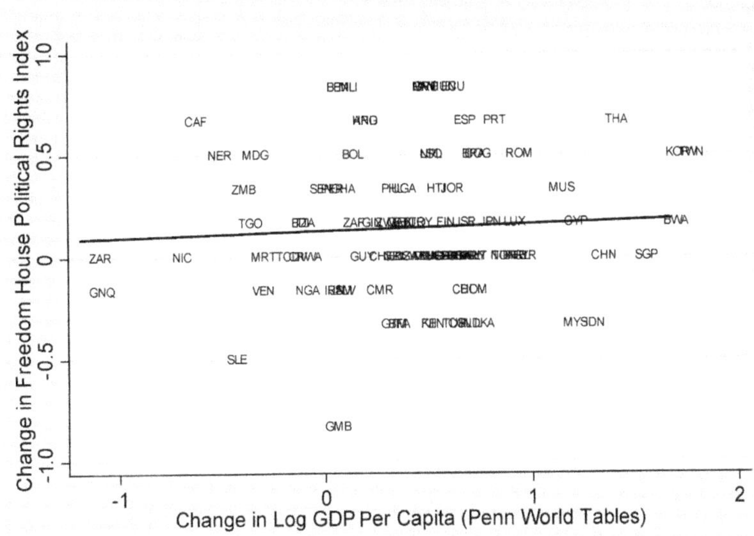

Figure 3.11. Democracy Growth and Income Growth 1970–1995.

and zero for those in the top two quintiles. These histograms make it clear that whereas the likelihood of transitioning to democracy is weakly correlated with income, there is a big difference between the fraction of rich and relatively poor democracies falling back to nondemocracy.

Although this is not the correct forum for reevaluating the existing empirical evidence, we emphasize that the patterns shown in Figures 3.5 through 3.10 do not correspond to causal effects of income and education on democracy and democratic transitions. More explicitly, these correlations do not establish that as a country becomes richer, it will necessarily tend to become more democratic. The major problem with a causal interpretation of these patterns is that countries that differ in income levels (or levels of educational attainment) also differ in histories and other institutional characteristics. Our recent work (Acemoglu, Johnson, Robinson, and Yared 2004) investigates this issue in detail and establishes that there is little causal effect of income (or education) on democracy or democratic transitions. Instead, other historical factors seem to determine both the economic and political development paths of various societies, leading to the types of correlations shown in Figures 3.5 through 3.10.

It is sufficient to give a glimpse of this pattern by showing how changes in income are related to changes in democracy during the period covered by Figures 3.5 through 3.10. This is shown in Figures 3.11 and 3.12 for the Freedom House and Polity indexes. In both figures, the horizontal axis shows the change in log GDP per capita between 1970 and 1995, and the vertical axis shows the change in

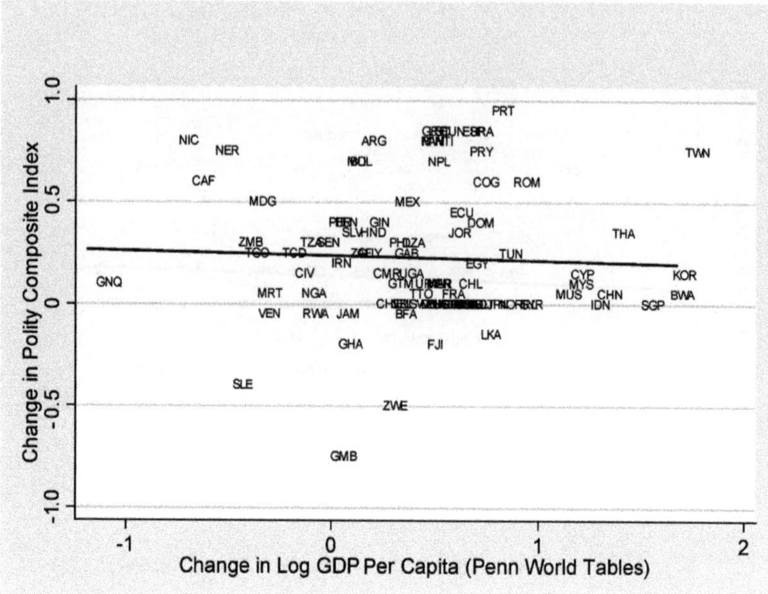

Figure 3.12. Democracy Growth and Income Growth 1970–1995.

the democracy score between the same dates (for the Freedom House and Polity indexes, respectively). This way of looking at the data is useful because it differences out potentially fixed characteristics that are simultaneously affecting income and democracy (thus bringing us closer to the causal relationship between income and democracy). Both figures show a clear pattern: there is no relationship between changes in income per capita and changes in democracy. In other words, although richer countries are more democratic, there is no evidence that countries that grow faster than others tend to become more democratic, at least over this period. A natural interpretation of the patterns shown in Figures 3.5 and 3.6 in light of these results is that they are largely driven by some fixed country characteristics. Consequently, conditional on these characteristics, countries that have grown faster during the past twenty-five to thirty years have not become more democratic.

Overall, a salient pattern in the data is the positive correlation between income and democracy, but this does not necessarily correspond to the causal effect of income on democracy. Therefore, part of the challenge to models of democracy and democratization is to understand how the world might have this positive correlation without a large causal effect. We return to this issue in Chapter 9.

3. Democracy, Inequality, and Redistribution

As discussed in Chapter 2, our approach to democracy emphasizes the role of social conflict, especially between different groups. One implication of this approach is that inter-group inequality should have an effect on the equilibrium

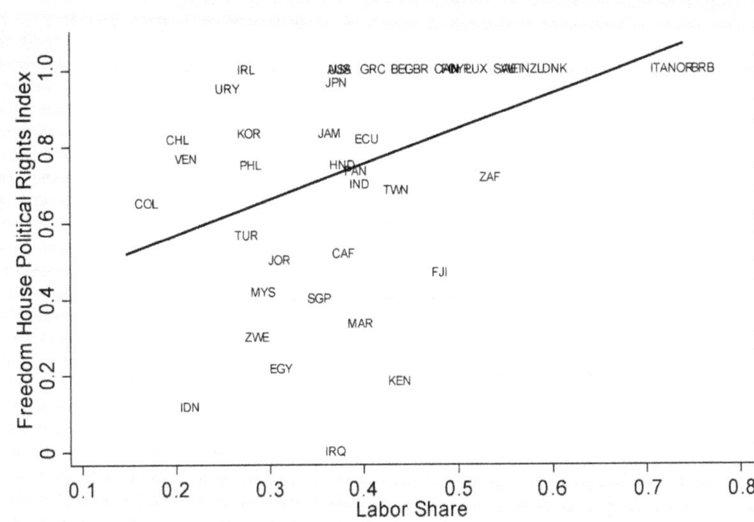

Figure 3.13. Democracy and Inequality 1990s.

of political institutions and thus on the likelihood that a society ends up as a democracy. The problem, however, is that the relevant notion of inter-group inequality is often difficult to measure (e.g., when it is between two different ethnic groups). Nevertheless, when the major conflict is between the rich and the poor, one variable that captures inter-group inequality is the share of labor income in GDP. The reasoning here is that, whereas the poorer segments of society obtain most of their income from labor, capital income (and sometimes land income) accrues largely to a smaller rich elite. Therefore, a high labor share corresponds to a low level of inter-group inequality when conflict is between rich and poor.

Figures 3.13 and 3.14 show the relationship between the labor share in the 1990s and the relevant democracy indexes. The labor share data is from the United Nations, is also used by Rodrik (1999), and covers only the manufacturing sector, so it may be less than fully representative for the entire economy. Both figures show a positive association between the labor share and democracy.

Figures 3.15 and 3.16 show the relationship between democracy and another measure of inequality: the Gini coefficient, which is the most common index of inequality in the literature and has a greater coverage of the various sectors of the economy than the labor share from the manufacturing sector (see Dollar and Kraay 2002 for more on these data). A higher value of the Gini coefficient corresponds to greater inequality. The relationship is similar to the one with the labor share, although less pronounced with the Polity data: countries that are more unequal and, consequently, have higher Gini coefficients tend to be less democratic.

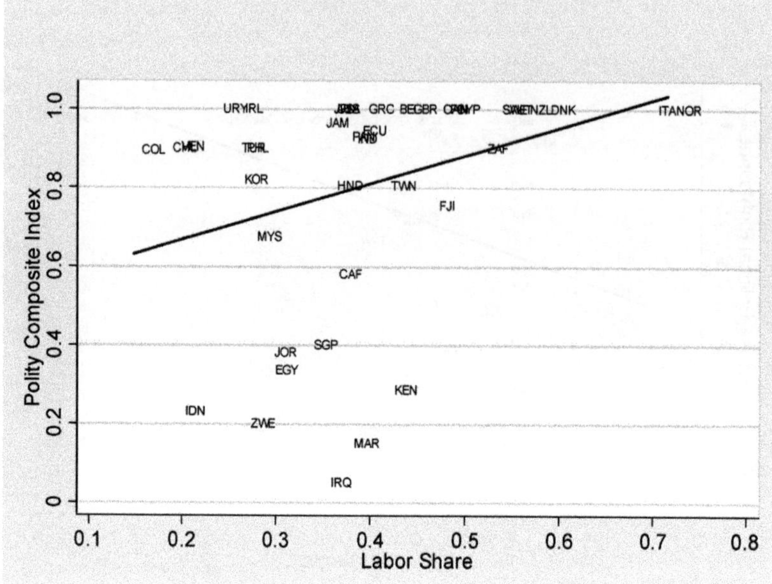

Figure 3.14. Democracy and Ineqeality 1990s.

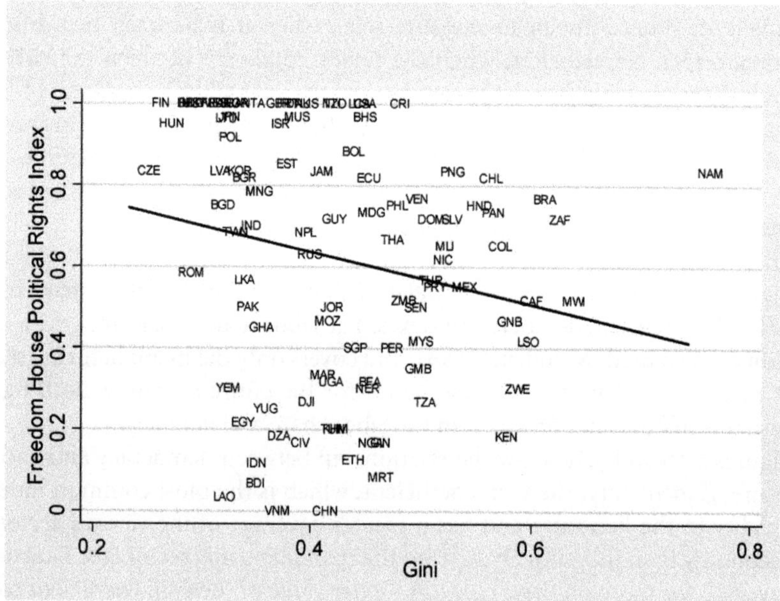

Figure 3.15. Democracy and Inequality 1990s.

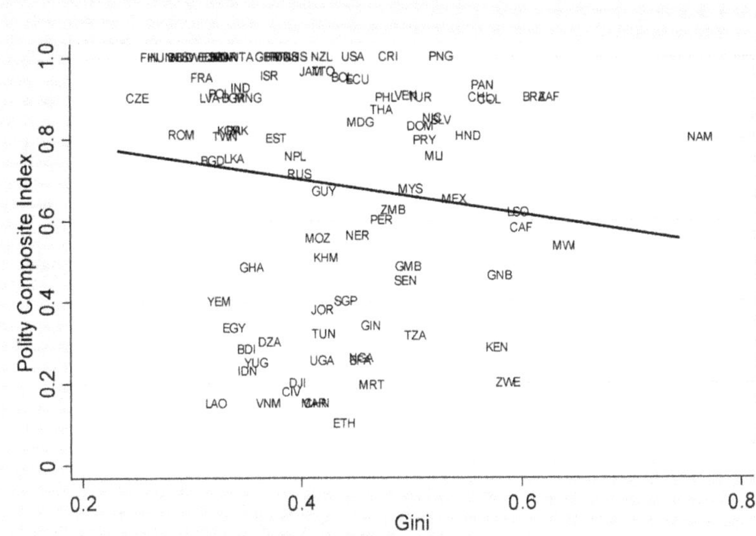

Figure 3.16. Democracy and Inequality 1990s.

As emphasized in the context of the relationship between income and democracy, these correlations do not correspond to the causal effect of labor share or inter-group inequality on democracy. Moreover, these correlations are not always robust to the inclusion of other variables in a regression model, and a relatively large literature has not reached a consensus on the relationship between inequality and democracy. Whereas the claim that democracy is not possible in highly unequal societies is common in the nonquantitative literature (e.g., Dahl 1971; Huntington 1991; and the review in Bollen and Jackman 1985), the empirical evidence is more mixed. Using cross-sectional econometrics, Bollen and Jackman (1985) found no relationship between measures of inequality and democracy. Muller (1988, 1995) presented empirical evidence suggesting that higher inequality made dictatorships more stable and reduced the propensity of a society to democratize, although his results were criticized for being nonrobust by Bollen and Jackman (1995). More recently, Przeworski et al. (2000) investigated the effects of three measures of inequality on transitions to and from democracy using probit analysis. The measures they used were the Gini coefficient, the ratio between the share of total income going to the richest 10 percent of the population and the share going to the poorest 10 percent (the higher this ratio is, the greater is the inequality), and the share of income produced by manufacturing that accrues to workers. They found no relationship between democratization and either of the first two measures of inequality, noting that (p. 120) "the durability of dictatorships is unaffected by income distribution." However, for the third measure, they

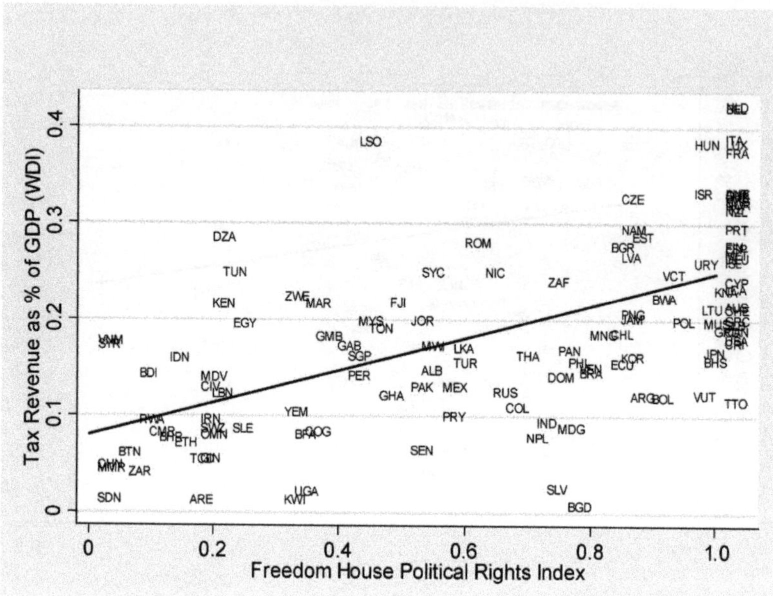

Figure 3.17. Democracy and Tax Revenue 1990s.

found (p. 122) "dictatorships ... are much more vulnerable when the functional distribution of income is more unequal." They also found that (p. 122) "democracies are less stable in societies that are more unequal to begin with, in societies in which household income inequality increases [when inequality is measured by the Gini coefficient or the ratio of top to bottom income shares], and in societies in which labor receives a lower share of value added in manufacturing." Using a similar methodological approach, Boix (2003) reports results in which higher inequality reduces the propensity of a society to democratize.

Other scholars have examined the relationship among inequality, revolution, and political instability, which is also relevant to our approach. Here again, the findings are mixed, although Muller and Seligson (1987) and Alesina and Perotti (1996) found that greater inequality leads to greater political instability (see Lichbach 1989 for a review of this literature).

The existing empirical literature is, therefore, rather contradictory and, more important, as already emphasized, focuses on correlations, not causal relationships. The correlations shown in Figures 3.13 through 3.16 are nonetheless informative. They suggest, for example, that models in which democracies are more redistributive and hence have a higher labor share, as well as models in which democracies can survive better in less unequal societies, can do a reasonable job of matching this pattern in the data.

Figures 3.17 and 3.18 further suggest that at least part of the positive correlation among democracy and labor income and the Gini coefficient might be due to the

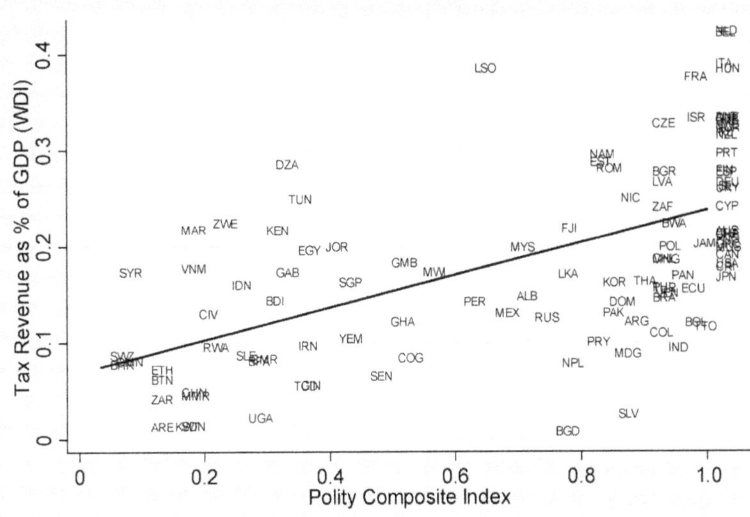

Figure 3.18. Democracy and Tax Revenue 1990s.

greater tendency for redistributive policies in democracies. These figures show a positive association between the share of tax revenues in GDP and the democracy scores during the 1990s. Again, this is a correlation and should not be interpreted as a causal relationship.[3]

The historical evidence is also consistent with the notion that the patterns of redistribution change after democratization. Here, we briefly discuss some of the evidence; the reader is referred to Lindert (2004), for a more detailed and satisfactory discussion of the European experience. Although Figures 3.17 and 3.18 emphasize the association between democracy and fiscal redistribution, in practice, many other instruments – ranging from labor-market policies to educational policies – appear to be important in governments' attempts to influence the distribution of income in society (DiNardo, Fortin, and Lemieux 1996; Wallerstein 1999).

In Britain, the Reform Acts of 1867–84 were a turning point in the history of the British state. In 1871, Gladstone reformed the civil service, opening it to public examination and thus making it meritocratic. Liberal and Conservative governments introduced a considerable amount of labor-market legislation, fundamentally changing the nature of industrial relations in favor of workers. From

[3] See Mulligan, Sala-i-Martin, and Gil (2003) for the argument that democracies do not redistribute more. See Rodrik (1999) for the original analysis of the link between democracy and labor share. For more details on the relationship between democracy and inequality, see Li, Squire, and Zou (1998). See also Persson and Tabellini (2003) and Persson (2003) on different policies pursued by democracies and different forms of democracies.

1906 to 1914, the Liberal Party, under the leadership of Asquith and Lloyd George, introduced the modern redistributive state to Britain, including health and unemployment insurance, government-financed pensions, minimum wages, and a commitment to redistributive taxation. As a result of the fiscal changes, taxes as a proportion of GNP more than doubled in the thirty years following 1870, and then doubled again in the subsequent thirty years. In the meantime, the progressivity of the tax system also increased (Lindert 2004).

Meanwhile, the educational system, which was either primarily for the elite or run by religious denominations during most of the nineteenth century, was opened up to the masses; the Education Act of 1870 committed the government to the systematic provision of universal education for the first time which was made free in 1891. The school-leaving age was set at eleven in 1893 and increased to twelve in 1899; special provisions for children of needy families were introduced (Mitch 1993). As a result of these changes, the proportion of ten-year-olds enrolled in school that stood at a disappointing 40 percent in 1870 increased to 100 percent in 1900 (Ringer 1979, p. 207). Finally, a reform act of 1902 led to a large expansion in the resources for schools and introduced the grammar schools that subsequently became the foundation of secondary education in Britain.

In France, the situation was similar. During the Second Empire, there was a significant expansion of government support for education; illiteracy fell from 39 to 29 percent of adults, and the primary-school enrollment rate increased from 51 to 68 percent (Plessis 1985, Table 14, p. 100). In 1881, the government abolished fees in public primary schools and, in 1882, it introduced seven years of compulsory education for children. The primary-school enrollment rate increased from 66 percent in 1863 to 82 percent in 1886. The "liberal" phase of the Second Empire saw significant labor-market legislation with strikes legalized in 1863, and unions were finally officially tolerated in 1868. Moreover, central-government expenditure as a percentage of GDP increased by one third from 9.4 percent in 1872 (a figure inflated by the Franco-Prussian War of 1870) to 12.4 percent in 1880 (Flora 1983).

In Germany, a large increase in redistribution in the 1920s was initiated by the Weimar state (Flora 1983). Also, in Sweden, major redistribution appears to have started only after democratization. Lindert's (1994) data show that before 1920, there was no redistribution in Sweden; after this date, it increased sharply. More generally, Lindert (2000b) shows that there is a strong historic relationship between democratization and educational expansion in Western Europe.

Overall, we can summarize our discussion, especially the relationship between democratization and educational reforms, by quoting Easterlin (1981, p. 14):

> . . . to judge from the historical experience of the world's 25 largest nations, the establishment and expansion of formal schooling has depended in large part on political conditions and ideological influences and a major commitment to mass education is frequently symptomatic of a major shift in political power and associated ideology in a direction conducive to greater upward mobility for a wider segment of the population.

4. Crises and Democracy

An important element of our theory of democratization, as discussed in Chapter 2, is that transitions to democracy (and, similarly, transitions away from democracy) are more likely to occur amid economic and political crises, when there is a transitory shift in political power. The reason goes to the heart of our framework: changes in political institutions take place as a way of turning transitory de facto political power into more durable de jure political power. This reasoning suggests that we may expect a correlation between severe crises and transitions to and from democracy.

Haggard and Kaufman (1995), in particular, emphasized that both democracies and nondemocratic regimes are destabilized by economic and political crises. They argue, for example, that "in Argentina, Bolivia, Brazil, Peru, Uruguay and the Philippines, democratic transitions occurred in the context of severe economic difficulties that contributed to opposition movements" (p. 45). Przeworski et al. (1996, p. 42), on the other hand, point out that: "the fragility of democracy . . . flows largely from its vulnerability in the face of economic crises." Przeworski et al. (2000, pp. 109–10) find that "most deaths of democracy are accompanied by some economic crisis; in twenty-eight out of thirty-nine instances, deaths of democracies were accompanied by a fall in income during at least one of the two preceding years." (See also Londregan and Poole 1990, 1996; and Gasiorowski 1995 on the relationship between crises and coups.) Our historical discussion in Chapter 1 and the following section also illustrates that many of the key transitions to democracy during both the nineteenth and twentieth centuries have happened in periods of unusual social unrest and turbulence. Here, we show some additional evidence consistent with this pattern.

Figures 3.19 and 3.20 show the likelihood of a democracy-to-nondemocracy transition and the likelihood of a nondemocracy-to-democracy transition They are constructed in a manner similar to Figures 3.9 and 3.10. The first figure comprises countries that were not democratic in 1970, 1975, 1980, 1985, 1990, and 1995 and separates them according to whether they had an economic crises in the preceding five years. An economic crisis is defined as an annual growth rate of GDP per capita less than −5 percent in any one of the preceding five years. The figure then shows the fraction of nondemocracies with and without economic crisis that have transitioned to democracy. Figure 3.20 performs the same exercise for transitions from democracy to nondemocracy. Both figures show that economic crises make transitions more likely. Overall, we interpret this pattern as supportive of the notion that regime transitions are more likely during times of crisis or turbulence.

5. Social Unrest and Democratization

Our approach to democratization, in fact, stresses not only the role of crises but also the importance of social unrest, the threat of revolution, and generally the de

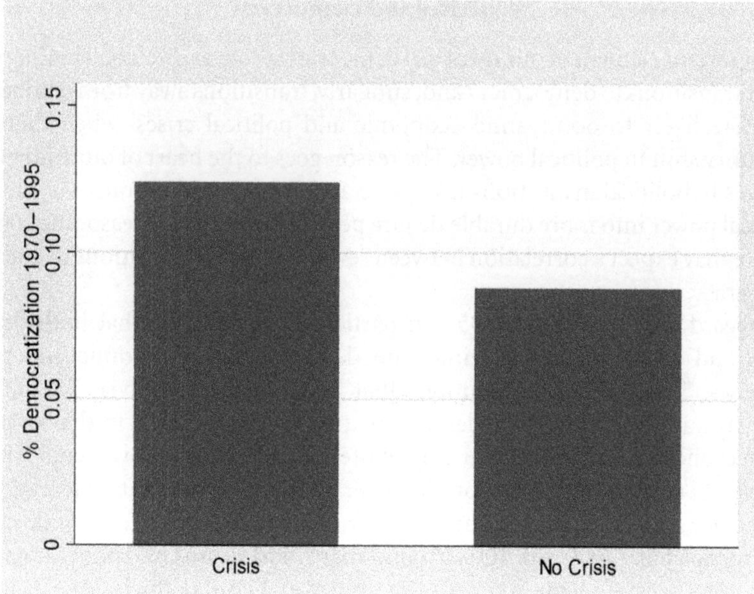

Figure 3.19. Transitions to Democracy and Crises 1970–1995.

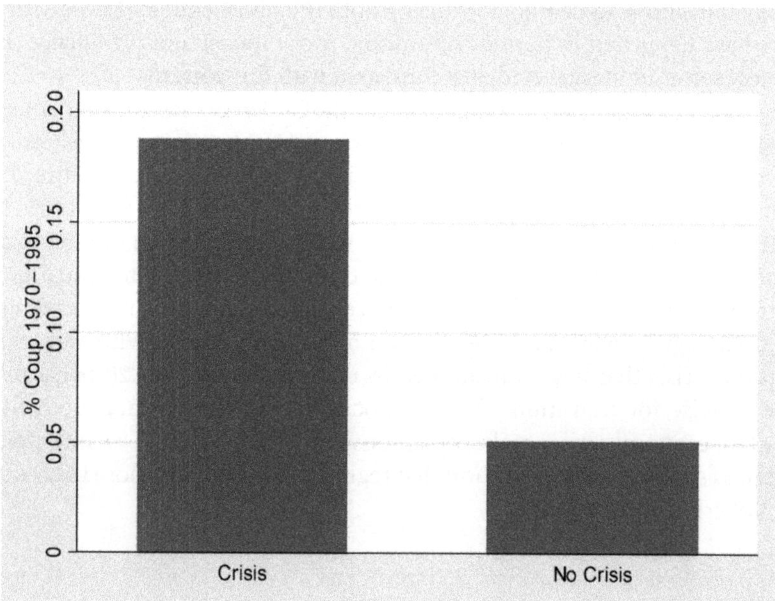

Figure 3.20. Transitions to Nondemocracy and Crises 1970–1995.

facto power of those without de jure political power in inducing a transition to democracy. In this section, we return to the historical discussion of the emergence of democracy in nineteenth-century Europe and twentieth-century America to discuss this issue (see Therborn 1977; Rueschemeyer, Stephens, and Stephens 1992; and Collier 1999 for overviews).

5.1 Democratizations in Nineteenth-Century Europe

In France, although democracy had flourished briefly after the revolution, it was quickly ended by the rise of the Jacobins and then Napoleon. After the fall of Napoleon, the absolutist monarchy was restored. Absolutism began to weaken after the 1830 revolution, which led to a highly restricted democratic regime in which property restrictions limited the electorate to about 0.75 percent of the population (Cole and Campbell 1989). The collapse of the Orleanist monarchy in the 1848 revolution led to the Second Republic, with the introduction of universal male suffrage in 1849 (Collier 1999, pp. 41–2). The effect of this was cut short, however, first by restrictions on voting rights introduced in 1850, disenfranchising 2.8 million men, and then by the coup of Louis Napoleon in 1851. Historians split this subsequent period into two phases: the "authoritarian" phase from 1852 to 1860 and the "liberal" phase from 1860 until the defeat of the French armies in the Franco-Prussian War of 1870. The defeat in the war led to further unrest (in particular, the Paris Commune) and to the collapse of the regime, making way for the Third Republic (Zeldin 1958; Plessis 1985; Price 1997). Finally, 1877, democracy with complete male suffrage was established, although other reforms, such as the secret ballot, were only introduced later in 1912 (Kreuzer 1996).

The history of modern democracy in Germany starts with the 1848 revolution, when nearly all German states significantly increased popular participation in government, again in the face of revolutionary pressures (Blackbourn 1998, Chapter 3). The effects of this democratization were strongly mitigated by institutional restrictions, however. This regime featured a three-class voting system and was controlled initially by Junker landlords, followed in the 1870s by the coalition of "iron and rye"; the Parliament could not appoint ministers or discuss foreign policy, and voting was oral. Although after 1870 all adult males over the age of twenty-five had the right to vote, voting was controlled in rural areas by the landlords (Gosnell 1930; Goldstein 1983). As Abrams (1995, p. 10) stated during this period "the German Empire was, in theory, a constitutional monarchy, yet in practice it was governed by a Prussian oligarchy." The final emergence of German democracy, the Weimar Republic in 1919, was in response to the severe threat of social disorder and revolution triggered by the collapse of the German armies on the Western Front in August 1918 (e.g., see the classic accounts in Gerschenkron 1943 and Mommsen 1981).

In Sweden, democracy arrived via a series of gradual franchise extensions, starting in 1866 with the creation of a bicameral parliament with First and Second Chambers. Universal male suffrage was introduced in 1909 in the First Chamber; however, true parliamentary government arrived only in 1918, when the political power of the Conservative Party and the monarchy were limited – once again, an outcome of unusual turbulence spurred by the end of the First World War and the severe economic crisis (Verney 1957). Tilton (1974) argues that

> . . . neither [of the first two reform acts] passed without strong popular pressure; in 1866 crowds thronged around the chamber while the final vote was taken, and the 1909 reform was stimulated by a broad suffrage movement [and] a demonstration strike. (p. 567)

The reform in 1909 had been preceded by strikes and demonstrations and, even though Sweden was not a participant in the First World War, the revolution in Russia and the situation in Germany forced the concession of democratic rights. In 1917, the Liberals and Social Democrats formed a coalition government and proposed full male suffrage, which was defeated by the Conservative-dominated Second Chamber. Collier (1999) explains that

> . . . it was only after the economic crisis of 1918 and ensuing worker protests for democracy led by the Social Democrats that the Reform Act was passed. Indeed, in November 1918, labor protests reached such a point as to be perceived as a revolutionary threat by Sweden's Conservative party and upper classes. (p. 83)

In all of these cases, the driving force behind political liberalization and the introduction of democratic measures is the threat of social disorder and, ultimately, revolution. Disorder was heightened by wars and other shocks to the social order.

5.2 Why in the Nineteenth Century?

Our approach so far explains the emergence of democracy but, in the European context, it does not answer the question of why the wave of democratizations started in the nineteenth century. The notion that democracy was a feasible set of political institutions goes back to ancient Greece and Rome and, at least by the seventeenth century in England, particularly during the Civil War, there were consistent demands for universal suffrage. A possible explanation for this emerges toward the end of the book, but even at this stage, it is worthwhile to see if the available evidence is consistent with the comparative statics we have already derived.

Before the nineteenth century, the disenfranchised segments of society were scattered in rural areas; therefore, we may think of the threat of revolution as less severe because it was very difficult for them to organize. Therefore, the combination of increased urbanization and factory employment may have been a key

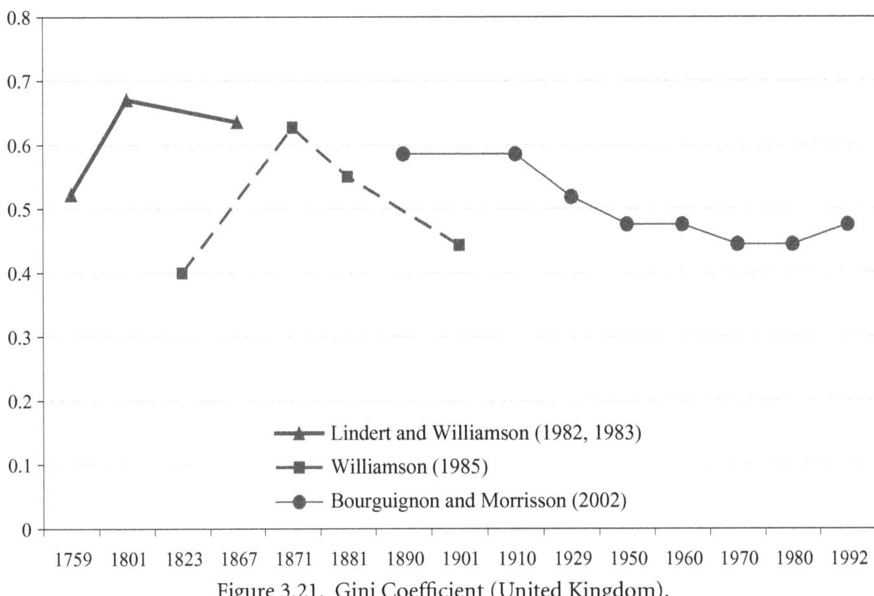

Figure 3.21. Gini Coefficient (United Kingdom).

factor in initiating the wave of democratization in nineteenth-century Europe. Changes in the structure of society and the economy during the early nineteenth century altered the balance of political power – in particular, making the exercise of de facto power by the politically disenfranchised much easier (Thompson 1963; Tilly 1995; and Tarrow 1998).

It is also undoubtedly true that the ideological changes that occurred during the Enlightenment, the French Revolution, and the U.S. War of Independence had the effect of changing people's ideas about the proper nature of government and the legitimacy of the old political order.

In the context of our approach so far, another potential answer is that inequality was more limited before the nineteenth century. Recall that when inequality is low, revolution is not a threat and even if it is, the elite can prevent revolution by promises of redistribution. Only with a sufficiently high level of inequality does democratization become a necessity. The limited data that exist on nineteenth-century inequality are consistent with the notion that inequality was rising until democratization (and then it started declining because of the redistribution following democratization). Much of this literature focuses to trying to discover whether there was a "Kuznets curve" historically, following Kuznets' (1955) conjecture that inequality first rises and then falls with economic development.

Data on income inequality for the nineteenth century are not extremely reliable. Figure 3.21 plots three different estimates of the historical evolution of the Gini coefficient in Britain. There is consensus among economic historians that income inequality in Britain fell sharply after the 1870s. There is also consensus that inequality rose in the century before this, although different scholars with different datasets found different timing for this rise. Lindert and Williamson (1982, 1983) found that this increase occurred before 1800 (see also Lindert and Williamson 1985; Lindert 1986, 2000a); Williamson (1985) found that it happened between 1800 and 1870. Other evidence (e.g., O'Rourke and Williamson 2002) is consistent with Williamson (1985). Whatever the case, the data on inequality are clearly consistent with the idea that inequality had risen in the century before 1867 and the Second Reform Act, and it may well have risen even before the First Reform Act. The evidence also suggests that inequality fell substantially after political reform.

Data for other countries are even more scarce. Morrisson (2000) surveyed the existing evidence and argued that Germany, France, and Sweden all went through a Kuznets curve. In Germany, inequality rose during the nineteenth century; most researchers place the peak around 1900. For example, Kuznets (1963) found that the income share of the top 5 percent went from 28 percent in 1873–80 to 32 percent in 1891–1900, stayed at 32 percent during 1901–10, and declined to 31 percent in 1911–13. Dumke (1991) found the same income share to be 28.4 percent in 1880, rising to 32.6 percent in 1900, and falling to 30.6 percent in 1913. During the Weimar Republic, inequality fell rapidly. Kraus (1981) records that by 1926, the income share of the top 5 percent had fallen by 6.2 percent. Overall, Morrisson (2000) argues that the Kuznets curve in Germany peaked in 1900, went flat, and started to fall in the 1920s. This date corresponds closely to the major democratization of 1918–19. Bourguignon and Morrisson's (2002) data show exactly this pattern.

For France, Morrisson (2000) and Morrisson and Snyder (2000) argued that inequality rose until 1870, with the income share of the top 10 percent peaking at around 50 percent. Inequality started to fall, however, in the 1870s; in 1890, the income share of the top 10 percent was down to 45 percent, falling further to 36 percent by 1929. The major political reforms of 1860–77 in France are, therefore, approximately around the peak of the Kuznets curve. The conventional wisdom about France has, to some extent, been challenged in recent research by Piketty (2003) on the twentieth century and by Piketty, Postal-Vinay, and Rosenthal (2003) on the nineteenth century. Using data on taxation returns, these authors found that inequality rose monotonically in the nineteenth century and only fell during the First and Second World Wars in the twentieth century.

Finally, Söderberg (1987, 1991) recorded that income inequality grew in Sweden, peaking just before the First World War, leveling off or falling slightly during the 1920s, and then falling rapidly thereafter. Once again, there is close correspondence between the decline in inequality and the extension of the franchise.

Overall, therefore, in Britain, France, Germany, and Sweden, the peak of the Kuznets curve appears to have followed democratization, which is in line with the mechanism proposed in this book.

5.3 The Latin American Experience

The evidence from the Latin American experience with democratization also supports the notion that the threat of revolution and social unrest was important and is broadly consistent with the comparative statics with respect to inequality. In Chapter 1, we discussed the Argentine case in which social conflict was important in the passing of the Sáenz Peña Law. In Chapter 2, we noted the views of Bushnell (1993) on the democratization in Colombia in the 1930s. We now look briefly at some other cases in more detail.

Historical studies of the movement toward democracy suggest an important role for social conflict. In Venezuela, a long period of *caudillismo* and political instability was ended by the dictatorship of Juan Vicente Gómez between 1908 and 1935. His military successors ruled until the first modern democracy was created in 1945. Levine (1973) describes the events leading up to democratization as follows:

> . . . after several days of fighting, a provisional revolutionary government was formed, with four members from Acción Democrática, two military officers, and one independent civilian. The three years that followed marked the introduction of a party system into Venezuela, abruptly ushering in an experiment with mass political democracy. (p. 89)

Democracy fell to a coup in 1948 but was reinstated in 1958 when the regime of General Pérez Jiménez collapsed in the midst of a widespread uprising. Levine (1989, p. 256) argues that redemocratization was in response to the unrest following economic depression and writes, "underground political forces, now united in a Junta Patriótica, mounted a wave of demonstrations and street fighting."

In Central America, the threat of social conflict and outright revolution has been a significant factor in inducing political elites to accede to democracy. For example, in Guatemala, General Jorge Ubico's thirteen-year dictatorship ended in 1944 when he was replaced by a junta led by General Federico Ponce. He was deposed the same year by an upsurge of pro-democratic sentiment and a student revolt, leading to the election of Juan Arévalo as president in 1945. He was followed in 1950 by Jacobo Arbenz, who was ousted by the coup of 1954. Redemocratization in Guatemala followed the same pattern and was a direct response to the eruption of conflict. Starting in 1982, the military acceded to a gradual redemocratization: Marco Cerezo was elected in 1985, followed by Jorge Serrano in 1990. This process continued after Serrano's attempted coup was foiled in 1993. Although these regimes were closely constrained by the military, the political liberalization was due to massive social unrest (Trudeau 1993).

In El Salvador, the picture is similar except without the brief early period of democracy (Baloyra 1982; Paige 1997). Rule was ceded by the coffee oligarchs to the military after the *matanza* insurrection of 1932. After 1962, democratic elections began but were closely controlled by the military and were subject to massive fraud. After a brief military interlude, redemocratization occurred in 1982 but in the midst of an extensive civil war, which only ended in 1992; 1994 was the first election in which the main left-wing group, the Frente Farabundo Martí para la Liberación Nacional (FMLN), contested power.

It is perhaps clearer that social conflict, often class and distributive conflict, has been behind most of the democratic collapses and coups in Latin America. This was a central theme of O'Donnell's (1973) seminal book, and Stepan's (1985) analysis of military coups in Chile, Uruguay, Argentina, and Brazil also echoes the same conclusion. He writes:

> The new authoritarianism in all four countries . . . was installed in an atmosphere of growing class conflict. In each country the bourgeoisie provided the social base for the new authoritarian regime, whose first political acts were the use of the coercive apparatus of the state to dismantle . . . working class organizations. (p. 318)

Drake (1996) similarly argues in his analysis of the role of labor in the dictatorships of Argentina, Brazil, Uruguay, Spain, and Portugal that

> most of the dictatorships arose out of the distributive struggle between capital and wages . . . Before the dawn of the dictatorships, working-class militance had begun to frighten property owners, who therefore abandoned liberal democracy. Losing profits, power, and legitimacy, the economic elites were rescued by the military . . . These right-wing, military based governments defended capitalism from populism, socialism, or communism by suppressing demands from the lower classes. They favored the private over the public, the wealthy over workers, capital accumulation over redistribution, hierarchy over equity. (pp. 3–4)

Another way of getting at the same issue is to look at how coups influence the value of different assets. For example, to the extent that democracy leads to redistribution and taxation of the assets of the rich (land and capital), we would expect the prices of these assets to fall with democracy and rise after a coup. Figure 3.22, constructed from data in Couyoumdjian, Millar, and Tocornal (1992), shows the real value of the stock-market index in Chile from 1928 to 1978. The real value of stocks declined continuously from the 1930s through to the coup of 1973, reaching its nadir with the election of Salvador Allende in 1970. The authors relate this secular decline to the increased intervention of the government in the economy, commenting that

> . . . the 1930–1960 period was scarcely auspicious for stock-market operations. It began with a deep depression, which finished in 1932. . . . From then on began an unequivocal process of deterioration, which had to do with the increasing state intervention in the economy, which, directly or indirectly, constrained free enterprise. It was limited in its development by price controls, tax increases, high inflation and other measures of distrust . . . Stock-market activity was not more than a reflection of the decreased participation of the private sector. (p. 309)

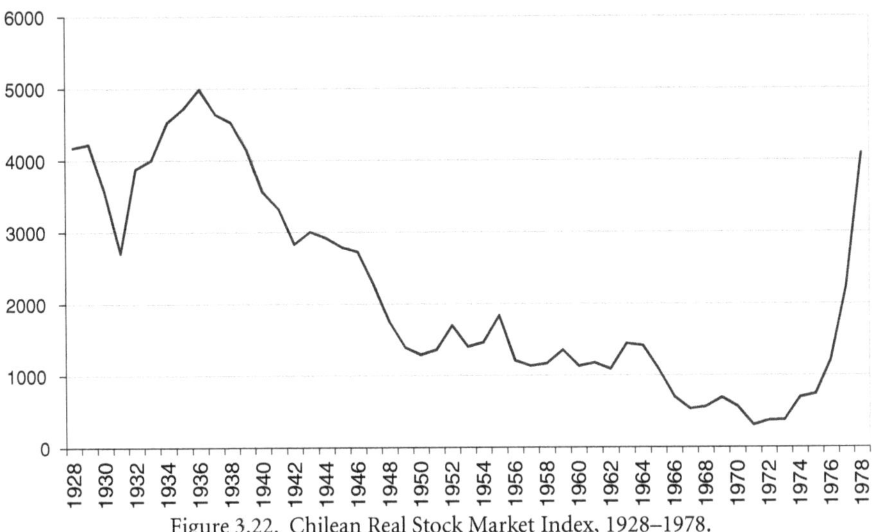

Figure 3.22. Chilean Real Stock Market Index, 1928–1978.

Then, in dramatic fashion, the value of the assets held by the rich recovered thirty years of losses in just five years. These data are consistent with an approach to the motivations of coups that emphasizes distributional conflict.

Collier (1999) recently argued for the importance of social pressure from the masses as a driving force behind many of the most recent redemocratizations. She argued that

> In . . . Peru, Argentina and Spain, massive labor protests destabilized authoritarianism and opened the way for the establishment of a democratically elected government. (p. 114)

She further argued for an important role for labor activism in inducing democratic transition in Bolivia, Uruguay, and Brazil. Even in Chile, apparently a case where the military withdrew without being pushed too hard, many scholars emphasize the reemergence of civil society during the 1980s. Drake (1998) argued that the reason Pinochet accepted the results of the plebiscite that ended the military regime was that

> . . . the foreseeable costs of maintaining the dictatorship probably would have included massive social and political disorder, class conflict, economic disruptions, radicalization of the left, draconian repression, escalating violence. (p. 89)

Much evidence is, therefore, consistent with the idea that, in Latin America, democracy was forced on political elites by the threat of revolution and by the collective action of the disenfranchised. Moreover, once democracy was created, elites often wanted and were frequently able to mount coups to take back power.

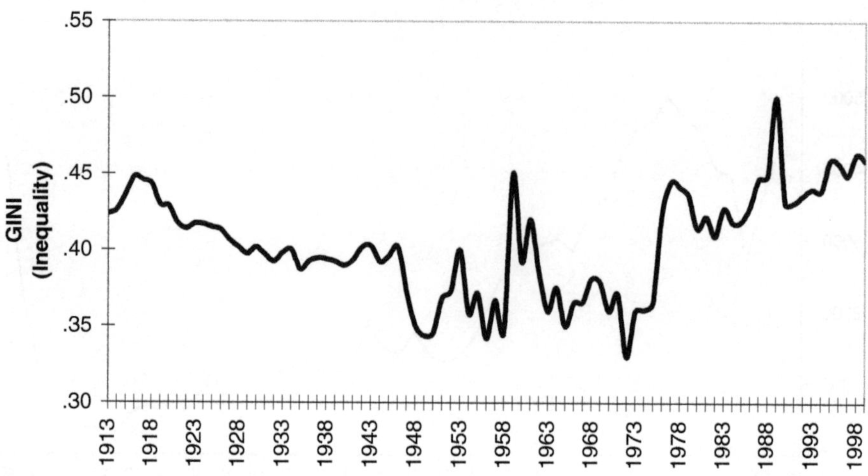

Figure 3.23. Gini Coefficient (Argentina). *Source*: Calvo, Torre, and Szwarcberg 2001.

Finally, following the European discussion, it is interesting to assess what is known about long-run trends in income distribution in Latin America. Unfortunately, much less is known about Latin America than Europe. In Figure 3.23, we plot the Gini coefficient for Argentina since the passing of the Sáenz Peña Law using data from Calvo, Torre, and Szwarcberg (2001). It shows that inequality has changed little in Argentina over the last century. Although the basic trend has been flat, the fluctuations have been interesting. After democratization in 1916, inequality began to fall consistently until the coup of 1930. After this, it was flat but then fell dramatically with the election of Perón's first government. The coup of 1955 led to a rapid increase in inequality, although this was unwound by the partially democratic regimes that assumed power after 1958. For example, Frondizi tried to court the Perónist vote by adopting pro-union policies. However, real democratization with Perón's second government after 1973 led to a further fall in inequality, and the coup of 1976 led to a dramatic increase in inequality. Other evidence supports this general pattern. For example, the share of wages in Argentinian national income, which was estimated to be around 28 percent at the time of the introduction of universal male suffrage, increased to 42 percent during the first ten years of democratic politics. Once democracy gave way to a dictatorship, the share of wages started to fall (Diaz-Alejandro 1970; Randall 1978, p. 29). Similarly, during Perón's first government, the share of wages in national income increased by more than 10 percent in the course of a few years, but all of this gain and more was lost during the military regimes of the 1970s (Di Tella and Dornbusch 1989). These movements are consistent with our framework. Democratization led to the incorporation of poorer groups into the polity and, consequently, resulted in policies designed to favor such groups. Many coups in

Argentina were clearly motivated by a desire to reverse such policies. These intentions and political forces show up in the data on income distribution. Democracy tended to promote equality, nondemocracy tended to promote inequality. The exception to this is the rapid rise of inequality since the 1990s under the presidencies of Menem, which abandoned the traditional pro-labor policies of the Perónists.

For Colombia, Berry and Urrutia (1976) and Londoño (1995) showed that inequality increased between 1938 and the mid-1960s and then fell monotonically thereafter until 1990. Interestingly, the period from 1948 to 1958 was one of nondemocracy. First, under the authoritarian semidemocratic Conservative regimes of Mariano Ospina Pérez and Laureano Gómez from 1948 until 1953, when opposition politicians were harassed and congress was closed, and then under the military until redemocratization in 1958.

Other facts on long-run income distribution can be deduced from work on the relationship between real wages and real rental rates of land (O'Rourke, Taylor and Williamson 1996; Williamson 1999; Bértola 2000; Bértola and Williamson 2003). These data suggest that in most Latin American countries, inequality rose from around the 1880s until The Great Depression. These authors argue that this was due to the incorporation of these primarily land-abundant countries into the world economy as exporters of agricultural goods. Interestingly, this rise in inequality was especially pronounced in countries such as Argentina and Uruguay, which were the most involved in international trade, and these were the countries that democratized first.

In the context of the Latin American experience, there are also many examples in which democracies have started important redistributive programs. Even in Costa Rica, a country with a relatively egalitarian history, Chalker (1995, p. 104) argued that "the most remarkable egalitarian measure in Costa Rica occurred in the 1960s and 1970s when the concentration in income distribution was reduced. Interestingly this was an outcome, rather than a cause of, democratic politics." Engerman, Mariscal, and Sokoloff (1998) establish more generally for Latin America that, as for Europe, there is a strong historical relationship between democratization and educational expansion.

6. The Literature

Our analysis of the emergence, consolidation, or collapse of democracy builds on a large and somewhat heterogeneous literature in political science and sociology and a small more recent literature using formal mathematical models by economists. There is a joke in economics that any statement you make is already in Marshall's *Principles of Economics*. Similarly, it is difficult to imagine making a claim about either democratization or consolidation that has not appeared somewhere in some form in the literature. For example, Huntington (1991, pp. 37–8) lists twenty-seven different factors that he claims have been said to promote democracy. Nevertheless, why anybody believes any particular causal claim is usually unclear, as are the causal mechanisms linking particular putative causes to outcomes. The great strength of the analytical approach we adopt is that these issues are crystal clear.

Theorizing about the issues we tackle in this book dates back at least to Aristotle and Plato and has become the center of much academic work since the studies of Lipset (1959) and Moore (1966). In this section, we describe how our work fits into the mainstream of the existing literature and outline what we think are our major contributions. As the book proceeds, we discuss extensively how our findings relate to existing work and particular theoretical and empirical claims made in the academic literature.

Lipset's (1959) work, inspired by "modernization" theory, was founded on the strong empirical correlation between per capita income and democracy. He argued that democracy emerged in society as it modernized, a process associated with rising urbanization, an increased importance of industry, higher educational attainment, and the increasing "complexity" of society. The work of Moore (1966), to some extent, challenged this focus on the unambiguous implications of modernization by emphasizing three "paths to the modern world," of which democracy was only one, the other two being fascism and communist revolution. Both scholars emphasized how underlying socioeconomic factors determined when democracy would emerge. Moore's work and the more recent contribution of Luebbert (1991) linked subsequent political regimes to initial social conditions, such as the class structure and the organization of agriculture, and to the strength of the bourgeoisie. For example, democracy emerged in Moore's theory when agriculture had commercialized and was no longer characterized by feudal or semifeudal labor relations, and where the bourgeoisie was strong.

These "structural" approaches came under attack from many political scientists in the 1970s, particularly Rustow (1970), Linz and Stepan (1978), and Linz (1978), as being too deterministic and apolitical. This criticism came with a change of focus from democratization to the collapse of democracy. The comparative project on the collapse of democracy overseen by Linz and Stepan was particularly important in reorienting the literature. They advocated (1978; p. ix) directing "systematic attention to the dynamics of the political process of breakdown." In their view, whether democracy collapsed was not determined by socioeconomic structures or conditions but was instead a result of specific choices by the relevant actors, both pro- and anti-democratic (Linz 1978, p. 4). More specifically, Linz (1978, p. 50) proposed that democracy collapses because it loses "legitimacy," and he argued that democracy collapses because of a failure of democratic politicians to solve political problems. Although the discussion of modernization by Lipset did not focus on choices by individuals or even groups, Moore's (1966) analysis does incorporate choices – for example, whether the bourgeoisie enters into a coalition with the aristocracy. Nevertheless, it is not clear in his analysis what determines whether such a choice is made.

Modernization theory was also attacked by O'Donnell (1973), who argued that the collapse of democracy in Latin America in the 1960s and 1970s undermined confidence in the income–democracy relationship and the idea that modernization promoted democracy. He pointed out that the military coups had happened in the richest Latin American countries – for example, Argentina, Uruguay, and Brazil.

In the 1980s, following contemporary events, research again refocused, this time back on democratizations. The most influential work was the "transitions" project overseen by O'Donnell, Schmitter, and Whitehead; their conclusions were presented in a highly influential book by O'Donnell and Schmitter (1986). They followed many of the methodological dicta of Linz and Stepan, arguing that structural explanations on democratizations were inadequate (1986, p. 4). O'Donnell and Schmitter's book presents a framework for clarifying the relevant processes that might lead to democratization and the various types of actors involved; for example, they made an influential distinction between the "hardliners" and the "softliners" in an authoritarian regime. The book then discusses various interactions between the relevant groups and the types of situations and dilemmas that might emerge between the end of an authoritarian regime and the initiation of democracy. All research in this tradition tends to emphasize that democracy is created by the will and decisions of individuals who are barely constrained by environmental factors (di Palma 1990 is perhaps the most extreme version of such a thesis). As such, the book does not really present an explanation of when democratization occurs, although it does, offer a few generalizations, the most famous of which is as follows:

> We assert that there is no transition whose beginning is not the consequence – direct or indirect – of important divisions within the authoritarian regime itself, principally along the fluctuating cleavage between hard-liners and soft-liners. (O'Donnell and Schmitter 1986, p. 19)

The most recent incarnation of this transitions literature and the focus of most political science research in the 1990s has been on democratic consolidation. Linz and Stepan's (1996) work is the most central. This literature emphasizes differences in the nature of democracy and the existence of different paths from authoritarian to democratic regimes. In an early paper, Stepan (1986) proposed the existence of ten alternative paths from nondemocratic regimes to democracy. Central is the idea that the form that democracy takes, once constructed, depends on the nature of the prior regime. For example, Linz and Stepan distinguish between four types of nondemocratic regime: authoritarian, totalitarian, post-totalitarian, and sultanistic. The type of democracy that emerges typically depends, in their view, on the type of nondemocratic regime initially in place. For example, the issues facing those wishing to create consolidated democracy in North Korea (totalitarian) are very different from those faced in the Congo (sultanistic) (Linz and Stepan 1996, p. 55).

The literature on democratic consolidation has also seen a resurgence in ideas about political culture and how this can be an important factor in determining consolidation (Almond and Verba 1963; Diamond 1999).

Other works have attempted to integrate both structural- and actor-based approaches to democracy and its consolidation. Huntington (1991) proposed a complex web of factors that influence democratization, and he argued that these vary according to which "wave" of democracy one considered. For instance, with respect to the First wave before the First World War, he emphasized modernization, urbanization, creation of a middle class, and decreasing inequality (p. 39). In the second wave his emphasis shifted to the impact of the Second World War and the collapse of empires (p. 40). With respect to the third wave, Huntington lists five factors as being important (pp. 45–6): (1) a crisis of authoritarian legitimacy created by economic recession induced by the oil shocks of the 1970s and the international debt crisis of the 1980s; (2) the income growth and increase in education experienced in the 1960s; (3) the change in the attitude of the Catholic church; (4) the changes in the attitudes of international institutions, the United States, and the Soviet Union; and (5) the "snowballing" or demonstration effects that led to contagion and the international dissemination of democracy. Huntington's discussion of the effects of income level on democracy differs little from Lipset's. He argues (p. 106) that democracy in the third wave was facilitated by "higher levels of economic well-being, which led to more widespread literacy, education and urbanization, a larger middle class, and the development of values and attitudes supportive of democracy." However, "the emergence of social, economic and external conditions favorable to democracy is never enough to produce democracy. Whatever their motives, some political leaders have to want it to happen" (p. 108).

Thus, the structural conditions are necessary but not sufficient for democratization to occur. Huntington's analysis of the process of democratization in many respects mirrors that of O'Donnell and Schmitter (1986). He outlines a set of stylized actors in the regime and the opposition and argues that democracy emerges when specific groups are strong or when specific sets of interactions occur (pp. 123–4, 142). Rather than provide a theory, Huntington uses this discussion to produce a taxonomy of different cases, and he focuses on three paths of democratization.

Closer to our work is that of Dahl (1971), who proposed a simple and appealing framework for understanding democratization. He argued that the basic issue with democratization is that

> From the perspective of the incumbents who currently govern, such a transformation carries with it new possibilities of conflict as a result of which their goals (and they themselves) may be displaced by spokesmen for the newly incorporated individuals, groups or interests.
>
> The problem of their opponents is the mirror image of the problem of the incumbents. . . .

> Thus the greater the conflict between government and opposition, the more likely that each will seek to deny opportunities to the other to participate effectively in policy making... the greater the conflict between the government and its opponents, the more costly it is for each to tolerate the other. (pp. 14–15)

Dahl's theory of democratization is that incumbents will democratize when either the cost of tolerating the opposition falls, so that they are prepared to enfranchise them, or the costs of suppression become too high (1971, pp. 15–16). He then makes a series of empirical claims about factors that are likely to influence these costs and, hence, the likelihood of democratization. In terms of mechanisms, Dahl emphasized that democracy arose when power was widely distributed in society, a situation he called a "pluralistic" order. It was when society became pluralistic – something induced, for example, by income growth and industrialization – that the costs of suppression became high and simultaneously, the costs of toleration became low.

In contrast to Moore's (1966) emphasis on the bourgeoisie and the middle classes, subsequent important and ambitious work – especially Therborn (1977) and Rueschemeyer, Stephens, and Stephens (1992) – noticed the important role that the poor and the working class played in the democratization process. In their theory, the working classes are pro-democratic and, when they are powerful enough, they can force democracy. Power relations are determined by three sets of forces (p. 5). As Rueschemeyer, Stephens, and Stephens noted:

> There is first the balance of power among different *classes and class coalitions*. This... is complemented by two other power configurations – the structure, strength, and autonomy of the *state apparatus* and its interrelations with civil society and the impact of *transnational power relations* on both the balance of class power and on state-society relations.

The main driving force behind democratization in their theory is capitalist development which increases the power of the working classes (p. 58).

Another important work is Haggard and Kaufman (1995), who concentrate on demonstrating the importance of economic crises for precipitating democratizations and then focus on the interaction among democratization, economic policy reform, and democratic consolidation. Their work suggests that the prime transmission mechanism between crises and democratic transitions is that crises breed social discontent against nondemocratic regimes. For instance, in their case studies,

> ... mounting economic difficulties encouraged opposition within the private sector and contributed to the mobilization of broader social and electoral movements. (p. 45)

They also found that

> "direct action campaigns" – anti-regime protests, general strikes, and demonstrations – also figured prominently in the authoritarian withdrawals. (p. 63)

An alternative theoretical approach to democratization stems from the sociological literature on the origins of state institutions. This argument, associated most with Tilly (1990) and applied recently to Africa by Herbst (2000), sees the origins of democracy in the process of state formation. Kings needed resources, particularly taxes, to fight wars. To induce elites to pay taxes, kings had to make concessions, one form of which was the creation of representative institutions. In this account, democracy emerges as a quid pro quo between kings and elites, in which elites are granted representation in exchange for taxes. In Africa, the lack of democracy is a consequence of the particular process of pre- and post-colonial state formation, which meant that political elites never had to make concessions to citizens in exchange for taxes to fight wars.

This research on state formation inspired an analyses of democratization by Bates and Lien (1985), Bates (1991), Rogowski (1998), and Tilly (2004). These scholars argued that democracy, like the origins of representative institutions more generally, is a concession from authoritarian rulers necessary to raise taxation. The more elastic is the tax base, the more difficult it is for authoritarian rulers to raise taxes without agreement, and the greater the likelihood of concessions – here, democracy. Hence, Bates (1991, p. 25) points out that democracy is less likely in an agrarian society – because land is easier to tax – than it is in a society dominated by physical or human capital. Moreover, he makes the argument that authoritarian rulers will be more willing to abide by democracy if they fear it less. He connects this to their economic power with respect to democracy – democrats cannot hurt previous elites if they have sufficient economic strength, perhaps because taxing the elite leads to a collapse in the economy. Rogowski (1998) similarly emphasizes the impact of the ability of citizens to exit as leading to democracy – a case in which voice prevents exit.

Finally, our work builds on the literature that emphasizes how political institutions can solve problems of commitment. The seminal paper is by North and Weingast (1989), and this has been a theme of a series of important papers by Weingast (1997, 1998).

7. Our Contribution

The ideas presented in this book build on the framework we introduced in Acemoglu and Robinson (2000a,b; 2001, 2002). There, we placed the issue of regime transitions within a framework of redistributive conflict and developed the basic idea of democracy as a credible commitment by the elites to avoid revolution and derived some of the important comparative static results – for instance, the inverted U-shaped relationship between inequality and democratization. Our research provides the first systematic formal analysis of the creation and consolidation of democracy.

Our analysis of these issues is in the tradition of formal political economy; therefore, we look for simple unified explanations of complex social phenomena.

As should be clear from the previous discussion, this is somewhat out of the mainstream of political science literature on regime transitions. Instead, this literature since the 1970s has followed the dictum of Linz and Stepan (1978, p. xi) that "the historicity of macro-political processes precludes the highly abstract generalizing of ahistorical social scientific models . . . applicable to all past times and any future cases." The lack of a theoretical framework with which to analyze regime transitions is even celebrated by some scholars, with O'Donnell and Schmitter (1986, p. 3) noting "We did not have at the beginning, nor do we have at the end of this lengthy collective endeavor, a 'theory' to test or to apply to the case studies and thematic essays in these volumes." They continue,

> if we ever had the temerity to formulate a theory of such processes, it would have to be a chapter in a much larger inquiry into the problem of "undetermined" social change, of large-scale transformations which occur when there are insufficient structural or behavioral parameters to guide and predict the outcome. Such a theory would have to include elements of accident and unpredictability, of crucial decisions taken in a hurry with inadequate information, of actors facing irresolvable ethical dilemmas and ideological confusions.

A recent survey of the literature on democratizations in the most prestigious journal in comparative politics, *World Politics*, noted that

> The literature on the third wave offers a number of general propositions about factors facilitating and obstructing democratization. The following are most notable:
>
> 1. There are few preconditions for the emergence of democracy.
> 2. No single factor is sufficient or necessary to the emergence of democracy.
> 3. The emergence of democracy in a country is the result of a combination of causes.
> 4. The causes responsible for the emergence of democracy are not the same as those promoting its consolidation.
> 5. The combination of causes promoting democratic transition and consolidation varies from country to country.
> 6. The combination of causes generally responsible for one wave of democratization differs from those responsible for other waves. (Shin 1994, p. 151)

It seems that the "general propositions" are that there are no general propositions. We do not disagree that democratizations, looked at in microdetail, are tremendously complex social phenomena. Nevertheless, could not the same be said of any issue that social scientists wish to understand? To develop any systematic understanding of the social world, one must proceed by simplifying (Occam's razor again) and abstracting from much of the details. Perhaps in this book we make the wrong decisions about which factors to emphasize and which to ignore, but whether we do can only be answered by the scientific and empirical usefulness of the theory and not by a priori assessments of how complicated the phenomena of democratization is.

In our terms, a general proposition about democratization would be an empirical claim, derived from a model with microfoundations, about what forces tend to lead to democratization. In our theory, many factors influence this: intergroup inequality, political institutions, structure of the economy, and nature and extent of globalization, to name a few. Our theory allows us to make comparative static predictions of the form: holding other things equal, a decrease in inequality makes a highly unequal society more likely to democratize. In a particular and highly unequal society, such as South Africa in the 1980s, democratization may be caused by falling inequality. Nevertheless, this does not mean that falling inequality is necessary or sufficient to induce democratization. In another highly unequal nondemocratic society, we might see inequality fall but democratization does not occur because something else changes as well (e.g., the extent of globalization changes) that decreases the appeal of democratization.

Despite the fact that our approach does not easily mesh with much mainstream research on regime transitions in political science, a close reading of the literature confirms that the distributional conflicts on which we focus are considered by all authors to be at the heart of understanding democratization and coups. For instance, although O'Donnell and Schmitter (1986) emphasized that transitions coincide with splits in the authoritarian regime, they recognized that authoritarian regimes only liberalize when they are forced to (pp. 16–17). In their conclusion, O'Donnell and Schmitter noted that

> . . . it is possible to offer a few generalizations. . . . First, all previously known transitions to political democracy have observed one fundamental restriction . . . the property rights of the bourgeoisie are inviolable. (1986, pp. 68–9)

This conclusion is not surprising given that (p. 52) "Most of the authoritarian regimes in our sample of countries have deliberately favored bourgeois interests." At other places in their work, they also made statements highly consonant with our approach. For instance, they argued that in democratization (p. 11), "the threat of violence and even frequent protests, strikes, and demonstrations are virtually always present," which is one of the building blocks of our approach. Interestingly, the analysis of democratic breakdown that emerges in Linz (1978) is also consistent with this basic idea (pp. 14–15, 20).

Our framework does, however, build on various themes in the literature. At the heart of our theory are trade-offs close to those discussed by Dahl (1971), although we place the trade-off between repression and democratization into a richer setting where political institutions have a real role because of how they influence the ability of actors to commit. Moore's (1966) work is also a clear inspiration for our research, both for the title of our book and our taxonomy of "paths of democratization" outlined in Chapter 1. We focus only on a subset of the issues that he did, however, because we do not extensively study revolutions and we completely ignore the issue of how fascism originates. Our economic focus also is different from his sociological focus, and our emphasis on methodological individualism means that we provide much more explicit microfoundations than he did. An obvious case is the connection between the strength of the middle class and democracy. We develop various explicit mechanisms via which this strength can influence the costs and benefits of democracy for different agents and, thus, the likelihood that it will be created.

Our work also has a similar relationship to that of scholars such as Therborn (1977) and Rueschemeyer, Stephens, and Stephens (1992). Although there are many common themes, our work is substantially different because we develop much more explicitly the mechanisms linking various factors to the rise and consolidation of democracy. Therborn and Rueschemeyer, Stephens, and Stephens see democratization as the result of capitalist development. They emphasize the effects of such development on the balance of class power more than Lipset did, but their account is based on the same empirical fact. However, they also fail to provide a mechanism for how capitalist development causes democracy. In our analysis, although capitalist development may increase the power of the poor to challenge a nondemocracy, it does not necessarily lead to democracy. For example, if such development allowed the citizens to make a permanent threat to the elite, then the elite would be able to avoid democratizing by credibly redistributing. Or, if capitalist development increased inequality sufficiently and did not make repression costly, it would encourage the elite to use repression rather than concede democratization. In our approach, it is the effect of capitalist development both on the strength of the citizens and the trade-off of the elite between repression and concession that determines the fate of democracy. Moreover, our analysis suggests that capital accumulation in itself may not be sufficient to induce democracy. Rather, it is changes in the structure of society's assets that may be crucial to changing the costs and benefits of democracy to the elite that lead to democratization.

These ideas point to an aspect of our work that is original and we believe important. No other authors have placed the issue of democratization in a context where the trade-offs among it, other types of concessions, and repression can be evaluated. As suggested in Chapter 2, we find a model that just says the poor want democracy and if they have more power they get it, to be too simple. Moreover, such a theory provides no real role for political institutions – surely, a critical step in explaining why and when democracy originates.

The closest thing to this is the distinction, initially made by O'Donnell and Schmitter (1986), between liberalization and democratization. In their schema, a process of liberalization always precedes democratization. By liberalization, they mean (p. 7) "the process of making effective certain rights that protect both individuals and social groups from arbitrary or illegal acts committed by the state or third parties. On the level of individuals these guarantees include the classical elements of the liberal: habeas corpus; sanctity of private home and correspondence; the right to be defended in a fair trial according to pre-established laws; freedom of movement, speech . . . and so forth." To the extent that such liberalization measures are valued by citizens, they constitute a concession of the type we have studied here (although obviously not a monetary one). Significantly, O'Donnell and Schmitter note that

> . . . liberalization and democratization are not synonymous, although their historical relationship has been close . . . without the accountability to mass publics and constituent majorities institutionalized under the latter, liberalization may prove to be easily manipulated and retracted at the convenience of those in government. (1986, p. 9)

The research of Moore (1966), Therborn (1977), and Rueschemeyer, Stephens, and Stephens (1992) is also problematical because they assume that political conflict is always along the lines of class. There is much evidence, however, that a richer conceptual framework is needed to provide a satisfactory general approach to democracy. The framework we develop applies to a much wider set of cases.

A long tradition from Moore (1966) and Dahl (1971) onward emphasizes that democracy is not feasible in agrarian societies. Rueschemeyer, Stephens, and Stephens (1992, p. 8) explain the reason for this in the following way: "The landed upper-class which were dependent on a large supply of cheap labor were the most consistently anti-democratic force. Democratization for them posed the possibility of losing their labor supply." Although this mechanism is plausible, the Latin American evidence is also consistent with landed interests opposing democracy because they anticipated losing their land. It is this idea that we develop more intensively, along with related ideas about how the cost of coups is influenced by the structure of assets.

We emphasize the fact that democracy is conceded in the face of potential conflict which is internal to a society (Therborn 1977; Rueschemeyer, Stephens, and Stephens 1992). Our reading of the historical literature suggests that the type of democratization that Collier (1999) calls an "elite project," where political elites create democracy for other reasons without external pressure, is such a rare event that it cannot be the basis of any useful generalizations. We also do not believe that the evidence is consistent with the notion that democracy arises as a by-product of state formation and the expansion of the fiscal base, possibly induced by external threats.

In contrast, the elite project approach, often associated with O'Donnell and Schmitter (1986), plays down the role of outside social pressure leading to democratization and instead emphasizes conflict within ruling authoritarian regimes. O'Donnell and Schmitter's elite splits are part of this and undeniably took place in many democratizations. Collier's use of this term is broader because she wants to use it also to capture some nineteenth-century democratizations that purportedly took place as nascent political parties extended voting rights to increase their support (the classic example being competition between Disraeli and Gladstone over the Second Reform Act of 1867). Our basic view is that elite splits are a manifestation of heterogeneity among the elite, but they are caused in the first place by the challenge of the disenfranchised citizens to the existing system. This challenge, combined with the intra-elite heterogeneity, leads to different attitudes toward democracy. We believe that this view is consistent with a close reading of O'Donnell and Schmitter and the case-study evidence on which their analysis is based. Haggard and Kaufman (1995) also recognize that splits in authoritarian elites may be important but also argue that these splits may be initiated by crises (pp. 31–2). In terms of Disraeli and Gladstone, as Chapter 8 makes clear, we believe this to be an unconvincing interpretation of events.

In terms of the recent literature on democratic consolidation, our work focuses on a narrower set of questions. Interestingly, in Linz and Stepan (1996), the reason for the path dependence that they argue exists in every democratization really hinges on the way that the nondemocratic legacy influences the difficulty of creating the different components of consolidation, such as the rule of law or a nonpatrimonial bureaucracy, which are outside the domain of our study, given our focus on a Schumpeterian definition of democracy. Although these questions are interesting, they are not within the scope of the questions asked in this book. What is central to our approach is the idea that the distribution of power in a democracy depends on many factors, including the structure of political institutions. If these vary, then so do the outcomes of democracy.

Because our approach is game theoretic, we obviously build on the literature that has attempted to use such an approach. This work began following the simple games of democratization sketched in Przeworski (1991), who used them to illustrate some of the conclusions reached by O'Donnell and Schmitter (1986). His approach has been developed by a number of scholars, including Gates and Humes (1997), Crescenzi (1999), and Sutter (2000). Other scholars have appealed to simple games, particularly the prisoner's dilemma, as metaphors for what happens when there is a coup (Cohen 1994) or a democratization (Colomer 2000).

Our emphasis on the economic motives of actors involved in creating and undermining democracy is shared by several of the recent key works – for instance, Przeworski (1991) and Haggard and Kaufman (1995). Haggard and Kaufman's approach is that

> we assume that the opportunities for political elites to mobilize political support or opposition will depend on how economic policy and performance affect the income of different social groups. Both aggregate economic performance and the distributive consequences of policy are crucial to politics everywhere, affecting the chances of both incumbents and oppositions. (pp. 6–7)

Nevertheless, the majority of game-theoretic models developed so far by political scientists are reduced form, generating few if any testable predictions, and failing to illuminate the causal mechanisms at work. By reduced form, we mean that the payoff to different players (e.g., from democracy or dictatorship) are represented as numbers or perhaps variables like x or y. Then, if I receive a payoff of 2 from democracy and 3 from dictatorship, I prefer dictatorship; alternatively, if x is my payoff from democracy and y my payoff from dictatorship, and $x > y$, then I prefer democracy. Such models do not reveal why any particular individual or group prefers the regime it does, nor do they allow one to derive testable predictions about the circumstances under which different outcomes arise. More problematical, following O'Donnell and Schmitter (1986), they define the preferences of individuals in terms of the actions they prefer. Thus, an agent is defined to be a hardliner because he prefers dictatorship. The same problem arises in the use of these ideas in Huntington (1991). Like O'Donnell and Schmitter, he does not explain why certain interactions occurred in some countries and not others, and he does not explain why pro-democratic actors were strong in some countries but weak in others. Moreover, it is again not really explained fundamentally why anybody is for or against a particular type of political regime. Ideally, an individual's preferences over regime outcomes ought to be derived from more fundamental preferences over income or other things, along with the implications of particular regimes for these preferences.

Possibly because of the reliance on reduced-form models, this game-theoretical literature has adopted the same dichotomy between structural and political approaches to explaining regime transitions first advocated by Linz and Stepan in the 1970s. For example, Colomer (2000), in a chapter entitled "Structural versus Strategic Approaches to Political Change," argues that

> Two basic approaches can be distinguished in the literature on regime change and transitions to democracy. One emphasizes the structural, socioeconomic or cultural requisites of democracy.... The other approach looks at political regimes as outcomes of strategic processes of change. The main role is given here to choices and interactions by the actors. (p. 133)

That such a dichotomy exists seems to be widely accepted by political scientists. Shin (1994) argues

> ... the establishment of a viable democracy in a nation is no longer seen as the product of higher levels of modernization, illustrated by wealth, bourgeois class structure, tolerant cultural values, and economic independence from external actors. Instead, it is seen more as a product of strategic interactions and arrangements among political elites, conscious choices among various types of democratic constitutions, and electoral and party systems. (pp. 138–9)

The framework we develop is game theoretic and individuals and groups behave strategically based on individual motivations and incentives. Yet, individuals function within social and economic systems that both constrain their actions and condition incentives. In fact, there is no dichotomy at all between structural and strategic approaches – they are one and the same.

Our approach, then, is to build much richer political-economy models from which we can derive empirical predictions about the incidence of democracy. We treat individuals' preferences as given but allow people to differ with respect to their income, wealth, the form in which they hold their wealth, or their options and alternatives. From these fundamentals, we derive individual preferences over regime types. Thus, if a member of the elite is a hardliner, it is because we can show that "hardline" behavior is optimal for him given his preferences, endowments, and opportunities. We do not define people by their behavior.

Although we know of no work of the same scope as ours, our results have been complemented by a number of other recent formal models of democratization. Most related is the research of Rosendorff (2001), who developed a model to argue that democratization occurred in South Africa because falling inequality made democracy less threatening for whites, an idea clearly related to one of the building blocks of our approach. Boix's (2003) recent book develops a simple static version of a democratization model derived from our papers (2001) and close to the model sketched by Dahl (1971), and applies it to historical instances of democratization, particularly in Switzerland and the United States. Because his book uses the framework we developed in our published articles, it suggests several of the comparative statics we analyze in this book. For instance, Boix verbally discusses ideas about how trade, exit, and the structure of the economy influence redistributive politics and thus democratization. The research of Ellman and Wantchekon (2000) is also related to our analysis of coups; they show how the threat of a coup may influence the policies that political parties offer in an election. This is one element of our analysis in Chapter 7. Other papers by Feng and Zak (1999), Justman and Gradstein (1999), and Conley and Temimi (2001) provide different formal models of democratization. Another stream in the political economy literature – including both nonformal work by Kiser and Barzel (1991) and Barzel (2001) and theoretical models by Green (1993), Weingast (1997), Gradstein (2002), Bueno de Mesquita, Morrow, Siverson, and Smith (2003) and Lizzeri and Persico (2004) – builds on the idea that democracy is voluntarily granted by political elites because it solves some sort of market failure or contractual incompleteness. For instance, Green (1993) argues that the creation of legislative institutions was a way for rulers to credibly signal information. The other research, though differing in details, is based on the idea that rulers face a severe commitment problem because they cannot use third parties to enforce their contracts. Creating democracy, therefore, can be Pareto-improving because, by giving away power, a ruler can gain credibility.

An alternative formal approach to democratization was proposed by Ades (1995), Ades and Verdier (1996), and Bourguignon and Verdier (2000). These papers assume that only wealthy citizens can vote and they study how, for a fixed-wealth threshold, changes in income distribution and economic development influence the extent of the franchise and, hence, the equilibrium policy. Another approach was developed by Ticchi and Vindigni (2003a), who analyze a model in which countries are engaged in interstate warfare and political elites democratize in order to give their citizens greater incentives to fight.

4 Democratic Politics

1. Introduction

In this chapter, we begin to analyze the factors that lead to the creation of democracy. As discussed in Chapter 2, our approach is based on conflict over political institutions, in particular democracy versus nondemocracy. This conflict results from the different consequences that follow from these regimes. In other words, different political institutions lead to different outcomes, creating different winners and losers. Realizing these consequences, various groups have preferences over these political institutions.

Therefore, the first step toward our analysis of why and when democracy emerges is the construction of models of collective decision making in democracy and nondemocracy. The literature on collective decision making in democracy is vast (with a smaller companion literature on decision making in nondemocracy). Our purpose is not to survey this literature but to emphasize the essential points on how individual preferences and various types of distributional conflicts are mapped into economic and social policies. We start with an analysis of collective decision making in democracies, turning to nondemocratic politics in Chapter 5.

The most basic characteristic of a democracy is that all individuals (above a certain age) can vote, and voting influences which social choices and policies are adopted. In a direct democracy, the populace would vote directly on the policies. In a representative democracy, the voters choose the government, which then decides which policies to implement. In the most basic model of democracy, political parties that wish to come to office attempt to get elected by offering voters a policy platform. It may be a tax policy, but it may also be any other type of economic or social policy. Voters then elect political parties, thereby indirectly choosing policies. This interaction between voters' preferences and parties' policy platforms determines what the policy will be in a democracy. One party wins the election and implements the policy that it promised. This approach, which we adopt for most of the book, builds on a body of important research in economics and political science, most notably by Hotelling (1929), Black (1948), and Downs (1957).

Undoubtedly, in the real world there are important institutional features of democracies missing from such a model, and their absence makes our approach only a crude approximation to reality. Parties rarely make a credible commitment to a policy, and do not run on a single issue but rather on a broad platform. In addition, parties may be motivated by partisan (i.e., ideological) preferences as well as simply a desire to be in office. Voters might also have preferences over parties' ideologies as well as their policies. There are various electoral rules: some countries elect politicians according to proportional representation with multimember districts, others use majoritarian electoral systems with single-member districts. These electoral institutions determine in different ways how votes translate into seats and, therefore, governments. Some democracies have presidents, others are parliamentary. There is often divided government, with policies determined by legislative bargaining between various parties or by some type of arrangement between presidents and parliaments, not by the specific platform offered by any party in an election. Last but not least, interest groups influence policies through nonvoting channels, including lobbying and, in the extreme, corruption.

Many of these features can be added to our models, and these refined models often make different predictions over a range of issues.[1] Nevertheless, our initial and main intention is not to compare various types of democracies but to understand the major differences between democracies and nondemocracies. For instance, although the Unites States has a president and Britain does not, nobody argues that this influences the relative degree to which they are democratic. Democracy is consistent with significant institutional variation. Our focus, therefore, is on simpler models of collective decision making in democracies, highlighting their common elements. For this purpose, we emphasize that democracies are situations of relative *political equality*. In a perfect democracy each citizen has one vote. More generally, in a democracy, the preference of the majority of citizens matter in the determination of political outcomes. In nondemocracy, this is not the case because only a subset of people have political rights. By and large, we treat nondemocracy as the opposite of democracy: whereas democracy approximates political equality, nondemocracy is typically a situation of *political inequality*, with more power in the hands of an elite.

Bearing this contrast in mind, our treatment in this chapter tries to highlight some common themes in democratic politics. Later, we return to the question of institutional variation within democracies. Although this does not alter the basic thrust of our argument, it is important because it may influence the type of policies that emerge in democracy and thus the payoffs for both the elites and the citizens.

[1] For example, it appears that, empirically, electoral systems with proportional representation lead to greater income redistribution than majoritarian institutions (see Austen-Smith 2000; Milesi-Feretti, Perotti, and Rostagno 2002; Persson and Tabellini 2003).

2. Aggregating Individual Preferences

In this subsection, we begin with some of the concepts and problems faced by the theory of social or collective choice, which deals with the issue of how to aggregate individual preferences into "society's preferences" when all people's preferences count. These issues are important because we want to understand what happens in a democracy. When all people can vote, which policies are chosen?

To fix ideas, it is useful to think of government policy as a proportional tax rate on incomes and some way of redistributing the proceeds from taxation. Generally, individuals differ in their tastes and their incomes, and thus have different preferences over policies – for example, level of taxation, redistribution, and public good provision. However, even if people are identical in their preferences and incomes, there is still conflict over government policy. In a world where individuals want to maximize their income, each person would have a clear preference: impose a relatively high tax rate on all incomes other than their own and then redistribute all the proceeds to themselves! How do we then aggregate these very distinct preferences? Do we choose one individual who receives all the revenues? Or will there be no redistribution of this form? Or some other outcome altogether?

These questions are indirectly addressed by Arrow's (1951) seminal study of collective decision making. The striking but, upon reflection, reasonable result that Arrow derived is that under weak assumptions, the only way a society may be able to make coherent choices in these situations is to make one member a dictator in the sense that only the preferences of this individual matter in the determination of the collective choice. More precisely, Arrow established an *(im)possibility theorem*, showing that even if individuals have well-behaved rational preferences, it is not generally possible to aggregate those preferences to determine what would happen in a democracy. This is because aggregating individual rational preferences does not necessarily lead to a social preference relation that is rational in the sense that it allows "society" to make a decision about what to do.

Arrow's theorem is a fundamental and deep result in political science (and economics). It builds on an important and simpler feature of politics: *conflict of interest*. Different allocations of resources and different social decisions and policies create *winners* and *losers*. The difficulty in forming social preferences is how to aggregate the wishes of different groups, some of whom prefer one policy or allocation whereas others prefer different ones. For example, how do we aggregate the preferences of the rich segments of society who dislike high taxes that redistribute away from themselves and the preferences of the poor segments who like high taxes that redistribute to themselves? Conflicts of interest between various social groups, often between the poor and the rich, underlie all of the results and discussion in this book. In fact, the contrast we draw between democracy and nondemocracy precisely concerns how they tilt the balance of power in favor of the elites or the citizens or in favor of the rich or the poor.

Nevertheless, Arrow's theorem does not show that it is always impossible to aggregate conflicting preferences. We need to be more specific about the nature of individuals' preferences and about how society reconciles conflicts of interest. We need to be more specific about what constitutes power and how this is articulated and exercised. When we do so, we see that we may get determinate social choices because, although people differ in what they want, there is a determinate balance of power between different individuals. Such balances of power emerge in many situations, the most famous being in the context of the Median Voter Theorem (MVT), which we examine in the next subsection.

To proceed, it is useful to be more specific about the institutions under which collective choices are made. In particular, we wish to formulate the collective-choice problem as a game, which can be of various types. For instance, in the basic Downsian model that we consider shortly, the game is between two political parties. In a model of dictatorship that we investigate in Chapter 5, the game is between a dictator and the disenfranchised citizens. Once we have taken this step, looking for determinate social choices is equivalent to looking for the Nash equilibrium of the relevant games.

3. Single-Peaked Preferences and the Median Voter Theorem

3.1 Single-Peaked Preferences

Let's first be more specific about individual preferences over social choices and policies. In economic analysis, we represent people's preferences by a utility function that allows them to rank various alternatives. We place plausible restrictions on these utility functions; for example, they are usually increasing (more is better) and they are assumed to be concave – an assumption that embodies the notion of diminishing marginal utility. Because we want to understand which choices individuals will make when their goal is to maximize their utility, we are usually concerned with the shape of the utility function. One important property that a utility function might have is that of being "single-peaked."

Loosely, individual preferences are single-peaked with respect to a policy or a social choice if an individual has a preferred policy; the farther away the policy is from this preferred point, in any direction, the less the person likes it. We can more formally define single-peaked preferences. First, with subsequent applications in mind, let us define q as the policy choice; Q as the set of all possible policy choices, with an ordering "$>$" over this set (again, if these choices are simply unidimensional [e.g., tax rates] this ordering is natural because it is simple to talk about higher and lower tax rates); and $V^i(q)$ as the *indirect utility function* of individual i where $V^i : Q \to \mathbb{R}$. This is simply the maximized value of utility given particular values of the policy variables. It is this indirect utility function that captures the induced preferences of i. The *ideal point* (sometimes called the "political bliss point") of this individual, q^i, is such that $V^i(q^i) \geq V^i(q)$

for all other $q \in Q$. Single-peaked preferences can be more formally defined as follows:

Definition 4.1 (Single-Peaked Preferences): Policy preferences of voter i are single-peaked if and only if:

$$q'' < q' < q^i \quad \text{or} \quad q'' > q' > q^i, \text{ then } V^i(q'') < V^i(q')$$

Strict concavity of $V^i(q)$ is sufficient for it to be single-peaked.[2]

It is also useful to define the median individual indexed by M. Consider a society with n individuals, the median individual is such that there are exactly as many individuals with $q^i < q^M$ as with $q^i > q^M$, where q^M is the ideal point of the median person.

To assume that people have single-peaked preferences is a restriction on the set of admissible preferences. However, this restriction is not really about the form or nature of people's intrinsic tastes or utility function over goods or income. It is a statement about people's induced preferences over social choices or policy outcomes (the choices over which people are voting, such as tax rates); hence, our reference to the "indirect utility function." To derive people's induced preferences, we need to consider not just their innate preferences but also the structure of the environment and institutions in which they form their induced preferences. It usually turns out to be the features of this environment that are crucial in determining whether people's induced preferences are single-peaked.

We often make assumptions in this book to guarantee that individual preferences are single-peaked. Is the restriction reasonable? Guaranteeing that induced preferences over policies are single-peaked entails making major restrictions on the set of alternatives on which voters can vote. These restrictions often need to take the form of restricting the types of policies that the government can use – in particular, ruling out policies in which all individuals are taxed to redistribute the income to one individual or ruling out person-specific transfers. Assuming preferences are single-peaked is again an application of Occam's razor. We attempt to build parsimonious models of complex social phenomena and, by focusing on situations where the MVT or analogues hold, we are making the assumption that, in reality, democratic decision processes do lead to coherent majorities in favor of or against various policies or choices. This seems a fairly reasonable premise.

[2] In fact, the weaker concept of strict quasiconcavity is all that is necessary for V^i to be single-peaked. However, in all examples used in this book, V^i is strictly concave so we do not introduce the notion of quasiconcavity. It is also possible to state the definition of single-peaked preferences with weak inequalities; e.g., if $q'' \leq q' \leq q^i$ or if $q'' \geq q' \geq q^i$, then $V^i(q'') \leq V^i(q')$. In this case, the corresponding concept would be quasiconcavity (or concavity). Such a formulation allows for indifference over policy choices (i.e., the utility function could be flat over a range of policies). We find it more intuitive to rule out this case, which is not relevant for the models we study in this book.

A large political science and political economy literature focuses on such single-peaked preferences. This is because single-peaked preferences generate the famous and powerful MVT, which constitutes a simple way of determining equilibrium policies from the set of individual preferences. In this book, we either follow this practice of assuming single-peaked preferences making use of the MVT or simply focus on a polity that consists of a few different groups (e.g., the rich and the poor) in which it is easy to determine the social choice (see Subsection 4.2). This is because our focus is not on specific democratic institutions that could aggregate preferences in the absence of nonsingle-peaked preferences but rather some general implications of democratic politics.

3.2 The Median Voter Theorem

Let's now move to an analysis of the MVT, originated by Black (1948). We can use the restrictions on preferences to show that individual preferences can be aggregated into a social choice. The MVT tells us not only that such a choice exists but also that the outcome of majority voting in a situation with single-peaked preferences will be the ideal point of the "median voter." There are various ways to state the MVT. We do this first in a simple model of direct democracy with an open agenda. In a direct democracy, individuals vote directly on pairs of alternatives (some $q, q' \in Q$); the alternative that gets the most votes is the winner. When there is an open agenda, any individual can propose a new pairwise vote pitting any alternative against the winner from the previous vote.

Proposition 4.1 (The Median Voter Theorem): *Consider a set of policy choices $Q \subset \mathbb{R}$; let $q \in Q$ be a policy and let M be the median voter with ideal point q^M. If all individuals have single-peaked preferences over Q, then (1) q^M always defeats any other alternative $q' \in Q$ with $q' \neq q^M$ in a pairwise vote; (2) q^M is the winner in a direct democracy with an open agenda.*

To see the argument behind this theorem, imagine the individuals are voting in a contest between q^M and some policy $\tilde{q} > q^M$. Because preferences are single-peaked, all individuals who have ideal points less than q^M strictly prefer q^M to $\tilde{q}$. This follows because indirect utility functions fall monotonically as we move away from the ideal points of individuals. In this case, because the median voter prefers q^M to $\tilde{q}$, this individual plus all the people with ideal points smaller than q^M constitute a majority, so q^M defeats $\tilde{q}$ in a pairwise vote. This argument is easily applied to show that any $\tilde{q}$ where $\tilde{q} < q^M$ is defeated by q^M (now all individuals with ideal points greater than q^M vote against $\tilde{q}$). Using this type of reasoning, we can see that the policy that wins in a direct democracy must be q^M – this is the ideal point of the median voter who clearly has an incentive to propose this policy.

Why does this work? When citizens have single-peaked preferences and the collective choice is one-dimensional, despite the fact that individuals' preferences differ, a determinate collective choice arises. Intuitively, this is because people can be separated into those who want more q and those who want less, and these groups are just balanced by the median voter. Preferences can be aggregated into a decision because people who prefer levels of q less than q^M have nothing in common with people who prefer levels of q greater than q^M. Therefore, no subset of people who prefer low q can ever get together with a subset of those who prefer high q to constitute an alternative majority. It is these "peripheral" majorities that prevent determinate social choices in general, and they cannot form with single-peaked preferences.

The MVT, therefore, makes sharp predictions about which policies win when preferences are single-peaked, and society is a direct democracy with an open agenda.

It is useful at this point to think of the model underlying Proposition 4.1 as an extensive form game. There are three elements in such a game (Osborne and Rubinstein 1994, pp. 89–90): (1) the set of players – here, the n individuals; (2) the description of the game tree that determines which players play when and what actions are available to them at each node of the tree when they have to make a choice; and (3) the preferences of individuals here captured by $V^i(q)$. (In game theory, preferences and utility functions are often called *payoffs* and *payoff functions*; we use this terminology interchangeably.) A player chooses a strategy to maximize this function where a strategy is a function that determines which action to take at every node in which a player has to make a decision.[3] A strategy here is simply how to vote in different pairwise comparisons. The basic solution concept for such a game is a Nash equilibrium, which is a set of n strategies, one for each player, such that no player can increase his payoff by unilaterally changing strategy. Another way to say this is that players' strategies have to be mutual best responses. We also extensively use a refinement of Nash equilibrium – the concept of subgame perfect Nash equilibrium – in which players' strategies have to be mutual best responses on every proper subgame, not just the whole game. (The relationship between these two concepts is discussed in Chapter 5.) Nevertheless, compared to the models we now discuss, the assumption of open agenda makes it difficult to write down the game more carefully. To do this, we would have to be more specific about who could propose which alternatives and when and how they make those decisions.

3.3 Downsian Party Competition and Policy Convergence

The previous example was based on a direct democracy, an institutional setting in which individuals directly vote over policies. In practice, most democratic societies

[3] Throughout this book, we consider only pure strategies.

are better approximated by representative democracy, where individuals vote for parties in elections and the winner of the election then implements policies. What does the MVT imply for party platforms?

To answer this question, imagine a society with two parties competing for an election by offering one-dimensional policies. Individuals vote for parties, and the policy promised by the winning party is implemented. The two parties care only about coming to office. This is essentially the model considered in the seminal study by Downs (1957), although his argument was anticipated to a large degree by Hotelling (1929).

How will the voters vote? They anticipate that whichever party comes to power, their promised policy will be implemented. So, imagine a situation in which two parties, A and B, are offering two alternative policies (e.g., tax rates) $q_A \in Q$ and $q_B \in Q$ – in the sense that they have made a *credible commitment* to implementing the tax rates q_A and q_B, respectively. Let $P(q_A, q_B)$ be the probability that party A wins power when the parties offer the policy platform (q_A, q_B). Party B, naturally, wins with probability $1 - P(q_A, q_B)$. We can now introduce a simple objective function for the parties: each party gets a rent or benefit $R > 0$ when it comes to power and 0 otherwise. Neither party cares about anything else. More formally, parties choose policy platforms to solve the following pair of maximization problems:

$$\text{Party } A: \max_{q_A \in Q} P(q_A, q_B)R \tag{4.1}$$

$$\text{Party } B: \max_{q_B \in Q} (1 - P(q_A, q_B))R$$

If the majority of the population prefer q_A to q_B, they will vote for party A and we will have $P(q_A, q_B) = 1$. If they prefer q_B to q_A, they will choose party B and we will have $P(q_A, q_B) = 0$. Finally, if the same number of voters prefer one policy to the other, we might think either party is elected with probability $1/2$, so that $P(q_A, q_B) = 1/2$ (although the exact value of $P(q_A, q_B)$ in this case is not important for the outcomes that the model predicts).

Because preferences are single-peaked, from Proposition 4.1 we know that whether a majority of voters will prefer tax rate q_A or q_B depends on the preferences of the median voter. More specifically, let the median voter again be denoted by superscript M; then, Proposition 4.1 immediately implies that if $V^M(q_A) > V^M(q_B)$, we will have a majority for party A over party B. The opposite obtains when $V^M(q_A) < V^M(q_B)$. Finally, if $V^M(q_A) = V^M(q_B)$, one of the parties will come to power with probability $1/2$. Therefore, we have

$$P(q_A, q_B) = \begin{cases} 1 & \text{if } V^M(q_A) > V^M(q_B) \\ \frac{1}{2} & \text{if } V^M(q_A) = V^M(q_B) \\ 0 & \text{if } V^M(q_A) < V^M(q_B) \end{cases} \tag{4.2}$$

The model we have developed can be analyzed as a game more explicitly than the direct-democracy model of the previous section. This game consists of the following three stages:

1. The two political parties noncooperatively choose their platforms (q_A, q_B).
2. Individuals vote for the party they prefer.
3. Whichever party wins the election comes to power and implements the policy it promised at the first stage.

There are $n + 2$ players in this game: the n citizens with payoff functions $V^i(q)$ and the two political parties with payoff functions given in (4.1). Individual voters do not propose policy platforms, only parties do so simultaneously at the first stage of the game. Parties have to choose an action $q_j \in Q$ for $j = A, B$, and citizens again have to vote. Thus, in this model, a subgame perfect Nash equilibrium would be a set of $n + 2$ strategies, one for each of the political parties and one for each of the n voters, which would determine which policies the parties offered and how individuals would vote. If such a set of strategies constituted an equilibrium, then it would have the property that neither party and no voters could improve their payoff by changing their strategy (e.g., by offering a different policy for parties or voting differently for citizens).

In the present model, however, we can simplify the description of a subgame perfect Nash equilibrium because, given a policy vector $(q_A, q_B) \in Q \times Q$, voters simply vote for the party offering the policy closest to their ideal point and, because preferences are single-peaked, the MVT implies that the winner of such an election is determined by (4.2). Hence, the only interesting strategic interaction is between the parties. More formally, we can solve the game by backward induction. To do this, we begin at the end of the game and work backward. Parties are committed to platforms, so whichever party wins implements the policy it offered in the election. Then (4.2) determines which party wins and, considering this at the initial stage of the game, parties choose policies to maximize (4.1).

This implies that a subgame perfect Nash equilibrium in this game reduces to a pair of policies (q_A^*, q_B^*) such that q_A^* maximizes $P(q_A, q_B^*)R$, taking the equilibrium choice of party B as given, and simultaneously q_B^* maximizes $(1 - P(q_A^*, q_B))R$, taking the equilibrium choice of party A as given. In this case, neither party can improve its payoff by choosing an alternative policy (or, in the language of game theory, by "deviating").

Formally, the following theorem characterizes the unique subgame perfect Nash equilibrium of this game:

Proposition 4.2 (Downsian Policy Convergence Theorem): *Consider a vector of policy choices $(q_A, q_B) \in Q \times Q$ where $Q \subset \mathbb{R}$, and two parties A and B that care only about coming to office, and can commit to policy platforms. Let M be the median voter, with ideal point q^M. If all individuals have single-peaked preferences over Q, then in the unique subgame perfect Nash equilibrium, both parties will choose the platforms $q_A^* = q_B^* = q^M$.*

Stated differently, both parties converge to offer exactly the ideal point of the median voter. To see why there is this type of policy convergence, imagine a configuration in which the two parties offered policies q_A and q_B such that $q_A < q_B \leq q^M$. In this case, we have $V^M(q_A) < V^M(q_B)$ by the fact that the median voters' preferences are single-peaked. There will therefore be a clear majority in favor of the policy of party B over party A; hence, $P(q_A, q_B) = 0$, and party B will win the election. Clearly, A has an incentive to increase q_A to some $q \in (q_B, q^M)$ if $q_B < q^M$ to win the election, and to $q = q^M$ if $q_B = q^M$ to have the chance of winning the election with probability 1/2. Therefore, a configuration of platforms such that $q_A < q_B \leq q^M$ cannot be an equilibrium. The same argument applies: if $q_B < q_A \leq q^M$ or if $q_A > q_B \geq q^M$, and so forth.

Next, consider a configuration where $q_A = q_B < q^M$. Could this be an equilibrium? The answer is no: if both parties offer the same policy, then $P(q_A, q_B) = 1/2$ (hence, $1 - P(q_A, q_B) = 1/2$ also). But, then, if A increases q_A slightly so that $q_B < q_A < q^M$, then $P(q_A, q_B) = 1$. Clearly, the only equilibrium involves $q_A = q_B = q^M$ with $P(q_A = q^M, q_B = q^M) = 1/2$ (hence, $1 - P(q_A = q^M, q_B = q^M) = 1/2$). This is an equilibrium because no party can propose an alternative policy (i.e., make a deviation) and increase its probability of winning. For instance, if $q_A = q_B = q^M$ and A changes its policy holding the policy of B fixed, we have $P(q_A, q_B) = 0 < 1/2$ for $q_A > q^M$ or $q_A < q^M$. Therefore, $q_A = q^M$ is a best response to $q_B = q^M$. A similar argument establishes that $q_B = q^M$ is a best response to $q_A = q^M$.

As noted, the MVT does not simply entail the stipulation that people's preferences are single-peaked. We require that the policy space be unidimensional. In the conditions of Proposition 4.1, we stated that policies must lie in a subset of the real numbers ($Q \subset \mathbb{R}$). This is because although the idea of single-peaked preferences extends naturally to higher dimensions of policy, the MVT does not.

Nevertheless, there are various ways to proceed if we want to model situations where collective choices are multidimensional. First, despite Arrow's theorem, it may be the case that the type of balance of power between conflicting interests that we saw in the MVT occurs also in higher dimensions. For this to be true in general, we need not simply state that preferences be single-peaked but also that the ideal points of voters be distributed in particular ways. Important theorems of this type are the work of Plott (1967) and McKelvey and Schofield (1987) (see Austen-Smith and Banks 1999, Chapter 5, for detailed treatment). There are also ideas related to single-peaked preferences, particularly the idea of value-restricted preferences, that extend to multidimensional policy spaces (e.g., Grandmont 1978). Restrictions of this type allow the sort of "balance of power" that emerges with the MVT to exist with a multidimensional policy space.

Second, once we introduce uncertainty into the model, equilibria often exist even if the policy space is multidimensional. This is the so-called probabilistic voting model (Lindbeck and Weibull 1987; Coughlin 1992; Dixit and Londregan 1996, 1998) analyzed in the appendix to this chapter.

Third, following Osborne and Slivinski (1996) and Besley and Coate (1997), once one assumes that politicians cannot commit to policies, one can establish the existence of equilibrium with many dimensions of policy. Intuitively, when politicians cannot commit to arbitrary policies to build majorities, many possibilities for cycling coalitions are removed.

We refer to the type of political competition in this subsection as Downsian political competition. The key result of this subsection, Proposition 4.2, resulting from this type of competition contains two important implications: (1) policy convergence – that is, both parties choose the same policy platform; and (2) this policy platform coincides with the most preferred policy of the median voter. As we show in the appendix, in non-Downsian models of political competition – for example, with ideological voters or ideological parties – there may still be policy convergence, but this convergence may not be to the most preferred policy of the median voter. There may also be nonconvergence, in which the equilibrium policy is partially determined by the preferences of political parties.

4. Our Workhorse Models

In this section, we introduce some basic models that are used throughout the book. As already explained, our theory of democracy and democratization is based on political and distributional conflict and, in an effort to isolate the major interactions, we use models of pure redistribution, where the proceeds of proportional taxation are redistributed lump sum to the citizens. In addition, the major conflict is between those who lose from redistribution and those who benefit from redistribution – two groups that we often conceptualize as the rich and the poor. Hence, a two-class model consisting of only the rich and the poor is a natural starting point. This model is discussed in the next three subsections. Another advantage of a two-class model is that something analogous to the MVT will hold even if the policy space is multidimensional. This is because the poor are the majority and we restrict the policy space so that no intra-poor conflict can ever emerge. As a consequence, no subset of the poor ever finds it advantageous to form a "peripheral" coalition with the rich. In this case, the policies preferred by the poor win over policies preferred by the rich. In Chapter 8, we extend this model by introducing another group, the middle class, and show how it changes a range of the predictions of the model, including the relationship between inequality and redistribution.

In addition to a model in which political conflict is between the rich and the poor, we want to examine what happens when conflict is based on other political identities. We introduce such a model in Subsection 4.4.

4.1 The Median Voter Model of Redistributive Politics

We consider a society consisting of an odd number of n citizens (the model we develop builds on the seminal papers of Romer 1975, Roberts 1977, and Meltzer and Richard 1981). Person $i = 1, 2, .., n$ has income y^i. Let us order people from poorest to richest and think of the median person as the person with median income, denoted y^M. Then, given that we are indexing people according to their incomes, the person with the median income is exactly individual $M = (n + 1)/2$. Let $\bar{y}$ denote average income in this society; thus,

$$\bar{y} = \frac{1}{n} \sum_{i=1}^{n} y^i \tag{4.3}$$

The political system determines a nonnegative tax rate $\tau \geq 0$ proportional to income, the proceeds of which are redistributed lump sum to all citizens. Moreover, this tax rate has to be bounded above by 100 percent – that is, $\tau \leq 1$. Let the resulting lump-sum transfer be T.

We also assume it is costly to raise taxes, so we introduce a general deadweight cost of taxation related to the tax rate. The greater the taxes, the greater are the costs. Economist Arthur Okun (1975) characterized these in terms of the metaphor of the "leaky bucket." Redistributing income or assets is a leaky bucket in the sense that when income or assets are taken from someone, as they are transferred to someone else, part of what was taken dissipates, like water falling through the leaks in a bucket. The leaks are due to the costs of administering taxes and creating a bureaucracy and possibly also because of corruption and sheer incompetence. More important, however, is that greater taxes also distort the investment and labor supply incentives of asset holders and create distortions in the production process. For these reasons, the citizens, who form the majority in democracy, determine the level of taxation and redistribution by trading off the benefits from redistribution and the costs from distortions (i.e., the leaks in the bucket).

Economists often discuss these distortions in terms of the "Laffer Curve," which is the relationship between the tax rate and the amount of tax revenues. The Laffer Curve is shaped like an inverted U. When tax rates are low, increasing the tax rate increases tax revenues. However, as tax rates increase, distortions become greater and eventually tax revenues reach a maximum. After this point, increases in the tax rate actually lead to decreases in tax revenues because the distortions created by taxation are so high.

In our model, these distortions are captured by an aggregate cost, coming out of the government budget constraint of $C(\tau)n\bar{y}$ when the tax rate is τ. Total income in the economy, $n\bar{y}$, is included simply as a normalization. We adopt this normalization because we do not want the equilibrium tax rate to depend in an arbitrary way on the scale of the economy. For example, if we vary $n\bar{y}$, we do not want equilibrium tax rates to rise simply because the costs of taxation are fixed while the benefits of taxation to voters increase. It seems likely that as $n\bar{y}$ increases, the costs of taxation also increase (e.g., the wages of tax inspectors increase), which is considered in this normalization. We assume that $C : [0, 1] \to \mathbb{R}_+$, where $C(0) = 0$ so that there are no costs when there is no taxation; $C'(\cdot) > 0$ so that costs are increasing in the level of taxation; $C''(\cdot) > 0$ so that these costs are strictly convex – that is, they increase faster as tax rates increase (thus ensuring that the second-order condition of the maximization problem is satisfied); and, finally, $C'(0) = 0$ and $C'(1) = 1$ so that an interior solution is ensured: the first says that marginal costs are small when the tax rate is low, and the second implies that costs increase rapidly at high levels of taxation. Together with the convexity assumption, both of these are plausible: they emphasize that the disincentive effects of taxation become substantial as tax rates become very high. Think, for example, of the incentives to work and to produce when there is a 100 percent tax rate on your earnings!

From this, it follows that the government budget constraint is as follows:

$$T = \frac{1}{n}\left(\sum_{i=1}^{n} \tau y^i - C(\tau) n\bar{y}\right) = (\tau - C(\tau))\,\bar{y} \tag{4.4}$$

which uses the definition of average income above (4.3). This equation emphasizes that there are proportional income taxes and equal redistribution of the proceeds, so higher taxes are more redistributive. For example, a higher τ increases the lump-sum transfer and, because rich and poor agents receive the same transfer but pay taxes proportional to their incomes, richer agents bear a greater tax burden.

All individuals in this society maximize their consumption, which is equal to their post-tax income, denoted by $\hat{y}^i(\tau)$ for individual i at tax rate τ. Using the government budget constraint (4.4), we have that, when the tax rate is τ, the indirect utility of individual i and his post-tax income are

$$\begin{aligned} V\left(y^i \mid \tau\right) &= \hat{y}^i\left(\tau\right) \\ &= (1-\tau)\,y^i + T \\ &= (1-\tau)\,y^i + (\tau - C(\tau))\,\bar{y} \end{aligned} \tag{4.5}$$

The indirect-utility function is conditioned only on one policy variable, τ, because we have eliminated the lump-sum transfer T by using (4.4). We also condition it on y^i because, for the remainder of the book, it is useful to keep this income explicit. Thus, we use the notation $V(y^i \mid \tau)$ instead of $V^i(\tau)$.

More generally, individuals also make economic choices that depend on the policy variables. In this case, to construct $V(y^i \mid \tau)$, we first need to solve for individual i's optimal economic decisions given the values of the policy variables and then define the induced preferences over policies, given these optimally taken decisions (Persson and Tabellini 2000, pp. 19–21).

It is straightforward to derive each individual i's ideal tax rate from this indirect-utility function. Recall that this is defined as the tax rate τ^i that maximizes $V(y^i \mid \tau)$. Under the assumptions made about $C(\tau)$, $V(y^i \mid \tau)$ is strictly concave and twice continuously differentiable. This tax rate can then be found simply from an unconstrained maximization problem, so we need to set the derivative of $V(y^i \mid \tau)$ with respect to τ equal to zero. In other words, τ^i needs to satisfy the first-order condition:

$$-y^i + \left(1 - C'(\tau^i)\right)\bar{y} = 0 \quad \text{and} \quad \tau^i > 0 \text{ or} \qquad (4.6)$$
$$-y^i + \left(1 - C'(\tau^i)\right)\bar{y} \leq 0 \quad \text{and} \quad \tau^i = 0$$

which we have written explicitly emphasizing complementary slackness (i.e., τ^i can be at a corner). In the rest of the book, we will not write such conditions out fully as long as this causes no confusion.

The assumption that $C''(\cdot) > 0$ ensures that the second-order condition for maximization is satisfied and that (4.6) gives a maximum. More explicitly, the second-order condition (which is derived by differentiating (4.6) with respect to τ) is $-C''(\tau^i)\bar{y} < 0$, which is always true, given $C''(\cdot) > 0$. This second-order condition also implies that $V(y^i \mid \tau)$ is a strictly concave function, which is a sufficient condition for it to be single-peaked.

We have written the first-order condition (4.6) in the Kuhn–Tucker form (Blume and Simon 1994, pp. 439–41) to allow for the fact that the preferred tax rate of agent i may be zero. In this case, we have a corner solution and the first-order condition does not hold as an equality. If $\tau^i > 0$, then (4.6) says that the ideal tax rate of voter i has the property that its marginal cost to individual i is equal to its marginal benefit. The marginal cost is measured by y^i, individual i's own income, because an incremental increase in the tax rate leads to a decline in the individual i's utility proportional to his income (consumption). The benefit, on the other hand, is $(1 - C'(\tau^i))\bar{y}$, which comes from the fact that with higher taxes, there will be more income redistribution. The term $(1 - C'(\tau^i))\bar{y}$ is the extra income redistribution, net of costs, generated by a small increase in the tax rate.

The conditions in (4.6) imply the intuitive result that rich people prefer lower tax rates and less redistribution than poor people. For a rich person, the ratio $y^i/\bar{y}$ is higher than it would be for a poor person. This means that for (4.6) to hold, $1 - C'(\tau^i)$ must be higher, so that $C'(\tau^i)$ must be lower. Because $C'(\tau^i)$ is an increasing function (by the convexity of $C(\cdot)$), this implies that the preferred tax rate must be lower. The model actually has a more specific prediction. For a person whose income is the same as the mean, (4.6) becomes $0 = -C'(\tau^i)$, which implies that $\tau^i = 0$ for such a person. Moreover, for any person with income $y^i > \bar{y}$, the Kuhn–Tucker conditions imply that there is a corner solution. Hence, people whose income is above average favor no income redistribution at all, whereas people with $y^i < \bar{y}$ favor a strictly positive tax rate, which is why we use the Kuhn–Tucker formulation.

To derive these comparative static results more formally, let us assume $\tau^i > 0$ and use the implicit function theorem (Blume and Simon 1994, p. 341) to write the optimal tax rate of individual i as a function of his own income, $\tau(y^i)$. This satisfies (4.6). The implicit function theorem tells us that the derivative of this function, denoted $\tau'(y^i)$, exists and is given by

$$\tau'(y^i) = -\frac{1}{C''(\tau(y^i))\bar{y}} < 0$$

Throughout the book, we appeal frequently to the implicit-function theorem to undertake comparative static analysis of the models we study. We undertake two types of comparative statics. First is the type we have just analyzed. Here, we use the conditions for an equilibrium to express a particular endogenous variable, such as the tax rate, as a function of the various exogenous variables or parameters of the model, such as the extent of inequality. Comparative statics then amounts to investigating the effect of changes in exogenous variables or parameters, such as inequality, on the value of the endogenous variable. (When inequality is higher, does the tax rate increase?) We often use the answers to such questions not just to derive predictions for what would happen within one country if inequality increased but also to compare across countries: Would a country where inequality was higher have a higher tax rate than a country with lower inequality?

We also conduct a different type of comparative statics. In game-theoretic models, various types of behavior may be equilibria in different types of circumstances. For instance, in the repeated prisoner's dilemma, cooperation forever may be an equilibrium if players value the future sufficiently. We derive conditions under which particular types of behavior – for instance, the creation of democracy – are an equilibrium. We then conduct comparative statics of these conditions to investigate which factors make democracy more or less likely to be created. When we do this, however, we are not directly investigating how a change in an exogenous variable (smoothly) changes the equilibrium value of an endogenous variable. Rather, we examine how changes in exogenous variables influence the "size of the parameter space" for which democracy is created. In essence, democracy can only be created in certain circumstances, and we want to know what makes such circumstances more likely.

We can now think of a game, the (Nash) equilibrium of which will determine the level of redistributive taxation. We can do this in the context of either a direct democracy or a representative democracy, but the most intuitive approach is the one we developed leading up to Proposition 4.2. This result implies that the equilibrium of the game will be for both political parties to propose the ideal point of the median voter, which will be the tax rate chosen in a democracy. The model has this prediction despite the fact that there is political conflict. Poor people would like high taxes and a lot of redistribution; rich people, those with greater than average income, are opposed to any redistribution. How can we aggregate these conflicting preferences? The MVT says that the outcome is the tax rate preferred by the median voter and, for most income distributions, the income of the median person is less than average income (i.e., $y^M < \bar{y}$). In this case, the median voter prefers a strictly positive tax rate τ^M that satisfies the first-order condition:

$$\frac{y^M}{\bar{y}} = 1 - C'(\tau^M)$$

The comparative statics of this condition follow from the discussion of (4.6). If y^M decreases relative to $\bar{y}$, then the median voter, who becomes poorer relative to the mean, prefers greater tax rates and more redistribution.

4.2 A Two-Group Model of Redistributive Politics

Although many of the results in this book follow from the previous model in which the income of each person is different, a useful simpler model is one in which there are just two income levels. Consider, therefore, a society consisting of two types of individuals: the rich with fixed income y^r and the poor with income $y^p < y^r$. To economize on notation, total population is normalized to 1; a fraction $1 - \delta > 1/2$ of the agents is poor, with income y^p; and the remaining fraction δ is rich with income y^r. Mean income is denoted by $\bar{y}$. Our focus is on distributional conflict, so it is important to parameterize inequality. To do so, we introduce the notation θ as the share of total income accruing to the rich; hence, we have:

$$y^p = \frac{(1-\theta)\bar{y}}{1-\delta} \quad \text{and} \quad y^r = \frac{\theta\bar{y}}{\delta} \tag{4.7}$$

Notice that an increase in θ represents an increase in inequality. Of course, we need $y^p < \bar{y} < y^r$, which requires that:

$$\frac{(1-\theta)\bar{y}}{1-\delta} < \frac{\theta\bar{y}}{\delta} \quad \text{or} \quad \theta > \delta$$

As in the last subsection, the political system determines a nonnegative income-tax rate $\tau \geq 0$, the proceeds of which are redistributed lump sum to all citizens. We assume that taxation is as costly as before and, from this, it follows that the government budget constraint is:

$$T = \tau\left((1-\delta)y^p + \delta y^r\right) - C(\tau)\bar{y} = (\tau - C(\tau))\,\bar{y} \tag{4.8}$$

With a slight abuse of notation, we now use the superscript i to denote social classes as well as individuals so, for most of the discussion, we have $i = p$ or r. Using the government budget constraint (4.8), we have that, when the tax rate is τ, the indirect utility of individual i and his post-tax income are:

$$V\left(y^i \mid \tau\right) = \hat{y}^i(\tau) = (1-\tau)\,y^i + (\tau - C(\tau))\,\bar{y} \tag{4.9}$$

As in the last subsection, all agents have single-peaked preferences and, because there are more poor agents than rich agents, the median voter is a poor agent. We can think of the model as constituting a game as in the previous subsection; democratic politics will then lead to the tax rate most preferred by the median voter: here, a poor agent. Notice that because they have the same utility functions and because of the restrictions on the form of tax policy (i.e., taxes and transfers are not person-specific), all poor agents have the same ideal point and vote for the same policy. Here, there is no need for coordination and no sort of collective-action problem (discussed in Chapter 5).

Let this equilibrium tax rate be τ^p. We can find it by maximizing the post-tax income of a poor agent; that is, by choosing τ to maximize $V(y^p \mid \tau)$. The first-order condition for maximizing this indirect utility now gives:

$$-y^p + \left(1 - C'(\tau^p)\right) \bar{y} = 0 \quad \text{with} \quad \tau^p > 0 \tag{4.10}$$

because $y^p < \bar{y}$. Equation (4.10), therefore, implicitly defines the most preferred tax rate of a poor agent and the political equilibrium tax rate. For reasons identical to those in the previous subsection, it is immediate that preferences are single-peaked.

Now, using the definitions in (4.7), we can write the equation for τ^p in a more convenient form:

$$\left(\frac{\theta - \delta}{1 - \delta}\right) = C'(\tau^p) \tag{4.11}$$

where both sides of (4.11) are positive because $\theta > \delta$ by the fact that the poor have less income than the rich.

Equation (4.11) is useful for comparative statics. Most important, consider an increase in θ, so that a smaller share of income accrues to the poor, or the gap between the rich and the poor widens. Because there is a plus sign in front of θ, the left side of (4.11) increases. Therefore, for (4.11) to hold, τ^p must change so that the value of the right side increases as well. Because $C''(\cdot) > 0$, when τ^p increases, the derivative increases; therefore, for the right side to increase, τ^p must increase. This establishes that greater inequality (higher θ) induces a higher tax rate, or, written mathematically using the implicit function theorem:

$$\frac{d\tau^p}{d\theta} = \frac{1}{C''(\tau^p)(1 - \delta)} > 0$$

It is also the case that total (net) tax revenues as a proportion of national income increase when inequality rises. Total net tax revenues as a proportion of national income are:

$$\frac{(\tau^p - C(\tau^p))\,\bar{y}}{\bar{y}} = \tau^p - C(\tau^p)$$

Notice that $d(\tau^p - C(\tau^p))/d\theta = (1 - C'(\tau^p)) \cdot d\tau^p/d\theta$. We know that higher inequality leads to higher taxes; that is, $d\tau^p/d\theta > 0$. Moreover, (4.11) implies that $C'(\tau^p) = (\theta - \delta)/(1-\delta) < 1$, so $1 - C'(\tau^p) > 0$, which then implies that $d(\tau^p - C(\tau^p))/d\theta > 0$. In other words, greater inequality leads to a higher proportion of net tax revenues in national income, as argued by Meltzer and Richard (1981) in the context of a slightly different model. In fact, it is straightforward to see that the burden of taxation on the rich is heavier when inequality is greater even if the tax rate is unchanged. Let us first define the burden of taxation as the net redistribution away from the rich at some tax rate τ. This is:

$$\text{Burden}(\tau) = C(\tau)\,\bar{y} - \tau\left(1 - \frac{\theta}{\delta}\right)\bar{y}$$

As inequality increases (i.e., θ increases), this burden increases, which simply reflects the fact that with constant average incomes, transfers are constant; and, as inequality increases, a greater fraction of tax revenues are collected from the rich. This observation implies that, even with unchanged tax rates, this burden increases and, therefore, with great inequality, the rich will be typically more opposed to taxation.

Finally, it is useful to conclude this subsection with a brief discussion of efficiency. In this model, taxes are purely redistributive and create distortionary costs as captured by the function $C(\tau^p)$. Whether democracy is efficient depends on the criterion that one applies. If we adopted the Pareto criterion (Green, Mas-Colell, and Whinston 1995, p. 313), the political equilibrium allocation would be Pareto optimal because it is impossible to change the tax policy to make any individual better off without making the median voter worse off – because the democratic tax rate maximizes the utility of the median voter, any other tax rate must lower his utility.

However, in many cases, the Pareto criterion might be thought of as unsatisfactory because it implies that many possible situations cannot be distinguished from an efficiency point of view. An alternative approach is to propose a stronger definition of social welfare, such as a utilitarian social welfare function, and examine if political equilibria coincide with allocations that maximize this function (Green, Mas-Colell, and Whinston 1995, pp. 825–31). The democratic political equilibrium here is inefficient compared to the utilitarian social optimum, which would involve no taxation. That taxation creates distortionary costs is a feature of most of the models we discuss throughout this book. In some sense, this is plausible because taxation creates disincentive effects, distorting the allocation of resources.

Its tendency to redistribute income with its potential distortions might suggest that democracy is inefficient relative to a regime that allocates political power to richer agents, who would choose less redistribution. Nevertheless, there are also plausible reasons in general for why greater redistribution might improve the allocation of resources. First, if we allowed people to get utility from public goods that were provided out of tax revenues, it is a standard result in median-voter models that the rich prefer too few public goods whereas the poor prefer too many (Persson and Tabellini 2000). In this case, depending on the shape of the income distribution, the level preferred by the poor may be closer to the social optimum, and democracy, giving political power to the poor, would improve the social efficiency of public goods provision.

Second, although we do not consider such models in this book, we can imagine a situation in which agents undertake investments in human capital, and the poor are credit-constrained and underinvest relative to the optimal amount. Then, redistributive taxation – even without public-good provision – by increasing the post-tax incomes of the poor may contribute to aggregate human-capital investments and improve the allocation of resources (Galor and Zeira 1993; Benabou 2000; Acemoglu and Robinson 2000a, 2002). Moreover, as we show later, democracy may in fact be more efficient than nondemocracy even when there are taxes raised in democracy. This is because nondemocracies may allocate resources to socially wasteful activities such as repression to stay in power, and the costs of taxation may well be less than the costs of repression.

4.3 Targeted Transfers

The model of redistributive politics we have analyzed so far places many restrictions on the form of fiscal policy. For instance, all agents receive the same amount of redistribution. As we suggested previously, allowing for completely arbitrary forms of redistribution quickly leads to a situation in which collective choices are not determinate. However, it is possible to introduce more complicated forms of redistribution without losing the determinateness of social choices, and the comparison of economies with different structures of taxation yields interesting results.

Most relevant in this context is an extension of the two-group model to allow for targeted transfers – that is, different levels of transfers for the rich and the poor. More concretely, after tax revenues have been collected, they may be redistributed in the form of a lump-sum transfer T_r that only goes to rich people, or a transfer T_p that only goes to poor people. This implies that the government budget constraint is now:

$$(1-\delta)T_p + \delta T_r = \tau\left((1-\delta)y^p + \delta y^r\right) - C(\tau)\bar{y} = (\tau - C(\tau))\,\bar{y} \tag{4.12}$$

The indirect utility of a poor person, in general, is:

$$V(y^p \mid \tau, T_p) = (1-\tau)y^p + T_p$$

This problem has a three-dimensional policy space because voting will be over the tax rate τ and the two transfers T_p and T_r but where one of these variables can be determined residually from the government budget constraint. This is why we condition the indirect-utility function $V(y^p \mid \tau, T_p)$ on only two of these variables with T_r following from (4.12). Because the policy space is now two-dimensional, the MVT does not apply. However, collective choices are determinate and the equilibrium policy will still be that preferred by the poor. The poor are more numerous and all prefer the same policy because targeted transfers, like lump-sum transfers, do not allow the formation of a coalition of the rich and a subset of the poor to overturn the majority formed by the poor.

To characterize the equilibrium, we can again think of the model as a game in which two political parties propose policy platforms. The unique Nash equilibrium involves both parties offering the ideal point of the poor. To see what this ideal point is, note that a poor agent clearly does not wish to redistribute to the rich; hence, $T_r = 0$. Hence, the intuitive outcome is that the poor choose τ to maximize:

$$\begin{aligned} V(y^p \mid \tau, T_p) &= (1-\tau)y^p + T_p \\ &= (1-\tau)y^p + \frac{(\tau - C(\tau))\,\bar{y}}{1-\delta} \end{aligned}$$

with first-order condition, $y^p(1-\delta) = (1 - C'(\tau^{pT}))\bar{y}$ gives an ideal point of (τ^{pT}, T_p^{pT}) where $\tau^{pT} > 0$. Here, we use the superscript T to indicate that τ^{pT} is the tax rate preferred by a poor agent when targeted transfers are allowed. Similarly, T_p^{pT} and T_r^{pT} are the preferred levels of transfers of a poor agent. Substituting for y^p, we see that τ^{pT} satisfies the equation:

$$\theta = C'(\tau^{pT}) \tag{4.13}$$

and because $T_r^{pT} = 0$ from the government budget constraint, we have $T_p^{pT} = (\tau^{pT} - C(\tau^{pT}))\bar{y}/(1-\delta)$.

The first important implication of this analysis is that the equilibrium tax rate in democracy with targeted transfers, τ^{pT}, is greater than the tax rate without targeted transfers, τ^p, given by (4.11). Mathematically, this follows from the fact that $\theta > (\theta - \delta)/(1-\delta)$. The intuitive reason for this is also simple: without targeted transfers, because redistribution goes both to the poor and the rich, each dollar of tax revenue creates lower net benefit for the poor than in the presence of targeted transfers. τ^{pT} and τ^p converge when $\delta \to 0$; that is, when the fraction of the rich in the population becomes negligible. This is natural; in this case, there are so few rich agents that whether they obtain some of the transfers is inconsequential.

More important than the comparison of the tax rates is the comparative statics of τ^{pT}. It can be seen that those are identical to the results obtained in the model without targeted transfers. In particular, greater inequality again increases taxes.

It is instructive to examine the burden of taxation on the elite in this model, which is now:

$$\text{Burden}^T(\tau) = \tau \frac{\theta}{\delta} \bar{y}$$

Obviously, $\text{Burden}^T(\tau) > \text{Burden}(\tau)$, where $\text{Burden}(\tau)$ was the burden of taxation defined in the previous subsection when there were no targeted transfers. Hence, the introduction of targeted transfers increases the burden of democracy on the rich. Moreover, as before, higher inequality increases this burden at unchanged tax rates.

An important implication of this result is that targeted transfers increase the degree of conflict in society. In particular, because with targeted transfers democracy charges higher taxes and redistributes the proceeds only to the poor, the rich are worse off than in democracy without targeted transfers. Furthermore, for similar reasons, nondemocracy is now worse for the poor. This is because, as discussed in Chapter 2, we can think of nondemocracy as the rule of an elite who we associate with the rich. In particular, and as we now show, in nondemocracy when targeted transfers are available, the rich elite would prefer to set positive taxes and redistribute the proceeds to themselves. In particular, their ideal point would be a vector (τ^{rT}, T_r^{rT}) (with T_p^{rT} following from (4.12)), where τ^{rT} satisfies the first-order condition $-y^r\delta + (1 - C'(\tau^{rT}))\bar{y} = 0$ if $\tau^{rT} > 0$ or $-y^r\delta + (1 - C'(\tau^{rT}))\bar{y} < 0$ and $\tau^{rT} = 0$. Unlike in the model without targeted transfers, the first-order condition for the rich does have an interior solution, with τ^{rT} implicitly defined by the equation:

$$1 - \theta = C'(\tau^{rT}) \tag{4.14}$$

which has a solution for some $\tau^{rT} > 0$. Hence, introducing targeted transfers makes nondemocracy better for the rich and worse for the poor.

The increased degree of conflict in society with targeted transfers has the effect of making different regimes more unstable – in particular, making democratic consolidation more difficult.

4.4 Alternative Political Identities

In the previous subsection, we allowed transfers to go to some subset of society, the poor or the rich. More generally, we are interested in what a democratic political equilibrium looks like when voting takes place not along the lines of poor versus rich but rather perhaps along the lines of ethnicity or another politically salient characteristic. There are few analytical studies in which researchers have tried to understand when socioeconomic class rather than something else, such as ethnicity, might be important for politics (Roemer 1998; Austen-Smith and

Wallerstein 2003). Our aim is not to develop a general model but rather to illustrate how democratic politics might work when other identities are salient and how this influences the comparative statics – for example, with respect to inequality, of the democratic equilibrium. In subsequent chapters, we use this model to discuss how our theory of the creation and consolidation of democracy works when political identities differ.

Consider, then, a model of pure income redistribution with rich and poor people but where people are also part of two other groups perhaps based on religion, culture, or ethnicity, which we call X and Z. Thus, some members of type X are relatively poor and some are relatively rich, and the same is true for type Z. To capture in a simple way the idea that politics is not poor versus rich but rather type X versus type Z, we assume that income is taxed proportionately at rate τ as usual but that it can be redistributed either as a transfer to type X, denoted T_X, or as a transfer to type Z, denoted T_Z. Let there be δ_X type Xs and δ_Z type Zs where $\delta_X + \delta_Z = 1$. We also introduce the notation δ^i_j for $i = p, r$ and $j = X, Z$ for the subpopulations. Throughout, we assume that $\delta_X > 1/2$ so that type Xs are in a majority and let y^i_j be the income of type $i = p, r$ in group $j = X, Z$.

The government budget constraint is:

$$\delta_X T_X + \delta_Z T_Z = (\tau - C(\tau))\, \bar{y}$$

where average income is defined as:

$$\bar{y} = \delta^p_X y^p_X + \delta^r_X y^r_X + \delta^p_Z y^p_Z + \delta^r_Z y^r_Z$$

where the total population size is again 1. To be more specific about incomes, we assume that group X gets a fraction $1 - \alpha$ of total income and group Z gets α. Thus, $\delta^p_X y^p_X + \delta^r_X y^r_X = (1 - \alpha)\bar{y}$ and $\delta^p_Z y^p_Z + \delta^r_Z y^r_Z = \alpha\bar{y}$. Income is distributed within the groups in the following way: $\delta^r_X y^r_X = \alpha^r_X (1 - \alpha)\bar{y}$ and $\delta^p_X y^p_X = (1 - \alpha^r_X)(1 - \alpha)\bar{y}$, so that α^r_X is the fraction of the income that accrues to the rich in group X. Similarly, we have $\delta^r_Z y^r_Z = \alpha^r_Z \alpha\bar{y}$ and $\delta^p_Z y^p_Z = (1 - \alpha^r_Z)\alpha\bar{y}$. We assume:

$$y^r_X > y^p_X, \text{ which implies } \frac{\alpha^r_X}{\delta^r_X} > \frac{1 - \alpha^r_X}{\delta^p_X}$$

$$y^r_Z > y^p_Z, \text{ which implies } \frac{\alpha^r_Z}{\delta^r_Z} > \frac{1 - \alpha^r_Z}{\delta^p_Z}$$

It is straightforward to calculate the ideal points of the four types of agents. Both poor and rich type X agents prefer $T_Z = 0$ and both may prefer $T_X > 0$. However, poor type Xs prefer more redistribution than rich type Xs. To see this, note that the preferred tax rates of poor and rich type Xs (conditional on $T_Z = 0$), denoted τ^p_X

and τ_X^r, satisfy the first-order conditions (with complementary slackness):

$$C'(\tau_X^p) = 1 - \frac{\delta_X y_X^p}{\bar{y}} \text{ if } \tau_X^p > 0 \quad \text{and} \quad C'(\tau_X^r) = 1 - \frac{\delta_X y_X^r}{\bar{y}} \text{ if } \tau_X^r > 0 \quad (4.15)$$

As usual, a priori we do not know if the solutions are interior or at a corner. The first-order condition for a rich agent can imply a positive tax rate when $\delta_X y_X^r/\bar{y} < 1$. Intuitively, in this model, redistribution is not from the rich to the poor but from one type of agent to another. Therefore, even rich people may benefit from this type of redistribution. If both tax rates τ_X^p and τ_X^r are interior, then $\tau_X^p > \tau_X^r$ follows from (4.15) so that the poor members of group X prefer higher tax rates and more redistribution. The ideal points of group Z are also easy to understand. All members of group Z prefer $T_X = 0$ and both may also prefer $T_Z > 0$, but poor members of Z prefer higher taxes and more redistribution than rich members of the group.

We now formulate a game to determine the tax rate in democracy. If we formulate the model as we have done so far in this chapter, where all issues are voted on simultaneously, then because the model has a three-dimensional policy space, it may not possess a Nash equilibrium. To circumvent this problem in a simple way, we formulate the game by assuming that the tax rate and the transfers are voted on sequentially. The timing of the game is as follows:

1. All citizens vote over the tax rate to be levied on income, τ.
2. Given this tax rate, voting takes place over T_X or T_Z, the form of the transfers to be used to redistribute income.

We solve this game by backward induction and show that there is always a unique subgame perfect Nash equilibrium. We focus on two types of equilibria. In the first, when $\delta_X^p > 1/2$, so that poor type Xs form an absolute majority, there is a unique equilibrium of this model that has the property that the equilibrium policy is τ_X^p, preferred by the poor type Xs.

In the second, $\delta_X^p < 1/2$, so that poor type Xs do not form an absolute majority, there is a unique equilibrium of this model that has the property that the equilibrium policy is τ_X^r, preferred by the rich type Xs.

To see why these are equilibria, we start by considering the first case. Solving by backward induction at the second stage, because $\delta_X > 1/2$, it is clear that a proposal to redistribute income only to Xs (i.e., propose $T_X > 0$ and $T_Z = 0$) will defeat a proposal to redistribute to Zs or to redistribute to both Xs and Zs. That this is the unique equilibrium follows immediately from the fact that Xs are in a majority. Next, given that only T_X will be used to redistribute, in the first stage of the game all agents have single-peaked preferences with respect to τ. The ideal point of all type Zs, given that subsequently $T_Z = 0$, is $\tau = 0$. The ideal points of poorer and richer members of X are τ_X^p and τ_X^r, as previously shown. When $\delta_X^p > 1/2$, poor Xs form an absolute majority and, hence, the median voter is a poor type

X. Because only T_X will subsequently be used to redistribute income, the MVT applies and the tax rate determined at the first stage of the game must be the ideal one for poor type Xs, τ_X^p. Therefore, in this case, there is a unique subgame perfect Nash equilibrium, which we denote $(\tau_X^p, T_Z = 0, T_X = (\tau_X^p - C(\tau_X^p))\bar{y}/\delta_X)$.

In the second case, where poor Xs are not an absolute majority, the difference is that the median voter is now a rich type X. Hence, the MVT implies that τ_X^r will be the tax rate determined at the first stage. Therefore, in this case, there is a unique subgame perfect Nash equilibrium $(\tau_X^r, T_Z = 0, T_X = (\tau_X^r - C(\tau_X^r))\bar{y}/\delta_X)$.

The equilibrium of this game does not depend on the timing of play. To see this, consider the following game in which we reversed the order in which the policies are voted on:

1. All citizens vote on the type of transfers, T_X or T_Z, to be used to redistribute income.
2. Given the form of income transfer to be used, all citizens vote on the rate of income tax, τ.

We can again see that there is a unique subgame perfect equilibrium, identical to the one we calculated previously. Begin at the end of the game where, given that either T_X or T_Z has been chosen, individuals vote on τ. In the subgame where T_X has been chosen, all agents again have single-peaked preferences over τ. Thus, when $\delta_X^p > 1/2$, the median voter is a poor member of X and the equilibrium tax rate chosen is τ_X^p. When $\delta_X^p < 1/2$, the median voter is a rich member of X and the equilibrium tax rate chosen is τ_X^r. In the subgame where T_Z has been chosen, because type Xs do not benefit from any redistribution, the ideal point of all Xs must be to set a tax rate of zero. Because type Xs are a majority, the equilibrium must have $\tau = 0$ because the median voter is a type X. Now, moving back to the first stage of the game, since Xs are in a majority, the outcome is that income will be redistributed only according to T_X. From this, we see that the unique subgame perfect equilibrium is identical to the one we analyzed before.

For our present purposes, the most interesting features of these equilibria are the comparative statics with respect to inequality. In both types of equilibria, an increase in inter-group inequality, in the sense that the income of type Xs falls relative to the income of type Zs, holding inequality within group Z constant, leads to higher tax rates and greater redistribution. If there is an increase in Zs income share, holding $\bar{y}$ constant, then both y_X^p and y_X^r will fall and both poor and rich type Xs favor higher taxes. To see this, we use the definitions of income and substitute them into (4.15):

$$C'(\tau_X^p) = 1 - \frac{\delta_X(1-\alpha_X^r)(1-\alpha)}{\delta_X^p} \quad \text{and} \quad C'(\tau_X^r) = 1 - \frac{\delta_X \alpha_X^r (1-\alpha)}{\delta_X^r}$$

where we assumed for notational simplicity that both first-order conditions have interior solutions. An increase in the share of income accruing to the Zs increases

α, which increases both τ_X^p and τ_X^r; that is:

$$\frac{d\tau_X^p}{d\alpha} = \frac{\delta_X(1 - \alpha_X^r)}{C''(\tau_X^p)\delta_X^p} > 0$$

that is, an increase in α increases the tax rate. Similarly, $d\tau_X^r/d\alpha > 0$.

However, such a change in income distribution does not map easily into the standard measures such as the Gini coefficient. Moreover, if there is a change in inequality that redistributes within groups (e.g., α_X^r increases [so that y_X^p falls and y_X^r rises]), then the comparative statics are different in the two equilibria. In the first, taxes will increase, whereas in the second, they will decrease.

It is worth pausing at this point to discuss the empirical evidence on the relationship between inequality and redistribution. Our model predicts that greater inequality between groups will lead to greater inter-group redistribution in democracy. However, because political identities do not always form along the lines of class, it does not imply that an increase in inequality – as conventionally measured by the Gini coefficient or the share of labor in national income – will lead to more measured redistribution. The empirical literature reflects this; for example, Perotti (1996) noted following the papers of Alesina and Rodrik (1994) and Persson and Tabellini (1994) that tax revenues and transfers as a fraction of GDP are not higher in more unequal societies.

Nevertheless, so far, this relationship has not been investigated with a careful research design. One obvious pitfall is that of reverse causality. Although Sweden is an equal country today, what we are observing is the result of seventy years of aggressive income redistribution and egalitarian policies (e.g., in the labor market). Indeed, existing historical evidence suggests that inequality has fallen dramatically during the last hundred years in Sweden.

There are also many potential omitted variables that could bias the relationship between inequality and redistribution, even in the absence of reverse causality. Stated simply, many of the institutional and potentially cultural determinants of redistribution are likely to be correlated with inequality. For example, Sweden is a more homogeneous society than either Brazil or the United States, and many have argued that the homogeneity of the population is a key factor determining the level of redistribution (Alesina, Glaeser, and Sacerdote 2001; Alesina and Glaeser 2004). Moreover, there may well be much more of a "taste for redistribution" in Sweden given that for most of the last seventy years, the country has been governed by socialists with a highly egalitarian social philosophy.

5. Democracy and Political Equality

Although the MVT is at the heart of this book and much positive political economy, there are, of course, many other theoretical approaches to modeling democratic politics. A useful way of thinking about these theories is that they imply different distributions of power in the society. The median-voter model is the simplest and perhaps the most naive setup in which each person has one vote. In the two-group model, numbers win and the citizens get what they want.

Nevertheless, as previously mentioned, in reality some people's preferences are "worth" more than others. There are many ways in which this can happen. First, preferences may be defined not just over income but people may also care about ideological positions associated with different political parties. Voters who are less ideological are more willing to vote according to the policies offered by different parties. Such voters, often called swing voters, therefore tend to be more responsive to policies and, as a result, the parties tailor their policies to them. To take an extreme situation, imagine that poor people are very ideological and prefer to vote for socialist parties, whatever policy the party offers. In this case, policy does not reflect the preferences of the poor because right-wing parties can never persuade the poor to vote for them; socialist parties already have their vote and, therefore, can design their policies to attract the votes of other groups, perhaps the rich. These ideas stem from the work on the probabilistic voting model by Lindbeck and Weibull (1987), Coughlin (1992), and Dixit and Londregan (1996, 1998). In this model, the preferences of all agents influence the equilibrium policy in democracy; the more a group tends to consist of swing voters, the more their preferences will count. Thus, for instance, if the rich are less ideological than the poor, it gives them considerable power in democracy even though they are in a numerical minority.

Second, equilibrium policy may be influenced not only by voting but also by campaign contributions and the activities of lobbies and special interests. In such a situation, groups that are represented by an organized special interest or who have more resources to channel through special interests tend to have more influence over policy than groups with less organization and resources. If the rich have an advantage in either of these dimensions, this allows their preferences to influence democratic policies. A model along these lines was developed initially by Becker (1983), which was greatly developed and extended by Grossman and Helpman (1996, 2001).

Third, so far, political parties have in a sense been perfect agents of the voters. In reality, however, political parties have objectives that are to some extent autonomous from those of citizens, and the policies they offer reflect them, not simply the wishes of the median voter. This is particularly true when, as first emphasized by Wittman (1983), there is uncertainty in the outcome of elections or, as shown by Alesina (1988), parties cannot commit to arbitrary policy platforms. When either of these is true, political parties' objectives, not simply the preferences of the voters, are important in influencing political outcomes. In this case, groups that can capture the agendas of political parties can influence democratic policy to a greater extent than their numbers would indicate.

Finally, and probably most interesting the Downsian model and many of its extensions, including models of probabilistic voting, feature a thin description of political institutions. The Downsian model introduced in this chapter is almost like a presidential election (although not in the United States because then we would have to introduce the electoral college). For example, we did not distinguish between electoral districts. If we wanted to use the model to capture the outcome of elections for the British Parliament, we would have to introduce such districts and model how the disaggregated vote share mapped into seat shares in Parliament. This may be significant because, as pointed out by Edgeworth in the nineteenth century and formalized by Kendall and Stuart (1950), small parties tend to be underrepresented in such majoritarian institutions. Thus, there is not a one-to-one relationship between vote share in aggregate and seat share in Parliament. Many other aspects of institutions might matter. For example, institutions influence voter turnout and also the abilities of minority groups to get what they want in legislatures.

This is interesting because the institutions matter for who has power in a democracy. Consider one specific example, motivated by the attention it has received in the political science literature: the difference between presidential and parliamentary democracy. As noted previously, Linz (1978, 1994) argued that presidential regimes tend to be more prone to coups; Przeworski et al. (2000) present econometric evidence consistent with this claim. The intuitive idea is that presidents, because they are elected in a popular vote, tend to represent the preferences of the median voter in society. On the other hand, Parliament may have to reconcile more diverse interests. In this case, if we compared the same country under these two different sets of institutions, we would expect the outcome with a president to be closer to that preferred by the citizens.

Motivated by these considerations, we use a simple reduced-form model parameterizing the political power of different groups in democracy. In the appendix to this chapter, we formally develop the first three of these ideas on modeling the distribution of political power in democracy and show how they map into the simple reduced-form model used here. Different specific models – whether they emphasize different institutional details, lobbying, relatively autonomous political parties, or the presence of swing voters – provide alternative microfoundations for our reduced form. Naturally, these details are also interesting and may be significant in specific cases; we discuss this as we proceed.

Let us now return to our basic two-class model with a unique policy instrument, the tax rate on income, τ. Given that the citizens are the majority (i.e., $1 - \delta > 1/2$), Downsian political competition simply maximized the indirect utility of the citizens, $V^p(\tau)$. In this model, the preferences of the elite are irrelevant for determining the tax rate. More generally, however, the elite will have some power and the equilibrium policy will reflect this. The simplest way of capturing this idea is to think of the equilibrium policy as maximizing a weighted sum of the indirect utilities of the elites and the citizens, where the weights determine how much the equilibrium policy reflects the preferences of the different groups. We call the weight of a group the "political power" of that group. Let those weights be χ and $1-\chi$ for the elites and the citizens, respectively. Then, the equilibrium tax rate would be that which maximizes:

$$\max_{\tau\in[0,1]} (1-\chi)(1-\delta)\left((1-\tau)y^p + (\tau - C(\tau))\bar{y}\right) \\ + \chi\delta\left((1-\tau)y^r + (\tau - C(\tau))\bar{y}\right)$$

which has a first-order condition (with complementary slackness).

$$-\left((1-\chi)(1-\delta)\,y^p + \chi\delta y^r\right) \\ + \left((1-\chi)(1-\delta)+\chi\delta\right)\left(1-C'(\tau)\right)\bar{y} = 0 \quad \text{if} \quad \tau > 0$$

This yields:

$$\frac{(1-\chi)(1-\theta)+\chi\theta}{(1-\chi)(1-\delta)+\chi\delta} = 1 - C'(\tau(\chi)) \tag{4.16}$$

where we define $\tau(\chi)$ to be the equilibrium tax rate when the political power parameter is χ.

It is instructive to compare Equations (4.16) and (4.11), which determined equilibrium policy in the two-class model with Downsian political competition. It is clear that the Downsian outcome is a special case of the current model for $\chi = 0$, in which case (4.16) becomes identical to (4.11) so that $\tau(\chi = 0) = \tau^p$. However, for all values of $\chi > 0$, the preferences of the elite also matter for equilibrium policies so that $\tau(\chi > 0) < \tau^p$. Moreover, the greater is χ, the more political power the elites have despite the fact that they are the minority. To see the implications of this, notice that if χ rises, then the left side of (4.16) increases. This implies that the right side must increase also so that $C'(\tau)$ must fall. Because $C'(\tau)$ is increasing in τ, this implies that τ falls. In other words, $d\tau(\chi)/d\chi < 0$. Thus, an increase in the power of the rich, or in their ability to influence the equilibrium policy in democracy through whatever channel, pulls the tax rate down and closer to their ideal point. The different models in the appendix provide different mechanisms by which the power of the elites is exerted and how the equilibrium tax rate responds as a result.

This is important because, so far, we have emphasized that democracies generate more pro-citizen policies than nondemocracies. If, in fact, we have that as $\chi \to 1$ and the tax rate generated by democratic politics tends to that most preferred by the elites, there will be little difference between democracies and nondemocracies. Our perspective is that there are often reasons for the elites to be powerful in democracies even when they are a minority, so $\chi > 0$ may be a good approximation of reality. Nevertheless, both the evidence discussed so far and introspection suggest that most democratic societies are far from the case where $\chi = 1$. As a result, democracies do not simply cater to the preferences of the rich the same way as would a typical nondemocracy.

6. Conclusion

In this chapter, we developed some basic models of democratic politics. We also discussed in detail the workhorse models and some of their properties that we use to characterize democracy in the remainder of the book. Our analysis focuses on the two-group model in conditions where either the MVT applies or where, when the policy space is multidimensional, the equilibrium policy is that preferred by the poor. We focus, therefore, on situations in which the median voter is a poor agent and his preferences determine what happens in a democracy. We also consider extensively three substantive extensions of this model. First, a three-class model in which the middle class enters as a separate group from the rich and the poor. We defer a formal introduction of this model until the first time it is used in Chapter 8. Second, the reduced-form model of democracy in which different groups "power" can vary depending on the nature of democratic institutions, on whether they are swing voters, whether they are an organized lobby, and so forth. In the appendix to this chapter, we discuss in detail different microfoundations for the power parameter χ but, for the rest of the book, we simply work with this reduced form rather than present detailed models in which institutions, lobbying, party capture, or probabilistic voting are explicitly introduced. Finally, the simple model in which political identities differ and can be different from those based purely on socioeconomic class or income level, and we analyze how this affects distributional conflict in society.

5 Nondemocratic Politics

1. Introduction

In this chapter, we discuss various issues that arise in thinking about policy determination in nondemocracy. For our purposes, the most basic distinction between a democracy and a nondemocracy is that the former is a situation of political equality: each citizen has one vote. As a result, in democracy, the preferences of all citizens matter in the determination of the political outcomes. In nondemocracy, this is not the case because only a subset of the people, an elite, has political rights. In principle, this could be any subset. Soviet socialism claimed to be the dictatorship of the proletariat and did not even consider "dictatorship" a word with pejorative connotations. Similarly, the dictatorship of Juvenal Habyarimana in Rwanda between 1973 and 1994 might be considered the dictatorship of a particular ethnic group, the Hutu. In Brazil between 1964 and 1985, there was a military dictatorship, with bureaucratic authoritarian and corporatist tendencies; this regime emphasized industrialization while also protecting the economic interests of the relatively rich and avoiding any radical – particularly agrarian – reforms. In contrast, the dictatorship of Mobutu Sese Seko in The Congo between 1965 and 1997 was a highly personalistic, kleptocratic regime, in which the main use of state power was to enrich Mobutu and his entourage. Despite these differences among nondemocracies (see Linz and Stepan 1996 for an influential taxonomy), our purpose is to emphasize the major difference between democracies and nondemocracies that we see as the extent of political equality.

In general, there are two features that shape economic policies in nondemocracies: first, the preferences of the group in power; and second, the constraints faced by that group. Everything else being equal, the group in power, the elite, choose policies that maximize its utilities. However, elites typically live in fear of being replaced by different social groups or by other individuals within the same group. Therefore, an important issue in nondemocracies is to ensure that no group is unhappy enough to attempt to overthrow the regime or take other political or economic actions detrimental to the utility of the group in power.

Our analysis in this chapter builds on the model of democracy described in Chapter 4. Thus, we think of a society composed of heterogeneous individuals. Nondemocracy is the rule of some subset of this society. In Chapter 4, we showed that democracy is the rule of the more numerous group, either the poor or, if political identities are along other lines, group X. Here, we think of nondemocracy as the rule of the less numerous group (either the rich or group Z).

To start, we focus on models in which nondemocracy is simply the rule of the rich. In many circumstances, this is a perfectly sensible postulate. For example, formal restrictions on suffrage have typically been on the poor: those with no assets, who have low income, or who are illiterate. There have also been racial restrictions on voting – for example, in the United States before the Civil War and in South Africa before the collapse of the apartheid system – but again, the racial groups disenfranchised have always been poor. Even apparently autonomous military regimes often serve the interests of the affluent, an obvious case being the Pinochet dictatorship in Chile between 1973 and 1990. Many other Latin American dictatorships in the twentieth century were induced by the threat of radical redistributive and social policies, for example, those in Argentina after 1930, after 1955, and again between 1976 and 1983. Other examples of coups against democracy aimed at avoiding radical policies are those in Venezuela in 1948, in Guatemala in 1954, and in Brazil in 1964. Although the regimes that took power after these coups were military, the coups themselves were induced by the threat of radical redistributive policies. Drake argues in this context that

> in many ways, the anti-labor stance of these despotisms defined their raison d'être . . . it motivated their seizure of power, legitimized their existence, marshalled their supporters and opponents, underlay their model of economic growth, drove their social policies, and propelled their political practices. That conflict with workers also substantially affected their tenure and terminations. (1996, p. 2)

To us, these examples suggest that there is often a close association between what nondemocratic regimes do and what the rich want. Nevertheless, as discussed in Chapter 2, our basic framework and many of the empirical results carry over to a situation in which nondemocracy is not simply the rule of the rich.

The models we develop in this chapter emphasize the interplay between elites' preferences and the constraints placed on them by the preferences of other groups – centrally the disenfranchised citizens – in society. Our aim is again to search for general tendencies that hold true across different types of nondemocratic regimes and to contrast those with the tendencies in a typical democracy. The dichotomous distinction we draw between democracy and nondemocracy, our desire to bring out the common elements within each regime, and our relentless reliance on Occam's razor may appear stark, even simplistic. Nevertheless, we believe that this is the correct way to make progress, and our conviction is that this dichotomy is useful for developing intuitive ideas about the forces that lead societies to have different political institutions.

2. Power and Constraints in Nondemocratic Politics

2.1 The Elites in Democratic Politics

We discussed in the previous chapter how the elites may be more powerful in democracy than their mere numbers suggest. We saw that a general model that allows the elites to have some power in democracy implies that the equilibrium tax rate is $\tau(\chi)$, where χ can be thought of as a measure of the power of the elites in democratic politics. In particular, consider the limit of $\chi \to 1$ in (4.16); in this case, the equilibrium policy will always be the policy preferred by the elites, which is τ^r.

We think of nondemocratic politics as similar to this limit. Because the society is not a well-functioning democracy, the wishes of the majority of the population are ignored, and policies are chosen to maximize the welfare of the elites. This discussion also highlights that, despite our dichotomous distinction between democracy and nondemocracy, we can think of a more continuous distinction between the two. A society is more democratic when the wishes of the majority are incorporated substantially into major policy choices. This corresponds to a situation in which χ is close to 0 in this model. Nondemocracy, on the other hand, is a situation in which the wishes of the majority are ignored in favor of the desires of a subpopulation, the elites. Here, this corresponds to the equilibrium in which $\chi \to 1$.

2.2 The Revolution Constraint

The previous discussion highlights how we can think of nondemocracy as a situation that maximizes the utility of the elites. However, nondemocracy, especially compared to the ideal of democracy, is neither egalitarian nor fair. Therefore, the citizens would have a constant desire to change the outcome, the policies, and the regime. What prevents them is the fact that the elites control the political institutions and military power in nondemocratic societies. Because of this control, they can maximize their utility but, given that they are the minority and would like to pursue policies not in line with the interest of the majority, there can also be certain constraints on the policies they want to pursue.

The major constraint that faces those controlling political power in nondemocracy is a danger that those excluded from political power might attempt to gain political power or to overthrow those who are in control.

In terms of the discussion in Chapter 2, recall that we distinguish between de jure political power and de facto political power. De jure political power is that which comes from political institutions. In contrast, de facto political power comes from the ability of one group to overwhelm the other, by fighting in a battle or through other means. In democracy, de jure political power rests with the citizens.

In nondemocracy, the citizens have no de jure political power; they are excluded from the political system. Nevertheless, they may have de facto political power by virtue of the fact that they are the majority, and they may be able to coordinate their actions to overthrow the existing regime. In the extreme, the citizens can undertake a *revolution* against a nondemocracy to change the political system to one that is more beneficial for them. We summarize the constraints placed on the elites by this type of de facto political power of the citizens by a *revolution constraint.*

In this subsection, we discuss the origins of the revolution constraint and the restrictions it places on the actions of the elites controlling the political system in nondemocracy. As a starting point, we discuss ways of formalizing revolutions and introduce concepts related to the collective-action problems that might arise in organizing the citizens so that they can exert de facto power. Throughout, we focus on the two-class model introduced in the last chapter to make the discussion more concrete. In this model, society is divided into rich elites and poor citizens, who are more numerous.

First, think about what happens after a revolution. By definition, a revolution in this environment corresponds to the citizens using their sheer numbers to overwhelm the elites in nondemocracy, taking control of the society and its wealth and income-generating assets. Hence, in some way, we are thinking of revolution leading to a postrevolutionary society in which the control passes from the elites to the citizens.

The simplest way to think of a postrevolutionary society is, therefore, one in which the citizens divide the resources of the economy. However, it is plausible that a violent event like a revolution creates significant turbulence and destruction and, consequently, reduces the productive capacity of the economy. So, let us think that after revolution, a fraction μ of the resources of the society are destroyed and the remainder can be divided among the citizens. This is clearly a simplification. Most revolutions do not act in such an egalitarian way by redistributing the resources of the postrevolutionary society only to the citizens. Some will invariably benefit more than others. Nevertheless, our purpose is not to develop a realistic theory of revolutions but rather to use the threat of revolution as a constraint on nondemocratic politics. For this reason, we again appeal to Occam's razor and model payoffs in the postrevolutionary society in the simplest way possible. Assuming that some of the resources of the economy are destroyed in the turbulence of the revolution and the rest are distributed in some way among the citizens is both a simple and appealing formulation for this purpose.

This assumption implies that after the revolution, each citizen (here, a poor agent) receives a net income of:

$$V^p(R, \mu) = \frac{(1-\mu)\bar{y}}{1-\delta} \tag{5.1}$$

because the total income they will divide among themselves is $(1-\mu)\bar{y}$, and there are $1-\delta$ of them. The notation $V^p(R, \mu)$ denotes the value (i.e., utility) to the citizen in a postrevolutionary society conditional on μ. Ignoring the collective-action problems discussed later, we can see that the revolution will be beneficial when the payoff given in (5.1) is greater than the payoff a citizen receives without revolution. Let τ^N denote the tax rate set by the elites, where N denotes nondemocracy, and suppose that without revolution, the elites simply set their most preferred tax rate, τ^r $(=0)$. Then, this payoff is:

$$V^p\left(y^p \,|\, \tau^N = \tau^r\right) = y^p \tag{5.2}$$

We say that the revolution constraint binds if (5.1) is greater than (5.2), or if:

$$\frac{(1-\mu)\bar{y}}{1-\delta} > y^p \tag{5.3}$$

We write this constraint with a strict inequality because we assume that if $(1-\mu)\bar{y}/(1-\delta) = y^p$, so that the citizens are indifferent between the political status quo and revolution, they do not revolt.[1] We adhere to this convention throughout the book.

An important feature of this inequality is that it compares the payoff from revolution to the payoff from the status quo. This comparison is conceptually the correct one for either the group as a whole or a "pivotal" agent who, by his or her participation, determines whether the revolution will succeed. Either interpretation is adequate for what follows, although other possibilities are also discussed in the next subsection.

Recalling the definitions from Chapter 4 in (4.7), the revolution constraint in (5.3) is equivalent to:

$$\theta > \mu \tag{5.4}$$

Our model of revolution is simple; nevertheless, it has two plausible features that are important for our discussion. First, the revolution constraint (5.4) is more likely to bind when the society is more unequal – that is, when θ is high. This is intuitive. In a more unequal society, the citizens receive only a small fraction of the resources; with a revolution, they can take control of all productive capacity (minus what is destroyed in the process of the revolution). It is, therefore, natural that revolution becomes more attractive for the citizens in a more unequal society. Second, the revolution is more attractive when $1-\mu$, the fraction of the output

[1] More formally, in the case of equality, the citizens would be indifferent between revolution and no revolution, and their choice should also be determined as part of the equilibrium. In the models studied throughout this book, there is no loss in generality in assuming that in case of equality, they do not revolt.

that remains to be distributed the postrevolutionary society, is high either for technological reasons or because the citizens have been able to successfully solve the collective-action problem.

2.3 Collective-Action Problems in Revolution

Before the revolution threat becomes a reality and, hence, before the revolution constraint becomes a constraint with which the elites have to deal, the citizens have to overcome the potential collective-action problems inherent in coordinating participation in revolutionary activity. The importance of collective-action problems in group decisions was highlighted by Olson (1965) in his classic book, *The Logic of Collective Action*, in which he analyzed the problems that groups have in convincing individuals to take actions that are costly for themselves but beneficial for the whole group. His analysis was applied to revolutions by Tullock (1971).

To see the potential collective-action problems in organizing a revolution, suppose, plausibly, that taking part in revolutionary activity or in the revolution itself is costly and denote this cost by $\varepsilon \bar{y}$. As usual, we normalize these costs by average income. This can include the actual cost of exerting effort for revolutionary activities, the implied costs posed by the danger of taking part in illegal activities, as well as costs of forfeited earnings due to the fact that revolutionary activities may replace working in the labor market. We first need to specify the circumstances under which a revolution attempt will succeed. Clearly, if none of the citizens take part in revolutionary activities, there will be no revolution. Suppose that we need at least a number $\xi^p \leq 1 - \delta$ of the citizens to take part in revolutionary activities for them to succeed.

Now consider the payoff to an agent who has taken part in revolutionary activities. This is given by the postrevolution payoff minus the cost of revolution activities; that is, $(1 - \mu)\bar{y}/(1 - \delta) - \varepsilon \bar{y}$ if the revolution succeeds and by $y^p - \varepsilon \bar{y}$ if the revolution fails. In contrast, the payoff of a citizen not taking part in revolutionary activities is $(1 - \mu)\bar{y}/(1 - \delta)$ or y^p in these two cases. The benefits are the same because a revolution is a public good in the sense that when it occurs, it changes the entire society and affects all citizens in the same way. Hence, whatever the outcome, the payoff for not taking part is always greater than the payoff for taking part in a revolution. Therefore, all citizens prefer to free-ride on others' revolutionary activities rather than incurring the costs themselves. The only obvious exception is when the agent making the decision between taking part and not taking part in revolutionary activities is "pivotal" in the sense that his or her participation would ensure or significantly increase the chance of success of the revolution and his or her nonparticipation would mean failure or a significantly reduced chance of success. Because there are numerous citizens, the action of a single one is typically not decisive for the outcome of the revolution. This introduces the famous collective-action or free-rider problem: no citizen should be willing to make the necessary investment in revolutionary activities and the threat of revolution will disappear.

The literature on the collective-action problem, including Olson's (1965) *The Logic of Collective Action*, identified a number of ways that groups can attempt to deal with collective-action problems, including the use of ideology and pecuniary benefits. Pecuniary benefits, in turn, can be usefully disaggregated into two categories: private benefits and exclusion.

First, groups may try to indoctrinate their members so that they view participation in activities that are beneficial for the group as a positive action that directly adds to their utility. In the case of citizens trying to organize revolutionary activities, this might mean that in addition to the cost $\varepsilon \bar{y}$, citizen i may view participation in revolutionary activities as bringing a nonpecuniary benefit of $\vartheta^i \bar{y}$. In this case, if the revolution succeeds, participation would have a payoff of $(1-\mu)\bar{y}/(1-\delta) + \vartheta^i \bar{y} - \varepsilon \bar{y}$ to citizen i, whereas nonparticipation would yield $(1-\mu)\bar{y}/(1-\delta)$. If the revolution fails, participation yields $y^p + \vartheta^i \bar{y} - \varepsilon \bar{y}$, whereas nonparticipation gives y^p. Hence, there will be participation in revolutionary activities by all citizens for whom $\vartheta^i - \varepsilon > 0$ and, if a critical mass of individuals derive sufficient ideological benefits, the revolution will take place. This type of indoctrination is clearly a common strategy by all revolutionary groups because, without it, revolutions typically do not succeed. We can then think of the leadership of a potential revolutionary group using this type of indoctrination when revolution is beneficial for the group as a whole – that is, when (5.3) holds.

Second, groups may attempt to generate private pecuniary benefits for those who participate in collective action. Consider first the strategy of providing private benefits to individuals, denoted by $b\bar{y}$, who take part in collective action. As we discuss shortly, most real-world revolutionaries try to generate private benefits, monetary or otherwise, for taking part in revolutionary activities that the participants can keep, even if the revolution fails. In this case, the return for taking part in collective action when the revolution succeeds would be $(1-\mu)\bar{y}/(1-\delta) + b\bar{y} - \varepsilon \bar{y}$, whereas that of not taking part would be $(1-\mu)\bar{y}/(1-\delta)$. When a revolution fails, the respective payoffs would be $y^p + b\bar{y} - \varepsilon \bar{y}$ and y^p. This implies that as long as $b > \varepsilon$, collective action would be rational for agents receiving the private benefits. Once again, we can think that when collective action – for example, revolution – is more beneficial for the group as a whole, the leadership of the group is more willing to provide private benefits to a critical mass; thus, we may expect private benefits to also encourage revolutionary activities more when (5.3) holds.

In practice, the most common strategy to deal with collective-action problems is "exclusion." Exclusion limits the benefits resulting from collective action to only those who take part in the action. The empirical literature illustrates the importance of exclusion in practice. For example, let the number of citizens taking part be ξ. Clearly, $\xi \leq 1-\delta$ because the total number of citizens is $1-\delta$. Moreover, suppose that the revolution will succeed if $\xi \geq \xi^p$. Assume that all citizens keep their own income whatever happens (including a successful revolution). In addition, if a revolution takes place, the income of the elites is distributed between all those who take part. In other words, each revolutionary agent will receive a total income of $y^p + (1-\mu)y^r/\xi$ as long as $\xi \geq \xi^p$. Then, given that revolutionary activity has a cost of $\varepsilon \bar{y}$, the revolution will take place as long as:

$$y^p + \frac{(1-\mu)y^r}{\xi^p} - \varepsilon \bar{y} > y^p \Rightarrow \frac{(1-\mu)y^r}{\xi^p} > \varepsilon \bar{y} \tag{5.5}$$

This condition implies that the maximum net gain from revolution should be greater than the cost of getting involved in revolutionary activities. The left-hand side is the maximum net gain because this is the gain to a citizen for taking part in revolution when the minimum number of agents necessary take part. Therefore, it maximizes the per-person gain. When condition (5.5) holds, there exists a revolutionary equilibrium with $\bar{\xi} > \xi^p$ agents taking part in revolution, and revolution succeeding,[2] where $\bar{\xi}$ is given by:

$$\frac{(1-\mu)\theta \bar{y}}{\bar{\xi}\delta} = \varepsilon \bar{y} \tag{5.6}$$

using the fact that $y^r = \theta \bar{y}/\delta$. That $\bar{\xi} > \xi^p$ immediately follows from the fact that (5.5) holds and the fact that the left-hand side of (5.6) is decreasing in ξ.

In this case, in which collective-action problems are present but are being solved by exclusion, we can think of the revolution constraint as corresponding to equation (5.5), or:

$$\theta > \frac{\varepsilon \bar{\xi} \delta}{1-\mu} \tag{5.7}$$

The results of interest that come from (5.7) are similar to the case in which the relevant constraint is given by (5.4). For example, in both cases, an increase in inter-group inequality parameterized as a rise in θ will make the revolution constraint more likely to hold. In the remainder of the book, we work with the simpler condition, (5.4).

Notice also another implication of using exclusion to solve the collective-action problem. We can think that a greater ξ^p corresponds to a more severe collective-action problem because more citizens need to participate in revolution for it to succeed and, therefore, more individuals need to be convinced to act for the group. In terms of the more reduced-form condition in (5.4), this is similar to a higher μ.

[2] There is another Nash equilibrium where, even though (5.5) is satisfied, there is a "coordination failure," so that no agent takes part in revolution because they all believe that nobody else will take part. In the remainder, we presume that the group is somehow able to solve the coordination problem – for example, due to the actions of its leaders – and avoids this less attractive equilibrium.

Therefore, we loosely talk of the level of μ reflecting both technological factors, related to how much of the productive capacity of the economy the citizens can make use of in a postrevolutionary society, and the severity of the collective-action problem.

Finally, the presence of the collective-action problem in revolution implies that the revolution constraint will not always be binding. It might be that the citizens are able to solve the collective-action problem during some periods but not others. Later, when we consider dynamic models, this is one of the sources of transitory political power for citizens in nondemocracy.

2.4 Evidence on the Collective-Action Problem

A rich empirical literature has investigated how the collective-action problem is solved in practice (e.g., the surveys in Lichbach 1995 and Moore 1995). Although there are different ways of classifying putative solutions to the collective-action problem (Lichbach 1995, pp. 20–1), most scholars emphasize, as we have done, the importance of ideology. Nevertheless, most of the empirical evidence is more about how private benefits and exclusion are used by those trying to organize collective action.

Popkin (1979) provides a seminal account of the solution to the collective-action problem in the Vietnamese revolution. He argues that "The problem of building support and overcoming free riders was . . . central to Viet Minh strategy" (p. 223). Their main tool was to break down large problems, such as mounting a revolution, into many small problems where individuals could see how their contribution was important and where each benefited directly. Popkin (1979, p. 262) argues, "one consideration in particular may have been crucial for effective mobilization of the peasantry . . . the initial organization of peasants focused on local goals and goods with immediate payoffs." This is similar to our model in which individuals get a private benefit of $b\bar{y}$, irrespective of the outcome of the action. When the Communists took over villages, they aimed at selectively providing what peasants wanted, such as land, in exchange for their participation. "Even when an organization produces divisible goods for individual consumption, there are collective goods aspects to the organization itself . . . it is possible to produce benefits for the peasants as well as a 'revolutionary surplus' which can then be used to support a supra-village organization and applied to broader organizational goals." An illustration of how this worked is given in Popkin (1979, p. 257):

> After land was redistributed and rents reduced in Cochinchina, peasants commonly went out of their way to warn Viet Minh cadres that French soldiers or agents were in the area; they did not risk free riding on warnings by waiting for someone else to notify the cadre.

Thus, once the Communist Party had framed the issues in the right way and used selective incentives, individuals found it rational to engage in collective action.

For example, Popkin notes that even though giving out land to peasants as private property was against the philosophical commitments of the Communists because they favored communal ownership and collective farms, they nevertheless gave land to peasants who cooperated with the revolution. He quotes a senior Communist official as saying

> . . . the system [private property] is far from perfect. . . . However, we have been obliged to stick to it because our entire political action among the peasants is based upon the right of each to individual property. We would have risked losing their support had we stopped breaking up landholdings. (p. 241)

The fact that one goal of the revolution was radical land reform and that land could be redistributed to those who took part and withheld from those who did not allowed the Viet Minh to use the strategy of exclusion to encourage people to take part in collective action.

Part of the strategy of the Viet Minh for solving the collective-action problem was also to exploit existing social networks and community institutions: "The Communists were forming small self-help fraternal organizations, one-fourth of whose members had been political prisoners. These organizations were built around friendship associations, groups to build straw huts, associations to celebrate the cult of the genii, and insurance systems" (Popkin 1979, p. 230; see also Woodside 1976, p. 179).

Several other informative case studies show the power of selective incentives in sustaining collective action. Kriger (1992) showed how participation in Zimbabwe's revolutionary war was driven by the expectation of personal gain. She interviewed people who had been members of Zimbabwe African National Union (ZANU) guerillas and found that they joined because they expected personal gain and, in particular, they expected to enhance their status within their local community. High-status people had to be coerced into joining ZANU.

The effectiveness of private benefits in stimulating collective action is graphically illustrated by evidence from the Rwandan genocide. In the comprehensive study by Human Rights Watch under the chief authorship of historian Alison Des Forges, there are many examples of how the Hutu political elite solved the collective-action problem inherent in mobilizing the Hutu population to massacre Tutsis. For instance,

> they (the Burgomasters) directed or permitted communal police, militia, or simply other citizens to burn down houses and to threaten the lives of those who refused to join in the violence. They also offered powerful incentives to draw the hesitant into killing. They or others solicited by them provided cash payments, food, drink and, in some cases, marijuana to assailants. They encouraged the looting of Tutsi property, even to the point of having the pillage supervised by the communal police. . . . In several places police reprimanded the people who wanted only to pillage and not to kill. . . . One of the most important resources for the burgomaster in enlisting participants was his authority to control the distribution of land, a much desired

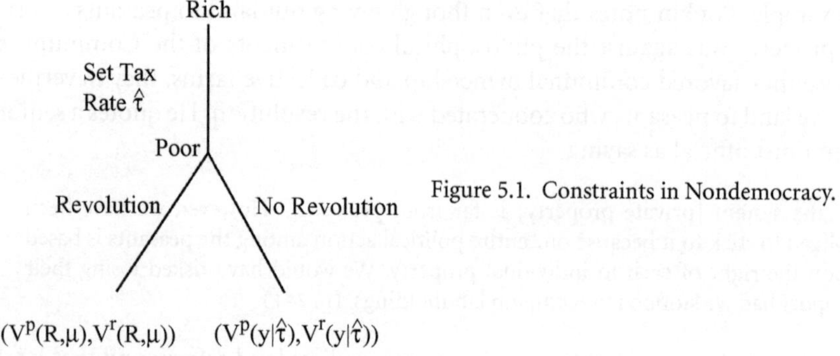

Figure 5.1. Constraints in Nondemocracy.

> and scarce source of wealth for the largely agricultural population. Hutu who had attacked Tutsi in the 1960's had acquired the field of their victims. A generation later, people again hoped to get more land by killing or driving Tutsi away. (Des Forges 1999, pp. 236–7)

No doubt, it is also true in the Rwandan case that ideology was important and the long-running animosity between the Hutu and Tutsi ethnic groups played an important role in the conflict. This evidence also suggests that another type of selective incentives – negative sanctions against those who failed to take part in the genocide – were also useful.

A key feature of our theoretical framework is that collective action is intrinsically transitory. Even with the use of ideology or incentives, solving the collective-action problem is difficult to begin with and very hard to sustain. The empirical literature also emphasizes that the difficulty of solving the collective action problem leads collective action to typically be transitory. Lichbach (1995, p. 17) notes "collective action, if undertaken on a short-term basis, may indeed occur; collective action that requires long periods of time does not. . . . Given that most people's commitments to particular causes face inevitable decline, most dissident groups are ephemeral, most dissident campaigns brief." This transitory nature of collective action is echoed by Tarrow (1991, p. 15), who notes "the exhaustion of mass political involvement," and Ross and Gurr (1989, p. 414) discuss political "burnout." Similarly, Hardin (1995) argues that

> . . . the extensive political participation of civil society receives enthusiastic expression only in moments of state collapse or great crisis. It cannot be maintained at a perpetually high level. (p. 18)

3. Modeling Preferences and Constraints in Nondemocracies

Let us now put the collective-action problem aside and start investigating the implications of the revolution constraint (5.4) binding on nondemocratic politics. To do so, consider the following game depicted in Figure 5.1. In writing about this game and others in the remainder of the book, we treat the elite and the poor as single players. In general, to specify what an equilibrium is in such a game, we would have to describe the payoff functions and strategies for all the elites and all the citizens. A Nash equilibrium would then entail a specification of strategies, one for each player, such that no member of the elite and no citizen could increase their payoff by changing their strategy. Nevertheless, this level of generality is redundant. All members of the elite are the same, as are all citizens. Moreover, as discussed previously, we assume that both groups have solved their collective-action problems. This justifies us in treating both groups collectively and talking about "the elite" and "the citizens" and examining an equilibrium stemming from interactions between these two groups. Nevertheless, in specifying payoffs, we do so at the individual level because even when the collective-action problem has been solved, behavior has to be individually rational.

In Figure 5.1, the elite move first and set the tax rate, τ^N. We use the notation $\hat{\tau}$ to refer to a specific value of τ^N set to avoid a revolution. After observing this tax rate, the citizens decide whether to undertake a revolution. If they do not, the game ends with payoffs:

$$V\left(y^p \middle| \tau^N = \hat{\tau}\right) = (1-\hat{\tau})y^p + \hat{T} = y^p + (\hat{\tau}(\bar{y} - y^p) - C(\hat{\tau})\bar{y}) \quad \text{and} \qquad (5.8)$$
$$V\left(y^r \middle| \tau^N = \hat{\tau}\right) = (1-\hat{\tau})y^r + \hat{T} = y^r + (\hat{\tau}(\bar{y} - y^r) - C(\hat{\tau})\bar{y})$$

where $\hat{T} = (\hat{\tau} - C(\hat{\tau}))\bar{y}$. These payoffs follow from redistribution in nondemocracy at the tax rate $\hat{\tau}$. The second equality in these equations rearranges the expression for $V\left(y^i \middle| \tau^N = \hat{\tau}\right)$ in a way particularly instructive for the remainder of the book. In particular, $\hat{\tau}\left(\bar{y} - y^i\right) - C(\hat{\tau})\bar{y}$ is the net amount of redistribution for $i = p, r$ so that $\hat{\tau}(\bar{y} - y^p) - C(\hat{\tau})\bar{y} > 0$ while $\hat{\tau}(\bar{y} - y^r) - C(\hat{\tau})\bar{y} < 0$; that is, the elite loses from income redistribution.

Alternatively, the citizens might choose to attempt a revolution, in which case we assume that the revolution always succeeds and they receive the payoffs:

$$V^p(R, \mu) = \frac{(1-\mu)\bar{y}}{1-\delta} \quad \text{and} \quad V^r(R, \mu) = 0$$

where the payoff to the citizens comes from the way we specified the revolution technology, and the elite receive nothing because all income is expropriated from them. What matters is not that the elite receives nothing but simply that what they receive is sufficiently low that they want to avoid revolution.

How do we solve a game like this? The answer is "backward induction," starting at the end of the game tree. This technique, which we appealed to in Chapter 4, is useful because it characterizes the subgame perfect Nash equilibria of the game. Subgame perfection is a refinement of the original Nash equilibrium concept, useful in games with sequential moves and in dynamic games. The key feature of such an equilibrium, noted originally by Selten (1975), is that it rules out Nash equilibria supported by noncredible threats "off the equilibrium path." By "off the equilibrium path," we mean that the equilibrium strategies are such that the threat will not be carried out – it remains just a threat. A noncredible threat is a threat that the player making it would not find optimal to actually undertake if called upon to do so.

To consider an extreme example, imagine that the citizens demand all the money of the elite or they will blow up the world, including themselves. Faced with this threat, it is optimal for the elite to give the citizens all of their money. This is one Nash equilibrium. However, it rests on the threat that if the elite refuses, the citizens will blow up the world. This threat is off the equilibrium path because the elite hand over their money and the citizens, therefore, do not have to carry out their threat. Imagine, however, that the elite refuses. Now, the citizens must decide whether to blow up the world. Faced with this situation, the citizens renege on their threat because, plausibly, it is better to get nothing from the elite than to kill themselves. Therefore, their threat is not credible, and the Nash equilibrium supported by this noncredible threat is not appealing. Fortunately, there is another more plausible Nash equilibrium in which the elite refuses to give the citizens anything and the citizens do not blow up the world. This second Nash equilibrium is indeed subgame perfect, whereas the first is not because it rests on noncredible threats. Given the importance in this book of the credibility of threats and promises, we make heavy use of the restriction that equilibria be subgame perfect.

We need to distinguish two cases. In the first, the revolution constraint (5.4) does not bind. This implies that even if the elite sets the tax rate most preferable for themselves, $\tau^N = \tau^r$, undertaking the revolution is not in the interests of the citizens. Then, in the subgame perfect equilibrium of the game, the elite anticipates that the revolution will never occur and, therefore, set their most preferred tax rate, $\tau^N = \tau^r = 0$.

The more interesting case for our exposition is the one in which (5.4) binds. Now, if the elite were to set $\tau^N = \tau^r$, it would be in the interest of the citizens to undertake a revolution. Anticipating this, the elite would try to make a concession – for example, change policy closer to that preferred by the citizens. In this context, this implies that they will set a tax rate sufficient to prevent the revolution. The first question to ask is, therefore, whether such a tax rate exists. The best tax rate from the point of view of the citizens is $\tau^N = \tau^p$, as given by (4.11) – after all, τ^p is the tax rate that the citizens would have set themselves, so the elite can never do better than setting this tax rate in trying to maximize the utility of the citizens. Thus, the question is whether:

$$y^p + (\tau^p(\bar{y} - y^p) - C(\tau^p)\bar{y}) \geq \frac{(1-\mu)\bar{y}}{1-\delta}$$

holds or, using the definitions in (4.7), whether:

$$\mu \geq \theta - (\tau^p(\theta - \delta) - (1-\delta)C(\tau^p)) \tag{5.9}$$

holds. We use a weak inequality because, as noted previously, we assume that if the citizens are indifferent between the status quo and revolution, then they do not revolt.

If (5.9) does not hold, then even the best tax rate for the citizens is not enough to prevent revolution. This might be because the citizens are well organized and have managed to fully solve the collective-action problem or because they can use the economy's productive resources quite productively after a revolution. Both of these scenarios translate into a low value of μ. Alternatively, (5.9) may fail to hold because taxation is costly, so even the best tax rate for the citizens is not sufficiently redistributive. In this case, the unique equilibrium involves the citizens undertaking a revolution.

The other case, which is arguably more interesting from the point of view of our analysis, is when (5.9) holds. In this case, a unique tax rate $\hat{\tau}$ exists such that $V\left(y^p \mid \tau^N = \hat{\tau}\right) = V^r(R, \mu)$ given by:

$$\mu = \theta - (\hat{\tau}(\theta - \delta) - (1 - \delta)C(\hat{\tau})) \tag{5.10}$$

It follows from (5.9) that this tax rate is such that $\hat{\tau} \leq \tau^p$. Therefore, in this case, the unique equilibrium involves the elite setting the tax $\hat{\tau}$ to prevent revolution.

The interesting feature of this simple game is that, despite the fact that the elite has complete control of formal political power in nondemocracy, they may have to deviate from their most preferred tax rate, τ^r, because there are other sources of political power in nondemocracy constraining their actions – in our formulation captured by the *revolution constraint*. This type of political power is de facto; the citizens are excluded from the political system, but they can pose an effective challenge from the outside. Fearing a revolution coming from this de facto political power of the citizens, the elite makes concessions and sets a tax rate that redistributes some of their resources toward the citizens.

Before stating the main result, we need to introduce a more formal definition of strategies. Let $\sigma^r = \{\tau^N\}$ be the actions taken by the elite, which consists of a tax rate $\tau^N \in [0, 1]$, in which the superscript N refers to nondemocracy. Similarly, $\sigma^p = \{\rho(\cdot)\}$ are the actions of the citizens that consist of a decision to initiate a revolution, $\rho(\tau^N)$ ($\rho = 1$ representing a revolution) where this decision is conditioned on the current actions of the elite who move before the citizens in the game according to the timing of events depicted in Figure 5.1. Hence, ρ is a function, $\rho : [0, 1] \to \{0, 1\}$. Then, a subgame perfect equilibrium is a strategy combination, $\{\tilde{\sigma}^r, \tilde{\sigma}^p\}$ such that $\tilde{\sigma}^p$ and $\tilde{\sigma}^r$ are best responses to each other in all proper subgames. We always use the tildes to represent a particular equilibrium.

Various strategy profiles can be in equilibrium, depending on the parameters. Nevertheless, for any specification of parameters, the equilibrium is unique. When $\theta \leq \mu$, the revolution constraint does not bind and the following strategies constitute an equilibrium: $\tau^N = 0$ and $\rho(\tau^N) = 0$ for all τ^N. According to these strategies, the elite sets the tax rate at zero and the citizens never revolt, whatever the tax rate is. Here, it does not matter what the elite does (i.e., $\rho = 0$ irrespective of τ^N) because the poor have a dominant strategy. Note the important property that strategies must specify behavior both on and off the equilibrium path. Even though the elite's strategy stipulates a zero tax rate, the citizens' strategy specifies what action to take for all tax rates, not just zero.

When $\theta > \mu$ and (5.9) does not hold, then the following strategy profile is the unique equilibrium: $\rho(\tau^N) = 1$ for all τ^N. In this case, even setting the tax rate τ^p will not stop a revolution so, whatever the elite does, the citizens revolt. The citizens again have a dominant strategy, this time to revolt irrespective of τ^N.

Finally and most interesting, when $\theta > \mu$ and (5.9) does hold, the following strategy profile is the unique equilibrium: $\tau^N = \hat{\tau}$ and $\rho(\tau^N) = 0$, for all $\tau^N \geq \hat{\tau}$; also off the equilibrium path, $\rho(\tau^N) = 1$ for all $\tau^N < \hat{\tau}$. Here, revolution is attractive if the elite makes no concessions, but because (5.9) holds, the citizens can be dissuaded from revolution by concessions, specifically by setting the tax rate $\hat{\tau}$ such that (5.10) holds. Note again the specification of behavior off the equilibrium path. The elite set the tax rate $\hat{\tau}$ and the citizens do not revolt if offered a tax rate $\tau^N \geq \hat{\tau}$. Nevertheless, the strategy of the citizen says that if offered a tax rate $\tau^N < \hat{\tau}$, they will revolt. It is this "threat" off the equilibrium path that induces the elite to give redistribution. This threat is credible because if the elite deviated and tried to get away with less redistribution, it would be optimal for the citizens to undertake revolution. The concept of subgame perfect Nash equilibrium explicitly imposes that such threats have to be credible.

Summarizing this analysis, we have the following:

Proposition 5.1: *There is a unique subgame perfect equilibrium* $\{\tilde{\sigma}^r, \tilde{\sigma}^p\}$ *in the game described in Figure 5.1, and it is such that:*

- *If (5.4) does not bind, then* $\tau^N = 0$ *and* $\rho(\tau^N) = 0$ *for all* τ^N.
- *If (5.4) binds and (5.9) does not hold, then* $\rho(\tau^N) = 1$ *for all* τ^N.
- *If (5.4) binds and (5.9) does hold, then* $\tau^N = \hat{\tau}$ *where* $\hat{\tau}$ *is given by (5.10), and* $\rho(\tau^N) = 0$, *for all* $\tau^N \geq \hat{\tau}$, *and* $\rho(\tau^N) = 1$ *for all* $\tau^N < \hat{\tau}$.

This discussion and Proposition 5.1, therefore, highlight how in nondemocracy equilibrium policies are determined by a combination of the preferences of the elite and the constraints that they face. When these constraints are absent or very loose, as in the case in which (5.4) does not bind, what matters is the preferences of the elite. When the constraints are tight (e.g., when (5.4) binds), the elite are constrained in the choices they can make.

Our model builds in a natural way on existing models of revolutions. This research – for example, Roemer (1985), Grossman (1991, 1994), Wintrobe (1998), and Bueno de Mesquita et al. (2003) – examines simple games where authoritarian regimes can be overthrown by the citizens and then make various types of responses, concessions such as cutting taxes and redistributing assets, or repression. Like our analysis, these papers abstract from the collective-action problem. Our main innovation comes later when we show how democratization can emerge when concessions are infeasible and when repression is too costly. To understand when concessions are or are not feasible, we need to examine their credibility.

4. Commitment Problems

4.1 Basic Issues

An important issue throughout this book is the inability of those controlling political power to commit not to use it. In other words, the problem is that when those with political power make promises to those without, the promises may sometimes be noncredible. This is important, in turn, because without such credible promises, those in power have fewer options open to them and, in particular, they may sometimes be unable to deal satisfactorily with crises, such as an immanent threat of revolution discussed in the previous section.

The issue of commitment is intimately linked to that of political power. To see this, consider a nondemocracy in which political power lies with the elites. For one reason or another – but, as we will see, most probably to avoid revolution – the elites would like to promise to choose policies in the future that are more to the liking of the citizens – for example, they might want to promise to redistribute income to the citizens. However, the elites hold political power in nondemocracy and, therefore, have the right to determine the level of taxes and transfers in the future. They can promise to make transfers in the future, but these promises may be noncredible. Tomorrow, they get to decide these transfers and, if it is not in their interest to be making them *tomorrow*, they will not make them. They get to decide whether to make the transfers tomorrow because they hold political power.

It is important to emphasize that the commitment problem arises from the potential de-coupling between the beneficiaries of the decisions and the identity of those holding political power. The transfers benefit the citizens; but, they are made by the elites, who are not the beneficiaries. On the contrary, they are the ones who bear the burden of any transfers. Therefore, typically it is not in their interest to make these transfers in the future and their promises of future transfers and redistribution are not credible. Contrast this with a situation in which political power is in the hands of the citizens. There is a congruence between the identity of those holding political power and those benefiting from the transfers. The citizens would certainly like to implement the transfers from the elites to themselves. This highlights that *commitment problems* arise when political power is not in the hands of the beneficiaries of the promised policies. In essence, those with political power cannot commit not to use it to renege on the promises made in the past.[3]

[3] Many scholars have emphasized the fact that a key feature of political economy is that there is no third party that can enforce the promises made by the state and that this leads to problems of commitment and endemic inefficiencies. This idea is discussed by North (1990) and Olson (1993), is central to the work of North and Weingast (1989) and Weingast (e.g., 1997, 1998), and is implicit in many other studies. See also Grossman and Noh (1994), Dixit (1996), Dixit and Londregan (1995), and Besley and Coate (1998) for discussions of how inability to commit generates inefficiencies in political outcomes.

Commitment problems are not only present in politics but also in all areas of social life. Almost all economic transactions have a temporal dimension. Traders typically deliver goods today but receive payment tomorrow. A commitment problem arises if customers promise to make a payment tomorrow but, when tomorrow comes, it is not in their interest to make the payment. In this case, they renege on their promises and fail to make the payment. Therefore, there is ample room for commitment problems in social and economic relations. However, in most instances, society has relatively low-cost ways of dealing with the most major potential commitment problems. To remove potential problems, we need to remove the freedom of customers to decide whether to make a payment tomorrow without facing any repercussions if they renege on their promise. As we saw, the problem is that whenever customers get to make such a decision in an unconstrained manner, they prefer not to make a payment (and thus keep the money in their pocket). There have to be some "constraints" on their actions or some potential repercussions (i.e., punishments) if they decide not to make the payment. There are three potential way to deal with these commitment problems: contracts, repeated transactions, and changing the identity of who gets to make the decision.

The most common way of dealing with potential commitment problems is to write enforceable contracts. For example, the trader could get the customer to sign a contract at the time of delivery stipulating that in a number of days, the customer will make a payment to the trader. What happens if the customer fails to make the payment? If the contract is in fact enforceable, there is an outside agency, typically a court of law, where the trader files a complaint that the customer broke the terms of the contract. This agency, after determining the truth of the claim, punishes the customer and forces him to make the payment, if possible. Contracts solve most potential commitment problems in an ideal world. However, even in the realm of purely economic transactions, we are far from this ideal world, and there are many problems with these types of contracts in economic transactions, including those stemming from asymmetries of information. They also include those related to the fact that certain important characteristics that one would like to contract upon, such as the quality of the good that the trader delivers to the customer, may not be "contractible" because the outside agency is unable to observe the true quality (the implications of this type of contracting problem is the topic of a large literature in organizational economics; for example, Williamson 1985 and Grossman and Hart 1986). However, potential problems with contracts are much more severe, even unsurpassable, when we come to the political arena.

An essential feature of this scenario is that when customers decide to renege on their promise, the outside agency steps in and "enforces the contract." Without such enforcement, the contract would be worth little. Customers would renege and suffer no repercussions. In economic transactions, such enforcement is sometimes difficult but essentially possible because there is "the state," with its monopoly of legitimate coercive power and the fact that it delegates this power to other agencies, such as the courts of law, so that they can enforce the contract. In the political realm, however, the groups that control political power are essentially "the state." Herein lies the problem. When it comes to contracts that the state or social groups controlling the state would like to write with others (e.g., the elites controlling political power in nondemocracy writing contracts with the citizens), they will, by definition, not be enforceable because groups controlling the state cannot *commit* not to use their power to renege on their promises and change the terms of the contract. This implies that contractual solutions are seldom useful in political-commitment problems because, most often, the agent violating the contract is precisely the party who is supposed to enforce it (Acemoglu 2003a).

The second possible solution is repeated game interactions. Customers may be deterred from reneging on their promises if they expect to do business with the same traders in the future, and the implicit (or explicit) agreement between them is that if the customers renege on their payments, they will no longer be able to trade in the future. Such repeated game interactions are an imperfect substitute for contracts. They are imperfect because they work only if behavior is sufficiently forward-looking and the rents generated by a continuing relationship are large enough for it to be worthwhile to customers to incur the costs of making the payments today – so that they receive those rents by trading in the future or face the punishment of being excluded from a potentially beneficial relationship. We discuss later how this type of repeated game interaction might help but often falls short.

This leaves us with the third possibility, which is to take the decision-making powers out of the hands of the customers. If whether the payment will be made is decided by the trader, not the customer, the problem will be solved. One way of doing so in the previous economic example is for the customer to give a postdated check to the trader, who will then cash it on the specified date. It is clearly in the interest of the trader to cash the check because the costs are borne by the customer, and she is the beneficiary herself. In other words, the commitment problem has been solved by removing the decoupling between the identities of the beneficiary of the action, the trader, and the person taking the action, the customer. Now, the trader is taking the action, and she will take the action that is in her interests, solving the commitment problem. Although such simple solutions are not available in the political arena, something similar in spirit may be the most useful remedy: change the identity of who has political power so that there is no longer a decoupling between the beneficiary of the policy and the identity of the group holding political power.

The commitment problem and how political institutions deal with it is essential for understanding the remainder of the book. In fact, as indicated in our Introduction, the key role of political institutions in our model is to regulate the future allocation of political power; democratization, a radical change in political institutions, arises as a way of transferring political power from the elites to the citizens. The need for such a transfer of power arises from the inherent commitment problem in politics. Like the customer not wanting to make a payment, the elites who hold political power in nondemocracy will not want to make any concessions, such as income transfers, to the citizens. Therefore, with the citizens excluded from the political system, promises of future redistribution and transfers made by the elites are noncredible. By transferring political power to the citizens, democratization is a way of making such promises credible. That democracy itself suffers from commitment problems is discussed in Chapter 7. In a democracy, the majority of citizens may enact policies highly unfavorable to the elites. In response, the elites may threaten to mount a coup, which democrats will wish to avoid by making concessions. Nevertheless, just as elites in nondemocracy may not be able to avoid revolution by making promises because they are not credible, in a democracy it may not be possible to avoid coups by making promises.

4.2 The Difficulty of Committing Not to Use Political Power

Before embarking on the formal analysis of commitment in political contexts, we discuss three extended historical examples of how it is difficult for those who possess political power to commit not to use it. We have seen interesting examples and some of the consequences in South Africa. In Chapter 1, we discussed how after the Soweto Uprising of 1976, the white government promised many concessions, including putting a stop to the creation of black homelands. However, once Soweto had been pacified and the threat dissipated, the white government reneged on its promises. Another interesting South African example emerges from the 1994 election. As it became evident how large a majority the ANC would have, its leaders became concerned that it should not be too large. For example, were the ANC to have more than 66 percent of the vote, it would be able to make unilateral changes to the constitution. The ANC, presumably because of its objective of creating a consolidated democracy that would prevent subversive action and perhaps capital flight by the white minority, preferred a more limited majority in the Parliament. Consequently, the ANC tried to avoid getting an electoral majority in the 1994 election that would have enabled it to rewrite the constitution. The constitution was an important part of securing democracy in South Africa, and the ANC understood that if it were able to rewrite it, they might not be able to stop themselves from doing so, a step with potentially disastrous consequences.

We focus on three other examples, all of which concern a state making concessions in the face of the threat of revolution. In all cases, the promise of these concessions worked in the sense that the revolution was aborted without the revolutionaries achieving a transfer of political power. Because of this and because of the transitory nature of de facto power, in all three cases the state reneged on its promises, which raises the natural question: Why would such promises stop a revolution? The natural reason is that in reality, and as the models we develop show, the actual extent of credibility is typically uncertain. Even though revolutionaries know there will be circumstances in which promises are reneged on, it may be better to gamble on such promises being upheld than to disregard the promises completely.

4.2.1 The Peasants Revolt of 1381

The Peasants' Revolt of 1381 was one of the most important popular rebellions in British history. Our account follows Hilton (1973), Dobson (1983), and Dyer (1984). It began as a local revolt in Essex and quickly spread across much of southeast England. In the end, an army of peasants marched on London, captured the Tower of London, killed the Archbishop of Canterbury and the King's Treasurer, and took their grievances directly to fourteen-year-old King Richard II at a famous meeting at Mile End.

The main background to the revolt was fallout from the Black Death. This epidemic in the 1340s greatly increased wages and led to many changes in feudal institutions beneficial to the peasants. However, during this period, there was a continual attempt by lords to reassert their powers, which led to many conflicts. Peasants wanted to be free of feudal labor restrictions, regulations, and taxes. The English state was also continually fighting expensive wars and, to help finance them, Richard II introduced a poll tax in 1380. This required everyone on the tax register to pay fivepence. It was the third time in four years that such a tax had been used. If peasants were unable to pay the tax in money, they had to pay in kind.

In May 1381, a tax collector arrived at the Essex village of Fobbing to find out why the people had not paid their poll tax; he was thrown out by the villagers. In June, soldiers arrived to establish law and order. They too were thrown out because the villagers of Fobbing had now organized themselves and many other local villages in Essex had joined them. The revolt quickly spread to the counties of Kent, Suffolk, Hertfordshire, and Norfolk. One man had emerged as the leader of the peasants: Wat Tyler from Kent. As the peasants from Kent and Essex marched to London, they destroyed tax records, tax registers, and government buildings.

By June 12, the Essex men were camped at Mile End, in fields just beyond Aldgate. On the following day, the Kentish men arrived at Blackheath. The authorities were unprepared and during the next few days, different bands of rebels from Essex and Kent were joined by some of London's poor. They set about attacking political targets in the city. They burned down the Savoy Palace, the home of John of Gaunt – Richard II's uncle and probably the most powerful magnate in the realm. They set fire to the Treasurer's Highbury Manor, opened prisons, and destroyed legal records.

On June 14, King Richard and a handful of lords and knights met the Essex peasants at Mile End. The peasants pledged their allegiance to Richard, and handed him a petition that asked for the abolition of villeinage, for labor services based on free contracts, and for the right to rent land at fourpence an acre. The king agreed to grant these demands. Remarkably, later that day, some peasants entered the Tower itself, invading the royal bedchambers and the privy wardrobe. While, in the Tower, the rebels took the Archbishop of Canterbury, the Chancellor, and John of Gaunt's physician into custody, dragging them onto Tower Hill and executing them. After these events, many of the Essex rebels began to disperse.

The next day, King Richard met the Kentish peasants at Smithfield. They demanded an end to all lordship beyond that of the king, that the Church's estates be confiscated and divided among the wider populace, and that there be only bishops throughout the whole kingdom. As before, the king agreed to all the demands put before him. However, the rebel leader, Wat Tyler, supposedly addressed the king with insolence and the mayor of London pulled Tyler from his horse and a squire killed him. The crowd prepared to rush the king and his men, but Richard confronted them. The death of Tyler and another promise by King Richard to give the peasants what they asked for were enough to send them home.

London was made safe from June 16, 1381 and, over time, the authorities gained control in all the regions that had experienced insurrection. King Richard issued a proclamation denying rumors that he had approved of what the rebels had done and, soon after, revoked the pardons he had granted them. A judicial enquiry followed and the king toured the areas that had experienced revolt. In Essex and Hertfordshire counties, the rebels were dealt with severely – many of the main leaders of the revolt were already dead; those who had survived were executed. As a chronicler at the time put it:

> Afterwards the King sent out his messengers into divers parts, to capture the malefactors and put them to death. And many were taken and hanged at London, and they set up many gallows around the City of London, and in other cities and boroughs of the south country. At last, as it pleased God, the King seeing that too many of his liege subjects would be undone, and too much blood spilt, took pity in his heart, and granted them all pardon, on condition that they should never rise again, under pain of losing life or members, and that each of them should get his charter of pardon, and pay the King as fee for his seal twenty shillings, to make him rich. And so finished this wicked war. (quoted in Oman 1906, pp. 200–203, 205)

King Richard did not keep any of his promises, claiming they were made under threat and, therefore, were not valid in law. The peasants' revolt is a classic example of how, once the threat vanishes, the promise of concessions can be reneged on because there was no change in the structure of de jure political power.

4.2.2 The Comunero Rebellion in New Grenada (Colombia)

Another classic example of reneging on promises comes from the Late Colonial Spanish Empire in Latin America. When the Bourbon dynasty assumed the Spanish throne in the early eighteenth century, it attempted to implement a large number of changes in colonial institutions, mostly with an eye to increasing the amount of taxes raised. This led to widespread discontent and two major revolts: the famous Tupac Amaru Rebellion in Peru (see Stavig 1999; Robins 2002) and the Comunero Rebellion in Colombia in 1781 (known during the colonial period as New Grenada).

We follow the definitive recent account of Safford and Palacios (2002); see also major works on the topic by Arcinegas (1938), Cardenas Acosta (1960), Phelan (1978), and Aguilera Peña (1985). Safford and Palacios note that

> innovations under the Spanish Bourbons helped sow the seeds of colonial rebellion. Administrative reform in the colonies meant . . . a conscious policy of preferring Spaniards to Creoles in filling high positions, a policy that further intensified colonials' irritation with the system. Attempts to increase tax collections provoked popular insurrection and tended to undermine the authority of Spanish officials. . . . The fiscal demands of war stirred substantial tax riots in New Grenada in the 1760's and full-scale rebellion in 1781. (2002, pp. 54–5)

In New Grenada,

> in the 1750's . . . administrators began to push for more effective revenue collection. A government monopoly of the sale of cane liquor . . . became a significant revenue earner. In the 1760's the royal government established monopoly control of the sale of tobacco. . . . Later officials . . . raised prices for both liquor and tobacco, and doubled existing sales tax exactions, among other impositions. (Safford and Palacios 2002, pp. 63–4)

The Comunero Rebellion began with protests in Bogotá in 1778 against the tobacco monopoly. Tobacco was widely grown by small farmers in New Grenada, and the monopoly gradually restricted the areas in which it could be grown to limit the supply and maximize returns to the royal government. The Guanentá region of northeast New Grenada (in the present-day department of Santander) was particularly hard hit. In 1780, riots broke out in Charalá, Mogotes, and Simacota. These actions induced no concessions from the government and the royal regent, Gutiérrez de Piñeres not only tightened the tobacco and cane liquor monopolies but also doubled the sales tax in the same year. These tax increases

> . . . were particularly grievous to the people in the Guanentá, as raw cotton and cotton yarn were among the commodities affected, and the Guanentá was the chief center of cotton weaving in the viceroyalty. For poor people in the Guanentá, these measures eliminated one of their chief measures of support, tobacco, and endangered a second, cotton weaving. (Safford and Palacios 2002, p. 65)

In addition, bad weather caused food shortages in the region and there was a serious outbreak of smallpox. Starting in March 1781, riots continually broke out in the region. Royal stores of tobacco and liquor were destroyed and the rebellion, although initiated by poor people, was soon organized by "men of middling fortune – butchers, weavers, cattle traders and small farmers"; moreover, "men of substance came to accept formal positions of leadership" (p. 66). In May, the rebels crushed a small force that Gutiérrez de Piñeres sent against them and support spread widely in northern and northeastern New Grenada. After this initial victory, the rebels, now calling themselves the Comuneros, marched south toward Bogotá and by the end of May, numbering perhaps fifteen thousand to twenty thousand, they were within reach of the capital.

By this time, Gutiérrez de Piñeres had fled the city and effective power was in the hands of Archbishop Caballero y Góngora. He immediately agreed to a list of thirty-five demands by the Comuneros, including the abolition of the new sales tax. The tobacco monopoly was to be ended. In short, as Safford and Palacios stated (2002, p. 67), "the implementation of all of these provisions would have meant the abandonment of virtually all of the new Bourbon revenue measures of the previous two decades." In addition, the Comuneros demanded the expulsion of Gutiérrez de Piñeres and the promotion of Creoles in the government.

Once the Archbishop had agreed to all of the demands, he was able to persuade the rebels to go home. However,

> After the fervor of rebellion cooled somewhat in the Guanentá, and reinforcements of royal troops arrived from Cartagena . . . the royal government carried out exemplary punishments. José Antonio Galán, who had persisted in rebellion after the capitulation of June 1781, and three other Comuneros were hanged in January 1782; their heads, hands and feet were placed on poles in public squares in the capital and towns that had figured prominently in the rebellion. Others . . . were sentenced to 200 lashes, public shame, and imprisonment in Africa. Landless peasants in the Guanentá were sent as colonists to the Isthmus on Panama. . . . Once the most severe punishments had been administered, royal officials . . . revoked the agreement with the Comuneros.

Thus, although the promise of concessions was sufficient to appease the Comuneros in June 1781, once the threat had subsided, the royal government reneged on its promises.

4.2.3 The 1905 Russian Revolution

Our final example is the 1905 Russian Revolution (Ascher 1988, 1992; Verner 1990; Rawson 1995). The revolution was precipitated by the disastrous military defeat of Russia at the hands of the Japanese, particularly the battle of Tsushima in May 1905, but it also reflected the many social tensions inherent in Russian society. Although the serfs had been freed in 1865, there were still many restrictions on their abilities to buy land or move, and conditions in the factories of the newly industrializing cities were very harsh. Attempts by workers to form trade unions were resisted by the factory owners. In 1903, a priest named Father Georgi Gapon succeeded in forming the Assembly of Russian Workers. Within a year, it had more than nine thousand members.

Gapon's movement gathered momentum in 1904 when rapid inflation caused by the war against Japan (which had started in February) led to a 20 percent decline in real wages. When four members of the Assembly of Russian Workers were dismissed at the Putilov Iron Works, Gapon called for industrial action. Over the next few days, more than 110,000 workers in St. Petersburg went on strike.

In an attempt to settle the dispute, Gapon made a personal appeal to Nicholas II and in January 1905 he drew up a petition outlining the workers' sufferings and demands. This petition demanded an eight-hour day; freedom to organize trade unions; improved working conditions; free medical aid; higher wages for women workers; elections to be held for a constituent assembly by universal, equal, and secret suffrage; freedom of speech, press, association, and religion; and an end to the war with Japan.

On January 22, Gapon led a demonstration to the Winter Palace in St. Petersburg to present the petition to the tsar. When the procession of workers reached the palace, it was attacked by the police and the Cossacks. More than hundred workers were killed and some three hundred were wounded. The incident, known as Bloody Sunday, started a series of events that became known as the 1905 Revolution. Strikes took place all over the country and the universities closed down when the entire student body staged a walkout to complain about the lack of civil liberties. Lawyers, doctor, engineers, and other middle-class workers established the Union of Unions and demanded a constituent assembly.

In June 1905, sailors on the battleship *Potemkin* protested against the serving of rotten meat. In response, the captain ordered that the ringleaders be shot. The firing squad refused to carry out the order and joined with the rest of the crew in throwing the officers overboard. The *Potemkin* mutiny spread to other units in the army and navy.

Industrial workers all over Russia went on strike and, in October 1905, the railwaymen went on strike, which paralyzed the entire Russian rail network. Later that month, Leon Trotsky and other Mensheviks established the St. Petersburg Soviet. Over the next few weeks, more than fifty soviets were formed throughout Russia.

Sergei Witte, the new Chief Minister, advised Nicholas II to make concessions. He eventually agreed and published the *October Manifesto*, which granted freedom of conscience, speech, meeting, and association. He also promised that in the future, people would not be imprisoned without trial. Finally, he announced that no law would become operative without the approval of a new organization called the Duma. Because this was only a consultative body, many Russians felt that the reform did not go far enough. Trotsky and other revolutionaries denounced the plan. In December 1905, Trotsky and the executive committee of the St. Petersburg Soviet were arrested. Nevertheless, the announcement of the concessions made in the *October Manifesto* had the effect of calming the country and undermining the revolutionary threat.

The First Duma was elected on the basis of indirect universal male suffrage. The peasants, the townsmen, and the gentry all elected their own representatives. Delegates from all provinces met in the provincial town and chose members of the Duma. However, since publication of the *October Manifesto*, Nicholas II had already made several changes in the composition of the Duma: he had created a state council, an upper chamber, of which he would nominate half its members. He also retained for himself the right to declare war, to control the Orthodox Church, and to dissolve the Duma. The tsar also had the power to appoint and dismiss ministers. Even before the First Duma met, Nicholas II was backtracking on the promises he had made in October.

Nevertheless, the First Duma had a left majority consisting of Socialist Revolutionaries, Mensheviks, Bolsheviks, Octobrists, and members of the Constitutional Democrat Party. At their first meeting in May 1906, members of the Duma put forward a series of demands, including the release of political prisoners, trade-union rights, and land reform. Nicholas II rejected all these proposals and dissolved the Duma in July 1906. In April 1906, Nicholas II had forced Witte to resign and replaced him with the more conservative Peter Stolypin. Stolypin attempted to provide a balance between the introduction of much needed social reforms, such as land reform, and the suppression of the radicals.

Elections for the Second Duma took place in 1907. Stolypin made changes to the electoral law and used his powers to exclude large numbers from voting. The new electoral law also gave better representation to the nobility and greater power to large landowners to the detriment of the peasants. Changes were also made to the voting in towns: those owning their own home elected more than half the urban deputies. This reduced the influence of the left but, when the Second Duma convened in February 1907, it still included many reformers. After three months of heated debate, Nicholas II dissolved the Duma on June 16, 1907.

The Third Duma met on November 14, 1907. The former coalition of Socialist Revolutionaries, Mensheviks, Bolsheviks, Octobrists, and the Constitutional Democrat Party were now outnumbered by the reactionaries and the nationalists. Unlike the previous Dumas, this one ran its full term of five years.

The 1905 Russian Revolution is our final example of how – without fundamental changes in the nature of de jure political power – promises can be reneged on. In response to the uprisings and unrest of 1905, Nicholas II made concessions including, to some extent, the creation of a democratic institution – the Duma. Yet, the Duma was not powerful enough to guarantee that Nicholas II would carryout his concessions; once the revolutionary moment had passed, Nicholas II duly reneged.

4.3 Modeling Commitment Problems in Nondemocracy

We now start laying the scene by introducing simple ways of modeling potential commitment problems in politics. Let us first return to the game shown in Figure 5.1, the key feature of which is that the elites decided the tax rate before the citizens made the revolution decision. Now imagine an alternative game shown in Figure 5.2, in which the citizens decide whether to make the revolution decision first; then, if there is no revolution, the elites set the tax rate. The difference

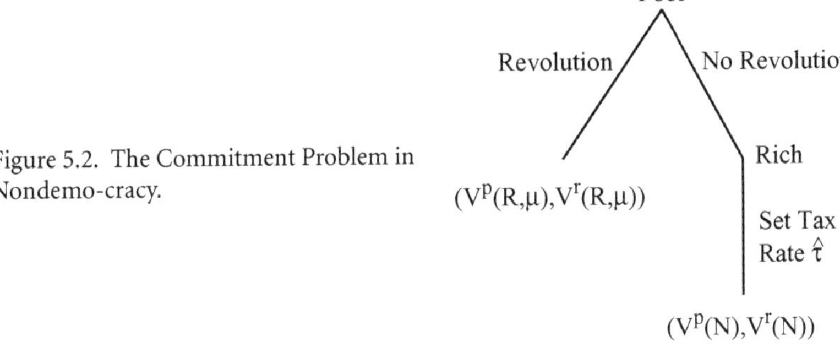

Figure 5.2. The Commitment Problem in Nondemo-cracy.

between the two games may appear minor, but there is, in fact, a major difference: in the game shown in Figure 5.1, there was no commitment problem. The elites set the tax rate before the revolution decision of the citizens and could use the tax rate to avoid the threat of revolution. Now, the elites no longer have that option because they set the tax rate after the revolution decision.

Let us analyze the subgame perfect equilibrium of this game. As usual, we do this by backward induction, starting in the last subgame, which is the one after the citizens decide not to undertake a revolution. In this subgame, the elites have to decide the tax rate, the tax rate gets implemented, and the game ends. Because there are no longer any constraints left, they simply choose their most preferred tax rate, $\tau^r = 0$, giving payoffs:

$$V^p(N) = V\left(y^p \middle| \tau^N = \tau^r\right) = y^p \quad \text{and} \tag{5.11}$$
$$V^r(N) = V\left(y^r \middle| \tau^N = \tau^r\right) = y^r$$

to the citizens and the elites. We use the notation $V^i(N)$ as the value to $i = p, r$ in nondemocracy when the elites set their ideal policy. Moving to the previous stage of the game, the citizens have to decide between revolution, which will yield them the payoff $V^p(R, \mu)$ as given by (5.1), or no revolution, which will give them the payoff $V^p(N) = V\left(y^p \middle| \tau^N = \tau^r\right)$. The former is greater whenever (5.4) holds, so the citizens undertake a revolution whenever (5.4) holds.

In specifying the equilibrium, we again use the notation $\sigma^p = \{\rho\}$ and $\sigma^r = \{\tau^N\}$. The citizens play first and choose $\rho \in \{0, 1\}$ (i.e., whether to revolt), while the elites play second and choose the tax rate τ^N. Because the elites only get to play if $\rho = 0$, we specify this as a choice (not a function) $\tau^N \in [0, 1]$. Then, a subgame perfect equilibrium is a strategy combination, $\{\tilde{\sigma}^r, \tilde{\sigma}^p\}$ such that $\tilde{\sigma}^p$ and $\tilde{\sigma}^r$ are best responses to each other in all proper subgames.

We can see that the following strategy profiles are the unique equilibria. When $\theta \leq \mu$, we have $\rho = 0$ and $\tau^N = 0$. In this equilibrium, the revolution constraint does not bind so the citizens do not revolt, and the elites set their preferred tax rate of zero. When $\theta > \mu$, then the following strategy profile is the unique equilibrium: $\rho = 1$. In this case, revolution is the optimal action and the poor undertake it. We now have the following proposition:

Proposition 5.2: *There is a unique subgame perfect equilibrium* $\{\tilde{\sigma}^r, \tilde{\sigma}^p\}$ *in the game described in Figure 5.2, and it is such that*

- *If (5.4) does not bind, then* $\rho = 0$ *and* $\tau^N = 0$.
- *If (5.4) binds, then* $\rho = 1$.

The results of this proposition are different from those of Proposition 5.1, and an equilibrium revolution happens for a much larger set of parameter values. This reflects the commitment problem of the elites. In the game described in the previous subsection, there was no commitment problem because the elites moved before the citizens had to decide whether to undertake a revolution. Now there is a serious commitment problem. To highlight the essence of this problem, think of the elites as "promising" redistribution to avoid revolution. However, this is not credible because, according to the game in Figure 5.2, they move after the revolution decision of the citizens, and whatever promise they make will not be credible.

This game illustrates the more general commitment problem outlined previously: those with political power – here, the elites – cannot promise to make transfers in the future as long as they hold onto their political power. In the game shown in Figure 5.2, the taxation decision of the elites was made after the revolution decision of the citizens; this implies that the elites have to promise to make transfers in the future. It is this promise about the future that is not credible. This is in some sense quite a reduced-form situation, however, because there is no real sense of present or future, and we can talk of promises only in a loose sense because the game does not really involve promises. We gradually enrich this game and use it as a building block for our analysis of democratization in Chapter 6. In the next section, we introduce a version of the simple game used throughout this book, which is in turn a simplification of a full dynamic game, introduced in the subsequent section.

5. A Simple Game of Promises

We have so far discussed the revolution constraint and how the elites can try to prevent revolution by making promises of redistribution, and we indicated why these promises may not be credible because the elites hold onto political power and, given their political power, they can renege on their promises. Two important elements are missing from this picture: (1) an effective threat of revolution is a rare event and occurs only when the citizens manage to solve the collective-action problem inherent in revolution; and (2) we have so far analyzed games in which either the elites move before the revolution decision and there is no commitment

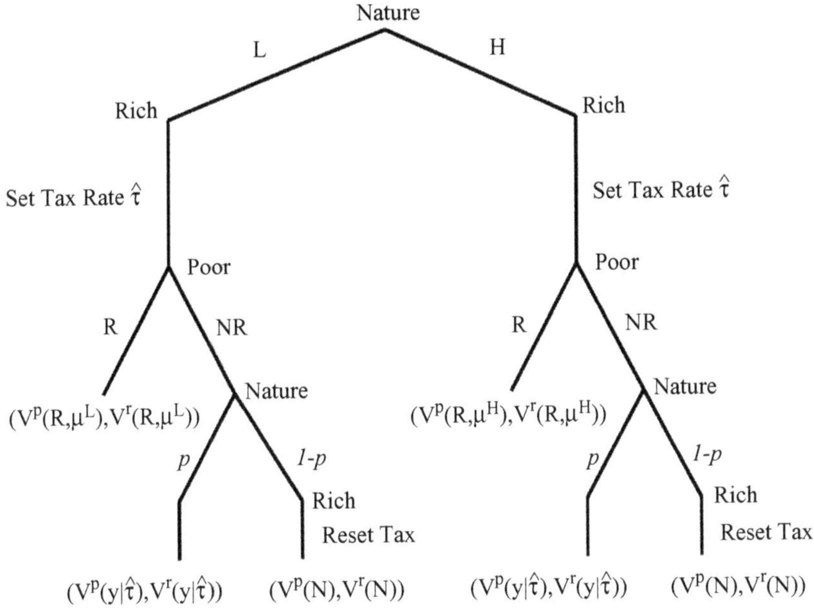

Figure 5.3. A Game of Promises.

problem, or they move after the revolution decision and there is no possibility of promises. Instead, we would like a game that has some possibility of promises by the elites, but these promises are only partially credible.

Figure 5.3 shows the simplest game incorporating these features. Nature moves first and selects between two threat states, low and high; $S = L$ or H. The motivation for introducing these two states is to emphasize that only in some situations is there an effective threat of revolution. In general, this could be because some circumstances are uniquely propitious for solving the collective-action problem – such as a harvest failure, a business-cycle depression, the end of a war, or some other economic, social, or political crisis. We assume that the effectiveness of the revolution threat differs between these two states. In particular, we assume that the payoff to the citizens from revolution in the state S is:

$$V^p\left(R, \mu^S\right) = \frac{(1-\mu^S)\bar{y}}{1-\delta} \tag{5.12}$$

where we think that the low-threat state corresponds to the case in which it is relatively costly for the citizens to solve the collective-action problem or face other problems in organizing revolution, so μ^L is high. To simplify the discussion, we take the extreme case in which $\mu^L = 1$. In contrast, in the high-threat state, the citizens are able to solve the collective-action problem relatively costlessly and/or the elites are not well organized in their defense, so there may be an effective threat of revolution, which we capture by assuming that $1 > \mu^H > 0$. Because μ^L does not play any real role in our analysis – indeed, we suppress this state later in the book to simplify the game trees – from now on, we use the notation $\mu^H = \mu$.

After nature reveals the threat state, the elites set the tax rate τ^N. Observing this tax rate, the citizens decide whether to undertake a revolution. So far, the game is not very different from the game in Figure 5.1. In fact, if it ended here, it would be almost identical, enriched only by having two states instead of one. However, after the revolution decision of the citizens, there is a continuation game capturing in reduced form the problems that those with political power will have in promising to undertake future actions that are not in their immediate interest. In particular, nature moves and determines whether the elites get to reset the tax from τ^N to a new rate different from that which they promised. More specifically, with probability p, the promise that the elites made to redistribute at the tax rate τ^N stands. But, with probability $1 - p$, the promise is void, and the elites get to reset the tax. We use $\bar{\tau}^N$ to denote this tax rate. At this point, because the opportunity to mount revolution has passed, the elites are unconstrained and set their most preferred tax, $\bar{\tau}^N = \tau^r$. We use the notation $\nu \in \{0, 1\}$ for nature's choice, with $\nu = 1$ indicating that the elites can reset the tax rate.

This continuation game after the revolution decision of the citizens is a reduced form way of modeling the inability of those with political power to commit to future redistribution and taxation decisions. When $p = 1$, there is no commitment problem and we have the situation depicted in Figure 5.1; whereas when $p = 0$, there is a complete inability to commit and we have the game shown in Figure 5.2. We can, therefore, use p as a way of parameterizing the ability of the nondemocratic regime to commit. In this game, there is no "future" in the proper sense because there is only one period of redistribution rather than an explicit difference between today and in the future. Nevertheless, the continuation game incorporates, in a relatively simple way, the possibility that after the threat of revolution is gone, the elites can backtrack from their promises. The next section shows that when we have a fully dynamic model in which the revolution threat recurs in the future, the model has a reduced form similar to the simpler game shown in Figure 5.3 that we are analyzing.

The relevant payoffs are as follows. If the citizens undertake a revolution, the payoffs are $V^p\left(R, \mu^S\right)$ given by (5.12) and $V^r\left(R, \mu^S\right) = 0$. If the elites get to reset the tax, they will choose their most preferred tax rate, τ^r, so the payoffs are $V^p(N)$ and $V^r(N)$ given by (5.11). If they are unable to reset the tax and the promised tax rate of τ^N stands, then the values of the two groups are $V\left(y^p \mid \tau^N\right)$ and $V\left(y^r \mid \tau^N\right)$ as given by (5.8). This implies that the expected payoffs at the time the elites make a promise to redistribute at τ^N are $(V^p(N, \tau^N), V^r(N, \tau^N))$, such that:

$$V^p(N, \tau^N) = y^p + p\left(\tau^N(\bar{y} - y^p) - C(\tau^N)\bar{y}\right) \quad \text{and} \tag{5.13}$$
$$V^r(N, \tau^N) = y^r + p\left(\tau^N(\bar{y} - y^r) - C(\tau^N)\bar{y}\right)$$

which take into account the fact that redistribution at the tax rate τ^N happens only with probability p, whereas with probability $1 - p$, the elites reset the tax to τ^r. Notice also that we are using the notation $V^i(N, \tau^N)$, which refers to the case in which the elites make a promise of redistribution at the tax rate τ^N. This is distinct from $V^i(N)$, which refers to the values when the elites are unconstrained. We use this type of notation throughout the book.

Therefore, after observing the promise of redistribution at the tax rate τ^N, the citizens have to make a comparison between $V^p(N, \tau^N)$ as given by (5.13) and the payoff from revolution $V^p(R, \mu^S)$ as given by (5.12). Clearly, $V^p(N, \tau^N) > V^p(R, \mu^L)$ for any τ^N by virtue of the fact that $\mu^L = 1$. Therefore, in the low state, $\mu^S = \mu^L$, the elites do not suffer a revolution; anticipating this, they make no concessions and simply set their most preferred tax rate, $\tau^N = \tau^r = 0$ (or, using our notation, $\tau^N(\mu^L) = \tau^r$).

In contrast, in the high-threat state $S = H$, the revolution constraint could be binding. As before, we say that the revolution constraint binds if $V^p(R, \mu^H) > V^p(N)$; that is, if the citizens receive more from revolution than they would when the elites set their most preferred tax rate in nondemocracy. Using (4.7) and (5.12), this revolution constraint is again equal to (5.4). If this revolution constraint does not bind, then even in the high state, the elites are unconstrained and, again, they set their most preferred tax rate. Suppose, on the other hand, that the revolution constraint binds (i.e., $\theta > \mu$). What happens then?

The elites would like to prevent revolution if at all possible. Whether they can do so depends on the value they can promise to the citizens. Clearly, the most favorable tax rate they can offer to the citizens is $\tau^N = \tau^p$, as given by (4.11). However, this is not as good as offering τ^p for certain because of the commitment problem. Whether the elites can prevent revolution depends on whether $V^p(N, \tau^N = \tau^p)$ is greater than $V^p(R, \mu^H)$. Written more explicitly, the key condition is whether:

$$y^p + p(\tau^p(\bar{y} - y^p) - C(\tau^p)\bar{y}) \geq \frac{(1-\mu)\bar{y}}{1-\delta}$$

recalling that μ^H takes the specific value μ, or whether:

$$\mu \geq \theta - p(\tau^p(\theta - \delta) - (1-\delta)C(\tau^p)) \tag{5.14}$$

If inequality is limited (i.e., θ is relatively low) or if there is a high probability that the promise made by the elites will be upheld (i.e., p is relatively high), then living under nondemocracy is not too bad for the citizens, and the condition (5.14) will hold and revolution can be avoided.

To analyze the model, let us determine a critical value of the revolution cost μ^* such that (5.14) holds as an equality:

$$\mu^* = \theta - p(\tau^p(\theta - \delta) - (1-\delta)C(\tau^p)) \tag{5.15}$$

Then, when $\mu > \mu^*$, we have $V^p(N, \tau^N = \tau^p) > V^p(R, \mu^H)$ or, in other words, (5.14) will hold. We can then define a $\hat{\tau} \leq \tau^p$ such that $V^p(N, \tau^N = \hat{\tau}) = V^p(R, \mu^H)$ so that the elites can prevent revolution by setting (i.e., by promising) this tax rate. Therefore, $\hat{\tau}$ satisfies

$$\mu = \theta - p(\hat{\tau}(\theta - \delta) - (1 - \delta)C(\hat{\tau})) \tag{5.16}$$

As before, we let σ^r and σ^p refer to the generic vector of actions. Here, $\sigma^r = \{\tau^N(\cdot), \bar{\tau}^N\}$ and $\sigma^p = \{\rho(\cdot, \cdot)\}$. Strategies are also conditioned on whether the state is low-threat or high-threat; thus, the strategy of the elites is a function $\tau^N : \{\mu^L, \mu^H\} \to [0, 1]$ (we use the notation $\{\mu^L, \mu^H\}$ instead of $\{1, \mu\}$ for clarity) and that for the citizens is a function $\rho : \{\mu^L, \mu^H\} \times [0, 1] \to \{0, 1\}$. Here, $\tau^N(\mu^S)$ is the taxation decision of the elites when the threat state is μ^S and $\rho(\mu^S, \tau^N)$ is the revolution decision when the state is μ^S and the elites chose the tax rate τ^N. In this game, the elites may play twice. If there is no revolution and nature chooses $\nu = 1$, then the elites get to reset the tax rate; however, because when $\nu = 0$ the elites do not get to play again, we represent this in σ^r by a choice $\bar{\tau}^N \in [0, 1]$ and not as a function of ν. Then, a subgame perfect equilibrium is a strategy combination, $\{\tilde{\sigma}^r, \tilde{\sigma}^p\}$ such that $\tilde{\sigma}^p$ and $\tilde{\sigma}^r$ are best responses to each other in all proper subgames.

When $\theta \leq \mu$, the following strategy profile is the unique equilibrium: for the elites, $\tau^N(\mu^S) = 0$; $\bar{\tau}^N = 0$; for the citizens, $\rho(\mu^S, \tau^N) = 0$ for all μ^S. Here, the revolution constraint binds in neither state, the elites never have to make any concessions, and the citizens never find it optimal to undertake a revolution.

When $\theta > \mu$ and $\mu < \mu^*$, the following strategy profile is the unique equilibrium: for the elites $\tau^N(\mu^L) = 0$ and $\bar{\tau}^N = 0$, and for the citizens $\rho(\mu^L, \tau^N) = 0$ and $\rho(\mu^H, \tau^N) = 1$ for all τ^N. Here, revolution is sufficiently attractive that concessions will not work. In words, this says that the strategy of the elites is that if the state is μ^L, they do not undertake any redistribution ($\tau^N = 0$), and the citizens' strategy implies that they do not undertake revolution in μ^L whatever tax rate is set ($\rho = 0$). If the state is μ^H, then it does not matter what tax rate the elites set because in this case, the citizens mount revolution ($\rho = 1$) whatever it is. To see that these strategies constitute an equilibrium, note that neither the elites nor the citizens could change their strategy and increase their payoff. For example, given that the citizens play $\rho(\mu^L, \tau^N) = 0$, then the elites cannot increase their payoff by setting any tax rate other than zero, so that $\tau^N(\mu^L) = \tau^r = 0$ is a best response. Similarly, given that $\mu^L = 1$, the citizens cannot increase their payoff by having a revolution.

When $\theta > \mu$ and $\mu \geq \mu^*$, the following profile constitutes the unique subgame perfect equilibrium: $\tau^N(\mu^L) = 0$, $\tau^N(\mu^H) = \hat{\tau}$ where $\hat{\tau} \in [0, \tau^p]$ is defined by $V^p(N, \tau^N = \hat{\tau}) = V^p(R, \mu^H)$, and $\bar{\tau}^N = 0$, and for the citizens $\rho(\mu^L, \tau^N) = 0$ and $\rho(\mu^H, \tau^N) = 0$ for $\tau^N \geq \hat{\tau}$. Also, off the equilibrium path, $\rho(\mu^H, \tau^N) = 1$ for $\tau^N < \hat{\tau}$.

We now have the following proposition summarizing the equilibrium of this game:

Proposition 5.3: *There is a unique subgame perfect equilibrium* $\{\tilde{\sigma}^r, \tilde{\sigma}^p\}$ *in the game described in Figure 5.3. Let* μ^* *and* $\hat{\tau}$ *be given by (5.15) and (5.16); then, in this equilibrium:*

- *If* $\theta \leq \mu$, *then* $\tau^N(\mu) = 0$, $\bar{\tau}^N = 0$, *and* $\rho(\mu, \tau^N) = 0$ *for all* τ^N *and* μ.
- *If* $\theta > \mu$, *then:*
  (1) *If* $\mu < \mu^*$, $\tau^N(\mu^L) = 0$, $\bar{\tau}^N = 0$, *and* $\rho(\mu^L, \tau^N) = 0$ *but* $\rho(\mu^H, \tau^N) = 1$ *for all* τ^N.
  (2) *If* $\mu \geq \mu^*$, $\tau^N(\mu^L) = 0$, $\tau^N(\mu^H) = \hat{\tau}$, $\bar{\tau}^N = 0$, *and* $\rho(\mu^L, \tau^N) = 0$, $\rho(\mu^H, \tau^N) = 0$ *for* $\tau^N \geq \hat{\tau}$ *and off the equilibrium path,* $\rho(\mu^H, \tau^N) = 1$ *for* $\tau^N < \hat{\tau}$.

This proposition gives a complete description of equilibrium strategies, including actions off the equilibrium path. To avoid statements of propositions becoming cumbersome, we can write Proposition 5.3 in an alternative, more intuitive form that is useful in the remainder of the book. In writing this, we abstract from actions off the equilibrium path.

Proposition 5.3 (alternative form): *There is a unique subgame perfect equilibrium* $\{\tilde{\sigma}^r, \tilde{\sigma}^p\}$ *in the game described in Figure 5.3. Let* μ^* *and* $\hat{\tau}$ *be given by (5.15), and (5.16); then, in this equilibrium:*

- *If* $\theta \leq \mu$, *then the revolution constraint is not binding, the elites never redistribute, and the citizens never undertake a revolution.*
- *If* $\theta > \mu$, *then the revolution constraint is binding in the high state. In this case:*
  (1) *If* $\mu < \mu^*$, *promises by the elites are insufficiently credible to avoid a revolution. In the low state, the elites do not redistribute and there is no revolution, but in the high state, a revolution occurs whatever tax rate the elites set.*
  (2) *If* $\mu \geq \mu^*$, *the elites do not redistribute in the low state and set the tax rate* $\hat{\tau}$ *in the high-threat state, just sufficient to stop a revolution. The citizens never revolt.*

The most important result for our analysis is the following: when the promise to redistribute by the elites is only imperfectly credible (i.e., p small), during unusual periods in which the citizens solve the collective-action problem, there will be an equilibrium revolution. A low p means that promises made by the elites are not very credible because there is a small probability that they will be upheld; with a relatively large probability, the elites will reset the tax once the threat of revolution disappears. This is the case, therefore, where because the elite have the de jure political power, their promises of redistribution in the future are not credible. Formally, μ^* is a decreasing function of p. The greater is p, the more credible is the promise of the elites to make concessions, the lower the costs of revolution must be for it to be attractive to the citizens.

Notice also that μ^* is increasing in θ. To see this, let us again use the implicit-function theorem and differentiate (5.15) with respect to θ:

$$\frac{d\mu^*}{d\theta} = 1 - p\tau^p - p((\theta - \delta) - (1 - \delta)C'(\tau^p))\frac{d\tau^p}{d\theta} > 0$$

To see why this expression is positive, first note that by the first-order condition that defines τ^p, (4.11), we have that $(1 - \delta)C'(\tau^p) = \theta - \delta$; hence, the second term in $d\mu^*/d\theta$ is zero. This is an example of the application of the envelope theorem (Green, Mas-Colell, and Whinston 1995, pp. 964–6). The result then follows from noting that because both p and τ^p are less than one, $1 - p\tau^p > 0$. This implies that a more unequal society has a higher threshold, which simply reflects the fact that revolutions are more attractive in more unequal societies, so the elites need future promises to be highly credible to avoid revolution.

An important prediction of Proposition 5.3 is, therefore, that others things being equal, revolutions happen in unequal societies and in societies where the political power of the elites makes it difficult for them to make credible commitments to future concessions (i.e., redistribution).

It is useful to reflect on how these results change if, as in Chapter 4, targeted transfers can be used. In this case, the elites can tax the citizens in nondemocracy. The first effect of this is to change the revolution constraint. The preferred tax rate of the elites is given in (4.14) and the revolution constraint becomes:

$$\frac{(1 - \mu)\bar{y}}{1 - \delta} > (1 - \tau^{rT})y^p$$

because the citizens pay taxes but get no redistribution. This implies:

$$\theta > \frac{\mu - \tau^{rT}}{1 - \tau^{rT}}$$

Because $(\mu - \tau^{rT})/(1 - \tau^{rT}) < \mu$, this immediately implies that revolution is attractive for the citizens at lower levels of inequality compared to before. Targeted transfers have one other implication: they allow the elites to make bigger transfers to the citizens, which reduces μ^*, allowing the elites to avoid revolution for a large part of the parameter space.

The static game analyzed in this section shows how the degree of credibility of promises affects whether the citizens prefer to live under nondemocracy, with political power in the hands of the rich elites, or undertake revolution. The other important feature of this game is that it has the same structure as many of the games we use to analyze the creation and then consolidation of democracy. There, exactly as in this game, those with political power try to make concessions and, if those concessions are credible, the existing regime will survive. If they are not credible, the regime will not survive; whether it falls to revolution or to a coup or whether there is an equilibrium transition to democracy arranged by the elites to avoid revolution depends on details of the game and on the circumstances we are trying to analyze.

6. A Dynamic Model

The analysis in the previous section shows how the degree of credibility of the promises made by the elite affects whether nondemocracy can overcome the constraints placed on it by revolutions, especially by the threat of a revolution during unusual periods in which the citizens solve the collective-action problem. However, the inability of the elites to commit to future redistribution was modeled in a reduced-form way by introducing the continuation game in which the elites, with some probability, were able to reset the tax away from that which they promised.

We now analyze a dynamic game that maps exactly into the simpler game of the previous section. The advantage of this game is that it captures the same issues in a more plausible and appealing way. Moreover, as mentioned in Chapter 2 and as discussed in detail in Chapter 6, the role of institutions in our theory is fundamentally intertemporal – they determine the future allocation of power. To model this, therefore, we need an intertemporal setup, which we now start developing.

The elites now can stay with the current taxes they set within one period, but they cannot commit to future redistribution – unless the future also poses an effective revolution threat. Therefore, the commitment problem takes a more natural form because it arises from the inability of those with political power to bind their hands in the future unless they relinquish their political power. This game is also the first example of a dynamic model and a prototype for the dynamic games analyzed throughout this book. Like those games, this one has a relatively simple recursive structure and we simplify it further by focusing on Markov perfect equilibria. Markov perfect equilibria are a subset of subgame perfect equilibria that are relatively easy to characterize (Fudenberg and Tirole 1991, pp. 501–35). The main difference is that, in general, in a repeated game, the actions that a player can take at any date can be a function of the entire history of the game up until that point. In a Markov equilibrium, we restrict this element of history dependence – indeed, actions at a particular date can only depend on the "state" of the game at that point (we discuss how to specify the state shortly). Nevertheless, the restriction to Markovian equilibria is really just a simplification of the model. To convince the reader, we look at non-Markovian strategies in the next section in which we characterize non-Markovian subgame perfect equilibria and compare them to the Markov equilibria we analyze in this section.

The total population is normalized to 1 with rich elites and poor citizens just as before, with fractions δ and $1-\delta$. But, we are now in a dynamic world, so the production structure outlined previously applies in every period. In particular, pre-tax incomes are constant and given by (4.7) at all dates. Individual utility is now defined over the discounted sum of post-tax incomes with discount factor $\beta \in (0, 1)$; therefore, for individual i at time $t = 0$, it is:

$$U^i = E_0 \sum_{t=0}^{\infty} \beta^t \hat{y}_t^i \tag{5.17}$$

which simply gives a discounted sum of the individual's income stream, with E_0 defined as the expectation based on the information set available at time $t = 0$.

If we restrict ourselves to sequences of events in which revolution never takes place, then (5.17) can be written more informatively:

$$U^i = E_0 \sum_{t=0}^{\infty} \beta^t \left((1-\tau_t)y^i + (\tau_t - C(\tau_t))\bar{y}\right) \tag{5.18}$$

where the second equality uses the expression for post-tax income (4.5), taking into account that tax rates are potentially time-varying, hence indexed by t. However, (5.18) only applies when there is no revolution along the equilibrium path. More generally, we should have:

$$U^i = E_0 \sum_{t=0}^{\infty} \beta^t \left[(1-\bar{\rho}_t)\left((1-\tau_t)y^i + (\tau_t - C(\tau_t))\bar{y}\right) + \bar{\rho}_t y_R^i\right]$$

where $\bar{\rho}_t = 1$ if there has been revolution at any time before t, and $\bar{\rho}_t = 0$ otherwise, and y_R^i is the income of individual i after revolution.

We denote the infinitely repeated discounted game under consideration here by the standard notation $G^{\infty}(\beta)$.

As in previous sections, the $1-\delta$ poor citizens have de facto political power and can pose a revolutionary threat. They can overthrow the existing regime in any period $t \geq 0$. If revolution is attempted, it always succeeds, but a fraction μ_t of the productive capacity of the economy is destroyed forever in the process. Therefore, if there is revolution at time t, each citizen receives a per-period return of $(1-\mu^S)\bar{y}/(1-\delta)$ in all future periods: total income in the economy is $(1-\mu^S)\bar{y}$ and is shared between $1-\delta$ agents. Here, after a revolution, μ^S is the value of μ_t at the date when the revolution took place (μ^H or μ^L). This implies that the state does not fluctuate once revolution has taken place. μ changes between two values, $\mu^H = \mu$ and $\mu^L = 1$, with $\Pr(\mu_t = \mu) = q$, irrespective of whether $\mu_{t-1} = \mu^H$ or μ^L.

The fact that μ fluctuates is crucial in modeling the limited ability of the elites to promise future redistribution. A change in μ corresponds to a change in the underlying environment, so the elites, who hold political power in nondemocracy, will optimize again. As a result, their promise to redistribute today may not materialize due to changes in circumstances tomorrow. A high value of μ means that revolution is very costly, whereas a low value of q implies that the threat of revolution is rare, perhaps because the citizens are unorganized. Fluctuations in the threat of revolution are the source of commitment problems arising from political power.

The timing of events within a period, say time t, can be summarized as follows.

1. μ_t is revealed.
2. The elites set the tax rate τ_t^N.
3. The citizens decide whether to initiate a revolution, denoted by ρ_t with $\rho_t = 1$ corresponding to revolution at time t. If there is revolution, they obtain the remaining $1 - \mu_t$ share of output in all future periods.

For Markov perfect equilibria, the crucial concept is that of the "state" of the game or the system, which is simply a complete specification of all payoff-relevant information. Here, the state of the system consists of the current opportunity for revolution, represented by either μ^L or μ^H. Let $\sigma^r = \{\tau^N(\cdot)\}$ be the actions taken by the elites when the state is $\mu_t = \mu^H$ or μ^L. This consists of a tax rate $\tau^N : \{\mu^L, \mu^H\} \to [0, 1]$. Similarly, $\sigma^p = \{\rho(\cdot, \cdot)\}$ is the action of the citizens, which consists of a decision to initiate revolution, ρ ($\rho = 1$ representing revolution) conditional on the current actions of the elites. Hence, as in the previous model $\rho : \{\mu^L, \mu^H\} \times [0, 1] \to \{0, 1\}$. Then, a Markov perfect equilibrium is a strategy combination, $\{\tilde{\sigma}^r, \tilde{\sigma}^p\}$ such that $\tilde{\sigma}^p$ and $\tilde{\sigma}^r$ are best responses to each other for all μ. Markov perfect equilibria are a subset of subgame perfect equilibria because they exclude any subgame perfect equilibria that feature non-Markovian strategies.

The advantage of the concept of Markov perfect equilibrium is that it incorporates the commitment problem in a simple way: given the state of the system, here the value of μ_t, each party plays the best strategy for itself, irrespective of any promises made before or how the game was played in the past. Therefore, this equilibrium concept already builds in the commitment problem: all players know that each will play whatever is in their interest in the future. The other convenient thing about this equilibrium concept is that it lends itself to a tractable analysis using Bellman equations (i.e., simple dynamic programming arguments; see Sargent 1987 and Stokey, Lucas, and Prescott 1989 for good introductions to dynamic programming and their uses in economics).

Let us start with the payoffs once there is revolution. We define $V^p(R, \mu^S)$ as the return to poor citizens if there is revolution starting in threat state $\mu^S \in \{\mu, 1\}$. Recall that only the value of μ^S at the time of revolution matters; after that, a fraction μ^S of the productive capacity of the economy is destroyed forever. This implies that the value of revolution starting in the state μ^S is:

$$V^p(R, \mu^S) = \frac{(1-\mu^S)\bar{y}}{1-\delta} + \beta\frac{(1-\mu^S)\bar{y}}{1-\delta} + \beta^2\frac{(1-\mu^S)\bar{y}}{1-\delta} + \cdots \tag{5.19}$$

which compounds all the future returns, taking into account that the future is discounted with discount factor $\beta < 1$. We have that:

$$V^p(R, \mu^S) = \frac{(1-\mu^S)\bar{y}}{(1-\delta)(1-\beta)}$$

To see this, we can write (5.19) as:

$$V^p(R, \mu^S) = \frac{(1-\mu^S)\bar{y}}{1-\delta} + \beta\left[\frac{(1-\mu^S)\bar{y}}{1-\delta} + \beta\frac{(1-\mu^S)\bar{y}}{1-\delta} + \cdots\right]$$

and then observe that the term within the square bracket to the right of this expression is nothing other than $V^p(R, \mu^S)$ itself. Thus, (5.19) can be written:

$$V^p(R, \mu^S) = \frac{(1-\mu^S)\bar{y}}{1-\delta} + \beta V^p(R, \mu^S) \tag{5.20}$$

and solving this for $V^p(R, \mu^S)$ gives the formula written previously and which we use in (5.21) below.

It is important to notice how the infinite horizon helps us analytically. What we have used here is the fact that after revolution has happened, we look into the future to sum up the benefits from revolution to the citizens. What (5.20) says is that looking into the infinite future from tomorrow on looks identical to looking into the infinite future today.

Also, because the rich elites lose everything, $V^r(R, \mu^S) = 0$. Next, recall that we also assumed $\mu^L = 1$; the citizens would never attempt revolution when $\mu_t = \mu^L$. Therefore, the only relevant value is the one starting in the state $\mu^H = \mu$, which is:

$$V^p(R, \mu^H) = \frac{(1-\mu)\bar{y}}{(1-\delta)(1-\beta)} \tag{5.21}$$

Let us next turn to the decision of the elites. First, consider the state $\mu_t = \mu^L$, where there is no threat of revolution, and let us try to calculate the value to the elites and to the citizens in this state, denoted by $V^r(N, \mu^L)$ and $V^p(N, \mu^L)$. We maintain the superscripts H and L on the μ's in the value functions to facilitate the exposition. The concept of Markov perfect equilibrium implies that irrespective of promises made in the past, in this state the elites choose whatever policy is in their best interest at that point. Because there is no threat of revolution, this must be to set $\tau^N = \tau^r$ and engage in no redistribution. However, the state $\mu_t = \mu^L$ in nondemocracy is not permanent. Next period, we could switch to $\mu_t = \mu^H$ and, in this case, the elites might have to engage in redistribution or there might be a revolution.

Let us denote the values to the elites and to the citizens in the state $\mu_t = \mu^H$ by $V^r(N, \mu^H)$ and $V^p(N, \mu^H)$. This implies that the relevant Bellman equations determining the values $V^r(N, \mu^L)$ and $V^p(N, \mu^L)$ can be written as:

$$V^r(N, \mu^L) = y^r + \beta\left[q V^r(N, \mu^H) + (1-q) V^r(N, \mu^L)\right] \tag{5.22}$$
$$V^p(N, \mu^L) = y^p + \beta\left[q V^p(N, \mu^H) + (1-q) V^p(N, \mu^L)\right]$$

These value functions have a form that recurs throughout the dynamic analysis in this book, so it is important to understand the reasoning behind them. We focus on the elites for concreteness.

The value functions in (5.22) say that the value to a member of the elite in a nondemocracy and in the state $\mu_t = \mu^L$ consists of two terms: (1) what happens today, the first term y^r; and (2) what is expected to happen tomorrow, or the continuation value, represented by the second term, $\beta\left[q V^r(N, \mu^H) + (1-q) V^r(N, \mu^L)\right]$. Today, given the decision $\tau^N = \tau^r$, there is no redistribution, and a member of the elite obtains y^r, which is the first term. The second term is multiplied by β because it starts tomorrow and, therefore, is discounted back to today by the discount factor β. Tomorrow, there is a new draw from the distribution of μ, and with probability $1-q$, the state μ^L recurs, so we have $\mu_{t+1} = \mu^L$. In this case, exactly the same reasoning as today implies that the value to an elite agent from that point onward is $V^r(N, \mu^L)$; hence, this term is multiplied by $1-q$ and included as part of the future value. The value $V^r(N, \mu^L)$ recurs because the world looking forward into the infinite future from state $\mu_t = \mu^L$ looks identical to the world looking forward into the infinite future from state $\mu_{t+1} = \mu^L$ (recall equation (5.20)). With the remaining probability, q, there is a change in the state, and we have $\mu_{t+1} = \mu^H$; in this case, we have a different value for a member of the elite tomorrow, denoted by $V^r(N, \mu^H)$.

The same argument also applies for citizens and gives the corresponding expression for $V^p(N, \mu^L)$, again consisting of two terms: what they receive today, y^p, and what they will receive tomorrow, $\beta\left[q V^p(N, \mu^H) + (1-q) V^p(N, \mu^L)\right]$.

The nice thing about the value functions in (5.22) is their "recursive" structure. Basically, the future is much like today, so the same value that applies today in the state μ^L also applies tomorrow if the state happens to be μ^L.

Naturally, (5.22) is not sufficient to characterize the equilibrium because we do not know what happens in the state $\mu_t = \mu^H$ or, in other words, we do not know what is $V^r(N, \mu^H)$ and, similarly, what is $V^p(N, \mu^H)$. In this state, there may be an effective threat of revolution. So, we must first check whether the revolution constraint is binding. To do so, we define $V^r(N)$ and $V^p(N)$ as the payoffs that would apply if society remains in nondemocracy all the time (i.e., no revolution) and the elites never redistribute to the citizens (i.e., $\tau^N = \tau^r$). We clearly have:

$$V^r(N) = y^r + \beta y^r + \beta^2 y^r + \cdots$$
$$= \frac{y^r}{1-\beta}$$

because the elites always receive the income y^r as there is no taxation, and this future income stream is discounted to the present at the discount factor β. Similarly:

$$V^p(N) = \frac{y^p}{1-\beta} \tag{5.23}$$

We say that the revolution constraint binds if the poor citizens prefer revolution in the state $\mu_t = \mu^H$ rather than to live in nondemocracy without any redistribution; that is, if:

$$V^p(R, \mu^H) > V^p(N)$$

where $V^p(R, \mu^H)$ is given by (5.21). Using the definitions in (4.7), the revolution constraint is equivalent to:

$$\theta > \mu \tag{5.24}$$

In other words, inequality needs to be sufficiently high (i.e., θ sufficiently high) for the revolution constraint to bind. If inequality is not that high so that we have $\theta \leq \mu$, there is no threat of revolution even in the state $\mu_t = \mu^H$, even with no redistribution ever. In this case, the elites always set their unconstrained best tax rate, $\tau^N = \tau^r$, and we have no revolution along the equilibrium path.

It is useful to recall the analysis of our "static" model in the previous section. The formula for the revolution constraint in the dynamic model (5.24) is identical to that in the static model (5.4). In both cases, they simply link inequality to the cost of mounting revolution. This is the basis of the parallel we draw between the static and dynamic models.

The more interesting case is the one in which the revolution constraint (5.24) binds. If, in this case, the elites set $\tau^N = \tau^r$ in the threat state $\mu_t = \mu^H$, there will be revolution. So, the elites make some concessions by setting a tax rate $\tau^N = \hat{\tau} > 0$. We denote the values to the elites and the citizens in the state $\mu_t = \mu^H$ when the elites set a tax rate $\hat{\tau}$ and are expected to do so in the future, and there is no revolution, by $V^r(N, \mu^H, \tau^N = \hat{\tau})$ and $V^p(N, \mu^H, \tau^N = \hat{\tau})$. At this tax rate, an agent of type i has net income of $(1 - \hat{\tau})y^i$, plus he receives a lump-sum transfer of $\hat{T}$. From the government budget constraint, this lump-sum transfer is $\hat{T} = (\hat{\tau} - C(\hat{\tau}))\bar{y}$, where $\hat{\tau}\bar{y}$ is total tax revenue and $C(\hat{\tau})\bar{y}$ is the cost of taxation.

By the same argument as before, we have the value functions $V^r(N, \mu^H, \tau^N = \hat{\tau})$ and $V^p(N, \mu^H, \tau^N = \hat{\tau})$ given by:

$$V^r(N, \mu^H, \tau^N = \hat{\tau}) = y^r + (\hat{\tau}(\bar{y} - y^r) - C(\hat{\tau})\bar{y}) + \beta\left[q V^r(N, \mu^H, \tau^N = \hat{\tau}) + (1-q)V^r(N, \mu^L)\right], \tag{5.25}$$

$$V^p(N, \mu^H, \tau^N = \hat{\tau}) = y^p + (\hat{\tau}(\bar{y} - y^p) - C(\hat{\tau})\bar{y}) + \beta\left[q V^p(N, \mu^H, \tau^N = \hat{\tau}) + (1-q)V^p(N, \mu^L)\right]$$

For the purpose of illustration, we focus on the value function for a member of the elite. The first term is now $y^r + (\hat{\tau}(\bar{y} - y^r) - C(\hat{\tau})\bar{y})$, which is his or her net income after taxation at the rate $\hat{\tau}$. The second term is again the continuation value, $\beta\left[q V^r(N, \mu^H, \tau^N = \hat{\tau}) + (1-q)V^r(N, \mu^L)\right]$. With probability q, the state μ^H arises again tomorrow and, in this case, the rich continue to set $\tau^N = \hat{\tau}$ and receive $V^r(N, \mu^H, \tau^N = \hat{\tau})$. With probability $1 - q$, the state switches to μ^L, and the corresponding value is $V^r(N, \mu^L, \tau^N = \hat{\tau})$. The entire term is multiplied by β to discount it to the present.

A similar argument underlies the expression for $V^p(N, \mu^H, \tau^N = \hat{\tau})$. A citizen receives a relatively high income today because there is redistribution at the rate $\hat{\tau}$. But, what happens in the future is uncertain. If the state remains at μ^H, redistribution continues. However, there is no guarantee and, in fact, the threat state could switch to μ^L where the threat of revolution disappears. As we saw previously, now irrespective of what they promise, the elites will stop redistributing and set $\tau^N = \tau^r$. Therefore, the expression for $V^p(N, \mu^H, \tau^N = \hat{\tau})$ already incorporates the potential "noncredibility" of the promise of future redistribution made today. Today's redistribution arises because the citizens have de facto political power: they have a relatively effective revolution threat and, if the elites do not make some concessions in the form of redistribution, they can overthrow the system. Political power, therefore, gets them additional income. This redistribution might cease tomorrow, however, if what gives political power to the citizens – the revolution threat – disappears. This is the essence of the problem of commitment in this society.

Note also at this point the similarity of the reasoning to that used in the simple game of the previous section. There, the elites made a promise to redistribute at the tax rate $\hat{\tau}$, but after the threat of revolution disappeared, nature decided whether they could reset the tax. Here, the elites can successfully redistribute to the citizens today, but what the citizens care about is not only redistribution today but also tomorrow, the day after tomorrow, and so on. Today's redistribution is supported by the citizens' political power: the threat of revolution. The elites might like to promise redistribution tomorrow, but when nature decides that the revolution threat disappears tomorrow (i.e., the state switches to μ^L with probability $1 - q$), they no longer keep their promise and cut taxes down to 0, $\tau^N = \tau^r$. Therefore, as claimed there, the simple game of the previous section was a reduced-form way of capturing the dynamic commitment problems being more carefully modeled here.

Returning to the analysis of the current game, we still need to determine the action of the citizens after the elites decide to redistribute at the tax rate $\hat{\tau}$ in the state μ^H. Clearly, they have a choice between no revolution, $\rho = 0$, and revolution, $\rho = 1$. If they decide to undertake revolution, then once the game reaches this point, the value functions for revolution, $V^r(R, \mu^H)$ and $V^p(R, \mu^H)$, will apply. Otherwise, we have $V^r(N, \mu^H, \tau^N = \hat{\tau})$ and $V^p(N, \mu^H, \tau^N = \hat{\tau})$. Moreover, clearly, a citizen will choose ρ depending on whether $V^p(N, \mu^H, \tau^N = \hat{\tau})$ or $V^p(R, \mu^H)$ is greater. Hence, we can write:

$$\rho \begin{cases} = 0 & \text{if } V^p(R, \mu^H) \leq V^p(N, \mu^H, \tau^N = \hat{\tau}) \\ = 1 & \text{if } V^p(R, \mu^H) > V^p(N, \mu^H, \tau^N = \hat{\tau}) \end{cases} \tag{5.26}$$

This decision calculus is the same for all citizens. In other words, a citizen takes part in revolution if he or she gets a higher return with revolution than with redistribution at the rate $\hat{\tau}$ today, which again can be thought of as a "semicredible promise of redistribution by the elites" – there will be redistribution today at the tax rate $\hat{\tau}$ and there might be tomorrow if nature determines that there is an effective threat of revolution tomorrow. We proceed by assuming in (5.26) that if $V^p(R, \mu^H) = V^p(N, \mu^H, \tau^N = \hat{\tau})$, then $\rho = 0$ so that indifference is broken by not undertaking revolution.

With ρ given by (5.26), we also have that:

$$V^r(N, \mu^H) = \rho V^r(R, \mu^H) + (1 - \rho) V^r(N, \mu^H, \tau^N = \hat{\tau}) \tag{5.27}$$
$$V^p(N, \mu^H) = \max_{\rho \in \{0,1\}} \left\{ \rho V^p(R, \mu^H) + (1 - \rho) V^p(N, \mu^H, \tau^N = \hat{\tau}) \right\}$$

As we know, the elites would like to prevent revolution if they can; the question is whether they will be able to do so. To answer this question, we need to see what is the maximum value that the elites can promise to the citizens. Clearly, this is when they set the tax most preferred by the citizens, τ^p, given by (4.11). Hence, the relevant comparison is between $V^p(R, \mu^H)$ and $V^p(N, \mu^H, \tau^N = \tau^p)$. If $V^p(N, \mu^H, \tau^N = \tau^p) \geq V^p(R, \mu^H)$, then a revolution can be averted but not otherwise.

As one would expect, the value function $V^p(N, \mu^H, \tau^N = \tau^p)$ crucially depends on q, the probability that the state will be μ^H in the future, because this is the extent to which redistribution recurs in the future (i.e., in one sense, how much future redistribution the rich elites can credibly promise). To derive an expression for $V^p(N, \mu^H, \tau^N = \tau^p)$, we substitute $V^p(N, \mu^H, \tau^N = \tau^p) = V^p(N, \mu^H)$ in (5.22) and note that (5.22) and (5.25) are two linear equations in two unknowns, the value functions $V^p(N, \mu^H, \tau^N = \tau^p)$ and $V^p(N, \mu^L)$. Solving these two equations, we find:

$$V^p(N, \mu^H, \tau^N = \tau^p) = \frac{y^p + (1 - \beta(1-q))(\tau^p(\bar{y} - y^p) - C(\tau^p)\bar{y})}{1-\beta} \tag{5.28}$$

Equation (5.28) has a straightforward interpretation: $V^p(N, \mu^H, \tau^N = \tau^p)$ is equal to the present discounted value of y^p, the pretax income of a citizen, plus the expected present value of net redistribution. Net redistribution is $\tau^p(\bar{y} - y^p) - C(\tau^p)\bar{y}$, but this only occurs when the state is μ^H, something that happens a proportion q of the time. However, in (5.28), $(\tau^p(\bar{y} - y^p) - C(\tau^p)\bar{y})$ is multiplied by $(1 - \beta(1-q))$, not by q. This reflects the fact that today we start in the state μ^H and, given that today is more important than the future because of discounting (i.e., because $\beta < 1$), the state μ^L, where there will be no redistribution, gets the weight $\beta(1-q)$, not $(1-q)$. As a result, the state μ^H received the remaining weight, $1 - \beta(1-q)$. (Expressed differently, because we start in the high state, the citizens receive transfers today and a fraction q of the time in the future, so the net present discounted value of the transfer is multiplied by $1 + \beta q/(1-\beta) = (1 - \beta(1-q))/(1-\beta)$.) Notice also that as $\beta \to 1$ (i.e., as discounting disappears), the weight of the state μ^H indeed converges to q.

Given this value function, we can see that revolution can be averted if $V^p(N, \mu^H, \tau^N = \tau^p) \geq V^p(R, \mu^H)$, or if:

$$\frac{y^p + (1 - \beta(1-q))(\tau^p(\bar{y} - y^p) - C(\tau^p)\bar{y})}{1-\beta} \geq \frac{(1-\mu)\bar{y}}{(1-\delta)(1-\beta)}$$

which can be simplified to:

$$\mu \geq \theta - (1 - \beta(1-q))(\tau^p(\theta - \delta) - (1-\delta)C(\tau^p)) \tag{5.29}$$

If this condition does not hold, even the maximum credible transfer to a citizen is not enough, and there will be revolution along the equilibrium path. We can now use (5.29) to define a critical value of μ^H, again denoted μ^* such that $V^p(N, \mu^H, \tau^N = \tau^p) = V^p(R, \mu^H)$, when $\mu^H = \mu^*$ or:

$$\mu^* = \theta - (1 - \beta(1-q))(\tau^p(\theta - \delta) - (1-\delta)C(\tau^p)) \tag{5.30}$$

where $\mu^* < \theta$. Naturally, we have that when $\mu \geq \mu^*$, $V^p(N, \mu^H, \tau^N = \tau^p) \geq V^p(R, \mu^H)$, and revolution is averted. Whereas when $\mu < \mu^*$, $V^p(N, \mu^H, \tau^N = \tau^p) < V^p(R, \mu^H)$, future transfers are expected to be sufficiently rare that even at the best possible tax rate for the citizens, there is not enough redistribution in the future, and the citizens prefer revolution rather than living under nondemocracy with political power in the hands of the elites.

It is also useful to point out that the expression in (5.30) is identical to that in (5.15) from the static model with $p = 1 - \beta(1 - q)$, again emphasizing the similarity between the two models.

As in the static model, when $\mu > \mu^*$, the elites can avert revolution by setting a tax rate $\hat{\tau} < \tau^p$. This tax rate is such that $V^p(N, \mu^H, \tau^N = \hat{\tau}) = V^p(R, \mu^H)$; that is, it just makes the citizens indifferent between revolution and living under nondemocracy with redistribution only during revolutionary periods. Using (5.21) and (5.28), we have that $\hat{\tau}$ is given by:

$$\mu = \theta - (1 - \beta(1 - q))(\hat{\tau}(\theta - \delta) - (1 - \delta)C(\hat{\tau})) \tag{5.31}$$

Putting all these pieces together, we have the key proposition of this section, which – although more complicated – in many ways mirrors Proposition 5.3. This is also a common feature of many of the games analyzed in this book. We start with the simpler reduced-form (static) model and then, most of the time, show that our results hold in a more satisfactory dynamic model.

To state the main result of this section more formally, we can appeal directly to the notation we used to specify the strategies before Proposition 5.3. There, actions were conditioned on whether μ was high or low, and now this is the crucial state variable. This implies that a Markov strategy in the repeated game under consideration has exactly the same form as the equilibrium strategies in the game whose equilibria were analyzed in Proposition 5.3. This enables us to state:

Proposition 5.4: *There, in a unique Markov perfect equilibrium $\{\tilde{\sigma}^r, \tilde{\sigma}^p\}$ of the game $G^\infty(\beta)$. Let μ^* and $\hat{\tau}$ be given by (5.30) and (5.31). Then, in this equilibrium:*

- *If $\theta \leq \mu$, the elites never redistribute and the citizens never undertake a revolution.*
- *If $\theta > \mu$, then we have:*
  (1) If $\mu < \mu^*$, promises by the elites are insufficiently credible to avoid a revolution. In the low state, the elites do not redistribute and there is no revolution, but in the high state, a revolution occurs whatever tax rate the elites set.
  (2) If $\mu \geq \mu^*$, the elites do not redistribute in the low state and set the tax rate $\hat{\tau}$ in the high-threat state, just sufficient to stop a revolution. The citizens never revolt.

Here, we used the intuitive alternative form for stating the proposition. The differences between Propositions 5.3 and 5.4 are the formula for μ^* and the fact that the strategies are now Markov strategies in a repeated game, not strategies in an extensive-form game.

It is interesting to focus on the cases where $\theta > \mu$. Starting with the elites in power, if $\mu < \mu^*$, then they set a zero tax rate when $\mu_t = \mu^L$; however, when the state transits to μ^H, they are swept away by revolution. The problem is that although the elites would like to stay in power by offering the citizens redistribution, they cannot offer today enough to make the present value of nondemocracy to the citizens as great as the present value of revolution. To avoid revolution, they would have to redistribute not just now but also in the future. Unfortunately, however, they cannot credibly promise to redistribute enough in the future and, as a result, the citizens find it optimal to revolt. In contrast, when $\mu \geq \mu^*$, the elites can prevent a revolution by redistributing. So, in the state $\mu_t = \mu^L$, they set $\tau^N = 0$, and when $\mu_t = \mu^H$, they set a tax rate, $\tau^N = \hat{\tau}$, just high enough to prevent a revolution.

This proposition, therefore, shows how in a dynamic setting the ability of the elites to transfer resources to the citizens – in other words, the "credibility" of their promises – depends on the future allocation of political power. When q is very low, the citizens may have de facto political power today because of an effective revolution threat, but they are unlikely to have it again in the future. In this case, any promises made by the elites are not credible, and the citizens prefer to use their political power to transform society toward one that is more beneficial for themselves. It is only when q is high, so that the de facto political power of the citizens is likely to recur in the future, that the promises made by the elites are sufficiently credible that a revolution can be averted.

There is an interesting paradox here. When q is high, so that the de facto political power of the citizens is more permanent, it is easier to avoid a revolution. This follows from the fact that μ^* defined by (5.30) is decreasing in q in the same way as μ^* defined by (5.15) is decreasing in p. This is because when the power of the citizens is not transitory, it is easier for the elites to make credible promises of redistribution in the future. This is somewhat counterintuitive because a simple intuition might have been that when the citizens were better organized and more powerful, revolution would have been more of a threat. This is not the case because the future threat of a revolution also enables more credible promises by the elites to stave off a revolution. Once we introduce democracy into the model, this feature of the equilibrium allows us to provide an interesting interpretation to some historical facts about the incidence of democracy (see Chapter 7).

Also, as in the last section, the critical threshold μ^* depends on the extent of inequality in society. In particular, the more unequal is society (i.e., the higher is θ), the higher is μ^* and the more likely are revolutions. The reason is simple: with greater inequality, revolution is more attractive, and a greater amount of credible redistribution is necessary to avert a revolution.

7. Incentive-Compatible Promises

The analysis in the previous section focused on Markov perfect equilibria, and showed how a revolution may arise as an equilibrium outcome. Because the political power of the citizens in the future was limited, any promise made by the elites when they keep political power in their own hands is imperfectly credible, and the citizens may prefer to take power today by revolution. An important ingredient of this scenario was the commitment problem: the elites find it optimal to revert back to their most preferred tax rate as soon as the threat of a revolution disappears. This was a consequence of our restricting attention to Markovian strategies because we imposed that, once the threat of revolution subsides, the elites would always choose the strategy that is in their immediate interests.

It is possible, however, that the elites can make certain other promises – for example, they might promise to redistribute in the future even if it is not in their immediate interests. They can support this promise by the implicit understanding that if they deviate from it, when the threat of revolution recurs again, the citizens would undertake a revolution, giving the elites a very low payoff. In other words, these promises could be supported by the threat of future punishments or by "repeated-game" strategies. Punishments correspond to actions that the citizens will take in the future (i.e., revolution), once the elites deviate from their prescribed behavior (i.e., renege on their promises), that will hurt the elites. When we allow players to play non-Markovian strategies, the result is the survival of nondemocracy for a larger set of parameter values. The important difference between Markovian and non-Markovian strategies is that the latter allow players to condition their actions at date t, not only on the state at that date but also on the previous history of play until that date.

This book does not enter into a lengthy discussion of the theory of repeated games, so the analysis is brief (see Fudenberg and Tirole 1991, Chapter 5, for more on repeated games; and Powell 2004 for an analysis of the circumstances under which punishment strategies can solve problems of commitment in a class of games close to those we study herein). What we want to show here is that this type of promise can go some way towards resolving commitment problems, but the underlying commitment problem will remain. It will still be the case that the elites cannot credibly promise arbitrarily large amounts of redistribution in the state where the revolution threat is not present and, as a result, the spirit of Proposition 5.4 applies even with non-Markovian strategies.

We now take a situation in which, in terms of Proposition 5.4, $\theta > \mu$ and $\mu < \mu^*$, so with the restriction to Markov perfect equilibria, the unique equilibrium involves a revolution. Let us see whether the elites can avert a revolution by using incentive-compatible promises supported by future punishments. To do this, we first find the maximum value that the elites can give to the citizens, once we consider potential punishment strategies. Because in general, repeated games have many subgame perfect equilibria, we focus on the subgame perfect equilibrium that is best for the elites. This subgame perfect equilibrium will prevent a revolution for the largest possible set of parameter values; however, there are other subgame perfect equilibria that also prevent a revolution for the same set of parameter values but give the citizens more. Nevertheless, this analysis of the specific equilibrium gives the flavor of what types of outcomes can be supported in non-Markovian equilibria.

Suppose also that we start when the state is μ^L. We first calculate the value to the elites if they redistribute at the rate $\tau^N = \tau^H \leq \tau^p$ in the state $\mu_t = \mu^H$ and at the rate $\tau^N = \tau^L \leq \tau^p$ in the state $\mu_t = \mu^L$ (because we are no longer looking at Markovian strategies, $\tau^L > 0$ is now possible). We also suppose for now that the citizens will not undertake a revolution (later, we impose this as a constraint on the tax vector). By the same arguments as in the previous section, this value is given by

$$V^r\left(N, \mu^L, \left[\tau^L, \tau^H\right]\right) = y^r + \left(\tau^L(\bar{y} - y^r) - C(\tau^L)\bar{y}\right) + \beta\left[qV^r\left(N, \mu^H, \left[\tau^L, \tau^H\right]\right) + (1-q)V^r\left(N, \mu^L, \left[\tau^L, \tau^H\right]\right)\right] \tag{5.32}$$

We are now using a different notation, $V^r\left(N, \mu^L, \left[\tau^L, \tau^H\right]\right)$, rather than $V^r(N, \mu^L)$ as we did in the previous section. This is because, while in the Markov Perfect Equilibrium, the elites always set $\tau^N = 0$ when $\mu_t = \mu^L$; this is no longer true. In particular, we are looking at situations in which the elites make credible promises of a tax rate of τ^L when $\mu_t = \mu^L$ and set a tax rate of τ^H when $\mu_t = \mu^H$. The new notation captures this. The term μ^L refers to the fact that we are in state $\mu_t = \mu^L$, and $[\tau^L, \tau^H]$ is the vector of promised taxes starting with the tax rate in the state $\mu_t = \mu^L$.

The intuition for (5.32) is straightforward: the first term, $y^r + (\tau^L(\bar{y} - y^r) - C(\tau^L)\bar{y})$, is again the current return to the elites, given that there is taxation at the rate τ^L. The second term is the continuation value, considering the fact that taxation changes to τ^H if the state switches to μ^H. By the same token, we also have:

$$V^r\left(N, \mu^H, \left[\tau^L, \tau^H\right]\right) = y^r + \left(\tau^H(\bar{y} - y^r) - C\left(\tau^H\right)\bar{y}\right) + \beta\left[qV^r\left(N, \mu^H, \left[\tau^L, \tau^H\right]\right) + (1-q)V^r\left(N, \mu^L, \left[\tau^L, \tau^H\right]\right)\right]$$

as the value starting in the state μ^H. Combining these two expressions, we obtain:

$$V^r\left(N, \mu^L, \left[\tau^L, \tau^H\right]\right) = \frac{y^r + (1-\beta q)\left(\tau^L(\bar{y} - y^r) - C\left(\tau^L\right)\bar{y}\right) + \beta q\left(\tau^H(\bar{y} - y^r) - C(\tau^H)\bar{y}\right)}{1-\beta} \tag{5.33}$$

as the value that the elites will receive if they adhere to their "promised" behavior summarized by the tax vector $\left[\tau^L, \tau^H\right]$. The key is whether this behavior is "incentive-compatible" for them – that is, whether they wish to deviate from it now or in the future.

What happens if they deviate? Clearly, the answer depends on how the citizens react. We want to see whether we can make the promise by the elites to redistribute at the tax rate $\tau^L > 0$ in state μ^L credible. It is more likely to be credible when deviation from it is less profitable or when deviation from this prescribed behavior is met by a severe punishment. The most severe punishment is that of revolution by the citizens when the opportunity occurs again (it is never profitable for the citizens to undertake revolution in the state $\mu_t = \mu^L$, because $\mu^L = 1$, so the threat to undertake such revolution in the state $\mu_t = \mu^L$ is not credible and, therefore, never part of a subgame perfect equilibrium). Consequently, the best way to ensure that the elites do not deviate from their promises is to threaten them (credibly) with as severe a punishment as possible – that is, revolution as soon as the state switches to $\mu_t = \mu^H$. So, there will be revolution the first time the state is $\mu_t = \mu^H$. What will happen until then? The elites are now deviating from their promised behavior so, in the meantime, they adopt the best policy for themselves, so $\tau^N = \tau^r = 0$. Thus, what we have is a value $V^r_d(N, \mu^L)$ for the elites, in which the subscript d denotes that they have deviated from their prescribed behavior. This value is given by the following recursion:

$$V^r_d(N, \mu^L) = y^r + \beta\left[q V^r(R, \mu^H) + (1-q)V^r_d(N, \mu^L)\right]$$

where we know that $V^r(R, \mu^H) = 0$. Using this fact, we have that:

$$V^r_d(N, \mu^L) = \frac{y^r}{1-\beta(1-q)} \tag{5.34}$$

This analysis immediately establishes that only redistribution at the rate τ^L in the state $\mu_t = \mu^L$, such that:

$$V^r\left(N, \mu^L, \left[\tau^L, \tau^H\right]\right) \geq V^r_d(N, \mu^L) \tag{5.35}$$

is credible. If the inequality were reversed, the elites would prefer to deviate and give the citizens no redistribution in the state μ^L, suffering the consequences rather than tax themselves at the rate τ^L now (and at the rate τ^H when the state becomes high). Therefore, (5.35) is necessary for redistribution at the tax rate τ^L to be "incentive-compatible" for the elites and thus a credible promise to the citizens. The tax rate $\tau^H \leq \tau^p$ in the state $\mu_t = \mu^H$ is automatically credible because we are looking at the part of the parameter space where $\mu < \mu^*$; therefore, any deviation by the elites from their promised actions in the high state can be immediately punished.

The subgame perfect equilibrium that is best for the elites, starting in the state μ^L, can be characterized as the solution to the following maximization problem:

$$\max_{\tau^L, \tau^H} V^r\left(N, \mu^L, \left[\tau^L, \tau^H\right]\right) \tag{5.36}$$

subject to (5.35) and

$$V^p\left(N,\mu^H,\left[\tau^L,\tau^H\right]\right)\geq V^p\left(R,\mu^H\right) \tag{5.37}$$

where $V^p\left(N,\mu^H,\left[\tau^L,\tau^H\right]\right)$ is the value to the citizens starting in the state μ^H from the tax vector $\left[\tau^L,\tau^H\right]$, and $V^p\left(R,\mu^H\right)$, as usual, is the value to the citizens from revolution in the state μ^H given by (5.21) in the previous section.

Whereas the first constraint ensures that the elites do not wish to renege on their promises, the second constraint requires that the citizens do not wish to undertake revolution in the high state.

The value $V^p\left(N,\mu^H,\left[\tau^L,\tau^H\right]\right)$ is obtained analogously to the values for the elites. In particular, we have the following value functions for the citizens. In the low state:

$$\begin{aligned}V^p\left(N,\mu^L,\left[\tau^L,\tau^H\right]\right)=&\ y^p+\left(\tau^L(\bar{y}-y^p)-C\left(\tau^L\right)\bar{y}\right)\\&+\beta\left[qV^p\left(N,\mu^H,\left[\tau^L,\tau^H\right]\right)\right.\\&\left.+(1-q)V^p\left(N,\mu^L,\left[\tau^L,\tau^H\right]\right)\right]\end{aligned}$$

and in the high state:

$$\begin{aligned}V^p\left(N,\mu^H,\left[\tau^L,\tau^H\right]\right)=&\ y^p+\left(\tau^H(\bar{y}-y^p)-C\left(\tau^H\right)\bar{y}\right)\\&+\beta\left[qV^p\left(N,\mu^H,\left[\tau^L,\tau^H\right]\right)\right.\\&\left.+(1-q)V^p\left(N,\mu^L,\left[\tau^L,\tau^H\right]\right)\right]\end{aligned}$$

Combining the two expressions, we obtain:

$$\begin{aligned}&V^p\left(N,\mu^H,\left[\tau^L,\tau^H\right]\right)\\&=\frac{y^p+\beta(1-q)\left(\tau^L(\bar{y}-y^p)-C\left(\tau^L\right)\bar{y}\right)+(1-\beta(1-q))\left(\tau^H(\bar{y}-y^p)-C(\tau^H)\bar{y}\right)}{1-\beta}\end{aligned} \tag{5.38}$$

Before providing a full solution to this maximization problem, it is straightforward to characterize the minimum value of μ^H such that a revolution can be averted. We denote this threshold by μ^{**} using an analogy with the threshold μ^* in the previous section. Formally, this threshold corresponds to the minimum value of μ^H such that the constraint set of the optimization problem is nonempty. When the constraint set is empty, this implies that there is no tax vector $\left[\tau^L,\tau^H\right]$ that is simultaneously credible and can convince the citizens not to undertake revolution, so there has to be an equilibrium revolution in the state μ^H.

To calculate this threshold, note that the largest value that τ^H can take is τ^p. Intuitively, in the high state, the elites are willing to give the maximum redistribution to avoid revolution. What about τ^L? Once $\tau^H=\tau^p$, τ^L is then given by treating the incentive-compatibility constraint of the elites, (5.35), as an equality. Therefore, the largest amount of redistribution that can credibly be promised is that which stems from levying the tax rate $\bar{\tau}'$ in the state $\mu_t = \mu^L$ such that either $V_d^r(N, \mu^L) = V^r(N, \mu^L, [\bar{\tau}', \tau^p])$ and $\bar{\tau}' \leq \tau^p$, or $\bar{\tau}' = \tau^p$. More specifically let $\bar{\tau}''$ be such that

$$\frac{y^r + (1 - \beta q)(\bar{\tau}''(\bar{y} - y^r) - C(\bar{\tau}'')\bar{y}) + \beta q(\tau^p(\bar{y} - y^r) - C(\tau^p)\bar{y})}{1 - \beta} = \frac{y^r}{1 - \beta(1 - q)}$$

Substituting for the definition of y^r and simplifying terms, we obtain:

$$\bar{\tau}''(\theta - \delta) + \delta C(\bar{\tau}'') = \frac{\beta q}{(1 - \beta q)} \left[\frac{\theta}{1 - \beta(1 - q)} - (\tau^p(\theta - \delta) + \delta C(\tau^p)) \right] \tag{5.39}$$

Then the maximum credible tax rate is $\bar{\tau}' = \min\{\bar{\tau}'', \tau^p\}$.

This tax rate, $\bar{\tau}'$, can be shown to be an increasing function of β; the more valuable the future, the less attractive it is for the elites to deviate from the promised behavior, so the higher is the maximum tax rate they can promise. This is intuitive and, in fact, a fundamental principle of analyses of repeated games; for players not to take the action in their immediate interest, the benefits from this action need to be counterbalanced by some other future considerations. Here, if they take these actions, they will be punished in the future. The more players discount the future or the less severe is the expected punishment, the more difficult it will be to convince them to adhere to these promises.

The important point highlighted by (5.39) is that the elites do not have unrestricted powers to make promises: they have a limited capability, supported by the threat of future punishments. Any promises they make will be credible only if it is in their interests to carry out this promise at the time. Here, some positive redistribution even without the threat of revolution might be in their interests because otherwise they know they will have to tolerate revolution later. Nevertheless, this threat of future punishments can support only a limited amount of redistribution (i.e., the elites cannot credibly promise a tax rate greater than $\bar{\tau}'$ in the low state).

This analysis then implies that the question of whether revolution can be averted boils down to whether the value to the citizens from redistribution at the tax rate $\bar{\tau}'$ in the state $\mu_t = \mu^L$ and at the tax rate τ^p in the state $\mu_t = \mu^H$, starting in the state $\mu_t = \mu^H$, is better than revolution for the citizens. Or, stated differently, this is equivalent to whether the tax vector $[\bar{\tau}', \tau^p]$ is in the constraint set of the maximization problem given by inequalities (5.35) and (5.37).

By analogy to the analysis in the previous section, we can see that the tax vector $[\bar{\tau}', \tau^p]$ is in the constraint set for all $\mu \geq \mu^{**}$, where μ^{**} is such that

$V^p(N, \mu^H, [\bar{\tau}', \tau^p]) = V^p(R, \mu^H)$ when $\mu^H = \mu^{**}$. More explicitly, the threshold μ^{**} is the solution to:

$$\mu^{**} = \theta - \beta(1-q)\left(\bar{\tau}'(\theta - \delta) - (1-\delta)C(\bar{\tau}')\right) \\ - (1 - \beta(1-q))(\tau^p(\theta - \delta) - (1-\delta)C(\tau^p)) \quad (5.40)$$

where $\bar{\tau}'$ is given by (5.39). It can be verified that $\mu^{**} > 0$.

Recall that, using the notation in this section, μ^* is defined by $V^p(N, \mu^H, [0, \tau^p]) = V^p(R, \mu^H)$, so for all $\bar{\tau}' > 0$, we have:

$$\mu^{**} < \mu^*$$

which is clear from formulas (5.30) and (5.40).

This implies that once we allow for the use of punishment strategies, there will be situations in which a revolution can be averted by incentive compatible promises but could not have been otherwise. This is true when $\mu \in [\mu^{**}, \mu^*)$. Nevertheless, since $\mu^{**} > 0$, there will still be situations (i.e., when $\mu < \mu^{**}$) in which the best that the elites can promise is not enough to avert a revolution.

This discussion leads to the main result of this section, which we informally state as the following:

Result: When we allow non-Markovian strategies, a revolution can be averted for all $\mu \geq \mu^{**}$. Here, $\mu^{**} < \mu^*$, which means that greater redistribution is now possible, but $\mu^{**} > 0$, which means that a revolution can happen if μ is sufficiently small.

To state the results of this section more carefully and to complete the characterization of the equilibrium, we must define what a strategy is in this game. The main difference with the previous section is that we have dropped the restriction to Markov strategies and now a strategy can depend not just on the state at any date t but also on the history of play up to that date. Let $\mathcal{H}^{t-1}$ denote the set of all possible histories of play up to $t-1$ with a particular history being denoted $h^{t-1} \in \mathcal{H}^{t-1}$. The actions of the elites and the citizens are now denoted by $\sigma^r = \{\tau^N(\cdot, \cdot)\}$ and $\sigma^p = \{\rho(\cdot, \cdot, \cdot)\}$, where $\tau^N(\mu_t, h^{t-1})$ is the tax rate set by the elites at date t when the current state is $\mu_t = \mu^H$ or μ^L and the observed history is h^{t-1}. Hence, $\tau^N : \{\mu^L, \mu^H\} \times \mathcal{H}^{t-1} \to [0, 1]$. Similarly, $\rho(\mu_t, \tau^N, h^{t-1})$ is the decision by the citizens to initiate a revolution conditional on the current state, the current actions of the elites, and the history. We have that $\rho : \{\mu^L, \mu^H\} \times [0, 1] \times \mathcal{H}^{t-1} \to \{0, 1\}$. Then, a subgame perfect equilibrium is a strategy combination, $\{\hat{\sigma}^r, \hat{\sigma}^p\}$, such that $\hat{\sigma}^r$ and $\hat{\sigma}^p$ are best responses to each other for all possible histories $h^{t-1} \in \mathcal{H}^{t-1}$ and prior actions taken within the same stage game.

When $\mu < \mu^{**}$, the following strategy profile is the unique subgame perfect equilibrium: $\tau^N(\mu_t, h^{t-1}) = 0$ for $\mu_t \in \{\mu^L, \mu^H\}$ and any h^{t-1}, $\rho(\mu^L, \cdot, h^{t-1}) = 0$ and $\rho(\mu^H, \cdot, h^{t-1}) = 1$ for any h^{t-1}. For this set of parameter values, a revolution is sufficiently attractive that concessions will not work; the first time μ^H arises there will be a revolution whatever the previous history of play or the current tax rate. Because the elites know this, they simply set zero taxes when μ^L occurs.

To understand the nature of the subgame perfect equilibrium when $\mu \geq \mu^{**}$, it is also useful to note that in this case there is an additional motive for the elites: "tax-smoothing." Intuitively, the elites want to deliver a given amount of redistribution to the citizens at the minimum cost to themselves. Because the cost of taxation given by the function $C(\cdot)$ is convex, this implies that taxes should exhibit as little variability as possible – in other words, they should be smooth.[4] This idea was first suggested by Barro (1979) in the context of optimal fiscal policy, but it applies equally here. Such tax-smoothing was not possible before because the elites could never promise to redistribute in the state μ^L. Now that this type of redistribution is possible, tax-smoothing also emerges as a possibility.

The tax-smoothing argument makes it clear that the cheapest way to the elite of providing utility of $V^p(R, \mu^H)$ is to set a constant tax rate, τ^S, such that:

$$V^p\left(N, \mu^H, \left[\tau^S, \tau^S\right]\right) = V^p(R, \mu^H) \tag{5.41}$$

or, more explicitly, τ^S is given by:

$$\begin{aligned} \mu = \theta - \beta(1-q)\left(\tau^S(\theta-\delta) - (1-\delta)C\left(\tau^S\right)\right) \\ - (1-\beta(1-q))\left(\tau^S(\theta-\delta) - (1-\delta)C(\tau^S)\right) \end{aligned} \tag{5.42}$$

Therefore, redistributing at this rate is the best possible strategy for the elites. The question is whether this tax vector is incentive-compatible – that is, whether it satisfies (5.35). The same arguments immediately imply that the vector $\left[\tau^S, \tau^S\right]$ will be incentive-compatible as long as $\tau^S \leq \bar{\tau}^S$ where $\bar{\tau}^S$ is given by:

$$\bar{\tau}^S(\theta-\delta) + \delta C\left(\bar{\tau}^S\right) = \frac{\beta q}{(1-\beta q)}\left[\frac{\theta}{1-\beta(1-q)} - \left(\bar{\tau}^S(\theta-\delta) + \delta C(\bar{\tau}^S)\right)\right] \tag{5.43}$$

which is similar to (5.39) with the vector $\left[\bar{\tau}^S, \bar{\tau}^S\right]$ replacing $[\bar{\tau}', \tau^P]$.

Then the question of whether perfect tax-smoothing can be achieved simply boils down to whether any tax rate $\tau^S \leq \bar{\tau}^S$ satisfies (5.41). Again, similar

[4] More explicitly, consider a pair of taxes, τ^L and $\tau^H > \tau^L$, that satisfy (5.37). Now imagine we construct a weighted average of these two taxes, $\tilde{\tau} = [\beta(1-q)\tau^L + (1-\beta(1-q))\tau^H]$. Inspection of (5.38) together with the (strict) convexity of $C(\cdot)$ immediately establishes that $V^p(N, \mu^H, [\tilde{\tau}, \tilde{\tau}]) > V^p(N, \mu^H, [\tau^L, \tau^H])$, so the tax vector $[\tilde{\tau}, \tilde{\tau}]$ also avoids revolution. Moreover, again by the convexity of $C(\cdot)$, $V^r(N, \mu^L, [\tilde{\tau}, \tilde{\tau}]) > V^r(N, \mu^L, [\tau^L, \tau^H])$, so the tax vector $[\tilde{\tau}, \tilde{\tau}]$ also gives higher utility to the elites. This establishes that tax-smoothing is preferable (if it is incentive-compatible).

arguments immediately establish that there exists a level of μ^H, here denoted $\bar{\mu}^S$ and given by:

$$\bar{\mu}^S = \theta - \beta(1-q)\left(\bar{\tau}^S(\theta-\delta) - (1-\delta)C\left(\bar{\tau}^S\right)\right) \\ - (1-\beta(1-q))\left(\bar{\tau}^S(\theta-\delta) - (1-\delta)C(\bar{\tau}^S)\right) \tag{5.44}$$

such that when $\mu \geq \bar{\mu}^S$, a perfectly smooth credible tax policy will prevent revolution.

Clearly, $\bar{\mu}^S > \mu^{**}$; on the other hand, $\bar{\mu}^S$ can be greater than or less than μ^*. When $\mu \geq \bar{\mu}^S$, the best possible subgame perfect equilibrium for the elites is a strategy combination that corresponds to the tax vector $[\tau^S, \tau^S]$ (which, by construction, prevents revolution at the lowest possible cost). More explicitly, let us define the history $\hat{h}^t$ such that $h^t = \hat{h}^t$ if for all $s \leq t$, $\tau^N(\mu^L, h^s) = \tau^S$, where τ^S is given by (5.41). Then, the subgame perfect equilibrium is given by the following strategy combination. For the elites:

$$\tau^N(\mu_t, h^{t-1}) = \begin{cases} \tau^S & \text{if } h^{t-1} = \hat{h}^{t-1} \\ 0 & \text{if } h^{t-1} \neq \hat{h}^{t-1} \end{cases} \tag{5.45}$$

for $\mu_t \in \{\mu^L, \mu^H\}$, and for the citizens: $\rho\left(\mu^L, \cdot, h^{t-1}\right) = 0$, and:

$$\rho\left(\mu^H, \tau^N, h^{t-1}\right) = \begin{cases} 0 & \text{if } h^{t-1} = \hat{h}^{t-1} \text{ and } \tau^N \geq \tau^S \\ 1 & \text{if } h^{t-1} \neq \hat{h}^{t-1} \text{ or } \tau^N < \tau^S \end{cases}$$

In this case, as before, strategies specify how a player will play even off the equilibrium path, which now includes all possible histories up to that point. In particular, here $\hat{h}^{t-1}$ denotes the equilibrium path. Then, as long as play is on this path, the elites set τ^S in both states and the citizens never revolt. However, if the elites ever set a tax rate less than τ^S, we will move along some history $h^{t-1} \neq \hat{h}^{t-1}$ and the strategies say that the first time the state is $\mu_t = \mu^H$, the citizens undertake revolution. How do we know that in such a situation it will actually be credible for the citizens to undertake revolution? This comes from (5.45), which states that if the elites find themselves setting the tax rate after some history different from $\hat{h}^{t-1}$, they set the tax rate to zero. Thus, the poor understand that if they do not undertake revolution following a deviation from the prescribed behavior, they will never get any redistribution from that point on in the game. Therefore, as long as the revolution constraint $\theta > \mu$ holds, it is optimal to undertake revolution following a deviation by the elites.

Finally, when $\mu \in [\mu^{**}, \bar{\mu}^S)$, revolution can be averted, but perfect-tax smoothing is no longer possible. In this case, it can be seen that the best subgame perfect equilibrium for the elites is a tax vector $\left[\hat{\tau}^L, \hat{\tau}^H\right]$, which is the solution to (5.36) and satisfies:

$$\hat{\tau}^L(\theta - \delta) + \delta C\left(\hat{\tau}^L\right) = \frac{\beta q}{(1 - \beta q)}\left[\frac{\theta}{1 - \beta(1 - q)} - \left(\hat{\tau}^H(\theta - \delta) + \delta C(\hat{\tau}^H)\right)\right] \quad (5.46)$$

and:

$$\begin{aligned} \mu = \theta - \beta(1 - q)\left(\hat{\tau}^L(\theta - \delta) - (1 - \delta)C(\hat{\tau}^L)\right) \\ - (1 - \beta(1 - q))\left(\hat{\tau}^H(\theta - \delta) - (1 - \delta)C(\hat{\tau}^H)\right) \end{aligned} \quad (5.47)$$

and the corresponding subgame perfect strategies are:

$$\tau^N(\mu^L, h^{t-1}) = \begin{cases} \hat{\tau}^L & \text{if } h^{t-1} = \hat{h}^{t-1} \\ 0 & \text{if } h^{t-1} \neq \hat{h}^{t-1} \end{cases}, \quad \tau^N(\mu^H, h^{t-1}) = \begin{cases} \hat{\tau}^H & \text{if } h^{t-1} = \hat{h}^{t-1} \\ 0 & \text{if } h^{t-1} \neq \hat{h}^{t-1} \end{cases}$$

$\rho(\mu^L, \cdot, h^{t-1}) = 0$, and:

$$\rho(\mu^H, \tau^N, h^{t-1}) = \begin{cases} 0 & \text{if } h^{t-1} = \hat{h}^{t-1} \text{ and } \tau^N \geq \hat{\tau}^H \\ 1 & \text{if } h^{t-1} \neq \hat{h}^{t-1} \text{ or } \tau^N < \hat{\tau}^H \end{cases}$$

Summarizing this discussion, we have the following:

Proposition 5.5: *Assume $\theta > \mu$. Let μ^{**} and $\bar{\mu}^S > \mu^{**}$ be given by (5.40) and (5.44). Then, the subgame perfect equilibrium that is best from the viewpoint of the elites, $\{\hat{\sigma}^r, \hat{\sigma}^p\}$, of the game $G^\infty(\beta)$ is such that:*

(1) If $\mu < \mu^{**}$, then $\tau^N(\mu_t, h^{t-1}) = 0$ for $\mu_t \in \{\mu^L, \mu^H\}$ and any h^{t-1}; and $\rho(\mu^L, \cdot, h^{t-1}) = 0$ and $\rho(\mu^H, \cdot, h^{t-1}) = 1$ for any $h^{t-1} \in \mathcal{H}^{t-1}$.

(2) If $\mu \geq \bar{\mu}^S$, $\tau^N(\mu_t, h^{t-1}) = \tau^S$ for $\mu_t \in \{\mu^L, \mu^H\}$ and $h^{t-1} = \hat{h}^{t-1}$, where τ^S is given by (5.42); $\tau^N(\mu_t, h^{t-1}) = 0$ for $\mu_t \in \{\mu^L, \mu^H\}$ and $h^{t-1} \neq \hat{h}^{t-1}$, $\rho(\mu^L, \tau^N, h^{t-1}) = 0$; $\rho(\mu^H, \tau^N, h^{t-1}) = 0$ for $h^{t-1} = \hat{h}^{t-1}$ and $\tau^N \geq \tau^S$; and $\rho(\mu^H, \tau^L, h^{t-1}) = 1$ for any $h^{t-1} \neq \hat{h}^{t-1}$ or $\tau^N < \tau^S$.

(3) If $\mu \in [\mu^{**}, \bar{\mu}^S)$, then $\tau^N(\mu^L, h^{t-1}) = \hat{\tau}^L$ and $\tau^L(\mu^H, h^{t-1}) = \hat{\tau}^H$ for $h^{t-1} = \hat{h}^{t-1}$ where $\hat{\tau}^L$ and $\hat{\tau}^H$ are given by (5.46) and (5.47); $\tau^N(\mu_t, h^{t-1}) = 0$ for $\mu_t \in \{\mu^L, \mu^H\}$ and $h^{t-1} \neq \hat{h}^{t-1}$; $\rho(\mu^L, \cdot, h^{t-1}) = 0$; $\rho(\mu^H, \tau^N, h^{t-1}) = 0$ if $h^{t-1} = \hat{h}^{t-1}$ and $\tau^N \geq \hat{\tau}^H$; and $\rho(\mu^H, \tau^N, h^{t-1}) = 1$ if $h^{t-1} \neq \hat{h}^{t-1}$ or $\tau^N < \hat{\tau}^H$.

The important point that emerges from Proposition 5.5 is that there is now a larger set of parameter values that allows the elites to avoid revolution. In other words, in societies with μ such that $\mu^{**} \leq \mu < \mu^*$, there will be equilibrium revolutions if we do not allow the elites to make incentive-compatible promises of redistribution in future low-revolution threat periods; however, these revolutions can be avoided once we allow such promises. Moreover, even when $\mu \geq \mu^*$, the elites can achieve a better outcome for themselves by smoothing taxes because of the possibility of using incentive-compatible promises.

Nevertheless, it is important to emphasize that the elites still have limited abilities to make credible promises. Only promises of redistribution at the tax rate τ^L that satisfy $V^r(N, \mu^L, [\tau^L, \tau^H]) \geq V_d^r(N, \mu^L)$ are incentive-compatible. This implies that in societies with $\mu < \mu^{**}$, the same considerations as in Proposition 5.4 apply and credible redistribution is not enough to convince the citizens to live under nondemocracy, and they will prefer alternative routes. Here, the only option open to them is a revolution. In Chapter 6, we see how the elites can try to convince them not to undertake a revolution by offering a change in political institutions to make future redistribution more credible. Democratization gives the citizens political power, thereby making much higher levels of future redistribution credible.

8. Conclusion

In this chapter, we developed our basic model of nondemocratic politics and introduced the fundamental issue of political commitment that underlies much of our approach. We studied how, in the face of the threat of collective action and revolution, a nondemocratic regime would want to make concessions to avoid being expropriated. Nevertheless, because revolutionary threats are intrinsically transitory, the promise of concessions may not be sufficiently credible. When the revolution threat dissipates, the regime may renege on its promises, as we illustrated with some historical examples. If citizens anticipate that the nondemocratic regime will renege on its promises, the regime may be swept away by a revolution.

We illustrated these ideas first in a static extensive-form game in which we introduced an exogenous probability that a promise by the regime will be kept. Although this model is useful and tractable, the exogenous probability of reneging is too reduced-form. For this reason, we also developed a richer dynamic model in which the regime can make promises for today but cannot make promises for the future. We showed how the qualitative results of the dynamic model are identical to those of the static model.

Nevertheless, the options we have allowed so far are restrictive: for example, might such a regime not have other instruments it could use other than policy concessions, such as income redistribution? The answer to this is yes, and in Chapter 6 we argue that democratization precisely arises as a credible concession by the elites to stop a revolution. By democratizing, the elites allow the citizens to set the tax rate not only today but also in the future, and this makes their concessions credible. However, even there our discussion are not complete. Rather than make any type of concession, the elites might try to use repression to avoid a revolution or having to democratize. Therefore, we also discuss the issue of the interaction among concessions, democratization, and repression in Chapter 6. Chapter 6 also discusses in more detail the conceptual foundations of our approach to democratization – in particular, stressing why institutional change can help solve commitment problems.

6 Democratization

1. Introduction

In this chapter, we motivate and develop our basic model of democratization. Individuals have preferences over different political institutions because they anticipate the different actions that political actors will take under these institutions – thus, the resulting different policies and social choices. In this sense, our analysis builds on our modeling of democracy and nondemocracy in the previous two chapters.

2. The Role of Political Institutions

Why do we need to talk about institutions at all? Why not simply say that the elites and the citizens have preferences over different policies, and political conflict between them results in a set of policies favoring one group or the other? We argue that there is more to the conflict between various social groups. Conflict over policies is static – it is about what happens today. Rational actors also care about the future. This is where political institutions – which are durable and, consequently, have the capacity to influence political actions and political equilibria in the future – come in. Therefore, we need to think seriously about political institutions in a dynamic setting; via this process, we can develop a theory of the emergence and, later, consolidation of democracy. Crucial to this is a notion of what political institutions do.

We emphasize that political institutions regulate the allocation of de jure political power. Political power is a measure of how influential a particular group (or individual) is in the political arena when there is conflict over which policy should be implemented. If the elites are the rich and if they are more powerful, we expect lower taxes, lower redistribution, and generally a range of policies favoring the rich rather than the poor. Political power is, therefore, inherent in every discussion of aggregating conflicting preferences. Various models of democracy aggregate those preferences differently and, therefore, as discussed in Chapter 4, they naturally allocate different amounts of political power to different groups. Nevertheless, critical to our approach is the assumption that, typically, the majority of citizens has more political power in a democratic rather than a nondemocratic society.

Forward-looking rational economic actors care not only about economic allocations and therefore policies today but also about the economic allocations and policies in the future. Therefore, political power is valuable and all groups would like to somehow ensure greater political power for themselves in the future. Political institutions can influence the allocation of de jure political power in the future by virtue of being *durable.* Our approach to institutions is based on the assumption that policies, even though they can sometimes be difficult to reverse, are generally easier to reverse than institutions. Therefore, democratization enables the citizens not only to be more powerful today but also in the future relative to an alternative regime that is nondemocratic. Hence, democratization is a way of transferring political power to the majority of citizens. If the citizens can secure democracy today, they will increase their de jure political power in the future because as long as democracy survives, they will have more say in the determination of economic and social policies.

How do the citizens ensure that society becomes democratic? They can do so only if they have sufficient political power. Clearly, starting from a situation of nondemocracy, the citizens are excluded from voting or, at the very least, their preferences matter only little. So how could they have political power? The answer is that political power is not only vested in the formal rules, it can also take the form of de facto political power. The citizens could have political power in nondemocracy if they pose a credible threat of revolution or significant social unrest that damages the economic and social interests of the elites who control de jure political power. Throughout this book, when we discuss political power, it includes both the power that comes from political institutions and the ability of the citizens to challenge the system or the ability of the elites to undertake a coup – that is, de facto ways of obtaining power. In other words, for our purposes, political power is anything that enables a social group to come close to its preferred policies, de jure or de facto.

However, our story is not yet complete. So far, what we have argued can be summarized diagrammatically as follows:

$$\begin{matrix}\text{political} \\ \text{power}_t\end{matrix} \Longrightarrow \begin{matrix}\text{political} \\ \text{institutions}_t\end{matrix} \Longrightarrow \begin{matrix}\text{political} \\ \text{institutions}_{t+1}\end{matrix} \Longrightarrow \begin{matrix}\text{de jure political} \\ \text{power}_{t+1}\end{matrix}$$

Groups that have political power today can introduce – or force others to introduce – political institutions that favor them. These political institutions persist and regulate the allocation of political power in the future. Therefore, democratization enables the citizens to increase their political power in the future.

But, why do the citizens need political institutions to ensure their political power tomorrow? After all, they have political power today.

In our theory, political institutions are particularly useful when de facto political power is *transitory* in the sense that who has more de facto political power today is generally different from who will have it tomorrow. This transitory nature might result from a variety of economic, social, and political shocks to the system. Indeed, we saw in Chapter 5 that the empirical literature on the collective-action problem emphasizes that even when the problem can be solved, such solutions tend to be transitory. The fact that a group has solved the collective-action problem today does not guarantee that it will manage to solve the problem tomorrow. There may be a recession today, creating political instability, giving an advantage to whichever group wants to use de facto means to influence political outcomes; however, recessions are often transitory; tomorrow there may be a boom.

Now imagine a situation in which the citizens have de facto political power today, but they expect not to have similar political power tomorrow. In this situation, they would demand a set of institutions that will *lock in* their political power. This is precisely what democratic institutions may do. The de facto power of the citizens that comes from an unusual event, such as a political crisis or the end of a war, becomes institutionalized and translated to future political power by the introduction of relatively free and fair elections in which the votes of all the citizens count, not just the elites.

There is one final step in our argument. Democratization is a move from nondemocracy to democracy and, in nondemocracy, the elites make the decisions. Therefore, democratization happens when the elites decide to "extend the franchise" and include wider segments of society in the decision-making process. This is not only a theoretical statement. As the discussion in the Introduction and Chapter 2 illustrated, almost all major moves toward democracy in nineteenth-century Europe and nineteenth- and twentieth-century America were extensions of the franchise by the existing political system to previously excluded segments of society.

Why would they do so? The answer is that the temporary de facto political power of the citizens in nondemocracy comes from actions they can take that are costly to the system, such as revolution or significant social unrest. The elites would like to prevent this and they are willing to make concessions in order to do so. But, the citizens care not only about allocations and policies today but also about those in the future. Therefore, typically, the elites have to make promises about future as well as current concessions. However, when the revolution threat subsides – the crucial transitory nature of de facto political power! – these promises may be broken. Consequently, the elites would like to make credible commitments. This is where the commitment value of institutions is relevant. Democratization ensures a credible transfer of political power to the majority of citizens, increasing the likelihood that the promises of the elites will be honored. Therefore, democratization occurs when the elites would like to make a credible commitment to future policies and they can do so only by relinquishing (part of their) political power, the de jure part, to the citizens.

Diagrammatically, our theory can be summarized as follows:

temporary political power for the citizens from threat of revolution or social unrest	$\Longrightarrow$	elites need to commit to future policies	$\Longrightarrow$	introduction of democracy	$\Longrightarrow$	more political power for the citizens in the future

3. Preferences over Political Institutions

In this section, we illustrate the basic conflict over political institutions, specifically democracy versus nondemocracy. With this purpose, let us return to the basic two-class model discussed in Chapter 4. Total population is normalized to 1, a fraction $1 - \delta > 1/2$ of the agents are poor with income y^p, and the remaining fraction δ are rich with income $y^r > y^p$. The rich are the elites and the poor are the citizens. Mean income is denoted by $\bar{y}$ and, as before, we use the notation θ to parameterize inequality. The incomes of poor citizens and rich elites are given by (4.7), and the preferred tax rate of a poor citizen satisfies (4.11).

We also use the notation for indirect utility introduced in Chapter 4: $V(y^i \mid \tau)$ denotes the utility of an agent with income level y^i when policy is given by τ. Now, define $V^p(D) \equiv V(y^p \mid \tau^p)$ as the indirect utility of a poor agent when the tax rate is equal to τ^p. Equivalently, in democracy, all the citizens have the same political preferences and they will vote for τ^p, so the equilibrium tax rate in democracy is τ^p. Therefore, $V(y^p \mid \tau^p)$ is also the indirect utility of a citizen in democracy, $V^p(D)$ (D is for democracy). Similarly, $V^r(D) \equiv V(y^r \mid \tau^p)$ is the indirect utility of a member of the elite in democracy. In nondemocracy, the most preferred tax rate of a member of the elite, $\tau^r = 0$, will result; therefore, $V^p(N) \equiv V(y^p \mid \tau^r)$ is the indirect utility of a citizen in nondemocracy (N is for nondemocracy) in which the equilibrium tax rate is $\tau^r = 0$. Finally, $V^r(N) \equiv V(y^r \mid \tau^r)$ is the indirect utility of an elite agent in nondemocracy.

We have that:

$$V^p(D) > V^p(N) \quad \text{while} \quad V^r(D) < V^r(N) \tag{6.1}$$

In other words, the citizens obtain higher utility and income in democracy, whereas the elites obtain higher income in nondemocracy. An immediate implication of this observation is that there is *conflict* over political institutions – that is, over whether the society should be democratic or nondemocratic. In democracy, the citizens get relatively higher benefits; the elites benefit in nondemocracy.

4. Political Power and Institutions

4.1 Institutions versus Policies

What is the difference between institutions and policies? In both political science and other social sciences, there is an implicit understanding that institutions and policies are significantly different objects. For example, few people would think that tax policy is an "institution," whereas whether there is a constitution or the society is democratic is generally seen as relating to institutions. So, what is the difference?

The Nobel–prize-winning economic historian Douglass North defines institutions as "the rules of the game in a society or, more formally . . . the humanly devised constraints that shape human interaction" (1990, p. 3). This definition of institutions is useful when we think of the broad set of institutions, encompassing many diverse social and political aspects underlying economic decisions, and the organization of economic and social activity. However, for our purposes, it might also be too broad. For us, the main difference between policies and institutions is their "durability" and the ability of institutions to influence the allocation of political power in the future. Policies are much easier to reverse, whereas institutions are more durable. Moreover, institutions determine how the political preferences of various groups are aggregated into social choices. Therefore, introducing a set of institutions today influences how powerful different social groups will be not only today but also tomorrow.

Their durability and ability to influence the allocation of power in the future make institutions valuable as a commitment device. Recall that the commitment problem in politics, discussed in Chapter 5, arises because the group in power, the elites, make promises for the future but honoring these promises later is not in their interests. They would rather renege and revert to a different course of action or choose different policies. We refer to this as a commitment problem because the group in power cannot *credibly promise* certain policies. The commitment problem is intimately linked to the fact that political power will be in the hands of a particular group in the future, and they can use this political power to revert to different policies instead of those they promised. This account also suggests that institutions could be useful as a *commitment device* because they influence the future allocation of political power. Stated simply, if a particular group wants to make a commitment to a course of action, what better way to make this credible than give more power to the party that wants to see this course of action implemented? In other words, the commitment problem emerges because there was a "decoupling" between those who had political power and those who benefited from the promised policies. Change the identity of who has political power and promises become credible.

We are not the first to emphasize the commitment value of institutions. Although this theme appears in many writings and is implicit in others (e.g., the literature on structure-induced equilibrium; see Shepsle 1979; Romer and Rosenthal 1978; and Shepsle and Weingast 1984), it is probably most clearly associated with the seminal paper by North and Weingast (1989). They argued that the establishment of the constitutional regime in Britain after the Glorious Revolution of 1688 provided commitment that the Crown would not repudiate its debt, thereby increasing its borrowing capacity. This led to fundamental changes in financial institutions and provided part of the preconditions for the Industrial Revolution.

What does this institutional change correspond to in practice? How is it achieving this commitment? Thinking about these questions clarifies the role of institutions in this specific context and, more generally, their role in our approach to political institutions and democratization. The first important feature is that institutions are durable. After the Glorious Revolution, the ruler could not revert back to the days when he had been able to arbitrarily manipulate debt and tax policy without the agreement of Parliament. The Glorious Revolution introduced regular parliaments (previously they had to be "called" by the king) and gave Parliament control over fiscal matters. Second, these institutions constrain the behavior of the ruler. It is this feature of the institutions that makes them a credible commitment to repay the debt.

North and Weingast's explanation is compelling and provides a good description of the various issues involved in one of the major examples of institutional change in European history. Why is it that these new institutions make repayment credible? Why, if Parliament was strong enough to remove from office the legitimate king, James II, did it need to alter institutions to ensure that future kings would not renege on their debt? A full exploration of the answer takes us to political power and the relationship between political power and institutions. When it deposed James II, Parliament used its de facto political power and that of the Dutch, who had sent an army to help. However, this situation was transitory; the Dutch were not going to send an army every time Parliament asked for it (for one thing, they were busy fighting the French). So, Parliament changed the political institutions in Britain to try to lock in their transitory de facto power. The new institutions allocated de jure political power to Parliament – if not completely, then much more so than previously. Moreover, this new allocation of power guaranteed that the king would not be able to default on his debt because much of it was held by Parliament, which therefore had an interest in making sure it was paid off (Stasavage 2003).

Similar issues will be important in our theory of democratization: the elites will be forced to democratize to prevent revolution by the disenfranchised. Once established, democracy will create durable changes in the political arena and these changes will constitute a sufficiently credible commitment to give the citizens power and the policies they want in the future.

4.2 Institutions and Commitment

Our discussion of North and Weingast (1989) raises a fundamental question: Why do institutions provide commitment at all? In our model, this is because de jure political institutions determine who can take which actions and when. For instance, in a democracy, policies are determined by majority voting, which means that the citizens can get what they want if the elites do not have de facto power to challenge the citizens. When democracy is created, the citizens understand that the institutions will give them de jure political power, which serves as a commitment to more pro-majority policies, even if they do not have de facto power in the future.

Moreover, there are natural reasons for why it will be costly to replace democracy once it has been created – most obviously because groups invest in particular sets of institutions (Brainard and Verdier 1997; Coate and Morris 1999; Acemoglu and Robinson 2001). To take one example, it was only after the Second Reform Act in 1867 in Britain that the Conservative and Liberal Parties began to organize themselves as mass parties and create the institutions needed to compete as national organizations. They created conservative and liberal clubs and countrywide networks of organizers who were needed to mobilize the new mass electorate. These are specific investments whose value would be destroyed if democracy ceases to function. This makes democracy persist because it gives people a greater incentive to fight for it ex post. Moreover, the creation of these organizations specific to democracy makes it easier to solve the collective-action problem once they have been created. These are fundamental reasons why democracy, once created, is difficult (though not impossible) to reverse and why it, as a set of political institutions, has commitment power.

4.3 Political Power

The discussion thus far emphasizes that political power has different facets. Obviously, political institutions bestow political power on those who control the presidency or the legislature. For example, the constitution of the United States allocates power to propose and make laws, which gives groups who are successful in elections the power to determine policies in their favor. Yet, there is clearly more to political power than this. Consider the case of Venezuela. Hugo Chávez was elected president by an overwhelming majority in 1998 and was able to closely control a process of rewriting the constitution in 1999, which increased his powers substantially. Chávez, therefore, has a lot of de jure political power. Yet, other groups, who neither control the presidency nor had any impact on the process of redrafting the constitution, also have significant de facto political power. Forces that oppose the policies that Chávez prefers – for example, the managers of the state oil company – can organize strikes that bring the economy to its knees, as they did for two months after December 2002. Political opponents can also organize street demonstrations to demand that the regime changes its policies, even if they have no de jure political power with which to influence such policies. Such economic decisions and collective actions are costly for the regime.

Nevertheless, such power to challenge regimes is, by nature, transitory. Although the striking oil workers imposed heavy costs on the economy and hurt the regime, they simultaneously hurt themselves and their families. Strikes must, by necessity, be transitory. Moreover, strikes are difficult to organize and sustain, and their power depends on other factors that change over time, such as the world price of oil. The power of the oil workers in Venezuela also depends on geopolitical factors and the fact that the United States imports 15 percent of its oil from Venezuela. This induces the U.S. administration to intervene in Venezuelan politics to keep the oil flowing. However, the nature of such interventions depends on the character of the U.S. administration, which changes over time, again making de facto power transitory.

One could argue that the threat of strikes or demonstrations is continually present, which would be sufficient to induce Chávez to change his policies. Yet, it is clear that Chávez did not make any concessions until these threats actually manifested in strikes and demonstrations. Generally, it will be unclear whether threats to organize strikes are credible because the actions of many people have to be coordinated and a strike may fail because the regime can organize strike-breaking activities. Even after a strike or demonstration has occurred, there is no guarantee that another one can be easily orchestrated in the future. These factors indicate why the opponents of Chávez were not content with policy concessions because they anticipate that they can be reversed. They would only be satisfied with the removal of the president and, thus, a change in the allocation of de jure power.

In the context of democratization, one of the best examples of the relationship between transitory shocks and switches in political power was pointed out by Therborn (1977), who observed that many democratizations took place following wars. This fits well with our theory because war is a time when the citizens, who comprise the armed forces, have significant temporary power until they are demobilized. This threat is clearly seen in the democratizations in countries such as Germany after the First World War.

An important point about de facto political power, therefore, is that it is not necessarily "stationary" – which group has political power changes over time because of economic and political shocks and social changes. We discussed earlier an example of transitory political power in our simple model of dictatorship. It is interesting that the transitory nature of de facto power has been explicitly noted in the transitions literature by O'Donnell and Schmitter (1986) who describe the dynamics of collective action in opposition to an authoritarian regime as follows:

> ... this wave crests sooner or later ... A certain normality is subsequently reasserted as some individuals and groups depoliticize themselves again, having run out of resources or become disillusioned, and as others de-radicalize themselves ... Still others simply become tired of constant mobilization and its intrusion into their private lives. (p. 26)

5. A Static Model of Democratization

We now build a model that features all the essential elements of our approach to democratization. As well as political conflict and the commitment role of institutions, this approach features transitory political power for the disenfranchised coming from a revolution threat. Under certain circumstances, the elites are induced to democratize as a credible commitment to future pro-citizen policies in order to prevent a revolution. In this chapter, we proceed by assuming that, once created, democracy is consolidated. We defer a study of coups against democracy to the next chapter.

There are two groups, the rich and the poor, with fractions δ and $1 - \delta$. The elites are the rich and the citizens are the poor, although in Section 9 we show that results of the analysis are robust to alternative structures of political identities. Individual preferences are defined over post-tax incomes, given by:

$$\hat{y}^i = (1 - \tau)\, y^i + (\tau - C(\tau))\, \bar{y}$$

and society starts in a nondemocracy in which government policy is decided by the elites.

Recall that when the elites have uncontested political power, they choose zero taxes and no redistribution of income (i.e., $\tau^r = 0$). In contrast, the most preferred tax rate for the citizens is $\tau^p > 0$, given by (4.11). The comparative statics of τ^p also play an important role. Recall from our previous discussion that a greater level of inter-group inequality (i.e., a higher level of θ) increases the desired tax rate of the citizens; hence, $d\tau^p/d\theta > 0$.

Let us now summarize the timing of the extensive-form game between the elites and the citizens in which the sequence of moves is depicted in the game tree in Figure 6.1. Following the discussion of the game depicted in Figure 5.3, we can conceive of the initial choice being made by "nature," which determines the value of a shock that affects how attractive it is to challenge the regime. However, as discussed in Chapter 5, in the static model there is no loss in suppressing the state L, dropping this branch from the tree, and simply focusing on the one state in which the nondemocratic regime is challenged. This being the case, we also suppress the notation H exactly as we did before. Hence, Figure 6.1 differs from Figure 5.3 in that the left side of the tree, that following the branch L, is dropped.

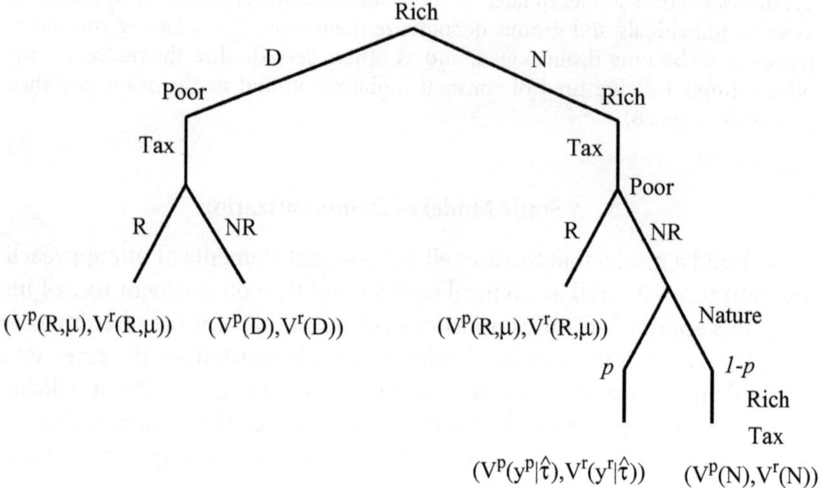

Figure 6.1. The Democratization Game.

The elites have political power initially and move before the citizens. They first decide whether to create a democracy, the branch labeled D, or not, the branch N. As in the last chapter, we denote the tax rate set by the elites in nondemocracy by τ^N and use the notation τ^D to refer to the tax set in democracy by the median voter. If the elites choose D, democracy is established and the median voter, a poor agent, sets the tax rate. If they do not democratize, then the tax rate is determined by the elites. Following this policy decision, the citizens decide whether to initiate revolution. Following the discussion in Chapter 5, revolutions generate private benefits for individuals who take part in them and there is, therefore, no collective-action problem. If revolution is attempted and a number $\xi^p \leq 1-\delta$ of the citizens take part, it always succeeds. After revolution, poor citizens expropriate the income of the elites. However, during revolution, a fraction $\mu > 0$ of the income of the economy is destroyed. A high value of μ implies that revolution is relatively costly.

These assumptions, as in the analysis of Chapter 5, imply that after revolution, each citizen receives a payoff of:

$$V^p(R,\mu) = \frac{(1-\mu)\bar{y}}{1-\delta} \tag{6.2}$$

The elites are expropriated in revolution and we assume that they receive nothing (i.e., $V^r(R,\mu) = 0$).

We again say that *the revolution constraint is binding* if the citizens obtain more in revolution than when the elites implement their ideal policy, τ^r. Therefore, the revolution constraint is binding if $V^p(R,\mu) = (1-\mu)\bar{y}/(1-\delta) > y^p$, or if:

$$\theta > \mu \tag{6.3}$$

As in Chapter 5, greater inequality (i.e., higher θ) makes the revolution constraint more likely to bind. Also, naturally, a low level of μ (i.e., greater income for the citizens after a revolution) makes revolution more attractive, and the revolution constraint (6.3) is more likely to bind. If the citizens undertake a revolution, branch R, then the game ends with payoffs to the citizens and to the elites of $(V^p(R, \mu), V^r(R, \mu))$.

If democracy has been created and there is no revolution, we are along the branch (D, NR). In this case, the game ends with the tax rate preferred by the median voter being implemented. In this case, the citizens and the elites obtain payoffs of $(V^p(D), V^r(D))$ where, as before:

$$V^p(D) = V\left(y^p \mid \tau^D = \tau^p\right) = y^p + \tau^p(\bar{y} - y^p) - C(\tau^p)\bar{y} \quad \text{and} \quad (6.4)$$

$$V^r(D) = V\left(y^r \mid \tau^D = \tau^p\right) = y^r + \tau^p(\bar{y} - y^r) - C(\tau^p)\bar{y}$$

The alternative is for the elites not to choose democratization and set the tax rate themselves. In this case, the issue is whether the elites can credibly commit to certain concessions. We again model this in a simple way by introducing a "continuation game" in which with probability $1 - p$ the elites can reset the tax rate, whereas with probability p, they cannot and the tax rate chosen before the revolution decision is implemented. This allows us to model the idea that in a nondemocratic society, the elites may make a promise of high redistribution in the future but cannot necessarily commit to it – the crucial transitory nature of de facto political power.

As discussed in Chapter 5, a more satisfactory approach is to have a repeated game, in which the elites can deliver the policy they promised today but can make no promises for the policies in the future, once the threat of revolution disappears. This is precisely the model we develop in Section 7, and we shall see that the current setup is similar to but, in many ways, much simpler than that dynamic game. Therefore, we prefer to start with this simpler setup to highlight the basic issues, returning to the more satisfactory framework later.

To prevent a revolution, the elites may try to set a tax rate $\tau^N = \hat{\tau}$, different from their ideal tax rate. This is the tax rate that will be effective when the elites do not democratize and are not able to reset the tax. Therefore, if the elites promise redistribution at the tax rate $\hat{\tau}$, the citizens choose not to revolt and nature does not allow the elites to reset the tax; the game ends with payoffs $V\left(y^p \mid \tau^N = \hat{\tau}\right)$ and $V\left(y^r \mid \tau^N = \hat{\tau}\right)$. In contrast, if nature allows the tax rate to be reset, the elites will set their most preferred tax rate, τ^r. In this case, the payoffs are $V^p(N)$ and $V^r(N)$, where:

$$V^p(N) = V\left(y^p \mid \tau^N = \tau^r\right) = y^p \quad \text{and} \quad V^r(N) = V\left(y^r \mid \tau^N = \tau^r\right) = y^r$$

Consequently, the expected payoffs from the promise of income redistribution can be written as $(V^p(N, \tau^N), V^r(N, \tau^N))$, such that:

$$V^p(N, \tau^N) = y^p + p\left(\tau^N(\bar{y} - y^p) - C(\tau^N)\bar{y}\right) \quad \text{and}$$
$$V^r(N, \tau^N) = y^r + p\left(\tau^N(\bar{y} - y^r) - C(\tau^N)\bar{y}\right)$$

which takes into account the fact that redistribution at the tax rate τ^N happens only with probability p. (Notice the difference between the notation $V^i(N)$, which refers to values when the society is nondemocratic and unconstrained, and $V^i(N, \tau^N)$, which refers to the case when the society is nondemocratic but the elites are forced to set a tax rate to avoid revolution. We use this type of notation later as well.)

We now analyze the subgame perfect equilibria of this extensive-form game. To do so, we start at the end of the game tree and apply backward induction, as in Chapter 5. We refer to the actions of the elites and the citizens as $\sigma^r = \{\phi, \tau^N, \bar{\tau}^N\}$ and $\sigma^p = \{\rho(\cdot), \tau^D\}$. The elites determine a tax rate $\tau^N \in [0, 1]$ and decide whether to create democracy $\phi \in \{0, 1\}$, where $\phi = 1$ indicates that democracy has been created. If there is no revolution and nature chooses $\nu = 1$, then the elites get to reset the tax rate. Because the elites do not make a decision when $\nu = 0$, we represent this as a choice $\bar{\tau}^N \in [0, 1]$. The citizens decide whether to initiate revolution, $\rho \in \{0, 1\}$ (with $\rho = 1$ representing revolution); this decision is conditioned on the actions of the elites; hence, $\rho : \{0, 1\} \times [0, 1] \to \{0, 1\}$. Here, $\rho(\phi, \tau^N)$ is the revolution decision when the elites make the democratization decision ϕ and set the tax rate τ^N. Finally, if $\phi = 1$, then democracy is created and the poor get to set the tax rate $\tau^D \in [0, 1]$. Then, a subgame perfect equilibrium is a strategy combination, $\{\tilde{\sigma}^r, \tilde{\sigma}^p\}$, such that $\tilde{\sigma}^p$ and $\tilde{\sigma}^r$ are best responses to each other in all proper subgames.

First, consider the situation in which the elites do not create democracy, promise a specific tax rate of $\tau^N = \hat{\tau}$, and there is no revolution. This generates expected payoffs of:

$$V^p(N, \tau^N = \hat{\tau}) = y^p + p\left(\hat{\tau}(\bar{y} - y^p) - C(\hat{\tau})\bar{y}\right) \quad \text{and} \tag{6.5}$$
$$V^r(N, \tau^N = \hat{\tau}) = y^r + p\left(\hat{\tau}(\bar{y} - y^r) - C(\hat{\tau})\bar{y}\right)$$

If $V^p(N, \tau^N = \hat{\tau}) \geq V^p(R, \mu)$, then such a concession would stop revolution. Following the analysis in Chapter 5, we can define μ^* such that at $\mu = \mu^*$, we have $V^p(R, \mu^*) = V^p(N, \tau^N = \tau^p)$; that is, the citizens get the same payoff from revolution as from the elites promising the best tax rate for them, τ^p. (Of course, $V^p(N, \tau^N = \tau^p) < V^p(D)$ because in the former case, the elites are only promising this tax, and their promise is realized only with probability p.) This critical value of the revolution cost, μ^*, is given from the equation $V^p(R, \mu^*) = V^p(N, \tau^N = \tau^p)$ by:

$$\mu^* = \theta - p\left(\tau^p(\theta - \delta) - (1 - \delta)C(\tau^p)\right) \tag{6.6}$$

When $\mu < \mu^*$, then revolution is not costly and we have from the definition of μ^* that $V^p(R, \mu) > V^p(N, \tau^N = \tau^p)$. Thus, even at the best tax rate, the promises of the elites are not sufficient to prevent revolution. The elites must, therefore, democratize to stop revolution. The strategy of democratization is feasible if democracy generates enough redistribution that the citizens do not revolt after democracy. This is the case when $V^p(D) \geq V^p(R, \mu)$, which is equivalent to:

$$\mu \geq \theta - (\tau^p(\theta - \delta) - (1 - \delta)C(\tau^p)) \tag{6.7}$$

When $\mu \geq \mu^*$, then revolution is sufficiently costly that the elites can prevent democratization by redistributing. In this case, they can stay in power by setting the tax rate at a level where the poor are just indifferent between revolting or not – that is, $\hat{\tau}$ satisfies $V^p(R, \mu) = V^p(N, \tau^N = \hat{\tau})$, which implies:

$$\mu = \theta - p(\hat{\tau}(\theta - \delta) - (1 - \delta)C(\hat{\tau}))$$

and they do not democratize.

Now we can see that there is a unique subgame perfect equilibrium; however, the character of this equilibrium depends on parameter configurations. First, when $\theta > \mu$ and $\mu \geq \mu^*$, the elites can stay in power by setting a tax rate $\hat{\tau}$. More interesting, the unique pair of strategies that constitute an equilibrium when $\theta > \mu$ and $\mu < \mu^*$ (and (6.7) holds) involve democratization by the elites to avoid revolution. It is useful to write the strategy profile for just this one case in full. Here, the following strategy profile is the unique equilibrium: for the elites, $\tau^N = 0$, $\phi = 1$, and $\bar{\tau}^N = 0$. For the citizens, $\rho(\phi = 0, \cdot) = 1$, $\rho(\phi = 1, \cdot) = 0$, and $\tau^D = \tau^p$. In this equilibrium, the elites create democracy and the citizens set the tax rate $\tau^D = \tau^p$. If democracy is created, then the citizens do not revolt ($\rho(\phi = 1, \cdot) = 0$); but, off the equilibrium path, the citizens play $\rho(\phi = 0, \cdot) = 1$ – that is, if democracy is not created, the citizens choose to mount a revolution. It is this credible threat of a revolution that induces the elites to democratize.

We now have the following result:

Proposition 6.1: *There is a unique subgame perfect equilibrium $\{\tilde{\sigma}^r, \tilde{\sigma}^p\}$ in the game described in Figure 6.1, and it is such that:*

- *If $\theta \leq \mu$, then the revolution constraint does not bind and the elites can stay in power without democratizing or redistributing income.*
- *If $\theta > \mu$, then the revolution constraint binds. In addition, let μ^* be defined by (6.6). Then:*
  - *(1) If $\mu \geq \mu^*$, the elites do not democratize and set the tax rate $\hat{\tau}$ to redistribute enough income to avoid a revolution.*
  - *(2) If $\mu < \mu^*$ and (6.7) holds, concessions are insufficient to avoid a revolution and the elites democratize.*
  - *(3) If $\mu < \mu^*$ and (6.7) does not hold, there is a revolution.*

The most important conclusion to be drawn from Proposition 6.1 is that democracy arises to avoid a revolution when the promises of the elites to make policy pro-citizen are not sufficiently credible. Note that the lower is p, the less credible are such promises, the higher is μ^* and the less likely it is that concessions will avoid a revolution. Thus, it is lack of credibility that forces the elites to democratize. Moreover, inequality must be sufficiently high ($\theta > \mu$) that a revolution becomes attractive in the first place. Before investigating the comparative statics of this model in detail and discussing more of its implications, we introduce repression.

6. Democratization or Repression?

So far, we have studied the trade-off between concessions and democratization when the citizens can challenge the power of a nondemocratic regime. However, as mentioned in Chapter 2, rather than make any type of concession, nondemocracies often respond with force to block political change. There are many examples of this. In December 1989, the Ceausescu regime in Romania attempted to block democratization by using the military. This tactic backfired when the army decided to side with the demonstrators, leaving only the secret police loyal to the regime. Similarly, in Tiananmen Square in June 1989 in China, the Communist Party used tanks to crush the pro-democracy movement rather than make any type of concession. Another relevant example is the military junta in Burma (Myanmar) maintaining its power by using force to repress all opposition. We now introduce repression into the model of the previous section and study the circumstances under which democracy emerges when repression is an option. The analysis initially begins by assuming that if the elites decide to repress the citizens, this always succeeds. In line with this assumption, O'Donnell and Schmitter (1986) noted:

> ...no transition can ever be forced purely by opponents against a regime which maintains the cohesion, capacity, and disposition to apply repression. (p. 21)

Nevertheless, later in this chapter we consider situations where repression may fail, in which case revolution can happen in equilibrium.

Pre-tax incomes are given by (4.7), except that now there can also be costs due to repression that affect net income. In particular, the post-tax net return of agent i is:

$$\hat{y}^i = \omega \Delta y^i + (1-\omega)\left((1-\tau)\, y^i + (\tau - C(\tau))\, \bar{y}\right) \qquad (6.8)$$

where Δ is the cost due to repression, with $\omega = 0$ denoting no repression and $\omega = 1$ denoting repression. We model the cost of repression as we did the cost of revolution. If the elites decide to repress, then all agents lose some fraction of their income in the period of repression. We assume that $\Delta = 1 - \kappa$, which makes the effective cost of repression equal to κy^i. We adopt the assumption that the citizens

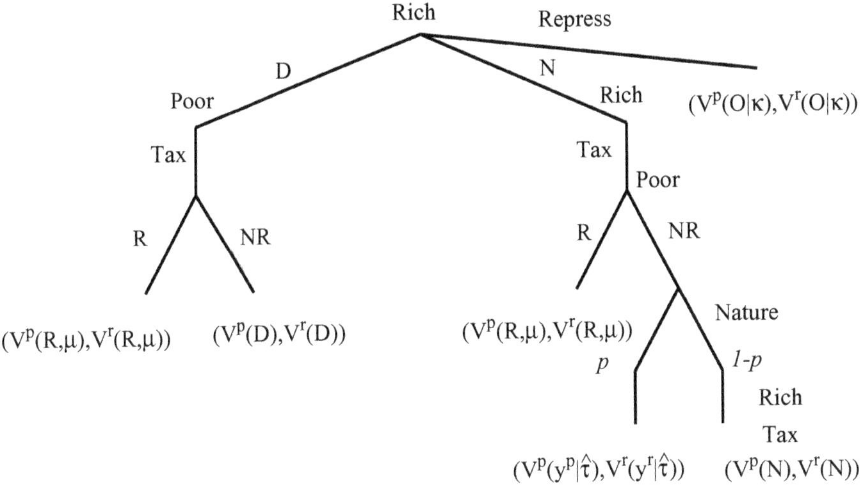

Figure 6.2. Democratization or Repression.

lose the same fraction of income as the elites only for symmetry; this plays no major role in the analysis because the repression decision is made by the elites.

The game is identical to that depicted in Figure 6.1 except that now the elites first choose among promising redistribution, using repression, or creating a democracy – see Figure 6.2. If they use repression, it always succeeds and the game tree ends with payoffs $(V^p(O \mid \kappa), V^r(O \mid \kappa))$, where the letter O refers to "oppression" (because R is already taken for revolution). With repression, the elites maintain power and can set their most preferred tax rate:

$$V^p(O \mid \kappa) = (1-\kappa)y^p \quad \text{and} \quad V^r(O \mid \kappa) = (1-\kappa)y^r$$

If the elites opt against repression, they can choose democracy, and the rest of the tree is the same as in Figure 6.1.

The analysis closely mirrors that of the previous section. First, the calculations leading to μ^* are unchanged so that, exactly as before, if $\mu \geq \mu^*$, the elites can maintain power by making concessions, whereas if $\mu < \mu^*$, they cannot. However, whatever the value of μ, the elites have the choice to repress. To understand what will happen in equilibrium, we have to compare the payoff to the elites from repressing to the payoff from democracy or concessions. Bearing this in mind, we can define two threshold levels for the cost of repression, $\hat{\kappa}$ and $\tilde{\kappa}$, such that the elites are indifferent between their various options at these threshold levels. More specifically, let $\hat{\kappa}$ be such that:

$$V^r(O \mid \hat{\kappa}) = V^r(N, \tau^N = \hat{\tau})$$

or, in other words,

$$\hat{\kappa} = \frac{p}{\theta}\left(\delta C(\hat{\tau}) - \hat{\tau}\,(\delta - \theta)\right) \tag{6.9}$$

Therefore, at $\hat{\kappa}$, the elites are indifferent between redistribution and repression. As a result, for all $\kappa < \hat{\kappa}$, they prefer repression to promising redistribution. Recall that κ is the fraction of income destroyed by repression so, the lower it is, the more attractive repression will be. This implies that one set of parameter configurations in which repression emerges is when $\mu \geq \mu^*$ and $\kappa < \hat{\kappa}$.

Next, define the other threshold such that:

$$V^r(O \mid \tilde{\kappa}) = V^r(D)$$

or, more explicitly,

$$\tilde{\kappa} = \frac{1}{\theta}\left(\delta C(\tau^p) - \tau^p\,(\delta - \theta)\right) \tag{6.10}$$

At $\tilde{\kappa}$, the elites are indifferent between democratization and repression. As a result, for all $\kappa < \tilde{\kappa}$, they prefer repression to democratization. Therefore, another set of parameter values in which repression will be an equilibrium outcome is when $\mu < \mu^*$ and $\kappa < \tilde{\kappa}$.

Both threshold levels $\hat{\kappa}$ and $\tilde{\kappa}$ are increasing in inequality – that is, increasing in θ. For example, totally differentiating (6.10), we have:

$$\frac{d\tilde{\kappa}}{d\theta} = -\frac{\delta}{\theta^2}\left(C(\tau^p) - \tau^p\right) + \frac{1}{\theta}\left(\delta C'(\tau^p) - \delta + \theta\right)\frac{d\tau^p}{d\theta} > 0$$

To see why this is so, notice that $(\tau^p - C(\tau^p))\,\bar{y}$ is the per capita transfer from the government budget constraint; we must have $C(\tau^p) - \tau^p < 0$, which gives $-\delta\left(C(\tau^p) - \tau^p\right)/\theta^2 > 0$. Next, $-\delta + \theta > 0$ follows from $y^r > y^p$ and we also know that $d\tau^p/d\theta > 0$. Hence, $d\tilde{\kappa}/d\theta > 0$.

That greater inequality increases $\hat{\kappa}$ and $\tilde{\kappa}$ is intuitive. Greater inequality makes redistribution more costly for the elites and, all else being equal, makes repression more attractive relative to democracy and relative to the promise of redistribution. This makes the elites more willing to undertake repression even if it is more costly.

We can now state a proposition outlining the nature of the equilibria in this game. To do this, we again adopt the intuitive approach. The nature of the strategies is similar to that discussed in Proposition 6.1, the only differences being that the elites initially have to decide whether to repress, $\omega \in \{0, 1\}$, and the revolution decision of the citizens is conditioned on ω in addition to ϕ and τ^N. Again, a subgame perfect equilibrium is a strategy combination $\{\tilde{\sigma}^r, \tilde{\sigma}^p\}$. Democracy results when $\theta > \mu$, $\mu < \mu^*$, and $\kappa \geq \tilde{\kappa}$.

We now have the following result:

Proposition 6.2: *There is a unique subgame perfect equilibrium* $\{\tilde{\sigma}^r, \tilde{\sigma}^p\}$ *in the game described in Figure 6.2, and it is such that:*

- *If* $\theta \leq \mu$, *then the revolution constraint does not bind and the elites can stay in power without repressing, redistributing, or democratizing.*
- *If* $\theta > \mu$, *then the revolution constraint binds. In addition, let* μ^* *be defined by (6.6) and* $\hat{\kappa}$ *and* $\tilde{\kappa}$ *be defined by (6.9) and (6.10). Then:*
  (1) *If* $\mu \geq \mu^*$ *and* $\kappa \geq \hat{\kappa}$, *repression is relatively costly and the elites redistribute income to avoid a revolution.*
  (2) *If* $\mu < \mu^*$ *and* $\kappa < \tilde{\kappa}$ *or* $\kappa \geq \tilde{\kappa}$ *and (6.7) does not hold, or if* $\mu \geq \mu^*$ *and* $\kappa < \hat{\kappa}$, *then the elites use repression.*
  (3) *If* $\mu < \mu^*$, *(6.7) holds, and* $\kappa \geq \tilde{\kappa}$, *concessions are insufficient to avoid a revolution and repression is relatively costly so the elites democratize.*

As in Proposition 6.1, democracy arises as a credible way to make policy more pro-citizen. Whether democratization will happen depends on the values of μ and κ. When $\theta > \mu$ and μ is lower than μ^*, revolution is relatively attractive and, given that the promises made by the elites are only imperfectly credible, it is unlikely that any tax rate that the elites promise before a revolution will ever be implemented. In this case, even when the elites offer the most desirable possible tax rate, τ^p, the citizens prefer revolution. Anticipating this, the elites must either repress or democratize to avoid being expropriated in a revolution. Repression is attractive when κ is relatively low, so democracy arises when a revolution is sufficiently remunerative to the citizens and repression costly enough to the elites. Repression is also used when the creation of democracy is insufficient to stave off a revolution.

When concessions do not work because they are not credible, the elites must democratize or repress. In Acemoglu and Robinson (2000b), we showed that there may be another important reason why concessions do not work. We developed a model in which the elites' strength and ability to repress is private information. Strong types can easily repress a revolution whereas weak types cannot. When faced with a revolution, we showed that there are circumstances where an elite that does not repress but instead makes concessions such as income redistribution may be inferred to be weak. In this case, concessions can actually encourage a revolution. We showed, therefore, that concessions are not used because of the information they may transmit to the citizens and the elites must repress or democratize.

6.1 Comparative Statics

We now investigate the comparative statics of the equilibrium in more detail. It is interesting to analyze the relationship between inequality and democratization.

For low levels of inequality, in particular for $\theta \le \mu$, democratization never occurs because the threat of revolution is not binding. Democratization, therefore, requires that the society be sufficiently unequal (i.e., $\theta > \mu$) so that revolution is a threat. Intuitively, in highly equal societies, the citizens do sufficiently well under the status quo distribution of assets that they never wish to contest power and democratization never occurs (unless, perhaps, as we discuss later in the chapter, the elites have a strong intrinsic preference for democracy that outweighs the loss from redistribution). Moreover, inequality has to be high enough that the promise of redistribution is not sufficient to stave off the revolutionary threat; in particular, $\theta > \theta^*$, where:

$$\mu = \theta^* - p(\tau^P(\theta^*)(\theta^* - \delta) - (1-\delta)C(\tau^P(\theta^*)))$$

Here, we use the notation $\tau^P(\theta^*)$ to emphasize that the tax rate preferred by the median voter depends on the extent of inequality. This needs to be considered when calculating the comparative statics. Clearly, $\theta^* > \mu$ because $p(\tau^P(\theta^*)(\theta^* - \delta) - (1-\delta)C(\tau^P(\theta^*))) > 0$. Therefore, an increase in inequality starting from low levels makes democratization more likely. From (6.7), we can define another critical value of θ, $\hat{\theta}$, such that:

$$\mu = \hat{\theta} - (\tau^P(\hat{\theta})(\hat{\theta} - \delta) - (1-\delta)C(\tau^P(\hat{\theta})))$$

where $\hat{\theta} > \theta^*$. This inequality follows from the fact that $p < 1$ and $\tau^P(\theta)(\theta - \delta) - (1-\delta)C(\tau^P(\theta))$ is increasing in θ. To see this latter result, note that the derivative of this expression is:

$$\frac{d\tau^P(\theta)}{d\theta}\left(\theta - \delta - (1-\delta)C'(\tau^P(\theta))\right) + \tau^P > 0$$

This is so because by the envelope theorem (i.e., the first-order condition that defines τ^P), $(\theta - \delta - (1-\delta)C'(\tau^P(\theta))) = 0$ and also $\tau^P > 0$. Thus, there is a range of inequality levels $\theta \in (\theta^*, \hat{\theta}]$ where democracy will be conceded, avoiding revolution.

However, when inequality is very high, $\hat{\kappa}$ and $\tilde{\kappa}$ are relatively high, and the elites prefer repression rather than suffer high levels of redistribution. Therefore, democratization only occurs for intermediate levels of inequality. The important theoretical point here is that the citizens prefer democracy to nondemocracy because it is more redistributive, and this preference becomes stronger as inequality increases. By the same token, the elites prefer nondemocracy, and they do so more intensely when inequality is higher and they expect more redistribution away from them in democracy. The higher the inequality, the more attractive nondemocracy is relative to democracy for the elites. Therefore, in a highly unequal society, the elites will use their resources to garner force and prevent revolution without democratizing.

For a given cost of repression, κ, we can implicitly define a critical threshold of inequality, $\tilde{\theta}(\kappa)$, such that

$$\kappa = \frac{1}{\tilde{\theta}(\kappa)}(\delta C(\tau^{p}(\tilde{\theta}(\kappa))) - \tau^{p}(\tilde{\theta}(\kappa))(\delta - \tilde{\theta}(\kappa)))$$

Then, democratization requires that inequality is less than this threshold, or $\theta \leq \tilde{\theta}(\kappa)$. Define $\theta^{\min} = \min\{\hat{\theta}, \tilde{\theta}(\kappa)\}$. We now state:

Corollary 6.1: *There is a nonmonotonic relationship between inequality and democratization. In particular, when $\theta \leq \theta^*$, the society remains nondemocratic and the elites maintain power; when $\theta > \theta^{\min}$, the society remains nondemocratic with repression. Democratization occurs when $\theta \in (\theta^*, \theta^{\min}]$.*

If $\hat{\theta} \leq \tilde{\theta}(\kappa)$, then before repression becomes attractive, (6.7) does not hold and – given that $\theta > \theta^*$ so that concessions do not work – the elites are forced to repress to avoid revolution. If $\hat{\theta} > \tilde{\theta}(\kappa)$, then when the critical level of inequality $\tilde{\theta}(\kappa)$ is reached, although it would be feasible to avoid revolution by democratizing, the elites find it more attractive to repress.

The results in Proposition 6.2, especially those in Corollary 6.1, may help us understand some comparative patterns of democratization discussed in Chapters 1 and 3. Although all Western European countries democratized by the early twentieth century, in parts of Latin America, such as Paraguay, Nicaragua, and El Salvador, dictatorial regimes survived practically the entire century by using repression to avoid democratization. This was also the case in African countries such as Zimbabwe (Rhodesia) until 1980 and South Africa until 1994. Such outcomes are explicable in our model because the extent of inequality in those societies made democratization very costly to the elites, leading them to prefer repression.

It may also be the case that repression was relatively cheap in those countries – for example, in Central America – because the disenfranchised were Amerindians who were ethnically distinct from the elites who were primarily descendents of Spaniards. Similarly, in Rhodesia and South Africa, the enfranchised were white whereas the disenfranchised and repressed were black Africans. In Chapter 2, Section 6.1, we discussed how the organization of civil society is important for democratization. If civil society is disorganized and ineffective, then it may be difficult to solve the collective-action problem to form threats to the existing regime, and any such attempt may be easier to repress. The long history of racial domination in both Central America and Southern Africa may be important in explaining the evolution of civil society. In Guatemala, for example, forced labor was still used until 1945, and government policies restricted labor mobility and the ability to organize collectively (McCreery 1994). In South Africa, the apartheid regime issued banning orders and pass laws and placed restrictions on the educational and career opportunities of black Africans. In both cases, these

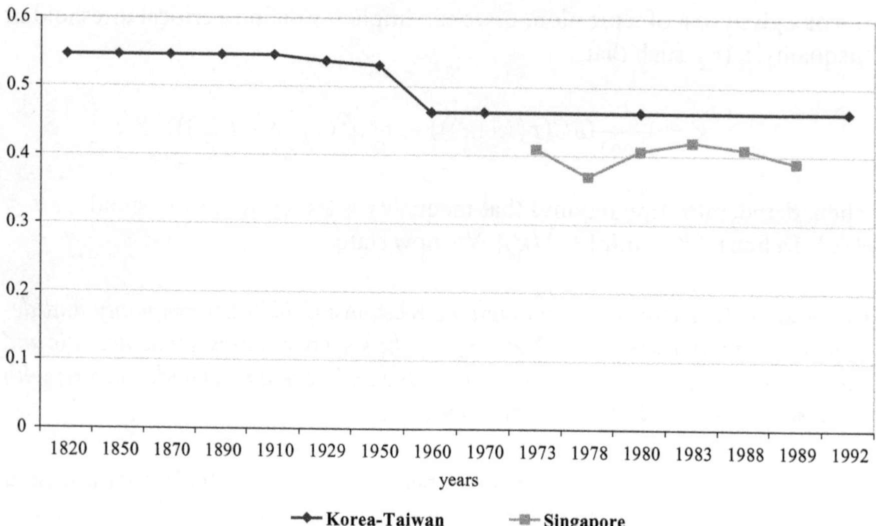

Figure 6.3. Gini Coefficient (Korea-Taiwan and Singapore). *Sources*: Singapore: Economic Growth Research, Deininger and Squire Data Set Korea-Taiwan: Bourguignon and Morrison (2002).

factors helped to fragment civil society and allowed the nondemocratic regimes to persist.

When the model is made even richer, the costs of repressing may also be influenced by such things as the form of wealth held by political elites. Later, we show that it may be significant that in all these countries, the political elites were primarily landowners. Indeed, the creation of democracy in these countries may have coincided with important changes in the elites' assets.

Proposition 6.2 also suggests the reason why there seem to be so few pressures toward political change in Singapore. For instance, Case (2002) notes

> ... "despite the emergence of a large middle class and suggestions that society is generally growing more participatory, social forces have failed to cumulate in any strong pressures for democracy." (p. 81)

Our analysis suggests that this absence may be due to the low levels of inequality in Singapore. Figure 6.3 shows data on inequality in Singapore from the Deininger and Squire dataset. This dataset, compiled by the World Bank,[1] gives measures of inequality only from 1973 because there are no historical data on inequality in Singapore from the colonial period. The data show that inequality has been persistently low in Singapore since independence and has shown no tendency to rise. Figure 6.3 also shows data from Bourguignon and Morrisson (2002) on the historical pattern of inequality in Taiwan and South Korea, two other Asian

[1] http://www.worldbank.org/research/growth/dddeisqu.htm.

countries that experienced delayed democratization. The picture is similar to that of Singapore, except for the large fall between 1950 and 1960 when agrarian reforms were implemented.

Finally, two recent empirical papers by Epstein, Bates, Goldstone, Kristensen, and O'Halloran (2004) and Papaioannou and Siourounis (2004) find tentative support for this nonmonotonic relationship between democratization and inequality that we first proposed in Acemoglu and Robinson (2001).

The costs of taxation also affect the form of the equilibrium and whether democratization will arise. When $C(\cdot)$, especially $C'(\cdot)$, is low, τ^p can be higher and there will be more redistribution in democracy. Although this makes democracy more attractive for the citizens, somewhat paradoxically it may also make it less likely to arise in equilibrium. This is because as the tax that the elites can promise increases, they can prevent revolution without democratization.

Finally, it is interesting to reflect on the role that (6.7) plays in Proposition 6.2. Repression is attractive to the elites when democracy threatens to enact policies that are very pro-citizen. However, if policies are insufficiently majoritarian, it is unlikely that (6.7) will hold; thus, the elites will be forced to repress when $\mu < \mu^*$ because democracy will not avoid revolution.

7. A Dynamic Model of Democratization

We now develop an infinite horizon model of democratization, the main motivation of which is that it allows us to model the issue of commitment to future policy in a more satisfactory way. The citizens demand democracy and changes in the structure of political institutions precisely because of the fact that such changes influence the allocation of political power in the future. Thus, the problems we are considering are inherently dynamic and intertemporal. In the static model, we had to model this by introducing a rather arbitrary assumption that the elites might be able to reoptimize after they had initially chosen their policy. We now show that results similar to those derived with this crude assumption flow naturally from the time structure of a repeated game.

The model is a direct extension of the one developed in Chapter 5, Section 6, and the one in the previous section. We adopt the same notation and again refer to the infinite horizon discounted repeated game as $G^{\infty}(\beta)$. There is again a total population of 1 with rich elites and poor citizens as before, with fractions δ and $1-\delta$. Initially, there is a nondemocracy, but the citizens can contest power through collective action, and in a democracy, the median voter will be a poor citizen. The structure of de facto power is exactly as in Chapter 5, Section 6, so that the cost of revolution is μ_t, where $\mu_t \in \{\mu^L, \mu^H\}$ and $\Pr(\mu_t = \mu^H) = q$ irrespective of whether $\mu_{t-1} = \mu^H$ or μ^L. We again normalize so that $\mu^L = 1$ and use the notation $\mu^H = \mu$.

The timing of the stage game is similar. In each period, the elites can decide whether to create democracy and whether to repress. If democracy is created, the median voter – a poor citizen – sets the tax rate. We assume that if democracy is created, it cannot be rescinded, so the society always remains a democracy. As before, we assume that if repression is chosen, revolution cannot be undertaken and the stage game is over for that period, with agents getting the repression payoffs.

As a result, utilities are now given by $U^i = E_0 \sum_{t=0}^{\infty} \beta^t \hat{y}_t^i$ where, as in the previous section, incomes are given by (6.8) and as in Chapter 5, U^i applies only when there is no revolution in equilibrium.

The timing of moves in the stage game is now as follows:

(1) The state $\mu_t \in \{\mu^L, \mu^H\}$ is revealed.
(2) The elites decide whether to use repression, $\omega \in \{0, 1\}$. If $\omega = 1$, the poor cannot undertake revolution and the stage game ends.
(3) If $\omega = 0$, the elites decide whether to democratize, $\phi \in \{0, 1\}$. If they decide not to democratize, they set the tax rate τ^N.
(4) The citizens decide whether to initiate revolution, $\rho \in \{0, 1\}$. If $\rho = 1$, they share the remaining income forever. If $\rho = 0$ and $\phi = 1$, the tax rate τ^D is set by the median voter (a poor citizen). If $\rho = 0$ and $\phi = 0$, the tax rate is τ^N.

We initially characterize Markov perfect equilibria of this game in which players are restricted to playing Markov strategies that are functions only of the current state of the game. Although the focus on Markovian equilibria is natural in this setting, for completeness in the next section, we drop the restriction to Markov strategies and discuss non-Markovian subgame perfect equilibria. As in Chapter 5, we show that this does not change the qualitative nature of our general results.

The state of the game consists of the current opportunity for revolution, represented by either μ^L or μ^H, and the political state P, which is either N (nondemocracy) or D (democracy). More formally, let $\sigma^r = \{\omega(\cdot), \phi(\cdot), \tau^N(\cdot)\}$ be the notation for the actions taken by the elites, and $\sigma^p = \{\rho(\cdot), \tau^D\}$ be the actions of the poor. The notation σ^r consists of a decision to repress $\omega : \{\mu^L, \mu^H\} \to \{0, 1\}$, or to create democracy $\phi : \{\mu^L, \mu^H\} \to \{0, 1\}$ when $P = N$, and a tax rate $\tau^N : \{\mu^L, \mu^H\} \to [0, 1]$ when $\phi = 0$ (i.e., when democracy is not extended). Clearly, if $\phi = 0$, P remains at N, and if $\phi = 1$, P switches to D forever; thus, we do not make these strategies explicit functions of the political state. The actions of the citizens consist of a decision to initiate revolution, $\rho : \{\mu^L, \mu^H\} \times \{0, 1\}^2 \times [0, 1] \to \{0, 1\}$ and possibly a tax rate $\tau^D \in [0, 1]$ when the political state is $P = D$. Here, $\rho(\mu, \omega, \phi, \tau^N)$ is the revolution decision of the citizens that is conditioned on the current actions of the elites, as well as on the state, because the elites move before the citizens in the stage game according to the timing of the previous events. Then, a Markov perfect equilibrium is a strategy combination $\{\tilde{\sigma}^r, \tilde{\sigma}^p\}$, such that $\tilde{\sigma}^p$ and $\tilde{\sigma}^r$ are best responses to each other for all μ_t and P.

We can characterize the equilibria of this game by writing the appropriate Bellman equations. Define $V^p(R, \mu^S)$ as the return to the citizens if there is revolution starting in state $\mu^S \in \{\mu^L, \mu^H\}$. This value is naturally given by:

$$V^p(R, \mu^S) = \frac{(1 - \mu^S)\bar{y}}{(1 - \delta)(1 - \beta)} \tag{6.11}$$

which is the per-period return from revolution for the infinite future discounted to the present. Also, because the elites lose everything, $V^r(R, \mu^S) = 0$ whatever is the value of μ^S. Moreover, recall that we have assumed $\mu^L = 1$, so $V^p(R, \mu^L) = 0$, and the citizens would never attempt revolution when $\mu_t = \mu^L$.

In the state (N, μ^L), the elites are in power and there is no threat of revolution; therefore, in any Markov perfect equilibrium, $\phi = \omega = 0$ and $\tau^N = \tau^r = 0$. This says simply that when the elites are in power and the citizens cannot threaten them, the elites do not repress and set their preferred tax rate, which is zero. Therefore, the values of the citizens and the elites, $i = p$ or r, are given by:

$$V^i(N, \mu^L) = y^i + \beta\left[q V^i(N, \mu^H) + (1 - q) V^i(N, \mu^L)\right] \tag{6.12}$$

Now, (6.12) says that the value to an agent of type i in a nondemocracy when there is no threat of revolution is equal to a payoff of y^i today, plus the expected continuation value discounted back to today (which is why it is multiplied by β). The payoff today is y^i because taxes are set at zero and everyone simply consumes their income. The continuation value consists of two terms; the second, $(1 - q)V^i(N, \mu^L)$, is the probability that μ^L arises tomorrow times the value of being in that state $V^i(N, \mu^L)$. In this case, tomorrow is the same as today, which is why the same value "recurs." The first term, $q V^i(N, \mu^H)$, is the probability that μ^H arises tomorrow multiplied by the value of that state $V^i(N, \mu^H)$. This value is different because now there is a potential threat to the regime. To see how this plays out, we need to understand what the value $V^i(N, \mu^H)$ looks like.

Consider the state (N, μ^H), where there is a nondemocracy but it is relatively attractive to mount a revolution. Suppose that the elites play $\phi = \omega = 0$ and $\tau^N = \tau^r$; that is, they neither create democracy nor repress nor redistribute to the citizens. Then, we would have:

$$V^p(N, \mu^H) = \frac{y^p}{1 - \beta}$$

The revolution constraint is equivalent to $V^p(R, \mu^H) > V^p(N, \mu^H)$, so that without any redistribution or democratization, the citizens prefer to initiate revolution when $\mu_t = \mu^H$. This is equivalent to $\theta > \mu$, which is identical to (6.3) in the previous section, and says that revolution becomes attractive when θ is sufficiently high (i.e., when inequality is sufficiently high).

Because revolution is the worst outcome for the elites, they will try to prevent it. They can do this in three different ways. First, the elites can choose to maintain political power, $\phi = 0$, but redistribute through taxation. In this case, the poor obtain $V^p(N, \mu^H, \tau^N)$ where τ^N is the specific value of the tax rate chosen by the elites. Second, the elites can create democracy. Third, the elites can use repression. Let $V^i(O, \mu \mid \kappa)$ be the value function of agent $i = p, r$ in state μ when the elites pursue the strategy of repression and the cost of repression is κ. We condition these values explicitly on κ to emphasize the importance of the cost of repression and to simplify notation when we later define threshold values.

If the elites create democracy or attempt to stay in power by redistributing, the citizens may still prefer revolution; thus:

$$V^p(N, \mu^H) = \omega V^p(O, \mu^H \mid \kappa) + (1-\omega) \max_{\rho \in \{0,1\}} \times \left\{\rho V^p(R, \mu^H) + (1-\rho)(\phi V^p(D) + (1-\phi) V^p(N, \mu^H, \tau^N))\right\}$$

where $V^p(D)$ is the return to the citizens in democracy. (Note here how the value of the citizens depends on the decision variables ω and ϕ of the elites). If $\omega = 1$, the elites choose to repress; the citizens cannot revolt and get the continuation value $V^p(O, \mu^H \mid \kappa)$. If $\omega = 0$, then what the citizens compare $V^p(R, \mu^H)$ to depends on the decision by the elites about creating democracy. If $\phi = 1$, then they choose between revolution and democracy. If $\phi = 0$, they choose between revolution and accepting the promise of redistribution at the tax rate τ^N.

We first focus on the trade-off for the elites between redistribution and democratization and then integrate repression into the analysis. The return to the citizens when the elites choose the redistribution strategy is:

$$V^p(N, \mu^H, \tau^N) = y^p + \tau^N(\bar{y} - y^p) - C(\tau^N)\bar{y} + \beta\left[q V^p(N, \mu^H, \tau^N) + (1-q) V^p(N, \mu^L)\right] \tag{6.13}$$

The elites redistribute to the citizens, taxing all income at the rate τ^N. The citizens, therefore, receive their income y^p from their own earnings and a net transfer of $\tau^N(\bar{y} - y^p) - C(\tau^N)\bar{y}$. If in the next period we are still in state $\mu_{t+1} = \mu^H$, redistribution continues. But, if the state switches to $\mu_{t+1} = \mu^L$, redistribution stops and the citizens receive $V^p(N, \mu^L)$. This captures our intuitive ideas that the elites cannot commit to future redistribution unless the future also poses an effective revolution threat.

The second strategy to prevent revolution is to democratize, $\phi = 1$. Because $1 - \delta > 1/2$, in a democracy the median voter is a citizen and the equilibrium tax rate is τ^p and $T = (\tau^p - C(\tau^p))\,\bar{y}$. The returns to the citizens and the elites in democracy are, therefore:

$$V^p(D) = \frac{y^p + \tau^p(\bar{y} - y^p) - C(\tau^p)\bar{y}}{1-\beta} \quad \text{and} \tag{6.14}$$

$$V^r(D) = \frac{y^r + \tau^p(\bar{y} - y^r) - C(\tau^p)\bar{y}}{1-\beta}$$

These expressions follow because in this chapter we are assuming that once created, democracy consolidates and there are never any coups.

Will democratization prevent revolution? The answer is not obvious. It might be that revolution in the state $\mu_t = \mu^H$ is so attractive that even democratization is not sufficient to prevent it. It is obvious that the condition for democratization to prevent revolution is $V^p(D) \geq V^p(R, \mu^H)$, which is exactly the condition we derived in Section 5 (i.e., (6.7)).

To determine whether the elites can prevent revolution with the redistribution strategy, let $V^p(N, \mu^H, \tau^N = \tau^p)$ be the maximum utility that can be given to the citizens without democratizing. This maximum utility is achieved by setting $\tau^N = \tau^p$ in (6.13). Therefore, combining (6.12) and (6.13), we obtain:

$$V^p(N, \mu^H, \tau^N = \tau^p) = \frac{y^p + (1 - \beta(1-q))\left(\tau^p(\bar{y} - y^p) - C(\tau^p)\bar{y}\right)}{1 - \beta} \tag{6.15}$$

(6.15) has a nice interpretation. It says that $V^p(N, \mu^H, \tau^N = \tau^p)$ is equal to the present discounted value of y^p, the pretax income of citizens, plus the expected present value of net redistribution from the elites to the citizens. Net redistribution is given by the expression $(\tau^p(\bar{y} - y^p) - C(\tau^p)\bar{y})$ but this only occurs today, and a proportion q of the time in the future when the state is μ^H. (The reason this leads to the expression $(1 - \beta(1-q))/(1-\beta)$ is exactly the same as the one discussed after (5.28) in Chapter 5.)

If $V^p(N, \mu^H, \tau^N = \tau^p) < V^p(R, \mu^H)$, then the maximum transfer that can be made when $\mu_t = \mu^H$ is not sufficient to prevent revolution. As long as (6.7) holds, $V^p(D) \geq V^p(R, \mu^H)$. It is clear that $V^p(N, \mu^H = 1, \tau^N = \tau^p) > V^p(R, \mu^H = 1)$ because revolution generates a zero payoff to the citizens forever. This implies that when $\mu^H = 1$, it must be the case that the value to the citizens of accepting redistribution at the rate τ^p in state μ^H is greater than the value of revolution. Also note that:

$$\begin{aligned} V^p(N, \mu^H = 0, \tau^N = \tau^p) &= y^p + (1 - \beta(1-q))\left(\tau^p(\bar{y} - y^p) - C(\tau^p)\bar{y}\right) \\ &< V^p(R, \mu^H = 0) = \frac{\bar{y}}{1 - \delta} \end{aligned} \tag{6.16}$$

so that the payoff from revolution must be greater when $\mu^H = 0$. Because $V^p(R, \mu^H)$ is monotonically increasing and continuous in μ, by the intermediate value theorem there exists a unique $\mu^* \in (0, 1)$, such that when $\mu^H = \mu^*$:

$$V^p(N, \mu^H, \tau^N = \tau^p) = V^p(R, \mu^H) \tag{6.17}$$

When $\mu < \mu^*$, concessions do not work so the elites are forced to either democratize or repress. When $\mu \geq \mu^*$, they can prevent revolution by temporary redistribution, which is always preferable to them when the alternative is democratization (because with democratization, redistribution is not temporary but rather permanent). In this case, the tax that the elites set, which we denote by $\hat{\tau}$, will be set exactly to leave the citizens indifferent between revolution and accepting concessions under a nondemocratic regime – that is, $\hat{\tau}$ satisfies the equation $V^p(N, \mu^H, \tau^N = \hat{\tau}) = V^p(R, \mu^H)$.

To determine equilibrium actions, we need to compare the payoffs to the elites from staying in power using redistribution and from democracy to the cost of repression. Without loss of generality, we limit attention to situations in which the elites play a strategy of always repressing rather than more complicated strategies of repressing sometimes and using redistribution other times (this also is without generality because of the "one-shot deviation" principle, discussed in greater detail in the next chapter; see also Fudenberg and Tirole 1991, pp. 108–10). By standard arguments, these values satisfy the Bellman equations:

$$V^i(O, \mu^H \mid \kappa) = \Delta y^i + \beta\left[q V^i(O, \mu^H \mid \kappa) + (1-q) V^i(N, \mu^L)\right] \quad (6.18)$$
$$V^i(N, \mu^L) = y^i + \beta\left[q V^i(O, \mu^H \mid \kappa) + (1-q) V^i(N, \mu^L)\right]$$

which takes into account that the cost of repression will only be incurred in the state where the revolution threat is active – that is, when $\mu_t = \mu^H$.

Together with the definition for Δ, the Bellman equations can be solved simultaneously to derive the values to the elites and the citizens from repression:

$$V^r(O, \mu^H \mid \kappa) = \frac{y^r - (1-\beta(1-q))\kappa y^r}{1-\beta} \quad \text{and} \quad (6.19)$$
$$V^p(O, \mu^H \mid \kappa) = \frac{y^p - (1-\beta(1-q))\kappa y^p}{1-\beta}$$

The value function $V^r(O, \mu^H \mid \kappa)$ has a clear interpretation: the payoff to the elites from a strategy of repression is the discounted sum of their income, $y^r/(1-\beta)$ minus the expected cost of repressing. The net present value of the cost of repressing is $(1-\beta(1-q))\kappa y^r/(1-\beta)$ for the elites because they pay this cost today and a fraction q of the time in the future.

To understand when repression occurs, we need to compare $V^r(O, \mu^H \mid \kappa)$ to $V^r(D)$ when $\mu < \mu^*$ and to $V^r(N, \mu^H, \tau^N = \hat{\tau})$ when $\mu \geq \mu^*$. As in the extensive-form game of the previous section, we now determine two threshold values for the cost of repression – this time called κ^* and $\bar{\kappa}$ – such that the elites are indifferent between their various options at these threshold levels. More specifically, let κ^* be such that the elites are indifferent between promising redistribution at the tax rate $\tau^N = \hat{\tau}$ and repression $V^r(O, \mu^H \mid \kappa^*) = V^r(N, \mu^H, \tau^N = \hat{\tau})$. This equality implies that:

$$\kappa^* = \frac{1}{\theta}\left(\delta C(\hat{\tau}) - \hat{\tau}(\delta - \theta)\right) \quad (6.20)$$

Similarly, let $\bar{\kappa}$ be such that at this cost of repression, the elites are indifferent between democratization and repression – that is, $V^r(O, \mu^H \mid \bar{\kappa}) = V^r(D)$, which implies that:

$$\bar{\kappa} = \frac{1}{\theta(1-\beta(1-q))}(\delta C(\tau^p) - \tau^p(\delta - \theta)) \tag{6.21}$$

It is immediate that $\bar{\kappa} > \kappa^*$; that is, if the elites prefer repression to redistribution, then they also prefer repression to democratization. Therefore, the elites prefer repression when $\mu \geq \mu^*$ and $\kappa < \kappa^*$ and also when $\mu < \mu^*$ and $\kappa < \bar{\kappa}$.

Given our previous analysis, the strategies that constitute equilibria in different parts of the parameter space can easily be constructed. Therefore, we have (as in Propositions 6.1 and 6.2, stated without specifying the full set of strategies):

Proposition 6.3: *There is a unique Markov perfect equilibrium $\{\tilde{\sigma}^r, \tilde{\sigma}^p\}$ in the game $G^\infty(\beta)$, and it is such that:*

- *If $\theta \leq \mu$, then the revolution constraint does not bind and the elites can stay in power without repressing, redistributing, or democratizing.*
- *If $\theta > \mu$, then the revolution constraint binds. In addition, let μ^* be defined by (6.17) and κ^* and $\bar{\kappa}$ be defined by (6.20) and (6.21). Then:*
  - *(1) If $\mu \geq \mu^*$ and $\kappa \geq \kappa^*$, repression is relatively costly and the elites redistribute income in state μ^H to avoid a revolution.*
  - *(2) If $\mu < \mu^*$ and $\kappa < \bar{\kappa}$, or $\kappa \geq \bar{\kappa}$ and (6.7) does not hold, or if $\mu \geq \mu^*$ and $\kappa < \kappa^*$, the elites use repression in state μ^H.*
  - *(3) If $\mu < \mu^*$, (6.7) holds, and $\kappa \geq \bar{\kappa}$, concessions are insufficient to avoid a revolution and repression is relatively costly. In this case, in state μ^H the elites democratize.*

Democracy arises only when $\mu < \mu^*$, repression is relatively costly (i.e., $\kappa \geq \bar{\kappa}$), and (6.7) holds. This critical threshold for the cost of repression, $\bar{\kappa}$, is increasing in inequality (increasing in θ); more specifically, we can again show by an argument identical to the one used in the last section that:

$$\frac{d\bar{\kappa}}{d\theta} > 0$$

Intuitively, when inequality is higher, democracy is more redistributive (i.e., τ^p is higher) and hence more costly to the rich elites, who are therefore more willing to use repression.

As also shown by the static model in the previous section, democracy emerges as an equilibrium outcome only in societies with intermediate levels of inequality. In very equal or very unequal societies, democracy does not arise as an equilibrium phenomenon. In very equal societies, there is little incentive for the disenfranchised to contest power and the elites do not have to make concessions, neither do they have to democratize. In very unequal societies, the elites cannot use redistribution to hang onto power; however, because in such a society democracy is very bad for the elites, they use repression rather than having to relinquish power. It therefore tends to be in societies with intermediate levels of inequality that democracy emerges. Here, inequality is sufficiently high for challenges to the political status quo to emerge, but not high enough that the elites find repression attractive. Thus, the intuition behind Corollary 6.2 applies in this model directly.

We show in the next section that even without the restriction to Markov perfect equilibria, similar results obtain: revolution can be stopped with temporary redistribution when $\mu \geq \tilde{\mu}^{**}$ where $\tilde{\mu}^{**} < \mu^*$ – hence, for a larger range of parameters – but if $\mu < \tilde{\mu}^{**}$, the elites cannot use concessions to avoid revolution.

Perhaps paradoxically, a high q makes franchise extension less likely. A high q corresponds to an economy in which the citizens are well organized so they frequently pose a revolutionary threat. Alternatively, if μ^L is sufficiently less than one, then even in this state, the elites have to redistribute to the citizens. In this case, a low value of μ^L would also lead to the same result. A naive intuition may have been that in this case franchise extension would be more likely. This is not the case, however, because with a frequent revolutionary threat, future redistribution becomes *credible*. When the citizens have the power to oversee the promises made to them, there is less need for the elites to undertake a change in institutions to increase the future political power of the citizens.

This result may explain why in the nineteenth century, Germany instituted the welfare state while allowing only a highly circumscribed democracy, whereas Britain and France democratized much more unconditionally. Social unrest against the existing system was as strong in Germany as it was in Britain and France. However, there were significant differences between the three countries in terms of the strength of the working class under the existing regime. Whereas there were no strong Socialist parties in Britain and France and trade unions were of little importance, the Social Democratic Party in Germany was by far the largest left-wing party in Europe at that time and the labor movement was strong (although not allowed to participate effectively in elections because of voting restrictions). For example, Nolan (1986, p. 354) explains the strength of the German workers movement as follows: "Although Britain experienced the first industrial revolution and France developed the first significant socialist associations, Germany produced the largest and best-organized workers' movement in the late nineteenth century." An alternative theory of democratization based purely on the strength of the working class would predict franchise extension in Germany before Britain and France. Proposition 6.3, which constructs a theory of democratization as a transfer of political power, in contrast, predicts that German elites should have had more flexibility in dealing with social unrest by promising future redistribution. This is also in part consistent with the actual evidence. Whereas Britain and France democratized and then increased redistribution toward the poor, Germany undertook redistribution without changing its nondemocratic regime. There is also little doubt that these redistributive measures were taken as a response to the potential revolutionary threat from the working class. Williamson (1998, p. 64), for example, writes that "the main aim of [the German] welfare programme was to avoid revolution through timely social reform and to reconcile the working classes to the authority of the state."

In addition, the distinction between the high and low state emphasizes that regime changes happen during unusual periods, perhaps economic crises or recessions. This is also in line with the evidence discussed in Chapter 3 (see also Acemoglu, Johnson, Robinson, and Yared 2004). Although in this book we capture these ideas using the reduced-form parameter μ so that the costs of revolution fluctuate directly, in Acemoglu and Robinson (2001) we showed how the same results follow from a model in which the cost of revolution is constant but total factor productivity fluctuates, as in standard models of the business cycle. In that model, changes in productivity change the opportunity costs of revolutions (and coups) and this has the same effects.

8. Subgame Perfect Equilibria

In the previous section, we characterized a subset of the subgame perfect equilibria of $G^{\infty}(\beta)$. In this section, we analyze our basic dynamic model of democratization without the restriction to Markovian strategies. More specifically, we look for subgame perfect equilibria. In general, there are many subgame perfect equilibria of this game that are supported by various history-dependent strategies and our analysis mirrors that of Chapter 5. We are interested in understanding the extent to which punishment strategies can make redistribution in state μ^L credible. Thus, we look for the best possible equilibrium for the elites, which will be the one that prevents democratization for the largest set of parameter values. Therefore, implicitly we are interested in the maximum possible amount of credible redistribution to the citizens in the nondemocratic regime. To simplify, we abstract from the use of repression, although this can be easily added. As in Chapter 5, Section 7, the analysis in this section focuses on showing that a cutoff level of μ, $\tilde{\mu}^{**} < \mu^*$ exists such that when $\mu \geq \tilde{\mu}^{**}$, there will be redistribution without democratization, preventing revolution. In contrast, when $\mu < \tilde{\mu}^{**}$, the equilibrium features democratization when $\mu_t = \mu^H$.

Exactly as in the analysis of Chapter 5, we study the circumstances under which the elites can redistribute at some tax rate $\tau^L > 0$ in state μ^L, thus avoiding the transition away from the nondemocratic regime even when $\mu < \mu^*$. There, we saw that the limitation on such redistribution was that it had to be incentive-compatible for the elite – that is, it had to be such that the payoff to the elites from redistributing according to the vector $[\tau^L, \tau^H]$, given by the value $V^r(N, \mu^L, [\tau^L, \tau^H])$, had to be greater than the payoff from deviating, $V^r_d(N, \mu^L)$.

There is only one substantive difference between the game we studied in Chapter 5 and this one: as long as (6.7) holds, when the nondemocratic regime collapses, there will be a transition to democracy. Therefore, the value $V_d^r(N, \mu^L)$ here takes into account that when the elites deviate in state μ^L, their "punishment" in state μ^H is democratization instead of revolution as before. This is because it is not a subgame perfect strategy for the citizens to threaten a revolution after the elites democratize because they obtain greater payoff from democracy than revolution. Consequently, if the elites democratize, it forestalls a revolution. This implies that the value $V_d^r(N, \mu^L)$ for the elites is given by the following recursion:

$$V_d^r(N, \mu^L) = y^r + \beta \left[q V^r(D) + (1-q) V_d^r(N, \mu^L)\right]$$

where $V^r(D)$ is as in (6.14).

As before, only redistribution at the tax vector $\left[\tau^L, \tau^H\right]$ such that:

$$V^r\left(N, \mu^L, \left[\tau^L, \tau^H\right]\right) \geq V_d^r(N, \mu^L)$$

is credible. In addition, it is obvious that the derivations leading up to $V^p\left(N, \mu^H, \left[\tau^L, \tau^H\right]\right)$ in (5.38) in Chapter 5 still apply. So, the incentive-compatibility constraint for the elites will only differ from before because of the change in $V_d^r(N, \mu^L)$.

As in Chapter 5, in general, the best equilibrium for the elites needs to consider the incentives to smooth taxes over time. However, to simplify the discussion and because the concept of tax-smoothing is not central to our analysis, we focus on characterizing the minimum value of μ^H such that the elites can avoid democratizing. We denote this $\tilde{\mu}^{**}$ such that when $\mu \geq \tilde{\mu}^{**}$, nondemocracy can be maintained with promises of redistribution. It is still the case that the maximum tax rate in the state μ^H is τ^p. So, we only need to find the maximum incentive compatible redistribution in state μ^L, which we now denote by $\tilde{\tau}'$. By an identical argument, it is given by:

$$V^r\left(N, \mu^L, \left[\tilde{\tau}', \tau^p\right]\right) = V_d^r(N, \mu^L)$$

Because $V^r(D) > 0$, the citizens can punish deviation less when the elites can democratize, which implies that deviation is more attractive for the elites. In consequence, it is immediate that $\tilde{\tau}' < \bar{\tau}'$, which satisfies (5.39).

In addition, because the value of revolution to the citizens is also the same, the formula for the critical value of the cost of revolution, $\tilde{\mu}^{**}$, must be identical to the one derived for μ^{**} in Chapter 5, with the value of $\bar{\tau}'$ derived there replaced by the new value of $\tilde{\tau}'$. Thus, the critical value $\tilde{\mu}^{**}$ can be easily found so that

$V^p\left(N, \mu^H, \left[\tilde{\tau}', \tau^p\right]\right) = V^p(R, \mu^H)$ at $\mu^H = \tilde{\mu}^{**}$. This is:

$$\tilde{\mu}^{**} = \theta - \beta(1-q)\left(\tilde{\tau}'(\theta - \delta) - (1-\delta)C\left(\tilde{\tau}'\right)\right) \\ - (1 - \beta(1-q))(\tau^p(\theta - \delta) - (1-\delta)C(\tau^p)) \tag{6.22}$$

The value of $\tilde{\mu}^{**}$ implied by (6.22) is greater than the value of μ^{**} in Chapter 5 because here, the potential punishments on the elites are less severe.

More important, it is clear that $\tilde{\mu}^{**} < \mu^*$ (where μ^* is given by (6.17)) and we have as before that if $\mu \geq \tilde{\mu}^{**}$, the elites can stay in power by redistributing. Equally important, when $\mu < \tilde{\mu}^{**}$, contrary to Chapter 5, there is no revolution because the elites have an extra instrument – they can democratize.

In summary, allowing the elites and the citizens to play non-Markovian strategies has implications in this model similar to those in Chapter 5. The threat of punishments by the citizens – in particular, the threat that they will undertake revolution – implies that some amount of redistribution can be sustained in state μ^L. It is interesting that this amount is actually lower here because the possibility for the elites to democratize limits the punishment that the citizens can inflict on them. Most important, however, is that the main thrust of the analysis of Chapter 5 applies. Although the ability to use punishment strategies increases the circumstances under which the elites can stay in power by making concessions, this does not eliminate the problem of credibility. When $\mu < \tilde{\mu}^{**}$, concessions do not work because of the absence of sufficient future credibility, and the elites will be forced to democratize.

9. Alternative Political Identities

We now return to the model in Chapter 4, Section 4.4, in which we considered political conflict along the lines not of socioeconomic class but in terms of group X versus group Z. Recall that when group X is the majority, and taxes and the form of transfers are determined sequentially by majoritarian voting, there are two types of subgame perfect equilibria. In both types, redistribution is from group Z to the more numerous group X and, if $\delta_X^p > 1/2$, the equilibrium tax rate will be the ideal point of poor members of X; if $\delta_X^p < 1/2$, the equilibrium tax rate will be the ideal point of rich members of group X. We now discuss how that model can be embedded in our static model of democratization presented in Section 6 of this chapter.

We think of nondemocracy as rule by group Z, who we will think of as the elites. Clearly, rule by the elites is no longer rule by the rich because some of the members of group Z are relatively poor. The first issue is the determination of the tax and transfer rates in nondemocracy and how key decisions, such as repression and democratization, are made. We assume that they are determined by majority voting in group Z, which implies that there are two cases to consider: one in which $\delta_Z^r > \delta_Z/2$ and one in which the opposite holds. In this section, we do not attempt a comprehensive analysis of all possible cases; we proceed by assuming $\delta_Z^r > \delta_Z/2$, which implies that it is the preferences of the rich members of Z that determine the social choices in nondemocracy. We also assume $\delta_X^p > 1/2$, thus dealing with only one of the democratic equilibria outlined in Chapter 4. With respect to the tax rate, we maintain the notation τ^N for nondemocracy.

All members of group Z prefer to set $T_X = 0$ and if there is no threat of revolution, then the unconstrained tax rate will be the one set by the median member of Z, a rich agent. Hence, the tax rate in nondemocracy is the ideal point of a rich member of Z, τ_Z^r, which satisfies the first-order condition:

$$C'(\tau_Z^r) = 1 - \frac{\delta_Z \alpha_Z^r \alpha}{\delta_Z^r} \qquad (6.23)$$

which we assume to have an interior solution and in which we have used the fact that $y_Z^r = \alpha_Z^r \alpha \bar{y}/\delta_Z^r$.

Therefore, in this case, redistribution goes from group X to group Z, with the equilibrium tax rate on income τ_Z^r. Moreover, no redistribution is given to group X, $T_X = 0$, and $T_Z = (\tau_Z^r - C(\tau_Z^r))\bar{y}/\delta_Z$. Clearly, members of group Z prefer nondemocracy to democracy, whereas the opposite is true for members of group X.

If the elites choose to repress, then we assume – following our analysis earlier in this chapter – that members of both Z and X incur costs of repression. The payoffs to members of group Z after repression are:

$$V_Z^p(O \mid \kappa) = (1 - \tau_Z^r)(1 - \kappa) y_Z^p + T_Z \quad \text{and} \qquad (6.24)$$
$$V_Z^r(O \mid \kappa) = (1 - \tau_Z^r)(1 - \kappa) y_Z^r + T_Z$$

These equations follow because if the elites use repression, they will stay in power and they will also be able to transfer income from group X to themselves. The optimal tax rate τ_Z^r is independent of κ. The payoffs to members of group X after repression are:

$$V_X^p(O \mid \kappa) = (1 - \tau_Z^r)(1 - \kappa) y_X^p \quad \text{and} \quad V_X^r(O \mid \kappa) = (1 - \tau_Z^r)(1 - \kappa) y_X^r$$

Imagine now that members of group X can engage in collective action and mount revolution against nondemocracy. Assume that this leads to the expropriation of all members of group Z but that, as in our main analysis, revolution is costly. Assume that after revolution, all income (not just the income of Z) is divided equally between members of group X. Because there is now heterogeneity within group X, we have to decide how to solve the social-choice problem that the group faces. To see where this problem originates, first note that the payoff to all members of group X from revolution is:

$$V_X^i(R,\mu) = \frac{(1-\mu)\bar{y}}{\delta_X}$$

for $i = p, r$, whereas without a revolution, the payoffs to the poor and rich members of X are $(1-\tau_Z^r)y_X^p$ and $(1-\tau_Z^r)y_X^r$. Thus, there are now two revolution constraints:

$$\frac{(1-\mu)\bar{y}}{\delta_X} > (1-\tau_Z^r)y_X^p \text{ for the poor} \quad \text{and}$$

$$\frac{(1-\mu)\bar{y}}{\delta_X} > (1-\tau_Z^r)y_X^r \text{ for the rich}$$

Recall that incomes are defined as $\delta_X^r y_X^r = \alpha_X^r(1-\alpha)\bar{y}$ and $\delta_X^p y_X^p = (1-\alpha_X^r)(1-\alpha)\bar{y}$, so that α_X^r is the fraction of the income of group X accruing to the rich in this group. Substituting these into the revolution constraints, we find

$$\frac{1-\mu}{\delta_X} > \frac{(1-\tau_Z^r)(1-\alpha_X^r)(1-\alpha)}{\delta_X^p} \text{ for the poor} \quad \text{and} \tag{6.25}$$

$$\frac{1-\mu}{\delta_X} > \frac{(1-\tau_Z^r)\alpha_X^r(1-\alpha)}{\delta_X^r} \text{ for the rich}$$

It is now immediate from the assumption that $y_X^r > y_X^p$, which implies $\alpha_X^r\delta_X^p > (1-\alpha_X^r)\,\delta_X^r$, that the revolution constraint binds first for the poor. Thus, there can be situations in which the poor in group X favor a revolution whereas the rich do not. We solve this social-choice problem by assuming that group X makes decisions according to majority voting, which implies that the preferences of the poor, because they are more numerous, determine whether a revolution takes place. An equivalent alternative would be to simply assume that the poor in group X can undertake a revolution on their own.

Faced with the threat of revolt by group X, the median voter of group Z wishes to make concessions by reducing the amount of redistribution toward himself and, in the limit, even giving redistribution to group X (i.e., set $T_X > 0$). As before, one can calculate the maximum amount of utility that group Z can credibly promise to group X. This involves setting $T_Z = 0$; setting the tax rate preferred by a poor member of X, τ_X^p; and setting $T_X = \left(\tau_X^p - C(\tau_X^p)\right)\bar{y}/\delta_X$. Considering that any promise of redistribution is only upheld with probability p, this gives members of X the expected payoffs:

$$V_X^p(N,\tau^N=\tau_X^p) = y_X^p + \frac{p}{\delta_X}\left(\tau_X^p(\bar{y}-\delta_X y_X^p) - C(\tau_X^p)\bar{y}\right) - (1-p)\tau_Z^r y_X^p \quad \text{and}$$

$$V_X^r(N,\tau^N=\tau_X^p) = y_X^r + \frac{p}{\delta_X}\left(\tau_X^p(\bar{y}-\delta_X y_X^r) - C(\tau_X^p)\bar{y}\right) - (1-p)\tau_Z^r y_X^r$$

These expressions incorporate the fact that with probability $1 - p$, the elites will be able to reset the tax rate and, therefore, because the revolution threat has passed, they will be able to set their preferred tax rate, τ_Z^r, and members of group X will get no redistribution.

We can use this to define a new μ^* such that if $\mu < \mu^*$, then concessions do not stop revolution. μ^* is defined by the equation $V_X^p(N, \tau^N = \tau_X^p) = V_X^p(R, \mu^*)$, which implies:

$$\mu^* = 1 - \frac{1}{\delta_X^p}\left[\delta_X(1 - \alpha_X^r)(1 - \alpha) + p\left(\tau_X^p\left(\delta_X^p - \delta_X(1 - \alpha_X^r)(1 - \alpha)\right)\right.\right.$$
$$\left.\left. - \delta_X^p C(\tau_X^p)\right) - (1 - p)\delta_X \tau_Z^r (1 - \alpha_X^r)(1 - \alpha)\right] \tag{6.26}$$

The first main point to emphasize is that similar to our analysis in the case of conflict between rich and poor, if $\mu < \mu^*$ defined by (6.26), then the elites cannot stay in power by offering redistribution or concessions; they either have to repress or democratize. Thus, the basic mechanism around which our book is built – namely, that promises may not be credible without fundamental changes in the structure of political power – functions no matter what the nature of political identities are.

All other trade-offs are qualitatively similar to before as well. For example, when $\mu < \mu^*$, whether the elites democratize depends on how costly democracy is compared to repression, whereas if $\mu \geq \mu^*$, the elites have to decide whether to make concessions or repress.

The main point of divergence is the comparative statics of this model, especially with respect to inequality. As discussed in Chapter 4, an increase in inter-group inequality can be captured by an increase in α. Consider the effects of α. If $\mu < \mu^*$, the trade-off for the elites is between democratization or repression. A higher α leads the median voter in group X to favor higher tax rates, which makes democracy worse for members of group Z, favoring repression. If $\mu \geq \mu^*$, higher α increases the amount of redistribution that the elites have to offer group X to make it indifferent between a revolution and nondemocracy, again favoring repression. These results, with respect to inter-group inequality, are basically the same as those derived in Section 5. Changes in inter-group inequality in this section, however, do not necessarily map into changes in observed measures of inequality.

Moreover, now consider the effects of an increase in α_Z^r, the share of group Z income that accrues to rich members of the group, holding α and α_X^r constant. An increase in α_Z^r unambiguously increases measured inequality. First, observe that when α_Z^r goes up, the equilibrium tax rate levied in nondemocracy falls. Second, because the left side of (6.25) does not change, the benefit from having a revolution does not change. Therefore, because the tax rate levied in nondemocracy falls, a revolution becomes less attractive even though measured inequality has certainly increased.

This brief analysis of conflict between two noneconomic groups illustrates that the basic mechanisms of democratization apply whichever political identities are relevant and also highlights that the comparative statics with respect to inequality may be quite different. This emphasizes that the robust predictions of our approach are those concerning the role of political institutions in affecting the future distribution of power when promises are not credible.

10. Targeted Transfers

We now briefly discuss how the introduction of targeted transfers (see Chapter 4, Section 4.3) changes our results in the static model of Section 5. What we showed there and in Chapter 5 was that allowing for targeted transfers increased the burden of democracy on the elites, making it worse for the elites but better for the citizens. At the same time, this effect is reinforced by the fact that the elites could redistribute from the citizens to themselves in nondemocracy. Thus, the burden of nondemocracy on the citizens increases. Citizens dislike nondemocracy more, whereas elites like it better and fear democracy more. More generally, when transfers can be targeted, there will be greater distributional conflict in society (not only between rich and poor but also between any groups) because those in power can use the fiscal system more effectively to redistribute resources to themselves.

The impact of increased conflict in our framework is obvious. First, targeted transfers make a revolution more attractive for the citizens because in nondemocracy, the citizens now pay taxes that are redistributed to the elites. The same argument also implies that nondemocracy is more attractive for the elites, and they are more willing to use repression.

This implies that whether transfers can be targeted, more generally the form of fiscal redistribution in society, will have important effects on equilibrium political institutions. Nevertheless, our framework does not make unambiguous predictions on whether targeted transfers make democracy more or less likely. Because they make the revolution threat stronger, they may force democratization, when temporary redistribution would have been sufficient without targeted transfers. However, because they make nondemocracy more attractive to the elites, they may also lead to repression, thereby preventing peaceful transitions to democracy.

11. Power of the Elites in Democracy

Let us now return to the class of models where we can discuss various types of democracies, giving different amounts of power to the citizens. Recall that in a fairly generic model of democratic politics, political competition in democracy between parties maximizes a weighted sum of different groups' utilities. In the context of the two-group model, this gives an equilibrium tax rate in democracy as a function of the parameter χ, which captures the weight on the utility of the elites. We used the notation $\tau(\chi)$ for this in Chapter 4 with $\tau(\chi = 0) = \tau^p$ and $d\tau(\chi)/d\chi < 0$. That is, as the power of the citizens in democracy declines, so does the equilibrium tax rate and the degree to which democracy redistributes income to the citizens. From this, it follows that:

$$\frac{dV^p(D)}{d\chi} < 0 \text{ and } \frac{dV^r(D)}{d\chi} > 0$$

The values of revolution and repression to the elites and the citizens are not affected by this modification in the modeling of democratic politics.

To study some of the implications of this model, we return to the simple static model of Section 6. Note first that the trade-off for the elites between repression and the promise of redistribution when $\mu \geq \mu^*$ is not altered by this new model of democracy. Therefore, we can concentrate on investigating the implications of χ for $\tilde{\kappa}$, the critical level of the cost of repression at which the elites are indifferent between repression and democracy. Recalling that the critical threshold for the cost of repression, $\tilde{\kappa}(\chi)$, which we now index by χ, is defined such that:

$$V^r(O \mid \tilde{\kappa}) = V^r(D)$$

we have that:

$$\tilde{\kappa}(\chi) = \frac{1}{\theta}\left(\delta C(\tau(\chi)) - \tau(\chi)(\delta - \theta)\right) \tag{6.27}$$

which is similar to (6.10), except that the equilibrium tax rate resulting from political competition with variable political power, $\tau(\chi)$, replaces the most preferred tax rate of the citizens, $\tau(\chi)$. Notice that

$$\frac{d\tilde{\kappa}(\chi)}{d\chi} = \frac{1}{\theta}\left(\delta C'(\tau(\chi)) - (\delta - \theta)\right)\frac{d\tau(\chi)}{d\chi} < 0$$

by the fact that the elites have higher incomes than the citizens, and that $d\tau(\chi)/d\chi < 0$. Thus, increases in χ, by making democracy less majoritarian, make repression less attractive for the elites. This implies that the ability to increase the power of the elites in democracy often enables a peaceful transition to democracy by making repression less attractive for the elites. Nevertheless, increasing χ is a double-edged sword because as the power of the elites in democracy goes up, democracy becomes less pro-citizen. It is only the fact that the welfare of the citizens is increased by democracy that makes democratization a feasible institutional change to avoid a revolution. When χ becomes too high, democracy is no longer a credible commitment to pro-citizen policies; to avoid a revolution, the elites have no choice but to use repression. To summarize this discussion:

Proposition 6.4: *In the model with variable power, an increase in χ starting from low values makes democracy less redistributive and makes repression less attractive for the elites. This makes democracy more likely. However, as χ increases further, (6.7) becomes less likely to hold and, therefore, it becomes less likely that democratization will stop a revolution, which induces the elites to choose repression again.*

Many interesting examples suggest the importance of Proposition 6.4. For example, the inability of the elites to compete successfully in democratic politics often leads to coups. As discussed in Chapter 1, many scholars argue that the inability of the Conservatives to compete with the Radicals in Argentina after implementation of the Sáenz Peña Law appears to be one of the factors behind the coup in 1930. Traditional elites were willing to grant full democracy, partially because they thought they would command a great deal of power under the new institutions. The failure of the Conservatives then shows that χ was smaller than had been thought at the time of democratization. In contrast, traditional political elites in Colombia have been successful in manipulating political institutions to sustain their power, even after the complete enfranchisement of males in 1936. In particular, by structuring the electoral rules in a way that discouraged entry by third parties, particularly Socialists, they were able to keep dissident factions within the parties and limit demands for radical redistributive policies (see Mazzuca and Robinson 2004). As noted previously, other factors facilitated this strategy in Colombia, particularly the fact that the distribution of land was more egalitarian than in other Latin American countries; thus, there was a substantial middle class with much less interest in redistribution (see Bergquist 2002).

This Colombian example suggests that, at least to some extent, manipulation of institutions can make χ endogenous. In support of this, Sáenz Peña also tried to manipulate the electoral system by introducing a system called the "incomplete list." Under this system, congressional candidates were elected in three member constituencies; however, only two members were elected from the party with the most votes, with the third allocated to the party with the second largest number of votes. Smith (1978, p. 11) notes that this "discriminated sharply against small parties, discouraged the formation of new movements, favored the established interests." This system was constructed as a way of guaranteeing one third of the seats to the Radicals as a concession to avoid further conflict with the anticipation that Conservatives would secure the two-thirds majority.

A fascinating example of an apparently successful manipulation of democracy is Pinochet's 1989 constitution. Pinochet lost a plebiscite that he had hoped would further extend the military government. He was faced with the decision about whether to actually democratize or instead ignore the results of the vote and stay in power by using force. In the end, he decided that democracy was the better option, but his preferences were clearly influenced by his success at "designing democracy." In particular, he managed to write into the electoral rules a systemic gerrymander that overrepresented Conservative groups (Londregan 2000); in our model, this increases χ and makes repression less attractive.

Another potentially important example is from Rokkan (1970), who argued that proportional representation was introduced in many Western European countries at the time of mass democratization by Conservatives trying to protect their power. In our framework, if Rokkan is right, then this switch in electoral rules may have played an important role in preserving democracy in such countries as Sweden, Belgium, and Norway (although Rokkan did not explain why the rule changes were permanent once the Socialists took power, as they did in Sweden and Norway; see Mazzuca and Robinson 2004).

The results in this section also throw some interesting light on the claims made in the comparative politics literature about how political elites try to "manage" transitions (e.g., Linz and Stepan 1996). For example, it is often argued that because the dictatorship in Argentina collapsed after the Falklands War in 1983, it had little ability to influence the design of democratic institutions. On the other hand, because the Brazilian dictatorship managed to organize a relatively orderly transition to democracy in 1985, it was able to significantly influence the form of political institutions and the outcomes in the nascent democracy. Our model shows that the ability to manipulate democracy may lead to a peaceful transition to democracy whereas otherwise there would have been repression. Thus, the fact that the Brazilian military was able to control the process of democratization in the 1980s may have actually facilitated it.

What explains why in some places the elites were able to install a limited democracy whereas in others they were not? What explains why in some circumstances the majority are willing to design institutions to limit their own power?

First, in many circumstances the relevant institutions may essentially be historically determined and difficult to change. By their nature, institutions tend to persist over time (Acemoglu, Johnson, and Robinson 2001, 2002) and, for the purpose of understanding regime dynamics, must be taken as given. An interesting example of this would be the fact that all Latin American countries have presidents. The consensus on the origins of presidentialism in Latin America is that when these countries became independent, they took the form of political institutions in the United States as a blueprint for how to organize a republic. Hence, they adopted presidential forms of democracy that have persisted over time.

Second, designing institutions involves both costs and benefits, both of which are uncertain. Take the decision of the ANC to build guarantees for whites into the South African constitution. This limited its power and, other things being equal, was undesirable from its point of view. One part of these concessions was the introduction of proportional representation. Reynolds (1999) notes:

> One of the least contentious issues throughout the entire negotiation process was the agreement of almost all the key players on the use of a proportional representation system (PR) to elect the Constitutional Assembly in 1994. The whites-only parliament had inherited the British single member district (SMD) plurality system . . . and it was long thought that the ANC would seek to maintain the system . . . because they perceived electoral advantage in doing so. (p. 183)

However, it was also clear to the ANC that an electoral system that underrepresented whites could be dangerously destabilizing. Reynolds (1999, p. 184) records that "the 1980 census showed whites to be in a majority in only five . . . districts . . . the ANC appreciated the way in which PR could facilitate an inclusive polity which would convert potentially anti-system minority parties into pro-system parties with incentives to play their democratic roles" and "the NP quickly realized that the existing SMD plurality system had the potential to devastate their seat winning abilities" (Reynolds 1999, p. 185). Not only did the ANC worry that the whites would be underrepresented, it also worried they would be overrepresented. For example, one problem with the SMD system was that "it would have given the ANC enough of a 'seat bonus to push them over the two-thirds threshold, giving them enough seats to write the permanent constitution alone" (Reynolds 1999, p. 185). As noted in Chapter 5, the ANC recognized that it was not advantageous to be able to independently rewrite the constitution. As a result, the ANC quickly agreed to switch to PR.

Whether the ANC would want to make such concessions would depend on its perception of the possible actions that the white minority could take. For example, if it expected the whites to sponsor a coup against democracy or flee the country with their wealth, building guarantees into the constitution would be more attractive. In reality, it is also uncertain whether any particular institutional guarantees work. For example, Robert Mugabe's regime in Zimbabwe has been able to override most of the checks and balances placed on it by the 1980 constitution, including the clauses designed to bolster the political power of the whites.

12. Ideological Preferences over Regimes

In our analysis so far, the only reason that agents care about political institutions is because of their different economic consequences. An alternative and complementary perspective is to recognize that individuals may also have ideological preferences over regimes. For example, after the Enlightenment in Europe, it may have been the case that the elites preferred democracy to nondemocracy for purely ideological reasons.

How does incorporating such ideological concerns change our analysis? At some level, a lot – at some other level, not that much. Of course, if ideological preferences are primary much of our analysis is not relevant. However, if ideological preferences are present, but not large enough to totally swamp the relevant economic concerns of individuals as well, much of our analysis and many of the insights developed so far continue to apply.

Let us introduce ideological concerns in our baseline model of democratization in Section 5 without repression. In particular, imagine that people's utility functions are additive in consumption and a term that captures an intrinsic preference for democracy. In democracy, the utilities of a poor citizen and rich elite agent who consume incomes y^p and y^r are $y^p + B_p \bar{y}$ and $y^r + B_r \bar{y}$, where we normalize by average income. Here, $B_p > 0$ and $B_r > 0$ capture the positive utility from living under democratic institutions. In contrast, if society is a nondemocracy, then agents do not receive these extra utility "benefits." All agents aim to maximize their expected utility.

In this model, the threat of revolution is not the only way democratization may arise. If B_r is relative large, then the elites prefer to democratize even though they could avoid doing so by redistributing income themselves. This was a result that we could never have before because democratization was always worse for the elites than making concessions. This corresponds to a "purely ideological" democratization, driven by the social values of the elites, arising when $V^r(D) \geq V^r(N, \tau^N = \hat{\tau})$.

To see how this new feature influences the model, note that because neither the revolution constraint nor the equation determining μ^* depends on the value from democracy, they are unchanged by the introduction of ideological preferences. The only difference is that before, democracy arose only if $\theta > \mu$ and $\mu < \mu^*$. Now it is possible that even if $\mu \geq \mu^*$, so that democratization could be avoided by concessions, the elites democratize. Moreover, even if $\theta \leq \mu$, so that the revolution constraint does not bind, B_r can be sufficiently large to ensure $V^r(D) \geq V^r(N)$, thus creating an ideology-driven democratization.

The crucial issue, naturally, is whether the elites have a strong enough preference for democracy. To study this, we need to define two cutoff levels: $\bar{B}$ is the cutoff level such that when $B_r \geq \bar{B}$, even when $\theta \leq \mu$, so that the threat of revolution does not bind, the elites democratize. This is clearly given by:

$$\bar{B} = \frac{1}{\delta}\left(\delta C\left(\tau^p\right) - \tau^p\left(\delta - \theta\right)\right)$$

in which the right-hand side is the net transfers away from the elites when the tax rate is the one that will be chosen in a democracy, τ^p. This is what the elites pay in democracy as net transfers away from them but, in return, they obtain the ideological benefit of having established democracy, B_r.

However, when $\theta > \mu$, the comparison is not between no taxation and democracy but rather between limited taxation and democracy. Therefore, the relevant threshold is:

$$\tilde{B} = \frac{1}{\delta}\left(\delta C\left(\tau^p\right) - \tau^p\left(\delta - \theta\right) + p\left(\hat{\tau}\left(\delta - \theta\right) - \delta C(\hat{\tau})\right)\right)$$

which takes into account that even without democracy, there will be net redistribution away from the elites equal to $\hat{\tau}\,(\delta - \theta) - \delta C(\hat{\tau}) < 0$ with probability p. Clearly, we have that:

$$\tilde{B} < \bar{B}$$

Analysis of these equations shows that both $\tilde{B}$ and $\bar{B}$ are increasing in θ: in other words, the higher is inequality, the higher are $\tilde{B}$ and $\bar{B}$. For example:

$$\frac{d\bar{B}}{d\theta} = \frac{1}{\delta}\left(\delta C'\left(\tau^{p}\right) - (\delta - \theta)\right)\frac{d\tau^{p}}{d\theta} - \frac{1}{\delta}(\delta - \theta) > 0$$

which follows immediately from noting that $-(\delta - \theta) > 0$ and recalling that $d\tau^{p}/d\theta > 0$. This is because with greater inequality, democracy is more costly for the elites (because it redistributes more away from them) and, as a result, their ideological preferences have to be stronger for them to prefer democracy to nondemocracy.

Finally, note that now, compared to (6.7), the condition that democracy prevents revolution is easier to satisfy because there is an extra utility benefit from democracy that does not accrue if there is revolution. Taking this into account, we can restate (6.7) as:

$$\mu \geq \theta - (\tau^{p}(\theta - \delta) - (1 - \delta)C(\tau^{p})) - B_p \tag{6.28}$$

We now have the following result:

Proposition 6.5: *There is a unique subgame perfect equilibrium such that:*

- *If $\theta \leq \mu$ and $B_r \leq \bar{B}$, then the revolution constraint does not bind and the elites stay in power without democratizing or redistributing income. If $B_r > \bar{B}$, and (6.28) holds, then the elites democratize.*
- *If $\theta > \mu$, then the revolution constraint binds. In addition, let μ^* be defined by (6.6). Then:*
  - *(1) If $\mu \geq \mu^*$, and $B_r \leq \tilde{B}$, the elites do not democratize and set the tax rate $\hat{\tau}$ to redistribute enough income to avoid a revolution.*
  - *(2) If $\mu < \mu^*$, or $\mu \geq \mu^*$ and $B_r > \tilde{B}$, and (6.28) holds, then the elites democratize.*
  - *(3) If (6.28) does not hold, there is a revolution.*

There are a couple of interesting points: (1) if ideological considerations are not important, our previous analysis applies identically because this implies that B_r is sufficiently small, so $B_r \leq \bar{B}$ and $B_r \leq \tilde{B}$ will be the relevant part of the parameter space, where the implications of Proposition 6.5 become identical to Proposition 6.1; and (2) when ideological considerations are sufficiently important, they may induce transitions to democracy that would not have taken place for purely economic reasons. Nevertheless, even in this case, economic incentives are potentially important. For example, both $B_r > \bar{B}$ and $B_r > \tilde{B}$ are more likely when inequality is low. As inequality increases, the redistribution away from the

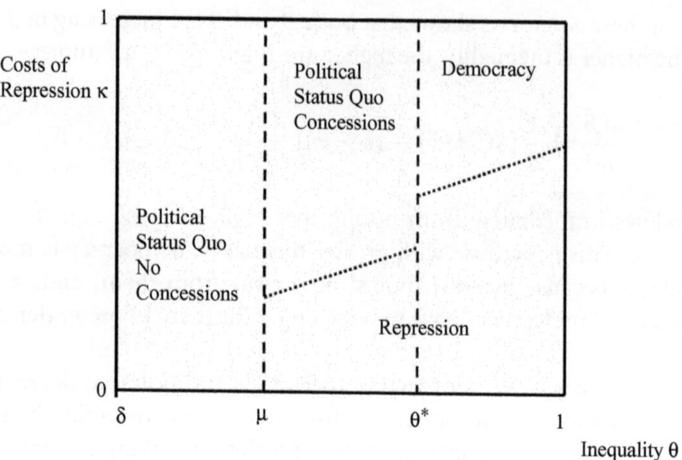

Figure 6.4. Concessions, Repression, or Democracy?

elites in democracy becomes larger, and for a given ideological benefit of democracy, these two conditions are less likely to hold.

13. Democratization in a Picture

We have now sufficiently developed our framework that we can rigorously construct Figure 2.1 from Chapter 2. We do this in the context of the static model of Figure 6.2 and assume that democracy is always sufficiently redistributive that it stops a revolution. Consider Figure 6.4. On the horizontal axis is inequality and on the vertical axis the cost of repression, is plotted. First note that when inequality is low – in particular, when $\mu > \theta$ – there is no threat of a revolution; this is the region to the left of the vertical line at μ in Figure 6.4. Next, note that whether a nondemocratic regime can stay in power by making policy concessions and redistributing income is also independent of κ and is thus another vertical line. This is derived from (6.6). We used the notation θ^* in Section 6.1 to refer to the critical level of inequality at which this equation is satisfied, which is shown on Figure 6.4. Therefore, we have two vertical lines that divide the box into three regions. On the left, is the political status quo with no repression. Next is a region where there are concessions but no need to create democracy. Finally, there is a region where inequality is so high that there will be revolution unless democracy is created or repression is used.

It now only remains to determine when the elites wish to repress. Consider the region where the elites can stay in power by redistributing. They will choose repression when $\kappa < \hat{\kappa}$, where $\hat{\kappa}$ is defined by (6.9). $\hat{\kappa}$ is an increasing function of θ when inequality is higher, the elites have to redistribute more when they make concessions, and repression is more attractive. Similarly, when democracy

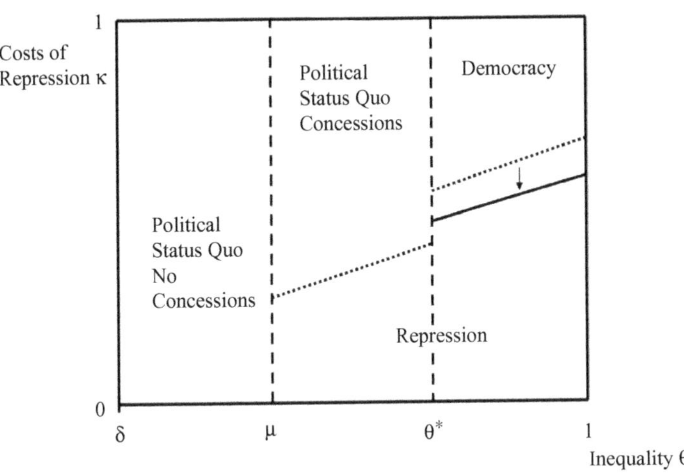

Figure 6.5. Manipulating Democracy. Making democracy less redistributive expands the region of democratization.

or repression is the relevant option, repression is optimal if $\kappa < \tilde{\kappa}$, where $\tilde{\kappa}$ is defined by (6.10). Finally, to complete the figure, note that for any value of θ, $\tilde{\kappa} > \hat{\kappa}$. This is so because democracy is always more redistributive than the promise of concessions. For clarity, only part of these functions are plotted in the figure.

We can do some interesting thought experiments in terms of these pictures. For example, we can introduce the possibility that a dictatorship can manipulate democracy to make it less pro-citizen. The only effect this has on the picture is to shift down $\tilde{\kappa}$, which implies that the cost of repression has to be less for it to be optimal – given that once democracy can be manipulated, it is less threatening to the elites. The effect of this is to expand the area in which we get democracy. This possibility is shown in Figure 6.5.

Finally, let us note that Figure 6.4 is the basis for Figure 2.1 in Chapter 2. The only difference is that we simplified Figure 2.1 by ignoring the possibility that nondemocratic regimes could stay in power by redistributing income. If we ignore this possibility in Figure 6.4, we erase the vertical line at θ^*, and we need to extend the upward sloping line that shows $\tilde{\kappa}$ as a function of θ. This results in Figure 6.6, which is the same as Figure 2.1.

14. Equilibrium Revolutions

We have so far assumed that repression definitely works and prevents a revolution. History is full of heavy-handed repression strengthening the threat of a revolution and ultimately leading to revolution or significant disruption. In this section, we briefly discuss the possibility that repression does not always work; in particular, assume that following repression, the citizens may actually revolt with

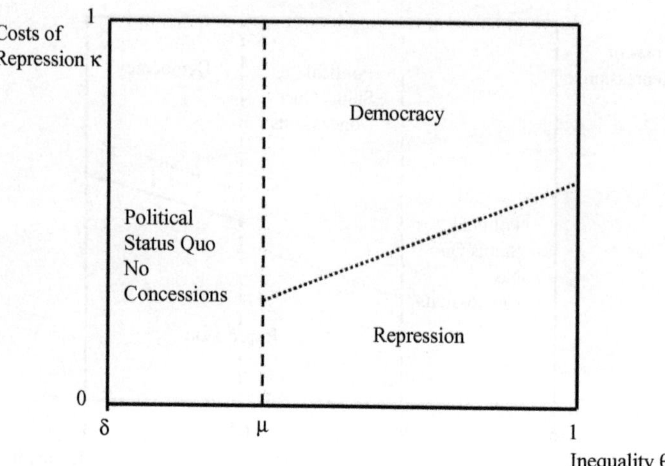

Figure 6.6. Democracy or Repression.

probability r. Thus, we allow repression to fail. To do this, we again develop the static extensive-form game model of Section 6 rather than the full-dynamic model. The game tree in Figure 6.7 draws this game. This modification, naturally, does not affect the payoffs from democracy and nondemocracy without repression. Moreover, it does not affect the circumstances under which the elites can stay in power by promising to make policy more pro-citizen. In consequence, the formula for μ^*

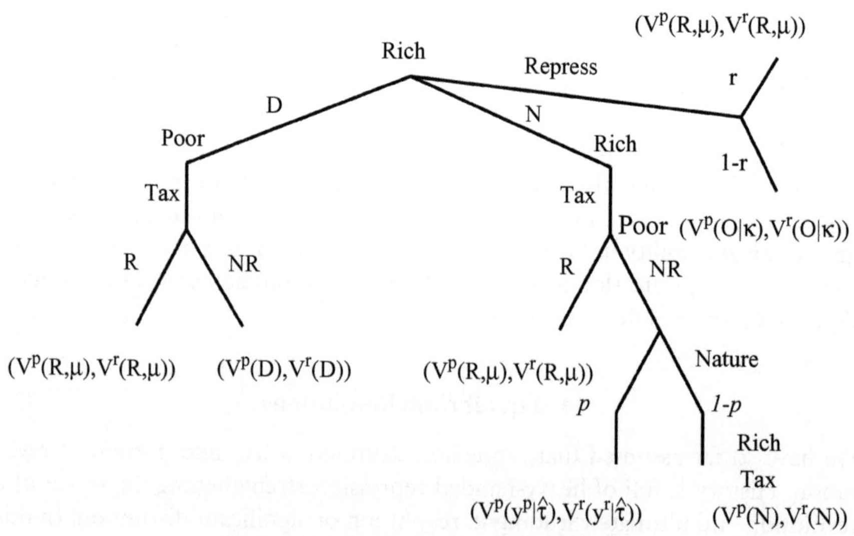

Figure 6.7. Democratization or Revolution.

is unchanged. However, allowing repression to fail does change the payoffs from repression. In particular, the value functions from repression are now given by:

$$V^p(O \mid \kappa) = (1-r)(1-\kappa)y^p + r\frac{(1-\mu)\bar{y}}{1-\delta} \quad \text{and}$$

$$V^r(O \mid \kappa) = (1-r)(1-\kappa)y^r$$

That is, with probability r, repression in the state fails and there will be revolution. In this case, both parties receive their payoffs from a revolution.

This changes the cutoff values for the cost of repression in an obvious way. More specifically, let $\hat{\kappa}(r)$ be the threshold that makes the elites indifferent between repression and redistribution. Thus:

$$V^r(O \mid \hat{\kappa}(r)) = V^r(N, \tau^N = \hat{\tau})$$

or, in other words:

$$\hat{\kappa}(r) = -\frac{r}{1-r} + \frac{p}{(1-r)\theta}\left[\delta C(\hat{\tau}) - \hat{\tau}\,(\delta-\theta)\right] \tag{6.29}$$

Next, define the threshold for the elites to be indifferent between repression and democratization as:

$$V^r(O \mid \tilde{\kappa}(r)) = V^r(D)$$

or, more explicitly:

$$\tilde{\kappa}(r) = -\frac{r}{1-r} + \frac{1}{(1-r)\theta}\left[\delta C(\tau^P) - \tau^P\,(\delta-\theta)\right] \tag{6.30}$$

where we index the threshold values by r. Clearly, $\hat{\kappa}(r) < \hat{\kappa}$ and $\tilde{\kappa}(r) < \tilde{\kappa}$, where $\hat{\kappa}$ and $\tilde{\kappa}$ are defined by (6.9) and (6.10). When it is possible that repression will fail, it has to be even cheaper for it to be optimal for the elites.

The fact that these cut-off values depend on the probability that repression will fail does not radically change the analysis, however. In particular, we can characterize the equilibria in this game with the following proposition, which is similar to Proposition 6.2. The main difference is that in the cases where the elites choose to repress, there is a revolution with probability r.

We now have the following result:

Proposition 6.6: *There is a unique subgame perfect equilibrium $\{\tilde{\sigma}^r, \tilde{\sigma}^p\}$ in the game described in Figure 6.7, and it is such that:*

- *If $\theta \leq \mu$, then the revolution constraint does not bind and the elites can stay in power without repressing, redistributing or democratizing.*
- *If $\theta > \mu$, then the revolution constraint binds. In addition, let μ^* be defined by (6.6) and $\hat{\kappa}(r)$ and $\tilde{\kappa}(r)$ be defined by (6.29) and (6.30). Then:*
  (1) If $\mu \geq \mu^*$ and $\kappa \geq \hat{\kappa}(r)$, then repression is relatively costly and the elites redistribute income to avoid a revolution.
  (2) If $\mu < \mu^*$ and $\kappa < \tilde{\kappa}(r)$ or $\kappa \geq \tilde{\kappa}(r)$ and (6.7) does not hold, or if $\mu \geq \mu^*$ and $\kappa < \hat{\kappa}(r)$, then the elites use repression. With probability r, repression fails and a revolution takes place.
  (3) If $\mu < \mu^*$, (6.7) holds, and $\kappa \geq \tilde{\kappa}(r)$, then concessions are insufficient to avoid a revolution and repression is relatively costly so the elites democratize.

This extension shows how equilibrium revolutions can emerge as a calculated risk by the elites to avoid democratization. It also predicts that revolutions are more likely when the society is highly unequal, so that despite the risk of a revolution, the elites choose repression rather than democratization.

15. Conclusion

In this chapter we built our basic model of democratization. To do this, we discussed in general terms why it is that political institutions, not simply political power, are important. We showed that to understand the role that political institutions play, we have to recognize the explicitly dynamic aspects of people's calculations. Institutions matter because they influence the future allocation of de jure political power; political actors wish to control and change institutions because they want to lock in their current political power. Because institutions influence the allocation of future political power, they also provide commitment – an aspect of institutions that is key to our theory.

We derived some basic predictions about the factors that lead to democracy under the working assumption that once created, democracy consolidates. So, when do democratizations occur? One important factor could be increasing inter-group inequality. We showed that democracy arises when inequality is sufficiently high that the disenfranchised want to contest power but not so high that the elites find it attractive to use repression. Consider a cross-section of societies. With low inequality, we would tend not to observe democracy. At higher levels of inequality, we would still not observe democracy because nondemocracies can maintain their power by engaging in temporary policy concessions to defuse potential challenges. As inequality gets even higher, we observe democracy. Even though the elites in a nondemocracy would like to use policy concessions to stay in power, current concessions in the absence of promised future concessions are not sufficient to stave off a revolution. However, if the elites maintain their monopoly of power, they cannot credibly promise such future concessions; thus, they have to give away their power – democratize – to avoid a revolution. However, as inequality gets even higher, democracy starts to become threatening for the elites because they will face highly adverse policies such as punitive rates of redistribution if they democratize. In consequence, repression begins to be attractive. Democratization is, therefore, not monotonically increasing in inter-group inequality, and we expect an inverse-U–shaped relationship between inequality and democracy, with democracy happening at intermediate levels of inequality.

Nevertheless, inter-group inequality is only part of the story, and we began to see how other factors influence the creation of democracy. For instance, we saw that the power of the elites in nondemocracy, and perhaps their ability to manipulate the form of democracy, can influence democratization. As we continue to develop our analysis, many other factors will enter this picture. There are important roles for the form that the elites hold their wealth; there are roles for the extent of globalization and the evolution of the international economy; and there is a key role for the middle class.

The analysis of this chapter suggests that there are interesting dynamic relationships between inequality and democracy, aspects of which we investigated in Acemoglu and Robinson (2000a, 2002). There we showed how rising inequality could – by tightening the revolution constraint – initially force the elites to democratize. After democracy is created, its redistributive nature could interact with the process of capital accumulation to lead to a subsequent fall in inequality. Thus, these papers showed how an endogenous process of capital accumulation, inequality, and democratization could account for the Kuznets curve like patterns of inequality discussed in Chapter 3.

Although it is not the main focus of our research, it is useful to briefly consider whether democratization promotes efficiency. Recall from Chapter 4 that the most useful way to discuss this is in terms of total surplus. If we simply used the Pareto criterion we would not be able to compare democracy with nondemocracy. In democracy, the citizens are better off; in nondemocracy, the elites are better off. The Pareto criterion cannot rank the two sets of institutions. However, we can make more progress with total surplus. Taking the simplest model in which the only type of policy is redistributive taxation, it is immediate that when repression is not used, total surplus is higher with nondemocracy. Redistribution, because it is costly, simply reduces total income and thus surplus. Because the elites do not support redistribution and they get their way in nondemocracy, democratization leads to a less efficient outcome. This conclusion is partly the result of the simplified model we used to communicate the basic ideas. First, if redistribution takes the form of investment in public goods rather than fiscal redistribution, the elites will wish to undersupply public goods (whereas the citizens wish to oversupply them). When there is inequality, the ideal point of neither coincides with the surplus-maximizing level of provision. In this case, democratization may increase efficiency by increasing the supply of public goods. Second, once nondemocracies stay in power by using repression, democracy begins to look more attractive from the efficiency point of view. Repression wastes resources simply to affect the distribution of resources between the elites and the citizens. In this case, democracy may be efficient even when redistributive taxation causes substantial distortions.

7 Coups and Consolidation

1. Introduction

So far, we studied situations in which democracy once created persists indefinitely – there are no reversals in the march toward democracy. The reality is quite different, however. There are many instances in which countries become less democratic and democratic regimes are overthrown by military coups, reverting to dictatorship.

The recent history of many Latin American countries is particularly marred by oscillations in and out of democracy. In Argentina, for example, universal male suffrage became effective in 1912, but it was soon overthrown by a coup in 1930 (see Chapter 1). Democracy was reinstated in 1946 but fell to a coup in 1955, re-created again in 1973, subverted again in 1976, and finally reinstalled in 1983. In between, several semidemocratic regimes fell to coups in 1943, 1962, and 1966. Why are there coups against democracy? Why has mass democracy been durable in many Northern European countries, and why has it been so difficult to consolidate this set of political institutions in less developed countries such as those in Latin America?

This chapter provides a framework for analyzing coups against democracy and then combines those ideas with the models developed in Chapter 6 to build a framework to analyze the creation and consolidation of democracy, as well as potential switches between democracy and nondemocracy.

In building our theory of coups, we emphasize the same economic and political incentives that featured prominently in understanding the creation of democracy. So far, we have emphasized that in democratic societies, the majority of the citizens are able to alter policies in their favor and against the interests of the elites. This makes the citizens pro-democratic while simultaneously giving the elites an incentive to oppose democracy. These contrasting incentives determine when and how democracy emerges. The same basic forces also determine the incentives for coups. Because the elites prefer nondemocracy to democracy, they may – under certain circumstances – support a coup against democracy that would lead to policies more favorable to themselves in the future.

Why undertake a coup rather than demand more pro-elite policies? The answer is the same as in the discussion about transitions to democracy: the elites not only care about policy today but also about policy in the future and, in democracy, future policies are decided by the median voter, who is not a member of the elite. Therefore, democracy can promise policies today to appease the elites but cannot commit to pro-elite policies in the future, especially if the political power that the elites have is transitory. Hence, a change in political institutions again emerges as a way of shaping future policies by changing the allocation of (de jure) political power.

One result of our analysis is that coups are more likely in societies where there is greater inequality between the elites and the citizens. The amount of redistribution away from the elites is increasing in the degree of inequality. Therefore, in an unequal society, the elites have more to gain by changing the regime than in a more equal society. As usual, whether this claim maps into a statement about inequality as conventionally measured depends on the identity of the elites and the citizens.

When we combine our theory of coups with our model of democratization, we obtain a dynamic framework that allows equilibrium democratizations and coups. In this framework, highly unequal societies may experience frequent switches between democracy and dictatorship. In nondemocracy, the citizens have much to gain by challenging the system, leading to frequent democratizations; in democracy, the elites are unhappy because of the high degree of redistribution and, in consequence, may undertake coups against the democratic regime. This insight suggests a reason why democracy has been relatively difficult to consolidate in Latin America, where many societies have significant economic inequality.

Our analysis also reveals a useful distinction between fully consolidated and semiconsolidated democracies. We say that a democracy is fully consolidated when there is never any effective coup threat. OECD countries are examples of fully consolidated democracies. An unconsolidated democracy is one that falls prey to coups. A semiconsolidated democracy can prevent coups, but it does so by changing the equilibrium policies from those that would have obtained in the absence of the coup threat. Therefore, semiconsolidated democracies live under the shadow of a coup, which is different from the situation in fully consolidated democracies where voters and parties can effectively ignore the threat of a coup in making their policy choices.

Another interesting result is a nonmonotonic relationship between inequality and income redistribution. Higher inequality typically leads to a greater amount of redistribution (with the caveats discussed in Chapter 4). However, in a model where there may be coups, highly unequal societies oscillate, between democracy and dictatorship, and thus do not redistribute as much as less unequal societies.

Also of interest is that in consolidated democracies, because the threat of coups is not important, there is little or no variability in the amount of redistribution. In contrast, highly unequal societies are either semiconsolidated or unconsolidated. In unconsolidated regimes, fiscal policy is more volatile because as a society fluctuates between different political regimes, the amount of fiscal redistribution changes. In semiconsolidated democracies, there are no equilibrium coups, but the amount of redistribution fluctuates to prevent coups from taking place. This pattern is consistent with the evidence presented by Gavin and Perotti (1997) that fiscal policy in Latin America is more variable than in Europe.

There is a major academic debate on the issue of how to define democratic consolidation and it leads back to the question of whether the Schumpeterian definition of democracy is the correct one. Linz and Stepan (1996) state that

> . . . we mean by a consolidated democracy a political situation in which . . . democracy has become "the only game in town." Behaviorally, democracy has become the only game in town when no significant political groups seriously attempt to overthrow the democratic regime. (p. 5)

Nevertheless, despite providing this initial definition, Linz and Stepan – in line with most of the recent political science literature – go on to add a number of other conditions that must be satisfied for a democracy to be consolidated. To be a consolidated democracy, a country must have:

> a state . . . if a functioning state exists, five other interconnected and mutually reinforcing conditions must also exist or be crafted for a democracy to be consolidated. First, the conditions must exist for the development of a free and lively civil society. Second, there must be a relatively autonomous and valued political society. Third, there must be a rule of law. . . . Fourth, there must be a state bureaucracy that is usable. . . . Fifth, there must be an institutionalized economic society. (p. 7)

The debate on consolidation revolves around what should be added or subtracted from lists like this (for which adjectives should be added to the word "democracy," see Collier and Levitsky 1997). Clearly, on this basis, many of the regimes that we would consider democratic are not consolidated (see Philip 2003 on Latin America, where there are probably no consolidated democracies in these terms). Although Linz and Stepan's initial definition is consistent with our approach, the subsequent conditions they impose are not.

Our use of the word *consolidation* instead builds on our Schumpetarian definition of democracy. As we argued before, this seems the natural place to start in building a theory of democracy, and this view echoes that of Schedler (1998) that:

> The term "democratic consolidation" should refer to expectations of regime continuity – and nothing else. Accordingly, the concept of a "consolidated democracy" should describe a democratic regime that relevant observers expect to last well into the future – and nothing else. (p. 103)

2. Incentives for Coups

We now consider a society in which democracy has been created and the preferences of the median voter determine the tax rate. We continue to use our two-group model and associate the elites with the rich and the citizens with the poor. The median voter in democracy is, therefore, a poor agent. In contrast to our previous analysis, however, we now consider the possibility that democracy may not last forever and, in fact, there may be a coup against democracy. Because of the pro-citizen policies – for example, income redistribution implied by democratic politics – in democracy, the citizens are relatively well off and the elites are worse off. This reasoning suggests that the greatest threat against democracy comes from the elites. Therefore, we model coups by focusing on the incentives of the elites to reduce redistribution by moving away from democracy to nondemocracy.

Many coups, especially in Latin America, had reducing redistribution as one of their major objectives and, in most cases, proceeded to reduce redistribution and change the income distribution significantly (see the evidence discussed in Chapter 3). Given that coups are generally undertaken by the military, our approach presumes that for various reasons, the military represents the interests of the elites more than those of the citizens. We believe this is a reasonable first pass; nevertheless, in practice, the objectives of the military are not always perfectly aligned with those of a single group and may have an important impact on the survival of democracy. Incorporating the role of the military in democratic consolidation into formal models of politics is a major area for future research, and we return to this topic briefly in the conclusion of the book.

In this chapter, we simply take as given the possibility that, at some cost, the elites can control the military and mount a coup against democracy, and we investigate the circumstances under which they would like to do so. From a modeling point of view, the interesting observation is that there is a parallel between the reasons of the citizens to want democracy and the reasons of the elites to want nondemocracy. Recall that the citizens demand a credible commitment to future pro-majority policies, and, therefore, a transition to democracy (and the elites were forced to give it to them) because they care about polices and social choices in the future as well as today and they only have temporary de facto political power. Similar reasoning applies in the case of transitions from democracy to nondemocracy. The elites want less pro-citizen policies, and they temporarily have political power to secure them. However, they care about future policies as well, and they know that once their temporary de facto power goes away, democracy will reintroduce the policies that it favors, such as higher taxes and income redistribution. Therefore, the way for the elites to secure the policies they prefer in the future as well as today is to change political institutions toward those that give them more de jure power – that is, a move from democracy toward nondemocracy.

There is much evidence that democrats would like to make concessions to the elites and the military to avoid coups, but the effectiveness of these is undermined by their lack of credibility. Nordlinger (1977) notes:

> . . . the military have intervened despite budgetary increases designed to stave off a coup, as in the 1973 coup against President Allende of Chile. Allende was overthrown despite military salary increases which were greater than those for equivalent civilian grades, better fringe benefits, and the purchase of additional equipment.[1] (p. 71)

There is one difference between the way we are modeling the transition from nondemocracy to democracy and the transition to nondemocracy: in the first case, the citizens had the option to undertake a revolution, and the elites created a democracy to prevent it. Here, the elites actually use their political power to mount a coup and change the system. This may appear like an asymmetry, but it is not essential to our results. We adopt this particular way of modeling transitions to and from democracy because we believe it provides a good approximation to reality: in most instances, democracy resulted from the elites democratizing, whereas the move from democracy to dictatorship is almost never consensual.

3. A Static Model of Coups

To model coups against democracy, consider the basic two-class model of Chapter 4, augmented to consider the possibility that the elites can mount a costly coup. We make identical assumptions about the agents and their incomes but now allow for costs due to coups. In particular, we have:

$$\hat{y}^i = \zeta \iota (S)\, y^i + (1 - \zeta) \left((1 - \tau)\, y^i + (\tau - C(\tau))\, \bar{y}\right) \tag{7.1}$$

where we use the convention that $\zeta = 0$ denotes no coup and $\zeta = 1$ denotes a coup. The notation $\iota(S)$ is the cost due to coup in state S. We model the costs of coups in exactly the same way as we modeled the costs of revolution and repression – a fraction of income gets destroyed. As in the static model in the previous chapter, we simply focus on the state where the coup is a threat and, hence, we suppress the notation for S. There are no costs if there is no coup; thus, if $\zeta = 0$, then $\iota = 1$. The relevant cost, therefore, is the value of ι when $\zeta = 1$, which we denote by $1 - \varphi$ where $0 < \varphi < 1$.

Figure 7.1 shows the game we use to analyze coups. Initially, because we are in a democracy, the median voter sets a tax rate, τ^D. If there is no threat of a coup from the elites, the citizens set their most preferred tax rate, τ^p, as given by (4.11). This results in payoffs $V^p(D)$ and $V^r(D)$, given by (6.4). Whether the elites mount a coup depends on the continuation value in democracy and nondemocracy. We allow the tax rate initially chosen by the citizens to be different from τ^p because

[1] For other examples, see Schmitter (1971, p. 484) and Cox (1976, pp. 207–8).

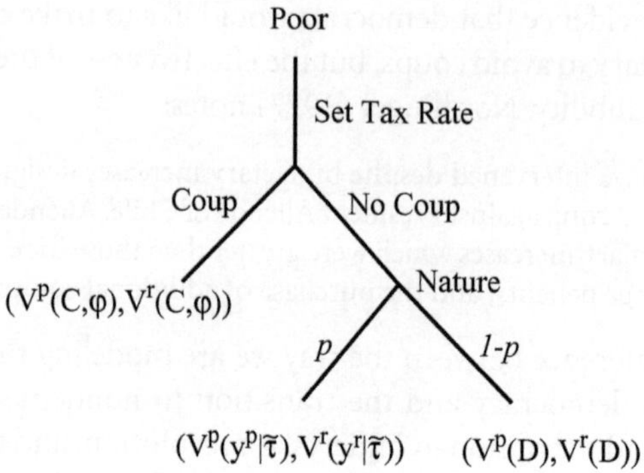

Figure 7.1. The Coup Game.

of the threat of a coup. After this, the elites decide whether to undertake the coup. If they do, the society switches to nondemocracy and the elites set the tax rate. Naturally, they choose their most preferred tax rate, $\tau^N = \tau^r$. As a result, the game ends with respective payoffs for the citizens and the elites[2]:

$$V^p(C,\varphi) = (1-\varphi)y^p \quad \text{and} \quad V^r(C,\varphi) = (1-\varphi)y^r \qquad (7.2)$$

Alternatively, if the elites decide not to undertake a coup, the political system remains democratic. In this case, nature moves one more time and determines whether the median voter – the politically decisive agent in democracy – gets to reset the tax rate from that promised by the citizens in the previous stage. As in our simple model of democratization, this captures the notion that we model in greater detail in the next section: a regime (even a democratic regime) cannot credibly commit to future taxes. More specifically, nature determines with probability p that the tax promised, denoted $\tilde{\tau}$, remains and the citizens and the elites receive values $V\left(y^p \mid \tau^D = \tilde{\tau}\right)$ and $V\left(y^r \mid \tau^D = \tilde{\tau}\right)$ where, as usual:

$$V\left(y^r \mid \tau^D = \tilde{\tau}\right) = y^p + \tilde{\tau}\left(\bar{y} - y^p\right) - C(\tilde{\tau})\bar{y} \quad \text{and}$$
$$V\left(y^r \mid \tau^D = \tilde{\tau}\right) = y^r + \tilde{\tau}\left(\bar{y} - y^r\right) - C(\tilde{\tau})\bar{y}$$

If, on the other hand, nature allows democracy to reset the tax, the median voter chooses a new tax rate, denoted by $\bar{\tau}^D$, leading to the values $V^p(D)$ and $V^r(D)$.

[2] We could write these values as $V^p(C,\varphi,\tau^N = \tau^r)$ and $V^r(C,\varphi,\tau^N = \tau^r)$ to emphasize that after a coup the elites get to set the tax rate and choose their ideal point. However, because it is immediate that $\tau^N = \tau^r$ in any subgame perfect equilibrium, we suppress this notation. Similar considerations apply to the values $V^p(D,\tau^D = \tilde{\tau},\bar{\tau}^D = \tau^p)$ and $V^r(D,\tau^D = \tilde{\tau},\bar{\tau}^D = \tau^p)$, where with probability $1-p$ the citizens choose the tax rate again and set $\bar{\tau}^D$. We also suppress the argument $\bar{\tau}^D = \tau^p$ from these value functions.

Therefore, the values resulting from a promise of less redistribution, only at the rate $\tilde{\tau}$, by the citizens in democracy are $V^p(D, \tau^D = \tilde{\tau})$ and $V^r(D, \tau^D = \tilde{\tau})$, such that:

$$V^p(D, \tau^D = \tilde{\tau}) = y^p + p(\tilde{\tau}(\bar{y} - y^p) - C(\tilde{\tau})\bar{y}) + (1 - p)(\tau^p(\bar{y} - y^p) - C(\tau^p)\bar{y}) \tag{7.3}$$

$$V^r(D, \tau^D = \tilde{\tau}) = y^r + p(\tilde{\tau}(\bar{y} - y^r) - C(\tilde{\tau})\bar{y}) + (1 - p)(\tau^p(\bar{y} - y^r) - C(\tau^p)\bar{y})$$

These expressions take into account that with probability $1 - p$, the citizens get to reset the tax, in which case they are unconstrained and choose their most preferred tax rate, $\bar{\tau}^D = \tau^p$.

We can now characterize the subgame perfect equilibrium of this game by backward induction. Essentially, the game has the same structure as our static democratization game in Chapter 6. The crucial issues are whether undertaking a coup is in the interest of the elites and whether the citizens can prevent a coup by promising concessions (in this case, to redistribute less toward themselves). The strategies are $\sigma^r = \{\zeta(\cdot), \tau^N\}$ and $\sigma^p = \{\tau^D, \bar{\tau}^D\}$. The actions of the citizens, who play first, consist initially of a tax rate $\tau^D \in [0, 1]$; also, if there is no coup and nature allows the tax rate to be reset, where we again use the notation $\nu = 1$, another tax rate $\bar{\tau}^D \in [0, 1]$. Here, the superscript D again indicates democracy. The actions of the elites are a coup decision $\zeta : [0, 1] \to \{0, 1\}$, where $\zeta(\tau^D)$ is the coup choice when the median voter sets the tax rate $\tau^D \in [0, 1]$, and if $\zeta = 1$, a decision about what tax rate to set, which we denote $\tau^N \in [0, 1]$. Then, a subgame perfect equilibrium is a strategy combination $\{\tilde{\sigma}^r, \tilde{\sigma}^p\}$, such that $\tilde{\sigma}^p$ and $\tilde{\sigma}^r$ are best responses to each other in all proper subgames.

Whether a coup is attractive for the elites given the status quo depends on whether the coup constraint, $V^r(C, \varphi) > V^r(D)$, binds. This states that a coup is more attractive than living under an unconstrained democracy. This coup constraint can be expressed as:

$$(1 - \varphi)y^r > y^r + (\tau^p(\bar{y} - y^r) - C(\tau^p)\bar{y})$$

or

$$\varphi < \frac{1}{\theta}(\delta C(\tau^p) - \tau^p(\delta - \theta)) \tag{7.4}$$

When this constraint does not bind, democracy is not redistributive enough, or coups are sufficiently costly that the elites never find a coup profitable. In this case, we refer to democracy as fully consolidated: there is never any effective threat against the stability of democracy. From (7.4), we can derive a critical level of the cost of a coup, denoted $\hat{\varphi}$, such that if $\varphi \geq \hat{\varphi}$ democracy is fully consolidated. This satisfies:

$$\hat{\varphi} = \frac{1}{\theta}\left(\delta C(\tau^P) - \tau^P(\delta - \theta)\right) \tag{7.5}$$

In contrast, when this constraint binds, democracy is not fully consolidated: if the citizens do not take an action, there will be a coup along the equilibrium path. The action that the citizens can take is to reduce the tax rate. The problem, however, is that they cannot perfectly commit to doing so because of the possibility of resetting the tax once the coup threat has subsided. Considering this possibility, the value to the elites of the citizens setting a tax rate of $\tilde{\tau}$ is $V^r(D, \tau^D = \tilde{\tau})$. This strategy of promising less distribution prevents the coup only if this value is greater than the return to the elites following a coup; that is, $V^r(D, \tau^D = \tilde{\tau}) \geq V^r(C, \varphi)$. In other words, only if:

$$y^r + p(\tilde{\tau}(\bar{y} - y^r) - C(\tilde{\tau})\bar{y}) + (1 - p)(\tau^P(\bar{y} - y^r) - C(\tau^P)\bar{y}) \geq (1 - \varphi)y^r$$

We can now define a threshold value for the cost of a coup, φ^*, such that when $\varphi < \varphi^*$, the promise of limited distribution by the citizens is not sufficient to dissuade the elites from a coup. Of course, the most attractive promise that the citizens can make to the elites is to stop redistribution away from them entirely – that is, $\tilde{\tau} = 0$ – therefore, we must have that at φ^*, $V^r(D, \tau^D = 0) = V^r(C, \varphi^*)$. Solving this equality gives the threshold value φ^* as:

$$\varphi^* = \frac{1 - p}{\theta}\left(\delta C(\tau^P) - \tau^P(\delta - \theta)\right) \tag{7.6}$$

Given this discussion, we can summarize the subgame perfect equilibrium of this game as follows:

Proposition 7.1: *There is a unique subgame perfect equilibrium $\{\tilde{\sigma}^r, \tilde{\sigma}^P\}$ in the game described in Figure 7.1. Let $\hat{\varphi}$ and φ^* be defined by (7.5) and (7.6). Then, in this unique equilibrium, we have:*

- *If $\varphi \geq \hat{\varphi}$, then democracy is fully consolidated and the citizens set their preferred tax rate $\tau^P > 0$ as given by (4.11).*
- *If $\varphi \in [\varphi^*, \hat{\varphi})$, then democracy is semiconsolidated. The citizens set a tax rate $\tau^D = \tilde{\tau}$ where $\tilde{\tau} \leq \tau^P$ such that $V^r(D, \tau^D = \tilde{\tau}) = V^r(C, \varphi)$.*
- *If $\varphi < \varphi^*$, then democracy is unconsolidated. There is a coup and the elites come to power and set their most preferred tax rate, $\tau^N = \tau^r$.*

The analysis shows how equilibrium coups can happen as a way for the elites to limit redistribution in the future. Notably, coups happen (when $\varphi < \varphi^*$) precisely because democracy has a limited potential to commit to low redistribution in the future. Then, the elites use their current (and temporary) political power to change political institutions so as to reduce future redistribution. The parallel to the discussion of democratization is obvious: again, equilibrium changes in political institutions happen as a way of regulating the future allocation of political power. There is also a parallel between repression and coups – both use force to avoid democracy, but they do so starting in different political states. This is why the comparative statics of coups are similar to those for repression.

The distinction between fully and semiconsolidated democracies is useful. Democracy is fully consolidated when the coup threat is never present, democracy is not really challenged, and the citizens can set their most preferred (unconstrained) tax rate, τ^p. A semiconsolidated democracy, on the other hand, would fall prey to a coup if it set the tax rate τ^p. It can only survive by making concessions to the elites to dissuade them from mounting a coup. Empirically, this notion of semiconsolidated democracy may help us explain some otherwise puzzling behavior: Wantchekon (1999), for example, argues that in El Salvador the parties representing the majority of citizens tried in the 1990s to reduce the amount of redistribution they offered in elections for fear of inducing a coup.

It is interesting to contrast our analysis with the claim of Przeworski (1991) that consolidated democracy necessitates that all groups, even the previous elites, have a sufficiently large chance of being in power. As Przeworski (1991) put it:

> . . . compliance depends on the probability of winning within the democratic institutions. A particular actor . . . will comply if the probability it attaches to being victorious in democratic competition . . . is greater than some minimum. . . . Democracy will evoke generalized compliance when all the relevant political forces have some specific minimum probability of doing well under the particular system of institutions. (pp. 30–1)

According to this argument, for democracy to be stable, all groups must have a sufficient chance of wielding power. If any group is completely excluded, they will be tempted to fight for power. This idea is widely accepted by political scientists (e.g., Weingast 1997). Colomer (2000, p. 10) reiterated this view when he wrote that "the establishment of democracy appears as a conventional agreement on new rules of the political game. Agreement is possible because democracy gives different actors reasonable expectations to gain or share power in some undetermined future."

In contrast, in our model of democracy, the elites can never win power because policies always cater to the preference of the median voter. However, this does not mean that the elites cannot get what they want in a democracy because even when they have no de jure power, they may have de facto power. For example, in a situation in which democracy is semiconsolidated, the policies of the citizens cater to the elites despite the fact that the elites do not form the government. Indeed, this is ironic because, according to Przeworski, if the elites cannot form a government, they will try to mount a coup and, hence, democracy is not consolidated. Yet, if they can overthrow the system by force, then they must have effective de facto power; this is exactly the situation in which they will be able to get what they want from the government without having to overthrow it. When the elites do not have de facto power, they do not get what they want from democracy but neither are they able to mount a coup. Przeworski's claim, therefore, is false in our model.

We now consider the comparative statics of coups with respect to inequality. First, we can implicitly define a critical threshold for inequality, $\tilde{\theta}$:

$$\varphi = \frac{1}{\tilde{\theta}} \left(\delta C(\tau^p(\tilde{\theta})) - \tau^p(\tilde{\theta})(\delta - \tilde{\theta}) \right)$$

such that when $\theta \leq \tilde{\theta}$, the coup constraint, (7.4), will not bind. In other words, this is the threshold level of inequality, such that when the inequality is less than this level, democracy is fully consolidated.

Next, using the definition of φ^*, we can determine $\bar{\theta}$ such that:

$$\varphi = \frac{1-p}{\bar{\theta}} \left(\delta C(\tau^p(\bar{\theta})) - \tau^p(\bar{\theta})(\delta - \bar{\theta}) \right)$$

Democracy is semiconsolidated when $\theta \leq \bar{\theta}$. Moreover, it is straightforward to check that $\bar{\theta} > \tilde{\theta}$. This discussion leads to the following corollary:

Corollary 7.1: *Consider a society with a fixed φ and p, and inequality given by θ. Then, there exist $\bar{\theta}$ and $\tilde{\theta} < \bar{\theta}$ such that*

- *When $\theta \leq \tilde{\theta}$, democracy is fully consolidated and the equilibrium tax rate is always τ^p.*
- *When $\theta \in (\tilde{\theta}, \bar{\theta}]$, democracy is semiconsolidated. It sets the tax rate $\tilde{\tau}$ so as to prevent a coup in this case.*
- *When $\theta > \bar{\theta}$, democracy is unconsolidated. There is a coup and the elites come to power and set the tax rate $\tau^N = \tau^r$.*

This analysis shows that coups tend to happen in more unequal societies. In less but still fairly unequal societies, democracy is semiconsolidated and survives only by making concessions to the elites in the form of lower taxes. The intuition for why inequality matters for coups is straightforward: coups happen in this model as a way for the elites to reduce future redistribution. Democracy is more redistributive when there is more inequality and, hence, more costly for the elites. Coups, therefore, become more attractive for them in an unequal society.

These comparative statics are consistent with the evidence in Chapter 3, which discussed a cross-country relationship between measures of inequality and democracy with more democratic societies tending to have lower inequality. In the previous chapter, we suggested that this might be because in more equal societies, repression was less attractive; thus, elites were more likely to create democracy.

Now we can see that once democracy is created in a more egalitarian society, it is more likely to consolidate.

4. A Dynamic Model of the Creation and Consolidation of Democracy

Our analysis so far treated democratization and consolidation of democracy separately. In particular, our simplifying assumption in analyzing democratization was that, once created, democracy is fully consolidated and is never challenged. In contrast, we saw how the elites may have an interest in reversing democracy to reduce redistribution away from themselves. How does the analysis change when agents realize that democracy can be reversed?

As was the case in the analyses in Chapter 6, we want to move away from the static structure of the game analyzed in the previous section in which the inability to commit to future actions was modeled by assuming a probability of the promised tax rate being reset.

Most important, the static model of the previous section does not enable an analysis of how equilibrium oscillations between different regimes can emerge. To deal with these issues, we revisit the infinite-horizon model first introduced in Chapter 5, and allow revolution, democratization, and coups.

As before, we consider an infinite-horizon model, denoted $G^{\infty}(\beta)$, with a population of size 1 divided into $1 - \delta > 1/2$ poor citizens, with the remaining δ forming a rich elite. Initially, political power is concentrated in the hands of the elites but the median voter is a poor agent. Agents' expected utility at time $t = 0$ is again given by $U^i = E_0 \sum_{t=0}^{\infty} \beta \hat{y}_t^i$. Here, if this is a nondemocracy, post-tax income $\hat{y}_t^i$ is given by (6.8); if this is a democracy, post-tax incomes are given by (7.1).

The collective-action technology via which the citizens can mount a revolution and the payoffs to a revolution are identical to those specified previously. In a democracy, the elites can attempt a coup. After the coup, all agents loses a fraction φ^S of their income, where the threat state is $S = H, L$ and $\varphi^H < \varphi^L$, and the political situation reverts back to the initial status quo with the elites controlling political power. Similar to the analysis of the revolution threat, we assume that in the low-threat state, the coup threat is not active, and we also set $\varphi^L = 1$. The relevant cost, therefore, is the cost to the elites in the state $S = H, \varphi^H = \varphi$, and only in this state will the elites want to mount a coup. We assume that $\Pr(\varphi_t = \varphi) = s$ and that both q and s are less than $1/2$ so that crises that facilitate the exercise of de facto power are relatively rare events.

If a coup is mounted, then $\mu_t = \mu^L$ at first so that there is no immediate revolution. Similarly, if democratization occurs, then democracy starts with the coup cost at 1, implying that democracy has at least some window of opportunity before a coup can occur. Finally, in each nondemocratic period the elites have to decide whether to democratize; if they do, the society becomes a democracy and the median voter, a citizen, sets the tax rate.

The timing of events within a period can be summarized as follows:

1. The state μ_t or φ_t is revealed.
2. The citizens set the tax rate, τ^D, if we are in democracy, and the elites set τ^N otherwise.
3. In a nondemocratic regime, the elites decide whether to repress, ω, or democratize, ϕ. In democracy, they decide whether to mount a coup, ζ. If they democratize or undertake a coup, the party that comes to power decides whether to keep the tax τ set at Stage 2 or to set a new tax rate.
4. If $P = N$ and $\omega = 0$, the citizens decide whether to initiate a revolution, ρ. If there is a revolution, they share the remaining income of the economy. If there is no revolution, the tax rate decided at Stage 2 or 3 gets implemented.
5. Incomes are realized and consumption takes place.

We again characterize the Markov perfect equilibria of this game in which strategies only depend on the current state of the world.[3] The state is either (D, φ^H), (D, φ^L), (N, μ^L), or (N, μ^H), where N denotes elites in power (i.e., nondemocratic regime) and D denotes democracy. Let $\sigma^r = \{\omega(\cdot), \phi(\cdot), \tau^N(\cdot), \zeta(\cdot), \tau^N\}$ be the notation for the actions taken by the elites, and $\sigma^p = \{\rho(\cdot), \tau^D(\cdot), \tau^D\}$ are the actions of the citizens. The notation σ^r consists of a decision to repress $\omega : \{\mu^L, \mu^H\} \rightarrow \{0, 1\}$ or to create democracy $\phi : \{\mu^L, \mu^H\} \rightarrow \{0, 1\}$ when $P = N$, and a tax rate $\tau^N : \{\mu^L, \mu^H\} \rightarrow [0, 1]$ when $\phi = 0$ (i.e., when democracy is not created). Clearly, if $\phi = 0$, P remains at N, and if $\phi = 1$, P switches to D. When $P = D$, the elites make a coup decision that is a function $\zeta : \{\varphi^L, \varphi^H\} \times [0, 1] \rightarrow \{0, 1\}$ where $\zeta(\varphi, \tau^D)$ is the coup decision when the state is φ and the median voter sets the tax rate τ^D. If $\zeta = 1$, then the political state switches to $P = N$ and the elites also get to reset the tax rate, $\tau^N \in [0, 1]$. The actions of the citizens consist of a decision to initiate revolution, $\rho : \{\mu^L, \mu^H\} \times \{0, 1\}^2 \times [0, 1] \rightarrow \{0, 1\}$. Here, $\rho(\mu, \omega, \phi, \tau^N)$ is the revolution decision of the citizens, which is conditioned on the current actions of the elites as well as the state. When $P = D$, the citizens set the tax rate, $\tau^D : \{\varphi^L, \varphi^H\} \rightarrow [0, 1]$.

Then, a Markov perfect equilibrium is a strategy combination, $\{\tilde{\sigma}^r, \tilde{\sigma}^p\}$ such that $\tilde{\sigma}^p$ and $\tilde{\sigma}^r$ are best responses to each other for all μ_t, φ_t, and P. As usual, we characterize the Markov perfect equilibria by writing the appropriate Bellman equations.

Let $V^i(D, \varphi^L)$ be the value of an agent of type $i = p, r$ when there is democracy and when the cost of mounting a coup is φ^L. Similarly, let $V^i(\varphi^H)$ be the value of agent i when the cost is φ^H (in which case there may be a switch to a nondemocratic regime as a result of a coup).

[3] In this chapter, we do not examine non-Markovian equilibria. See Powell (2004) for a study of subgame perfect equilibria in a simplified version of the model presented here.

When the state is (D, φ^L), there are no constraints on the median voter, so he will choose the tax rate $\tau^D = \tau^p$. The returns to the citizens and the elites are:

$$V^i(D, \varphi^L) = y^i + \tau^p(\bar{y} - y^i) - C(\tau^p)\bar{y} + \beta\left[s V^i(\varphi^H) + (1-s) V^i(D, \varphi^L)\right] \tag{7.7}$$

for $i = p, r$ and, as before, $\tau^p(\bar{y} - y^i) - C(\tau^p)\bar{y}$ represents the net amount of redistribution at tax rate τ^p faced by agent i.

Next, consider the state (D, φ^H) in which the poor may set a tax rate different from the one they prefer in an attempt to prevent a coup. Denote the values in the state (D, φ^H) when the tax rate is τ^D by $V^i(D, \varphi^H, \tau^D)$, which are given as:

$$\begin{aligned} V^i(D, \varphi^H, \tau^D) = {} & y^i + \tau^D(\bar{y} - y^i) - C(\tau^D)\bar{y} \\ & + \beta\left[s V^i(D, \varphi^H, \tau^D) + (1-s) V^i(D, \varphi^L)\right] \end{aligned} \tag{7.8}$$

Clearly, $\tau^D(\bar{y} - y^p) - C(\tau^D)\bar{y} \leq \tau^p(\bar{y} - y^p) - C(\tau^p)\bar{y}$ and $\tau^D(\bar{y} - y^r) - C(\tau^D)\bar{y} \geq \tau^p(\bar{y} - y^r) - C(\tau^p)\bar{y}$, for $\tau^D \leq \tau^p$.

After observing the tax rate τ^D, the elites may still decide to mount a coup, so the values in the state (D, φ^H) are not necessarily equal to $V^i(D, \varphi^H, \tau^D)$. Instead, we denote them by $V^i(\varphi^H)$, such that:

$$\begin{aligned} V^r(\varphi^H) &= \max_{\varsigma \in \{0,\}} \left\{\varsigma(V^r(N, \mu^L) - \varphi y^r) + (1-\varsigma) V^r(D, \varphi^H, \tau^D)\right\} \\ V^p(\varphi^H) &= \varsigma(V^p(N, \mu^L) - \varphi y^p) + (1-\varsigma) V^p(D, \varphi^H, \tau^D) \end{aligned} \tag{7.9}$$

where recall that $\varsigma = 1$ implies a coup. The first line of (7.9) says that the value $V^r(\varphi^H)$ for the elites in the high-threat state depends on their own choice about whether to mount a coup. In making this decision, they compare the value from not mounting a coup and accepting a concession of a tax rate of τ^D from the citizens, which is $V^r(D, \varphi^H, \tau^D)$, to the value from mounting a coup. This value is $V^r(N, \mu^L) - \varphi y^r$, which is the value of being in nondemocracy when there is no threat of a revolution, $V^r(N, \mu^L)$, minus the cost of a coup φy^r. The second line states that the value for the citizens in this state, $V^p(\varphi^H)$, also depends on what the elites do. If $\varsigma = 1$, then the citizens find themselves in a nondemocracy and their continuation value is $V^p(N, \mu^L)$, minus the cost of the coup φy^p; whereas if $\varsigma = 0$, there is no coup, democracy persists, and the citizens' value is $V^p(D, \varphi^H, \tau^D)$.

We now derive the *coup constraint*, a generalization of the static coup constraint of the game in the previous section to this dynamic setup. This constraint immediately follows from (7.9) by checking when a coup is attractive, provided that the median voter sets his or her preferred tax rate $\tau^D = \tau^p$. It is, therefore:

$$V^r(N, \mu^L) - \varphi y^r > V^r(D, \varphi^H, \tau^D = \tau^p) \tag{7.10}$$

This coup states that a coup occurs if the gain to the elites of capturing political power and reducing taxation, $V^r(N, \mu^L) - V^r(D, \varphi^H, \tau^D = \tau^p)$, is greater than the cost of the coup, φy^r.

We can now determine a critical value of φ, denoted $\hat{\varphi}$, such that as long as $\varphi \geq \hat{\varphi}$, a coup is never beneficial for the elites, even if the citizens tax at $\tau^D = \tau^p$ in state (D, φ^H). This critical value clearly satisfies inequality (7.10) as an equality with $\tau^D = \tau^p$. Therefore:

$$\hat{\varphi} = \frac{V^r(N, \mu^L) - V^r(D, \varphi^H, \tau^D = \tau^p)}{y^r} \tag{7.11}$$

In words, this equation specifies that the critical threshold is such that the loss of current income for the elites is equivalent to the discounted loss of living forever under democracy with the tax rate most preferred by the citizens, $V^r(D, \varphi^H, \tau^D = \tau^p)$, versus undertaking a coup and switching to a nondemocratic regime, which gives the value $V^r(N, \mu^L)$.

However, (7.11) is not informative unless we obtain expressions for $V^r(N, \mu^L)$ and $V^r(D, \varphi^H, \tau^D = \tau^p)$. The return to the elites of always remaining in democracy with a tax rate $\tau^D = \tau^p$ is simply:

$$V^r(D, \varphi^H, \tau^D = \tau^p) = \frac{y^r + \tau^p(\bar{y} - y^r) - C(\tau^p)\bar{y}}{1 - \beta} \tag{7.12}$$

We next compute the value of nondemocracy to the elites $V^r(N, \mu^L)$. First, with the standard arguments, we have:

$$V^i(N, \mu^L) = y^i + \beta\left[qV^i(N, \mu^H) + (1 - q)V^i(N, \mu^L)\right] \tag{7.13}$$

for $i = p$ or r, where $V^i(N, \mu^H)$ refers to values in nondemocracy when $\mu_t = \mu^H$. In this expression, we already used the fact that when $\mu_t = \mu^L (= 1)$, the elites choose no redistribution in a nondemocratic regime.

Next, because society starts in a nondemocracy, if a coup ever happens, then democratization must have previously arisen. Thus, it is natural to assume that we are in the part of the parameter space where if coups happen and the state moves to $\mu_t = \mu^H$, then following a coup, a redemocratization must take place and, therefore, it must take place again when $\mu_t = \mu^H$. Therefore, we can impose $V^r(N, \mu^H) = V^r(D, \varphi^L)$.

The issue, however, is that once democracy has been reached again, the state (D, φ^H) will also be reached, and we have to make some conjectures about whether there will be another coup. However, the logic of dynamic programming dictates that what conjectures we make about future coups are not important. In other words, we can compute $V^r(N, \mu^L)$ and $V^r(D, \varphi^L)$ in two different ways, with identical implications for the threshold $\hat{\varphi}$. In the first, and possibly more natural way, we assume that once (D, φ^H) has been reached, there will be another coup. The second way looks only at a "one-shot deviation" (see Fudenberg and Tirole 1991, pp. 108–10) and assumes that, even though the elites undertake a coup today, in the future they will never again do so, and democracy would survive even in the state (D, φ^H).

To illustrate the working of the model and this principle, we now derive the critical value $\hat{\varphi}$ using both approaches. Let us start with the first; in that case, the relevant values can be written as:

$$V^r(N, \mu^L) = y^r + \beta\left[qV^r(D, \varphi^L) + (1-q)V^r(N, \mu^L)\right] \tag{7.14}$$

and

$$\begin{aligned} V^r(D, \varphi^L) = {} & y^r + \tau^P(\bar{y} - y^r) - C(\tau^P)\bar{y} \\ & + \beta\left[s(V^r(N, \mu^L) - \varphi y^r) + (1-s)V^r(D, \varphi^L)\right] \end{aligned} \tag{7.15}$$

Notice that (7.14) imposes a switch to democracy in the state (N, μ^H) for reasons discussed previously (i.e., we are in the part of the parameter space in which there is an equilibrium switch to democracy). On the other hand, (7.15) imposes that whenever state (D, φ^H) comes, there will be a coup; hence, there is a switch to nondemocracy, giving the value $V^r(N, \mu^L) - \varphi y^r$ to the elites, which takes into account the fact that they incur the cost of coup, φy^r. To solve for $V^r(N, \mu^L)$, we treat (7.14) and (7.15) as two equations in two unknowns, $V^r(N, \mu^L)$ and $V^r(D, \varphi^L)$, which we can solve for $V^r(N, \mu^L)$.

Substituting this into (7.10), using (7.12), and solving for φ gives the critical value as:

$$\hat{\varphi} = \frac{1}{\theta}\left(\frac{\delta C(\tau^P) - \tau^P(\delta - \theta)}{1 - \beta(1-q)}\right) \tag{7.16}$$

The second method of looking at one-shot deviations is often simpler. In this case, because a coup takes place only once and never again, when democracy is reached, there will never again be a coup despite the fact that the citizens always tax at the rate τ^P. This implies that in (7.14), we have:

$$V^r(D, \varphi^L) = \frac{y^r + \tau^P(\bar{y} - y^r) - C(\tau^P)\bar{y}}{1-\beta}$$

Substituting this into (7.14), we can solve for $V^r(N, \mu^L)$, which gives:

$$V^r(N, \mu^L) = \frac{(1-\beta(1-q))y^r + \beta q(\tau^P(\bar{y}-y^r) - C(\tau^P)\bar{y})}{(1-\beta)(1-\beta(1-q))}.$$

Substituting this into (7.10), using (7.12), and solving for φ gives the same critical value as in (7.16).

When $\varphi \geq \hat{\varphi}$, the coup threat does not play a role and democracy is fully consolidated. The tax rate, $\tau^D = \tau^P$, is always determined by the usual trade-off for the median voter, balancing transfers against the deadweight losses of taxation. Observe that $d\hat{\varphi}/d\theta > 0$, which implies that a more unequal society is less likely to achieve a fully consolidated democracy. This is intuitive because a greater level of inequality makes democracy less attractive for the elites and generalizes results from the static model.

We can next determine the value of the cost of coup, φ^*, such that if $\varphi \geq \varphi^*$, the citizens can stop a coup by setting a low enough tax rate in the state (D, φ^H) (or, conversely, when $\varphi < \varphi^*$, even a policy of setting $\tau^D = 0$ in state φ^H does not stop a coup). Because the lowest tax rate that the citizens can set is $\tau^D = 0$, φ^* is given by $V^r(N, \mu^L) - V^r(D, \varphi^H, \tau^D = 0) = \varphi^* y^r$.

Combining (7.7) and (7.8) and setting $V^r(\varphi^H) = V^r(D, \varphi^H, \tau^D = 0)$, we can calculate the value of always remaining in democracy for the elites. From this, we define:

$$V^r(D, \varphi^H, \tau^D = 0) = \frac{y^r + \beta(1-s)(\tau^P(\bar{y}-y^r) - C(\tau^P)\bar{y})}{1-\beta}$$

as the maximum value that the median voter can credibly commit to give to a member of the elite under democracy.

To solve for $V^r(N, \mu^L)$, we use the one-shot deviation approach again. To do this, we work with (7.14) and substitute $V^r(N, \mu^H) = V^r(D, \varphi^L)$. As before, we assume that a coup is only undertaken once and if there is redemocratization, there is never a coup again. However, the formula for $V^r(N, \mu^L)$ is different because when democracy is re-created after a coup, it will be a democracy in which the median voter sets $\tau^D = 0$ when $\varphi_t = \varphi^H$. Hence:

$$V^r(D, \varphi^L) = \frac{y^r + (1-\beta s)(\tau^P(\bar{y}-y^r) - C(\tau^P)\bar{y})}{1-\beta}$$

Using this in (7.14), we find:

$$V^r(N, \mu^L) = \frac{(1-\beta(1-q))y^r + \beta q(1-\beta s)(\tau^P(\bar{y}-y^r) - C(\tau^P)\bar{y})}{(1-\beta)(1-\beta(1-q))}$$

Therefore, $V^r(\varphi^H) = V^r(N, \mu^L) - \varphi y^r$ implies:

$$\varphi^* = \frac{1}{\theta}\left(\frac{\beta(q+s-1)\left(\tau^P(\delta-\theta) - \delta C(\tau^P)\right)}{1-\beta(1-q)}\right) \tag{7.17}$$

where $\tau^P(\delta-\theta) - \delta C(\tau^P) < 0$ and $q+s-1<0$, so φ^* is decreasing in q and s. If q is high, then a nondemocratic regime following a coup will be short-lived because a revolutionary threat will reoccur quickly. This reduces the expected benefits from a coup. Similarly, if s is high, the coup constraint binds regularly and because in this state the elites pay relatively low taxes, democracy is less costly to them. Also, clearly, $\varphi^* < \hat{\varphi}$.

More important for the focus of this chapter is that $d\varphi^*/d\theta > 0$: higher inequality decreases the threshold φ^* and makes a coup more likely because in an unequal society, the elites lose more under democracy.

If $\varphi \geq \varphi^*$, then democracy is semiconsolidated: the citizens can avoid a coup by reducing the tax rate below τ^P in state (D, φ^H) and setting $\tau^D = \tilde{\tau} \leq \tau^P$ such that:

$$V^r(N, \mu^L) - \varphi y^r = V^r(D, \varphi^H, \tau^D = \tilde{\tau}) \tag{7.18}$$

Although society always remains democratic, the threat of a coup is still important and influences taxes: the tax rate $\tilde{\tau}$ is less than τ^P, which the citizens would have set in the absence of this threat. Now $V^r(D, \varphi^H, \tau^D = \tilde{\tau})$ is solved from the equations:

$$\begin{aligned} V^r(D, \varphi^H, \tau^D = \tilde{\tau}) &= y^r + \tilde{\tau}(\bar{y} - y^r) - C(\tilde{\tau})\bar{y} \\ &\quad + \beta\left[s V^r(D, \varphi^H, \tau^D = \tilde{\tau}) + (1-s) V^r(D, \varphi^L)\right] \end{aligned} \tag{7.19}$$

$$\begin{aligned} V^r(D, \varphi^L) &= y^r + \tau^P(\bar{y} - y^r) - C(\tau^P)\bar{y} \\ &\quad + \beta\left[s V^r(D, \varphi^H, \tau^D = \tilde{\tau}) + (1-s) V^r(D, \varphi^L)\right] \end{aligned}$$

which gives:

$$V^r(D, \varphi^H, \tau^D = \tilde{\tau}) = \frac{y^r + (1-\beta(1-s))\left(\tilde{\tau}(\bar{y} - y^r) - C(\tilde{\tau})\bar{y}\right)}{1-\beta} + \frac{\beta(1-s)\left(\tau^P(\bar{y} - y^r) - C(\tau^P)\bar{y}\right)}{1-\beta}$$

To calculate $V^r(N, \mu^L)$, we again use (7.14). The one-shot deviation approach implies that we should replace $V^r(D, \varphi^L)$ in (7.14) with the value of democracy to the elites when the citizens set the tax rate $\tau^D = \tilde{\tau}$ when $\varphi_t = \varphi^H$ and set

$\tau^D = \tau^p$ when $\varphi_t = \varphi^L$. This value is just $V^r(D, \varphi^L)$, calculated from (7.19):

$$V^r(D, \varphi^L)$$
$$= \frac{y^r + \beta s(\tilde{\tau}(\bar{y} - y^r) - C(\tilde{\tau})\bar{y}) + (1 - \beta s)(\tau^p(\bar{y} - y^r) - C(\tau^p)\bar{y})}{1 - \beta}$$

Using this to solve for $V^r(N, \mu^L)$ from (7.14), we find:

$$V^r(N, \mu^L) = \frac{(1 - \beta(1 - q))y^r + \beta^2 qs(\tilde{\tau}(\bar{y} - y^r) - C(\tilde{\tau})\bar{y})}{(1 - \beta)(1 - \beta(1 - q))} + \frac{\beta q(1 - \beta s)(\tau^p(\bar{y} - y^r) - C(\tau^p)\bar{y})}{(1 - \beta)(1 - \beta(1 - q))},$$

and substituting the results of these calculations into (7.18), we find that the tax rate $\tilde{\tau}$ is given implicitly by the equation:

$$\varphi = \frac{1}{\theta}\left(\frac{(\beta(1 - q - s) - 1)(\tilde{\tau}(\delta - \theta) - \delta C(\tilde{\tau}))}{1 - \beta(1 - q)} + \frac{\beta(q + s - 1)(\tau^p(\delta - \theta) - \delta C(\tau^p))}{1 - \beta(1 - q)}\right)$$

Implicit differentiation shows that $\tilde{\tau}$ is decreasing in θ: $d\tilde{\tau}/d\theta < 0$, so higher inequality reduces the tax rate that is required to prevent a coup.

If $\varphi < \varphi^*$, democracy is unconsolidated; even a strategy of setting $\tau^D = 0$ by the citizens will not prevent a coup. In this case, the society reverts back to a nondemocratic regime when $\varphi_t = \varphi$. The citizens would like to prevent such an outcome, and if they could, they would promise lower tax rates in the future. However, such promises are not credible because future tax rates are determined in future political equilibria; once the threat of coup disappears, the tax rate rises back to τ^p. Forward-looking elites, realizing this, prefer a coup, even though this is a costly outcome for society as a whole.

This discussion generalizes the circumstances described in Section 3 under which coups take place. The concepts of fully and semiconsolidated democracies naturally arise in the dynamic context as well. Nevertheless, now that we have a fully dynamic model, we can integrate the analysis of coups with that of democratizations, which we could not do in the static model.

Consider the state (N, μ^H). If the citizens did not attempt revolution in this state, the elites would stay in power forever and set $\tau^N = 0$, so the citizens would receive utility equal to $y^p/(1 - \beta)$. In contrast, with revolution in state $\mu_t = \mu^H$, they would obtain $V^p(R, \mu^H) = (1 - \mu)\bar{y}/(1 - \delta)(1 - \beta)$, the per-period return from revolution for the infinite future discounted to the present. Recall that revolution is an absorbing state in the sense that once revolution occurs, society stays like that forever and that only the value of μ at the time of a revolution matters. Hence, the per-period return is constant over time (this also implies that in the state $\mu_t = \mu^L (= 1)$, a revolution never occurs). To reduce the number of cases to be considered, we now impose $\theta > \mu$, which implies that when $\mu_t = \mu^H (= \mu)$, the revolution threat is binding.

In case of a revolution, the elites lose everything; that is, $V^r(R, \mu^H) = 0$. They will therefore attempt to prevent it at all costs. They can do this in three different ways. First, they can democratize, $\phi = 1$, giving the citizens their return under democracy, $V^p(D, \varphi^L)$. Second, they can use repression, giving citizens the value $V^p(O, \mu^H \mid \kappa)$, which is identical to the value we derived in the previous chapter. Third, they can choose to maintain political power, $\phi = 0$, but redistribute through taxation. In this case, the elites impose a tax rate τ^N and give the citizens a return $V^p(N, \mu^H, \tau^N)$, where:

$$V^i(N, \mu^H, \tau^N) = y^i + \tau^N \left(\bar{y} - y^i\right) - C(\tau^N)\bar{y} + \beta[q V^i(N, \mu^H, \tau^N) + (1-q) V^i(N, \mu^L)] \tag{7.20}$$

So, agent i receives income y^i from his or her own earnings and also a net income transfer $\tau^N \left(\bar{y} - y^i\right) - C(\tau^N)\bar{y}$. If in the next period we are still in state $\mu_{t+1} = \mu^H$, then redistribution continues. But, if in the next period the economy switches to $\mu_{t+1} = \mu^L$, redistribution stops. This captures the notion that the elites cannot commit to future redistribution unless the future also poses an effective revolution threat. Also, $\tau^N \leq \tau^p$; that is, the elites will not tax themselves at a rate higher than τ^p because this is the rate that maximizes redistribution to a citizen. If this tax rate is not sufficient to stop a revolution, then no tax rate $\tau^N \in [0, 1]$ will do so.

With either democratization or redistribution by the elites, the citizens may still prefer a revolution. Thus, given the actions ϕ and τ^N of the elites, the value to the citizens in the state (N, μ^H) is:

$$V^p(N, \mu^H) = \omega V^p(O, \mu^H \mid \kappa) + (1-\omega) \max_{\rho \in \{0,1\}} \times \left\{\rho V^p(R, \mu^H) + (1-\rho)(\phi V^p(D, \varphi^L) + (1-\phi) V^p(N, \mu^H, \tau^N))\right\}$$

Combining (7.13) and (7.20), we calculate the maximum utility that can be given to the citizens without democratizing. This involves the elites setting the tax rate $\tau^N = \tau^p$ when there is a threat of a revolution so that the continuation value for the citizens is $V^p(N, \mu^H, \tau^N = \tau^p)$. This value satisfies:

$$V^p(N, \mu^H, \tau^N = \tau^p) = \frac{y^p + (1 - \beta(1-q)) \left(\tau^p \left(\bar{y} - y^p\right) - C(\tau^p)\bar{y}\right)}{1-\beta} \tag{7.21}$$

which is, of course, the same as (6.15) derived in the previous chapter. The citizens compare (7.21) to $V^p(R, \mu^H)$. This defines a critical value of μ^H:

$$\mu^* = \theta - (1 - \beta(1-q))\left(\tau^p(\theta - \delta) - (1-\delta)C(\tau^p)\right) \tag{7.22}$$

such that $V^p(N, \mu^H, \tau^N = \tau^p) = V^p(R, \mu^H)$ when $\mu^H = \mu^*$. For $0 < \mu < \mu^*$, a revolution is so attractive for the citizens in state $\mu_t = \mu^H$ that even the maximum amount of redistribution by the elites cannot stop it. Democratization is, therefore, the only option left to the elites. Also:

$$\frac{d\mu^*}{d\theta} = 1 - (1 - \beta(1-q))\frac{d\left(\tau^p(\theta - \delta) - (1-\delta)C(\tau^p)\right)}{d\theta} > 0$$

such that high inequality increases the revolution threshold because the citizens are worse off in a nondemocratic regime. Citizens are now willing to undertake a revolution when the cost of doing so is higher.

For $\mu \geq \mu^*$, democratization can be avoided by redistributing to the citizens in state (μ^H, N). In this case, the tax rate that the elites have to set to avoid a revolution is $\tau^N = \hat{\tau}$, such that $V^p(N, \mu^H, \tau^N = \hat{\tau}) = V^p(R, \mu^H)$, which is decreasing in μ and increasing in θ (i.e., increasing in the level of inequality).

Having determined the conditions under which a nondemocratic regime can stay in power by making concessions and when a democracy is or is not consolidated, it remains to consider the implications of repression. Our assumptions about repression are identical as before so that the payoffs from repression are given by (6.18). Again, there are two situations to consider. If $\mu \geq \mu^*$, then a nondemocratic regime never needs to democratize, in which case repression is used in equilibrium if it is cheaper than making policy concessions. The conditions under which this is so and, indeed, the threshold level κ^* at which the elites are indifferent between promising redistribution at the tax rate $\hat{\tau}$ and repression, are identical to those derived previously. In particular, κ^* is again given by (6.20). If $\mu < \mu^*$, then the elites cannot use concessions to stay in power and they compare the cost of repression to the cost of democracy. In the previous analysis, the cost of democracy was uniquely defined because we assumed that democracy was fully consolidated. However, this is not the case now and the cost of democracy to the elites and, therefore, the attractiveness of repression, depends on the nature of democracy.

If $\varphi \geq \hat{\varphi}$ so that democracy is fully consolidated, then the threshold at which the elites are just indifferent between repression and democratization is $\bar{\kappa}$ given by (6.21). If $\varphi \in [\varphi^*, \hat{\varphi})$, then democracy is partially consolidated and when a coup is threatened, the tax rate is cut. In this case, we can define a threshold level $\kappa(\varphi)$ such that the elites are just indifferent between repressing and creating a semiconsolidated democracy. To see the formula for this, first recall that the value of repression is $V^r(O, \mu^H \mid \kappa)$ given by (6.19) in Chapter 6. The value of being in an unconsolidated democracy is $V^r(D, \varphi^L)$, which satisfies (7.14) and (7.15). Thus, $\kappa(\varphi)$ is such that $V^r(O, \mu^H \mid \kappa(\varphi)) = V^r(D, \varphi^L)$. The higher φ, the more costly a coup, the higher the tax in this state, and the greater the cost of creating democracy to the elites. Hence, $\kappa(\varphi)$ is a strictly increasing function of φ because as φ increases, the burden of democracy increases for the elites and they are more inclined to use repression. Finally, if $\varphi < \varphi^*$, democracy is unconsolidated and we can define a threshold $\check{\kappa}$ such that elites are just indifferent between repressing and creating an unconsolidated democracy.

We restrict attention to the area of the parameter space where democratization prevents revolution; that is, $V^p(D, \varphi^L) \geq V^p(R, \mu^H)$. Because democracy is not necessarily an absorbing state, the value function $V^p(D, \varphi^L)$ takes into account the future possibility of coups. The value to the citizens of a semiconsolidated democracy is higher than that of a democracy subject to coups, so it suffices to ensure that the value to the citizens of an unconsolidated democracy is greater than $V^r(R, \mu^H)$. To derive a formula for the value of a citizen of an unconsolidated democracy, we use (7.7) and (7.13) with $V^p(N, \mu^H) = V^p(D, \varphi^L)$ and $V^p(\varphi^H) = V^p(N, \mu^L)$, giving:

$$V^p(N, \mu^L) = y^p + \beta\left[q V^p(D, \varphi^L) + (1-q) V^p(N, \mu^L)\right]$$

$$V^p(D, \varphi^L) = y^p + \tau^p(\bar{y} - y^p) - C(\tau^p)\bar{y} + \beta\left[s(V^p(N, \mu^L) - \varphi y^p) + (1-s) V^p(D, \varphi^L)\right]$$

which are the same as (7.14) and (7.15) from the point of view of the citizens. Solving for $V^p(D, \varphi^L)$, we find:

$$V^p(D, \varphi^L) = \frac{y^p\left((1-\varphi\beta s)(1-\beta(1-q)) + \beta s\right)}{(1-\beta(1-s))(1-\beta(1-q)) - \beta^2 sq} + \frac{(1-\beta(1-q))(\tau^p(\bar{y} - y^p) - C(\tau^p)\bar{y})}{(1-\beta(1-s))(1-\beta(1-q)) - \beta^2 sq}$$

and the condition $V^p(D, \varphi^L) \geq V^p(R, \mu^H)$ is therefore equivalent to:

$$\frac{(1-\beta+\beta(q+s))(1-\theta)(1-\varphi\beta s)}{1-\beta+\beta(q+s)} + \frac{(1-\beta(1-q))(\tau^p(\theta-\delta) - (1-\delta)C(\tau^p))}{1-\beta+\beta(q+s)} \geq 1-\mu$$

which is a condition on the parameters that we simply assume holds. As with the corresponding condition in Chapter 6, this holds when democracy is sufficiently redistributive. This leads to an interesting trade-off: a highly redistributive democracy leads to political instability, but if the potential for redistribution is too limited, democratization does not prevent a revolution.

We can now establish the following result:

Proposition 7.2: *There is a unique Markov perfect equilibrium* $\{\tilde{\sigma}^r, \tilde{\sigma}^p\}$ *in the game* $G^\infty(\beta)$. *Let* $\hat{\varphi}, \varphi^*, \kappa^*, \bar{\kappa}, \kappa(\varphi)$, *and* $\breve{\kappa}$ *be as defined previously. Then, in this equilibrium:*

- *If* $\mu \geq \mu^*$, *the society remains nondemocratic. When* $\mu_t = \mu^L, \tau^N = \tau^r$ *and there is no redistribution. If* $\kappa < \kappa^*$, *then when* $\mu_t = \mu^H$, *the rich use repression. If* $\kappa \geq \kappa^*$, *then when* $\mu_t = \mu^H, \tau^N = \hat{\tau}$, *such that* $V^p(N, \mu^H, \tau^N = \hat{\tau}) = V^p(R, \mu^H)$.
- *If* $\mu < \mu^*$, *then:*

(1) *If* $\varphi \geq \hat{\varphi}$ *and* $\kappa \geq \bar{\kappa}$, *we are in a fully consolidated democracy. The society switches to democracy the first time* $\mu_t = \mu^H$ *and remains democratic thereafter, and taxes are always given by* $\tau^D = \tau^p$.

(2) *If* $\varphi^* \leq \varphi < \hat{\varphi}$ *and* $\kappa \geq \kappa(\varphi)$, *we are in a semi-consolidated democracy. The society switches to democracy the first time* $\mu_t = \mu^H$ *and remains democratic thereafter. When* $\varphi_t = \varphi^L, \tau^D = \tau^p$. *When* $\varphi_t = \varphi^H$, *democracy sets the tax rate* $\tau^D = \tilde{\tau} < \tau^p$ *such that* $V^r(N, \mu^L) - \varphi\bar{y} = V^r(\varphi^H, D, \tau^D = \tilde{\tau})$.

(3) *If* $\varphi < \varphi^*$ *and* $\kappa \geq \breve{\kappa}$, *we are in an unconsolidated democracy. The society continuously switches regimes. In a nondemocratic regime, when* $\mu_t = \mu^L$, *the elites set* $\tau^N = \tau^r$; *when* $\mu_t = \mu^H$, *they democratize. In a democracy, when* $\varphi_t = \varphi^L, \tau^D = \tau^p$; *when* $\varphi_t = \varphi^H$, *there is a coup.*

(4) *If* $\varphi \geq \hat{\varphi}$ *and* $\kappa < \bar{\kappa}$, *or* $\varphi^* \leq \varphi < \hat{\varphi}$ *and* $\kappa < \kappa(\varphi)$, *or if* $\varphi < \varphi^*$ *and* $\kappa < \breve{\kappa}$, *when* $\mu_t = \mu^L, \tau^N = \tau^r$, *and there is no redistribution and when* $\mu_t = \mu^H$, *the elites use repression to stay in power.*

The main message from Proposition 7.2 is that democracy again arises because the elites cannot commit to future policies while they maintain a monopoly of political power. However, once created, democracy is not necessarily consolidated. Despite the fact that rational individuals anticipate that coups against democracy may occur in the future, the creation of democracy may nevertheless stop a revolution in the same way as described in Chapter 6. This is because to mount a coup, the elites must have de facto power and whether they will have it in the future is uncertain. This being the case, the citizens value the creation of democracy, which moves de jure power in their direction even when they understand that democracy may not be permanent.

We now discuss the conditions in the proposition in more detail. In the first type of equilibrium where $\mu \geq \mu^*$ a revolution is sufficiently costly that, given the amount of inequality and the value of q, the elites can avoid it by redistributing. Therefore, in state $\mu_t = \mu^L$, the elites set their preferred tax rate of zero (i.e., $\tau^N = \tau^r = 0$), whereas in state μ^H, if repression is sufficiently costly, they redistribute by setting the tax rate $\tau^N = \hat{\tau}$, which is just enough to stop a revolution. If repression is relatively cheap, however, the elites respond to the threat of a revolution by repressing the citizens. In this equilibrium, there is never democratization and the amount of redistribution is relatively limited (or zero) if the elites choose repression. If redistribution takes place, inequality nonetheless increases the level of redistribution in this regime because the elites are forced to choose higher taxes to prevent a revolution in the state (N, μ^H).

Consider what happens when $\mu < \mu^*$. When the society transits into state μ^H, the elites can no longer maintain their political power via redistribution and must either repress or democratize. There are four types of equilibria depending on the values of φ and κ. The first possibility is that $\varphi \geq \hat{\varphi}$ and $\kappa \geq \bar{\kappa}$. Democracy, once created, is fully consolidated and repression is sufficiently costly that democracy will be created even though the elites know that the citizens will always set $\tau^D = \tau^p$ from then on. In this type of society, the amount of redistribution is at its highest level, there is little or no fiscal volatility, and the threat of a coup plays no role once the society becomes democratic. We interpret this case as similar to the situation in most OECD countries. It is more likely to arise when θ is low – that is, when the society is fairly equal as long as $\theta > \mu$ so that the revolution constraint binds.

The second possibility is that $\varphi^* \leq \varphi < \hat{\varphi}$ and $\kappa \geq \kappa(\varphi)$. Then, democracy is semiconsolidated and only survives by making concessions in some states. In particular, if in democracy the citizens were to set a tax rate τ^p in the state (D, φ^H), a coup would occur. The citizens avoid this by setting a lower tax $\tau^D = \tilde{\tau}$ in state (D, φ^H), which is just sufficient to dissuade the elites from mounting a coup. Although the society always remains democratic, it is in some sense "under the shadow of a coup," because the threat of a coup keeps overall redistribution below the level of a fully consolidated democracy.

The third type of equilibrium involves $\varphi < \varphi^*$ and $\kappa \geq \check{\kappa}$ so that democracy is unconsolidated: when the state moves to φ^H, a coup is relatively attractive for the elites and cannot be halted by reducing taxes. As a result, the economy fluctuates randomly between democracy and nondemocracy. More specifically, when repression is not attractive, the economy starts with the elites in power and they set $\tau^N = \tau^r$. Whenever the state moves to μ^H, they democratize, after which the citizens set $\tau^D = \tau^p$. But, as soon as the state goes from (D, φ^L) to (D, φ^H), the elites mount a coup, regain political power, and set $\tau^N = 0$. The variability of policy is, therefore, highest in this equilibrium, and the amount of redistribution is less than in the second and third case but more than in the first case. Higher inequality increases redistribution in this regime because it increases the tax rate when there is democracy, whereas there is never any redistribution in nondemocracy. In this case, when the citizens are in power, they set the maximum tax rate, fully anticipating that redistribution will eventually come to an end as a result of a coup. This result may help to explain the existence of highly redistributive but relatively short-lived populist regimes in Latin America (e.g., see Kaufman and Stallings 1991).

The final type of equilibrium involves repression by the elites to maintain the nondemocratic regime. This arises in various circumstances if the cost of repression is sufficiently low. Because $\bar{\kappa} > \kappa(\varphi) > \check{\kappa}$, repression is most attractive for the elites when they anticipate that they will have to create a fully consolidated democracy. It is interesting, therefore, that our analysis suggests it is more likely that an unconsolidated rather than a fully or semiconsolidated democracy will be created.

As with democratizations, coups happen only in the high state, which can be interpreted as a relatively unlikely or unusual state. In this context, one appealing interpretation is that the high state corresponds to periods of recession or economic crises. During such crises, undertaking a coup may be less costly because society is in disarray and a proportional loss of income or output due to turbulence and political instability may be less severe because output is already low. This interpretation – which suggests that regime changes, particularly coups, are more likely during recessionary periods – is in line with the broad patterns in the data. Many coups happen during recessions or during periods of economic difficulties, such as those in Brazil in 1964, Chile in 1973, and Argentina in 1976 (see the evidence in Chapter 3). The relationship between volatility and coups suggests that a possible reason for the greater success of richer societies in consolidating democracy is their economic stability (Acemoglu and Zilibotti 1997).

Four other conclusions can be drawn from this analysis. The first links inequality to regime changes. An increase in θ increases μ^*, φ^*, $\hat{\varphi}$, κ^*, $\bar{\kappa}$, $\kappa(\varphi)$, and $\check{\kappa}$. Thus, higher inequality makes revolutions, coups, and repression all more attractive. As in the model of Chapter 6, which assumed that democracy was always consolidated, there is an inverted-U–shaped relationship between inequality and democratization. Highly equal or highly unequal societies are unlikely to democratize. Rather, it is societies at intermediate levels of inequality in which we observe democratization. The model of this chapter predicts that having democratized, democracy is also more likely to consolidate in more equal societies. Thus, we might expect to see very equal societies, such as Singapore, remain nondemocratic. Societies with higher levels of inequality will democratize and become fully or semiconsolidated democracies, whereas societies with greater inequality may democratize but be unconsolidated. These two cases may fit the historical evolution of Britain and Argentina. Finally, a very inegalitarian society may never democratize in the first place, which fits the South African experience. Of course, these statements apply relative to other things being equal.

The second conclusion pertains to the link between inequality and redistribution. To see this, fix the cost of a coup φ and define $\theta^H > \theta^L$ such that $\varphi = \hat{\varphi}(\theta^L)$ and $\varphi = \varphi^*(\theta^H)$. Moreover, suppose that $\mu < \mu^*(\theta^H)$. When $\theta < \theta^L, \varphi \geq \hat{\varphi}(\theta)$, so inequality is sufficiently low that democracy is fully consolidated. Now consider an increase in inequality (i.e., an increase in θ). This increases redistribution at first as in the standard models of voting over redistribution (e.g., Meltzer and Richard 1981) because $d\tau^p/d\theta > 0$. However, as θ rises above θ^L, democracy is no longer fully consolidated but rather semiconsolidated (i.e., $\varphi \in [\varphi^*(\theta), \hat{\varphi}(\theta))$). In this case, the citizens are forced to reduce taxes from τ^p to $\tilde{\tau}$ in the state (D, φ^H), so overall redistribution falls. In fact, in a semiconsolidated democracy, the relationship between inequality and taxation is ambiguous. The average tax rate is $\tau^a = (1-s)\tau^p + s\tilde{\tau}$. The tax rate τ^p is increasing in inequality while $\tilde{\tau}$ is decreasing. If the cost of taxation $C(\tau)$ is highly convex, then the second effect dominates and the average tax rate falls as inequality rises. Intuitively, higher inequality makes a coup more attractive for the elites so, to prevent the coup, the citizens have to reduce the tax rate substantially in the state φ, leading to lower redistributive taxation on average. As inequality increases further, we have $\theta > \theta^H$ so $\varphi < \varphi^*$, and democracy is now unconsolidated with lower overall redistribution than both in fully and semiconsolidated democracies. Therefore, there is a nonmonotonic relationship between inequality and redistribution, with societies at intermediate levels of inequality redistributing more than both very equal and very unequal societies.

The third implication of our analysis is related to fiscal volatility. The relationship between fiscal volatility and inequality is likely to be increasing. Within each regime, higher inequality leads to more variability. Moreover, higher inequality makes unconsolidated democracy, which has the highest amount of fiscal variability, more likely. This may help explain why fiscal policy has been more volatile in Latin America than in the OECD countries (Gavin and Perotti 1997).

The fourth implication of our analysis is that the costs of redistribution also have an impact on the equilibrium political system. Suppose that the cost of taxation becomes less convex, so that $C(\tau^p)$ is unchanged but $C'(\tau^p)$ decreases. Because deadweight losses from taxation are now lower, the median voter chooses a higher level of taxation. However, as τ^p increases, so will $-(\tau^p(\bar{y} - y^r) - C(\tau^p)\bar{y})$; therefore, democracy becomes more costly to the elites and less likely to be consolidated. This implies that in societies where taxation creates less economic distortions – for example, where a large fraction of the GDP is generated from natural resources – democracies may be more difficult to consolidate. This result has an obvious parallel to the result discussed later; that is, targeted transfers also make coups more likely. These two results together imply that a more efficient or flexible fiscal system may not always be preferable once its implications for the political equilibrium are considered.

Although we do not consider them in this book, the implications of social mobility for regime transitions were investigated in the model of this chapter by Leventoğlu (2003a,b), building on work by Wright (1996) and Benabou and Ok (2001). She shows that when there is social mobility – in the sense that an individual who is poor at t may be rich at date $t+1$ and vice versa – and when taxation decisions are "sticky" – in the sense that the tax rate set today influences future tax rates – then the rate of social mobility has important implications for regime transitions. Consider the preferred tax rate in democracy of the poor median voter. The main result here is that a poor person who expects to be rich in the future prefers a lower rate of taxation than a poor person who expects to remain poor. Hence, the greater the extent of social mobility, the less support there is politically for high taxes and the less redistributive is democracy. As a result, democracy is more willingly conceded by the elites and more likely to be consolidated because coups are less attractive in a society with high rates of social mobility. This may help to explain why a country like the United States in the nineteenth century, which had high rates of social mobility, was able to consolidate its (white male) democracy.

5. Alternative Political Identities

We now return briefly to the model of Chapter 4, in which we considered political conflict along the lines not of socioeconomic class but in terms of group X versus group Z. In the previous chapter, the basic results concerning the mechanisms leading to democracy and the circumstances under which democracy would be created were unchanged in this situation. The main difference was that some of the comparative statics, particularly with respect to inequality, were different.

This model can be extended directly to coups and the study of democratic consolidation. When group X is the majority, democratic redistribution goes from group Z to group X, with the equilibrium amount of redistribution being determined either by the preferences of the poor or rich members of group X depending on whether δ_A^p is greater or less than 1/2. Nondemocracy is rule by group Z and, for simplicity, we assumed that in nondemocracy the tax rate is determined by majority voting in group Z. The equilibrium tax rate is that preferred by the median voter of group Z; in Chapter 6, we considered the case where this median voter was rich. Clearly, members of group Z prefer nondemocracy to democracy, whereas the opposite is true for members of group X.

Imagine now that we are in democracy (rule by group X) but that members of group Z can mount a coup to reinstall nondemocracy – the rule of group Z. The mechanics of the models of this chapter can be applied to this situation. Imagine that the coup decision is made by majority voting within group Z so that the median voter of Z, a rich agent, will make the decision. Facing the threat of a coup, both poor and rich members of group X wish to make a concession by reducing the amount of redistribution from Z to X. Yet, such concessions are not necessarily credible for the same reasons in our analysis; hence, group Z may wish to mount a coup to recover power and induce a credible commitment to pro-Z policies. The basic mechanisms that lead to coups, therefore, are independent of the nature of political identities. Nevertheless, it is easy to construct examples in which the comparative statics with respect to measured inequality are different from those we have so far emphasized in this chapter.

6. Targeted Transfers

We now briefly discuss the implications of targeted transfers for coups and democratic consolidation. In Chapter 6, we showed that allowing for targeted transfers leads to greater political instability because it increases the stakes of the political game. Democracy is better for the citizens and worse for the elites. Simultaneously, nondemocracy is better for the elites and worse for the citizens.

In the context of coups, this implies that the presence of targeted transfers increases the desire of the elites to mount a coup and tends to make democracy less consolidated. For instance, in the context of the static model of this chapter, the introduction of targeted transfers increases the critical thresholds $\hat{\varphi}$ and φ^*, implying that the elites will be willing to undertake coups even when they are more costly. This follows because without a coup, the citizens tax the elites more and once the elites take power via a coup, they can tax the citizens – something they could not do before – which increases the benefit from undertaking a coup.

It is interesting that, different from the discussion of democracy in the previous chapter, now targeted transfers unambiguously increase the likelihood of coups against democracy. This is because inter-group inequality makes democracy less attractive for the elites. In contrast, the implications of inter-group inequality on democratization were ambiguous because it affected both the revolution constraint and the willingness of the elites to use repression.

Finally, the effect of targeted transfers on coups suggests that a more flexible fiscal system may be "counterproductive" because of its impact on the political equilibrium.

7. Power in Democracy and Coups

Our basic analysis implies that the origins of coups against democracy lie in the redistributive policies of democracy. An interesting question, therefore, is how alternative arrangements in democracy affect the likelihood of coups. To answer this question, we return to the static model of Section 3 and introduce our richer model of democracy, which can bestow some power to the elites. In the context of our two-class model, this gives a solution for the tax rate $\tau(\chi)$, where χ is the weight of the elites. When $\chi = 0$, we have our basic model of democracy, in which the poor agent is the median voter and chooses his or her most preferred tax rate, so $\tau(\chi = 0) = \tau^p$. In Chapter 4, $\tau(\chi)$ was implicitly defined by the first-order condition (4.16) and this implied that $d\tau(\chi)/d\chi < 0$. That is, as the power of the citizens in democracy declines, so does the equilibrium tax rate and the degree to which a democracy redistributes income away from the elites.

The important implication of this model and the analysis of Chapter 6 was that as χ increases, the power of the elites in democratic politics increases, and the value they obtain in democracy is greater. So, we have $dV^p(D, \chi)/d\chi < 0$ and $dV^r(D, \chi)/d\chi > 0$. Consequently, it is easy to see that the addition of variable power has important effects on the coup constraint in our basic extensive-form game of coups. Recall that the coup constraint is $V^r(C, \varphi) > V^r(D, \chi)$, or (7.4). The higher χ, the better is democracy for the elites and the less likely is it that (7.4) will bind. Hence, an increase in χ above 0 can lead an unconsolidated democracy to become semiconsolidated. Moreover, a further increase in χ can lead the society to become a fully consolidated democracy. We can also see how (7.6) depends on χ and we can derive a new critical threshold $\varphi^*(\chi)$:

$$\varphi^*(\chi) = \frac{1-p}{\theta}(\delta C(\tau^p(\chi)) - \tau(\chi)(\delta - \theta))$$

Because $\varphi^*(\chi < 1) < \varphi^*(\chi = 1)$, as the power of the elites increases, it becomes less attractive to mount coups and it becomes more likely that democracy is consolidated.

Proposition 7.3: *In the model with variable political power, an increase in χ makes it less likely that the coup constraint will bind and more likely that the society will have a consolidated democracy.*

This result implies that the citizens in an unconsolidated democracy may wish to limit their own power and bolster that of the elites. Although this reduces their income, other things being equal, it can also remove the threat of a coup. An obvious way for the citizens to do this is to change institutions in such a way as to overrepresent the elites in democracy – give them more power than their numbers alone merit. Nevertheless, even if it is feasible for the citizens, it does not mean that they will choose to do so. In reality, whether a coup will take place or succeed if it is attempted is uncertain. Faced with such uncertainty, the citizens may not want to increase the power of the elites in democracy because it will reduce the payoff of the citizens forever, whereas the coup may fail and the threat vanish in the future. Hence, there is a trade-off in designing institutions that avoids coups. This implies that even when institutions can be designed freely to increase the power of the elites in democracy, it is not always optimal for democrats to undertake such actions; as a result, coups sometimes occur in equilibrium.

As emphasized in Chapter 6, however, many of the relevant institutions are the outcome of long historical processes and highly persistent. By their nature, institutions are difficult to change and it is unrealistic, therefore, to imagine that democrats or even nondemocrats can freely optimize over the structure of political institutions at any date. Indeed, it is interesting that examples of institutional engineering to bolster the power of the elites, such as the Zimbabwean constitution of 1980 or the negotiated settlement that ended apartheid in South Africa, happen only in the context of rather large ruptures in society. Other attempts to redesign institutions, such as the putative shift from a presidential to a parliamentary regime in Brazil after the end of the military dictatorship, typically fail.

The relationship between the institutional structure and the consolidation of democracy has also been emphasized in the political science literature. For example, Rueschemeyer, Stephens, and Stephens (1992) note that:

> once democracy was installed, the party system became crucial for protecting the interests of the dominant classes and thus keeping them from pursuing authoritarian alternatives. Democracy could be consolidated only where there were two or more strong competing political parties at least one of which effectively protected dominant class interests, or where the party system allowed for direct access of the dominant classes to the state apparatus. (p. 9)

They later note (p. 10), "democracy . . . could be consolidated only if the interests of the capitalist classes were not directly threatened by it." We have already discussed two important historical examples of the importance of the party system and the consolidation of democracy: in Argentina before the coup in 1930 and in helping to explain the long democratic history of Colombia. This is obviously an important area for future research.

The idea that has attracted the most attention in this context is that presidential democracies are more prone to coups (Linz 1978, 1994). Przeworski et al. (2000) find that the evidence supports this claim; they conclude:

> it is clear that presidential democracies are less durable than parliamentary ones. This difference is not due to the wealth of the countries in which these institutions are observed, nor to their economic performance. Neither is it due to any of the political conditions under which they functioned. Presidential democracies are simply more brittle under all economic and political conditions. (p. 136)

This empirical evidence, therefore, fits well with the idea that presidential democracies are unstable because a president tends to represent the preferences of the median voter. With a parliamentary regime, there are often coalition governments and the preferences of the citizens do not necessarily find full expression in the equilibrium policy. This means that parliamentary regimes may not be so threatening to the elites. In contrast, in a presidential system, more radical policies may come onto the political agenda because they appeal to a presidential candidate trying to gain the support of a majority of the population.

8. Consolidation in a Picture

We are now in a position to rigorously derive Figure 2.2 used in the introduction. This figure shows the relationship between inequality and the cost of a coup. For simplicity in Chapter 2, we did not make a distinction between fully and semiconsolidated democracy, so as with our discussion in Chapter 6, we first build the full picture and then show how it can be simplified to derive the figures in Chapter 2. Consider Figure 7.2: on the horizontal axis is θ, on the vertical axis

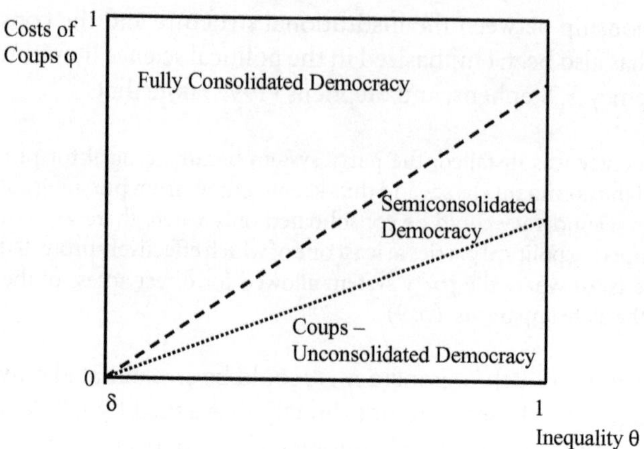

Figure 7.2. Consolidation or Coups?

is φ. The first thing to plot is the coup constraint. We can write this now as:

$$\varphi = \frac{1}{\theta}\left(\delta C(\tau^{p}) - \tau^{p}(\theta - \delta)\right) \tag{7.23}$$

If $\theta = \delta$, so there is complete equality, then (7.23) implies that $\varphi = 0$. With no inequality, even when the cost of a coup is zero, the elites are indifferent between a coup and democracy. Intuitively, when there is no inequality, there is no income redistribution and thus no incentive for a coup, even if it is costless. Thus, (7.23) starts at the origin and is increasing – as inequality rises, coups become attractive and for the elites to be indifferent, the cost of a coup must be rising. One can see that as inequality rises to $\theta = 1$, we have $\varphi = \delta C(\tau^{p}(\theta = 1)) - \tau^{p}(\theta = 1)(1 - \delta) = \delta(C(1) + 1) - 1 < 1$ because $\tau^{p}(\theta = 1) = 1$. To the right of this line, inequality is relatively high compared to the cost of coups and, as a consequence, coups will be attractive. To the left is the region of fully consolidated democracy. To distinguish between the situations of semiconsolidated and unconsolidated democracy, consider the function:

$$\varphi = \frac{1 - p}{\theta}\left(\delta C(\tau^{p}) - \tau^{p}(\theta - \delta)\right)$$

which shows pairs of θ and φ at which the elites are just indifferent between mounting a coup and accepting the promise of the best possible concession under democracy. It is immediate that this function again goes through the origin, is increasing, and when $\theta = 1$, we have $\varphi = (1 - p)(\delta(C(1) + 1) - 1) < 1$. In Figure 7.2, the implications of this are shown in terms of these two new regions. From Figure 7.2 it is easy to get to Figure 2.2; we just drop the function that determines the boundary line between semiconsolidated and unconsolidated democracies.

9. Defensive Coups

So far, we have focused on coups in democracy that are aimed at limiting redistribution away from the elites. Another plausible idea is that the elites support coups when they are afraid that democracy will fall to a revolution. We can think of such coups as "defensive" in the sense that those supporting coups view them as a defense against a much worse outcome for themselves: a revolution. Such a scenario may arise when a revolution against democracy is easier than a revolution against nondemocracy. We now discuss a model exhibiting these features.

To model defensive coups, consider a variant of our basic static model. Again, the citizens who have control of politics in democracy move first and decide on the tax rate. After this tax rate, the elites decide whether to undertake a coup. We now assume, however, that after the elites' decision, the citizens may decide to undertake a revolution, which is different than before. The return from a revolution differs between the two states but also depends on whether there has been a coup. So, we denote this by $\mu(\zeta)$ when the coup decision is ζ

The crucial assumption, which we view as plausible, is that:

$$\mu(\zeta = 0) < \mu(\zeta = 1)$$

which means that it is easier and more effective to take revolutionary action against democracy than against nondemocracy (recall that the cost of a revolution is μ). Although there could be exceptions – for example, when a nondemocratic regime is unfair and brutal, thus helping the citizens to solve their collective-action problems as a reaction to its injustices – it must typically be the case that overthrowing democracy is easier than a well-organized military regime.

How does this affect our results? We first simplify the analysis by assuming that $\mu(\zeta = 1) \to 1$, so that following a coup, there is no effective revolution threat. We can now write the relevant value functions. When democracies are unconstrained, we have the values $V^p(D)$ and $V^r(D)$ given by (6.4). After a coup, we have (7.2) as in Section 7.3, which for the current purpose incorporates the fact that the revolution threat disappears after a coup. The values of the promise of less redistribution under democracy are identical to what they were in (7.3). In addition, we have the values from a revolution, similar to those in Chapter 6:

$$V^p(R, \mu(\zeta)) = \frac{(1 - \mu(\zeta))\bar{y}}{1 - \delta}$$

which condition the return from a revolution on whether there is a coup.

Here, we informally outline the results from this model. First, if $\mu(\zeta = 0) \to 1$, then the basic proposition, Proposition 7.1, applies. There is no effective revolution threat against democracy, and the coup decision is taken simply by trading-off the costs of redistribution against the cost of a coup.

However, if $\mu(\zeta = 0) < 1$, then there are new results from this model. Naturally, there will be a coup whenever there was a coup before, but there might also be a coup in some additional cases. To see this, first compare:

$$V^p(R, \mu(\zeta = 0)) = \frac{(1 - \mu(\zeta = 0))\bar{y}}{1 - \delta}$$

to:

$$V^p(D, \tau^D = \tilde{\tau}) = y^p + p(\tilde{\tau}(\bar{y} - y^p) - C(\tilde{\tau})\bar{y}) \\ + (1 - p)(\tau^P(\bar{y} - y^p) - C(\tau^P)\bar{y})$$

with $\tilde{\tau}$ being the tax rate that prevents a coup. This reduction in the tax rate is necessary because otherwise the elites will necessarily undertake a coup. However, given this reduction in the tax rate, democracy is less attractive for the citizens, and it can be the case that:

$$V^p(R, \mu(\zeta = 0)) > V^p(D, \tau^D = \tilde{\tau})$$

If this is the case, the elites anticipate that the citizens will undertake a revolution rather than live in this democracy, which is not very redistributive toward themselves; because a revolution is the worst outcome for them, the elites prefer to undertake a coup to prevent a revolution.

We can think of this as a "defensive coup" because the elites are not undertaking the coup to reduce redistribution but rather to prevent a revolution. Many military coups against democracy in Latin America claimed that they were there to protect the capitalist system or even democracy from a revolution – a salient case being Chile in 1973. This model shows that there might be some truth to those claims.

Nevertheless, it is interesting that there is still an important interaction between this and redistribution. We have that:

$$V^p(R, \mu(\zeta = 0)) > V^p(D, \tau^D = \tilde{\tau})$$

but it might still be the case that:

$$V^p(R, \mu(\zeta = 0)) < V^p(D)$$

That is, a revolution would not have been attractive for the citizens if democracy were not trying to defend itself against a coup! Therefore, the reason why a revolution might become a threat in the first place is the fact that the coup constraint is preventing democratic politics from catering to the wishes of the citizens.

10. Conclusion

In this chapter, we introduced a model of coups. We showed how to integrate this theory of coups with our theory of democratization in Chapter 6. This extended model allows us to study the conditions under which democracy is not only created but also consolidated – surely a question of equal importance. Many democracies, once created, quickly collapse, so here we built a framework to understand why. We showed that many of the same issues that arose in modeling democratization arise in studying democratic consolidation. In particular, coups arise because democrats cannot credibly promise not to use their power to enact pro-citizen and anti-elite legislation and policies. To avoid this, the only solution is for the elites to take power – to mount a coup.

We showed how whether democracy was consolidated depended on inter-group inequality, although whether this comparative static maps into a statement about observed measures of inequality depends on the nature of political identities. When political conflict is between the poor and the rich, we expect, for example, higher inequality to lead to more coups. We also showed that the power of the elites mattered for democratic consolidation. If the elites have sufficient power, they do not need to undertake coups. This suggests that there might be institutional solutions to avoiding coups, just as we argued that democracy is an institutional solution to avoid revolutions. Perhaps democrats could alter institutions and by doing so give more power in democracy to the elites. This would limit the power of democracy, but it might help consolidate it; democracy would be consolidated but limited. Nevertheless, there are dangers inherent in such a strategy, even if it is feasible. If democrats, in their desire to consolidate democracy, give the elites too much power, then the democracy that they consolidate may be so limited in its ability to transform society that it is not stable because the mass of citizens may push for a revolution and more radical social and political change.

These are only the initial empirical lessons from the model. In the next three chapters, we discuss many other factors that can be important for determining whether democracy consolidates.

8 The Role of the Middle Class

1. Introduction

In Part 4, we put the basic models of democratization and coups to work in a number of different settings. To keep things simple, we do this only in the context of our basic extensive-form static game in which the commitment problem is modeled in a reduced-form way. Our aim is to show the utility of the framework we developed for thinking about why some countries are democratic and others are not and illustrate some ways in which the framework can be enriched and extended. We also keep the analysis and statements of results more informal than in the book so far. For instance, we do not present formal specifications of strategies, although it will be straightforward to fill in the details from the analysis already presented.

In this chapter, we extend our framework by allowing for a third group with interests intermediate to those of the elites and the great mass of citizens. For simplicity, we call this group the middle class. Our model has focused on the political conflict between the elites and the citizens. Clearly, real-world societies do not correspond to our simple model with only two groups. Just as the distinctions between the elites and the citizens and the rich and the poor are useful as a tractable device for developing ideas, so is the three-class model (another application of Occam's razor). Because many individuals see themselves as part of a "middle class" distinct from the rich and the poor, and because political scientists believe that decisive voters in democracy are often from the middle class, we believe this approach is useful.

A long tradition in social science, including Moore's (1966) *Social Origins of Dictatorship and Democracy*, views third classes such as the middle class – or, what Moore called, following Marxist terminology, the *bourgeoisie* – as the key actor in the processes that ultimately lead to democracy. Moore suggested that only societies with a sufficiently strong bourgeoisie would become democratic, whereas societies in which landowners were strong enough that the emerging bourgeoisie had to enter into an alliance with them would turn into dictatorships.

Scholars within the modernization tradition have also stressed the importance of the middle class (e.g., Lipset 1959; Dahl 1971). Huntington (1991) suggests the key role of the middle class in reducing the distributional conflicts that make democracy unstable. He argues

> ... economic development promotes the expansion of the middle class.... Democracy is premised... on majority rule, and democracy is difficult in a situation of concentrated inequalities in which a large, impoverished majority confronts a small, wealthy oligarchy. (p. 66)

Similarly, the literature on Latin American dictatorships and democratic consolidation emphasizes the important role played by the middle class. We have seen this in our discussion on the role of the Radical party in the history of democracy in Argentina and also discussed the idea that the relatively large middle class in countries such as Colombia and Costa Rica may help to explain why these countries have an unusually democratic political history compared to most of their neighbors.

Motivated by these issues, in this chapter we extend our analysis of political conflict based on the citizens versus the elites by including the middle class. We show how this changes the main results from our basic approach and in what sense the middle class plays an important role in the process of the creation and consolidation of democracy. In this chapter, instead of referring to the elites and the citizens, we refer to these three groups as the rich, the middle class, and the poor. We use this language because we investigate various situations, some in which we can think of the middle class as forming a coalition with the poor against the rich and some in which the middle class forms a coalition with the rich against the poor, thus becoming part of the "elite." In this case, the composition of the elites could include the middle class so, to avoid confusion, we drop this language from this chapter.

We start with an analysis of the emergence of partial democracy – that is, a situation in which only a limited segment of society participates in voting.[1] This segment typically includes the elites and the middle class, while the poor are excluded because of income or literacy restrictions on voting. Although democracy emerged in some Latin American or African countries as a direct move from nondemocracy toward universal mass suffrage (see Chapters 1 and 3), European democracy emerged more gradually. Our three-class model enables an analysis of such incremental democratizations. In particular, when the threat of revolution from the disenfranchised comes as a result of a coalition between the middle class and the poor, it may be beneficial for the rich elites to break

[1] Because partial democracy is less than full democracy, we could refer to it as a form of nondemocracy. Recall from Chapter 2, however, that the focus of our analysis is to understand the forces that push a society toward or away from democracy. Although most of our analysis has focused on contrasting full democracy with the rule of some elites, we can therefore study the move from political control by the rich to a partial democracy – which includes also the middle class – as an instance of democratization.

the coalition by extending voting rights only to the middle class. Because the middle class is, by definition, richer than the poor, it is easier to dissuade from revolution.

The next step is to analyze the move from a partial to a full democracy. Here, we distinguish between two different approaches. The first, which is often invoked when explaining the 1867 Second Reform Act in Britain, is that competition among elites (e.g., between the rich and the middle class) led to the extension of democratic rights by one of the groups to increase its likelihood of remaining in power. According to this story, Tory Prime Minister Disraeli introduced a Radical reform, enfranchising a large group of the population, to strengthen his party in its competition against the Liberals led by Gladstone. We show how this type of intra-elite competition can be modeled within this framework but then also argue that it is unlikely to provide a satisfactory explanation for either the British or other cases of transition from partial to full democracy. Instead, as in our baseline model of Chapter 6, the revolutionary threat from the disenfranchised poor appears to have been important both in the British and other cases we have studied.

Inspired by this, we use our three-class model to analyze the response of a partial democracy to a threat of a revolution from the poor. More specifically, we model the situation as one in which the rich and the middle class have voting rights and the poor challenge the system. Once again, the promises of the existing regime to redistribute in the future are not fully credible because with de jure political power in the hands of the rich and the middle class, they will revert to policies they prefer once the threat of a revolution subsides. Therefore, full democracy emerges as a way to change the future distribution of political power, thus creating a credible commitment to future pro-poor policy. The new results in this instance involve the role of the middle class: if the middle class is sufficiently poor, even partial democracy will generate policies (e.g., rates of redistributive taxation) that are close to those the poor prefer. In this case, the poor expect relatively pro-poor policies in the future even if the exact promises made to them while they have an effective threat of revolution are not kept. Here, greater inequality in the form of a relatively poor middle class may make full democracy less likely by enabling the existing regime to commit to policies relatively attractive to the poor without having to actually give the poor democratic rights.

The most interesting new results from our analysis of the role of the middle class come when we introduce the option to use repression. We learned in Chapter 6 that a highly unequal society may not democratize because with high levels of inequality, democracy would adopt policies that are radically different to those preferred by the rich. Anticipating this, the rich are willing to use repression to prevent democratization. In a model of redistributive taxation, the poor, who constitute a majority in democracy, are in favor of high rates of income redistribution. However, if the middle class is sufficiently large, the median voter in a full democracy could be a middle-class agent; moreover, if the middle class is relatively affluent, this median voter would choose only limited redistribution. Therefore, a relatively large and affluent middle class acts as a buffer between the rich and the poor and limits redistribution. By ensuring that policies are not too far from those preferred by the rich, it discourages the rich from using repression and makes democracy more likely.

The discussion of the middle class as a buffer focuses on a model in which, initially, the rich are in power and are considering extending voting rights to the rest of the population, which includes the middle class and the poor. An alternative scenario, relevant in many Latin American examples, is that a nondemocracy represents the interests of the rich and the middle class and has to decide whether to move to a democracy with the poor also included in the system. In this case, which we can also think of as a movement from partial to full democracy, the model provides a way to formalize the often-discussed distinction between softliners and hardliners in the political science literature. According to many qualitative accounts (e.g., O'Donnell and Schmitter 1986), when nondemocratic regimes are challenged, there are often divides between hardliners who want to use force to keep the system going and softliners who want to administer a smooth transition to democracy. Transitions to democracy take place when softliners become more influential within the existing regime. In our framework, a natural divide exists between the rich and the middle class. Because the rich have more to lose from the policies adopted by a democracy, they are more pro-repression than the middle class. For an interesting set of parameter values, there will be repression when the rich, who correspond to hardliners, are more influential within nondemocracy but peaceful transition to democracy when the middle class, the softliners, is more influential.

Finally, in Section 7 we analyze coups. We show that the role of the middle class can mirror its role in reducing the inclination of the rich to repress to avoid democratizing. If the median voter in democracy is a middle-class agent and if the middle class is relatively affluent, this mitigates the antirich impact of democracy and makes coups less attractive for the rich. The fact that the middle class can be a buffer between the rich and the poor, therefore, may help consolidate democracy as well as create it in the first place.

Overall, therefore, the analysis in this chapter reveals that the middle class plays an important role in the emergence of democracy in a number of ways: (1) it can be the driving force for democracy, especially for the emergence of partial democracy; (2) it can be in favor of the poor being included in the political arena, facilitating a move from partial to full democracy; (3) perhaps most interesting, it can act as a buffer between the rich and the poor by ensuring that democracy will not be very antirich and, therefore, dissuading the rich from using repression or mounting coups; and (4) when it is in power together with the rich, it can play the role of softliners arguing against repression and in favor of a transition to democracy, which is less costly for the middle class than for the rich.

2. The Three-Class Model

We first generalize our basic two-group model of Chapter 4 to allow for a third income group. There are three groups of agents: the rich of size δ^r, the middle class of size δ^m, and the poor of size δ^p. We normalize total population to 1 as before, thus $\sum_i \delta^i = 1$, and assume that $\delta^p > \delta^m > \delta^r$; that is, the poor are the most populous followed by the middle class, and the rich constitute the smallest group in the population. Also, we denote average income by $\bar{y}$ as before, and introduce the notation that:

$$y^r = \frac{\theta^r}{\delta^r}\bar{y},\ y^m = \frac{\theta^m}{\delta^m}\bar{y},\quad \text{and} \quad y^p = \frac{\theta^p}{\delta^p}\bar{y} \tag{8.1}$$

This implies that group i has a share θ^i of the economy's total income and, naturally, $\sum_i \theta^i = 1$. Moreover, we assume that:

$$\frac{\theta^r}{\delta^r} > \frac{\theta^m}{\delta^m} > \frac{\theta^p}{\delta^p} \tag{8.2}$$

so that the rich are richer than the middle class, which is in turn richer than the poor.

As before, we assume that the political system determines a nonnegative income tax rate $\tau \geq 0$, the proceeds of which are redistributed lump sum, and there is an aggregate cost of taxation $C(\tau)\bar{y}$. Nevertheless, as we showed in Chapter 4, one can easily introduce group-specific transfers without altering the thrust of the results; hence, the setup used here is only for simplicity.

Given this setup, we can define the most preferred tax rates of rich, middle-class, and poor agents. For any group, the most preferred tax rate is that which maximizes $\hat{y}^i$; therefore, the most preferred tax rate of group i satisfies the following condition that we write in the Kuhn–Tucker form to allow for the possibility of a corner solution: $-y^i + (1 - C'(\tau^i))\bar{y} = 0$ and $\tau^i > 0$, or $-y^i + (1 - C'(\tau^i))\bar{y} \leq 0$ and $\tau^i = 0$. Substituting for the definitions of incomes, we write these two conditions as:

$$\left(\frac{\delta^i - \theta^i}{\delta^i}\right) - C'(\tau^i) = 0 \quad \text{and} \quad \tau^i > 0 \quad \text{or} \tag{8.3}$$

$$\left(\frac{\delta^i - \theta^i}{\delta^i}\right) - C'(\tau^i) \leq 0 \quad \text{and} \quad \tau^i = 0$$

Because $y^r > \bar{y}$ by definition, we have that for the rich, (8.3) holds as an inequality and $\tau^r = 0$ as before. Moreover, because $\bar{y} > y^p$, the most preferred tax rate of the poor is positive (i.e., $\tau^p > 0$), given by:

$$\left(\frac{\delta^p - \theta^p}{\delta^p}\right) = C'(\tau^p) \tag{8.4}$$

The most preferred tax rate of the middle class could be zero or positive depending on whether y^m is greater or less than mean income $\bar{y}$. In most real-world income distributions, the rich are sufficiently rich that the median is less than the mean, so we assume that $\theta^m/\delta^m < 1$ or $\bar{y} > y^m$. Therefore, we have that τ^m is given by:

$$\left(\frac{\delta^m - \theta^m}{\delta^m}\right) = C'(\tau^m) \tag{8.5}$$

and $\tau^m > 0$. This assumption allows us to focus on the most interesting case. However, by virtue of the fact that the middle class is richer than the poor (i.e., $\theta^m/\delta^m > \theta^p/\delta^p$), we also have that:

$$\tau^p > \tau^m$$

so that the middle class always prefers lower taxes than the poor.

We can apply the analysis of Chapter 4 to determine the democratic equilibrium of this model. Consider the game where two "Downsian" political parties noncooperatively offer tax policies in an attempt to win an election. There is majority voting. Because all individuals have single-peaked preferences, the MVT (Median Voter Theorem) applies and the unique equilibrium involves both parties offering the policy preferred by the median voter. The nature of the democratic political equilibrium then depends crucially on the relative sizes of the three groups. In particular, the previous assumption that $\delta^p > \delta^m > \delta^r$ immediately implies $\delta^r < 1/2$, so the rich are not the majority. This leaves us with two interesting cases:

1. $\delta^p < 1/2$, so the poor are not the majority either, and the median voter is a middle-class agent. In that case, majority voting leads to the most preferred policy of the middle class, τ^m.
2. $\delta^p \geq 1/2$, so the poor are the majority and majority voting generates their most preferred policy, τ^p.

We now separately analyze these two cases.

First, suppose that $\delta^p \geq 1/2$. Then, the poor are the majority and democratic politics will lead to their most preferred tax rate, τ^p, as given by (8.4). The comparative statics of this equilibrium are similar to those of the two-class model, but what matters now is θ^p, which is a measure of the gap between the poor and average income, not necessarily the gap between the poor and the rich. For example, when θ^p declines so that the poor become relatively poorer, their most preferred tax rate, τ^p, increases; in other words, $d\tau^p/d\theta^p < 0$. However, this can happen while the gap between the rich and the poor remains constant. For example, we could have a simultaneous decline in θ^p and θ^r, compensated by an increase in θ^m. In this case, the poor would still vote for and obtain higher taxes, but they are not poorer relative to the rich; they are simply poorer relative to average income.

This observation already shows that the relationship between inequality and the equilibrium policy now depends on exactly what measure of inequality we use. For example, a common measure in the literature is the Gini coefficient or the standard deviation of the logarithm of individual income. Now consider a change in income distribution such that the middle class becomes poor (i.e., θ^m falls) and the rich become richer (i.e., θ^r increases) without any change in θ^p or $\bar{y}$. In this model with $\delta^p \geq 1/2$, this has no effect on the equilibrium rate of taxation, whereas according to both measures, income inequality has increased. In fact, if $y^m < \bar{y}$, according to the more rigorous and demanding definition of a mean-preserving spread (Rothschild and Stiglitz 1970, 1971), we have a more unequal distribution – one that is a mean-preserving spread of the original one, meaning that the distribution now has more weight in the tails than the original distribution. Similarly, if we used the measure of inequality that is the gap between the rich and the poor (e.g., the often-used measure of the ratio of 90th and 10th percentiles of the income distribution), again inequality has increased, but there is no effect on the equilibrium policy chosen. Instead, this model makes a specific prediction: the equilibrium policy should depend on the gap between the poor and average incomes. However, this prediction does not necessarily map into a relationship between policy and a standard measure of inequality.

Next, consider the case in which $\delta^p < 1/2$ so that the poor are not the absolute majority and the median voter is from the middle class. In this case, the political equilibrium is given by the tax rate that maximizes the indirect utility of a middle-class agent. The political equilibrium tax rate is given by (8.5). The comparative statics of this equilibrium tax rate are similar to those of the most preferred tax rate of the poor. In particular, we have:

$$\frac{d\tau^m}{d\theta^m} < 0$$

so that when the middle class becomes poorer relative to the average, it desires higher taxes.

Now, the relationship between measures of inequality and tax rates is even more nuanced. For example, consider a change in the distribution that reduces θ^p so that the poor become poorer, simultaneously increasing θ^m and θ^r. Most measures would show this as an increase in inequality, but the equilibrium tax rate actually declines.

We now use this three-class framework to look at what new factors the middle class might bring into the study of the creation and consolidation of democracy.

3. Emergence of Partial Democracy

As already discussed, the Western European experience shows a gradual move toward democracy: first, the middle class was incorporated into the political system and then later the poor. Chapter 6 analyzed a simple game between the enfranchised and the disenfranchised. So, at some level, this might be thought of as a model of a radical move to democracy starting from nondemocracy. Although the Latin American experience might be approximated by a game like this, the Western European experience also suggests that an analysis of how democracy may arise gradually, which factors might play a role in the enfranchisement of the middle class, and which factors determine later democratizations in which the poor are also given the vote would be useful. Even in Latin America, there were often restrictions that stopped people who were illiterate from voting (e.g., until 1936 in Colombia and 1970 in Chile). Because literate people tend to be richer than illiterate people, the extension of voting rights only to males who were literate is similar to a situation in which voting rights are extended only to the middle class and not the poor.

Now consider a situation in which the middle class is disenfranchised and poses a revolutionary threat, just as the poor did in the Chapter 6 analysis. Although during recent times a revolutionary threat from the middle class may appear farfetched, early democratizations in Europe – like those in Britain during the first half of the nineteenth century – were in response to significant social unrest from the middle segments of the society. In Latin America, the situation was often similar. For example, the Radical party in Argentina that organized a series of uprisings in the late nineteenth century with the aim of creating democracy was essentially an urban-based middle-class movement (Alonso 2000).

To model this issue, assume that the middle class and the poor jointly pose a revolutionary threat but, if the middle class withdraws from this process, the poor cannot undertake a successful revolution. Hence, a middle class and poor coalition is required for revolution to be a threat. This might be because in many instances, it is members of the middle class who are more educated and have access to more opportunities and who, therefore, play leadership roles in organizing extralegal and revolutionary activities.

The rest of the setup is similar to the static game in Chapter 6; for the moment, therefore, we do not allow the rich to use repression. Figure 8.1 draws the game tree. There are two new elements: (1) the rich now have two democratization decisions: partial and full; and (2) the key revolution decision is by the middle class because if it withdraws from the revolutionary coalition, revolution is assumed not to take place. To keep the game tree relatively simple, we have therefore suppressed the revolution action by the poor. We have also tried to keep the tree as simple as possible by expressing the payoffs in terms of vectors. Hence, the payoff $V^i(R, \mu) = (V^p(R, \mu), V^m(R, \mu), V^r(R, \mu))$, and so forth.

We can analyze this game by backward induction again, but we now need to define values for all three groups; for revolution and partial and full democracy;

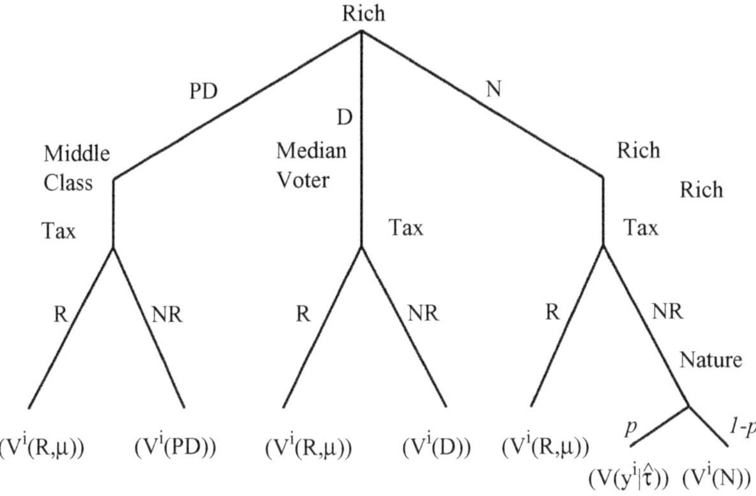

Figure 8.1. Partial Enfranchisement and the Middle Class.

as well as for promised redistribution under the existing system, in which the rich control de jure political power.

We assume that returns from a revolution are similar to before except that now the middle class and the poor share the returns. As in our previous model, we focus the analysis on a state in which a revolution is a threat. Therefore, we have:

$$V^p(R,\mu) = V^m(R,\mu) = \frac{(1-\mu)\bar{y}}{\delta^p + \delta^m} \tag{8.6}$$

as the return to undertaking a revolution for the poor and the middle class. If they undertake a revolution, a fraction μ of the economy's income is destroyed and the remainder is distributed between the poor and the middle class, which make up a total of $\delta^p + \delta^m$ agents. As before, we have that $V^r(R,\mu) = 0$.

The revolution constraint is binding if both the middle class and the poor prefer revolution to the status quo under the existing system, or if

$$V^p(R,\mu) = V^m(R,\mu) = \frac{(1-\mu)\bar{y}}{\delta^p + \delta^m} > y^p \text{ and } > y^m$$

Because $y^m > y^p$, if the revolution threat is binding for the middle class, it will be so for the poor. Therefore, the revolution constraint is:

$$\mu < 1 - \left(\frac{\delta^p}{\delta^m} + 1\right)\theta^m \tag{8.7}$$

This condition behaves in an intuitive way. When θ^m falls, the income share of the middle class falls, which increases inequality in the sense of the relationship between middle-class and average income. This increases the right-hand side of (8.7) and makes it more likely that it is greater than μ.

As before, the rich may meet the threat of a revolution by promising redistribution, which is only a partially credible promise because they have a chance to reset the tax with probability $1 - p$ once the revolution threat has subsided. The values to the three different groups, when the rich keep political power and promise redistribution at the tax rate τ^N, are:

$$V^i(N, \tau^N) = y^i + p\left(\tau^N\left(\bar{y} - y^i\right) - C(\tau^N)\bar{y}\right) \tag{8.8}$$

for $i = p, m, r$.

On the other hand, if the rich choose partial democracy, PD, only the middle class is enfranchised and, by the assumption that $\delta^p > \delta^m > \delta^r$ in this partial democracy, the rich are the minority, and the preferred tax rate of the middle class will be implemented. In general, we use the notation τ^{PD} for the tax rate set in partial democracy. However, for now, the values $V^i(PD)$ take into account that $\tau^{PD} = \tau^m$, the ideal tax rate for a middle-class agent. Therefore, we have:

$$V^i(PD) = y^i + \left(\tau^m\left(\bar{y} - y^i\right) - C(\tau^m)\bar{y}\right) \tag{8.9}$$

Finally, the values in democracy depend on whether the median voter is a poor or a middle-class agent. Recall that this depends on whether δ^p is less than or greater than 1/2. Therefore, write

$$V^i(D) = y^i + \left(\tau^D\left(\bar{y} - y^i\right) - C(\tau^D)\bar{y}\right) \tag{8.10}$$

where

$$\tau^D = \begin{cases} \tau^m & \text{if } \delta^p < 1/2 \\ \tau^p & \text{if } \delta^p \geq 1/2 \end{cases} \tag{8.11}$$

This immediately shows that if $\delta^p < 1/2$, full and partial democracy leads to the same tax rate and to the same allocation. Therefore, the rich are indifferent between full and partial democratization in this case. On the other hand, when $\delta^p \geq 1/2$, because the value to the rich, $V(y^r \mid \tau^D)$, is strictly decreasing in τ^D and because $\tau^p > \tau^m$, we have that $V^r(PD) > V^r(D)$.

As in the Chapter 6 analysis, the crucial issue is going to be whether the promise of redistribution can prevent a revolution. If it can, the rich prefer this to partial or full democratization. For a revolution to be prevented, we need that:

$$V^m(N, \tau^N) \geq V^m(R, \mu) \tag{8.12}$$

or

$$V^p(N, \tau^N) \geq V^p(R, \mu). \tag{8.13}$$

Because $V^p(R, \mu) = V^m(R, \mu)$ and by the fact that the middle class is richer than the poor, $V^m(N, \tau^N) > V^p(N, \tau^N)$, (8.12) is easier to satisfy than (8.13) and the rich simply try to satisfy this and convince the middle class not to partake in revolution. The highest value the rich can offer to the middle class is clearly when they set the tax rate most preferred by the middle class, τ^m. Therefore, for the promise of redistribution to prevent a revolution, we need:

$$V^m(N, \tau^N = \tau^m) \geq V^m(R, \mu)$$
$$y^m + p(\tau^m(\bar{y} - y^m) - C(\tau^m)\bar{y}) \geq \frac{(1-\mu)\bar{y}}{\delta^p + \delta^m}$$

Define μ^* such that this condition holds as an equality or, in other words:

$$\mu^* = 1 - \frac{(\delta^p + \delta^m)}{\delta^m}(\theta^m + p(\tau^m(\delta^m - \theta^m) - \delta^m C(\tau^m))) \tag{8.14}$$

Finally, we also need a condition similar to Chapter 6 when partial or full democratization is sufficient to prevent a revolution. This means that these options should make a revolution unattractive for either the middle class or the poor. The same argument as before means that a revolution is less attractive for the middle class so the relevant condition is for it. Moreover:

$$V^m(PD) \geq V^m(D)$$

because in partial democracy the middle class sets its most preferred tax rate. Therefore, it is sufficient to have $V^m(PD) \geq V^m(R, \mu)$, or:

$$\frac{1}{\delta^m}(\theta^m + \tau^m(\delta^m - \theta^m) - \delta^m C(\tau^m)) \geq \frac{1-\mu}{\delta^p + \delta^m} \tag{8.15}$$

Given this discussion, we have the following result, which is a direct generalization of the results of Chapter 6:

Proposition 8.1: *In the game described above, there is a unique subgame perfect equilibrium. Let μ^* be defined by (8.14). Then:*

- *If (8.7) does not bind, the rich set their most preferred tax rate, $\tau^N = \tau^r$.*
- *If (8.7) binds and (8.15) fails to hold, there is a revolution.*
- *If (8.7) binds and $\mu \geq \mu^*$, the rich prevent democratization by setting the tax rate $\tau^N = \hat{\tau}$ such that $V^m(N, \tau^N = \hat{\tau}) = V^m(R, \mu)$.*
- *Finally, if (8.7) binds, (8.15) holds, and $\mu < \mu^*$, then the rich democratize. If, in addition, $\delta^p \geq 1/2$, the rich choose partial democratization, and if $\delta^p < 1/2$, they are indifferent between partial and full democratization.*

Much of the intuition of this proposition is the same as for Proposition 6.1 in Chapter 6. Institutional change again arises as a way of transferring political power from one group to another to guarantee certain policies in the future. Here, partial democracy transfers power from the rich to the middle class, thereby ensuring that the middle class obtains redistribution in the future. The new features are the choice between partial and full democratization and the fact that this proposition can help explain why early in the nineteenth century, democracy was extended first to the middle class and not to the entire disenfranchised population. Proposition 8.1 also helps to explain why in many situations only people who were literate were given political rights, with people who were illiterate were excluded from such rights.

If this model with (8.7), (8.15), $\mu < \mu^*$, and $\delta^p < 1/2$ is a good approximation to reality, it provides one justification for the role ascribed by scholars to the middle class: early democratization was spearheaded by the middle class; including the middle class in the system, with partial democratization, was the cheapest way for the rich to prevent social unrest.

The comparative statics with respect to inequality are worth emphasizing. Parallel to the results of Proposition 6.1, a lower fraction of income accruing to the middle class makes the revolution constraint (8.7) more likely to hold because the right side of (8.7) is decreasing in θ^m. To see the influence of θ^m on μ^*, we must totally differentiate (8.14), giving:

$$\frac{d\mu^*}{d\theta^m} = -\frac{(\delta^p + \delta^m)}{\delta^m}\left(1 - p\tau^m + ((\delta^m - \theta^m) - \delta^m C'(\tau^m))\frac{d\tau^m}{d\theta^m}\right) < 0$$

Because from (8.5) we have $(\delta^m - \theta^m) - \delta^m C'(\tau^m) = 0$ (another application of the envelope theorem) and $1 - p\tau^m > 0$, $d\mu^*/d\theta^m < 0$ follows. Thus, if the share of income going to the middle class increases, μ^* falls, which implies that the rich can use concessions to buy off the middle class for a larger range of parameter values.

This highlights that the relevant concept of inequality is not the gap between the poor and the rich (as in Chapter 6). The (marginal) social class that poses the revolutionary threat now and that needs to be dissuaded from revolution is the middle class, so what matters is how much it is obtaining in the existing regime. Therefore, the crucial measure of "inequality" now is how rich is a middle-class individual relative to the rest of the society, or θ^m. As a result, the poorer the middle class relative to average income, the less well off it is under the existing regime and the more attractive a revolution is for them. Hence, when it is poorer, the middle class needs to receive a credible commitment of future redistribution, a move toward partial democracy.

4. From Partial to Full Democracy

The previous section discussed how partial democracy may emerge by extending the reasoning of our basic model in Chapter 6. We now turn to the reasons why partial democracy might extend political rights to the poor. We start with a model of intra-elite conflict, implicit in some of the discussions of the Second Reform Act in Britain. We then turn to a model of revolutionary threat from the poor leading to a transition to full democracy, which is more similar to our basic approach in Chapter 6.

4.1 Intra-Elite Conflict and Transition to Full Democracy

The view that intra-elite conflict is important in the transition toward democracy is, in part, inspired by the British experience, where the competition between Disraeli and Gladstone was a major factor in political reform.

In 1866, Russell's Liberal government proposed a relaxation of the property restrictions on voting. This measure was defeated by a coalition of Conservatives led by Disraeli and right-wing Liberals, the "Adullamites," who thought the extension too generous. The Liberal government then collapsed and Disraeli formed a minority administration (with only 290 Members of Parliament as opposed to 360 outside the administration). Disraeli then proposed an even more radical extension of voting rights than the initial Liberal measure, and it was Disraeli's measure that then passed.

How can we make sense of these events? One possibility is to argue that politicians have a strong preference to stay in power and may extend the franchise with the expectation that the newly enfranchised will return the favor by voting for their party (e.g., see Himmelfarb 1966, who argues this for the British case; see the general discussion in Collier 1999). In this interpretation, Disraeli extended the franchise – something he had initially opposed – because he decided that the newly enfranchised would vote Conservative.

Another view, which is potentially more interesting and more in line with our approach based on economic incentives, is that including the poor segments of the society in the political arena might strengthen one social group at the expense of another; therefore, the extension of the franchise to the poor is a strategic move to affect future political equilibria. In the class of models we are analyzing, including the poor in the political system would benefit the middle class relative to the rich; for this reason, the middle class might try to push for further democratization to increase its political power. If we apply this interpretation to the British experience, we have to argue that the Tory Party under Disraeli was more representative of the middle class than rich landowning classes, which may not be realistic. In any case, we argue that this approach does not provide an entirely satisfactory explanation for the transition from partial to full democracy. Nevertheless, it is useful to understand how this argument could be formally developed.

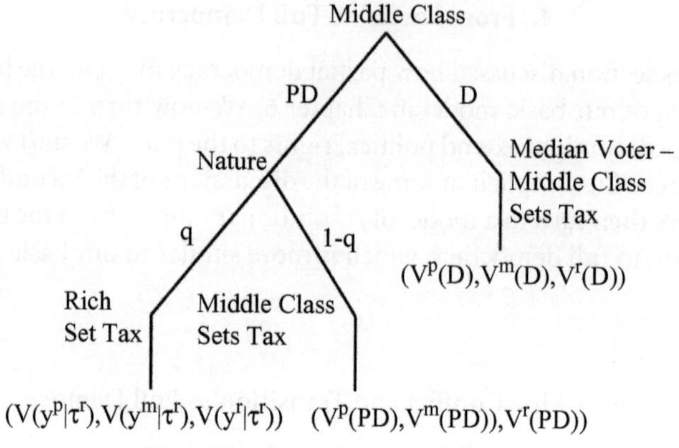

Figure 8.2. Disraeli versus Gladstone.

To formalize these ideas, consider the game depicted in Figure 8.2. The underlying political considerations are that in a partial democracy, where only the rich and the middle class are enfranchised, the rich may gain power with some probability – say, $q > 0$. The motivation for this is that in a restricted democracy, even if the middle class is more numerous than the rich, lobbying and other types of influence activities are effective in controlling the political system, which sometimes allows the rich to control the outcomes. In a full democracy, we assume that numerical superiority dominates (it is difficult to lobby or bribe a large number of people), and we assume $\delta^p < 1/2$ so that the median voter is a middle-class agent who we assume determines the policy outcomes. The game starts with the middle class in power, but it is afraid of losing power to the rich in partial democracy, with probability q. Therefore, if it keeps the system as it is, it will obtain its most preferred tax rate, τ^m, with probability $1 - q$, but $\tau^N = 0$ with probability q. The corresponding expected payoff is, therefore:

$$V^m(PD) = y^m + (1-q)(\tau^m(\bar{y} - y^m) - C(\tau^m)\bar{y})$$

In contrast, if the middle class extends the franchise to the poor, they become the median voter and their payoff is:

$$V^m(D) = y^m + (\tau^m(\bar{y} - y^m) - C(\tau^m)\bar{y})$$

Knowing that by including the poor in the political system, they will become the median voter, the middle class extends the franchise and administers a transition to full democracy. This ensures that it obtains its most preferred tax rate.

The reasoning underlying institutional change is again similar to our baseline argument: a particular group, now the middle class, has power today but it is transitory. Therefore, it wants to change institutions so as to lock in its political power. Before, the relevant institutional change was for the poor to obtain the vote so that they became powerful themselves. Here, the middle class wants to include the poor in the system so that the poor counterbalance the rich, ensuring that the middle class becomes more powerful.

Although this intra-elite competition view is interesting, it does not receive much support from the historical evidence in the British case. The Conservatives lost the 1868 election immediately after having passed the franchise extension (and the Liberal Party lost the election of 1885 after pushing through the Third Reform Act in 1884). So, if the strategy was aimed at winning elections, it was clearly a failure. Although the fact that the Conservatives lost the election does not prove that franchise extension was not aimed at winning elections, other aspects of this reform also appear inconsistent with a strategy of maximizing Conservative votes. In particular, as a result of the split over the Corn Laws, support for the Conservative Party was essentially concentrated in rural areas, with Tory landowners exerting substantial control over the electorate in the absence of a secret ballot. The reform measure passed under Disraeli increased the voting population by only 45 percent in counties compared to 145 percent in the boroughs, effectively ensuring a Conservative defeat in the subsequent elections.

The notion that the Liberals and Conservatives were prepared to extend the franchise simply to keep their party in power is not completely persuasive either. Instead, both parties were fundamentally opposed to extending the franchise further. Between 1859 and 1865, the Liberal Prime Minister Palmerston – who was opposed to franchise extension – and the Conservative leader Lord Derby colluded so that the issue of suffrage would never be raised in Parliament (Lee 1994, p. 138). During this period, Disraeli himself was an implacable opponent to political reform. In opposing reform in 1859, he said:

> If you establish a democracy, you must in due season reap the fruits of a democracy. You will in due season have great impatience of the public bodies combined in due season with great increase of the public expenditure. You will in due season reap the fruits of such united influence. You will in due season have wars entered into from passion, and not from reason; and you will in due season submit to peace ignominiously sought and ignominiously obtained, which will diminish your authority and perhaps endanger your independence. You will, in due season, with a democracy find that your property is less valuable and that your freedom is less complete. (quoted in Lang 1999, pp. 81–2).

Overall, the most plausible interpretation of the interparty rivalry in Britain during the 1860s and 1870s was that, whereas both parties regarded the extension of voting rights as inevitable due to mounting social pressure, they clearly saw that it could be structured in ways that were more or less advantageous to themselves. This created a complicated "end game." Cowling (1967, p. 89) argues that the Conservative Party supported Disraeli in 1867 because if the act failed, "the Liberals might then do precisely what Derby and Disraeli had striven in 1866 to prevent their doing – carry Reform on their own lines." In fact, Disraeli's first move upon becoming prime minister was to introduce a *less* generous franchise extension, but he realized that this would not gain majority support. He then switched to the more radical proposal that he could pass by gaining the support of a heterogeneous group of Liberals. The one triumph of the 1867 reform for Disraeli was the fact that it limited the redistribution of seats away from the counties to the boroughs, which would have been even more substantial otherwise. This strategy reduced the impact of the franchise extension for the Conservative Party and its constituency. Smith (1966, p. 97) agrees and argues that "Derby and Disraeli . . . in 1867, did not determine to trust the people, or put their faith in a Conservative democracy. They did what they felt they had to do, to satisfy the popular agitation and reconcile the upper strata of the working classes to the established political system."

Other cases of nineteenth-century democratization in Europe also do not offer much support for the view that the transition to full democracy was a way for one subgroup of the elites to increase its own vote share. For example, in the German case, the threat of revolution appeared to be the main factor. With army units in revolt and the economy collapsing in Germany in 1918–19, the former political elites attempted to prevent revolution by generating a transition that would cause minimal damage to their interests.

In France, there were more distinct subsets within elites. Orleanists and Legitimists formed separate factions within the monarchist camp; the Republicans, although democratic, were basically middle class and not in favor of universal male suffrage in 1848. When the monarchy collapsed in 1848, these groups had to concede to the demands of the revolutionaries. The same is true for the period after 1870. The conflict at the time, particularly the Commune, forced democracy along the lines of 1848. Although no group within the elites was committed to universal male suffrage, they were forced to reintroduce it.

The Swedish case is perhaps the most similar to Britain. In 1906, the Liberal Party's first-ever government fell after failing to pass a law introducing universal male suffrage. The reform measure of 1909 was then passed by the Conservative government under Lindman. As with Disraeli in 1867, "Lindman and his Conservative ministry that took office a year after the Liberals' 1906 failure saw an opportunity to pass a political reform on its own terms" (Collier 1999, p. 84). Although male suffrage was conceded in one house, the Conservatives kept control over the other through the maintenance of multiple voting and taxpayer suffrage. As with the British case, this pattern of events was not the result of attempts by the Conservatives to gain votes but rather a damage-limitation exercise in the face of mounting social pressure for a full democracy.

4.2 The Threat of Revolution and Transition to Full Democracy

So, if the move from partial to full democracy was not the result of intra-elite competition, what was the cause? Our answer, perhaps not surprisingly, is again

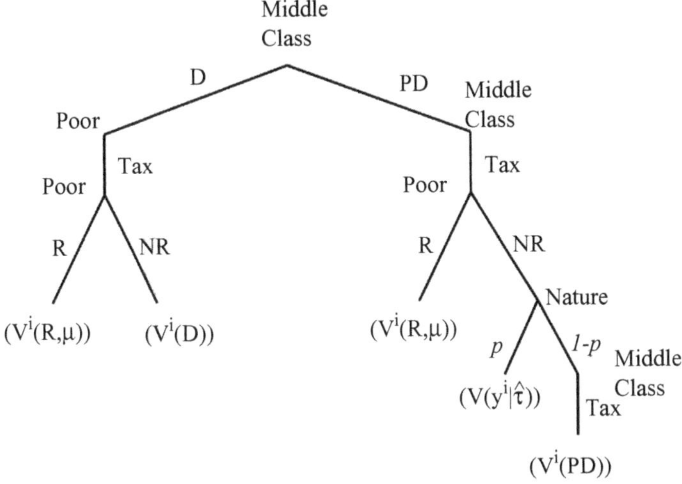

Figure 8.3. From Partial to Full Democracy.

the threat of revolution from the disenfranchised poor. As Chapter 1 illustrates, there was significant political and social unrest during the years leading to the Second Reform Act in Britain. In Chapter 3, we discussed evidence suggesting that in many other countries political reforms were frequently driven by similar forces. We therefore believe that we need a model along the lines of those in Chapter 6 to understand transition from partial to full democracy.

Let us now analyze how a society might transition from partial to full democracy because the poor form an effective challenge or pose a revolutionary threat. The underlying economic model is the same as our basic three-class model described previously.

How is this model different from that of Chapter 6? The main differences are that without further institutional change, we are in a world with partial democracy; the middle class is politically decisive with respect to the tax rate in partial democracy; and, given $\bar{y} > y^m$, there is going to be positive taxation and therefore redistribution toward the poor, even when they are excluded from the political system. Figure 8.3 draws the game tree. The revolution threat now comes from the poor and takes the same form as in Chapter 6. After revolution, the poor share the remaining income and the middle class and the rich receive nothing. Specifically, if there is revolution, we have:

$$V^p(R, \mu) = \frac{(1-\mu)\bar{y}}{\delta^p}$$

and $V^m(R, \mu) = V^r(R, \mu) = 0$.

It is important that without further democratization, we are in partial democracy, so the relevant values are as in (8.9). This implies that the revolution constraint is now different because the existing system is redistributing at the tax rate

τ^{PD}. In particular, in this case the revolution constraint would require:

$$V^p(R, \mu) > V^p(PD)$$

which is equivalent to:

$$\mu < 1 - \theta^p - (\tau^m(\delta^p - \theta^p) - \delta^p C(\tau^m)) \tag{8.16}$$

In addition, partial democracy can now promise to tax at a rate τ^{PD} greater than τ^m, in the same way that the rich promised higher redistribution in nondemocracy to stave off a revolution. The difference is that if those holding political power, the middle class and the rich, get a chance to reset the tax, they will not go down to zero taxation but rather to the most preferred tax rate of the median enfranchised voter, who is now a middle-class agent. Therefore, the values to the three social groups following a promise of future redistribution by the existing regime are as follows:

$$\begin{aligned} V^i(PD, \tau^{PD}) = y^i &+ p\left(\tau^{PD}\left(\bar{y} - y^i\right) - C(\tau^{PD})\bar{y}\right) \\ &+ (1-p)\left(\tau^m\left(\bar{y} - y^i\right) - C(\tau^m)\bar{y}\right) \end{aligned} \tag{8.17}$$

for $i = p, m, r$, where we incorporate the fact that if the middle class gets to reset the tax rate, then it chooses its preferred rate and sets τ^m. Following our previous analysis, we can now determine a critical level, μ^*, so that at μ^*, we have:

$$V^p(PD, \tau^{PD} = \tau^p) = V^p(R, \mu^*)$$

or:

$$\begin{aligned} \mu^* = 1 - \theta^p - (&p(\tau^p(\delta^p - \theta^p) - \delta^p C(\tau^p)) \\ &+ (1-p)(\tau^m(\delta^p - \theta^p) - \delta^p C(\tau^m))) \end{aligned} \tag{8.18}$$

There is an important new feature for future reference: μ^* is decreasing in τ^m. Intuitively, when the existing regime is more redistributive, it is easier to convince the poor with promises of future redistribution because even when the existing regime gets a chance to reset the tax, there will be some redistribution. This implies that when the middle class favors more redistribution, it is easier to convince the poor not to undertake a revolution. In consequence, it is easier to avoid democratizing.

Finally, we need to check that transition to full democracy prevents a revolution. This discussion shows that when $\delta^p < 1/2$, full democracy also implements the most preferred tax rate of a middle-class agent. Therefore, in this case, full democracy is no different than partial democracy. The more interesting case is when $\delta^p \geq 1/2$, so that the median voter in full democracy is a poor agent, and democracy leads to the most preferred tax rate of the poor, τ^p. In this case, the condition for full democratization to prevent revolution is $V^p(R, \mu) \leq V^p(D)$, which is equivalent to:

$$\mu \geq 1 - \theta^p - (\tau^p(\delta^p - \theta^p) - \delta^p C(\tau^p)) \tag{8.19}$$

Given this discussion, we can state:

Proposition 8.2: *In the game described in Figure 8.3, there is a unique subgame perfect equilibrium such that:*

- *If (8.16) does not bind, then partial democracy sets the most preferred tax rate of the middle class,* $\tau^{PD} = \tau^m$.
- *If (8.16) binds and (1)* $\delta^p \geq 1/2$ *and (8.19) fails to hold, or (2)* $\delta^p < 1/2$ *and* $\mu < \mu^*$*, then there is revolution.*
- *If (8.16) binds and* $\mu \geq \mu^*$*, then the existing regime prevents transition to full democracy by promising to redistribute at the tax rate* $\tau^{PD} = \hat{\tau}$ *such that* $V^p(PD, \tau^{PD} = \hat{\tau}) = V^p(R, \mu)$.
- *Finally, if (8.16) binds, (8.19) holds,* $\delta^p \geq 1/2$*, and* $\mu < \mu^*$*, then transition to full democracy happens as a credible commitment to future redistribution toward the poor.*

For the most part, the results of this proposition are similar to those of Proposition 6.1. However, there is an important new result. We know from our results that τ^m is higher when the middle class is relatively poor (i.e., when θ^m/δ^m is low). However, our analysis shows that a high level of τ^m makes partial democracy more attractive for the poor and decreases μ^*. As a result, societies in which the middle class is relatively poor may be able to stave off the threat of a revolution without having to fully democratize. Here, it is the middle class that is pivotal in nondemocracy (or partial democracy) and if it reneges on any promised concession it offers the poor, it will revert to its preferred polity, τ^m. If the middle class is relatively poor, τ^m will not be too far from τ^p, the policy preferred by the poor. In this case, the fact that the middle class may not be able to commit to offering τ^p is less important, a revolution less attractive, and democracy less likely to arise. Therefore, this model suggests that full democratization is more likely not only when the poor are poor but also when the middle class is relatively rich. This result is certainly in line with scholars who have argued for the importance of the strength and affluence of the middle class in democratization.

5. Repression: The Middle Class as a Buffer

In this section, we revisit the simple game analyzed in Section 3 in which both the middle class and the poor are disenfranchised but make the alternative assumption that the revolution threat is posed by the poor. In reality, both the middle class

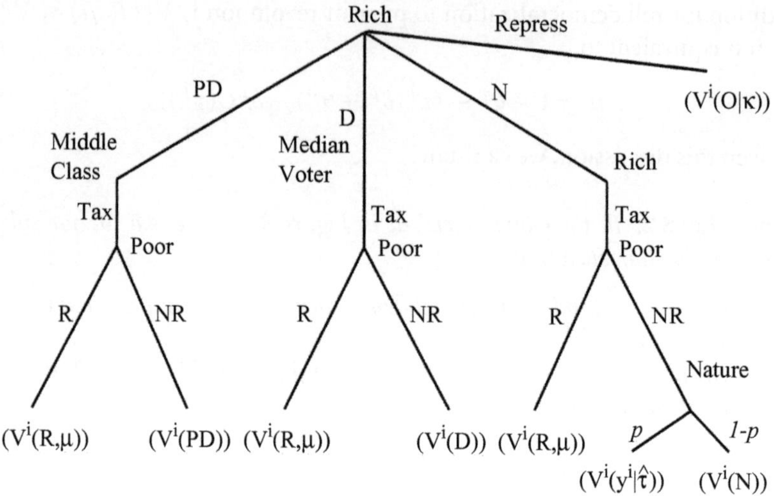

Figure 8.4. The Middle Class as a Buffer.

and the poor pose threats when they are excluded from political power. What matters is which group is pivotal. In the previous section, we considered the situation in which both the middle class and the poor were disenfranchised but the middle class was pivotal. Here, we investigate the alternative scenario: as in our basic model of democratization of Chapter 6, the rich have to satisfy the poor to prevent a revolution. Crucially, however, we reintroduce the possibility that the rich can use repression to prevent a revolution. The key question is: When will the rich prefer repression rather than democratization?

In this model, the presence of the middle class may act as a buffer between the rich and the poor and allow society to avoid repression. Therefore, repression is more likely to arise in societies in which the middle class is small or relatively poor.

The underlying model is the same as our basic three-class model. Agents again value posttax income but, in addition, there are the potential costs of repression if the rich choose the repression strategy. More specifically, the utility of an agent of class i now takes the form given in (6.8).

Figure 8.4 draws the game tree. The rich have two democratization options: partial and full. Also, the key revolution decision is now by the poor (they can undertake revolution even without help from the middle class). In addition, we still have the feature that the promise to redistribute by the rich is imperfect because they can get to reset the tax after the threat of revolution has subsided with probability $1 - p$, which implies that any tax set initially will stay with probability p.

We assume that the returns from revolution are similar to before but because the poor are the main revolutionary element, we assume for the sake of simplicity that they share the returns only among themselves. So, the return to the poor from undertaking a revolution is:

$$V^p(R,\mu) = \frac{(1-\mu)\bar{y}}{\delta^p} \tag{8.20}$$

The middle class and the rich obtain nothing after a revolution, so $V^m(R,\mu) = V^r(R,\mu) = 0$.

The revolution constraint is binding if the poor prefer revolution to no redistribution under the existing system or if $V^p(R,\mu) = (1-\mu)\bar{y}/\delta^p > y^p$. The revolution constraint can be written as:

$$\theta^p < 1 - \mu \tag{8.21}$$

As before, the rich may meet the revolution threat by promising redistribution, which is only a partially credible promise because they have a chance to reset the tax with probability p once the threat has subsided. The values to the three different groups, when the rich keep political power and promise redistribution at the tax rate $\hat{\tau}$, are given by (8.8) evaluated at $\tau^N = \hat{\tau}$.

If the rich choose partial democracy, PD, only the middle class is enfranchised and by the assumption that $\delta^p > \delta^m > \delta^r$, in this partial democracy the rich are a minority and the most preferred tax rate of the middle class is implemented. By assumption, this tax rate, τ^m, is strictly positive. Therefore, we have the values $V^i(PD)$ given by (8.9).

Finally, the values in democracy depend on whether the median voter is a poor or a middle-class agent. Recall that this depends on whether δ^p is less than or greater than 1/2. These values are given by (8.10) with the tax rate determined by (8.11). As before, if $\delta^p < 1/2$, then $V^r(PD) = V^r(D)$, but when $\delta^p \geq 1/2$, we have $V^r(PD) > V^r(D)$.

As in the Chapter 6 analysis and in Section 3, the crucial issue is whether the promise of redistribution can prevent revolution. But now, in contrast to when the middle class was the politically pivotal group, it is the poor that need to be placated to avoid revolution. Thus, for revolution to be prevented, we need that:

$$V^p(N,\tau^N) \geq V^p(R,\mu) \tag{8.22}$$

Because the highest value that the rich can offer to the poor is clearly when they set the tax rate most preferred by the poor, τ^p, this is equivalent to:

$$V^p(N,\tau^N = \tau^p) \geq V^p(R,\mu)$$

Define μ^* such that this condition holds as an equality or, in other words:

$$\mu^* = 1 - \theta^p - p\left(\tau^p(\delta^p - \theta^p) - \delta^p C(\tau^p)\right). \tag{8.23}$$

The rich can now also try to prevent revolution by undertaking a partial democratization. Following partial democratization, the median voter is a middle-class agent and chooses a tax rate of $\tau^{PD} = \tau^m$. This strategy prevents revolution if:

$$V^p(PD) \geq V^p(R, \mu)$$

or if:

$$\mu \geq 1 - \theta^p - (\tau^m(\delta^p - \theta^p) - \delta^p C(\tau^m)) \tag{8.24}$$

Finally, we need to look at payoffs from repression, which are:

$$V^i(O \mid \kappa) = (1 - \kappa)y^i \quad \text{for} \quad i = p, m, r \tag{8.25}$$

The analysis is similar to before and, in particular, we need to determine threshold values for the cost of repression such that the rich are indifferent between repression and their other alternatives. Denote these threshold values by $\hat{\kappa}$ and $\tilde{\kappa}(\tau)$ such that the rich are indifferent between their various options at these threshold levels. The second threshold is conditioned on the tax rate that will result in either democracy, τ^D, or partial democracy, τ^{PD}. More specifically, we have:

$$V^r(O \mid \hat{\kappa}) = V^r(N, \tau^N = \hat{\tau})$$

where $\hat{\tau}$ is such that $V^p(N, \tau^N = \hat{\tau}) = V^p(R, \mu)$. In other words:

$$\hat{\kappa} = \frac{p}{\theta^r}(\delta^r C(\hat{\tau}) - \hat{\tau}(\delta^r - \theta^r)) \tag{8.26}$$

Therefore, at $\hat{\kappa}$, the rich are indifferent between redistribution and repression. As a result, for all $\kappa < \hat{\kappa}$, they prefer repression to promising redistribution. This implies that one set of parameter configurations in which repression emerges is when $\mu \geq \mu^*$ and $\kappa < \hat{\kappa}$.

Next, define the threshold for the elites to be indifferent between democratization and repression by $\tilde{\kappa}(\tau)$ as a function of the tax rate in democracy:

$$V^r(O \mid \tilde{\kappa}(\tau)) = V^r(D) \tag{8.27}$$

or:

$$V^r(O \mid \tilde{\kappa}(\tau)) = V^r(PD) \tag{8.28}$$

These two conditions both imply the same formula:

$$\tilde{\kappa}(\tau) = \frac{1}{\theta^r}(\delta^r C(\tau) - \tau(\delta^r - \theta^r)) \tag{8.29}$$

where $\tau = \tau^D$ if the value of repression is equated to the value of full democracy (i.e., (8.27)) or $\tau = \tau^{PD}$ if the value of partial democracy is relevant (i.e., (8.28)).

At $\tilde{\kappa}(\tau)$, the rich are indifferent between repression and either partial or full democratization, which leads to the tax rate $\tau \in \{\tau^D, \tau^{PD}\}$. As a result, for all $\kappa < \tilde{\kappa}(\tau)$, they prefer repression to democratization. Therefore, another set of parameter values in which repression is an equilibrium outcome is when $\mu < \mu^*$ and $\kappa < \tilde{\kappa}(\tau)$:

Proposition 8.3: *Assume that (8.19) holds. In the game described in Figure 8.4, there exists a unique subgame perfect equilibrium. Let μ^*, $\tilde{\kappa}(\tau)$, and $\hat{\kappa}$ be as defined above. Then:*

- *If (8.21) does not bind, the rich set their preferred tax rate, $\tau^N = \tau^r$.*
- *It (8.21) binds. Then:*
  (1) *If $\mu < \mu^*$ and (8.24) holds, $\delta^p \geq 1/2$, and $\kappa \geq \tilde{\kappa}(\tau^{PD})$, the rich undertake a partial democratization.*
  (2) *If $\mu < \mu^*$, (8.24) does not hold, $\kappa \geq \tilde{\kappa}(\tau^D)$, and $\delta^p \geq 1/2$, the rich fully democratize.*
  (3) *If (1) $\mu < \mu^*$, (8.24) does not hold, and $\delta^p < 1/2$; or (2) $\mu < \mu^*$, (8.24) does not hold, $\kappa < \tilde{\kappa}(\tau^D)$, and $\delta^p \geq 1/2$; or (3) $\mu < \mu^*$, (8.24) holds, and $\kappa < \tilde{\kappa}(\tau^{PD})$; or (4) $\mu \geq \mu^*$ and $\kappa < \hat{\kappa}$, then the rich use repression.*
  (4) *If $\mu \geq \mu^*$ and $\kappa \geq \hat{\kappa}$, the rich prevent democratization by promising to redistribute by setting the tax rate $\tau^N = \hat{\tau}$ such that $V^p(N, \tau^N = \hat{\tau}) = V^p(R, \mu)$.*

To understand the main result in this proposition, note that when the revolution constraint binds there are several possibilities. First, the rich are unable to use concessions to maintain power ($\mu < \mu^*$), but (8.24) holds and $\delta^p \geq 1/2$. This implies that a partial democratization is sufficient to avoid revolution essentially because the middle class prefers more redistribution than the rich. Moreover, because $\delta^p \geq 1/2$, full democratization would bring the poor to power, something the rich would like to avoid if possible. In this case partial democratization occurs if $\kappa \geq \tilde{\kappa}(\tau^{PD})$ so that repression is relatively costly. Second, full democratization arises because neither concessions nor partial democratization works (i.e., $\mu < \mu^*$ and (8.24) does not hold) and repression is relatively costly (i.e., $\kappa \geq \tilde{\kappa}(\tau^D)$). Because $\delta^p \geq 1/2$ and (8.19) holds, the creation of full democracy leads to a tax rate of τ^p, which avoids revolution. The third situation is where repression arises. This happens in four types of situations. First, concessions to the poor again do not work, (8.24) does not hold, and $\delta^p < 1/2$. In this case partial democracy is insufficiently redistributive to avoid revolution. Moreover, full democratization leads to the median voter being a member of the middle class, and since this would lead to a tax rate τ^m the failure of (8.24) to hold implies that this will also lead the poor to revolt. In this case the rich have no option but to repress if they want to avoid a revolution. Second, again neither concessions nor partial democratization can avoid a revolution, but since $\delta^p \geq 1/2$ and (8.19) holds full democratization does. Nevertheless, when $\kappa < \tilde{\kappa}(\tau^D)$ repression is preferred to full democracy. Thirdly, concessions do not work but partial democracy does and $\kappa < \tilde{\kappa}(\tau^{PD})$. Here, though partial democracy would be sufficient to avoid a revolution the rich find it better to repress than enfranchise the middle class. The fourth case is where concessions work but repression is cheaper ($\mu \geq \mu^*$ and $\kappa < \hat{\kappa}$). The final case is the familiar one where concessions do work and repression is relatively costly so that the rich maintain power by setting a tax rate sufficiently high to placate the poor.

This proposition is similar to Proposition 6.2. The main difference is that now one of the two key thresholds, $\tilde{\kappa}(\tau)$, depends on the size and the level of income of the middle class. It is obvious that $\tilde{\kappa}(\tau)$; is increasing in τ; therefore, a higher level of the tax rate in democracy, τ, makes repression more attractive for the rich. Taxes in democracy are higher when the median voter is a poor agent (i.e., $\delta^p \geq 1/2$), which corresponds to the case in which the middle class is small so that the poor are decisive in democracy, or when the median voter is a middle-class agent (i.e., $\delta^p < 1/2$) but is relatively poor and likes higher taxes.

Therefore, a relatively large and affluent middle class may make democracy less costly for the rich and may act as a buffer between the poor and the rich, making repression less likely. Conversely, when the middle class is small or poor, the rich may be more inclined to undertake repression. The caveat "may" is necessary because this need not always be the case. For instance, if θ^m increases, τ^m falls, and (8.24) becomes less likely to hold. If $\mu < \mu^*$, (8.24) ceases to hold, and $\delta^p < 1/2$, then the rich switch to repression because neither partial nor full democracy is redistributive enough to stop revolution.

6. Repression: Softliners versus Hardliners

The previous section discussed a model in which the rich had to choose between repression and democratization to prevent a revolutionary threat from the poor, who were until then excluded from the political system. We also presumed that the middle class, like the poor, was outside the system. Therefore, democratization gave the middle class as well as the poor political power and, in this way, the middle class played an important role in affecting the trade-off between repression and democratization. With a large and relatively rich middle class, the rich anticipated that they would not face high taxes in democracy and were more likely to democratize rather than repress.

In this section, we analyze a similar game; however, both the rich and the middle class are part of the ruling coalition and they have to decide jointly whether to promise redistribution to the poor under the existing regime, democratize, or repress. The key insight of the analysis is that the rich are always more in favor of repression than the middle class. This has a simple reason: the rich have more to lose than the middle class from redistributive taxation.

This difference between the attitudes of the rich and the middle class toward repression provides a way to formalize the often-made distinction between softliners and hardliners in dictatorships. It is argued, especially in the context of Latin American and Southern European transitions to democracy, that there is often a split within the elites controlling dictatorships: hardliners wish to use force to prolong the dictatorship; softliners try to administer a soft landing to democracy.

But who are hardliners and softliners? Elites in nondemocratic regimes are obviously heterogeneous, but what are important sources of heterogeneity? Our three-class model provides a simple answer by mapping the softliners into middle-class agents and the hardliners into rich agents. We show in Chapter 9 that there can be other splits – for example, between landowners and capitalists along the same lines – but for now our focus is with the three-class model in which the only difference is in the levels of income, not from which types of activities these incomes are being generated.

The economic model is the same as before with three groups of agents. In nondemocracy, when the rich and the middle class have different preferences, we have to propose a way to aggregate their diverging preferences, specifically with respect to the decision about whether to repress the poor. In this chapter so far when we modeled partial democracy, we considered it a situation in which the preferences of the middle class determined the policy outcome, at least if unconstrained by the threat of revolution. Here, we adopt a different approach that allows the preferences of both the rich and the middle class to matter. We assume policy decisions in nondemocracy are made according to a utilitarian social-welfare function, meaning that repression takes place if the repression decision maximizes the weighted sum of utilities of the rich and the middle class.

There are various ways in which such an approach can be justified, but it is a natural extension of our model in Chapter 4 in which the parameter χ represented the power of the elites in democracy. We argued and substantiated this argument in the appendix to the chapter that many models of democratic politics boiled down to different microfoundations for χ. In general, therefore, we can think of the democratic tax rate as maximizing a weighted sum of utilities, with the median-voter model being a special case with $\chi = 0$. Analogous reasoning suggests that we can treat the intra-elite preference-aggregation problem in the same way and imagine that the repression decision was simply that which maximizes a weighted sum of utilities of the rich and the middle class. For instance, we can think of elite control as a limited type of democracy (e.g., most European and Latin American countries before the creation of universal suffrage) in which political parties compete only for the votes of members and factions of the elites. For simplicity and without affecting our main results, we proceed by assuming that the weights on the preferences of different subsets of the elites are the same so that the repression decision simply maximizes the sum of utilities of the elites.

There is again the democratization option and the feature that the promise to redistribute by the rich is imperfectly credible because the elites can reset the tax rate after the threat of a revolution has subsided with probability $1 - p$.

We assume that returns from a revolution are similar to before, with the poor sharing the returns only among themselves. The return to the poor from undertaking a revolution is $V^p(R, \mu) = (1 - \mu)\bar{y}/\delta^p$, with $V^m(R, \mu) = V^r(R, \mu) = 0$.

As usual, the revolution constraint is binding if the poor prefer a revolution to the existing system or if $(1 - \mu)\bar{y}/\delta^p > y^p$. The relevant revolution constraint can be written as:

$$1 - \mu > \theta^p \tag{8.30}$$

In this section, we assume that this condition holds.

The values to the three different groups when the existing system is maintained and redistribution at the tax rate τ^{PD} is promised are given again by $V^i(PD, \tau^{PD})$ in (8.17). Because both the rich and the middle class are part of the ruling coalition, we refer to this regime as partial democracy.

The values in full democracy depend on whether the median voter is a poor or a middle-class agent. Recall that this depends on whether δ^p is less than or greater than 1/2. Here, we assume that $\delta^p \geq 1/2$, so:

$$V^i(D) = y^i + \left(\tau^p\left(\bar{y} - y^i\right) - C(\tau^p)\bar{y}\right)$$

As in our previous analysis and in Chapter 6, the promise of redistribution is only imperfectly credible and it prevents a revolution only if $V^p(PD, \tau^{PD}) \geq V^p(R, \mu)$. Again, we can determine a critical value, μ^*, such that at μ^*, we have:

$$V^p(PD, \tau^{PD} = \tau^p) = V^p(R, \mu^*)$$

To simplify the discussion, we are going to focus on the case in which $\mu < \mu^*$ so that the promise of redistribution is not sufficient to prevent a revolution. The choice is, therefore, between democratization and repression. The payoffs from repression are given by (8.25).

We again determine two threshold values, but now one refers to the rich and the other to the middle class, making the respective group indifferent between democratization and repression. Let these two critical values be $\tilde{\kappa}^r$ and $\tilde{\kappa}^m$ for the rich and the middle class, respectively. They are defined by:

$$V^r(O \mid \tilde{\kappa}^r) = V^r(D) \quad \text{and} \quad V^m(O \mid \tilde{\kappa}^m) = V^m(D)$$

or, more explicitly:

$$\tilde{\kappa}^r = \frac{1}{\theta^r}\left(\delta^r C(\tau^P) - \tau^P\left(\delta^r - \theta^r\right)\right) \tag{8.31}$$

$$\tilde{\kappa}^m = \frac{1}{\theta^m}\left(\delta^m C(\tau^P) - \tau^P\left(\delta^m - \theta^m\right)\right)$$

As before, the rich prefer repression to democratization when $\kappa < \tilde{\kappa}^r$ and the middle class prefers repression to democratization when $\kappa < \tilde{\kappa}^m$.

It is important that because $\theta^r/\delta^r > \theta^m/\delta^m$ by the fact that the rich are richer than the middle class, we have that $\tilde{\kappa}^m < \tilde{\kappa}^r$; thus, for $\kappa \in [\tilde{\kappa}^m, \tilde{\kappa}^r)$, the rich want to use repression whereas the middle class prefers democratization to repression. In this region, therefore, the preferences of the two factions of the elites diverge. In this case, repression is chosen if:

$$\delta^r V^r(O \mid \kappa) + \delta^m V^m(O \mid \kappa) > \delta^r V^r(D) + \delta^m V^m(D)$$

or if:

$$\begin{aligned} &\delta^r(1-\kappa)y^r + \delta^m(1-\kappa)y^m \\ &\quad > \delta^r\left(y^r + \tau^P(\bar{y} - y^r) - C(\tau^P)\bar{y}\right) + \delta^m\left(y^m + \tau^P(\bar{y} - y^m) - C(\tau^P)\bar{y}\right) \end{aligned}$$

Now, substituting for the definitions of y^r and y^m and dividing through by $\bar{y}$, we find that repression is chosen if:

$$\kappa < \frac{1}{(\theta^r + \theta^m)}\left(\delta^r C(\tau^P) - \tau^P\left(\delta^r - \theta^r\right) + \delta^m C(\tau^P) - \tau^P\left(\delta^m - \theta^m\right)\right)$$

Using the definitions of $\tilde{\kappa}^r$ and $\tilde{\kappa}^m$, we also have:

$$\kappa < \tilde{\kappa}^e = \frac{\theta^r \tilde{\kappa}^r + \theta^m \tilde{\kappa}^m}{(\theta^r + \theta^m)}$$

where $\tilde{\kappa}^e \in (\tilde{\kappa}^m, \tilde{\kappa}^r)$. If $\kappa < \tilde{\kappa}^e$, the preferences of the rich determine that repression will be used, whereas if $\kappa \geq \tilde{\kappa}^e$, it is the preferences of the middle class that win and democracy is created even though the rich would prefer to use repression when $\kappa \in [\tilde{\kappa}^e, \tilde{\kappa}^r)$.

As before, we also need to ensure that democratization prevents revolution; the condition for this is (8.19). This analysis leads to the following proposition:

Proposition 8.4: *Assume that $\delta^p \geq 1/2$, $\mu < \mu^*$, $1 - \mu > \theta^p$, and (8.19) holds so that democratization prevents revolution. Then, in the unique subgame perfect equilibrium:*

- *If $\kappa \geq \tilde{\kappa}^r$, then both the rich and the middle class prefer democratization to repression, and democratization occurs as a credible commitment to future redistribution.*
- *If $\kappa < \tilde{\kappa}^m$, then both the rich and the middle class prefer repression to democratization, and they use repression to prevent a revolution.*
- *If $\kappa \in [\tilde{\kappa}^m, \tilde{\kappa}^r)$, the rich prefer repression to democratization, whereas the middle class prefers democratization to repression. If $\kappa < \tilde{\kappa}^e$, the elites use repression to avoid democratizing, whereas if $\kappa \geq \tilde{\kappa}^e$, they democratize.*

This proposition, especially the case in which $\kappa \in [\tilde{\kappa}^m, \tilde{\kappa}^r)$, captures the different attitudes of the softliners (here, the middle class) and the hardliners (here, the rich). The hardliners have more to lose from democratization and prefer to use repression even when softliners prefer a transition to democracy.

This model can be used to formalize the idea that democratizations occur when the elites "split." To see this, consider the case in which $\kappa < \tilde{\kappa}^m$, so that initially both factions of the elites favor repression. Now consider a situation in which κ increases. For instance, the costs of repression may increase because the end of the Cold War moves the international community in a more prodemocratic manner, or democratizations in neighboring countries make repression less feasible. In this case, κ can move into the region in which $\kappa \in [\tilde{\kappa}^m, \tilde{\kappa}^r)$. Initially, the rich still favor repression whereas now the middle class swings in favor of democracy. Here, the elites split in the sense that different segments now prefer different policies. Nevertheless, as long as $\kappa \in [\tilde{\kappa}^m, \tilde{\kappa}^e)$, the preferences of the rich dominate and repression is used in equilibrium. However, if κ increases above $\tilde{\kappa}^e$, even though the rich still favor repression, the preferences of the middle class dominate and democratization occurs. At this point, the split in the elites leads to a democratization but only when the power of the middle classes is sufficiently large within the elites. In our model of preference aggregation (i.e., the utilitarian social-welfare function), as κ increases, both groups become less in favor of repression, which can lead to a switch in the decision of the elites even when the rich still prefer repression.

It is also interesting that the disagreement between the rich and the middle class regarding repression becomes stronger when the middle class is relatively poor. When the middle class is relatively richer (i.e., when θ^m/δ^m is higher), they also have more to lose from redistribution in democracy and they become more favorable toward repression.

7. The Role of the Middle Class in Consolidating Democracy

In this section, we switch attention from the creation of democracy and examine how the middle class may play an important role in democratic consolidation. We show how a large and relatively rich middle class might help consolidate democracy. Intuitively, when the median voter is a middle-class agent, democracy is less redistributive and becomes even less so when the middle class becomes richer. As democracy becomes less redistributive, the rich have less to gain by changing the regime and democracy becomes more likely to survive.

Let us now return to the three-class model. The basic setup is identical to before. We assume that the median voter in a full democracy is a member of the middle class and prefers the tax rate $\tau^m > 0$. This implies that the values $V^i(D)$ satisfy (8.10) with $\tau^D = \tau^m$. The rich have to decide whether to mount a coup; the payoffs after a coup are:

$$V^i(C, \varphi) = (1 - \varphi)y^i \quad \text{for} \quad i = p, m, r$$

As before, the median voter may meet the threat of a coup by promising redistribution, which is only a partially credible promise because has a chance to reset the tax with probability p once the coup threat has subsided. The values to the three different groups when there is democracy and a promise of redistribution at the tax rate, $\tau^D \leq \tau^m$, are:

$$\begin{aligned} V^i(D, \tau^D) = y^i &+ p\left(\tau^D\left(\bar{y} - y^i\right) - C(\tau^D)\bar{y}\right) \\ &+ (1 - p)\left(\tau^m\left(\bar{y} - y^i\right) - C(\tau^m)\bar{y}\right) \end{aligned}$$

Whether a coup is attractive for the rich given the status quo depends on whether the coup constraint, $V^r(C, \varphi) > V^r(D)$, binds. This coup constraint can be expressed as:

$$\varphi < \frac{1}{\theta^r}\left(C(\tau^m)\delta^r - \tau^m(\delta^r - \theta^r)\right) \tag{8.32}$$

When this constraint does not bind, democracy is not redistributive enough or coups are sufficiently costly that the rich never find a coup profitable. In this case, we refer to democracy as fully consolidated: there is never any effective threat against the stability of democracy. It is clear that (8.32) is easier to satisfy than (7.4) because $\tau^m < \tau^p$. Because the middle class is richer, it prefers less taxation, and this makes coups less attractive to the rich. Moreover, the greater θ^m, the lower is τ^m and the cheaper a coup must be for it to be attractive to the rich.

When this constraint binds, democracy is not fully consolidated: if the middle class does not take action, there will be a coup along the equilibrium path. The action that it can take is to reduce the fiscal burden that democracy places on the rich or, in other words, reduce the tax rate. The value to the rich of the middle-class setting a tax rate of $\tilde{\tau}$ is $V^r(D, \tau^D = \tilde{\tau})$. This strategy of promising less distribution prevents the coup only if this value is greater than the return to the rich following a coup (i.e., $V^r(D, \tau^D = \tilde{\tau}) \geq V^r(C, \varphi)$). In other words, democracy survives only if:

$$\varphi \leq \frac{p}{\theta^r}(\delta^r C(\tilde{\tau}) - \tilde{\tau}(\delta^r - \theta^r)) + \frac{(1-p)}{\theta^r}(\delta^r C(\tau^m) - \tau^m(\delta^r - \theta^r))$$

As in our analysis of the basic static consolidation game in Chapter 7, we now define a threshold value φ^{**} such that when $\varphi < \varphi^{**}$, the promise of limited redistribution by democracy is not sufficient to dissuade the rich from a coup. Of course, the most attractive promise that can be made to the rich is to stop redistribution away from them (i.e., $\tau^D = 0$); therefore, we must have that at φ^{**}, $V^r(D, \tau^D = 0) = V^r(C, \varphi)$. Solving this equality gives the threshold value φ^{**} as:

$$\varphi^{**} = \frac{(1-p)}{\theta^r}(\delta^r C(\tau^m) - \tau^m(\delta^r - \theta^r)) \tag{8.33}$$

Given this discussion, we can summarize the subgame perfect equilibrium of this game as follows:

Proposition 8.5: *In the game described above, there is a unique subgame perfect equilibrium such that:*

- *If the coup constraint (8.32) does not bind, the coup threat is weak, democracy is fully consolidated, and the middle class sets its most preferred tax rate,* $\tau^m > 0$.
- *If the coup constraint (8.32) binds and* $\varphi \geq \varphi^{**}$*, then democracy is semiconsolidated. The middle class sets a tax rate,* $\tilde{\tau} < \tau^m$*, such that* $V^r(D, \tau^D = \tilde{\tau}) = V^r(C, \varphi)$.
- *If the coup constraint (8.32) binds and* $\varphi < \varphi^{**}$*, then democracy is unconsolidated. There is a coup, the rich come to power, and set their most preferred tax rate,* $\tau^D = \tau^r$.

The main insight that this model adds is that the preferred tax rate of the middle class is now crucial in the coup constraint and the definition of (8.33).

Moreover, it is easy to see that $\varphi^{**} < \varphi^*$ derived in Section 7.1. Taxes in democracy are higher when the median voter is a poor agent (i.e., $\delta^p \geq 1/2$) which corresponds to the case in which the middle class is small or when the median voter is a middle-class agent (i.e., $\delta^p < 1/2$) but is relatively poor and likes higher taxes. Both of these cases make coups more attractive to the rich. Therefore, a relatively large and affluent middle class makes democracy less costly for the rich and acts as a buffer between the poor and the rich, making coups less likely and thus helping to consolidate democracy.

8. Conclusion

In this chapter, we introduced a third group into our analysis, the middle class. We focused the discussion on situations in which sociopolitical conflict was along the lines of socioeconomic class. We used this model to generate some interesting new insights consistent with some of the claims made in the political science and sociology literature on the importance of the middle class for democracy. Although we investigated various phenomena in this chapter, including how the introduction of the middle class allowed us to provide a simple model of how "splits in the elites" might work, there are two main results that we believe may be the most significant.

First, a strong and large middle class may aid democratization because it is less in favor of radical policies than the poor. Hence, if the rich are convinced that democracy is controlled by the interests of middle-class agents, they have less to fear from democracy and are less inclined to use repression to avoid it. This may occur either because the middle class grows numerically and, thus, the median voter becomes a middle-class agent or the median voter is already middle class and the middle class becomes richer (and, thus, prefers less redistribution). It is also interesting that other theories of the distribution of power in democracy, such as those discussed in the appendix to Chapter 4, emphasize that the political power of the middle class in democracy is often greater than its number would indicate. The most famous example of this is "Director's law of income redistribution" (Stigler 1970), which claims that the preponderance of redistributive policies in democracy actually favor the middle class and not the poor. Although there are no definitive microfoundations for this claim and it is contentious empirically, it can be formalized in various ways. For instance, Persson and Tabellini (2000, pp. 57–8) show in a probabilistic voting model (see the appendix to Chapter 4, Section 2) how, if the middle class is less ideological than the poor and the rich, then its preferences are critical in determining the policies adopted in democracy. An alternative approach would be to assume in the context of a lobbying model (Grossman and Helpman 2001; appendix to Chapter 4, Section 3) that the middle class is better able to solve the collective-action problem than other groups.

Second and related a strong middle class may encourage democratic consolidation. The mechanism by which it does so is similar to that by which it helps to promote democratization. If the middle class is sufficiently influential in democratic politics, then democracy is not too costly for the rich; as a result, coups are less attractive. Hence, a strengthening of the middle class, in terms of an increase in either its size, political power, or relative income, may lead to the consolidation of a previously unconsolidated democracy. There is, of course, a natural caveat here: if the middle class becomes too rich, then it becomes indistinguishable from the rich and, therefore, will not be able to play the critical role of buffer between the rich and the poor.

Overall, the models in this chapter suggest that a third group, the middle class or the bourgeoisie, can play important roles in democratization. It can do so because it alters the nature of political conflict. Although scholars in the democratization literature have certainly suggested that the middle class can play an important role in democracy, they have not provided microfoundations for these claims. In this chapter, we showed that extending our framework to three groups provides natural microfoundations for the importance attributed to the middle class.

9 Economic Structure and Democracy

1. Introduction

So far, we have taken the determination of the level and distribution of income as exogenous. In this chapter, we endogenize the level and distribution of income. Instead of being directly endowed with income, people have various endowments of assets: land, labor, and physical and human capital. We introduce a technology, an aggregate production function, that determines how these factors of production can be combined to produce output. We also introduce key economic institutions, specifically property rights and competitive markets, that determine the rates of return on various assets.

Why would any of this matter? Intuitively, the structure of the economy or economic institutions could be important if they influence the trade-off between democracy and nondemocracy for the elites or the benefits of democracy as opposed to revolution for the citizens. There are many reasons why this might be so. First, the structure of the economy might influence the costs of revolution, repression, or coups. Second, the structure of the economy may also influence the nature of redistributive politics between different groups, something that our framework links to the creation and consolidation of democracy. We investigate both sets of ideas in this chapter. The models analyzed also allow us to consider some of the most salient claims in the political science and sociology literature about democracy. For instance, the claim that democracy can never be sustained in a primarily agrarian society, or at least one where the elites are large landowners, is common in the literature from Moore (1966), and Dahl (1971), to Rueschemeyer, Stephens, and Stephens (1992). Yet, the microfoundations of this claim are unclear. The models in this chapter help isolate mechanisms that may induce such a connection.

There seem to be a number of plausible reasons for why the costs of coups and repression might be related to the structure of the economy. Most important, repression and coups are costly because they disrupt economic life. Production in a modern capitalist economy requires input from many diverse firms, and much of this is not coordinated centrally or consciously but rather organized by the invisible hand of the market, as well as the visible hand of established firms. Moreover, most of these economic relationships are based on some type of implicit trust. At the simplest level, the employer knows that the workers will show up the following day and the workers know that when they show up, there will be work for them and they will be paid. More important, each firm trusts that its suppliers will provide it with the materials necessary for production and that customers and firms downstream are there to purchase those products. Even more important, there is an implicit trust in the quality of the goods and services provided. Employers believe that workers will not only show up but also exert appropriate amounts of effort, and suppliers will supply not just any odd materials but materials of sufficient quality to enable production. Finally, customers trust that they will be buying relatively high quality products, not things that would be unattractive for them to consume. Any sudden eruption of violence, any turmoil transforming the political system, any situation heightening the already existing conflicts in society also disrupts the economic structure, the relationships of trust, the cooperation that is the essence of capitalist production. In a related discussion, Dahl (1971) notes the

> . . . enormous limitations, costs and inefficiencies of violence, coercion and compulsion in managing an advanced society where incentives and complex behavior are needed that cannot be manipulated by threats of violence. (p. 79)

There are also analogous ideas in the literature on military politics. For instance, Finer (1976) argues that military governments cannot run complex industrial societies because the costs would be too high. He notes

> as an economy advances, as the division of labour becomes more and more extensive, as the secondary and then the tertiary services expand, and as the society requires the existence of a professional bureaucracy, of technicians . . . so the army ceases to be able to rule by its own resources alone. (p. 17)

These ideas suggest why repression and coups are costly. The reasoning emphasizes the breakdown of complex economic relations, which are important for capitalist production. Although the same relationships are present in agrarian production, they are clearly less important. Quality issues are less paramount when it comes to agricultural products than in manufacturing. In a less developed and less industrialized economy, there are fewer complex relationships of buyer and supplier networks and less reliance on investments in skills and relationship-specific capital. These considerations naturally suggest that repression and coups become more costly in economies where production techniques are capital-intensive, both physical and human, rather than land-intensive.

Of equal importance is that the structure of the economy may influence the form of political conflict and the redistributive implications of democracy for the elites. For instance, landowners may have more to lose in democracy than industrialists. Recall that our entire approach is based on the presumption that the citizens have the political power to set policy to favor themselves in democracy. One factor that may limit the ability of the citizens to get the policies they want in democracy is that the elites may have power out of proportion to their numbers (e.g., through lobbying or the control of parties, as analyzed in the appendix to Chapter 4). But, there is an equally important economic factor that limits what the citizens can do, which we referred to as the Laffer Curve in Chapter 4. It is easiest to discuss this in the context of income redistribution. If taxes are very high, this stifles economic activity and creates such deep economic distortions that there is not much output left. Therefore, democracy is naturally restrained in applying high taxes, trying to ensure that these taxes do not distort the allocation of resources too much and do not induce the elites to withdraw their assets from economic activity, thus reducing tax revenues. But, the extent to which these considerations apply to capital and to land differs significantly. A high tax rate on land at most encourages landowners to leave their lands empty, but there is not much more they can do. In contrast, physical capital is more elastically supplied or more mobile: tax capital at a higher rate and there will not be much accumulation; capital holders will invest their money in nontaxable sectors or take it abroad where it will not be taxed (a possibility we discuss in detail in Chapter 10). Human capital is probably in the most elastic supply because it is useless unless people exert effort which they will not be prepared to do if tax rates becomes too high. This implies that democracy naturally applies higher taxes on landowners than physical or human capital owners in an effort to maximize redistribution without creating too many distortions. Similarly, democracy in many unequal societies at first turns to asset redistribution and, because land is much easier and probably less distortionary to redistribute than physical capital, land reform is a way of dealing with the most severe inequities. Human capital is, of course, impossible to redistribute. Again, landowners have more to lose from democracy than capitalists or industrialists.

These ideas imply that elites who are heavily invested in land are typically more willing to use force to preserve nondemocracy or ensure a transition back to nondemocracy than elites who are invested in physical or human capital. This may be because repression and coups are less costly in such a society and, therefore, the costs of opposing or undermining democracy are lower relative to the benefit from doing so (which is the avoidance of pro-citizen, anti-elite policies such as redistributive taxation). Or it may be that the benefits of avoiding democracy are greater for landowners because they expect their income to be taxed at a higher rate or even their assets to be redistributed in land reforms.

A final consideration may be that landowners are typically richer than industrialists or those with human capital, especially in relatively poor countries that are at the margin of becoming democratic or at the relevant threshold of economic and political development where they could be democratic but still have not consolidated their democracies. Therefore, in terms of our analysis in Chapter 8, landowners correspond to the rich and industrialists and people with high human capital correspond to the middle class. Landowners lose more from taxation because they are richer; hence, everything else being equal, they are more in favor of actions to prevent democracy. Nevertheless, in this chapter, we examine the implications of economic structure holding inequality constant so as to focus more clearly on the other mechanisms described previously.

We conclude this chapter by outlining how the ideas discussed herein might be useful in understanding the relationship between economic and political development.

2. Economic Structure and Income Distribution

We now introduce an explicit economic structure that enables us to endogenize income distribution and discuss the political implications of different factor endowments. We want this structure to include labor (as the source of income for the citizens), physical capital, and land. To simplify, we abstract from human capital in most of the analysis and return to its implications in Section 10. We consider a fully competitive economy with a unique final consumption good, produced via the aggregate production function:

$$Y = F(K, L, N)$$

where K is the capital stock, L is total amount of productive land, and N is the labor force. Y is aggregate output, that is the physical quantity that people have to consume. All of these factors are fully employed and we assume that the production function F exhibits constant returns to scale, so that when all three factors are doubled, total output is doubled. Constant returns to scale is important because it implies that all revenues from production are distributed as income to the factors of production, capital, land, and labor. Fully competitive markets imply that all factors of production will be paid their marginal products. Holding institutions constant, inequality results because these marginal products differ and there are different scarcities for different factors.

The simplest way to provide a microfoundation for the framework used so far is to assume that the aggregate production function takes the special Cobb–Douglas form:

$$Y = (K + \sigma L)^{\theta} N^{1-\theta} \tag{9.1}$$

where $0 < \theta < 1$ and $\sigma > 0$. As will become clear when we calculate the distribution of income in this model, the choice of $1 - \theta$ as the power to which N is raised is chosen deliberately to relate this model to those used so far.

Two features are implicit in this function. First, there is a limited amount of substitution between labor and the other factors of production (more precisely, the elasticity of substitution between labor and the other factors is exactly equal to

1). Second, there is a much higher level of substitution between capital and land. Both of these assumptions are plausible. For instance, they imply that the share of labor in national income is constant when income grows as a result of capital accumulation, whereas the share of land falls and the share of capital rises. This is roughly consistent with empirical evidence.

Let us examine this in greater detail. First, we assume like before that there are $1-\delta$ citizens and now these agents correspond to wage earners. Hence, $N = 1-\delta$, and we can write the production function as:

$$Y = (K + \sigma L)^{\theta}(1-\delta)^{1-\theta}$$

Moreover, the remaining δ agents, who constitute the elites, do not own any labor, and each of them holds a fraction δ of total capital stock, K, and a fraction δ of total land stock, L.

We assume that the final good Y is the numeraire (i.e., its price is normalized to 1). Throughout, all other prices are therefore relative to the price of the final good. Exploiting the fact that in competitive markets all factors of production are paid their full marginal products, we have the following expressions for factor prices:

$$w = (1-\theta)\left(\frac{K+\sigma L}{1-\delta}\right)^{\theta} \tag{9.2}$$

$$r = \theta\left(\frac{K+\sigma L}{1-\delta}\right)^{\theta-1}$$

$$v = \sigma\theta\left(\frac{K+\sigma L}{1-\delta}\right)^{\theta-1}$$

Here, w denotes the wage rate, r the return to capital, and v the rental rate of land. These prices are all "real" or relative prices because they are measured in terms of the final good.

The shares of national income accruing to three factors are given as:

$$s_N \equiv \frac{wN}{Y} = 1-\theta \tag{9.3}$$

$$s_K \equiv \frac{rK}{Y} = \theta\frac{K}{K+\sigma L}$$

$$s_L \equiv \frac{vL}{Y} = \theta\frac{\sigma L}{K+\sigma L}$$

It is interesting that the share of national income accruing to labor is a constant equal to $1-\theta$. This stems directly from the functional form of the Cobb-Douglas production function (9.1). For example, even if capital accumulates and from

(9.2) real wages increase, the share of labor in national income is nevertheless constant. At the same time, the share of capital in national income increases and that of land declines.

Now, total income is $(K + \sigma L)^{\theta}(1 - \delta)^{1-\theta}$ and because total population is 1, this is also average income $\bar{y}$. Hence:

$$\bar{y} = (K + \sigma L)^{\theta}(1 - \delta)^{1-\theta} \tag{9.4}$$

Exploiting the fact that citizens only have labor income, we can derive an expression for the income of a citizen, denoted y^p:

$$y^p = (1 - \theta)\left(\frac{K + \sigma L}{1 - \delta}\right)^{\theta} = \frac{(1 - \theta)(K + \sigma L)^{\theta}(1 - \delta)^{1-\theta}}{1 - \delta} \tag{9.5}$$
$$= \left(\frac{1 - \theta}{1 - \delta}\right)\bar{y}$$

which is the exact expression for y^p used throughout the book.

Recall that, for now, we are assuming that all members of the elite are homogeneous and own both capital and land. Therefore, we have:

$$y^r = \frac{rK + vL}{\delta} = \frac{\theta}{\delta}(K + \sigma L)^{\theta}(1 - \delta)^{1-\theta} = \frac{\theta}{\delta}\bar{y} \tag{9.6}$$

as the expression that gives the income of a member of the elite.

We assume that the parameters are such that average incomes are less than the incomes of the rich or, in other words, $\delta < \theta$, which is identical to the assumption made in the model in which incomes are exogenous.

3. Political Conflict

We now show how our previous analyses of policy determination in democracy can be adapted to this more complex economic model. As before, all individuals have utility functions that are linear in consumption and, because people consume all their income, they aim to maximize income. Again, we assume that there are two policy instruments: a tax rate proportional to income and a lump-sum transfer that all agents receive. As before, it is costly to redistribute income. Although we now have a model with a richer set of underlying institutions, we assume these to be exogenous in the analysis of this chapter, although in Section 9 we discuss how they could enter into the analysis.

The utility of an individual i is now $(1 - \tau)y^i + T$ or $i = p, r$, where the government budget constraint again implies that:

$$T = \delta\tau y^r + (1 - \delta)\tau y^p - C(\tau)\bar{y} = (\tau - C(\tau))\bar{y}$$

Incorporating the costs of taxation, we have the indirect utility of a poor agent as $V(y^p \mid \tau) = (1 - \tau)y^p + (\tau - C(\tau))\bar{y}$. The first-order condition of maximizing this indirect utility is identical to that which we derived before and, because we know from Chapter 4 that preferences are single-peaked, we can apply the median-voter theorem to determine the (unconstrained) democratic equilibrium tax rate, again denoted τ^p. Using the fact that the incomes of the poor are given by (9.5) and average income is given by (9.4), this equilibrium tax, τ^p, is identical to the baseline tax rate in Chapter 4: namely, (4.11).

4. Capital, Land, and the Transition to Democracy

In this section, we embed the economic and political models of the previous two sections into our basic democratization model of Chapter 6, Section 6, which incorporated repression. The first issue we examine is how the structure of the economy influences the costs of repression. Following our previous discussion, we assume that repression creates costs for the elites depending on the sources of their income – in particular, whether they rely more on income from capital or income from land. As already discussed, it is plausible to presume that the disruption associated with putting down the threat of a revolution and an uprising by the citizens is more costly for industrialists, factories, and commerce than for land and landowners. As a result, when land is important for the elites, they are more willing to bear the cost of repression to avoid democratization. In a society in which income from capital becomes more important than income from land, it is more likely that the potential costs of repression exceed those of democracy and the elites prefer to give democracy to the dissatisfied citizens rather than use force against them.

Given the parallels to the analysis we conducted before, we simply outline the model here. The rich elites have to decide whether to repress, democratize, or promise redistribution; if there is no repression, no democratization, and no revolution, nature decides once more whether the elites get to reset the tax they have promised. The game tree for this model is identical to Figure 6.2.

The underlying economic model is the same as the one described in Section 2. The elites own capital and land. Moreover, all members of the elite have identical endowments so there is no heterogeneity among the elites (we return later to the distinction between industrialists and landowners). As before, the payoff to the citizens from revolution is $V^p(R, \mu) = (1 - \mu)\bar{y}/(1 - \delta)$, whereas the elites always have $V^r(R, \mu) = 0$.

Repression is costly for the elites. So far, because income was exogenously determined, we simply assumed that repression (and coups) destroyed some fraction of income. The previous arguments, however, suggest that it may be more useful to imagine conflict actually destroying capital – this is what we assume in this chapter. However, all the results of this chapter apply when it is income that is destroyed as long as the fraction of income coming from capital that is destroyed is larger than the fraction that comes from land. Moreover, it can be verified that all results of previous chapters could be restated if we allow assets rather than income to be destroyed by repression, revolution, or coups.

Consequently, if the elites choose to repress to avoid revolution and democratization, they will lose a fraction κ_K of the capital stock and a fraction κ_L of land. Moreover, we assumed:

$$\kappa_K \geq \kappa_L$$

To reduce notation, we set $\kappa_L = \kappa$ and $\kappa_K = \varrho\kappa$ where $\varrho \geq 1$.

The values to the citizens and to the elites if there is democracy are given by:

$$V^p(D) = w + \tau^p(\bar{y} - w) - C(\tau^p)\bar{y} \tag{9.7}$$

$$= \frac{1}{1-\delta}(1 - \theta + \tau^p(\theta - \delta) - (1-\delta)C(\tau^p))(K + \sigma L)^\theta(1-\delta)^{1-\theta}$$

$$V^r(D) = \frac{rK + vL}{\delta} + \tau^p\left(\bar{y} - \frac{rK + vL}{\delta}\right) - C(\tau^p)\bar{y}$$

$$= \frac{1}{\delta}(\theta + \tau^p(\delta - \theta) - \delta C(\tau^p))(K + \sigma L)^\theta(1-\delta)^{1-\theta}$$

where the factor prices w, r, and v are given by (9.2) and the most preferred tax rate of the citizens is τ^p. These expressions take into account that once there is democratization, the citizens set their most preferred tax rate unconstrained.

If, on the other hand, the elites choose repression, the payoffs are:

$$V^p(O|\kappa) = (1-\theta)\left(\frac{(1-\varrho\kappa)K + \sigma(1-\kappa)L}{1-\delta}\right)^\theta \tag{9.8}$$

$$V^r(O|\kappa) = \frac{\theta}{\delta}((1-\varrho\kappa)K + \sigma(1-\kappa)L)^\theta(1-\delta)^{1-\theta}$$

Finally, the elites could offer redistribution under the existing regime without democratizing and without resorting to repression. The best they can do in this case is offer redistribution at the favorite tax rate of the citizens, τ^p, given by (4.11); in this case, the values are:

$$V^p(N, \tau^N = \tau^p) = \frac{1}{1-\delta}(1 - \theta + p(\tau^p(\theta - \delta) - (1-\delta)C(\tau^p))) \times (K + \sigma L)^\theta(1-\delta)^{1-\theta} \tag{9.9}$$

$$V^r(N, \tau^N = \tau^p) = \frac{1}{\delta}(\theta + p(\tau^p(\delta - \theta) - \delta C(\tau^p)))(K + \sigma L)^\theta(1-\delta)^{1-\theta}$$

which incorporates the fact that this promise is realized only with probability p.

As before, if $\theta \leq \mu$, the revolution threat is absent. The more interesting case for this discussion is the one in which $\theta > \mu$ which, for simplicity, we assume to be the case. The promise to redistribute prevents a revolution if we have that $V^p(N, \tau^N = \tau^p) \geq V^p(R, \mu)$. Using the same arguments as those in Chapter 6, this is equivalent to $\mu \geq \mu^*$, in which μ^* is given by (6.6).

If $\mu < \mu^*$, the elites cannot prevent a revolution by promising redistribution, so they have to resort either to democratization or repression. We assume as usual that $V^p(D) \geq V^p(R, \mu)$ so that democratization prevents a revolution; the formula for this is identical to (6.7).

When do the elites prefer repression? This depends on whether $\mu \geq \mu^*$. When $\mu \geq \mu^*$, the relevant comparison is between redistribution and repression because, for the elites, redistribution is always preferable to democratization when it is feasible. The case that is more interesting is when $\mu < \mu^*$ so that there is a trade-off between repression and democratization. In this case, the elites simply compare $V^r(D)$ and $V^r(O|\kappa)$ as given by (9.7) and (9.8). It is clear that they prefer repression if $V^r(D) < V^r(O|\kappa)$ or if:

$$\theta + \tau^p(\delta - \theta) - \delta C(\tau^p) < \theta \left(\frac{(1 - \varrho\kappa)K + \sigma(1 - \kappa)L}{K + \sigma L} \right)^\theta \tag{9.10}$$

It is useful to rewrite (9.10) in terms of the capital-to-land ratio, $k = K/L$. This gives:

$$\theta + \tau^p(\delta - \theta) - \delta C(\tau^p) < \theta \left(\frac{(1 - \varrho\kappa)k + \sigma(1 - \kappa)}{k + \sigma} \right)^\theta \tag{9.11}$$

as the condition under which repression takes place. We say that when k is higher, the economy is more "capital-intensive," whereas low values of k correspond to relatively "land-intensive" societies. Equation (9.11) makes it clear that capital intensity of a society is a crucial determinant of whether repression is attractive for the elites. The key comparative statics arising from this condition are discussed in the next section. For now, we summarize the analysis in the following proposition:

Proposition 9.1: *Assume that (6.7) holds, $\theta > \mu$, and $\mu < \mu^*$, where μ^* is given by (6.6). Then, we have that:*

- *If (9.11) does not hold, democratization happens as a credible commitment to future redistribution by the elites.*
- *If (9.11) holds, the elites use repression to prevent a revolution.*

This proposition is therefore similar to the main results in Chapter 6. The interest here is that whether the condition determining if repression is desirable, (9.11), holds, depends on how capital-intensive the economy is (i.e., the level of k).

The easiest way to see this is to consider the case where $\varrho = 1$ so that the costs of repression fall equally on capital and land. In this case, we have the following proposition:

Proposition 9.2: *Consider the game with $\varrho = 1$. Then, (9.11) is independent of k so the political equilibrium is unaffected by the capital intensity of the economy.*

In contrast, if $\varrho > 1$, it is straightforward to verify that (9.11) is less likely to hold as k increases. Therefore, let us define k^* such that:

$$\theta + \tau^p(\delta - \theta) - \delta C(\tau^p) = \theta \left(\frac{(1 - \rho\kappa)k^* + \sigma(1 - \kappa)}{k^* + \sigma} \right)^{\theta} \tag{9.12}$$

Then we can state:

Corollary 9.1: *Consider a society described by the game with $\varrho > 1$ and define k^* by (9.12). Then, in the unique subgame perfect equilibrium, we have that if $k < k^*$, then the elites will meet the threat of a revolution with repression, and if $k \geq k^*$, they will democratize in response to the threat of a revolution.*

This corollary is the main result of this section. It shows that a more capital-intensive society is more likely to become democratic. This is because the use of force by the elites is more costly in such a society compared to a land-intensive society or, expressed differently, capital investments make the elites more prodemocractic than land holdings (i.e, as discussed in the next section industrialists are more prodemocratic than landowners).

5. Costs of Coup on Capital and Land

We now move to extend these ideas to coups. Because of the parallels between using repression and mounting coups, there appear to be natural reasons for these costs to also depend on how capital-intensive the economy is. In particular, suppose that during a coup a certain fraction of the productive assets of the economy gets destroyed. Let the fraction of physical capital destroyed be φ_K and land be φ_L if a coup is undertaken. It is natural to think that:

$$\varphi_K \geq \varphi_L$$

In other words, the disruptions associated with a coup are more destructive to capital than to land. The reasons that this is plausible are similar to those discussed previously. Coups and the associated turbulence and disruption lead to the breakdown of complex economic relations. These are much more important for capitalist production than agrarian production. This is natural because there is less concern about the quality of products in agriculture than in manufacturing.

Moreover, the importance of complex relationships between buyer and supplier networks, and of investments in skills and in relationship-specific capital, is far greater in more industrialized activities. Therefore, land will be hurt less than capital as a result of a coup.

Let $\varphi_L = \varphi$ and $\varphi_K = \xi\varphi$ where $\xi \geq 1$. Given this assumption, we can write the incomes after coups as:

$$\tilde{y}^p = (1-\theta)\left(\frac{(1-\xi\varphi)K + \sigma(1-\varphi)L}{1-\delta}\right)^{\theta} \tag{9.13}$$

$$\tilde{y}^r = \frac{\theta}{\delta}((1-\xi\varphi)K + \sigma(1-\varphi)L)^{\theta}(1-\delta)^{1-\theta} \tag{9.14}$$

Clearly, both expressions are less than the corresponding ones before the coup, (9.5) and (9.6), because the disruptions associated with a coup typically lead to the destruction of a certain fraction of the productive assets of an economy.

Armed with this specification of the costs of coups, we can now analyze the impact of economic structure on coups and democratic consolidation. The game tree for the model in this section is identical to the one depicted in Figure 7.1.

Whether the elites wish to mount a coup depends on the continuation value in democracy and nondemocracy. Faced with the threat of a coup, the median voter wishes to make a concession to avoid a coup (i.e., set $\tau^D < \tau^p$). After this, the elites decide whether to undertake the coup. If they do so, society switches to nondemocracy and the elites set the tax rate. Naturally, after a successful coup, they choose their most preferred tax rate, $\tau^N = 0$. As a result, the game ends with respective payoffs for the citizens and the elites, $V^p(C,\varphi) = \tilde{y}^p$ and $V^r(C,\varphi) = \tilde{y}^r$, where $\tilde{y}^p$ and $\tilde{y}^r$ are given by (9.13) and (9.14). Alternatively, if the elites decide not to undertake a coup, the political system remains democratic and with probability $1-p$, the median voter may get to reset the tax from that promised by the citizens in the previous stage. Therefore, with probability p, the tax promised by the citizens, τ^D, remains, and the citizens and the elites receive values $V\left(y^p \mid \tau^D\right)$ and $V\left(y^r \mid \tau^D\right)$, where:

$$V\left(y^r \mid \tau^D\right) = \frac{1}{1-\delta}\left(1-\theta+\tau^D(\theta-\delta)-(1-\delta)C(\tau^D)\right) \times (K+\sigma L)^{\theta}(1-\delta)^{1-\theta} \quad \text{and}$$

$$V\left(y^r \mid \tau^D\right) = \frac{1}{\delta}\left(\theta+\tau^D(\delta-\theta)-\delta C(\tau^D)\right)(K+\sigma L)^{\theta}(1-\delta)^{1-\theta}$$

If, on the other hand, nature allows democracy to reset the tax, the citizens and the elites both receive the values pertinent to (unconstrained) democracy, $V^p(D)$ and $V^r(D)$, as given by (9.7). Therefore, the values resulting from a democratic promise of lower taxation at the rate τ^D are $V^p(D, \tau^D)$ and $V^r(D, \tau^D)$, such that:

$$V^p(D, \tau^D) = \frac{1}{1-\delta}\left[1 - \theta + p\left(\tau^D(\theta - \delta) - (1-\delta)C(\tau^D)\right)\right. \tag{9.15}$$
$$\left. + (1-p)(\tau^p(\theta-\delta) - (1-\delta)C(\tau^p))\right](K + \sigma L)^\theta (1-\delta)^{1-\theta}$$
$$V^r(D, \tau^D) = \frac{1}{\delta}\left[\theta + p\left(\tau^D(\delta - \theta) - \delta C(\tau^D)\right)\right.$$
$$\left. + (1-p)(\tau^p(\delta-\theta) - \delta C(\tau^p))\right](K + \sigma L)^\theta (1-\delta)^{1-\theta}$$

These expressions take into account that with probability $1 - p$, the citizens get to reset the tax, the coup decision is already a bygone and, consequently, they choose their most preferred tax rate, τ^p.

We can now characterize the subgame perfect equilibrium of this game by backward induction. Whether a coup is attractive for the elites depends on whether the coup constraint, $V^r(C, \varphi) > V^r(D)$, binds. This states that a coup is more attractive than living under an unconstrained democracy. This coup constraint can be expressed as:

$$\theta + \tau^p(\delta - \theta) - \delta C(\tau^p) < \theta\left(\frac{(1-\xi\varphi)k + \sigma(1-\varphi)}{k+\sigma}\right)^\theta \tag{9.16}$$

where we again write the expression in terms of the capital intensity of the economy $k = K/L$. When this constraint does not bind, coups are sufficiently costly that the elites never find a coup profitable – democracy is fully consolidated. Equation (9.16) is fairly intuitive and responds to changes in parameters in the way expected. For example, a greater democratic tax rate, τ^p, makes it more likely to hold because only the left-hand side depends on τ^p and is decreasing in it. A greater level of φ makes it less likely to hold because a greater fraction of the assets of the elites is destroyed in the process of a coup.

In contrast, when this constraint binds, the democratic regime is not fully consolidated: if the citizens do not deviate from their most preferred to tax rate, there will be a coup along the equilibrium path. Therefore, we can define a critical value of the fraction of assets destroyed in a coup, denoted φ^*, such that when $\varphi < \varphi^*$ (i.e., a coup is not too costly), the promise of limited redistribution by the citizens is not sufficient to dissuade the elites from a coup. Of course, the most attractive promise that the citizens can make to the elites is to stop redistribution away from them totally (i.e., $\tau^D = 0$). Therefore, we must have that at φ^*, $V^r(D, \tau^D = 0) = V^r(C, \varphi^*)$, or:

$$\varphi^* = \left[1 - \left(1 + \frac{(1-p)}{\theta}(\tau^p(\delta - \theta) - \delta C(\tau^p))\right)^{\frac{1}{\theta}}\right]\left(\frac{k+\sigma}{\xi k + \sigma}\right) \tag{9.17}$$

This expression implies as usual that a higher level of τ^p makes democracy worse for the elites and, therefore, increases φ^*; that is, the elites are willing to undertake more costly coups when τ^p is higher. We now have the following result:

Proposition 9.3: *In the game described above, there is a unique subgame perfect equilibrium such that:*

- *If the coup constraint (9.16) does not bind, democracy is fully consolidated and the citizens set their most preferred tax rate,* $\tau^p > 0$.
- *If the coup constraint (9.16) binds and* $\varphi \geq \varphi^*$, *democracy is semiconsolidated. The citizens set a tax rate,* $\tau^D = \tilde{\tau} < \tau^p$, *such that* $V^r(D, \tau^D = \tilde{\tau}) = V^r(C, \varphi)$.
- *If the coup constraint (9.16) binds and* $\varphi < \varphi^*$, *democracy is unconsolidated. There is a coup, the elites come to power, and set their most preferred tax rate,* $\tau^N = 0$.

The novel part of this result is that the likelihood of a coup is now affected by the economic structure – in particular, whether society is capital- or land-intensive. However, the only reason the degree of capital intensity affects the propensity of the elites to mount coups is that different fractions of capital and land are destroyed in the process of the coup (i.e., $\varphi_K > \varphi_L$) To emphasize this, we state an analogous result to Proposition 9.2:

Proposition 9.4: *Consider this game with* $\xi = 1$. *Then, (9.16) is independent of* k, *so the political equilibrium is unaffected by the capital intensity of the economy.*

The proof of this result follows from (9.17) because when $\xi = 1$, the term $(k + \sigma)/(\xi k + \sigma) = 1$ and cancels from the right side. This proposition states that in the model here there is no link between economic structure and capital intensity when costs of coups are the same for capital and land holders.

This picture changes substantially when $\xi > 1$, however. With a greater cost of coups on capital than land, (9.16) implies that as k increases, the coup constraint becomes less tight and from (9.17), φ^* decreases. This implies that we can define two threshold levels $\hat{k}$ and k^* such that at $k = \hat{k}$, (9.16) holds with equality. On the other hand, $k = k^*$ is such that when democracy promises $\tau^D = 0$, the elites are indifferent between a coup and living in democracy. Naturally, $k^* < \hat{k}$. This discussion establishes the next result:

Corollary 9.2: *Consider a society described by this game and assume that* $\xi > 1$. *Let* $\hat{k}$ *and* k^* *be as described. In the unique subgame perfect equilibrium, we have that if* $k < k^*$, *then society is an unconsolidated democracy. If* $k^* \leq k < \hat{k}$, *then society is a semiconsolidated democracy. If* $k \geq \hat{k}$, *then society is a fully consolidated democracy.*

Therefore, in a land-intensive society where k is low, there will be coups during periods of crises. However, when the structure of production is different – that is, when capital is relatively more important in the production process and in the asset portfolios of the elites, as captured by the threshold level of capital intensity k^* – then coups no longer happen along the equilibrium path and democracy persists. But, because $k < \hat{k}$, democracy is not a fully consolidated political institution and survives only by making concessions to the elites who pose an effective coup threat. As society becomes even more capital-intensive and k increases, it eventually becomes a fully consolidated democracy without the shadow of a coup affecting equilibrium tax rates and redistributive policies.

This model, therefore, illustrates how the structure of the economy, in particular the extent of capital-intensity, influences the propensity of democracy to consolidate. The underlying idea is that in a more industrialized society with a greater fraction of the assets of the elites in the form of physical capital, the turbulence and disruption associated with coups – like those created by repression – are more damaging. In consequence, coups as well as repression are less attractive in a capital-intensive society.

6. Capital, Land, and the Burden of Democracy

An even more important channel via which the economic structure may affect democracy is that the elites' attitudes toward democracy also vary with the structure of the economy because there are typically different burdens of taxation on capital and land. In this section, we analyze a model with this feature. For brevity, we focus only on coups and democratic consolidations. Given the results in the preceding two sections, it is clear that the analysis of transition to democracy is similar; factors discouraging coups also discourage repression, facilitating transition to democracy.

The key in this section is that because land is supplied more inelastically, when allowed, the citizens impose higher taxes on land than on capital. Thus, everything else being equal, the elites are more opposed to democracy when land is more important for their incomes. This gives us another reason for land-intensive economies to be less likely to consolidate democracy (and also to transition to democracy).

Let us now discuss this issue by assuming that there can be separate taxes on income from different sources: in particular, a tax rate on capital income, τ_K, and one on income from land, τ_L. Throughout, we simplify the discussion by assuming that there is no tax on labor income (i.e., the tax on labor, τ_N, is equal to 0). Clearly, the citizens would not like to tax their own incomes but, more generally, in a nondemocratic regime, the elites might like to tax the citizens and redistribute to themselves (as in discussions of targeted transfers in previous chapters). To simplify the exposition, we ignore this possibility by restricting attention to the case in which $\tau_N = 0$.

How do we model the costs of taxation when there are separate taxes on capital income and land income? The costs of taxation originate, in large part, from the fact that factors of production are supplied elastically. For example, labor taxation is "costly" because individuals take more leisure instead of supplying work to the market. There are two aspects to these costs, both of them relevant for this discussion. First, as less labor is supplied to the market, measured income and therefore tax revenues decline. This constitutes a cost for those who use tax revenues because there are fewer revenues now. Second, there is also a cost of allocative efficiency; without the taxation, labor was being allocated to its best use: market work. Taxation discourages this and creates a distortion by creating an incentive for time to be reallocated away from its most efficient uses, forcing it to be used where it is less valuable, in leisure or home production. Capital taxation is similarly costly, especially because capital can flee to other activities, or even abroad, and avoid taxes. Again, this response of capital is costly both because there are substantially less revenues from taxation and the allocation of capital between various activities is distorted. More generally, in all cases, distortions from taxation result because in its effort to avoid taxes, each factor is not being allocated to its most productive use, and measured market income on which taxes are collected is declining. It is also important that both of these costs relate to the "elasticity of the supply" of various factors. When a factor is supplied inelastically, it cannot be easily withdrawn from market activity; hence, measured income does not change and there are few distortions. Thinking of the supply elasticities as the major factor determining the costs of taxation immediately reveals that taxing capital should be more costly than taxing land. After all, capital can easily go to other sectors, but land is set in its place; at best, it can be withdrawn to inactivity.

Motivated by these considerations, we think that when the tax on capital is τ_K, there is a cost of taxation equal to $C_K(\tau_K)rK$; when the tax on land is τ_L, the cost of taxation is $C_L(\tau_L)vL$. As before, we assume that both of these functions are continuous, differentiable, and convex. Moreover, we impose the usual boundary condition that $C'_L(0) = C'_K(0) = 0$ and a slightly different boundary condition $C'_L(1) > 1$ and $C'_K(1) > 1$ (the reason for this difference becomes clear later). The crucial assumption we make is that:

$$C'_L(\tau) < C'_K(\tau) \quad \text{for all} \quad \tau > 0$$

This assumption implies that the marginal cost of taxing capital is always higher than the marginal cost of taxing land, which is equivalent to capital being supplied more elastically than land. The important implication of this assumption is that the citizens would like to impose greater taxes on land than on capital.

To further simplify the discussion, we now depart in one more respect from our baseline model. As in our targeted transfers model, we assume that in addition to lump-sum transfers, there are transfers targeted to specific groups – in particular, to the citizens, T_p – as well as a lump-sum transfer to the elites, T_r.

Given all these pieces, we can write the total post-tax incomes of the elites and the citizens as follows:

$$\hat{y}^p = w + T_p$$

$$\hat{y}^r = (1 - \tau_K)\frac{rK}{\delta} + (1 - \tau_L)\frac{vL}{\delta} + T_r$$

which incorporates our assumption that all capital and land are equally owned by each member of the elite, and there are δ of them.

The government budget constraint can now be written as:

$$\delta T_r + (1 - \delta)T_p = \tau_K rK - C_K(\tau_K)rK + \tau_L vL - C_L(\tau_L)vL \qquad (9.18)$$

The left-hand side of (9.18) is total expenditure on transfers. T_r is the lump-sum transfer that members of the elite receive and is thus multiplied by δ; T_p is the transfer to a citizen and is thus multiplied by $1 - \delta$. The right-hand side is total tax revenue from the taxation of capital and land. At the tax rates τ_K, τ_L, capital owners pay a total of $\tau_K rK$ in tax and landowners pay $\tau_L vL$. From these amounts, we subtract the costs of taxation, $C_K(\tau_K)rK$ and $C_L(\tau_L)vL$.

Given the availability of a targeted transfer to themselves, the citizens would simply redistribute all the income they raise from capital and land using this targeted transfer; hence, we have $T_r = 0$ in democracy.

Next, because the citizens are no longer taxing themselves, their most preferred taxes are those that maximize the net tax receipts, the right-hand side of (9.18) – in other words, the citizens would now like to be at the top of the Laffer Curve, which relates total tax revenue to tax rate. Therefore, the citizens' most preferred taxes can be computed simply by solving the following maximization problem:

$$\max_{\tau_K, \tau_L} \{\tau_K rK - C_K(\tau_K)rK + \tau_L vL - C_L(\tau_L)vL\}$$

The first-order conditions are straightforward and give the most preferred taxes for the poor, τ_K^p, τ_L^p, implicitly as:

$$C_K'\left(\tau_K^p\right) = 1 \qquad (9.19)$$

$$C_L'\left(\tau_L^p\right) = 1$$

which maximize their net tax revenues. The assumption that $C_L'(\tau) < C_K'(\tau)$ immediately implies that $\tau_K^p < \tau_L^p$.

We next compute the net burden of democratic taxation on the elites. As in Chapter 4, we define the burden as the net amount of redistribution away from the elites. Because they receive no transfers now, this is simply equal to taxes they pay; hence:

$$\text{Burden}\left(\tau_K^p, \tau_L^p\right) = \tau_K^p rK + \tau_L^p vL$$

Using (9.3), we can write this relative to total income and in terms of capital intensity as:

$$\mathcal{B} \equiv \frac{\text{Burden}\left(\tau_K^p, \tau_L^p\right)}{Y} = \tau_K^p \frac{k}{k+\sigma} + \tau_L^p \frac{\sigma}{k+\sigma} \tag{9.20}$$

First, note that from (9.19), the tax rates τ_K^p and τ_L^p are independent of k. Then, (9.20) implies that as the economy becomes more capital-intensive, the burden of democracy on the elites will decrease. This reflects the fact that capital is less attractive to tax than land. Analytically, the burden of taxes, $\mathcal{B}$, is decreasing in capital intensity:

$$\frac{d\mathcal{B}}{dk} = \frac{\tau_K^p}{k+\sigma} - \frac{\tau_K^p k + \tau_L^p \sigma}{(k+\sigma)^2} < 0$$

which follows immediately from the fact that $\tau_K^p < \tau_L^p$. This result implies that elites are less opposed to democracy for another reason when they are invested more in capital than in land; this is because democracy taxes capital less than it taxes land.

There is another interesting interpretation of $\tau_K^p < \tau_L^p$. So far, we have emphasized the different tax rates imposed on incomes generated by land and capital. Another possibility is redistribution of assets. Because asset redistribution has not been explicitly considered in this chapter, we might think that the potential for asset redistribution is also incorporated into these taxes τ_K^p and τ_L^p. Are there any reasons to think that the potential for asset redistribution is different for capital and for land? The answer is yes. Although democracy can easily redistribute land via land reform, redistribution of capital is more difficult because capital, in the form of factories, is not easily divisible. More important, when these factories are taken away from their owners and given to new parties, they typically are not very productive. This is because the complex relationships necessary for capitalist production – the specific investments, and the know-how – are all in the hands of the original owners and difficult or even impossible to transfer. One could argue that rather than redistribute the capital itself, shares in firms could be redistributed; yet, the modern theory of the firm (Hart 1995) suggests precisely that the incentives of agents within a firm depend on the ownership structure so that capital cannot be arbitrarily redistributed without damaging productivity. Indeed, if capital markets are perfect, one would expect the initial ownership structure to be efficient (although if they are not, then the effects of redistribution are more complex; e.g., Legros and Newman 1996).

Land is much easier to redistribute without creating distortions. When land is taken from big landowners and redistributed to agrarian workers, the loss of efficiency may not be significant and, in fact, according to some estimates, there might even be a gain in efficiency because many of the big farms are owned by major landowners who farm more land than is efficient (Binswanger, Deininger, and Feder 1995 discuss evidence that land reforms may have efficiency gains; Besley and Burgess 2000 show that land reforms in India have had little adverse effect on aggregate economic performance). This suggests that land reform is often an attractive policy tool for democracies to achieve their fiscal objectives without creating major distortions. Naturally, this implies a greater burden of democracy on landowners than on capital owners. This consideration implies that when land is a more important asset of the rich, they have more to fear from democracy and typically they expect greater redistribution away from them and a greater burden. This could be captured by our result that $\tau_K^p < \tau_L^p$.

We now put these two pieces together and analyze the likelihood of coups in a world with different taxes on capital and land. Consider the economic model described herein and the political model depicted by the game in Figure 7.1. We further simplify the discussion by assuming that the same fractions of capital and land are destroyed in the process of a coup (i.e., $\varphi_K = \varphi_L$ or that $\xi = 1$). This assumption isolates the channel we want to emphasize in this section.

If the citizens get to set their most preferred taxes and transfers, taxes on capital and land are given by (9.19), and we also have $T_r = 0$. This implies that the transfer to each citizen is given by:

$$T_p^p = \frac{\tau_K^p r K - C_K\left(\tau_K^p\right) r K + \tau_L^p v L - C_L\left(\tau_L^p\right) v L}{1-\delta}. \tag{9.21}$$

The superscript p on T_p^p indicates that it is the preferred value of the citizens. Therefore, the corresponding values are those in an unconstrained democracy:

$$V^p(D) = w + T_p^p \tag{9.22}$$

$$V^r(D) = \left(1 - \tau_K^p\right)\frac{rK}{\delta} + \left(1 - \tau_L^p\right)\frac{vL}{\delta}$$

with factor prices w, r, and v given by (9.2); with τ_K^p and τ_L^p given by (9.19); and T_p^p given by (9.21).

Whether the elites mount a coup depends on the continuation values in democracy and nondemocracy. The citizens again set taxes on capital and labor income, which are potentially different from their most preferred tax rates, τ_K^p and τ_L^p, denoted by $\tilde{\tau}_K$ and $\tilde{\tau}_L$. The corresponding redistribution to a citizen is:

$$\tilde{T}_p^p = \frac{\tilde{\tau}_K r K - C_K(\tilde{\tau}_K) r K + \tilde{\tau}_L v L - C_L(\tilde{\tau}_L) v L}{1-\delta} \tag{9.23}$$

That the citizens would decide to cut taxes on capital and land rather than redistribute lump sum to the elites is obvious because these taxes are distortionary.

If we had allowed labor income to be taxed, the citizens could find it optimal to tax themselves and transfer resources to the elites to avoid a coup.

After this, the elites decide whether to undertake the coup. If they do, society switches to nondemocracy, and the elites set the tax rate. Naturally, they choose their most preferred tax rates, $\tau_K^N = \tau_L^N = 0$. As a result, the game ends with respective payoffs for the citizens and the elites, $V^p(C, \varphi)$ and $V^r(C, \varphi)$, where:

$$V^p(C, \varphi) = (1-\theta)(1-\varphi)^\theta \left(\frac{K+\sigma L}{1-\delta}\right)^\theta \tag{9.24}$$

$$V^r(C, \varphi) = \frac{\theta}{\delta}(1-\varphi)^\theta (K+\sigma L)^\theta (1-\delta)^{1-\theta} = \frac{\theta}{\delta}(1-\varphi)^\theta Y$$

Alternatively, if the elites decide not to undertake a coup, the political system remains democratic. In this case, nature moves one more time and determines whether democracy gets to reset the tax from that promised by the citizens in the previous stage. As before, this continuation game captures the fact that democracy may be unable to commit to less redistribution (i.e., to not adopting pro-citizen policies) once the threat of a coup disappears. Nature determines with probability p that the tax rates promised by the citizens remain, and the citizens and the elites receive values $V\left(y^p \mid \tau_K^D = \tilde{\tau}_K, \tau_L^D = \tilde{\tau}_L\right)$ and $V\left(y^r \mid \tau_K^D = \tilde{\tau}_K, \tau_L^D = \tilde{\tau}_L\right)$, where:

$$V\left(y^r \mid \tau_K^D = \tilde{\tau}_K, \tau_L^D = \tilde{\tau}_L\right) = w + \tilde{T}_p^p$$

$$V\left(y^r \mid \tau_K^D = \tilde{\tau}_K, \tau_L^D = \tilde{\tau}_L\right) = (1-\tilde{\tau}_K)\frac{rK}{\delta} + (1-\tilde{\tau}_L)\frac{\nu L}{\delta}$$

where $\tilde{T}_p^p$ is given by (9.23).

If, on the other hand, nature allows democracy to reset the tax, they both receive the (unconstrained) democracy values, $V^p(D)$ and $V^r(D)$, as given by (9.22). Therefore, the values resulting from a promise of less redistribution only at the tax rates $(\tilde{\tau}_K, \tilde{\tau}_L)$ by the citizens in democracy are $V^p(D, \tau_K^D = \tilde{\tau}_K, \tau_L^D = \tilde{\tau}_L)$ and $V^r(D, \tau_K^D = \tilde{\tau}_K, \tau_L^D = \tilde{\tau}_L)$, such that:

$$V^p\left(D, \tau_K^D = \tilde{\tau}_K, \tau_L^D = \tilde{\tau}_L\right) = w + (1-p)T_p^p + p\tilde{T}_p^p \tag{9.25}$$

$$V^r\left(D, \tau_K^D = \tilde{\tau}_K, \tau_L^D = \tilde{\tau}_L\right) = \left(1 - p\tilde{\tau}_K - (1-p)\tau_K^p\right)\frac{rK}{\delta} + \left(1 - p\tilde{\tau}_L - (1-p)\tau_L^p\right)\frac{\nu L}{\delta}$$

with w, r, and ν given by (9.2); τ_K^p and τ_L^p given by (9.19); T_p^p given by (9.21); and $\tilde{T}_p^p$ given by (9.23). These expressions take into account that with probability

$1 - p$, the citizens get to reset the tax, in which case they are unconstrained and choose their most preferred taxes τ_K^P and τ_L^P, as given by (9.19).

We can now characterize the subgame perfect equilibrium of this game by backward induction. The crucial issues are whether undertaking a coup is in the interests of the elites and whether the citizens can prevent a coup by promising concessions.

Whether a coup is attractive depends on whether the coup constraint, $V^r(C, \varphi) > V^r(D)$, binds. The answer is yes when the burden of taxation on the elites is sufficiently high. Using (9.22) and (9.24), the coup constraint can be expressed as:

$$(1-\varphi)^{\theta} > \left(1-\tau_K^P\right)\frac{k}{k+\sigma} + \left(1-\tau_L^P\right)\frac{\sigma}{k+\sigma} \tag{9.26}$$

When this constraint does not bind, democracy is fully consolidated.

In contrast, when this constraint binds, democracy is not fully consolidated: if the citizens do not take an action, there will be a coup along the equilibrium path. The action that the citizens can take is to reduce the burden that democracy places on the elites by reducing taxes on both capital and land. In particular, the best that the citizens can do is promise zero taxes on both $V^r(D, \tau_K^D = 0, \tau_L^D = 0)$ to the elites. As in the previous analysis, we can then define a threshold value for φ, φ^*, such that when $\varphi < \varphi^*$, the promise of limited distribution by the citizens is not sufficient to dissuade the elites from a coup. Therefore, we must have that at φ^*, $V^r(D, \tau_K^D = 0, \tau_L^D = 0) = V^r(C, \varphi^*)$. Solving this equality gives the threshold value φ^* as:

$$\varphi^* = 1 - \left(\left(1-(1-p)\tau_K^P\right)\frac{k}{k+\sigma} + \left(1-(1-p)\tau_L^P\right)\frac{\sigma}{k+\sigma}\right)^{\frac{1}{\theta}} \tag{9.27}$$

Given this discussion, we can summarize the subgame perfect equilibrium of this game as follows:

Proposition 9.5: *In the game described above, there is a unique subgame perfect equilibrium such that:*

- *If the coup constraint (9.26) does not bind, democracy is fully consolidated. The citizens set their most preferred tax rates on capital and land, $\tau_K^P > 0$ and $\tau_L^P > 0$, as given by (9.19).*
- *If the coup constraint (9.26) binds and $\varphi \geq \varphi^*$, democracy is semiconsolidated. The citizens set taxes below τ_K^P and τ_L^P.*
- *If the coup constraint (9.26) binds and $\varphi < \varphi^*$, democracy is unconsolidated. There is a coup, the elites come to power, and set their preferred tax rates, $\tau_K^N = \tau_L^N = 0$.*

Let us again define two threshold levels of capital intensity $\hat{k}$ and k^*, such that as the economy passes these threshold levels, it first becomes a semiconsolidated and then a fully consolidated democracy. These threshold values are:

$$k^* = \frac{\left(\left(1-(1-p)\tau_L^p\right)\right)-(1-\varphi)^\theta\right)\sigma}{(1-\varphi)^\theta-\left(1-(1-p)\tau_K^p\right)} \tag{9.28}$$

and

$$\hat{k} = \frac{\left(\left(1-\tau_L^p\right)-(1-\varphi)^\theta\right)\sigma}{(1-\varphi)^\theta-\left(1-\tau_K^p\right)} \tag{9.29}$$

Then, Corollary 9.2 applies exactly as before with k^* and $\hat{k}$ as given by (9.28) and (9.29). The result is, therefore, similar to before: as capital and industry become more important relative to land and agriculture, the elites become less averse to democracy and the threat against democracy diminishes. The reason this happens is different from before, however. In the model of the previous section, the burden of democracy was independent of the composition of assets of the elites; their different attitudes toward coups originated from the different costs that the disruption due to a coup would cause. Perhaps more important in practice is that not all segments of the elite suffer equally in democracy. This section emphasizes this by constructing a model in which land is taxed more heavily (or perhaps redistributed more radically by land reform); therefore, the elites have more to fear from democracy when land is an important source of income for them. As the degree of capital intensity increases, their opposition to democracy declines and consolidation is more likely.

The implications of the model in this section carry over immediately to democratization. Because the burden of democracy falls more heavily on landowners than on capitalists, as the capital intensity of the economy increases, repression becomes less attractive relative to democracy and democratization becomes more likely to arise. Indeed, by analogy to the previous analysis, there exists a level of capital intensity that is sufficiently high to ensure that repression is never attractive to the elites.

7. Conflict between Landowners and Industrialists

The previous analysis showed how the increased capital intensity of an economy made coups against democracy less likely. To simplify the discussion, we allowed the composition of assets to change but we assumed that the elites were homogeneous, with each member holding the same share of capital and land. In practice, there are distinct groups – landowners and industrialists – and certain groups are more opposed than others to democracy. Such distinctions are an enduring theme of the literature stemming from Moore (1966) and have emerged in the more recent literature on democratization under the guise of "hardliners" and "softliners." In the previous chapter, we discussed how the distinction between a hardliner and a softliner could be given some content and microfoundations in the context of a model with both rich and middle-class agents. Nevertheless, in Chapter 8, incomes were still exogenous and the only difference between such agents was their income level.

The models of this chapter provide another approach to this issue. In particular, because both the costs of repression and coups fall more heavily on capital holders than land holders and the burden of democracy is greater on the latter than the former, we expect capitalists and industrialists to be less opposed to democracy than landowners. Thus, we can imagine situations in which the elites split, capitalists are in favor of conceding democracy, and landowners are opposed to it.

Although the discussion of hardliners and softliners in the political science literature has been restricted to discussions of transition to democracy, the underlying logic suggests that such a distinction ought to be important for democratic consolidation as well. There is heterogeneity among those opposed to democracy; when splits occur among these groups, how their preferences are aggregated is crucial in determining whether democracy survives. Therefore, we follow the previous two sections in focusing on how capital intensity influences democratic consolidation in circumstances where the elites are heterogeneous. This provides some contrast to the Chapter 8 analysis in which elite heterogeneity was discussed only in the context of democratization.

In this section, we use the same model as in the previous section but with three groups of agents, workers, landowners, and industrialists. We denote the number of industrialists by δ^k and landowners by δ^l, such that $\delta^k + \delta^l = \delta$. All capital is held by industrialists and all land is held by landowners. We also continue the analysis of the previous section by assuming that there are no differential costs of a coup for landowners (i.e., $\xi = 1$), but there are different tax rates imposed on them by the poor workers. The political situation is again described by a similar game. The citizens first decide to set taxes on capital and land, τ_K^D and τ_L^D, and they may want to offer promises $\tilde{\tau}_K$ and $\tilde{\tau}_L$, which differ from their ideal tax rates. Then, if the elites decide not to undertake a coup, there is another move by nature, capturing the commitment problem of democracy: with probability $1 - p$, the citizens get to reset taxes from $\tilde{\tau}_K$ and $\tilde{\tau}_L$.

To discuss what the elites want to do, however, we have to propose a way of aggregating the preferences of the capitalists and the landowners. As discussed before there are various ways to do this, but here we follow the model of Chapter 8, Section 6, in which we aggregated the preferences of the rich and the middle class by assuming that decisions were determined using a utilitarian social-welfare function. We make the same assumption here so that the elites are in favor of a coup if this decision maximizes the sum of utilities of the elites – landowners plus industrialists.

The payoffs are also different now because there are three groups. If the outcome of the game is democracy, the citizens set their most preferred tax rates given by

(9.19), and the payoffs to the citizens, the industrialists (capitalists), and the landowners are, respectively:

$$V^p(D) = w + T_p$$
$$V^k(D) = \left(1 - \tau_K^p\right)\frac{rK}{\delta^k} + T_r$$
$$V^l(D) = \left(1 - \tau_L^p\right)\frac{\nu L}{\delta^l} + T_r$$

with w, r, and ν given by (9.2), and because a democracy chooses $T_r = 0$, T_p given by (9.21). Here, we are assuming that capital and land are equally owned within each faction of the elites. We have simplified the notation by writing $V^k(D)$ as the value to all industrialists and $V^l(D)$ as the value to all landowners, and we do so with all the value functions in this section.

If, on the other hand, there is a coup, industrialists and landowners come to power and, in this case, we assume that they jointly choose taxes and transfers. This results in no taxation but, in the process of the coup, a fraction φ of the capital stock and land is destroyed. Therefore, the payoffs to a worker, an industrialist, and a landowner are:

$$V^p(C, \varphi) = (1-\theta)(1-\varphi)^\theta\left(\frac{K + \sigma L}{1-\delta}\right)^\theta$$
$$V^k(C, \varphi) = \theta(1-\varphi)^\theta(K + \sigma L)^{\theta-1}(1-\delta)^{1-\theta}\frac{K}{\delta^k}$$
$$V^l(C, \varphi) = \theta(1-\varphi)^\theta(K + \sigma L)^{\theta-1}(1-\delta)^{1-\theta}\sigma\frac{L}{\delta^l}$$

In specifying these payoffs to a coup, we impose that in nondemocracy established after a coup, there is no taxation of the elites. It is possible that industrialists might be in favor of setting $\tau_L^N > 0$ and $T_r > 0$, taxing landowners to redistribute to themselves. Similarly, landowners may be in favor of taxing industrialists. However, such taxation would be determined here by maximizing the same welfare function that determined whether a coup takes place, and the utilitarian form of the objective function ensures that such taxation never occurs in equilibrium.

Finally, the expected payoffs when the poor promise redistribution at the tax rates $\tau_K^D = \tilde{\tau}_K$ and $\tau_L^D = \tilde{\tau}_L$ – taking into account that they have to adhere to this promise with probability p – are:

$$V^p(D, \tau_K^D = \tilde{\tau}_K, \tau_L^D = \tilde{\tau}_L) = w + (1-p)T_p^p + p\tilde{T}_p^p$$
$$V^k(D, \tau_K^D = \tilde{\tau}_K) = \left(1 - p\tilde{\tau}_K - (1-p)\tau_K^p\right) r\frac{K}{\delta^k}$$
$$V^l(D, \tau_L^D = \tilde{\tau}_L) = \left(1 - p\tilde{\tau}_L - (1-p)\tau_L^p\right) \nu\frac{L}{\delta^l}$$

Parallel to the previous analysis, we can again define a coup constraint and threshold values for φ such that the elites are indifferent between a coup and living in democracy. If coups are more costly than this critical level, then we are in a fully consolidated democracy. These values now depend on the balance of political power within the elites. We first define the basic coup constraints that imply that $V^k(C, \varphi) > V^k(D)$ and $V^l(C, \varphi) > V^l(D)$. These are, respectively:

$$\theta(1-\varphi)^{\theta}(K+\sigma L)^{\theta-1}(1-\delta)^{1-\theta} > \left(1-\tau_K^p\right) r \tag{9.30}$$

and

$$\theta(1-\varphi)^{\theta}(K+\sigma L)^{\theta-1}(1-\delta)^{1-\theta}\sigma > \left(1-\tau_L^p\right) v \tag{9.31}$$

If these constraints hold, then democracy must make some type of concession in the high state to avoid a coup and, therefore, is not fully consolidated.

Therefore, we write the constraints $V^k(C, \varphi) > V^k(D, \tau_K^D = 0)$ and $V^l(C, \varphi) > V^l(D, \tau_L^D = 0)$, which show when a coup will take place even when the poor make the best possible concession they can promise. These conditions determine the conditions under which democracy is semiconsolidated. From this, we have the constraint under which industrialists prefer a coup rather than accept the best possible concession from the citizens:

$$\theta(1-\varphi)^{\theta}(K+\sigma L)^{\theta-1}(1-\delta)^{1-\theta} > \left(1-(1-p)\tau_K^p\right) r \tag{9.32}$$

and a constraint that shows the circumstances under which the best possible concession to landowners is worse for them than mounting a coup:

$$\theta(1-\varphi)^{\theta}(K+\sigma L)^{\theta-1}(1-\delta)^{1-\theta}\sigma > \left(1-(1-p)\tau_L^p\right) v \tag{9.33}$$

recall that these are evaluated at $\tau_K^D = 0$ and $\tau_L^D = 0$.

To see under which circumstances a coup will take place we have to study whether a coup maximizes a utilitarian welfare function of the elites. It will do so if:

$$\delta^k V^k(C, \varphi) + \delta^l V^l(C, \varphi) > \delta^k V^k(D, \tau_K^D = 0) + \delta^l V^l(D, \tau_L^D = 0)$$

Here, $\delta^k V^k(C, \varphi) + \delta^l V^l(C, \varphi)$ is the sum of the utilities of industrialists and landowners when the elites mount a coup against democracy. The notation $\delta^k V^k(D, \tau_K^D = 0) + \delta^l V^l(D, \tau_L^D = 0)$ is the sum of utilities when industrialists and landowners accept the best possible concession and do not mount a coup. It can be the case that $V^l(C, \varphi) > V^l(D, \tau_L^D = 0)$ so that landowners are in favor of a coup, whereas $V^k(C, \varphi) < V^k(D, \tau_K^D = 0)$ so that industrialists are against it. Now:

$$\begin{aligned}&\delta^k V^k(C,\varphi)+\delta^l V^l(C,\varphi)\\&\quad=\theta(1-\varphi)^\theta(K+\sigma L)^{\theta-1}(1-\delta)^{1-\theta}\left(\delta^k\frac{K}{\delta^k}+\delta^l\sigma\frac{L}{\delta^l}\right)\\&\quad=\theta(1-\varphi)^\theta(K+\sigma L)^\theta(1-\delta)^{1-\theta}=\theta(1-\varphi)^\theta Y\end{aligned}$$

Similarly:

$$\begin{aligned}&\delta^k V^k(D,\tau_K^D=0)+\delta^l V^l(D,\tau_L^D=0)\\&\quad=\delta^k\left(1-(1-p)\tau_K^p\right)r\frac{K}{\delta^k}+\delta^l\left(1-(1-p)\tau_L^p\right)\nu\frac{L}{\delta^l}\end{aligned}$$

Thus, a coup occurs when democracy makes the best possible promise it can (i.e., $\tau_K^D=0$, $\tau_L^D=0$) if:

$$\theta(1-\varphi)^\theta Y>\left(1-(1-p)\tau_K^p\right)rK+\left(1-(1-p)\tau_L^p\right)\nu L \qquad (9.34)$$

A coup occurs when democracy makes no concessions when:

$$(1-\varphi)^\theta Y>\left(1-\tau_K^p\right)rK+\left(1-\tau_L^p\right)\nu L \qquad (9.35)$$

Note that (9.35) is the same equation as (9.26). Moreover, (9.34) implies exactly the same critical value for the cost of a coup φ^* given in (9.27). Thus, the analysis of Proposition 9.5 applies in this case. For example, we can define critical levels of capital intensity, k^* and $\hat{k}$, such that if $k<k^*$, a coup will occur. For $k\in[k^*,\hat{k})$, democracy can survive by making concessions and is therefore semiconsolidated, whereas if $k\geq\hat{k}$, democracy is fully consolidated.

It is interesting that situations now emerge where the interests and preferences of the elites diverge. Because $\tau_K^p<\tau_L^p$, landowners are naturally more inclined to have a coup than industrialists. However, as capital intensity increases, industrialists gain in power relative to landowners; therefore, the coup decision increasingly reflects their interests (i.e., because they lose less from democracy, they are less inclined to mount coups). Thus, we can have an interesting situation in which there is a split in the elites. Landowners want a coup but industrialists do not; the preferences of the industrialists dominate when the capital intensity becomes high enough.

What matters here is not simply that the elites as a whole are becoming more pro-democratic as the economy develops and capital and industry become more important. In contrast and somewhat more realistically, there are divisions within the elites; the old aristocratic landowners are always more opposed to democracy because they pay a greater price and fear an even greater price in the future from democratic politics. Their attitudes are not changing very fast but with industrialization, the structure of the economy is changing, new factions of the elite are becoming more powerful, and industrialists have more to lose from coups and less to fear from democracy. As these new segments gain more power, democracy has less to fear from the elites. This result follows from the fact that as capital intensity increases, the intensity of preference of the different elite factions changes with industrialists becoming increasingly opposed to a coup and landlords less in favor. Relative intensity of preference maps into relative political power.

8. Industrialists, Landowners, and Democracy in Practice

How do the perspectives developed in this chapter help us understand cross-country differences in the creation and consolidation of democracy? The comparison between Latin America and Western Europe is particularly telling. When European countries such as Britain and France moved toward full democracy in the 1870s, they were primarily urban societies; when Brazil, Guatemala, and Venezuela democratized in the 1940s, they were primarily rural. In the European cases, although democracy created redistribution of income and economic and social policies that favored the poor, no radical program of asset redistribution emerged. Although European socialists certainly talked about the "socialization of the capital stock," it was never actually proposed as a serious electoral strategy, except perhaps in the context of nationalization of industry. Yet, nationalization, at least in the British case, was often of industries that had heavy losses and whose owners were always compensated. Serious redistribution of capital took place only after communist revolutions. In Latin America, however, the newly enfranchised rural poor demanded agrarian reform – the wholesale redistribution of land (Lapp 2004). This happened consistently in Latin American democratizations except in the more urbanized countries such as Argentina and Uruguay, where politics had evolved around a rural-versus-urban cleavage.[1] The response to demands for radical land redistribution in Brazil in 1964, Guatemala in 1954, Venezuela in 1948, and Chile in 1973 was a coup. Thus, the notion that industrialists, because they have less to fear from redistribution, are less anti-democratic than landowners seems consistent with the cross-country historical experience.

The idea that industrialists and landowners may have different preferences toward democracy can also help explain the dynamics of democratization in Central America in the 1990s. In El Salvador, for instance, economic diversification took place after the 1940s with new import substitution industries in the towns and a move from coffee to cotton (Williams 1986; Paige 1997). Because cotton was more mechanized, there was significant shedding of rural labor and workers moved to towns and urban areas. The concentration of people in urban areas seems

[1] For example, the support of Perón in Argentina was mostly urban and his policies aimed at redistributing from the rural sector to Buenos Aires. Clearly, as in the British and other Western European cases, urban workers were not interested in land redistribution.

to have added considerably to the political instability of the country. Moreover, a new breed of industrialists invested in cotton and industry emerged. This new elite suffered much heavier losses from the fighting and was central to the push for compromise that began in the 1980s. Thus, the idea that repression is more costly for industrialists fits well with the Central American evidence, as does the idea that increasing political power of industrialists can lead to a split in the regime and democratization.

Wood (2000) presents an interesting extension of these ideas to South Africa, arguing that a similar transformation took place with white landowners becoming less important relative to industrialists who benefited less from the apartheid regime (because they were hurt by the restriction stopping Africans accumulating human capital) and also lost more through repression and the international sanctions placed on South Africa.

9. Economic Institutions

The analysis in this chapter (and, for that matter, this entire book) took the structure of economic institutions as given. Nevertheless, it is clear that if those with political power can alter such institutions, it may have important implications for democracy. Imagine, for instance, that instead of markets being competitive, those in power could intervene and distort markets. In nondemocracy run by capital owners and landowners, the elites could intervene to reduce wages, perhaps by creating monopsonies in the labor market. In nondemocracy, this would increase the share of national income going to capital and land, reducing what accrued to labor to below $1 - \theta$. In such a society, democratization would not only lead to taxation policies that the elites would not like, it would also undermine their preferred economic institutions. For example, once the citizens – who get their income from supplying their labor – dominate democratic politics, they have an incentive to pass laws undermining the market power of industrialists and landowners. Indeed, they have an incentive to increase their own market power, perhaps by facilitating the formation of trade unions, introducing unemployment insurance, minimum wages, and firing costs. This would have the effect of reducing θ in democracy. Democratization in Britain in the nineteenth century led to important changes in labor-market legislation, switching bargaining power away from employers and toward workers (see Chapter 3).

The effect of allowing labor-market and other economic institutions to be endogenized in this way is to make the elites more antidemocratic and the citizens more prodemocratic. Thus, revolution becomes more attractive because, as in our models with targeted transfers, the nondemocratic status quo becomes worse for the citizens. Simultaneously, democracy becomes worse for the elites and they will therefore be more inclined to use repression to avoid it. Clearly, once democracy has been created, the ability to manipulate economic institutions also increases the incentive of the elites to mount coups. In essence, allowing economic institutions to be endogenous generates results similar to the model with targeted transfers. It increases the stakes from any particular set of political institutions and tends to make society more conflictual and more unstable.

Although we do not analyze models of endogenous economic institutions in this book, in reality it is an important issue. For example, in the work of Moore (1966) and his many followers, great emphasis is placed on the organization of agriculture. Moore argued that one of the forces that facilitated democracy in Britain was the fact that agriculture was highly commercialized with relatively free factor markets. As we discussed previously, predemocratic labor-market institutions in Britain certainly tried to reduce the bargaining power of workers – for example, by banning trade unions, but they were a long cry from the situation in Eastern Europe. Britain was one of the first countries in Europe to witness a collapse of feudalism, whereas in Eastern Europe it lived on until the middle of the nineteenth century. Moore contrasted the situation in Britain with the "labor-repressive" agriculture in Eastern Europe. This distinction makes sense in our framework when economic institutions are endogenous. In Britain, political elites in the nineteenth century, although they certainly anticipated changes in economic institutions, had much less to lose from democratization than the elites of Russia or Austria-Hungary.

Moore's discussion also suggests another connection between land-intensive societies and democratization. It is possible that labor-repressive economic institutions – and, in the extreme, slavery – are less inefficient and/or feasible in conjunction with agricultural technology. For example, this is the standard argument about why slaves were used primarily in the Southern United States before the Civil War (Fogel and Engerman 1974; Eltis 2000). Although we do not know of microfoundations for this claim, it certainly seems consistent with much evidence and would provide another link, this time via economic institutions, between capital-intensive societies and democracy – labor repression is simply less possible or attractive for industrialists.

Although in Moore's study, one might take nineteenth-century Britain to be relatively capital-intensive and Russia to be land-intensive, there is much variation that comes from differences in economic institutions even in land-intensive societies. These ideas can also help explain the intra–Latin American variation. Take Central America, for example. Despite being highly specialized in the same economic activities, particularly coffee, there are large differences in the paths of political development experienced by different Central American countries (Williams 1994; Paige 1997). For example, Nicaragua had one of the most pernicious personalistic dictatorships, that of the Somoza family, throughout most of the twentieth century, until it fell to the Sandinista Revolution of 1979. In Guatemala and El Salvador, such a kleptocratic regime did not emerge; instead, landed elites kept a close grip on power with the support of the military. This grip on power loosened only briefly in Guatemala in the 1940s and in El Salvador in the late 1920s. In both countries, elites took the path of repression rather than democracy; as a result, they had to fight sustained guerilla wars. These wars ended through negotiation in the 1990s, but certainly in Guatemala, the same elites still maintain considerable political power. On the other hand, neighboring Costa Rica is perhaps the most democratic nation in Latin America and has been a democracy since 1948; even before then, it experienced relatively democratic and nonrepressive regimes.

What can explain these differing outcomes? One clear factor is the absence of large landed estates in Costa Rica (Williams 1994; Gudmundson 1995; Paige 1997; Yashar 1997; Lehoucq 1998; Nugent and Robinson 2000; Wood 2000; Mahoney 2001). There, coffee was grown by smallholders and in the early and mid-nineteenth century, the state passed a series of "homestead acts" that basically gave away coffee-growing land to anyone who wanted to farm it. Conversely, in the other Central American countries, the expansion of the world economy in the late nineteenth century led not to homestead acts but to a series of large expropriations of lands by political elites and those with political connections. This led not to a smallholder society like Costa Rica but rather to the creation of large estates and higher land inequality. Most scholars see the different forms of agricultural organization, the existence of a "landed elite," in most of Central America but its absence in Costa Rica as a key to explaining the different paths of political development in those countries.

The situation in relatively democratic Colombia is remarkably similar to that in Costa Rica. In Costa Rica and Colombia, political elites concentrated much more on finance and the purchase and export of the crop rather than coffee production (see Paige 1997 and Mahoney 2001 on Costa Rica; see Palacios 1980 and Nugent and Robinson 2000 on Colombia). One outcome was that labor-market institutions were considerably more "labor-repressive" in Guatemala and El Salvador. Forced labor was in operation in Guatemala until the initial creation of democracy in 1945, something that did not survive the early 1820s in Colombia. The importance of this for democracy was that in Guatemala and El Salvador, the elites invested in land also anticipated losing their preferred labor-market institutions if they democratized, as indeed they did in Guatemala in 1945.

More generally, the literature on comparative development within the Americas is predicated on the idea that initial conditions in Spanish and Portuguese colonies led to economic institutions that were designed to extract rents from indigenous peoples and control colonial elites (Lockhart and Schwartz 1983; Coatsworth 1993; Engerman and Sokoloff 1997; Acemoglu, Johnson, and Robinson 2001, 2002, 2004). These institutions, such as forced labor, absence of well-defined property rights or equality before the law, and highly mercantilistic policies, persisted over time. They appear to have played a major role in the inability of Latin American countries to industrialize during the nineteenth century. They also help explain why inequality became so high. Long-run economic divergence within the Americas is, therefore, at least in part explained by the persistence of different economic institutions, the origins of which lie in different initial conditions in the colonies (e.g., the population density of indigenous peoples).

These arguments suggest that particular sets of economic institutions persist over long periods. Indeed, if institutions did not persist, they would hardly be able to structure social, economic, and political life in the way that they do. This also suggests that not all or even most economic institutions can freely be changed when political regimes change. Despite the interesting examples of correlations among democratizations, coups, and changes in economic institutions that we discuss in this section, this is a primary reason that we have not analyzed them in detail. The situation here is similar to the discussion in Chapter 6 about political institutions. Once created, institutions – both political and economic – have strong tendencies to persist (see Acemoglu, Johnson, and Robinson 2001 for a discussion of explanatory mechanisms). In any society, the institutions that currently exist are the outcome of complex historical processes. In Guatemala and Britain, at one level, there were important changes in economic institutions at the time of democratization; at another level, there were significant historically determined differences in economic institutions. This means that in proposing an explanation for why democratization occurred more rapidly in Britain than in Guatemala, it is useful to treat these differences in economic institutions parametrically. Ultimately, however, one would wish to develop a theory for which the joint evolution of economic and political institutions are accounted. Such a theory is beyond the scope of this book but is an exciting area for future research (see Acemoglu, Johnson, and Robinson 2004 for the outline of such a theory). Finally, the relationship between economic institutions and the political regimes that support them provides another link between inequality and political development; for example, societies with economic institutions favoring a narrow elite may remain nondemocratic and, in turn, continue to maintain such economic institutions and generate high levels of inequality, whereas other societies may transition to democracy and choose more egalitarian economic institutions.

10. Human Capital

The models in this chapter showed that in a society that was more (physical) capital-intensive, repression and coups become more costly and democracy becomes less radical and threatening. As a consequence, such societies ought to democratize more readily and be more prone to consolidate their democracies. Over the past half-century, land and even physical capital have become less important and human capital and technology even more important. Indeed, Goldin (2001) refers to the twentieth century as the "human capital century." In this section, therefore, we extend the analysis of this chapter by focusing on what happens to democracy when human capital comes to dominate the economy.

Human capital – the skills, knowledge, and education embodied in individuals – enters naturally into these mechanisms. First, the burden of repression or coups often falls on the indviduals who are killed during conflict. It is easier to damage or kill a human than to destroy a piece of land or a machine. Thus, we might anticipate that human capital suffers the greatest losses from repression, violence, and coups. Second, human capital is, of course, impossible to redistribute. Moreover, even the income generated from human capital is costly to tax because, unlike the output of a machine, the output generated from human capital only occurs if individuals exert effort. Effort is difficult to monitor; therefore, it is difficult for the government to force people to use their human capital, and it is easily dissuaded by high rates of income taxation. Thus, a democracy in a society where productive assets are dominated by human capital as opposed to physical capital or land is likely to be much less redistributive.

This discussion immediately suggests that it is straightforward to apply an analysis similar to the previous one with $h = H/K$ as the human-capital intensity of the society rather than $k = K/L$, the physical-capital intensity of the society. Greater human-capital intensity of the elites makes them less willing to use force against democracy, moreover, it reduces the burden of democracy because human capital is more difficult to tax than physical capital or land. Both of these channels imply that as human capital becomes more important, democracy becomes more likely to arise and consolidate.

In addition, as human capital becomes more important, we can think of the middle class (as in the analysis of Chapter 8) becoming richer and more numerous, which tends to make democracy more likely.

Therefore, our analysis suggests a number of reasons for major interactions between human capital and democracy, providing useful channels to understand the empirical relationships shown in Chapter 3: specifically, Figures 3.7 and 3.8.

11. Conjectures about Political Development

The relationships between capital, both physical and human, and land intensity and democracy that we investigated in this chapter allow us to make some conjectures about the relationship between economic and political development. Although recent theories of economic growth sometimes emphasize the process of growth simply as an increase in the level of income of society, economic development is more than that. With economic development, productive relationships change significantly; both workers and firms migrate from rural areas to cities; physical capital and then later human capital and technology become more important; and the entire economic structure becomes transformed. These themes were developed by earlier theorists of economic development – for instance, Singer (1949), Rosenstein-Rodan (1949), Nurkse (1953), Lewis (1954), Myrdal (1957), and especially Kuznets (1966). They were formalized to some extent by Murphy, Shleifer, and Vishny (1989); Matsuyama (1992); and Acemoglu and Zilibotti (1997, 1999).

Thus, economic development and increases in per capita income come along with changes in the structure of the economy that are related to the concept of capital intensity that we used in this chapter. This perspective suggests that as an economy develops, capital becomes more important than land, industry becomes more important than agriculture, and our political framework suggests that opposition to and threats against democracy weaken. We might expect that countries with higher per capita income would also be more capital-intensive and that this would generate an empirical relationship between per capita-income and democracy.

Such a relationship, first documented by Lipset (1959), is one of the most important "facts" in political economy. As Chapter 3 showed, this is a robust correlation in cross-country data. However, there is as yet no real theoretical explanation for this empirical fact. Lipset traced the origins of his explanation to Aristotle and argued, like Aristotle, that "only in a wealthy society in which relatively few citizens lived in real poverty could a situation exist in which the mass of the population could intelligently participate in politics and could develop the self-restraint necessary to avoid succumbing to the appeals of irresponsible demagogues" (1959, p. 75). According to this view, the relationship between income and democracy reflects the fact that only in relatively rich countries are the citizens sufficiently "mature" and well informed enough to live the more complex lives associated with democracy. More recent scholars have focused on testing the robustness of this relationship rather than proposing explanations for it.

The models developed in this book before the current chapter were constructed to be deliberately agnostic on this question because we designed them to give results that are invariant to the level of per capita income (e.g., by normalizing the costs of taxation). However, the results in this chapter may provide a plausible microfoundation for the relationship between economic and political development. They suggest that as an economy develops, factors of production accumulate, and per capita income rises, it is the change in the structure of the economy toward a more capital-intensive endowment of assets that leads to democracy and its consolidation.

At this stage, this is only a conjecture lacking empirical support. Indeed, because the empirical work on the determinants of democracy has yet to convincingly establish that there is a causal effect of income on democracy, an investigation of the implications of mechanisms in this chapter for political development is an area for future research. It is plausible that the correlation in the data could be due to another omitted variable. Recall the discussion of the impact of economic institutions on democracy in the previous section. There, we argued that the different economic institutions in Guatemala, compared to Britain, may help explain why Guatemala historically has been so much less democratic than Britain. Obviously, the first-order effect of economic institutions is on economic incentives and performance. Thus, these differences in economic institutions may also explain why Guatemala is much poorer than Britain (Acemoglu, Johnson, and Robinson 2001). In this account, per capita income and democracy are positively correlated, but there is no causal relationship between the two. In fact, both are caused by something else: economic institutions (Acemoglu, Johnson, Robinson, and Yared 2004).

12. Conclusion

In this chapter, we developed a model in which the level and distribution of income are endogenous and showed how the structure of the economy may help to determine the creation and consolidation of democracy. We emphasized that how important physical and human capital are compared to land in the production process – what we called the capital intensity of the economy – can influence the costs of both repression and coups and the burden of democracy for elites. This occurs because (1) repression and the use of force is more costly for capitalists and industrialists than it is for landowners; and (2) democracies will rationally tax land and the income from land at higher rates than capital and the income from capital. The ideas presented are tentative and have not been empirically tested; nevertheless, they are consistent with many case studies, historical material, and mainstream approaches to the theory of economic development. They are also consistent with the observed correlation between per capita income and measures of democracy.

Although we did not explicitly analyze the issue in this chapter, it is important that these results do not depend on the nature of political identities. Even if political conflict were along the lines of ethnic groups X and Z rather than socioeconomic classes, greater capital intensity would have similar consequences for democracy. To see how capital intensity influences democracy, assume that the elites of each group own capital and land, whereas the rest just have their labor. Even if conflict is between ethnic groups, greater capital intensity still reduces the desire of the larger group X to redistribute away from the smaller group Z because this will now be more expensive. This result is true as long as there are some capital owners and landowners in group Z. This reduces the incentives of group Z to mount coups once democracy has been created. Further, in nondemocracy, which here is rule by group Z, greater capital intensity makes repression more costly for Z, which facilitates democratization for the reasons discussed.

It is interesting to compare the results of this chapter with those of Chapter 8 in which we contrasted the attitudes of the very rich and the middle class to democracy. We saw there that, consistent with the emphasis of Moore, the middle class is more pro-democractic because – given that their incomes are lower than those of the rich – they have less to lose than the rich from democratic taxation. As a result, they were less willing than the rich to support repression to avoid democratization. The analysis in Chapter 8 showed that the same considerations made the middle class more opposed to coups against democracy than the rich, who had more to gain from a switch to nondemocracy. The problem with those analyses was that there were no explicit economic bases corresponding to the labels "middle class" and "rich," making it difficult to link economic changes to these potential changes in political attitudes. In this chapter, rather than focusing on these broad distinctions between the middle class and the rich, we emphasize the differences between industrialists and landowners. As with the middle class, industrialists have less to lose from democracy and perhaps more to lose from disruption and violence than landowners.

10 Globalization and Democracy

1. Introduction

In this chapter, we discuss how globalization of the world economy might affect democracy. The framework developed so far shows how the emergence and survival of democracy depends on the distribution of income and, by this channel, factor prices. Globalization, in the form of increased international trade and/or increased financial integration, affects factor prices and income levels, and hence, it may have an important effect on democracy.

Many scholars have conjectured the existence of different connections between globalization and democracy, and the recent empirical literature in political science has begun to investigate some of the links. This literature finds significant correlations between democratizations and changes in the international economy. For example, Quinn (1997, 2002) shows that since the 1960s, measures of democracy averaged across countries are highly correlated with measures of capital and current account liberalization. Yet, this literature (Kubota and Milner 2005) has focused on the effects of democracy on international liberalization (seen as a subset of more general liberalization).

To discuss the potential effects of globalization on democracy, we distinguish three dimensions of "globalization":

- increased international trade (market integration)
- increased financial integration
- increased political integration

In this chapter, we treat these different facets of globalization as exogenous to a specific country and not amenable to control by politicians. Although whether a country is influenced by globalization is often – at least to some extent – under the control of domestic politicians, an important component of the recent wave of globalization is the decline in the costs of international trade and greater integration of the world economy, which politicians can do little to halt. Therefore, an analysis of the implications of exogenous globalization on political equilibrium is a useful starting point.

More international trade typically tends to close the gaps in goods and factor prices across countries (Dixit and Norman 1980; Feenstra 2003). Specifically, in the absence of international trade, locally abundant factors have lower prices. For example, if a country is abundant in labor and scarce in capital, it will have lower wages and higher returns to capital than is true on average in the world. International trade, therefore, increases wages and reduces interest rates in such a country. Both consolidation of democracy against the threat of coups and transitions to democracy are problems for relatively poorer countries that have not attained a stage in which democracy is fully consolidated. Recall, for example, from Chapter 3 that richer countries are typically democracies; it is the poorer countries that are nondemocratic or have a high risk of suffering a coup against democracy. Poor countries are also typically abundant in labor and scarce in capital. International trade, therefore, should reduce the income gap between the poor who earn their living from labor and the rich who are the capital holders.

In the context of our models of politics, the reduction in the gap between the incomes of the poor and the rich implies reduced political conflict. For example, with a smaller gap between the rich and the poor, the poor have less reason to vote for highly redistributive policies and democracy is less of a threat to the rich. Therefore, international trade reduces the intensity of the conflict between the rich and the poor or, as it is sometimes stated in the popular press, globalization might weaken "class conflict." With less intense conflict between the rich and the poor and lower taxes in democracy, the rich are less willing to incur the costs of a coup to revert back to nondemocracy, and democracy is more likely to consolidate. Therefore, globalization might contribute to democratic consolidation in developing nations. The same argument also implies that because democracy is less costly for the rich, nondemocratic societies that sustain themselves through repression might also be more likely to democratize; in this case, globalization should also contribute to democratization around the world. However, we should be careful in these conclusions because, as pointed out in Chapter 6, the relationship between inequality and democratization is in fact nonmonotonic. Consequently, the effects of changes in inequality on democratization depend on where we are in this relationship. If we start from a situation of relative equality, then greater equality – by removing the threat of revolution – can actually impede the creation of democracy. Nevertheless, when thinking of the consolidation of democracy, it is natural to presume that greater inequality destabilizes the democratic institutions in a relatively poor society, so we should expect a reduction in inequality induced by international trade to make democracy more durable once created – even if its general effect on the creation of democracy might be ambiguous. Overall, the exact effect of international trade on democracy is an empirical question, and we view the models in this chapter as most useful in framing future empirical investigations.

Globalization has the opposite effect on factor prices in rich countries. Whereas wages increase and the returns to capital fall in the labor-abundant developing nations, wages should fall and returns to capital should increase in the capital-rich nations, such as the OECD economies. Should we expect a greater likelihood of coups against democracy in the OECD countries? We believe the answer is no: because the OECD societies are already fully consolidated democracies, a marginal increase in democratic redistribution will not push them into the position of unconsolidated democracies.

This discussion is predicated on the presumption that increased international trade reduces inequality in developing countries, especially narrowing the gap between capital holders and labor. This is a prediction of most trade models (especially the celebrated Heckscher–Ohlin model) when the nondemocratic countries are scarce in physical capital and abundant in labor relative to the rest of the world. But, in practice, some of the nondemocratic countries joining the world economy may be abundant in land (e.g., Argentina and Chile in the early twentieth century). In this case, international trade may increase the return to land and, through the mechanisms emphasized in Chapter 9, make democratization and democratic consolidation less likely.

Another important caveat is that international trade not only affects the relative price of capital and labor but also the relative price of human capital (i.e., returns to skills). Less developed nations are typically scarce in skilled labor, and we should expect increased trade integration to reduce the skill premium in those countries. However, recent experience in many of those countries has been an increase in the returns to skill and a greater gap between the more and the less educated workers. The literature in economics explains this fact by the associated diffusion of skill-biased technologies to less developed nations, increasing the marginal product of skilled workers. Therefore, we also briefly discuss a model in which trade integration increases the returns to skills and show that even though this may increase overall inequality, it might again help democratic consolidation. We can think of the skilled workers as corresponding to the "middle class" and, as discussed in Chapter 8, with a richer middle class, democracy is less redistributive and may be more likely to consolidate.

Another aspect of globalization is increased financial integration. We also show in this chapter that increased financial integration in the world economy may affect the creation and survival of democracy. For this purpose, it is important to distinguish between the effects of capital inflows to less developed and capital-scarce nations, which follows increased financial integration and the possibility of capital flight from those nations. Capital inflows, just like increased international trade, reduce returns to capital in the capital-scarce countries and increase wages. Therefore, the effects of financial integration through this channel are similar to those of increased international trade: they reduce the income gap between the rich and the poor and, by this channel, may help the consolidation and creation of democracy.

The possibility of capital flight may also help democracy but this time through a different mechanism. In a closed economy, without the possibility that capital may be invested abroad, the elasticity of capital supply is relatively low: capital holders can consume their capital rather than invest it or perhaps invest it in nontaxable activities (in the "informal sector"), which may have much lower productivity. In contrast, with increased financial integration, high taxes may encourage capital holders to take their capital out of the country and invest it in other markets where taxes are lower and where the risk of expropriation is absent. In other words, financial integration increases the elasticity of capital supply. Realizing this, democracy imposes lower taxes on capital and is generally forced to be less redistributive. Therefore, financial integration also reduces redistribution in democracy because of the potential flight of capital. Anticipating this, the rich have less to fear from democracy, are more willing to accept it rather than use repression, and are less willing to undertake a coup against democracy when a window of opportunity arises. As a result, financial integration may also help the creation and consolidation of democracy.

Lastly, globalization also comes with increased political integration, which may affect the costs of coups through various channels. Most important, with increased political integration, countries may face greater sanctions from other democratic nations if they suffer a coup against democracy. Through this channel, globalization might help democratic consolidation. In addition, greater political integration may also help the development of civil society in less developed nations and increase the cost of coups and contribute to democratic consolidation.

Overall, our analysis in this chapter reveals that there may be important links between globalization and the emergence and consolidation of democracy. An interesting possibility is that these links may help to explain waves of democratizations or coups. By a wave, we mean a concurrent move toward or away from democracy in a number of nations. Waves toward democracy may have occurred historically – for example, in the period before the First World War, after the Second World War, and since the 1970s (Huntington 1991; Markoff 1996). It is interesting that there is a close correlation between these waves of democratization and upsurges in globalization; indeed, it is natural to think of globalization as being a phenomenon simultaneously impacting many nations and thus as a potential explanatory variable.

As noted previously, many scholars have discussed the relationship between globalization and democracy and our analysis makes several important contributions. First, to our knowledge, no one has previously suggested that increased international trade can influence the creation or consolidation of democracy through the channels we discuss (namely, the impact on factor prices and, hence, the distribution of income).

Second, Bates and Lien (1985), Bates (1991), Rogowski (1998), Newman and Robinson (2002), and Boix (2003) note that the possibility of exit from a nation might promote democracy, but they do not offer an analysis of the full political equilibrium when international trade affects the structure of inequality and the options of various parties in the political game.

Third, by placing the idea of exit into a standard economic model of factor mobility, we discover other important effects – for example, the distributional impacts of capital inflow. Although there is a huge literature in economics on the impacts of globalization, both increased trade and financial integration (Prasad et al. 2002), it has only just begun to link these forces to institutional change. Scholars such as Rodrik (1997) and Garrett (1998) emphasized the idea that increasing globalization limits the policy scope for national governments, but they do not suggest that this may influence the equilibrium structure of institutions. We show that globalization may have important effects for democracy.

Fourth, most of the literature in political science has focused on ideas about geopolitics and the ideological diffusion of democracy (Kopstein and Reilly 2000; Maxfield 2000).

The results presented in this chapter are suggestive but have yet to be tested empirically. Moreover, whether the mechanisms we discuss promote democracy depends on which part of the parameter space we are. This was discussed previously with respect to the effects of increased trade integration on inequality, and the same applies to the effect of financial integration. We see it as a theoretical possibility, although probably not the empirically relevant case, that by reducing inequality, increased trade integration may consolidate nondemocratic regimes.

Finally, globalization may reduce the scope for democracy to set majoritarian policies by so much that the creation of democracy fails to promote stability. If democracy delivers nothing to the citizens, then revolution becomes attractive for them and repression becomes attractive for the elites. In such a circumstance, globalization does not promote democracy.

2. A Model of an Open Economy

To study the links between globalization and democracy, we use a version of the model from Chapter 9 with capital, land, and labor. We focus on a single country, which is first taken to be closed to international trade. Then we look at the case in which the country integrates into the world economy and starts trading goods with other countries.

As in Chapter 9, we assume there is an aggregate production function but instead of this directly taking capital, land, and labor as inputs, we assume that three different intermediate goods are used as inputs. As before, let Y be the output of the final good that is consumed and let Y_K, Y_L, and Y_N be the amounts of the three intermediate goods used in the production of Y. The aggregate production function is again assumed to be Cobb–Douglas:

$$Y = (Y_K + \sigma Y_L)^{\theta} Y_N^{1-\theta} \tag{10.1}$$

and we assume, as before, that $0 < \theta < 1$ and $\sigma > 0$.

In a closed economy with no trade, intermediate goods are themselves produced by domestic factors of production; the subscripts on the intermediate goods indicate that one is capital-intensive, Y_K; another is land-intensive, Y_L; and the last is labor-intensive, Y_N. In an open economy, intermediate goods are traded internationally. On the production side, in the simplest possible world, all three goods are produced using only their respective factors; therefore, domestic production of each intermediate good is given by:

$$\begin{aligned} Y_K &= K \\ Y_L &= L \\ Y_N &= 1-\delta \end{aligned} \tag{10.2}$$

exploiting the fact that there are $1-\delta$ workers. The remaining δ agents, who constitute the elites, do not own any labor, and each holds fractions δ of the total capital stock, K, and the total land stock, L.

When there is no international trade, this world is identical to the one in Chapter 9. More formally, without international trade, the country in question has to use its domestic production of capital, land, and labor-intensive intermediate goods to produce output. Substituting (10.2) into (10.1), we have that:

$$Y = (K + \sigma L)^{\theta} (1-\delta)^{1-\theta}$$

which is identical to the aggregate production function specified in Chapter 9.

We assume that all markets, both for intermediate inputs and factors of production, are perfectly competitive. We set the price of final output to be 1 and use this good as the numeraire. The prices for the three intermediate goods are denoted by p_K, p_L, and p_N. To determine these prices, we examine the cost-minimization problem of a firm choosing input demands to minimize the cost of production. Formally, a firm solves the problem:

$$\min_{Y_K, Y_L, Y_N} \{p_K Y_K + p_L Y_L + p_N Y_N\}$$

subject to:

$$Y = (Y_K + \sigma Y_L)^{\theta} Y_N^{1-\theta}$$

Here, $p_K Y_K + p_L Y_L + p_N Y_N$ is the total cost of using the three intermediate goods. This is a simple constrained-optimization problem. To solve it, we form the Lagrangean function:

$$\mathcal{L} = p_K Y_K + p_L Y_L + p_N Y_N - \lambda \left[(Y_K + \sigma Y_L)^{\theta} Y_N^{1-\theta} - Y \right]$$

and derive the first-order conditions with respect to the three choice variables Y_K, Y_L, and Y_N. These are:

$$\begin{aligned}\lambda\theta\,(Y_K+\sigma Y_L)^{\theta-1}\,Y_N^{1-\theta} &= p_K \\ \lambda\theta\sigma\,(Y_K+\sigma Y_L)^{\theta-1}\,Y_N^{1-\theta} &= p_L \\ \lambda(1-\theta)\,(Y_K+\sigma Y_L)^{\theta}\,Y_N^{-\theta} &= p_N\end{aligned} \tag{10.3}$$

From these, we derive:

$$\frac{p_K}{p_N}=\frac{\theta}{1-\theta}\frac{Y_N}{Y_K+\sigma Y_L} \quad \text{and} \quad \frac{p_K}{p_L}=\frac{1}{\sigma} \tag{10.4}$$

where the first follows from dividing the first and third equations in (10.3), and the second follows from dividing the first two equations in (10.3). These equations imply that:

$$p_K=\frac{p_L}{\sigma}=\theta\left(\frac{Y_N}{Y_K+\sigma Y_L}\right)^{1-\theta} \quad \text{and} \quad p_N=(1-\theta)\left(\frac{Y_N}{Y_K+\sigma Y_L}\right)^{-\theta} \tag{10.5}$$

Because one unit of each factor is used to produce its respective goods and factor markets are competitive, each factor is paid the value of its marginal product – that is:

$$w=p_N, \quad r=p_K, \quad \text{and} \quad v=p_L$$

where w denotes the wage rate, r the return to capital, and v the rental rate of land. In the closed economy, we use (10.2) together with (10.5) to obtain:

$$\begin{aligned}p_K &= \theta\left(\frac{K+\sigma L}{1-\delta}\right)^{\theta-1} \\ p_L &= \sigma\theta\left(\frac{K+\sigma L}{1-\delta}\right)^{\theta-1} \\ p_N &= (1-\theta)\left(\frac{K+\sigma L}{1-\delta}\right)^{\theta}\end{aligned} \tag{10.6}$$

and, therefore, the relevant closed-economy factor prices are identical to those in Chapter 9 and given in (9.2). This is, of course, not surprising given the previous observation that the two models are identical for the case of the closed economy. Consequently, factor shares are also the same as before and given by (9.3). Exactly as before, we have that incomes of the poor citizens and of the elites and average incomes are given by (9.4), (9.5), and (9.6). We again make an assumption ensuring that the elites are richer than average (i.e., $\theta > \delta$). Thus, the elites are homogeneous and each owns capital and land in equal amounts. The citizens simply own their own labor. We focus in this chapter on situations in which political conflict is along the lines of socioeconomic class. Nevertheless, as is clear from our previous analysis, many of the results apply when political conflict is along other lines; we return briefly to this issue in the conclusion of this chapter.

We again assume there is a single tax rate on income, irrespective of its source. This tax rate creates the standard distortions captured by the function $C(\tau)\bar{y}$. Then, the most preferred tax rate by a citizen, τ^p, is given by an equation identical to before.

2.1 Factor Prices and Incomes in an Open Economy

Now assume that this country joins the world trading system and can trade with all other countries in the world without any friction. We think of this increased trade integration as one aspect of "globalization." Because there is only a single produced good, there is no incentive for countries to trade it. However, there may be incentives for countries to trade the intermediate goods that are inputs to the production of the final good because they are produced using factors of production with which countries may be differentially endowed. For now, we assume that factors of production cannot be traded (i.e., there is no capital mobility and no migration). Instead of simply using domestic stocks of capital, land, and labor to produce intermediate goods, a country can trade with the rest of the world, sell its supplies of capital-, land-, and labor-intensive intermediate goods at world prices, and attain a different level of production of the final good. If world prices of capital-, land-, and labor-intensive goods are denoted, respectively, by $\underline{p}_N$, $\underline{p}_K$, and $\underline{p}_L$ (underlined variables always refer to the open economy), then the budget constraint of this country is:

$$\underline{p}_K Y_K + \underline{p}_L Y_L + \underline{p}_N Y_N = \underline{p}_K K + \underline{p}_L L + \underline{p}_N (1 - \delta)$$

The left-hand side of the equation is the total expenditure of this country on intermediate goods at world prices; the right-hand side is the total revenue that this country raises by selling its production of intermediate goods at world prices (considering the production functions given by (10.2)).

How are these world prices determined? The answer is not essential for this discussion. We simply assume that the prices are determined in some world-market equilibrium, and we take it such that:

$$\underline{p}_K = \frac{\underline{p}_L}{\sigma} = \theta \Psi^{\theta - 1} \quad \text{and} \quad \underline{p}_N = (1 - \theta)\Psi^{\theta} \tag{10.7}$$

where we can think of Ψ as the ratio of the sum of capital and land relative to labor in the world economy. In (10.6), what mattered for the determination of domestic prices was the ratio of $K + \sigma L$ to $1 - \delta$; this is what is meant by "the ratio of the sum of capital and land relative to labor." In the world economy, we can think of the same ratio mattering but where the relevant totals are the world stocks of factors, not just the stocks in one country. For example, if all countries of the world trade and there are no tariffs or trading frictions, we have that:

$$\frac{\underline{p}_K}{\underline{p}_N} = \frac{\theta}{1-\theta} \frac{\sum_j N_j}{\sum_j K_j + \sigma \sum_j L_j}$$

where N_j is total labor supply in country j, K_j is the capital stock, and L_j is the stock of land. In this case, we have that Ψ is equal to the sum of the capital-and-land-to-labor ratios across the world – i.e.,

$$\Psi = \frac{\sum_j K_j + \sigma \sum_j L_j}{\sum_j N_j}$$

If, on the other hand, there are tariffs or trading frictions, Ψ differs from this ratio. Whether this is the case is not central for the analysis in this chapter.

Our focus is with the emergence and consolidation of democracy in nondemocratic societies. Nondemocratic societies are typically poorer and, therefore, they are more abundant in labor than capital. Therefore, it is natural to think that the country in question is relatively scarce in capital. Stating this as an assumption, we have:

$$\Psi > \frac{K + \sigma L}{1 - \delta} \tag{10.8}$$

The most important implication of this assumption is seen by comparing (10.7) with (10.6), which implies that after trade opening, the price of the labor-intensive intermediate good increases in the country in question (which is presumed throughout to be a relatively labor-abundant country). Intuitively, this country is relatively abundant in labor compared to the world economy, which depresses the price of the labor-intensive intermediate good when there is no international trade. International trade pulls the price of the labor-intensive good to the world level.

Once these prices are given, factor rewards in this economy are again given by the relevant value of marginal products, now evaluated at these world prices; therefore:

$$\underline{w} = \underline{p}_N, \quad \underline{r} = \underline{p}_K, \quad \text{and} \quad \underline{v} = \underline{p}_L \tag{10.9}$$

This implies that international trade also increases wages relative to capital and land returns. These changes in relative factor prices are the main channel by which international trade has an impact on whether democracy emerges or consolidates.

It is also noteworthy that we are implicitly imposing *factor price equalization.* That is, with Ψ interpreted as the world capital-and-land-to-labor ratio and $\underline{p}_N$, $\underline{p}_K$, and $\underline{p}_L$ as the world prices, factor prices given by (9.2) would be the same as factor prices in other countries. Nevertheless, whether factor-price equalization holds is also not important for this analysis. What matters is simply that after trade opening, the price of the abundant factor increases relative to other factor prices and that for the country in question, a relatively poor country, the abundant factor is labor. This is a feature of many trade models even when factor-price equalization does not hold, as well as the standard Heckscher–Ohlin model with factor-price equalization. The important implication of this change in factor prices is that inequality declines after trade. Existing evidence is broadly consistent with the notion that wages are higher in capital-abundant countries (Trefler 1985; Leamer 1998; Romalis 2004), but there is also evidence that the recent increase in international trade has raised the incomes of higher skilled workers more; we discuss these implications next.

Combining (10.7) and (10.9), we have that post-trade factor prices are given by:

$$\begin{aligned} \underline{w} &= (1-\theta)\Psi^{\theta} \\ \underline{r} &= \theta\Psi^{\theta-1} \\ \underline{v} &= \sigma\theta\Psi^{\theta-1} \end{aligned} \tag{10.10}$$

Equation (10.8) implies that wages are higher and the returns to land and capital are lower than under autarky.

Using these factor prices, post-trade incomes are:

$$\underline{y}^p = (1-\theta)\Psi^{\theta}$$

and

$$\underline{y}^r = \frac{\theta}{\delta}\Psi^{\theta-1}(K+\sigma L)$$

and average income in this case is:

$$\underline{\bar{y}} = \Psi^{\theta-1}((1-\theta)(1-\delta)\Psi + \theta(K+\sigma L)) \tag{10.11}$$

Using these expressions, we obtain the most preferred (unconstrained) tax rate of the citizens as $\underline{\tau}^p$, which again satisfies the usual first-order condition:

$$\frac{\underline{y}^p}{\underline{\bar{y}}} = 1 - C'(\underline{\tau}^p) \quad \text{or} \tag{10.12}$$

$$\frac{1-\theta}{(1-\theta)(1-\delta)+\theta\frac{K+\sigma L}{\Psi}} = 1 - C'(\underline{\tau}^p)$$

By (10.8), $\frac{K+\sigma L}{\Psi} < 1-\delta$, so

$$\frac{1-\theta}{(1-\theta)(1-\delta)+\theta\frac{K+\sigma L}{\Psi}} > \frac{1-\theta}{1-\delta}$$

and

$$\underline{\tau}^p < \tau^p$$

where $\underline{\tau}^p$ is the preferred tax rate of the citizens after trade, given by (10.12), and τ^p is their most preferred tax rate before trade. Thus, the citizens, whose income comes from supplying labor, prefer to set lower taxes after trade. This implies that after globalization, democracy becomes less redistributive because globalization reduces income inequality.

3. Political Conflict – Democratic Consolidation

We now incorporate this economic model into our political models. We begin with an analysis of democratic consolidation. The analysis mirrors those before, especially those in Chapter 9, Section 5, and the game tree in Figure 7.1 captures the strategic situation. We assume that a fraction φ of both capital and land is lost during a coup, so there are no differential costs depending on asset composition. We define two different coup constraints – one before and one after trade – and two threshold levels for φ, which we denote φ^* and $\tilde{\varphi}$, for before and after trade.

This discussion implies that the values from democracy before trade are given by (9.7). Similarly, before trade, the values to citizens and to the elites following a coup are given by (9.24).

The coup constraint before trade, $V^r(C,\varphi) > V^r(D)$, is identical to the one we derived before in (9.16) with $\xi = 1$:

$$\theta + \tau^p(\delta-\theta) - \delta C(\tau^p) < \theta(1-\varphi)^\theta \tag{10.13}$$

After trade, the values from democracy change because of the changes in factor prices and are given by:

$$\underline{V}^p(D) = \Bigg[(1-\theta)\Psi + \underline{\tau}^p\left(\theta\left(K+\sigma L\right) - (1-\theta)\delta\Psi\right) - C(\underline{\tau}^p)\left(\theta\left(K+\sigma L\right) + (1-\theta)(1-\delta)\Psi\right)\Bigg]\Psi^{\theta-1} \tag{10.14}$$

$$\underline{V}^r(D) = \Bigg[\frac{\theta}{\delta}\left(K+\sigma L\right) + \underline{\tau}^p\left((1-\theta)(1-\delta)\Psi - \frac{1-\delta}{\delta}\theta\left(K+\sigma L\right)\right) - C(\underline{\tau}^p)\left(\theta\left(K+\sigma L\right) + (1-\theta)(1-\delta)\Psi\right)\Bigg]\Psi^{\theta-1}$$

Similarly, coup values are:

$$\underline{V}^p(C,\varphi) = (1-\theta)\Psi^{\theta} \tag{10.15}$$

$$\underline{V}^r(C,\varphi) = \frac{\theta}{\delta}(1-\varphi)\left(K+\sigma L\right)\Psi^{\theta-1}$$

The coup constraint after trade is, therefore, $\underline{V}^r(C,\varphi) > \underline{V}^r(D)$, which can be written as:

$$\theta + \delta\underline{\tau}^p\left(\frac{(1-\theta)(1-\delta)\Psi}{(K+\sigma L)} - \frac{(1-\delta)}{\delta}\theta\right) - \delta C(\underline{\tau}^p)\left(\theta + \frac{(1-\theta)(1-\delta)\Psi}{(K+\sigma L)}\right) < \theta(1-\varphi) \tag{10.16}$$

It is straightforward to check that the coup constraint after trade, (10.16), binds less often than the coup constraint before trade, (10.13). This occurs for two reasons. First, as shown in the previous subsection, after trade, taxes are lower; therefore, democracy is less costly to the elites. Second, with trade, a coup is more costly to the elites because they are price-takers; therefore, destruction of the fraction φ of their assets is not shared with workers. Stated differently, in a closed economy, once the assets of the elites are destroyed, wages fall and the returns to capital and land increase. This implies that income of the elites falls less than proportionately. In contrast, the returns to capital and land are given by international prices in the open economy, so the incomes of the elites fall proportionally as a result of the coup. This is shown mathematically by comparing the right-hand side of (10.16), which is $\theta(1-\varphi)$, to the right-hand side of (10.13), which is $\theta(1-\varphi)^{\theta} > \theta(1-\varphi)$. As a result, a coup is now more costly to the elites.

Similarly, we examine the circumstances when promises of policy concessions by the citizens are just sufficient to avoid a coup, given that such policies are implemented only with probability p (i. e., our basic static coup game of Chapter 7).

To do this, we calculate the threshold values for the cost of a coup before trade, φ^*, and after trade, $\underline{\varphi}^*$, using the best offer that the citizens can promise the elites. For this, the values of the promise of no redistribution (i.e., $\tau^D = 0$) in a democracy, considering that they are upheld only with probability p, are:

$$V^p(D, \tau^D = 0) = \frac{1}{1-\delta}(1 - \theta + (1-p)(\tau^p(\theta - \delta) - (1-\delta)C(\tau^p)))(K + \sigma L)^\theta (1-\delta)^{1-\theta} \tag{10.17}$$

$$V^r(D, \tau^D = 0) = \frac{1}{\delta}(\theta + (1-p)(\tau^p(\delta - \theta) - \delta C(\tau^p)))(K + \sigma L)^\theta (1-\delta)^{1-\theta}$$

which follow from (9.15). The corresponding values after trade are:

$$\underline{V}^p(D, \tau^D = 0) = [(1-\theta)\Psi + (1-p)\underline{\tau}^p(\theta(K+\sigma L) - (1-\theta)\delta\Psi) - (1-p)C(\underline{\tau}^p)(\theta(K+\sigma L) + (1-\theta)(1-\delta)\Psi))]\Psi^{\theta-1}$$

$$\underline{V}^r(D, \tau^D = 0) = \left[\frac{\theta}{\delta}(K+\sigma L) + (1-p)\underline{\tau}^p \times \left((1-\theta)(1-\delta)\Psi - \frac{1-\delta}{\delta}\theta(K+\sigma L)\right) - (1-p)C(\underline{\tau}^p)(\theta(K+\sigma L) + (1-\theta)(1-\delta)\Psi)\right]\Psi^{\theta-1}$$

The closed economy threshold value φ^* is defined by setting $V^r(D, \tau^D = 0) = V^r(C, \varphi)$ and, hence, is given by:

$$\varphi^* = 1 - \left(1 + \frac{(1-p)}{\theta}(\tau^p(\delta - \theta) - \delta C(\tau^p))\right)^{\frac{1}{\theta}} \tag{10.18}$$

which is naturally identical to (9.17) with $\xi = 1$. The relevant threshold level after trade, $\underline{\varphi}^*$, is in turn given by $\underline{V}^r(D, \tau^D = 0) = \underline{V}^r(C, \underline{\varphi}^*)$; hence:

$$\underline{\varphi}^* = (1-p)\left(\delta C(\underline{\tau}^p)\left(1 + \frac{(1-\theta)(1-\delta)\Psi}{\theta(K+\sigma L)}\right) - \delta\underline{\tau}^p\left(\frac{(1-\theta)(1-\delta)\Psi}{\theta(K+\sigma L)} - \frac{(1-\delta)}{\delta}\right)\right) \tag{10.19}$$

The same argument we used to show that (10.16) binds less often implies that:

$$\underline{\varphi}^* < \varphi^*$$

This says that, once the economy is open to international trade, coups have to be less costly to be attractive. Therefore, this comparison establishes the following proposition:

Proposition 10.1: *Consider the economic model and the political game described above and define* φ^* *by (10.18) and* $\underline{\varphi}^*$ *by (10.19). Then:*

- *If* $\varphi < \underline{\varphi}^*$*, there are coups both before and after trade opening.*
- *If* $\varphi \geq \varphi^*$*, there are no coups either before or after trade opening.*
- *If* $\underline{\varphi}^* \leq \varphi < \varphi^*$*, there are coups before trade opening but not after.*

This proposition, therefore, shows how globalization might help to consolidate democracy. As the discussion suggests, there are two reasons for this. First, under the hypothesis that condition (10.8) holds (the country in question is labor-abundant relative to the world), trade opening increases the returns to labor and therefore to the poorer segments of society, relative to the returns to capital and land. Via this channel, increased international trade reduces equilibrium taxes. With lower taxation, democracy is more likely to survive. We think of this channel as loosely corresponding to a reduction in class conflict between the elites and the citizens. Such conflict is less in a more globalized economy, at least under the assumptions of this standard model.

The second reason relates to changes in the costs of a coup as a result of trade opening. In a closed economy, the costs of a coup are shared between the elites and the citizens because of general equilibrium price effects. More explicitly, the destruction of part of the stocks of capital and land reduces wages and increases the returns to capital and land because capital and land now become "scarcer." This general equilibrium price effect partly offsets the reduction in the income accruing to capital and land. In an open economy, factor prices are given, and capital owners and landowners bear the full burden of the destruction of their asset stocks, which also tends to make coups less attractive.

4. Political Conflict – Transition to Democracy

That increased international trade makes democracy less redistributive also has implications for the transition to democracy. Recall that a barrier to the transition to democracy is the fear of the elites that democracy will be highly anti-elite. This fear may make them choose repression rather than democratization. If international trade makes democracy less redistributive, it should alleviate concerns of the elites and they may now prefer to concede democracy rather than use repression to quell a potential revolutionary threat.

To analyze the issues, we return to the model of democratization in the presence of a revolutionary threat – specifically, the version used in Chapter 9 in which capital, land, and labor were introduced as three productive factors. The underlying economic model is the same as the one described earlier, and we look at it before and after trade opening. The extensive-form game depicted in Figure 6.2 captures the strategic setup.

We start with nondemocracy and assume that the citizens have a potential revolutionary threat. After revolution and before trade opening, the payoff to the citizens from revolution is:

$$V^p(R, \mu) = \frac{(1-\mu)\bar{y}}{1-\delta} \tag{10.20}$$

with $\bar{y}$ given by (9.4). After trade, we have instead:

$$\underline{V}^p(R, \mu) = \frac{(1-\mu)\underline{\bar{y}}}{1-\delta}$$

with $\underline{\bar{y}}$ given by (10.11). Both before and after trade, the elites get zero after revolution.

If the elites choose to repress to avoid either a revolution or democratization, we assume they lose a fraction κ of their capital and land. This assumption about the costs of repression mirrors our assumptions about the costs of coups. The rest of the setup is the same as before. In particular, values to the citizens and to the elites if there is a democratization are given by (9.7) before trade and by (10.14) after trade.

If the elites choose repression before trade, the payoffs are:

$$V^p(O\,|\kappa) = (1-\theta)(1-\kappa)^\theta \left(\frac{K+\sigma L}{1-\delta}\right)^\theta = \left(\frac{1-\theta}{1-\delta}\right)(1-\kappa)^\theta Y \tag{10.21}$$

$$V^r(O\,|\kappa) = \frac{\theta}{\delta}(1-\kappa)^\theta\,(K+\sigma L)^\theta\,(1-\delta)^{1-\theta} = \frac{\theta}{\delta}(1-\kappa)^\theta Y$$

which correspond to (9.8) with $\varrho = 1$.

After trade, the values from repression change in a way similar to the values from a coup. In particular, we have:

$$\underline{V}^p(O\,|\kappa) = (1-\theta)\Psi^\theta \tag{10.22}$$

$$\underline{V}^r(O\,|\kappa) = \frac{\theta}{\delta}(1-\kappa)\,(K+\sigma L)\,\Psi^{\theta-1}$$

Finally, the elites could offer redistribution under the existing regime without democratizing and without resorting to repression. The best they can do in this case is offer redistribution at the favorite tax rate of the citizens, τ^p; in this case, the values are identical to those in (9.9). Similarly, after trade, we have:

$$\underline{V}^p(N, \tau^N = \underline{\tau}^p) = \big[(1-\theta)\Psi + p\underline{\tau}^p\,(\theta\,(K+\sigma L) - (1-\theta)\delta\Psi) \\ - pC(\underline{\tau}^p)\,(\theta\,(K+\sigma L) + (1-\theta)(1-\delta)\Psi)\big]\,\Psi^{\theta-1}$$

$$\underline{V}^r(N, \tau^N = \underline{\tau}^p) = \left[\frac{\theta}{\delta}(K+\sigma L) + p\underline{\tau}^p\left((1-\theta)(1-\delta)\Psi - \frac{1-\delta}{\delta}\theta\,(K+\sigma L)\right)\right. \\ \left. - pC(\underline{\tau}^p)\,(\theta\,(K+\sigma L) + (1-\theta)(1-\delta)\Psi)\right]\Psi^{\theta-1}$$

which take into account that after trade, the most preferred tax rate of the citizens is $\underline{\tau}^p$, given by (10.12).

To simplify the discussion in this section, we assume that the revolution constraint always binds; that is, $\theta > \mu$ without trade and:

$$\frac{\theta(K+\sigma L - (1-\delta)\Psi)}{(1-\theta)(1-\delta)\Psi + \theta(K+\sigma L)} > \mu$$

with trade. Moreover, democracy is always (before and after trade) sufficiently redistributive that it prevents a revolution.

More important we assume that:

$$V^p(R, \mu) > V^p(N, \tau^N = \tau^p) \\ \underline{V}^p(R, \mu) > \underline{V}^p(N, \tau^N = \underline{\tau}^p) \tag{10.23}$$

These conditions imply that promise of temporary redistribution is not going to be sufficient to prevent revolution. This ensures that we are in the part of the parameter space in which the trade-off is between democratization and repression and greater inequality makes democracy less acceptable to the elites (without this assumption, we may be on the other side of the nonmonotonic relationship between inequality and democratization).

With these assumptions, the analysis of the political equilibrium is straightforward. Before trade, the relevant condition for the elites to prefer democracy is:

$$V^r(D) \geq V^r(O\,|\kappa)$$

This condition defines a closed economy cutoff level κ^* such that for all $\kappa \geq \kappa^*$, the elites prefer democratization to repression. More explicitly, κ^* is given by $V^r(D) = V^r(O\,|\kappa^*)$, or by:

$$\kappa^* = 1 - \left(\frac{1}{\theta}\,(\theta + \tau^p\,(\delta-\theta) - \delta C(\tau^p))\right)^{\frac{1}{\theta}} \tag{10.24}$$

Similarly, after trade, we need to check that for the open economy:

$$\underline{V}^r(D) \geq \underline{V}^r(O\,|\kappa)$$

so that we have a new threshold defined by $\underline{V}^r(D) = \underline{V}^r(O\,|\underline{\kappa}^*)$:

$$\underline{\kappa}^* = \delta C(\underline{\tau}^p)\left(\frac{(1-\theta)(1-\delta)\Psi}{\theta(K+\sigma L)} + 1\right) - \delta\underline{\tau}^p\left(\frac{(1-\theta)(1-\delta)\Psi}{\theta(K+\sigma L)} - \frac{(1-\delta)}{\delta}\right) \tag{10.25}$$

which, of course, is almost identical to the formula in (10.19).

For all $\kappa \geq \underline{\kappa}^*$, the elites prefer democratization rather than using repression in an open economy. The same argument as before immediately establishes that:

$$\underline{\kappa}^* < \kappa^*$$

and for the same reasons. After trade opening, democracy is less costly because the poor now prefer lower taxes, $\underline{\tau}^p$, as given by (10.12) rather than τ^p. In addition, repression is more costly to the elites in an open economy because the costs that stem from the loss in their productive capital and land from a coup are borne only by them. This is, again, because factor prices are given by world prices; therefore, capital and land do not become more valuable after the disruption caused by repression destroys part of them.

This discussion establishes a parallel proposition to Proposition 10.1, as follows:

Proposition 10.2: *Consider the economic model and the political game described above and define κ^* by (10.24) and $\underline{\kappa}^*$ by (10.25):*

- *If $\kappa < \underline{\kappa}^*$, the elites use repression to prevent revolution and democratization both before and after trade opening.*
- *If $\kappa \geq \kappa^*$, there is democratization both before and after trade opening.*
- *If $\underline{\kappa}^* \leq \kappa < \kappa^*$, the elites use repression to prevent revolution and democratization before trade opening but there is democratization after trade opening.*

This proposition shows that for similar reasons to those that allowed globalization to aid democratic consolidation, globalization may also facilitate a transition to democracy. Globalization makes democracy less redistributive and also increases the costs of using force to prevent transitions to democracy. Through both channels, democratization becomes more attractive relative to repression. Consequently, this model suggests that international trade reduces political conflict by reducing inequality and, via this channel, makes democracy more likely.

4.1 Implications of Land Abundance

This analysis is predicated on the assumption that (10.8) holds, which, in practice, implies that the country in question is abundant in labor (and scarce in capital).

Although this seems a reasonable assumption for many nondemocratic countries joining the world economy, there are countries such as Argentina and Chile at the beginning of the last century in which the most abundant factor was land. In this case, the exact converse of (10.8) holds, and international trade increases the relative income of the elites.

The implications for the political equilibrium are obvious from this analysis, and we state this simply as the following corollary:

Corollary 10.1: *Consider the economic model described above and suppose the converse of (10.8) holds. Then, trade opening makes democratization and democratic consolidation less likely.*

This corollary is useful in stressing that the implications of international trade for the political equilibrium depend on its implications for factor prices. Although we emphasized the equalizing role of international trade based on the presumption that labor is the abundant factor in many nondemocratic countries, in certain cases international trade can increase the price of land and the incomes of the elites, thereby potentially making repression and coups more attractive for them. Whether this is so is an empirical question we leave for future research.

5. Financial Integration

Another dimension of globalization is increased financial integration. We now analyze how increased financial integration affects the consolidation of democracy and the likelihood of the use of repression to prevent transition to democracy.

We distinguish between two cases, referred to as the "capital-in" and "capital-out" cases. Capital-in is the usual case in which increased financial integration leads to capital flows toward the capital-scarce country. Capital-out, on the other hand, refers to the case in which capital may fly from the less developed country, despite the fact that the country is more capital-scarce, because of heavy taxation there. We analyze these two cases separately because they emphasize different mechanisms.

5.1 Capital-in and Democracy

Consider the same model as in the previous section, but assume that there is no trade in intermediate goods. Instead, we investigate the implications of factor mobility – specifically, capital mobility. Again, we think that the country in question is less intensive in $K + \sigma L$ than the rest of the world, for which the ratio of capital and land to labor is again denoted by Ψ.

Now imagine that there is financial integration and this country opens to capital flows from abroad and for now assume that there is no possibility of capital outflows. The only difference from this economic model is that now domestic production of intermediate goods is given by:

$$
\begin{aligned}
Y_K &= K + K' \\
Y_L &= L \\
Y_N &= 1 - \delta
\end{aligned}
\tag{10.26}
$$

where K' is the amount of capital owned by foreigners invested in the production of capital-intensive goods in this country. We assume that foreign capital can be invested in this country without any costs.

The same arguments now imply that domestic prices are given by:

$$
\underline{p}'_K = \frac{\underline{p}'_L}{\sigma} = \theta \left(\frac{K + K' + \sigma L}{1 - \delta} \right)^{\theta - 1} \quad \text{and} \quad \underline{p}'_N = (1 - \theta) \left(\frac{K + K' + \sigma L}{1 - \delta} \right)^{\theta}
\tag{10.27}
$$

and factor prices are:

$$
\underline{w}' = \underline{p}'_N, \quad \underline{r}' = \underline{p}'_K, \quad \text{and} \quad \underline{v}' = \underline{p}'_L
$$

where $\underline{w}'$ denotes the wage rate, $\underline{r}'$ is the return to capital, and $\underline{v}'$ is the rental rate of land all after financial integration. Combining these equations, we obtain:

$$
\begin{aligned}
\underline{w}' &= (1 - \theta) \left(\frac{K + K' + \sigma L}{1 - \delta} \right)^{\theta} \\
\underline{r}' &= \theta \left(\frac{K + K' + \sigma L}{1 - \delta} \right)^{\theta - 1} \\
\underline{v}' &= \sigma\theta \left(\frac{K + K' + \sigma L}{1 - \delta} \right)^{\theta - 1}
\end{aligned}
\tag{10.28}
$$

Because we assumed that the country in question is scarce in capital relative to the world, it is reasonable to expect that $K' > 0$, so that with capital account opening, capital flows into rather than out of the country in question. This generally is the case as long as taxes in this country are not too high relative to taxes abroad. To highlight the forces at work in this subsection we assume that foreign capital is excepted from taxation and from the costs of a coup and also ignore taxation of foreign capital abroad. Then the world rate of return on capital is $\underline{r} = \theta\Psi^{\theta-1}$ and with $K' = 0$, $\underline{r}' > \underline{r}$ encouraging capital inflows until the domestic gross rate of return on capital is $\underline{r}' = \underline{r}$.

This implies that $\underline{w}'$ is also equal to $\underline{w}$ as given by (10.10) and therefore from the analysis above the coup threshold in the economy with capital inflows is given by $\underline{\varphi}^*$ in (10.19). This establishes a version of Proposition 10.1.

Proposition 10.3: *Consider the economic model and the democratic consolidation game described above and define φ^* by (10.18) and $\underline{\varphi}^*$ by (10.19):*

- *If $\varphi < \underline{\varphi}^*$, there are coups both before and after financial integration.*
- *If $\varphi \geq \varphi^*$, there are no coups either before or after financial integration.*
- *If $\underline{\varphi}^* \leq \varphi < \varphi^*$, there are coups before financial integration but not after.*

Therefore, just like trade opening, financial integration makes democracy less redistributive. This implies that the elites have less to fear from democracy and are less willing to undertake a coup. In addition, with financial integration, factor prices again move toward world prices (i.e., returns to labor increase and those to capital decline), and coups again become more costly after financial integration. (Recall that before financial integration, coups also increase the return to capital and land but after financial integration they do not.) Both of these effects make democratic consolidation more likely after financial integration. The additional effect highlighted herein is that financial integration may also encourage the median voter in democracy to choose lower taxes to attract more capital and increase wages. This effect is discussed in greater detail in the next subsection.

Similarly, financial integration by making democracy less redistributive and the use of force against democracy more costly may help the transition to democracy. Therefore, as long as the choice for the elites is between democratization and repression, we could also state a proposition similar to Proposition 10.2; however, we refrain because the analogy is immediately apparent.

5.2 Capital-out

The previous subsection showed how financial integration can help democratic consolidation and the transition to democracy through a channel similar to the effect of increased international trade: by affecting the income gap between the elites and the citizens and by influencing the cost of using force against democracy. However, the more important role of financial integration may be the potential threat that capital may fly out and leave the country if taxed too heavily. To put this in context, imagine a Latin American country before financial integration. If capital is taxed heavily, it can withdraw into the informal sector or the elites may decide to consume more and save less. This is what we capture with our cost of taxation, $C(\tau)$. After financial integration, however, there is another option. If capital holders are taxed heavily, they can take their capital to Panama or the Cayman Islands, where taxes are lower. This increases the elasticity of capital with respect to taxes and affects how much taxation democracy would like to impose on the elites. In this subsection, we analyze the implications of this potential capital-out channel on the consolidation of democracy. To simplify the analysis and highlight the implications of the capital-out mechanism, we now abstract from capital inflows; therefore, after financial integration, factor prices do not change.

Assume that we start with the economic model described previously and there is no trade in goods or financial flows, so factor prices are given by (9.2). The rate of return to capital is now $\theta\left((K+\sigma L)/(1-\delta)\right)^{\theta-1}$ and with the tax rate, τ, the net return is:

$$r(1-\tau) = (1-\tau)\theta\left(\frac{K+\sigma L}{1-\delta}\right)^{\theta-1}$$

If capital flies out, it has a (net) rate of return $\underline{r}$. We assume that:

$$(1-\tau^p)\theta\left(\frac{K+\sigma L}{1-\delta}\right)^{\theta-1} < \underline{r}$$

Therefore, if the citizens set their unconstrained tax rate, τ^p, capital will fly out. As long as capital is sufficiently important in the income of the elites and therefore in the tax revenues that the citizens collect from the elites, the citizens would not want to tax incomes at such a high rate that capital holders take their money outside the country. Therefore, in equilibrium, they have to set the lower tax rate, $\bar{\tau}^p$, such that:

$$r(1-\bar{\tau}^p) = (1-\bar{\tau}^p)\theta\left(\frac{K+\sigma L}{1-\delta}\right)^{\theta-1} = \underline{r} \tag{10.29}$$

Given this lower tax rate, democracy becomes less costly and more likely to be consolidated. Similarly, it also is less attractive for the elites to use repression to avoid having to democratize.

More formally, after financial integration, the returns from democracy are now given by:

$$\begin{aligned}
\underline{V}^p(D) &= \frac{1}{1-\delta}\left(1-\theta+\bar{\tau}^p(\theta-\delta)-(1-\delta)\,C(\bar{\tau}^p)\right)(K+\sigma L)^\theta\,(1-\delta)^\theta \\
\underline{V}^r(D) &= \frac{1}{\delta}\left(\theta+\bar{\tau}^p\,(\delta-\theta)-\delta C(\bar{\tau}^p)\right)(K+\sigma L)^\theta\,(1-\delta)^{1-\theta}
\end{aligned} \tag{10.30}$$

which are simply (9.7) evaluated at the tax rate, $\bar{\tau}^p$. We again use the notation $\underline{V}$ to refer to values in the open economy. Because the tax rate that applies after financial integration, $\bar{\tau}^p$ as given by (10.29), is lower than that which applies before financial integration, τ^p as given by (4.11), we have that:

$$\underline{V}^r(D) > V^r(D)$$

That is, democracy is better for the elites after financial integration.

Similarly, imagine the values of democracy to the citizens and elites when the citizens promise to set a tax rate of zero, with this promise upheld with probability p. From (9.15), these are now given by:

$$\underline{V}^p(D, \tau^D = 0)$$
$$= \frac{1}{1-\delta}(1-\theta+(1-p)(\bar{\tau}^p(\theta-\delta)-(1-\delta)C(\bar{\tau}^p)))(K+\sigma L)^\theta(1-\delta)^{1-\theta}$$

$$\underline{V}^r(D, \tau^D = 0) = \frac{1}{\delta}(\theta+(1-p)(\bar{\tau}^p(\delta-\theta)-\delta C(\bar{\tau}^p)))(K+\sigma L)^\theta(1-\delta)^{1-\theta}$$

These expressions, once again, take into account that if democracy gets to reset taxes, the median voter sets the lower tax, $\bar{\tau}^p$, instead of τ^p because at the higher tax, τ^p, capital will fly out of the country.

Even after financial integration, the costs of coups are not different because after a coup, there is no taxation and, therefore, no capital flight. As a result, the values after a coup are still given by (9.24). We again define φ^* by (10.18) as the threshold value before financial integration (i.e., at $\varphi = \varphi^*$); we have $V^r(D, \tau^D = 0) = V^r(C, \varphi)$. Also define $\underline{\varphi}^*$ as the corresponding threshold after financial integration – that is, such that at $\varphi = \underline{\varphi}^*$, we have:

$$\underline{V}^r(D, \tau^D = 0) = V^r(C, \underline{\varphi}^*)$$

which implies that:

$$\underline{\varphi}^* = 1 - \left(1 + \frac{(1-p)}{\theta}(\bar{\tau}^p(\delta-\theta) - \delta C(\bar{\tau}^p))\right)^{\frac{1}{\theta}} \tag{10.31}$$

That democracy is less redistributive after financial integration immediately implies that:

$$\underline{\varphi}^* < \varphi^*$$

Consequently, in the current model, Proposition 10.3 again applies but because of the effects of financial integration through the potential of capital flight rather than through capital inflow. Therefore, financial integration again may help democratic consolidation but now through as somewhat different channel. After financial integration, democracy does not find it optimal to impose as high taxes because such taxes would induce capital holders to take their assets abroad.

Because democracy is expected to be less redistributive, the elites do not have as much to gain from a coup and democracy is more likely to survive even during periods of crisis.

A similar argument also applies to transitions to democracy. Consider the transition to democracy game discussed in the previous subsection and recall that the values to the citizens and the elites from repression are still given by (10.21). Make the same assumptions as in the previous subsection so that concessions by nondemocracy do not work; after financial integration, the elites prefer democratization to repression if:

$$\underline{V}^r(D) \geq V^r(O \mid \kappa)$$

where $\underline{V}^r(D)$ is defined by (10.30). This condition defines a different cutoff level, now denoted by $\underline{\kappa}^*$, such that for all $\kappa \geq \underline{\kappa}^*$, the elites prefer democratization to repression after financial integration. More explicitly, $\underline{\kappa}^*$ is given by:

$$\underline{\kappa}^* = 1 - \left(\frac{1}{\theta}\left(\theta + \bar{\tau}^p(\delta - \theta) - \delta C(\bar{\tau}^p)\right)\right)^{\frac{1}{\theta}} \tag{10.32}$$

which is simply (10.24) with τ^p replaced by $\bar{\tau}^p$. That $\bar{\tau}^p < \tau^p$ immediately implies:

$$\underline{\kappa}^* < \kappa^*$$

where κ^* is given by (10.24). Because the presence of financial integration makes democracy less bad for the elites, repression has to be cheaper for it to be optimal.

As long as the choice for the elites is between democratization and repression, this analysis leads to a proposition paralleling Proposition 10.2, where now financial integration – by again making democracy less redistributive – may lead to democratization in circumstances in which without financial integration the elites would have preferred repression. We do not state this proposition because its logic is clear and its implications are identical to the results already stated herein.

6. Increased Political Integration

Another dimension of globalization is increased political integration. In a more globalized world, there are closer political links between nations. A common view is that the increased integration of Eastern European nations with the European Community has been an important element in their smooth transition to democracy and in the rapid consolidation of their democracies. Supporting this view is a finding that the post-Communist societies that are geographically closer to Western Europe (e.g., closer to Berlin) are more democratic (Kopstein and Reilly 2000).

A natural reason for this is that through various channels, greater political integration between democratic and nondemocratic societies increases the costs of using force to prevent democracy. The reasons might vary, ranging from potential sanctions or boycotts by democratic nations if there is a coup against democracy, to the destruction of trading relationships. Another complementary channel would be that with greater political integration, civil society in nondemocratic nations or in unconsolidated democracies becomes stronger, increasing the cost of coups or repression.

In a reduced-form way, we capture all of these ideas by supposing that the cost of using force against democracy – more specifically, the cost of coups – increases after political integration. In particular, assume that after political integration, a coup leads to the destruction of a fraction $\hat{\varphi} > \varphi$ of the asset stock of the elites, whereas before political integration, the same fraction was φ. This implies that after political integration, the values to the citizens and the elites following a coup are:

$$\hat{V}^p(C,\varphi) = (1-\theta)(1-\hat{\varphi})^\theta \left(\frac{K+\sigma L}{1-\delta}\right)^\theta \tag{10.33}$$

$$\hat{V}^r(C,\varphi) = \frac{\theta}{\delta}(1-\hat{\varphi})^\theta (K+\sigma L)^\theta (1-\delta)^{1-\theta}$$

instead of (9.24). We can now state the following proposition:

Proposition 10.4: *Consider the models underlying Propositions 10.1 and 10.3. Once political integration takes place, the cost of a coup is higher, and a society is more likely to be a consolidated democracy.*

This proposition, therefore, shows how political integration may have effects similar to those induced by increased international trade and financial integration. However, although these effects ultimately have similar implications, they work through a different channel. They discourage coups by making them more costly because of international pressure and sanctions or because of the induced development in civil society that follows from closer political links among democratic and nondemocratic nations.

7. Alternative Assumptions about the Nature of International Trade

Propositions 10.1 and 10.2 illustrate that globalization in the form of increasing integration of markets for goods may promote both the creation and consolidation of democracy. These results, however, stem from the structure of the models we wrote down. Most models of international trade have the implication that trade promotes the income of the poor in developing countries (who we are associating with the citizens) because such countries are typically labor-abundant. However, as already alluded to, the empirical evidence is somewhat equivocal about whether increased trade in fact promotes equality in poor countries. Also, it could be that some developing countries, such as Argentina or Chile, are in fact land-abundant and not labor-abundant. In this case, increased globalization has the effect of increasing the rate of return on land. This not only increases inequality but it also raises the incomes of the asset holders who, as we argued extensively in Chapter 9, have most to lose from democracy.

Here, we sketch a different type of trade model, motivated by a salient empirical pattern in the recent data: in many of the less developed nations opening to trade during the past twenty five years, returns to skills and, therefore, income inequality, have actually increased (Leamer 1995, 1998; Cragg and Epelbaum 1996; Attanasio, Goldberg, and Pavcnik 2004). This is the opposite of the prediction of the simple Heckscher – Ohlin trade model because the less developed nations in question are relatively scarce in skilled workers. So, everything else being equal, trade opening should reduce the skill premium in those countries. A lengthy discussion of why returns to skill appear to have increased in these countries is beyond the scope of this book, but there are some natural conjectures. Most important, there is wide consensus that many of the important advances in technology during the past twenty five years have been relatively "skill-biased," meaning that they favored skilled workers and, everything else being equal, tended to increase the skill premium (e.g., Acemoglu 2002). Most of these technologies are embedded in machines produced in the United States and in some OECD economies. Less developed countries can make use of these technologies only if they import the relevant machines from the United States, and other rich nations. This implies that when they are closed to international trade, less developed nations typically do not use these machines. The important implication for this analysis is that trade opening now comes with a change in the technology of production toward more skill-biased technology, increasing returns to skill. So, there will be a technology effect counteracting and perhaps dominating the standard Heckscher – Ohlin effect of trade reducing the skill premium in less developed nations (Acemoglu 2003b; Thoenig and Verdier 2003).

What are the implications of this for democracy? The discussion so far, which was based on our two-class model, might suggest that implications of the spread of skill-biased technology to less developed nations is the opposite of what we emphasized: an increase in inequality and, therefore, a force acting against the creation and consolidation of democracy. This is certainly one possible conclusion; however, other potential forces may be at work. The increase in the returns to skills and, more generally, the increased role of human capital in the modern economy (discussed in Chapter 9) can be interestingly analyzed in our three-class model. In the context of that model, we can think of skilled workers as constituting the backbone of the middle class. This implies that trade opening, associated with the transfer of skill-biased technology, increases the income of the middle class. As discussed in Chapter 8, the middle class can act as an important buffer between the rich and the poor, and an increase in the income of the middle class may help the creation and consolidation of democracy. This is because the median voter in democracy may be a member of the middle class, and an increase in the income of the median voter (relative to mean income) reduces the propensity of democracy to be anti-rich. With less radical policies adopted in democracy, the rich have less to fear from democracy and are less willing to use force to prevent democratization or create a switch to nondemocracy.

To highlight these issues, we briefly return to our basic model from Chapter 8. In that model there are three groups of agents; the rich of size δ^r, the middle class of size δ^m, and the poor of size δ^p. We normalize total population to 1 as before; thus, $\sum_i \delta^i = 1$. We assume that $\delta^p > \delta^m > \delta^r$; that is, the poor are the most numerous, then the middle class, and the rich comprise the smallest group in the population. Also, we denote average income by $\bar{y}$ as before and let incomes be given as in (8.1) where (8.2) holds so that the rich are richer than the middle class, who are in turn richer than the poor.

To simplify the analysis along the lines of the discussion in Chapter 8, we assume that $\delta^p < 1/2$, so that the poor do not constitute an absolute majority and a middle-class agent is the median voter. Moreover, suppose that $\theta^m < \delta^m$ or $\bar{y} > y^m$, so that the middle class is less rich than mean income and would like to impose some amount of redistributive taxation. As in Chapter 8, the amount of redistribution preferred by the median voter – therefore, that which results in an unconstrained democracy – is given by the tax rate τ^m, which satisfies (8.5).

Now consider the basic political game discussed in Chapter 8 in which the society is nondemocratic with the poor and the middle class excluded from voting. Because of a potential revolution threat, the rich are considering democratization or the use of force (repression) – the promise of limited redistribution is not credible. As in the previous analysis, there is a cutoff level for the cost of repression, $\tilde{\kappa}(\tau^D)$, given by (8.29). When the cost of repression, κ, is equal to $\tilde{\kappa}(\tau^D)$, the rich are indifferent between democratization and the use of force. They prefer repression whenever $\kappa < \tilde{\kappa}(\tau^D)$. It is clear from (8.5) that an increase in the income share of the middle class reduces τ^m and, therefore, decreases $\tilde{\kappa}(\tau^D)$.

Opening to international trade and the associated transfer of skill-biased technology by increasing the incomes of the middle class may reduce redistribution in democracy and help induce a transition to democracy. In particular, suppose that after trade opening, because technology becomes more skill-biased, θ^m increases to $\hat{\theta}^m$ and, as a result, the most preferred tax rate by the middle class falls to $\hat{\tau}^m$ given from (8.5) implicitly by $(\delta^m - \hat{\theta}^m)/\delta^m = C'(\hat{\tau}^m)$. This implies that the new threshold for the rich to be indifferent between repression and democratization becomes:

$$\hat{\kappa} = \frac{1}{\hat{\theta}^r}\left(\delta^r C(\hat{\tau}^m) - \hat{\tau}^m\left(\delta^r - \hat{\theta}^r\right)\right) \tag{10.34}$$

where $\hat{\theta}^r$ is the share of the rich in incomes after trade and $\hat{\theta}^r < \theta^r$ because $\hat{\theta}^m > \theta^m$. Clearly, we have

$$\hat{\kappa} < \tilde{\kappa}(\tau^D)$$

Then, we can state the following:

Proposition 10.5: *Consider the transition to democracy game described above. The society starts nondemocratic with the poor and the middle class excluded from voting. Define $\tilde{\kappa}(\tau^D)$ by (8.29) and $\hat{\kappa}$, which applies after opening to international trade and the transfer of skill-biased technologies by (10.34). Then, we have that:*

- *If $\kappa < \hat{\kappa}$, the rich use repression to prevent a revolution and democratization both before and after trade opening and transfer of technology.*
- *If $\kappa \geq \tilde{\kappa}(\tau^D)$, there is democratization both before and after trade opening and transfer of technology.*
- *If $\hat{\kappa} \leq \kappa < \tilde{\kappa}(\tau^D)$, the rich use repression to prevent a revolution and democratization before trade opening and transfer of technology, but there is democratization after trade opening and transfer of technology.*

This proposition shows how the recent wave of globalization and increased international trade may again make democracy more likely but this time through a different channel. Because of the transfer of skill-biased technologies from the richer nations associated with trade opening, the income share of the middle class increases; with a richer middle class, democracy becomes less redistributive and the rich are more willing to democratize.

A similar argument can be developed to show that with a richer middle class acting as a buffer in the conflict between the rich and the poor, democracy is also less likely to fall to a coup. Therefore, through this channel, previously nonconsolidated democracies are also more likely to consolidate.

8. Conclusion

In this chapter, we examined how globalization influences whether a country becomes a democracy and, once democratic, whether it remains that way. Our main objective was to show that broadening our analysis in this way generates a rich set of predictions. Many are conditional on the impact of trade and factor mobility on income distribution. Because the empirical literature on this topic is highly unsettled, we cannot use the models of this chapter to claim definitively whether globalization is or is not good for democracy. Settling this issue requires careful and intensive empirical investigation, which is an important area for future research.

It is also useful to repeat a caveat that we raised previously when discussing the power of the elites in democracy and the effects of manipulating democracy on its creation and consolidation. We have seen that greater capital mobility – by making democracy less threatening to the elites – may lead to the creation of a consolidated democracy. However, it is also true, as with any effect that reduces the scope for collective choices in a democracy to deviate from those preferred by the elites, that greater capital mobility implies that democracy is less able to deliver what the majority of the citizens want. In such circumstances, increased globalization may reduce the ability of democracy to improve the welfare of the majority. The extent of this is also a topic for empirical investigation.

11 Conclusions and the Future of Democracy

In this book, we proposed a framework for thinking about why some societies are democratic whereas others are not. We emphasized the two related aspects of this question: (1) why some societies become democratic in the first place, and (2) why some democracies persist and consolidate whereas others collapse. In this chapter, we revisit what we have learned, discuss some of the areas where we believe our framework can usefully be extended, and discuss what our model implies for the future of democracy.

1. Paths of Political Development Revisited

We now revisit the four narratives of political development that we outlined in Chapter 1. How does our framework help to account for these differing paths?

1.1 Britain

What explains why Britain followed a path of gradual democratization and why democracy was so easy to consolidate in Britain? At some level, the answer from our analysis is clear: the parameters – in particular, the nature of political and economic institutions, the structure of the economy, the collective-action problem, and the costs and benefits of revolution – were such that there was a sufficient threat of a revolution in predemocratic Britain and the elites could not defuse those pressures without democratization. They also did not find it beneficial to use repression to prevent democratization. However, this answer is incomplete. We also need to understand how Britain came to have the parameters that it did in the nineteenth and twentieth centuries. We now discuss which of these parameters were more important in understanding the British case and how they evolved.

In the seventeenth century, a series of political conflicts was won by those interested in introducing political institutions that limited the de jure power of the monarchy. This change in political institutions greatly improved economic institutions. By reducing the risk of state predation, property rights became more stable. De jure political power in the new system was in the hands of people with commercial and capitalistic interests; this led to large induced changes – for instance, in capital and financial markets – that were important for economic expansion.

The reason that these institutional changes arose in Britain appears to be twofold. First, at the start of the early modern period, Britain had political institutions that limited the powers of the monarchs more than in other places (Ertman 1997). Why this was so seems to be the outcome of a complex historical process of the building of dynasties and invasions. Second, significant changes took place in the structure of the economy that greatly strengthened the interest of various groups, particularly capitalistic farmers (the so-called gentry) and merchants, in different economic institutions. Also significant was the early collapse of feudal institutions in Britain (Brenner 1976). These changes increased the de facto power of these same interests, which critically influenced the outcome of the Civil War and the Glorious Revolution (Tawney 1941; Brenner 1993; Acemoglu, Johnson, and Robinson 2005). For example, merchants who became rich from trade in the colonies were able to play critical roles in both conflicts on the side of Parliament.

The outcome of the seventeenth-century conflicts in Britain was a set of economic institutions that gave property rights to a broad set of people (Thompson 1975). The result was the ending of the Malthusian cycle and the beginning of modern economic growth. Yet, the structural changes that consequently began (e.g., urbanization and the rise of the factory system) had further implications for the distribution of de facto political power. In particular, they began to make the exercise of de facto power by the poor and politically disenfranchised much easier (Tilly 1995 and Tarrow 1998 document the changing qualitative nature of collective action during this period). The rise in the de facto political power of the poor made the existing regime unsustainable and necessitated a change in political institutions in their favor to defuse the threat of revolution. This was to tilt the future allocation of de jure political power and, consequently, to ensure future economic institutions and policies consistent with the interests of the poor. This is exactly what the process of democratization did. Political tensions were also exacerbated by the rise in inequality, which (see Chapter 3) most scholars believe took place in the first half of the nineteenth century.

Beginning in 1832, the British political elites made a series of strategic concessions aimed at incorporating the previously disenfranchised into politics because the alternative was seen to be social unrest, chaos, and possibly revolution. The concessions were gradual because in 1832 social peace could be purchased by buying off the middle class. Moreover, the effect of the concessions was diluted by the specific details of political institutions, particularly the continuing unrepresentative nature of the House of Lords. Although challenged during the 1832 reforms, the House of Lords provided an important bulwark for the wealthy against the potential of radical reforms emanating from a democratized House of Commons. Later, as the working classes reorganized through the Chartist movement and subsequently through trade unions, further concessions had to be made. The Great War and its fallout sealed the final offer of full democracy.

Why did the elites in Britain create a democracy? Many other countries faced the same pressures and the political elites decided to repress the disenfranchised rather than make concessions to them. The problem with repression is that it is costly: it risks destroying assets and wealth. In the urbanized environment of nineteenth-century Europe (Britain was 70 percent urbanized at the time of the Second Reform Act), the disenfranchised masses were relatively well organized and therefore difficult to repress. Moreover, industrialization and the policy of free trade after the 1840s based on Britain's comparative advantages had led to an economy based on physical and, increasingly, human capital. Such assets are easily destroyed by repression and conflict, making repression an increasingly costly option for the elites. Because capital is more difficult to redistribute, the elites in Britain found the prospect of democracy less threatening and were easier to convince to accept it.

Repression is attractive not just when it is relatively cheap but also when there is much at stake. Our discussion suggests that the changes in economic and political institutions that allowed sustained economic growth to emerge also made democracy much less of a concern to the British elites.

Nevertheless, democracy did bring changes in economic institutions away from those preferred by the elites. In the nineteenth century, economic institutions – particularly in the labor market – disadvantaged the poor. For example, trade unions were illegal and as late as 1850, British workers trying to organize a union could be shipped to the penal colony in Tasmania, Australia. As discussed in Chapter 3, this practice and many others changed, particularly after 1867 when economic institutions were altered to cater to the demands of the newly enfranchised. Although important for the working of the British economy in the nineteenth century, the implications of these changes were much less damaging to the elites than the potential of the freeing of rural labor markets or the threat of land reform in an economy dominated by landed elites. In fact, compared to the changes in economic institutions faced by the elites in Russia or Austria-Hungary in the nineteenth century or those in Guatemala and El Salvador in the twentieth century, the changes in Britain were relatively easy for the elites to accept.

What about the promise of redistribution to prevent democratization? The political elites in Britain seem not to have seriously considered mass income redistribution as an alternative to democracy, although they certainly anticipated that democracy might lead to it. Perhaps, as Stephens understood, promises to redistribute could not be believed. It is significant, for example, that the Chartists' petition that gained the most attention from Parliament was presented in 1848 in the midst of the European revolutions. With such a threat of revolution, the political elites had to be seen as listening; however, as long as they maintained power, they would only listen as long as the threat was present – the Chartist movement produced only transitory threats. Consequently, perhaps it is not surprising that promises of redistribution to defuse the social unrest were not first on the agenda in Britain.

Finally, why did democracy in Britain consolidate so easily? Our framework suggests that this was influenced by many of the same factors discussed in the context of democratization. It consolidated because coups were too expensive and, in any case, democracy was not radical enough to pose a sufficient threat to the traditional elites. Democracy eventually brought major changes in British society but it took half a century and had to wait until the full effect of educational reforms were manifested. The elites never faced the type of threats common in democratizations elsewhere in the world, such as radical asset redistribution. Under these circumstances, our approach suggests that the elites should have been less opposed to democracy and, indeed, they were.

1.2 Argentina

Many of the same forces that led to democracy in Britain seem to have been in operation in Argentina. As in Britain, democracy in Argentina was induced by a series of revolts stimulated by economic and financial crises. Also as in Britain, the process of democratization took place in the context of rapidly rising inequality and economic growth. Yet, Argentina democratized with different underlying political and economic institutions than in Britain. The economy relied on agricultural exports and the boom in world trade, rather than decreasing, increased the value of the assets of the rich elites: land (O'Rourke, Taylor, and Williamson 1996). Moreover, because the economy was less diversified, it was more susceptible to instability and more volatile, creating windows of opportunity to induce political change. The landed elites, although forced to concede democracy, did not like it and were able to undermine it during the crisis surrounding the onset of The Great Depression.

In addition, political and economic institutions did not facilitate democracy. Unlike those that emerged in Britain after 1688, political institutions placed fewer constraints on the use of political powers, particularly those of the president, as witnessed by the actions of Yrigoyen in the 1920s and Perón in the 1940s. With respect to economic institutions, Argentina shared to some extent the legacy of other Spanish colonies that had been based on the exploitation of indigenous peoples. Although this legacy was minor relative to countries such as Bolivia or Guatemala, the underlying set of economic institutions – particularly with respect to access to land – increased the stakes from political conflict.

During the 1930s and 1940s, a highly polarized situation arose in which urban working classes, which dominated democratic politics, aimed to redistribute income toward themselves. Such a situation was intolerable to the rural elites and increasingly to the military, which came to adopt a rabid anti-Perónist stance. Given the structure of the economy, the costs of coups against democracy were tolerable and were exceeded by potential benefits of the nondemocratic regime, especially given the threat of radical redistributive and populist policies in democracy. Although all sides attempted to structure institutions in their favor – for example, in 1912 and again in the late 1950s when the military sponsored the introduction of proportional representation in the hope that it would lead to the fragmentation of the Perónist party – none of these measures managed to make democracy more acceptable to the elites.

Is democracy now consolidated in Argentina? Our analysis gives some reason for hope. The substantial increase in globalization – in particular, the capital mobility brought by the financial integration since the mid-1970s – implies that democracy may be much less of a threat to the elites interests than it has been historically. Perhaps more important, Argentina is a relatively highly educated society and the increase in the value of human capital has created a strong middle class that can act as a major buffer in the conflict between the rich and the poor. Consequently, democracy was stable in the 1990s despite a significant rise in inequality, suggesting that the underlying political equilibrium has changed. Moreover, one of the long-run effects of the economic policies implemented by the military after 1976 is that the economic base of the left and organized labor is much weaker in Argentina than it used to be, which is an explanation for the radical shift in the economic and social policies of the Perónist party in the 1990s. Paradoxically, this shift may be beneficial for the poor segments of society, because, given the shift in policies, democracy may at last be consolidated in Argentina.

1.3 Singapore

Why has Singapore not democratized? Our analysis suggests a rather simple answer. Singapore is a very equal society. There are no traditional wealthy landed elites and the economy relies on external capital and businesses. Most people, therefore, appear to be relatively happy with the status quo – at least, not so unhappy that they want to engage in serious and potentially costly collective action to induce a major change in political institutions. There is little to gain relative to what they already have.

By the same token, however, the current elites of the PAP have little to lose other than power. The PAP primarily consists of successful middle-class people and has remained relatively open in the sense that it has tried to co-opt people of talent and potential opponents. Although it is undoubtedly linked to the rich elites that exist in Singapore, none are likely to face expropriation of their assets or wealth. Although the political elites would likely lose their considerable rents from office holding, this is unlikely to be sufficient to justify a long period of repression to keep their privileged positions. Our analysis, therefore, also suggests that Singapore should eventually become a consolidated democracy. At some point, there will be pressure from a segment of the population for more representative political institutions; at that point, the elites and the PAP will not find it profitable to use repression to prevent democracy.

1.4 South Africa

Why was democracy so long delayed in South Africa and what triggered its final creation? The historical situation here could not be more different from that in Singapore. The white elites of South Africa had much to lose from democracy that historically would surely have led to large demands for land reform, the redistribution of wealth, and a massive restructuring of economic institutions away from those that benefited the rich white elites.

The state of South Africa was founded as a settler colony similar in many ways to those in North America or Australia. Yet, unlike in the United States, the indigenous peoples did not die off from imported diseases, which led to a situation in which the indigenous Africans became the labor force that the rich white elites could employ cheaply and control with coercive methods (Lundahl 1992). In this environment, the whites not only made no concessions to the Africans, they also even created a philosophy (i.e., apartheid) to justify the unequal distribution of resources in society. Repression was relatively cheap and feasible in South Africa because of the apartheid philosophy and because it was aimed at one easily identifiable racial group.

Yet, the apartheid regime was ultimately unsustainable. As the economy developed, the African majority became more vital to the sustenance of the white economy. They became increasingly hostile to their predicament and politically mobilized. In response, the white regime used intense repression, being prepared to ban, imprison, torture, and murder to maintain its hegemony. Yet, even this could not work indefinitely. The profitability of the apartheid economy gradually declined because of external sanctions and the disruptions caused by repression. Moreover, as the world changed, not only did apartheid become less internationally acceptable after the end of the Cold War, a globalized economy also meant that the rich white elites had less to fear from democracy. As land became less important and mobile capital more important, the threat of a radical African majority dissipated. It addition, the concessions that the white regime made during the 1970s – in particular, the legalization of African trade unions – reduced many of the economic rents that apartheid had created for the whites. This reduction meant that the whites had less to lose from the loss of political control. Indeed, as Rosendorff (2001) noted in exactly this context, inequality fell from the mid-1970s onward. Finally, the whites, in conjunction with the ANC, were able to negotiate a structure of political institutions that gave the whites sufficient confidence in a democratic future that they were willing to stop fighting and allow democratization.

Nevertheless, there is always uncertainty about what the future holds. For instance, the attempt to induce democratic consolidation through constitutional engineering in Zimbabwe has not been a great success. It is interesting that in his assessment of the future for democracy in South Africa, Thompson (1995, p. 275) notes there is "one great structural threat to democracy in South Africa: The lack of a well educated skilled labor force – the consequence of the abysmal state of education in South Africa." Our analysis in Chapter 9 suggests that this may indeed be a problem.

2. Extensions and Areas for Future Research

Like any social-science theory, ours is highly simplified. To focus on mechanisms that we think are important, we abstracted from many details as well as other potentially important mechanisms. This means that there are alternative approaches to some of the basic issues we addressed and also that we excluded other forces that may be important to include for a complete theory of the creation and consolidation of democracy.

First, our framework concentrated on social conflict as the main driving force that leads to different political institutions. Changes in political institutions occur not because of unanimity but because the side that favors change becomes more powerful and manages – at least temporarily – to impose its preferences. In Chapter 3, we briefly discussed some alternative approaches to democratization: for instance, the ideas of Bates (1991), Rogowski (1998), Herbst (2000), and Tilly (2004) that democracy emerges from the process of state formation, or the ideas of Bueno de Mesquita et al. (2003) and Lizzeri and Persico (2004) that democracy is voluntarily created by political elites because it leads to different equilibrium public policies that makes everyone better off. Although we believe that the major patterns of democratization and democratic consolidation cannot be explained only by these alternative interpretations, these are ultimately potentially complementary approaches, and empirical work must determine the relative importance of different mechanisms. As discussed in Chapter 3, empirical work on the determinants of the creation and consolidation of democracy has not progressed beyond correlations with little attention to the identification of causal relationships or isolating truly exogenous sources of variation. Thus far, there has been no serious attempt to discriminate among different mechanisms leading to democratization (Acemoglu, Johnson, Robinson, and Yared 2004).

In addition to examining and testing alternative hypotheses, there are several important areas in which more theoretical work appears to be a high priority. Five important areas that we initially planned to discuss were omitted to keep the book length manageable.

The first is the role of the military. In our baseline model, the only actors are different groups, and we considered that these groups could engage directly in conflict. In reality another institution, the military, plays a crucial role in revolutions, repression, and coups. Implicitly, we assumed that the military did not act as an autonomous actor but instead formed a coalition either with the elites (in the case of repression or coups) and perhaps with the citizens (in the case of a revolution). Nevertheless, there is a widespread claim in political science that the military often intervenes not on behalf of a social group but with its own interests in mind. It is also clear that in developing societies, the military is very powerful relative to other social and economic groups. An important priority for research, therefore, is to develop a theory of military politics to better grasp when the military sides with a particular group and when it may become relatively autonomous from social groups. Although there is a rich case-study literature on the military (Huntington 1964; Finer 1976; Nordlinger 1977; Rouquie 1987; Stepan 1988; Fitch 1998; Loveman 1999), there are as yet few generalizations about the objectives and behavior of the military; only Ticchi and Vindigni (2003b) have tried to use the methodological approach we adopt in this book and the tools of game theory to examine the military.

The study of the military is related to another major research area in comparative politics. In Chapter 5, we presented a "bare-bones" model of nondemocratic politics; our analysis abstracted from differences in nondemocratic regimes. Yet, much of the political science literature precisely focuses on providing different taxonomies of nondemocratic regimes (e.g., Linz and Stepan 1996). Moreover, much research argues that the type of nondemocratic regime helps to determine the potential for the creation and consolidation of democracy. Whether this is true is ultimately an empirical question, but it is certainly a distinct possibility (Geddes 1999a,b). In this book, we chose to emphasize what we believe is the key distinction between democracy and nondemocratic regimes: the extent of political equality. Nevertheless, introducing richer models of the institutional structure of nondemocracy will undoubtedly generate many new insights.

The second major area omitted from our analysis but clearly of central importance to understanding the dynamics of democracy is the variations in democratic institutions. A large theoretical and empirical literature emphasizes the differences between different types of democracies: for example, presidential versus parliamentarian and between those that use proportional representation as opposed to majoritarian electoral institutions (e.g., Cox 1997; Lijphart 1999; Persson and Tabellini 2000, 2003; Persson, Roland, and Tabellini 2000). Although in the appendix to Chapter 4 we provide some different microfoundations for the parameter χ, the most interesting approach is to relate it to the more detailed structure of political institutions. Throughout the book, we gave examples of how the details of democratic institutions are important for the feasibility and durability of democracy. However, the formal literature is only at the beginning of a research agenda to develop models of how the types of electoral systems or whether a democracy is presidential or parliamentary influence the incentives of politicians or citizens. The choice of the equilibrium form of democratic institutions and how this influences the feasibility of democracy is an exciting area for the years ahead. Our analysis suggests that the detailed institutional structure – because of the way it influences how preferences are aggregated – will be important in determining how political conflicts take place and thus in whether democracy is created or consolidated.

The third area in which more theoretical work is needed is within the context of what we called alternative political identities. A vast amount of political economy conceptualizes conflict along socioeconomic or class lines, but there is also a widespread understanding that this is not always the case. Although we have tried to show that our main results regarding the circumstances of when democracy arises and consolidates do not depend on the nature of political identities, having a richer model should generate many new empirical predictions. An important area for research is not just the implications of political identities but also their formation and how this depends on the institutional structure. To illustrate, historians of Africa have shown how some important current ethnic identities in Africa that are salient in political conflicts are actually an outcome of incentives created during the colonial period (e.g., Horowitz 1985 on the Ibo in Nigeria and Ranger 1991 on the Shona of Zimbabwe).

A fourth important area for future research is collective action and revolution. In Chapter 5, we discussed the collective-action problem and argued that the available empirical evidence suggested it is circumvented by revolutionaries providing private benefits to those who take part in revolution. This inspired the model we developed and used throughout the text. Nevertheless, developing a deeper understanding of collective action is a fascinating area for future research, both theoretical and empirical. We also modeled "postrevolution societies" in the crudest way. Our justification is that revolutions (except for a brief discussion in Chapter 6) are off the equilibrium path. However, developing a better understanding of what happens in revolutions and how institutions subsequently evolve is an important topic that may generate new predictions about the creation and consolidation of democracy. As with military politics, there is a rich case-study literature on revolutions that can be the starting point for developing models and more explicitly testable hypotheses.

Finally, and perhaps most important, the future literature must provide richer models of the workings of economy and the form of economic institutions than presented in this book. A particularly exciting area for future research is the investigation of the interactions between endogenous economic and political institutions. Although in Chapter 9 we endogenized the distribution of income and discussed the important role played by economic institutions, we did not develop explicit models in which economic institutions were determined or changed over time. Moreover, we only examined situations in which income was determined by stocks of assets that were constant. In reality, capital accumulates over time and technology changes. Incorporating these dynamics of growth and accumulation into our framework is an important step (Acemoglu and Robinson 2000a, 2002; Jack and Lagunoff 2003). Such extensions will also help to explain why there may be path dependence in political institutions, which many scholars believe to be the case.

3. The Future of Democracy

The objective of this book is to develop and present a parsimonious framework to analyze democratic and nondemocratic politics and the transitions between those regimes. Our analysis is mostly aimed at understanding a relatively abstract picture of complex social phenomena. Although any simple framework makes predictions about the future at its own peril, it is useful to reflect on the future of democracy given the framework we developed herein.

Several issues are important in thinking about whether democracies around the world will be consolidated and how they will transform themselves from what they are today. First, the world is experiencing an increased importance of *human capital* relative to land and physical capital for two reasons: (1) typical citizens of both developed and developing nations are more educated today than they were fifty years ago; and (2) technology throughout the twentieth century appears to have relied more on the skills and the human capital of the workers (or to have been skill-biased), thus increasing the importance of human capital in the labor market (Acemoglu 2002). Although greater returns to human capital may increase inequality in certain instances (e.g., as in the U.S. economy during the past thirty years), it generally helps to close the gap between the elites and the citizens and creates a large middle class in many less developed nations that are nondemocratic or live in unconsolidated democracies. As this gap closes and a middle class emerges, we expect less distributional conflict and more stable democracies not only in societies where political conflict has been between the rich and the poor but also where political conflict is along other lines. The recent past has witnessed many accounts of the "end of class warfare" (e.g., Fukayama 1992). We are not predicting an end to political conflict anytime soon but rather that with a greater role for human capital, the conflict will be less charged and intense.

Second, we now live in a highly *globalized world economy*. For reasons already discussed, we believe that greater international economic and financial links may promote and consolidate democracy. Again, conflict between the elites and the majority of citizens will remain in the global world economy, but globalization may take the most disruptive weapons from both sides' arsenal in this fight. The citizens do not want to pursue the most populist and redistributive policies, making the elites more secure in democracy. The elites are much more averse to coups and disruptions.

Third, the *end of the Cold War* implies that the implicit economic and political support that many nondemocratic regimes received has come to an end, making the transition to democracy easier and coups against democracy more difficult (although there is a danger that the war against terrorism might offset the potential benefits of the end of the Cold War).

These three factors imply that the future of democracy is bright. Democracy is much more likely to triumph against nondemocracy today than in the past, both in places where it has not arrived and where it has not been consolidated yet.

Yet, given these developments, do we expect democracy to change its nature in this new era? Our argument has been that democracy is pro-majority, even possibly pro-poor. This is mainly a relative statement, comparing democracy to a typical nondemocratic regime. We also noted that there are reasons why, in democracy, the elites may be powerful even if democracy is generally more pro-majority than nondemocracy. There are two reasons to expect that, in time, the elites may become more powerful in democracy.

First, the most important sources of extra power for the elites in democracy are their control of the party system and, thus, the political agenda and their ability to form an effective lobby against certain policies. Do we expect the elites to be able to do so more effectively in the future? There are two reasons for suspecting that the answer may be yes. With the increased bright future for democracy, the elites – especially in the current unconsolidated democracies – have to come to terms with living in democracy. In this case, they may as well do their best to influence democratic politics. Therefore, the returns to the elites for increasing their power in democracy may now be greater.

Perhaps more important, as democracy matures, there may be a greater opportunity for organized groups, which potentially include the elites or certain segments thereof, to become more powerful. The argument that interest groups become stronger over time in democratic societies was first developed by Mancur Olson in his classic 1982 political economy treatise, *The Rise and Decline of Nations*. Olson pointed out that as time goes by, cooperation and trust form between different members of influential lobbies and, perhaps more important, these lobbies more effectively capture the major branches of the government and the political system. In the context of democratic politics, one of the interest groups that may become stronger and come to dominate much of politics is the elite. If so, we might expect democracies to become less pro-majority in time. The fact that new democracies appear to have been more redistributive than mature democracies throughout the twentieth century and the observation that conservative parties have become stronger in many well-established democracies during the past forty years is consistent with this notion.

This relates to the *Iron Law of Oligarchy* formulated by the sociologist Robert Michels in his classic 1911 book, *Political Parties*. Michels claimed that all organizations, particularly political parties – even socialist ones – tended to be captured by whoever ran them; those people then came to be incorporated into the elites. He argued that this meant democracy had little chance of radically changing society because, at best, it simply replaced one elite with another. In no case would this lead to radical majoritarian social changes. If this law is true, then a natural process of elite capture reduces the radical threat of democracy.

Second, there is also a different side to the increased importance of human capital (including skill-biased technical change) and greater globalization. By reducing distributional conflict, these economic developments are weakening many of the organizations that have played an important role in supporting the majority and policies favoring the majority. The organizations losing strength include traditional social democratic parties and labor unions. This is most visible in much of the Anglo-Saxon world, especially the United States and the United Kingdom, where labor unions today are much weaker and the traditional left parties have become generally opposed to income redistribution.

If these changes become more widespread around the world, we may expect the elites and conservative parties to become more powerful and democracy to become less redistributive in the future, especially if new forms of representation for the majority – in both the political sphere and the workplace – do not emerge. Thus, democracy will become more consolidated; however, for those who expect democracy to transform society in the same way as British democracy did in the first half of the twentieth century, it may be a disappointing form of democracy.

12 Appendix to Chapter 4: The Distribution of Power in Democracy

1. Introduction

In this appendix, we discuss the models that underpin the analysis of distribution of political power in democracy in the last section of Chapter 4. There we argued that, under some circumstances, the equilibrium policy in democracy could be thought of as maximizing a weighted sum of the indirect utilities of the rich and the poor. We now develop a series of models that can provide microfoundations for those claims and clarify what those "circumstances" are.

2. Probabilistic Voting Models

2.1 Probabilistic Voting and Existence of Equilibrium

Before we discuss the probabilistic voting model, it is useful to revisit the nonexistence of voting equilibria in models without single-peaked preferences. Recall that the MVT applies only when the policy space is single-dimensional and preferences are single-peaked. Although in this book we obtained a lot of mileage from models that satisfy these assumptions, many real-world situations – where there are cross-cutting coalitions and multidimensional differences – do not. In these situations in which the MVT does not apply, the party competition game often does not have an equilibrium in terms of pure strategies. Although in these situations mixed-strategy equilibria exist, it is often unappealing to think of parties mixing over their platforms. The probabilistic voting model first introduced by Lindeck and Weibull (1987) is useful not only as an alternative approach to policy determination but also because it provides a potential way out of the nonexistence problems that arise in the standard model.

To appreciate the contribution of the probabilistic voting model, it is useful to reconsider the source of nonexistence problems with nonsingle-peaked preferences. The source of the problem is illustrated in (4.2), which links the probability of winning an election for a party to the preferences of the median voter, when preferences are single-peaked. We repeat this equation as specifying the probability that party A offering platform q_A will win against party B offering policy q_B:

$$P(q_A, q_B) = \begin{cases} 1 & \text{if } V^M(q_A) > V^M(q_B) \\ \frac{1}{2} & \text{if } V^M(q_A) = V^M(q_B) \\ 0 & \text{if } V^M(q_A) < V^M(q_B) \end{cases} \tag{12.1}$$

where M denotes the median voter. The important feature of this equation is that the probability that party A wins is a *discontinuous* function of its policy; as q_A varies, this probability jumps from 0 to 1/2 and then to 1. To illustrate the reason, suppose that the policy vector in question, q, is unidimensional and that the median voter M's preferences are single-peaked, with his or her most preferred policy denoted by q^M. Then, when the two parties offer the policies q_A and q_B such that $q_A = q_B + \varepsilon < q^M$, where ε is a small positive number (in the limit, infinitesimally small). The median voter prefers party A, which is offering a policy closer to his or her preferred point. Now imagine that party B changes its policy by a small amount, increasing it by 2ε. This causes the median voter to prefer party B and because the party that attracts the median voter wins the election, this change in policy causes a discontinuous change in $P(q_A, q_B)$ from 1 to 0.

To guarantee the existence of pure strategy, Nash equilibria requires continuity of payoff functions in all strategies (as well as strategy sets to be bounded, closed, and convex and the payoff functions to be quasiconcave in their own strategies; e.g., Fudenberg and Tirole 1991, Theorem 1.2, p. 34). As this discussion illustrates, the Downsian party-competition model does not satisfy these assumptions. Nevertheless, discontinuities do not necessarily lead to nonexistence, but they do imply that we cannot establish existence under general conditions. In fact, as the analysis in Chapter 4 established, with single-peaked preferences the Downsian model generates a unique equilibrium (even though the objective functions of the political parties are not continuous). This demonstrates that continuity is sufficient to guarantee the existence of an equilibrium, but it is not necessary – an equilibrium can exist even if behavior is discontinuous. However, the discontinuity of the objective functions leads to nonexistence when preferences are not single-peaked or the policy space is multidimensional.

How can we ensure the existence of an equilibrium? One way is to smooth out the discontinuities in the payoff functions – in this context, the probability that party A wins the election, $P(q_A, q_B)$. This is what the probabilistic voting approach does.

The idea of the probabilistic voting approach is that an equation like (12.1) should apply at the individual level (for individual voting decisions) but because of heterogeneities at the individual level and random shocks to preferences, the probability that party A wins the election should be a smooth function of its platform. Specifically, let $p^i(q_A, q_B)$ be the probability that individual i votes for party A offering policy q_A rather than party B offering policy q_B. This is given by the following equation, similar to (12.1):

$$p^i(q_A, q_B) = \begin{cases} 1 & \text{if } V^i(q_A) > V^i(q_B) \\ \frac{1}{2} & \text{if } V^i(q_A) = V^i(q_B) \\ 0 & \text{if } V^i(q_A) < V^i(q_B) \end{cases} \tag{12.2}$$

Why would $P(q_A, q_B)$ differ from $p^i(q_A, q_B)$? The most common approach in the literature is to presume that there are some nonpolicy-related reasons for uncertainty in individuals' preferences (either related to "ideology" or to the "valance" of the politicians), so that individual voters have slightly different preferences (e.g., Lindbeck and Weibull 1987; Coughlin 1992; Persson and Tabellini 2000). As a result, when aggregated over individuals, $P(q_A, q_B)$ will be a smooth function of policy platforms, and a small change in policy only gets a small response in terms of aggregate voting behavior. This is the approach we develop next. Our particular interest in this model is not only for the technical reason that an equilibrium may exist where otherwise it would not, but also because the probabilistic voting model incorporates different ideas about who has power in a democracy.

2.2 Probabilistic Voting and Swing Voters

Let the society consist of N distinct groups of voters (i.e., all voters within a group have the same economic characteristics). Examples would be the rich and the poor in the two-class model, or the rich, the middle class, and the poor in the three-class model.

There is electoral competition between two parties, A and B, and let π_j^n be the fraction of voters in group n voting for party j where $j = A, B$, and let λ^n be the share of total voters in group n and, naturally, $\sum_{n=1}^N \lambda^n = 1$. Then, the expected vote share of party j is

$$\pi_j = \sum_{n=1}^{N} \lambda^n \pi_j^n$$

Under Downsian electoral competition, because all voters in n have the same economic preferences, π_j^n is given by (12.2), and jumps discontinuously from 0 to 1 because voters in group n always vote with certainty for the party that promises the policy that they prefer more. As summarized in Proposition 4.2, this type of Downsian electoral competition leads to the policy most preferred by the median voter. We now see how different outcomes emerge when ideological differences are incorporated in voting behavior.

Instead, imagine that an individual i in group n has the following preferences:

$$\tilde{V}^{ni}(q, j) = V^n(q) + \tilde{\sigma}_j^{ni} \tag{12.3}$$

when party j comes to power, where q is a vector of economic policies chosen by the party in power. Assume that $q \in Q \subset \mathbb{R}^S$ so that q is an S-dimensional vector. Here, $V^n(q)$ is the indirect utility of agents in group n as before and captures their economic interests. All individuals in a particular group have the same $V^n(q)$. In addition, the term $\tilde{\sigma}_j^{ni}$ can be interpreted as nonpolicy-related benefits that the individual receives from party j. The most obvious source of these preferences would be ideological. So, this model allows individuals within the same economic group to have different ideological or idiosyncratic preferences.

Now defining the difference between the two parties' ideological benefits for individual i in group n by $\tilde{\sigma}^{ni} \equiv \tilde{\sigma}_B^{ni} - \tilde{\sigma}_A^{ni}$, the voting behavior of individual i can be represented by an equation similar to (12.2):

$$p^{ni}(q_A, q_B) = \begin{cases} 1 & \text{if } V^n(q_A) - V^n(q_B) > \tilde{\sigma}^{ni} \\ \frac{1}{2} & \text{if } V^n(q_A) - V^n(q_B) = \tilde{\sigma}^{ni} \\ 0 & \text{if } V^n(q_A) - V^n(q_B) < \tilde{\sigma}^{ni} \end{cases} \tag{12.4}$$

Because this equation makes it clear that all that matters is the difference between the two ideological benefits, we work directly with $\tilde{\sigma}^{ni}$. Let the distribution of this differential benefit $\tilde{\sigma}^{ni}$ within group n be given by the smooth cumulative distribution function F^n defined over $(-\infty, +\infty)$, with the associated probability density function f^n. Then, (12.4) immediately implies:

$$\pi_A^n = F^n(V^n(q_A) - V^n(q_B)) \tag{12.5}$$

Furthermore, and somewhat differently from before, suppose that parties maximize their expected vote share.[1] In this case, party A sets this policy platform q_A to maximize:

$$\pi_A = \sum_{n=1}^{N} \lambda^n F^n(V^n(q_A) - V^n(q_B)) \tag{12.6}$$

Party B faces a symmetric problem, which can be thought of as minimizing π_A. Equilibrium policies then are determined as the Nash equilibrium of a game in

[1] In Chapter 4, the parties' objectives function was to come to power; thus, they simply wanted their vote share to be greater than 1/2. The assumption here is that they wish to maximize their vote share. This assumption is adopted to simplify the discussion.

which both parties make simultaneous policy announcements to maximize their vote share.

We first look at the first-order condition of party A with respect to its own policy choice, q_A, taking the policy choices of the other party, q_B, as given. This requires:

$$\sum_{n=1}^{N} \lambda^n f^n(V^n(q_A) - V^n(q_B))\nabla V^n(q_A) = 0$$

where $\nabla V^n(q_A)$ denotes the gradient vector of the function $V^n(q_A)$; that is,

$$\nabla V^n(q_A) = \left(\frac{\partial V^n(q_A)}{\partial q_{A1}}, \ldots, \frac{\partial V^n(q_A)}{\partial q_{AS}}\right)^T$$

and the superscript T denotes the transpose of the vector $\nabla V^n(q_A)$. So, in other words, the derivative of the vote share in (12.6) needs to be equal to zero with respect to each component of the policy vector q.

This first-order condition characterizes a maximum when the second-order condition is also satisfied. The second-order sufficient condition is for the matrix:

$$\sum_{n=1}^{N} \lambda^n f^n(V^n(q_A) - V^n(q_B)) \cdot \nabla^2 V^n(q_A) \qquad (12.7)$$
$$+ \sum_{n=1}^{N} \lambda^n \frac{\partial f^n(V^n(q_A) - V^n(q_B))}{\partial q_A} (\nabla V^n(q_A)) \cdot (\nabla V^n(q_A))^T$$

to be negative definite, in which $\nabla^2 V^n(q_A)$ denotes the Hessian of the function $V^n(q_A)$ evaluated at the policy vector, q_A.

This condition is satisfied if voter utilities are concave functions of platforms, so that $\nabla^2 V^n(q_A)$ is negative definite and the density of ideological differences is not increasing sharply – or, specifically, if it is similar to a uniform distribution. Although ensuring that the second-order conditions hold in general is difficult, here, we follow the literature on probabilistic voting and assume that they do.

Because the problem of party B is symmetric, it also promises the same policy; hence, in equilibrium, we have policy convergence with $q_A = q_B$.[2] Therefore,

[2] There may also exist asymmetric equilibria in which the two parties choose different platforms.

$V^n(q_A) = V^n(q_B)$ and equilibrium policies, announced by both parties, are given by:

$$\sum_{n=1}^{N} \lambda^n f^n(0) \nabla V^n(q_A) = 0 \tag{12.8}$$

Equation (12.8), which gives equilibrium policies, also corresponds to the solution to the maximization of the following weighted utilitarian social-welfare function:

$$\sum_{n=1}^{N} \chi^n \lambda^n V^n(q) \tag{12.9}$$

where

$$\chi^n = f^n(0)$$

are the weights that different groups receive in the social-welfare function. We state this result as the following proposition for future reference:

Proposition A.1. (Probabilistic Voting Theorem): *Consider a set of policy choices Q, let $q \in Q \subset \mathbb{R}^S$ be a policy vector, and let preferences be given by (12.3) as a function of policy and which party is in power, with the distribution function of $\tilde{\sigma}^{ni}$ being F^n. Then, equilibrium policy if it exists is given by q^* that maximizes the weighted utilitarian social-welfare function (12.9).*

There are two features worth emphasizing here. First, an equilibrium exists as long as the second-order conditions in (12.7) are satisfied; we do not need single-peaked preferences and now the policy space, Q, can be a subset of $\mathbb{R}^S$ for $S > 1$, no longer necessarily unidimensional. Therefore, the probabilistic voting model partially avoids the nonexistence problems associated with either the failure of single-peakedness or the multidimensionality of policy spaces. This is a result of the smoothing of the individual-level discontinuities by aggregation.

Second, and more important, this model gives us a way to parameterize the different political power of various groups. If the $f^n(0)$'s, the density of ideological biases between parties' at the point where both parties' platforms give the same utility (i.e., at $V^n(q_A) = V^n(q_B)$) are identical across groups, (12.9) becomes exactly the utilitarian social-welfare function. The actual equilibrium in this political economy game differs from the maximization of this utilitarian social welfare function because different groups have different sensitivities to policy. For example, imagine two groups n and n' such that n is more "ideological," meaning that there are individuals in this group with strong preferences toward party A or party B. This corresponds to the distribution function F^n having a relatively large amount of weight in the tails. In contrast, imagine that group n' is not very ideological and the majority of the group votes for the party that gives them slightly better economic policies. This corresponds to having relatively little weight in the tails of $F^{n'}$ and, therefore, a significant value of $f^{n'}(0)$. In this case, voters from group n' become the "swing voters" receiving more weight in the political competition game because they are more responsive to changes in policies. Intuitively, tilting policies in favor of groups that are more likely to be responsive to policies (rather than ideological issues) is more attractive to the parties as a strategy for winning votes, so in the political equilibrium, policies are more responsive to the swing group's preferences.

This discussion has immediate implications for our two-class workhorse model. Although the poor are more numerous, it does not follow that political parties offer a policy platform that is the ideal point of the poor because in the probabilistic voting model, it is not just "mere numbers" that count. When there is ideology, what also matters is how willing voters are to switch their allegiance from one party to the other. This typically means that political parties consider the preferences of the rich as captured by our reduced-form model in the text where the political process maximized a weighted utilitarian social-welfare function similar to (12.9). In this context, we can also think of changes in the weight of the rich χ^r (or with the microfoundations here $f^r(0)$) affecting how redistributive democratic politics will be.

3. Lobbying

The models discussed so far allow only the votes of the citizens to affect policies. In practice, different groups, especially those that can organize as a lobby, make campaign contributions or pay money to politicians to induce them to adopt a policy that they prefer. In this section, we develop a simple lobbying model and investigate how this affects the determination of equilibrium policies.

With lobbying, political power comes not only from voting but also from other sources, including whether various groups are organized, how many resources they have available, and their marginal willingness to pay for changes in different policies. The most important result is that even with lobbying, equilibrium policies look like the solution to a weighted utilitarian social-welfare maximization problem.

We now develop a baseline model of lobbying from Grossman and Helpman (1996, 2001). Imagine again that there are N groups of agents, each with the same economic preferences. The utility of an agent in group n, when the policy q is implemented, is equal to:

$$V^n(q) - \gamma^n(q)$$

where $V^n(q)$ is the usual indirect utility function and $\gamma^n(q)$ is the per-person lobbying contribution from group n. We allow these contributions to be a function of the policy implemented by the politician; to emphasize this, it is written with q as an explicit argument.

To obtain sharp results, we now abstract entirely from electoral politics and assume that there is already a politician in power. Suppose that this politician has a utility function of the following from:

$$G(q) \equiv \sum_{n=1}^{N} \lambda^n \gamma^n(q) + a \sum_{n=1}^{N} \lambda^n V^n(q) \tag{12.10}$$

where, as before, λ^n is the share of group n in the population. The first term in (12.10) is the monetary receipts of the politician and the second term is utilitarian aggregate welfare. Therefore, the parameter a determines how much the politician cares about aggregate welfare. When $a = 0$, he or she only cares about money; when $a \to \infty$, he or she acts as a utilitarian social planner. One reason that politicians might care about aggregate welfare is because of electoral politics; for example, in the last subsection, the vote share that he or she receives might depend on the welfare of each group (Grossman and Helpman 1996).

Now consider the problem of an individual i in group n. By contributing some money, he or she might be able to sway the politician to adopt a policy more favorable to his or her group. But he or she is one of many members in his or her group, and there is the natural free-rider problem associated with any type of collective action (see Chapter 5). Consequently, he or she might let others make the contribution and simply enjoy the benefits. This is the typical outcome if groups are unorganized (e.g., there is no effective organization coordinating their lobbying activity and excluding noncontributing members from some of the benefits). On the other hand, organized groups might be able to collect contributions from their members to maximize group welfare.

We think that of the N groups of agents, $L < N$ of those are organized as lobbies and can collect money among their members to further the interests of the group. The remaining $N - L$ are unorganized and make no contributions. Without loss of any generality, let us rank the groups such that groups $n = 1, \ldots, L$ are the organized ones.

The lobbying game takes the following form: every organized lobby n simultaneously offers a schedule $\gamma^n(q) \geq 0$, which denotes the payments they would make to the politician when policy q is adopted. After observing the schedules, the politician chooses q. The important assumption is that contributions to politicians (i.e., campaign contributions or bribes) can be conditioned on the actual policy that is implemented by the politicians. This assumption may be a good approximation to reality in some situations but in others, lobbies might simply have to make upfront contributions and hope that they help the parties that are expected to implement policies favorable to them to get elected.

This is a potentially complex game because various different agents (here, lobbies) are choosing functions (rather than scalars or vectors). Nevertheless, noticing the fact that this looks like an auction model along the lines of the work by Bernheim and Whinston (1986), it can be shown that the equilibrium has a simple form.

In particular, the following proposition can be established[3]:

Proposition A.2 (Grossman–Helpman Lobbying Equilibrium): *In the lobbying game described above, contribution functions for groups* $n = 1, 2 \ldots L$, $\{\hat{\gamma}^n(\cdot)\}_{n=1,2..L}$ *and policy* q^* *constitute a subgame perfect Nash equilibrium if:*

1. $\hat{\gamma}^n(\cdot)$ *is feasible in the sense that* $0 \leq \hat{\gamma}^n(q) \leq V^i(q)$.
2. *The politician chooses the policy that maximizes his welfare; that is,*

$$q^* \in \arg\max_{q \in Q} \left\{ \sum_{n=1}^{L} \lambda^n \hat{\gamma}^n(q) + a \sum_{n=1}^{N} \lambda^n V^n(q) \right\} \tag{12.11}$$

3. *There are no profitable deviations for any lobby,* $n = 1, 2, \ldots, L$*; that is,*

$$q^* \in \arg\max_{q \in Q} \left\{ \lambda^n V^n(q) - \lambda^n \hat{\gamma}^n(q) + \sum_{n'=1}^{L} \lambda^{n'} \hat{\gamma}^{n'}(q) + a \sum_{n'=1}^{N} \lambda^{n'} V^{n'}(q) \right\} \tag{12.12}$$

Although this proposition at first looks complicated, it is quite intuitive. Condition 1 is simply feasibility; negative contributions are not allowed and no group would pay in amounts that would give negative utility.

Condition 2 has to hold in any subgame perfect equilibrium because the politician chooses the policy after the lobbies offer their contribution schedules. This condition simply states that given the lobbies' contribution schedules, the politician chooses the policy that maximizes his or her objective.

Condition 3 is the most important restriction on the equilibrium. If this condition did not hold, then the lobby could change its contribution schedule and improve its welfare.

To establish this result, we can reason as follows. Suppose to obtain a contradiction that this condition does not hold for lobby $n = 1$ and, instead of q^*, some $\hat{q}$ maximizes (12.12). Denote the difference in the values of (12.12) for $n = 1$ evaluated at q^* and $\hat{q}$ by $\Delta > 0$ (which is strictly positive by the hypothesis that

[3] Grossman and Helpman (2001) also prove that for each lobby n, there exists a policy $\hat{q}^n \in \arg\max_{q \in Q}(\sum_{n'=1}^{L} \lambda^{n'} \hat{\gamma}^{n'}(q) + a \sum_{n'=1}^{N} \lambda^{n'} V^{n'}(q))$, which satisfies $\hat{\gamma}^n(\hat{q}^n) = 0$. This means that the equilibrium contribution function of each lobby is such that there exists a policy that makes no contributions to the politician and gives him or her the same utility. If this condition were not true, the lobby could reduce all its contributions and still induce the same behavior. This feature of the equilibrium is not important for the results we highlight here; hence, it is relegated to this footnote.

(12.12) is violated). Then, consider the following contribution schedule for lobby $n = 1$:

$$\tilde{\gamma}^1(q) = \frac{1}{\lambda^1}\left(\sum_{n=1}^{L}\lambda^n\hat{\gamma}^n(q^*) + a\sum_{n=1}^{N}\lambda^n V^n(q^*) - \sum_{n=2}^{L}\lambda^n\hat{\gamma}^n(q) - a\sum_{n=1}^{N}\lambda^n V^n(q) + \varepsilon c^1(q)\right)$$

where $c^1(q)$ is a continuous positive function reaching its strict maximum at $q = \hat{q}$. Basically, this schedule is designed by lobby 1 to induce the politician to choose $\hat{q}$ instead of q^* and, by design, it ensures greater utility for the politician at $\hat{q}$ than at q^*. To see this, suppose that with this new schedule, the politician chooses q^*; in this case, the payoff is:

$$\begin{aligned} G(q^*) &= \sum_{n=2}^{L}\lambda^n\hat{\gamma}^n(q^*) + a\sum_{n=1}^{N}\lambda^n V^n(q^*) + \left(\sum_{n=1}^{L}\lambda^n\hat{\gamma}^n(q^*) + a\sum_{n=1}^{N}\lambda^n V^n(q^*)\right. \\ &\quad \left. - \sum_{n=2}^{L}\lambda^n\hat{\gamma}^n(q^*) - a\sum_{n=1}^{N}\lambda^n V^n(q^*) + \varepsilon c^1(q^*)\right) \\ &= \sum_{n=1}^{L}\lambda^n\hat{\gamma}^n(q^*) + a\sum_{n=1}^{N}\lambda^n V^n(q^*) + \varepsilon c^1(q^*) \end{aligned}$$

On the other hand, if the politician chooses $\hat{q}$, the payoff is:

$$\begin{aligned} G(\hat{q}) &= \sum_{n=2}^{L}\lambda^n\hat{\gamma}^n(\hat{q}) + a\sum_{n=1}^{N}\lambda^n V^n(\hat{q}) + \sum_{n=1}^{L}\lambda^n\hat{\gamma}^n(\hat{q}) + \left(\sum_{n=1}^{L}\lambda^n\hat{\gamma}^n(q^*)\right. \\ &\quad \left. + a\sum_{n=1}^{N}\lambda^n V^n(q^*) - \sum_{n=2}^{L}\lambda^n\hat{\gamma}^n(\hat{q}) - a\sum_{n=1}^{N}\lambda^n V^n(\hat{q}) + \varepsilon c^1(\hat{q})\right) \\ &= \sum_{n=1}^{L}\lambda^n\hat{\gamma}^n(q^*) + a\sum_{n=1}^{N}\lambda^n V^n(q^*) + \varepsilon c^1(\hat{q}) \end{aligned}$$

This immediately shows that for any $\varepsilon > 0$, $G(\hat{q}) > G(q^*)$. In fact, because $c^1(q)$ is maximized at $q = \hat{q}$, the politician strictly prefers the policy $q = \hat{q}$ to any other feasible alternative, when faced with this contribution schedule for any $\varepsilon > 0$.

The change in the welfare of lobby 1 as a result of changing its strategy from $\hat{\gamma}^1$ to $\tilde{\gamma}^1$ is:

$$\Delta - \varepsilon c^1(q)$$

Because $\Delta > 0$, for small enough ε, the lobby gains from this change, showing that the original allocation could not have been an equilibrium.

The results in Proposition A2 appear far from the simple weighted utility maximization of Chapter 4. We next see that they in fact imply weighted utility maximization. Suppose that the contribution functions, the $\hat{\gamma}$s, are differentiable. In practice, restricting to differentiable functions might be a simplifying assumption, although Bernheim and Winston (1986) showed that differentiable contribution functions have the desirable property of being robust to mistakes (or perturbations) and to coalition formation.

With differentiability, the politician's maximization problem in (12.11) implies the following first-order condition for every policy choice, q_s, within the vector q:

$$\sum_{n=1}^{L} \lambda^n \frac{\partial \hat{\gamma}^n(q)}{\partial q_s} + a \sum_{n=1}^{N} \lambda^n \frac{\partial V^n(q)}{\partial q_s} = 0 \text{ for all } s = 1, 2, .., S$$

Similarly, from each lobby's optimization, (12.12):

$$\lambda^n \frac{\partial V^n(q)}{\partial q_s} - \lambda^n \frac{\partial \hat{\gamma}^n(q)}{\partial q_s} + \sum_{n'=1}^{L} \lambda^{n'} \frac{\partial \hat{\gamma}^{n'}(q)}{\partial q_s} + a \sum_{n'=1}^{N} \lambda^{n'} \frac{\partial V^{n'}(q)}{\partial q_s} = 0$$

$$\text{for all } s = 1, 2, .., S \text{ and } n = 1, 2, .., L$$

These two sets of first-order conditions basically state that both the politician and the lobbies are equating marginal cost to marginal benefits. For the politician, the benefits are increased contributions, whereas the costs are deviations from the social-welfare maximizing objective. For the lobby, the benefits are policies more in line with their interests, whereas the costs are increased contributions.

Combining these two first-order conditions, we obtain:

$$\frac{\partial \hat{\gamma}^n(q)}{\partial q_s} = \frac{\partial V^n(q)}{\partial q_s} \tag{12.13}$$

for all $s = 1, 2, .., S$ and $n = 1, 2, .., L$. Intuitively, at the margin each lobby is willing to pay for a change in policy exactly as much as this policy brings them in terms of additional return. For this reason, the equilibrium of this type of lobbying game with differentiable contribution functions are sometimes referred to as "truthful," in the sense that the contribution functions reflect the marginal benefits of policies to the lobbies.

The advantage of (12.13) is that it enables us to establish our main objective: the political equilibrium with lobbying can be characterized as a solution to maximizing the following function:

$$\sum_{n=1}^{L} \lambda^n V^n(q) + a \sum_{n=1}^{N} \lambda^n V^n(q) \tag{12.14}$$

with respect to q.

In other words, the equilibrium maximizes a weighted social-welfare function, with individuals in unorganized groups getting a weight of a and those in organized group receiving a weight of $1 + a$. Intuitively, $1/a$ measures how much money matters in politics and, the more money matters, the more weight groups that can lobby receive. As $a \to \infty$, we converge to the utilitarian social-welfare function. Therefore, we can state the following proposition:

Proposition A.3: *The lobbying game with full commitment on the side of the politicians and differentiable contribution functions leads to equilibrium policies that maximize the weighted utilitarian social-welfare function (12.14).*

It is also useful to discuss the implications of the lobbying model for the two-class model. In a model with political divisions between the rich and the poor, it may be reasonable to think that, under certain circumstances, the rich are more organized and can form an effective lobby to influence policies. Specifically, we return to our baseline model and assume that the poor are unorganized but the rich are able to form an effective lobby. The results in this subsection imply that the lobbying equilibria are given by maximizing:

$$\max_{\tau} a(1-\delta)((1-\tau)y^p + \tau\bar{y} - C(\tau)\bar{y}) + (1+a)\delta((1-\tau)y^r + \tau\bar{y} - C(\tau)\bar{y})$$

which has a first-order condition that can be written, again with complementary slackness, as:

$$\frac{a(1-\theta) + (1+a)\theta}{a(1-\delta) + (1+a)\delta} \leq 1 - C'(\tau) \text{ and } \tau \geq 0 \tag{12.15}$$

As $a \to \infty$, we obtain the case of maximizing the utilitarian social-welfare function. As $a \to 0$, equilibrium policy simply maximizes the utility of the rich agents, who become more influential in democratic politics because of their organized lobby. It is interesting, that in this case, irrespective of the value of a, we have that $\tau = 0$, because even with the utilitarian social-welfare function, there should be no distortionary taxation, as discussed previously.

More interesting, it is possible to combine elements from the probabilistic voting model, where different groups have different amounts of political power, and the lobbying model. For example, we could have that equilibrium policy is given by:

$$q^* = \arg\max_q \left(\sum_{n=1}^{L} \lambda^n V^n (q) + a \sum_{n=1}^{N} \lambda^n \chi^n V^n (q) \right)$$

where χ^ns are political-power parameters coming from electoral politics.

Let us apply this model to our two-class model of redistribution and suppose that the rich are organized as a lobby and the poor are not. We can see immediately that there will be redistributive taxation (i.e., $\tau > 0$) if the poor are sufficiently powerful in electoral politics (e.g., $\chi^p > \chi^r$) so as to offset the effects of the power of the rich that derive from their lobbying activities.

4. Partisan Politics and Political Capture

Another important approach to democratic politics incorporates the idea that political parties have broader objectives than simply winning power. First, political parties may also have ideologies, which would also have an effect on equilibrium policies. Second, an important question is whether certain groups can capture the political agenda (e.g., via lobbying as in the previous section) and how this could be influential in democratic politics. In this section, we introduce ideological parties (i.e., partisan politics) and show how they affect the implications of the Downsian political competition model; we also use this model to discuss issues of political capture. As long as there are no issues of probabilistic voting (i.e., ideological considerations on the side of voters), the predictions of the model of Downsian political competition apply as before, and there are strong forces toward convergence of policies to the preferences of the median voter. However, when there are either ideological considerations on the side of voters as well or problems of commitment on the side of parties, the ideological preferences of parties will also affect equilibrium policy. This provides another channel through which the reduced-form model of the distribution of political power in democracy can arise and another reason why certain groups may influence equilibrium policy more than their voting numbers suggest (i.e., because they are able to capture the agendas of political parties).

4.1 Electoral Competition with Partisan Parties

In the basic Downsian model of political competition, the objective functions of the parties were given by (4.1), which only valued the rent from coming to power. By ideological or partisan parties, we mean those that have preferences over policies as well as whether they come to power.

To formalize these notions, imagine a single dimension of policy, again denoted q from a convex and compact subset Q of $\mathbb{R}$, and let there be two parties A and

B. We now replace (4.1) with:

$$\text{Party } A: \max_{q_A \in Q} \{P(q_A, q_B)(R + W_A(q_A)) + (1 - P(q_A, q_B)) W_A(q_B)\} \quad (12.16)$$

$$\text{Party } B: \max_{q_B \in Q} \{(1 - P(q_A, q_B))(R + W_B(q_B)) + P(q_A, q_B) W_B(q_A)\}$$

where $W_A(q)$ and $W_B(q)$ denote the "utility functions" of parties A and B, and R is a rent from being in office, which is assumed to be nonnegative. Parties now maximize their "expected utility," taking into account the voting behavior of the citizens as summarized by the function $P(q_A, q_B)$. This expected utility consists of their ideological preferences over policies that are implemented and the rent from coming to office.

To start, we consider the case where $P(q_A, q_B)$ is given by (12.1): for example, because preferences are single-peaked and there are no ideological considerations on the side of the voters (we later come to probabilistic voting and thus to more smooth versions of (12.1)).

Suppose that the utility functions of the parties are smooth and strictly quasi-concave (i.e., single-peaked), with ideal policies q^A and q^B; that is,

$$q^A = \arg\max_{q_A \in Q} W_A(q_A) \quad \text{and} \quad q^B = \arg\max_{q_B \in Q} W_B(q_B)$$

In other words, $\partial W_A(q^A)/\partial q_A = 0$ and $\partial W_B(q^B)/\partial q_B = 0$.

A model of partisan politics along these lines was first formalized by Wittman (1983), who used it to argue that there may not be policy convergence when parties have ideological biases. We also use this model to discuss issues of capture of the political agenda by one of the groups.

Finally, we assume that both parties choose their policies (i.e., policy platforms) simultaneously. Therefore, the predictions of this model can be summarized by the corresponding Nash equilibrium, in which each party chooses the policy that maximizes its utility given the policy of the other party. Nash equilibrium policy platforms, (q_A^*, q_B^*), satisfy the following conditions:

$$q_A^* = \arg\max_{q_A \in Q} \{P(q_A, q_B^*)(R + W_A(q_A)) + (1 - P(q_A, q_B^*)) W_A(q_B^*)\}$$

and, simultaneously:

$$q_B^* = \arg\max_{q_B \in Q} \{(1 - P(q_A^*, q_B))(R + W_B(q_B)) + P(q_A^*, q_B) W_B(q_A^*)\}$$

Intuitively, these conditions state that in a Nash equilibrium, taking q_B^* as given, q_A^* should maximize party A's expected utility. At the same time, it must be true that taking q_A^* as given, q_B^* should maximize B's expected utility.

The problem in characterizing this Nash equilibrium is that the function $P(q_A, q_B)$, as shown by (12.1), is not differentiable. Nevertheless, it is possible to establish the following proposition, which was first proven by Calvert (1985) and shows that even with partisan politics, there is policy convergence; it is typically to the most preferred point of the median voter:

Proposition A.4 (Policy Convergence with Partisan Politics): *Consider the partisan-politics model described above, with ideal points of the two parties q^A and q^B, and the ideal point of the median voter q^M. Suppose also that the probability of party A winning the election is given by $P(q_A, q_B)$, as in (12.1). Then:*

- *If $R > 0$, or if $q^A \geq q^M \geq q^B$, or if $q^B \geq q^M \geq q^A$, the unique equilibrium involves convergence of both parties to the median (i.e., $q_A = q_B = q^M$), and each party wins the election with probability* $1/2$.
- *If, on the other hand, $R = 0$ and q^A and q^B are both to the left or to the right of q^M, there is no convergence to the median. In particular, when $V^M(q^A) > V^M(q^B)$, the equilibrium policy is q^A and when $V^M(q^A) < V^M(q^B)$, the equilibrium policy is q^B.*

Therefore, the basic result is that although there can be exceptions when there are no rents from coming to office and both parties have the same type of ideological bias, there are strong forces toward policy convergence. As the following discussion illustrates, the source of these powerful forces is (12.1), which implies that the policy that comes closer to the median voter's preferences will win relative to another policy.

Proposition A.4 is relatively straightforward to prove and here we simply provide an outline and the basic intuition. Start with the first case in which the preferences of the median voter are intermediate with respect to the ideal points of the two parties. Consider first the situation in which $q_A = q^M \neq q_B$. Then, we have that $P(q_A, q_B) = 1$, and party A is winning for sure. The utility of party B is given by $W_B(q^M)$. Now imagine a deviation by party B to $q_B = q^M$. We have that $P(q_A, q_B) = 1/2$, so the utility of party B changes to $R/2 + W_B(q^M) > W_B(q^M)$; hence, the deviation is profitable, and $q_A = q^M \neq q_B$ cannot be an equilibrium. (In the case in which $R = 0$, the argument is different, and now party A can change its policy to something slightly away from q^M toward its ideal point q^A, still win the election, and implement a policy closer to its preferences.)

Similarly, consider a situation in which $q_A \neq q^M \neq q_B$ and suppose without loss of any generality that $q^A > q^M > q^B$ and $V^M(q_A) > V^M(q_B)$, so that we again have $P(q_A, q_B) = 1$. It is clear that we must have $q_A \geq q^M$; otherwise, party A could find a policy q'_A such that $V^M(q'_A) > V^M(q_B)$ and $q'_A \geq q^M$ preferable to any $q_A \in (q^M, q_B)$. But then party B is obtaining utility $W_B(q_A)$ and by changing its policy to $q_B = q^M$, it obtains utility $R + W_B(q^M)$ if $q_A > q^M$ and $R/2 + W_B(q^M)$ if $q_A = q^M$. By the fact that $q_A \geq q^M$, both of these are greater than its initial utility, $W_B(q_A)$; hence, no policy announcements with $q_A \neq q^M \neq q_B$ can be an equilibrium. Therefore, the equilibrium must have $q_A = q_B = q^M$ – that is, convergence to the median. Intuitively, the median voter's ideal point is preferable to each party relative to the other party's ideal point and, moreover, increases their likelihood of coming to power. Therefore, no policy other than the median voter's ideal point can ever be implemented in equilibrium.

Next, we consider the case in which $q^B > q^A > q^M$ (other configurations give analogous results). Now, suppose that we have $q_A = q^A$. What should party B do? Clearly, any policy $q_B > q^A$ loses the election. On the other hand, $q_B = q^A$ wins the election with probability $1/2$ and is preferable. But, in fact, party B can do better. It can set $q_B = q^A - \varepsilon$, which is closer to the median voter's preferences and, by the fact that voters' preferences are single-peaked, this is preferable to q^A and therefore wins the election for party B. Although this policy is worse for party B than q^A (because $q^B > q^A$), for ε small enough, the difference is minuscule, whereas the gain in terms of the rent from coming to power is first-order. This argument only breaks down when $R = 0$ and, in this case, the best that party B can offer is $q_B = q^A$ (or any other policy $q_B > q^A$ for that matter because it does not care about coming to power; in either case, q^A is the equilibrium policy).

Therefore, the policy convergence to the median is a rather strong force that demonstrates that the assumption about objectives of parties in the Downsian model is not as restrictive as it may first appear. However, there can be exceptions, especially when rents from coming to power are nonexistent.

4.2 Electoral Competition with Partisan Parties and Probabilistic Voting

Nevertheless, these results depend crucially on the form of the $P(q_A, q_B)$ function, which created strong returns to being closer to the most preferred point of the median voter. In the previous discussion we learned that in the presence of ideological considerations on the side of the voters, $P(q_A, q_B)$ can become a continuous function. If that is the case, then policy convergence breaks down. To understand this, suppose that $P(q_A, q_B)$ is a continuous and differentiable function and suppose that it reaches its maximum for each party at q^M (i.e., being closer to the median voter's preferences is still beneficial in terms of the probability of being elected – the fact that we make this point which maximizes winning probabilities the median voter's ideal point is simply a normalization without any consequences). In that case, the Nash equilibrium of the policy competition game between the two parties is a pair of policies (q_A^*, q_B^*) such that the following first-order conditions hold:

$$\frac{\partial P(q_A^*, q_B^*)}{\partial q_A}(W_A(q_A^*) + R - W_A(q_B^*)) + P(q_A^*, q_B^*)\frac{\partial W_A(q_A^*)}{\partial q_A} = 0 \quad (12.17)$$

$$-\frac{\partial P(q_A^*, q_B^*)}{\partial q_B}(W_B(q_B^*) + R - W_B(q_A^*)) - (1 - P(q_A^*, q_B^*))\frac{\partial W_B(q_B^*)}{\partial q_B} = 0$$

The first term on both lines is the gain in terms of the utility of winning times the change in the probability of winning in response to a policy change. The second term is the product of the current probability of winning times the gain in terms of improvements in the party's utility because of the policy change. When these two marginal effects are equal to each other, each party is playing its best response. When both parties are playing their best responses, we have a Nash equilibrium.

Although (12.17) characterizes the Nash equilibrium implicitly for any function $P(q_A, q_B)$, it is not informative unless we put more structure on this function. To do this, let us follow the analysis of probabilistic voting above and assume that parties maximize their vote shares given by (12.6), $\pi_A = \sum_{n=1}^{N} \lambda^n F^n(V^n(q_A) - V^n(q_B))$. In that case, the equilibrium condition for party A in (12.17) can be written as:

$$\sum_{n=1}^{N} \lambda^n f^n(V^n(q_A^*) - V^n(q_B^*)) \frac{\partial V^n(q_A^*)}{\partial q_A} (W_A(q_A^*) + R - W_A(q_B^*)) \quad (12.18)$$

$$+ \sum_{n=1}^{N} \lambda^n F^n(V^n(q_A^*) - V^n(q_B^*)) \frac{\partial W_A(q_A^*)}{\partial q_A} = 0$$

with a similar condition for party B.

The interest of the partisan-politics model is that under some circumstances, it also leads to the reduced-form model of the distribution of political power in democracy used in Chapter 4, potentially giving more power to the rich than the MVT. To highlight this possibility in the simplest way, we next assume that both parties have preferences aligned with those of one of the social groups (for example in our two-class model, the rich). We denote this group that has captured the platforms of both parties by "1." Then, we have that:

$$W_A(q) = W_B(q) = V^1(q)$$

In that case, the equilibrium is again symmetric, and, using (12.18), we obtain the equilibrium policy, in this case denoted q^*, satisfying:

$$\sum_{n=1}^{N} \lambda^n f^n(0) R \frac{\partial V^n(q^*)}{\partial q} + \frac{\partial V^1(q^*)}{\partial q} \sum_{n=1}^{N} \lambda^n F^n(0) = 0$$

implying

$$\sum_{n=1}^{N} \lambda^n f^n(0) R \frac{\partial V^n(q^*)}{\partial q} + \frac{1}{2} \frac{\partial V^1(q^*)}{\partial q} = 0$$

where the second line uses the fact that in equilibrium, each party comes to power with probability 1/2; thus, $\sum_{n=1}^{N} \lambda^n F^n(0) = 1/2$.

This analysis then implies that the equilibrium policy is the solution to maximizing the weighted utilitarian social-welfare maximization:

$$\sum_{n=1}^{N} \chi^n \lambda^n V^n(q) \tag{12.19}$$

where

$$\chi^1 = f^1(0)R + \frac{1}{2}, \text{ and } \chi^n = f^n(0)R \text{ for } n \geq 2$$

In other words, the group whose preferences are represented by the party platforms has a greater weight in politics. The model also highlights that this effect is more likely to be pronounced when parties do not value coming to power (i.e., R is small), whereas when coming to office matters to the parties, the results are similar to the baseline probabilistic voting model.

This provides another potential interpretation for the reduced-form model of democratic politics in Chapter 4, where the equilibrium policy was the solution to a weighted utilitarian social-welfare maximization problem. We summarize this result as the following proposition:

Proposition A.5 (Policy Nonconvergence with Partisan Politics and Probabilistic Voting): *Suppose that $P(q_A, q_B)$ is a continuous function because of probabilistic voting, and political parties represent the preferences of one of the groups. Then, the political equilibrium is given by maximizing the weighted utilitarian social-welfare function (12.19), which places greater weight on the social group whose preferences are reflected in the party platforms.*

The reason this proposition is important is that it suggests that certain groups can be quite powerful in democratic politics if they can manage to control the ideological leanings of the parties. In terms of our two-class model, we can think of democratic politics sometimes as captured by the rich – for example, because they control the political parties.

4.3 Commitment and Convergence

An important assumption so far is that parties announce policy platforms and then they can commit to the policies they announced in those platforms. This way, parties could basically compete by varying the policies that they implement when in office. However, as emphasized by Alesina (1988), Osborne and Slivinski (1996), and Besley and Coate (1997), the assumption of commitment is not necessarily plausible. In these one-shot models, what is there to stop the politicians from changing policies to their ideal point once they come to power? Nothing; there is no potential punishment. (There would be some punishment if we were in the world with repeated elections, but this is beyond the scope of our treatment.)

To see what happens when we remove this commitment assumption, consider the model of the previous section but assume that parties can choose whichever policy they like when they come to office. Suppose also that $P(q_A, q_B)$ is given by (12.1). Announcements before the election are nothing more than cheap talk and in a subgame perfect equilibrium, voters realize that once they come to power, parties implement their ideal points. Therefore, they simply compare $V^n(q^A)$ and $V^n(q^B)$ and vote for whichever party has an ideal point closer to theirs. The result is that the party with an ideal point closer to that of the median voter wins. Therefore, we have the following proposition:

Proposition A.6 (Policy Nonconvergence with Partisan Politics and No Commitment): *Suppose that there is no commitment to policy platforms in this model of partisan politics. Then, in the unique equilibrium, we have that if $V^M(q^A) > V^M(q^B)$, party A comes to power with probability 1 and the equilibrium policy is q^A; if $V^M(q^B) > V^M(q^A)$, party B comes to power with probability 1 and the equilibrium policy is q^B; and if $V^M(q^A) = V^M(q^B)$, each party comes to power with probability 1/2 and the equilibrium policy is q^A with probability 1/2 and q^B with probability 1/2.*

Consequently, in this model of partisan politics without commitment, we see that parties' policy preferences matter even more. This implies that the control of the political agenda and the parties' internal structures becomes more important in determining equilibrium policies and, thus, more valuable when parties cannot perfectly commit to policies at the election stage. In this case, if both parties' platforms are totally captured by a social group, equilibrium policies are always at the ideal point of one of those groups. For example, consider a situation in which the poor control one political party and the rich the other. If the ideal point of the rich is closer to the ideal point of the median voter, the equilibrium democratic policy is always the ideal point of the rich.

In summary, the models discussed in this appendix provide a microfoundation for the reduced-form model of political power used at the end of Chapter 4. The models suggest that the rich may have more power in some democracies because they either are less ideological in their voting than the poor or have been able to form effective lobbies for their interests or are able to capture or influence party platforms.

Bibliography

Abrams, Lynn (1995) *Bismarck and the German Empire, 1871–1918*; New York: Routledge.

Acemoglu, Daron (2002) "Technical Change, Inequality, and the Labor Market," *Journal of Economic Literature*, 40, 7–72.

Acemoglu, Daron (2003a) "Why Not a Political Coase Theorem?" *Journal of Comparative Economics*, 31, 620–52.

Acemoglu, Daron (2003b) "Patterns of Skill Premia," *Review of Economic Studies*, 70, 199–230.

Acemoglu, Daron, Simon Johnson, and James A. Robinson (2001) "The Colonial Origins of Comparative Development: An Empirical Investigation," *American Economic Review*, 91, 1369–401.

Acemoglu, Daron, Simon Johnson, and James A. Robinson (2002) "Reversal of Fortune: Geography and Institutions in the Making of the Modern World Income Distribution," *Quarterly Journal of Economics*, 118, 1231–94.

Acemoglu, Daron, Simon Johnson, and James A. Robinson (2005) "The Rise of Europe: Atlantic Trade, Institutional Change and Economic Growth," *American Economic Review*, 95, 546–79.

Acemoglu, Daron, Simon Johnson, and James A. Robinson (2004) "Institutions as the Fundamental Cause of Long-Run Growth," NBER Working Paper #10481, forthcoming in Philippe Aghion and Steven Durlauf (eds.), *Handbook of Economic Growth*; Amsterdam: North-Holland.

Acemoglu, Daron, Simon Johnson, James A. Robinson, and Pierre Yared (2004) "Income and Democracy," Unpublished Paper.

Acemoglu, Daron, and James A. Robinson (2000a) "Why Did the West Extend the Franchise? Growth, Inequality, and Democracy in Historical Perspective," *Quarterly Journal of Economics*, CXV, 1167–99.

Acemoglu, Daron, and James A. Robinson (2000b) "Repression or Democratization?" *European Economic Review*, 44, 683–93.

Acemoglu, Daron, and James A. Robinson (2001) "A Theory of Political Transitions," *American Economic Review*, 91, 938–63.

Acemoglu, Daron, and James A. Robinson (2002) "The Political Economy of the Kuznets Curve," *Review of Development Economics*, 6, 183–203.

Acemoglu, Daron, and Fabrizio Zilibotti (1997) "Was Prometheus Unbound by Chance? Risk, Diversification, and Growth," *Journal of Political Economy*, 105, 709–51.

Acemoglu, Daron, and Fabrizio Zilibotti (1999) "Information Acquisition in Development," *Journal of Economic Growth*, 4, 5–38.

Ades, Alberto (1995) "Economic Development with Endogenous Political Participation," *Economics and Politics*, 7, 93–117.

Ades, Alberto, and Thierry Verdier (1996) "The Rise and Fall of Elites: A Theory of Economic Development and Social Polarization in Rent-Seeking Societies," CEPR Discussion Paper #1495.

Aguilera Peña, Mario (1985) *Los Comuneros: Guerra Social y Lucha Anticolonia*, Bogotá: Universidad Nacional de Colombia.

Alesina, Alberto (1988) "Credibility and Political Convergence in a Two-Party System with Rational Voters," *American Economic Review*, 78, 796–805.

Alesina, Alberto, and Roberto Perotti (1996) "Income Distribution, Political Instability, and Investment," *European Economic Review*, 40, 1203–25.

Alesina, Alberto, and Dani Rodrik (1994) "Distributive Politics and Economic Growth," *Quarterly Journal of Economics*, 109, 465–90.

Alesina, Alberto, Edward Glaeser, and Bruce Sacerdote (2001) "Why Doesn't the United States Have a European-Style Welfare State?" *Brookings Papers on Economic Activity*, Fall 2001, 187–278.

Alesina, Alberto, and Edward Glaeser (2004) *Fighting Poverty in the U.S. and Europe: A World of Difference*; New York: Oxford University Press.

Almond, Gabriel A., and Sidney Verba (1963) *The Civic Culture; Political Attitudes and Democracy in Five Nations*; Princeton: Princeton University Press.

Alonso, Paula (2000) *Between Revolution and the Ballot Box: The Origins of the Argentine Radical Party in the 1890s*; New York: Cambridge University Press.

Altimir, Oscar (1986) "Estimaciones de la Distribucion del Ingreso en la Argentina, 1953–1980," *Desarollo Económico*, 25, 521–66.

Aminzade, Ronald (1993) *Ballots and Barricades: Class Formation and Republican Politics in France, 1830–1871*; Princeton: Princeton University Press.

André, Catherine, and Jean-Philippe Platteau (1997) "Land Relations under Unbearable Stress: Rwanda Caught in the Malthusian Trap," *Journal of Economic Behavior and Organization*, 34, 1–47.

Arcinegas, German (1938) *Los Comuneros*; Bogotá: Editorial ABC.

Arrow, Kenneth J. (1951) *Social Choice and Individual Values*; New York: Wiley.

Ascher, Abraham (1988) *The Revolution of 1905*, Volume 1; Stanford: Stanford University Press.

Ascher, Abraham (1992) *The Revolution of 1905*, Volume 2; Stanford: Stanford University Press.

Attanasio, Orazio, Pinelopi K. Goldberg, and Nina Pavcnik (2004) "Trade Reforms and Wage Inequality in Colombia," *Journal of Development Economics*, 74, 331–66.

Austen-Smith, David (2000) "Income Redistribution under Proportional Representation," *Journal of Political Economy*, 108, 1235–69.

Austen-Smith, David, and Jeffrey S. Banks (1999) *Positive Political Theory I: Collective Preferences*; Ann Arbor: University of Michigan Press.

Austen-Smith, David, and Michael Wallerstein (2003) "Redistribution in a Divided Society," Northwestern University, J. L. Kellogg School of Management, CMS-EMS Discussion Paper #1362.

Baloyra, Enrique A. (1982) *El Salvador in Transition*; Chapel Hill: University of North Carolina Press.

Barro, Robert J. (1979) "On the Determination of the Pubic Debt," *Journal of Political Economy*, 87, 940–71.

Barro, Robert J. (1997) *The Determinants of Economic Growth: A Cross-Country Empirical Study*; Cambridge, MA: MIT Press.

Barro, Robert J. (1999) "The Determinants of Democracy," *Journal of Political Economy*, 107, S158–S183.

Barro, Robert J., and Jong-Wha Lee (2000) "International Data on Educational Attainment: Updates and Implications," CID Working Paper #42.

Barzel, Yoram (2001) *A Theory of the State: Economic Rights, Legal Rights, and the Scope of the State*; New York: Cambridge University Press.

Bates, Robert H. (1991) "The Economics of Transition to Democracy," *PS: Political Science and Politics*, 24, 24–7.

Bates, Robert H., and Da-Hsiang D. Lien (1985) "A Note on Taxation, Development and Representative Government," *Politics and Society*, 14, 53–70.

Beard, Charles A. (1913) *An Economic Interpretation of the Constitution of the United States*; New York: The Free Press.

Becker, Gary S. (1983) "A Theory of Competition among Pressure Groups for Political Influence," *Quarterly Journal of Economics*, 98, 371–400.

Benabou, Roland (2000) "Unequal Societies: Income Distribution and the Social Contract," *American Economic Review*, 90, 96–129.

Benabou, Roland, and Efe Ok (2001) "Social Mobility and the Demand for Redistribution: The POUM Hypothesis," *Quarterly Journal of Economics*, 116, 447–87.

Bergquist, Charles (2002) "The Left and the Paradoxes of Colombian History," Unpublished Paper; Department of History, University of Washington at Seattle.

Bernheim, B. Douglas, and Michael Whinston (1986) "Menu Auctions, Resource Allocation, and Economic Influence," *Quarterly Journal of Economics*, 1010, 1–31.

Berry, Albert R., and Miguel Urrutia (1976) *Income Distribution in Colombia*; New Haven: Yale University Press.

Bértola, Luis (2000) *Ensayos de historia economica: Uruguay y la region en la economia mundial, 1870–1990*; Montevideo: Ediciones Trilce.

Bértola, Luis, and Jeffrey G. Williamson (2003) "Globalization in Latin America before 1940," NBER Working Paper #9687.

Besley, Timothy, and Robin Burgess (2000) "Land Reform, Poverty Reduction and Growth: Evidence from India," *Quarterly Journal of Economics*, 115, 389–430.

Besley, Timothy F., and Steven T. Coate (1997) "An Economic Model of Representative Democracy," *Quarterly Journal of Economics*, 112, 85–114.

Besley, Timothy F., and Steven T. Coate (1998) "Sources of Inefficiency in a Representative Democracy: A Dynamic Analysis," *American Economic Review*, 88, 139–56.

Binswanger, Hans P., Klaus Deininger, and Gershon Feder (1995) "Power, Distortions, Revolt and Reform in Agricultural Land Relations," in Jere Behrman and T. N. Srinivasan (eds). *The Handbook of Development Economics*, Volume III; Amsterdam: North-Holland.

Black, Duncan (1948) "On the Rationale of Group Decision-Making," *Journal of Political Economy*, 56, 23–34.

Blackbourn, David (1998) *The Long Nineteenth Century: A History of Germany, 1780–1918*; New York: Oxford University Press.

Blume, Lawrence, and Carl P. Simon (1994) *Mathematics for Economists*; New York: W.W. Norton & Co.

Boix, Carles (2003) *Democracy and Redistribution*; New York: Cambridge University Press.

Boix, Carles, and Sebastián Rosato (2001) "A Complete Data Set of Political Regimes, 1800–1999," Unpublished, Department of Political Science, University of Chicago.

Bollen, Kenneth A. (1979) "Political Democracy and the Timing of Development," *American Sociological Review*, 44, 572–87.

Bollen, Kenneth A. (1990) "Political Democracy: Conceptual and Measurement Traps," *Studies in Comparative International Development*, 25, 7–24.

Bollen, Kenneth A. (2001) "Cross-National Indicators of Liberal Democracy, 1950–1990" [computer file]. 2nd ICPSR version. Chapel Hill, NC: University of North Carolina [producer], 1998. Inter-university Consortium for Political and Social Research [distributor].

Bollen, Kenneth A., and Robert W. Jackman (1985) "Political Democracy and the Size Distribution of Income," *American Sociological Review*, 60, 438–57.

Bollen, Kenneth A., and Robert W. Jackman (1995) "Income Inequality and Democratization Revisited: A Comment on Muller," *American Sociological Review*, 60, 983–89.

Bourguignon, François, and Thierry Verdier (2000) "Oligarchy, Democracy, Inequality, and Growth," *Journal of Development Economics*, 62, 285–313.

Bourguignon, François, and Christian Morrisson (2001) "Data Sources for Inequality among World Citizens, 1820–1992,"Unpublished, www.delta.ens.fr/XIX.

Bourguignon, François, and Christian Morrisson (2002) "Inequality among World Citizens, 1820–1992," *American Economic Review*, 92, 727–44.

Bowman, Larry W. (1991) *Mauritius: Democracy and Development in the Indian Ocean*; Boulder: Westview Press.

Brainard, Lael, and Theirry Verdier (1997) "The Political Economy of Declining Industries: Senescent Industry Collapse Revisited,"*Journal of International Economics*, 42, 221–38.

Bratton, Michael, and Nicolas van de Walle (1997) *Democratic Experiments in Africa: Regime Transitions in Comparative Perspective*; New York: Cambridge University Press.

Brenner, Robert (1976) "Agrarian Class Structure and Economic Development in Pre-industrial Europe," *Past and Present*, 70, 30–75.

Brenner, Robert (1993) *Merchants and Revolution: Commercial Change, Political Conflict, and London's Overseas Traders, 1550–1653*; Princeton: Princeton University Press.

Briggs, Asa (1959) *Chartist Studies*; London: Macmillan.

Bueno de Mesquita, Bruce D., James D. Morrow, Randolph M. Siverson, and Alastair Smith (2003) *The Logic of Political Survival*; Cambridge, MA: MIT Press.

Bunce, Valerie (2003) "Rethinking Recent Democratization: Lessons from the Postcommunist Experience," *World Politics*, 55, 167–192.

Burkhart, R. E., and Michael S. Lewis-Beck (1994) "Comparative Democracy–The Economic Development Thesis," *American Political Science Review*, 88, 903–10.

Bushnell, David (1993) *The Making of Modern Colombia: A Nation in Spite of Itself*; Berkeley: University of California Press.

Calvert, Randall L. (1985) "Robustness of the Multidimensional Voting Model: Candidate Motivations, Uncertainty, and Convergence," *American Journal of Political Science*, 29, 69–95.

Calvo, Ernesto, Juan Carlos Torre, and Mariela Szwarcberg (2001) "The New Welfare Alliance," Unpublished; Department of Political Science, Universidad di Tella, Buenos Aires.

Cardenas Acosta, Pablo E. (1960) *El Movimiento Comunal de 1781 en el Nuevo Reino de Granada*, 2 Volumes; Bogota: Editorial Kelly.

Case, William (2002) *Politics in South-East Asia: Democracy or Less*; Richmond: Cruzon Press.

Cavarozzi, Marcelo (1986) "Political Cycles in Argentina since 1955," in Guillermo O'Donnell, Philippe C. Schmitter, and Lawrence Whitehead (eds.). *Transitions from Authoritarian Rule: Latin America*; Baltimore: Johns Hopkins University Press.

Chalker, Cynthia H. (1995) "Elections and Democracy in Costa Rica," in Mitchell A. Seligson and John A. Booth (eds.). *Elections and Democracy in Central America Revisited*; Chapel Hill: University of North Carolina Press.

Coate, Stephen, and Stephen E. Morris (1999) "Policy Persistence," *American Economic Review*, 89, 1327–36.

Coatsworth, John H. (1993) "Notes on the Comparative Economic History of Latin America and the United States," in Walter L. Bernecker and Hans Werner Tobler (eds.). *Development and Underdevelopment in America: Contrasts in Economic Growth in North and Latin America in Historical Perspective*; New York: Walter de Gruyter.

Cohen, Youssef (1994) *Radicals, Reformers, and Reactionaries: The Prisoner's Dilemma and the Collapse of Democracy in Latin America*; Chicago: University of Chicago Press.

Cole, Alistair, and Peter Campbell (1989) *French Electoral Systems and Elections since 1789*; Aldershot: Gower Press.

Collier, David (1979) *The New Authoritarianism in Latin America*; Princeton: Princeton University Press.

Collier, David, and Steven Levitsky (1997) "Democracy with Adjectives," *World Politics*, 49, 430–51.

Collier, Ruth Berins (1999) *Paths Towards Democracy: The Working Class and Elites in Western Europe and South America*; New York: Cambridge University Press.

Colomer, Josep M. (2000) *Strategic Transitions: Game Theory and Democratization*; Baltimore: Johns Hopkins University Press.

Conley, John P., and Akram Temimi (2001) "Endogenous Enfranchisement When Groups' Preferences Conflict," *Journal of Political Economy*, 109, 79–107.

Coughlin, Peter J. (1992) *Probabilistic Voting Theory*; New York: Cambridge University Press.

Couyoumdjian, Juan Ricardo, Rene Millar, and Josefina Tocornal (1992) *Historia de la Bolsa de Comercio de Santiago, 1983–1993. Un siglo del mercado de valores en Chile*; Santiago: Bolsa de Comercio de Santiago.

Cowling, Maurice (1967) *Disraeli, Gladstone and Revolution*; New York: Cambridge University Press.

Cox, Gary W. (1997) *Making Votes Count*; New York: Cambridge University Press.

Cox, Thomas S. (1976) *Civil-Military Relations in Sierra Leone: A Case Study of African Soldiers in Politics*; Cambridge, MA: Harvard University Press.

Cragg, Michael I., and Mario Epelbaum (1996) "Why Has Wage Dispersion Grown in Mexico?" *Journal of Development Economics*, 51, 99–116.

Crescenzi, Mark J. C. (1999) "Violence and Uncertainty in Transitions," *Journal of Conflict Resolution*, 43, 192–212.

Dahl, Robert A. (1971) *Polyarchy: Participation and Opposition*; New Haven: Yale University Press.

Darvall, Frank O. (1934) *Popular Disturbances and Public Order in Regency England*, Oxford: Oxford University Press.

Des Forges, Alison (1999) *"Leave None to Tell the Story": Genocide in Rwanda*; New York: Human Rights Watch.

Diamond, Larry J. (1992) "Economic Development and Democracy Reconsidered," *American Behavioral Scientist*, 35, 450–99.

Diamond, Larry J. (1999) *Developing Democracy: Towards Consolidation*; Baltimore: Johns Hopkins University Press.

Diaz-Alejandro, Carlos (1970) *Essays on the Economic History of the Argentine Republic*; New Haven: Yale University Press.

Di Nardo, John E., Nicole M. Fortin, and Thomas Lemieux (1996) "Labor Market Institutions and the Distribution of Wages, 1973–1992: A Semiparametric Approach," *Econometrica*, 65, 1001–44.

Di Palma, Giuseppe (1990) *To Craft Democracies*; Berkeley: University of California Press.

di Tella, Guido, and Rudiger Dornbusch (1989) *The Political Economy of Argentina, 1946–83*; Pittsburgh: University of Pittsburgh Press.

Dixit, Avinash K. (1996) *The Making of Economic Policy: A Transaction Cost Politics Perspective*; Cambridge, MA: MIT Press.

Dixit, Avinash K., and John B. Londregan (1995) "Redistributive Politics and Economic Efficiency," *American Political Science Review*, 89, 856–866.

Dixit, Avinash K., and John B. Londregan (1996) "The Determinants of Success of Special Interest in Redistributive Politics," *Journal of Politics*, LVIII, 1132–55.

Dixit, Avinash K., and John B. Londregan (1998) "Ideology, Tactics, and Efficiency in Redistributive Politics," *Quarterly Journal of Economics*, CXIII, 497–530.

Dixit, Avinash K., and Victor Norman (1980) *Theory of International Trade: A Dual, General Equilibrium Approach*; New York: Cambridge University Press.

Dobson, R. B. (1983) *The Peasants' Revolt of 1381*; 2nd Edition. London: Macmillan.

Dollar, David, and Art Kraay (2002) "Growth Is Good for the Poor," *Journal of Economic Growth*, 7, 195–225.

Downs, Anthony (1957) *An Economic Theory of Democracy*; New York: Harper & Row.

Drake, Paul W. (1996) *Labor Movements and Dictatorships: The Southern Cone in Comparative Perspective*; Baltimore: Johns Hopkins University Press.

Drake, Paul W. (1998) "The International Causes of Democratization, 1974–1990," in Paul W. Drake and Mathew D. McCubbins (eds.). *The Origins of Liberty*; Princeton: Princeton University Press.

Dumke, Rolf (1991) "Income Inequality and Industrialization in Germany 1850–1945," in Y. Brenner et al. (eds.). *Income Distribution in Historical Perspective*; New York: Cambridge University Press.

Dyer, Christopher C. (1984) "The Social and Economic Background to the Rural Revolt of 1381," from Rodney H. Hilton and T. H. Aston (eds.). *The English Rising of 1381*; New York: Cambridge University Press.

Easterlin, Richard A. (1981) "Why Isn't the Whole World Developed?" *Journal of Economic History*, 41, 1–19.

Ellman, Matthew, and Leonard Wantchekon (2000) "Electoral Competition under the Threat of Political Unrest," *Quarterly Journal of Economics*, 115, 499–531.

Eltis, David (2000) *The Rise of African Slavery in the Americas*; New York: Cambridge University Press.

Engerman, Stanley L., and Kenneth L. Sokoloff (1997) "Factor Endowments, Institutions, and Differential Growth Paths among New World Economies," in Stephen Haber (ed.). *How Latin America Fell Behind*; Stanford: Stanford University Press.

Engerman, Stanley L., Elisa Mariscal, and Kenneth L. Sokoloff (1998) "Schooling, Suffrage, and the Persistence of Inequality in the Americas, 1800–1945," Unpublished Paper; Department of Economics, UCLA.

Epstein, David L., Robert H. Bates, Jack Goldstone, Ida Kristensen, and Sharyn O'Halloran (2004) "Democratic Transitions," Harvard University, J.F.K. School of Government, CID Working Paper No. 101.

Ertman, Thomas (1997) *Birth of the Leviathan: Building States and Regimes in Medieval and Early Modern Europe*; New York: Cambridge University Press.

Evans, Eric J. (1996) *The Forging of the Modern State: Early Industrial Britain, 1783–1870*, 2nd edition; New York: Longman.

Feenstra, Robert C. (2003) *Advanced International Trade: Theory and Evidence*; Princeton: Princeton University Press.

Feinstein, Charles H. (1988) "The Rise and Fall of the Williamson Curve," *Journal of Economic History*, 48, 699–729.

Feng, Yi, and Paul K. Zak (1999) "The Determinants of Democratic Transitions," *Journal of Conflict Resolution*, 43, 162–177.

Finer, Samuel E. (1976) *The Man on Horseback: The Role of the Military in Politics*, 2nd edition; Baltimore: Penguin.

Fitch, J. Samuel (1998) *The Armed Forces and Democracy in Latin America*; Baltimore: Johns Hopkins University Press.

Flora, Peter (1983) *State, Economy, and Society, 1815–1975*; Frankfurt: Campus-Verlag.

Fogel, Robert W. (1989) *Without Consent or Contract: The Rise and Fall of American Slavery*; New York: Norton.

Fogel, Robert W., and Stanley L. Engerman (1974) *Time on the Cross: The Economics of American Negro Slavery*; Boston: Little, Brown.

Fudenberg, Drew, and Jean Tirole (1991) *Game Theory*; Cambridge, MA: MIT Press.

Fukuyama, Francis (1992) *The End of History and the Last Man*; New York: Free Press.

Galor, Oded, and Omer Moav (2003) "Das Human Kapital: A Theory of the Demise of the Class Structure," Unpublished. http://www.econ.brown.edu/fac/Oded_Galor/.

Galor, Oded, and Joseph Zeira (1993) "Income Distribution and Macroeconomics," *Review of Economic Studies*, 40, 35–52.

Garrard, John (2002) *Democratization in Britain: Elites, Civil Society, and Reform since 1800*; Basingstoke: Palgrave.

Garrett, Geoffery (1998) *Partisan Politics in the Global Economy*; New York: Cambridge University Press.

Gasiorowski, Mark J. (1995) "Economic Crises and Political Regime Change: An Event History Analysis," *American Political Science Review*, 89, 882–97.

Gates, Scott, and Brian D. Humes (1997) *Games, Information, and Politics*; Ann Arbor, MI: University of Michigan Press.

Gavin, Michael, and Roberto Perotti (1997) "Fiscal Policy in Latin America," *NBER Macroeconomics Annual*, edited by Benjamin Bernanke and Julio Rotemberg; Cambridge, MA: MIT Press.

Geddes, Barbara (1999a) "What Do We Know about Democratization after Twenty Years?" *Annual Review of Political Science*, 2, 115–44.

Geddes, Barbara (1999b) "The Effect of Regime Type on Authoritarian Breakdown: Empirical Test of a Game Theoretic Argument," Unpublished. Department of Political Science, UCLA.

Gerschenkron, Alexander (1943) *Bread and Democracy in Germany*; Berkeley: University of California Press.

Gibbons, Robert (1992) *Game Theory for Applied Economists*; Princeton: Princeton University Press.

Goldin, Claudia (2001) "The Human Capital Century and American Leadership: Virtues of the Past," *Journal of Economic History*, 61, 263–92.

Goldstein, Richard J. (1983) *Political Repression in Nineteenth Century Europe*; London: Croon Helm.

Gosnell, Harold F. (1930) *Why Europe Votes?* Chicago: University of Chicago Press.

Gradstein, Mark (2002) "Political Inequality and Institutional Quality," Unpublished Paper. Ben-Gurion University.

Grandmont, Jean-Michel (1978) "Intermediate Preferences and Majority Rule," *Econometrica*, 46, 317–30.

Green, Edward J. (1993) "On the Emergence of Parliamentary Government: The Role of Private Information," *Federal Reserve Bank of Minneapolis Quarterly Review*, 17, 1–12.

Green, Jerry R., Andreu Mas-Colell, and Michael D. Whinston (1995) *Microeconomic Theory*; New York: Oxford University Press.

Grossman, Gene, and Elhanan Helpman (1996) "Electoral Competition and Special Interest Politics," *Review of Economic Studies*, 63, 265–86.

Grossman, Gene, and Elhanan Helpman (2001) *Special Interest Politics*; Cambridge, MA: MIT Press.

Grossman, Gene, and Elhanan Helpman (2002) "Managerial Incentives and the International Organization of Production," NBER Working Paper #9403.

Grossman, Herschel I. (1991) "A General Equilibrium Model of Insurrections," *American Economic Review*, 81, 912–21.

Grossman, Herschel I. (1994) "Production, Appropriation, and Land Reform," *American Economic Review*, 84, 705–12.

Grossman, Herschel, and Suk Jae Noh (1994) "Proprietary Public Finance and Economic Welfare," *Journal of Public Economics*, 53, 187–204.

Grossman, Sanford J., and Oliver D. Hart (1986) "The Costs and Benefits of Ownership: A Theory of Vertical and Lateral Integration," *Journal of Political Economy*, 94, 691–719.

Gudmundson, Lowell (1995) "Lord and Peasant in the Making of Modern Central America," in Evelyn Huber and Frank Safford (eds.). *Agrarian Structure and Political Power*; Pittsburgh: University of Pittsburgh Press.

Haggard, Stephan, and Robert R. Kaufman (1995) *The Political Economy of Democratic Transitions*; Princeton: Princeton University Press.

Hardin, Russell (1982) *Collective Action*; Baltimore: Johns Hopkins University Press.

Hardin, Russell (1995) *All For One*; Princeton: Princeton University Press.

Harrison, Royden (1965) *Before the Socialists: Studies in Labour and Politics, 1861–1881*; London: Routledge Keegan and Paul.

Hart, Oliver D. (1995) *Firms, Contracts, and Financial Structure*; New York: Oxford University Press.

Hayes, William A. (1982) *The Background and Passage of the Third Reform Act*; Oxford: Oxford University Press.

Helpman, Elhanan, and Paul R. Krugman (1989) *Trade Policy and Market Structure*; Cambridge, MA: MIT Press.

Herbst, Jeffrey I. (1988) "Prospects for Revolution in South Africa," *Political Science Quarterly*, 103, 665–85.

Herbst, Jeffrey I. (2000) *States and Power in Africa: Comparative Lessons in Authority and Control*; Princeton: Princeton University Press.

Heston, Alan, Robert Summers, and Bettina Atten (2002) *Penn World Tables Version 6.1.* Center for International Comparisons at the University of Pennsylvania (CICUP).

Hilton, Rodney H. (1973) *Bond Men Made Free: Medieval Peasant Movements and the English Rising of 1381*; New York: Viking Press.

Himmelfarb, Gertrude (1966) "The Politics of Democracy: The English Reform Act of 1867," *Journal of British Studies*, 6, 97–138.

Hirschman, Albert O. (1970) *Exit, Voice and Loyalty*; Cambridge, MA: Harvard University Press.

Hirschman, Albert O. (1978) "Exit, Voice, and the State," *World Politics*, 31, 90–107.

Hobbes, Thomas (1996) *Leviathan*; New York: Cambridge University Press.

Horowitz, Donald L. (1985) *Ethnic Groups in Conflict*; Berkeley: University of California Press.

Horowitz, Donald L. (1992) *A Democratic South Africa? Constitutional Engineering in a Divided Society*; Berkeley: University of California Press.

Hotelling, Harold (1929) "Stability in Competition," *Economic Journal*, 39, 41–57.

Huff, W. G. (1994) *The Economic Growth of Singapore: Trade and Development in the Twentieth Century*; New York: Cambridge University Press.

Huntington, Samuel P. (1964) *The Soldier and the State: The Theory and Politics of Civil-Military Relations*; Cambridge, MA: Belknap Press of Harvard University Press.

Huntington, Samuel P. (1968) *Political Order in Changing Societies*; New Haven: Yale University Press.

Huntington, Samuel P. (1991) *The Third Wave: Democratization in the Late Twentieth Century*; Norman, OK: University of Oklahoma Press.

Jack, William, and Roger Lagunoff (2003) "Dynamic Enfranchisement," Department of Economics, Georgetown University. http://www.georgetown.edu/faculty/lagunoff/franch10.pdf.

Jennings, Ivor (1961) *Party Politics*; New York: Cambridge University Press.

Justman, Moshe, and Mark Gradstein (1999) "The Industrial Revolution, Political Transition, and the Subsequent Decline in Inequality in 19th Century Britain," *Explorations in Economic History*, 36, 109–27.

Kaufman, Robert R., and Barbara Stallings (1991) "The Political Economy of Latin American Populism," in Rudiger Dornbusch and Sebastian Edwards (eds.). *The Macroeconomics of Populism in Latin America*; Chicago: University of Chicago Press.

Kendall, M. G., and A. Stuart (1950) "The Law of the Cubic Proportion in Election Results," *British Journal of Sociology*, 1, 183–96.

Keyssar, Alexander (2000) *The Right to Vote: The Contested History of Democracy in the United States*; New York: Basic Books.

Kiser, Edgar, and Yoram Barzel (1991) "The Origins of Democracy in England," *Rationality and Society*, 3, 396–422.

Kolb, Glen L. (1974) *Democracy and Dictatorship in Venezuela 1945–1958*; Hamden: Shoestring Press.

Kopstein, Jeffery, and David A. Reilly (2000) "Geographic Diffusion and the Transformation of the Postcommunist World," *World Politics*, 53, 1–37.

Kraus, Franz (1981) "The Historical Development of Income Inequality in Western Europe and the United States," in Peter Flora and Arnold J. Heidenheimer (eds.). *The Development of the Welfare State in Europe and America*; New Brunswick, NJ: Transactions Books.

Kreuzer, Marcus (1996) "Democratization and Changing Methods of Electoral Corruption in France from 1815 to 1914," in Walter Little and Eduardo Posada-Carbó (eds.) *Political Corruption in Europe and Latin America*; London: Macmillan.

Kriger, Norma J. (1992) *Zimbabwe's Guerilla War: Peasant Voices*; New York: Cambridge University Press.

Kubota, Keiko, and Helen V. Milner (2005) "Why the Move to Free Trade? Democracy and Trade Policy in the Developing Countries?" forthcoming in *International Organization Winter Edition.*

Kuznets, Simon S. (1955) "Economic Growth and Income Inequality," *American Economic Review*, 65, 1–28.

Kuznets, Simon S. (1963) "The Distribution of Income by Size," *Economic Development and Cultural Change*, 11, 1–80.

Kuznets, Simon S. (1966) *Modern Economic Growth: Rate, Structure, and Spread*; New Haven: Yale University Press.

Lang, Sean (1999) *Parliamentary Reform, 1785–1928*; New York: Routledge.

Lapp, Nancy D. (2004) *Landing Votes: Representation and Land Reform in Latin America*; New York: Palgrave Macmillan.

Leamer, Edward E. (1995) "International Trade Theory: The Evidence," in James Levinson, Gene M. Grossman, and Kenneth Rogoff (eds.). *The Handbook of International Economics*, Volume III; Amsterdam: North-Holland.

Leamer, Edward E. (1998) "In Search of Stolper–Samuelson Effects on U.S. Wages," in Susan M. Collins (ed.). *Imports, Exports, and the U.S. Worker*; Washington, DC: Brookings Institution Press.

Lee, Stephen J. (1994) *Aspects of British Political History, 1815–1914*; New York: Routledge.

Legros, Patrick, and Andrew F. Newman (1996) "Wealth Effects, Distribution and the Theory of Organization," *Journal of Economic Theory*, 70, 312–41.

Lehoucq, Fabrice E. (1998) *Instituciones democráticas y conflictos políticos en Costa Rica*; Heredia: Editorial UNA.

Leventoğlu, Bahar (2003a) "Social Mobility and Political Transitions," Unpublished. Department of Political Science, SUNY Stony Brook, http://www.sunysb.edu/polsci/.

Leventoğlu, Bahar (2003b) "Social Mobility, Middle Class and Political Transitions," Unpublished. Department of Political Science, SUNY Stony Brook, http://www.sunysb.edu/polsci/.

Levine, Daniel H. (1973) *Conflict and Political Change in Venezuela*; Princeton: Princeton University Press.

Levine, Daniel H. (1989) "Venezuela: The Nature, Sources and Prospects for Democracy," in Larry J. Diamond, Juan J. Linz and Seymour M. Lipset (eds.). *Democracy in Developing Areas: Latin America*; Boulder: Lynne Rienner.

Lewis, Arthur W. (1954) "Economic Development with Unlimited Supplies of Labour," *Manchester School of Economic and Social Studies*, 22, 139–91.

Li, Hongyi, Lyn Squire, and Heng-fu Zou (1998) "Explaining International and Intertemporal Variations in Income Inequality," *Economic Journal*, 108, 26–43.

Lichbach, Mark I. (1989) "An Evaluation of 'Does Economic Inequality Breed Political Conflict?' Studies," *World Politics*, 41, 431–70.

Lichbach, Mark I. (1995) *The Rebel's Dilemma*; Ann Arbor: University of Michigan Press.

Lijphart, Arend (1999) *Patterns of Democracy: Government Forms and Performance in Thirty-Six Countries*; New Haven: Yale University Press.

Lim, Linda, Pang Eng Fong, and Roland Findlay (1993) "Singapore," in Ronald Findlay and Stanislaw Wellisz, *Five Small Open Economies*; New York: Oxford University Press.

Lindbeck, Assar, and Jörgen Weibull (1987) "Balanced-Budget Redistribution as the Outcome of Political Competition," *Public Choice*, LII, 272–97.

Lindert, Peter H. (1986) "Unequal English Wealth since 1670," *Journal of Political Economy*, 94, 1127–1162.

Lindert, Peter H. (1994) "The Rise in Social Spending, 1880–1930," *Explorations in Economic History*, 31, 1–37.

Lindert, Peter H. (2000a) "Three Centuries of Inequality in Britain and America," in Anthony B. Atkinson and François Bourguignon (eds.). *Handbook of Income Distribution*; Amsterdam: North-Holland.

Lindert, Peter H. (2000b) "The Political Economy of Comparative Mass Education in Europe before 1914," Unpublished. University of California at Davis, Agricultural History Center.

Lindert, Peter H. (2004) *Growing Public: Social Spending and Economics Growth since the Eighteenth Century*, two volumes; New York: Cambridge University Press.

Lindert, Peter H., and Jeffrey G. Williamson (1982) "Revising England's Social Tables, 1688–1812," *Explorations in Economic History*, 19, 385–408.

Lindert, Peter H., and Jeffrey G. Williamson (1983) "Reinterpreting Britain's Social Tables, 1688–1913," *Explorations in Economic History*, 20, 94–109.

Lindert, Peter H., and Jeffrey G. Williamson (1985) "Growth, Equality, and History," *Explorations in Economic History*, 22, 341–77.

Linz, Juan J. (1978) *Crisis, Breakdown and Re-equilibration*; Baltimore: Johns Hopkins University Press.

Linz, Juan J. (1994) "Presidential or Parliamentary Democracy: Does It Make a Difference?" in Juan J. Linz and Arturo Valenzuela (eds.). *The Failure of Presidential Democracy*; Baltimore: Johns Hopkins University Press.

Linz, Juan J. (2000) *Totalitarian and Authoritarian Regimes*; Boulder: Lynne Rienner.

Linz, Juan J., and Alfred Stepan (1978) *The Breakdown of Democratic Regimes*; Baltimore: Johns Hopkins University Press.

Linz, Juan J., and Alfred Stepan (1996) *Problems of Democratic Transition and Consolidation: Southern Europe, South America, and Post-Communist Europe*; Baltimore: Johns Hopkins University Press.

Lipset, Seymour M. (1959) "Some Social Prerequisites for Democracy: Economic Development and Political Legitimacy," *American Political Science Review*, 53, 69–105.

Lipset, Seymour M., and Gary Marks (2000) *It Didn't Happen Here: Why Socialism Failed in the United States*; New York: W.W. Norton & Co.

Lizzeri, Alessandro, and Nicola Persico (2004) "Why Did the Elites Extend the Suffrage? Democracy and the Scope of Government, with an Application to Britain's 'Age of Reform,'" *Quarterly Journal of Economics*, 119, 707–65.

Llavador, Humberto, and Robert J. Oxoby (2003) "Partisan Competition, Growth and Franchise," Unpublished. Department of Economics, Universitat Pompeu Fabra.

Lockhart, James, and Stuart B. Schwartz (1983) *Early Latin America*; New York: Cambridge University Press.

Londoño, Juan-Luis (1995) *Distribución del Ingreso y Desarollo Económico: Colombia en el Siglo XX*; Fedesarollo: TM Editores, Bogotá.

Londregan, John B. (2000) *Legislative Institutions and Ideology in Chile*; New York: Cambridge University Press.

Londregan, John B., and Keith T. Poole (1990) "Poverty, the Coup Trap, and the Seizure of Executive Power," *World Politics*, 42, 151–83.

Londregan, John B., and Keith T. Poole (1996) "Does High Income Promote Democracy?" *World Politics*, 49, 1–30.

Loveman, Brian (1999) *For la Patria: Politics and the Armed Forces in Latin America*; Wilmington: SR Books.

Luebbert, Gregory (1991) *Liberalism, Fascism or Social Democracy: Social Classes and the Political Origins of Regimes in Interwar Europe*; New York: Oxford University Press.

Lundahl, Mats (1992) *Apartheid in Theory and Practice: An Economic Analysis*; Boulder; Westview Press.

Maddison, Angus (1995) *Monitoring the World Economy, 1820–1992*; Paris, France: Development Centre of the Organization for Economic Co-operation and Development.

Maddison, Angus (2001) *The World Economy: A Millennial Perspective*; Paris, France: Development Centre of the Organization for Economic Co-operation and Development.

Mahoney, James (2001) *The Legacies of Liberalism: Path Dependence and Political Regimes in Central America*; Baltimore: Johns Hopkins University Press.

Manin, Bernard (1997) *The Principles of Representative Government*; New York: Cambridge University Press.

Markoff, John (1996) *Waves of Democracy: Social Movements and Political Change*; Thousand Oaks, CA: Pine Forge Press.

Marshall, Alfred (1920) *Principles of Economics*, 8th edition; London: Macmillan and Co. Limited.

Marshall, Monty G., and Keith Jaggers (2004) "Political Regime Characteristics and Transitions, 1800–2002," Polity IV Project, University of Maryland.

Matsuyama, Kiminori (1992) "A Simple Model of Sectoral Adjustment," *Review of Economic Studies*, 59, 375–88.

Maxfield, Sylvia (2000) "Capital Mobility and Democratic Stability," *Journal of Democracy*, 11, 95–106.

Mazzuca, Sebastián L., and James A. Robinson (2004) "Power and Proportionality," Unpublished. Department of Government, Harvard.

McCreery, David J. (1994) *Rural Guatemala, 1760–1940*; Stanford: Stanford University Press.

McGuire, Robert A. (1988) "Constitution Making: A Rational Choice Model of the Federal Convention of 1787," *American Journal of Political Science*, 32, 483–522.

McKelvey, Richard D., and Norman Schofield (1987) "'Generalized Symmetry Conditions at a Core Point," *Econometrica*, 55, 923–34.

McLaren, John E. (2000) "Globalization and Vertical Structure," *American Economic Review*, 90, 1239–54.

Meltzer, Allan H., and Scott F. Richard (1981) "A Rational Theory of the Size of Government," *Journal of Political Economy*, 89, 914–27.

Michels, Robert [1911] (1962) *Political Parties: A Sociological Study of the Oligarchical Tendencies of Modern Democracy*; New York: The Free Press.

Milesi-Ferretti, Gian Maria, Roberto Perotti, and Massimo Rostagno (2002) "Electoral Systems and Public Spending," *Quarterly Journal of Economics*, 117, 609–57.

Milne, Robert S., and Diane K. Mauzy (1990) *Singapore: The Legacy of Lee Kuan Yew*; Boulder: Westview Press.

Milne, Robert S., and Diane K. Mauzy (2002) *Singapore Politics under the People's Action Party*; New York: Routledge.

Mitch, David (1993) "The Role of Human Capital in the First Industrial Revolution," in Joel Mokyr (ed.). *The British Industrial Revolution: An Economic Perspective*; San Francisco: Westview Press.

Mommsen, Wolfgang J. (1981) "The German Revolution 1918–1920: Political Revolution and Social Protest," in R. Bessle and E. J. Feuchtwanger (eds.). *Social Change and Political Development in Weimar Germany*; London: Croon Helm.

Moore, Barrington (1966) *The Social Origins of Dictatorship and Democracy: Lord and Peasant in the Making of the Modern World*; Boston: Beacon Press.

Moore, Will H. (1995) "Rational Rebels: Overcoming the Free-Rider Problem," *Political Research Quarterly*, 48, 417–54.

Morrisson, Christian (2000) "Historical Evolution of Income Distribution in Western Europe," in Anthony B. Atkinson and François Bourguignon (eds.). *Handbook of Income Distribution*; Amsterdam: North-Holland.

Morrisson, Christian, and Wayne Snyder (2000) "The Income Inequality of France in Historical Perspective," *European Review of Economic History*, 4, 59–84.

Muller, Edwin N. (1988) "Democracy, Economic Development, and Income Inequality," *American Sociological Review*, 53, 50–68.

Muller, Edwin N. (1995) "Economic Determinants of Democracy," *American Sociological Review*, 60, 966–982.

Muller, Edwin N., and Mitchell A. Seligson (1987) "Inequality and Insurrections," *American Political Science Review*, 81, 425–51.

Mulligan, Casey B., Xavier Sala-i-Martin and Richard Gil (2003) "Do Democracies Have Different Public Policies than Nondemocracies?" NBER Working Paper #10040.

Murphy, Kevin J., Andrei Shleifer, and Robert W. Vishny (1989) "Industrialization and the Big Push," *Journal of Political Economy*, 97, 1003–26.

Myrdal, Gunnar (1957) *Economic Theory and Under-Developed Regions*; London: Duckworth.

Namier, Lewis (1961) *The Structure of Politics at the Accession of George III*; London: Macmillan.

Newman, Andrew F., and James A. Robinson (2002) "Globalization and Democracy," Unpublished. Department of Government, Harvard University.

Nolan, Brian (1986) "Economic Crisis, State Policy and Working-Class Formation in Germany, 1870–1900" in Ira Katznelson and Aristide R. Zolberg (eds.). *Working-Class Formation: Nineteenth-Century Patterns in Western Europe and the United States*; Princeton: Princeton University Press.

Nordlinger, Eric A. (1977) *Soldiers in Politics: Military Coups and Governments*; Englewood Cliffs, NJ: Prentice-Hall.

North, Douglass C. (1981) *Structure and Change in Economic History*; New York: W.W. Norton & Co.

North, Douglass C. (1990) *Institutions, Institutional Change, and Economic Performance*; New York: Cambridge University Press.

North, Douglass C., and Robert P. Thomas (1973) *The Rise of the Western World: A New Economic History*; Cambridge, UK: Cambridge University Press.

North, Douglass C., and Barry R. Weingast (1989) "Constitutions and Commitment: The Evolution of Institutions Governing Public Choice in Seventeenth-Century England," *Journal of Economic History*, 49, 803–32.

Nugent, Jeffery B., and James A. Robinson (2000) "Are Endowments Fate?" CEPR Discussion Paper #3206.

Nurkse, Ragnar (1953) *Problems of Capital Formation in Underdeveloped Countries*; New York: Oxford University Press.

O'Brien, Patrick K. (1993) "Political Preconditions for the Industrial Revolution," in Patrick K. O'Brien and R. Quinault (eds.). *The Industrial Revolution and British Society*. New York: Cambridge University Press.

O'Donnell, Guillermo (1973) *Modernization and Bureaucratic Authoritarianism: Studies in South American Politics*; Berkeley: University of California, Institute for International Studies.

O'Donnell, Guillermo (1978) "Permanent Crisis and the Failure to Create a Democratic Regime: Argentina 1955–1966," in Juan J. Linz and Alfred Stepan (eds.). *The Breakdown of Democratic Regimes: Latin America*; Baltimore: Johns Hopkins University Press.

O'Donnell, Guillermo (1994) "Delegative Democracy," *Journal of Democracy*, 5, 55–69.

O'Donnell, Guillermo, and Philippe C. Schmitter (1986) *Transitions from Authoritarian Rule: Tentative Conclusions about Uncertain Democracies*; Baltimore: Johns Hopkins University Press.

O'Meara, Dan (1996) *Forty Lost Years: The Apartheid State and the Politics of the National Party, 1948–1994*; Athens: Ohio University Press.

O'Rourke, Kevin H., Alan M. Taylor, and Jeffery G. Williamson (1996) "Factor Price Convergence in the Late 19th Century," *International Economic Review*, 37, 499–530.

O'Rourke, Kevin H., and Jeffery G. Williamson (1999) *Globalization and History*; Cambridge, MA: MIT Press.

O'Rourke, Kevin H., and Jeffery G. Williamson (2002) "From Malthus to Ohlin: Trade, Growth and Distribution since 1500," NBER Working Paper #8955.

Oatley, Thomas (1999) "How Constraining is Capital Mobility? The Partisan Hypothesis in an Open Economy," *American Journal of Political Science*, 43, 1003–27.

Okun, Arthur M. (1975) *Equality and Efficiency, The Big Trade-off*; Washington, DC: Brookings Institution Press.

Olson, Mancur C. (1965) *The Logic of Collective Action; Public Goods and the Theory of Groups*; Cambridge, MA: Harvard University Press.

Olson, Mancur C. (1982) *The Rise and Decline of Nations: Economic Growth, Stagflation, and Social Rigidities*; New Haven: Yale University Press.

Olson, Mancur C. (1993) "Dictatorship, Democracy, and Development," *American Political Science Review*, 87, 567–75.

Oman, Charles (1906) *The Great Revolt of 1381*; Oxford: Clarendon Press.

Osborne, Martin J., and Ariel Rubinstein (1994) *A Course in Game Theory*; Cambridge, MA: MIT Press.

Osborne, Martin J., and Al Slivinski (1996) "A Model of Political Competition with Citizen-Candidates," *Quarterly Journal of Economics*, 111, 65–96.

Paige, Jeffery M. (1997) *Coffee and Power: Revolution and the Rise of Democracy in Central America*; Cambridge, MA: Harvard University Press.

Palacios, Marco (1980) *Coffee in Colombia, 1850–1970: An Economic, Social, and Political History*; New York: Cambridge University Press.

Papaioannou, Elias, and Gregorios Siourounis (2004) "Economic and Social Factors Driving the Third Wave of Democratization," Unpublished. London Business School.

Perotti, Roberto (1996) "Growth, Income Distribution and Democracy: What the Data Say," *Journal of Economic Growth*, 1, 149–87.

Persson, Torsten (2003) "Consequences of Constitutions," NBER Working Paper #10170.

Persson, Torsten, and Guido Tabellini (1994) "Is Inequality Harmful for Growth?" *American Economic Review*, 84, 600–21.

Persson, Torsten, and Guido Tabellini (2000) *Political Economics: Explaining Economic Policy*; Cambridge, MA: MIT Press.

Persson, Torsten, and Guido Tabellini (2003) *The Economic Effects of Constitutions: What Do the Data Say?* Cambridge, MA: MIT Press.

Persson, Torsten, Gerard Roland, and Guido Tabellini (2000) "Comparative Politics and Public Finance," *Journal of Political Economy*, 108, 1121–61.

Phelan, John Leddy (1978) *The People and the King: The Comunero Revolution in Colombia, 1781*, Madison: University of Wisconsin Press.

Philip, George (2003) *Democracy in Latin America*; Cambridge, UK: Polity.

Piketty, Thomas (2003) "Income Inequality in France, 1901–1998," *Journal of Political Economy*, 111, 1004–42.

Piketty, Thomas, Gilles Postal-Vinay, and Jean-Laurant Rosenthal (2003) "Wealth Concentration in a Developing Economy: Paris and France, 1807–1994," Unpublished. CEPREMAP, http://pythie.cepremap.ens.fr/~piketty/Papers/Piketty2003a.pdf.

Plessis, Alain (1985) *The Rise and Fall of the Second Empire, 1852–1871*; New York: Cambridge University Press.

Plott, Charles R. (1967) "A Notion of Equilibrium and Its Possibility under Majority Rule," *American Economic Review*, 57, 787–806.

Popkin, Samuel L. (1979) *The Rational Peasant: The Political Economy of Rural Society in Vietnam*; Berkeley: University of California Press.

Potter, Anne L. (1981) "The Failure of Democracy in Argentina 1916–1930: An Institutional Perspective," *Journal of Latin American Studies*, 13, 83–109.

Powell, Robert (2004) "The Inefficient Use of Power: Costly Conflict with Complete Information," *American Political Science Review*, 98, 231–41.

Prasad, Eswar, Kenneth Rogoff, Shang-jin Wei, and M. Ayhan Kose (2002) "Effects of Financial Globalization on Developing Countries: Some Empirical Evidence," International Monetary Fund: March 17, 2003. Available at: http://www.imf.org/external/np/res/docs/2003/031703.pdf.

Price, Robert M. (1991) *The Apartheid State in Crisis: Political Transformation in South Africa 1975–1990*; New York: Oxford University Press.

Price, Roger (1997) *Napoleon III and the Second Empire*; New York: Routledge.

Przeworski, Adam (1991) *Democracy and the Market*; New York: Cambridge University Press.

Przeworski, Adam, Michael Alvarez, José A. Cheibub, and Fernando Limongi (1996) "What Makes Democracy Endure?" *Journal of Democracy*, 7, 39–55.

Przeworski, Adam, Michael Alvarez, José A. Cheibub, and Fernando Limongi (2000) *Democracy and Development: Political Institutions and Material Well-Being in the World: 1950–1990*; New York: Cambridge University Press.

Przeworski, Adam, and Fernando Limongi (1997) "Modernization: Theory and Facts," *World Politics*, 49, 155–83.

Putnam, Robert H. (with Robert Leonardi and Raffaella Nanetti) (1993) *Making Democracy Work; Civic Traditions in Modern Italy*; Princeton: Princeton University Press.

Quinn, Dennis P. (1997) "The Correlates of Change in International Financial Regulation," *American Political Science Review*, 91, 531–51.

Quinn, Dennis P. (2002) "Democracy and International Financial Liberalization," Unpublished. Department of Political Science, Georgetown University.

Randall, Laura J. (1978) *An Economic History of Argentina in the Twentieth Century*; New York: Columbia University Press.

Ranger, Terence (1991) "Missionaries, Migrants and the Manyika: The Invention of Ethnicity in Zimbabwe," in Leroy Vail (ed.). *The Creation of Tribalism in Southern Africa*; Berkeley: University of California Press.

Rawson, Don C. (1995) *Russian Rightists and the Revolution of 1905*; New York: Cambridge University Press.

Reynolds, Andrew (1999) *Electoral Systems and Democratization in Southern Africa*; New York: Oxford University Press.

Ringer, Fritz (1979) *Education and Society in Modern Europe*, Bloomington: University of Indiana Press.

Roberts, Kevin W.S. (1977) "Voting over Income Tax Schedules," *Journal of Public Economics*, 8, 329–40.

Robins, Nicholas A. (2002) *Genocide and Millennialism in Upper Peru: The Great Rebellion of 1780–1782*; Westport: Praeger.

Robinson, James A., and Kenneth L. Sokoloff (2003) "Historical Roots of Inequality in Latin America," Chapter 5 of *Inequality in Latin America and the Caribbean: Breaking with History?* World Bank.

Rock, David J. (1987) *Argentina, 1516–1987: From Spanish Colonization to the Falklands War*; Berkeley: University of California Press.

Rodan, Gary (1997) "Singapore in 1996: Extended Election Fever," *Asian Survey*, 37, 175–80.

Rodan, Gary (1998) "Singapore in 1997: Living with the Neighbours," *Asian Survey*, 38, 177–82.

Rodrik, Dani (1997) *Has Globalization Gone Too Far?* Washington, DC: Institute of International Economics.

Rodrik, Dani (1999) "Democracies Pay Higher Wages," *Quarterly Journal of Economics*, CXIV, 707–38.

Rodrik, Dani, and Francisco Rodriguez (2000) "Trade Policy and Economic Growth: A Skeptic's Guide to the Cross-National Evidence," in Ben S. Bernanke and Kenneth S. Rogoff (eds.). *NBER Macroeconomic Annual*; Cambridge, MA: MIT Press.

Roemer, John E. (1995) "Rationalizing Revolutionary Ideology: A Tale of Lenin and the Tsar," *Econometrica*, 53, 85–108.

Roemer, John E. (1998) "Why the Poor Don't Expropriate the Rich in Democracies," *Journal of Public Economics*, 70, 399–424.

Rogowski, Ronald (1998) "Democracy, Capital, Skill, and Country Size: Effects of Asset Mobility and Regime Monopoly on the Odds of Democratic Rule," in Paul W. Drake and Mathew D. McCubbins (eds.). *The Origins of Liberty*; Princeton: Princeton University Press.

Rokkan, Stein (1970) *Citizens, Elections, Parties; Approaches to the Comparative Study of the Processes of Development*; New York: McKay.

Romalis, John (2004) "Factor Proportions and the Structure of Commodity Trade," *American Economic Review*, 94, 67–97.

Romer, Thomas (1975) "Individual Welfare, Majority Voting and the Properties of a Linear Income Tax," *Journal of Public Economics*, 7, 163–8.

Romer, Thomas, and Howard Rosenthal (1978) "Political Resource Allocation, Controlled Agendas and the Status Quo," *Public Choice*, 33, 27–43.

Romero, Luis Alberto (2002) *A History of Argentina in the Twentieth Century*; University Park: Pennsylvania State University Press.

Rosendorff, B. Peter (2001) "Choosing Democracy," *Economics and Politics*, 13, 1–29.

Rosenstein-Rodan, Paul (1943) "Problems of Industrialization in Eastern and Southeastern Europe," *Economic Journal*, 53, 202–11.

Ross, Jeffrey I., and Tedd R. Gurr (1989) "Why Terroism Subsides: A Comparative Study of Canada and the United States," *Comparative Politics*, 21, 405–26.

Rothschild, Michael, and Joseph E. Stiglitz (1970) "Increasing Risk I: A Definition," *Journal of Economic Theory*, 4, 225–43.

Rothschild, Michael, and Joseph E. Stiglitz (1971) "Increasing Risk II: Its Economic Consequences," *Journal of Economic Theory*, 5, 66–84.

Rouquie, Alain (1987) *The Military and the State in Latin America*; Berkeley: University of California Press.

Rueschemeyer, Dietrich, Evelyn H. Stephens, and John D. Stephens (1992) *Capitalist Development and Democracy*; Chicago: University of Chicago Press.

Rustow, Dankwart C. (1970) "Transitions to Democracy: Toward a Dynamic Model," *Comparative Politics*, 2, 337–63.

Sachs, Jeffrey D., and Andrew Warner (1995) "Economic Reform and the Process of Global Integration," *Brookings Papers on Economic Activity*, 1–118.

Safford, Frank, and Marco Palacios (2002) *Colombia: Fragmented Land, Divided Society*; New York: Oxford University Press.

Sargent, Thomas J. (1987) *Dynamic Macroeconomic Theory*; Cambridge, MA: Harvard University Press.

Schedler, Andreas (1998) "What Is Democratic Consolidation?" *Journal of Democracy*, 9, 91–107.

Schmitter, Philippe C. (1971) "Military Intervention, Political Competitiveness and Public Policy in Latin America: 1950–1967," in Morris Janowitz and Jacques van Doorn (eds.). *On Military Intervention*; Rotterdam: Rotterdam University Press.

Schumpeter, Joseph A. (1942) *Capitalism, Socialism and Democracy*; New York: Harper & Brothers.

Scott, James C. (1976) *The Moral Economy of the Peasant*; New Haven: Yale University Press.

Searle, Geoffrey R. (1993) *Entrepreneurial Politics in Mid-Victorian Britain*; Oxford: Oxford University Press.

Selten, Reinhard (1975) "Reexamination of the Perfectness Concept for Equilibrium Points in Extensive Games," *International Journal of Game Theory*, 4, 25–55.

Sen, Amartya K. (1970) *Collective Choice and Social Welfare*; Amsterdam: North-Holland.

Shepsle, Kenneth A. (1979) "Institutional Arrangements and Equilibria in Multidimensional Voting Models," *American Journal of Political Science*, 23, 27–59.

Shepsle, Kenneth A., and Barry R. Weingast (1984) "Uncovered Sets and Sophisticated Voting Outcomes with Implications for Agenda Institutions," *American Journal of Political Science*, 28, 49–74.

Shin, Don Chull (1994) "On the Third Wave of Democratization: A Synthesis and Evaluation of Recent Theory and Research," *World Politics*, 47, 135–70.

Siavelis, Peter M. (2000) *The President and Congress in Postauthoritarian Chile: Institutional Constraints to Democratic Consolidation*; University Park: Pennsylvania State University Press.

Singer, H. W. (1949) "Economic Progress in Underdeveloped Countries," *Social Research*, 16, 1–11.

Smith, F. B. (1966) *The Making of the Second Reform Bill*; Cambridge, UK: Cambridge University Press.

Smith, Peter H. (1978) "The Breakdown of Democracy in Argentina, 1916–1930," in Juan J. Linz and Alfred Stepan (eds.). *The Breakdown of Democratic Regimes: Latin America*; Baltimore: Johns Hopkins University Press.

Söderberg, Johan (1987) "Trends in Inequality in Sweden, 1700–1914," Historical Social Research, 58–78.

Söderberg, Johan (1991) "Wage Differentials in Sweden, 1725–1950," in Y. Brenner et al. (eds.). *Income Distribution in Historical Perspective*; New York: Cambridge University Press.

Starr, Harvey (1991) "Democratic Dominoes: Diffusion Approaches to the Spread of Democracy in the International System," *Journal of Conflict Resolution*, 35, 356–81.

Stasavage, David (2003) *Public Debt and the Birth of the Democratic State: France and Great Britain 1688–1789*; New York: Cambridge University Press.

Stavig, Ward (1999) *The World of Tupac Amaru: Conflict, Community, and Identity in Colonial Peru*; Lincoln: University of Nebraska Press.

Stepan, Alfred (1985) "State Power and the Strength of Civil Society in the Southern Cone of Latin America," in Peter B. Evans, Dietrich Rueschemeyer, and Theda Skocpol (eds.). *Bringing the State Back In*; New York: Cambridge University Press.

Stepan, Alfred (1986) "Paths Toward Redemocratization: Theoretical and Comparative Considerations," in Guillermo O'Donnell, Philippe Schmitter, and Lawrence Whitehead (eds.). *Transitions from Authoritarian Rule: Comparative Perspectives*; Baltimore: Johns Hopkins University Press.

Stepan, Alfred (1988) *Rethinking Military Politics: Brazil and the Southern Cone*; Princeton: Princeton University Press.

Stevenson, John (1979) *Popular Disturbances in England, 1700–1870*; New York: Longman.

Stigler, George J. (1970) "Director's Law of Public Income Redistribution," *Journal of Law and Economics*, 13, 1–10.

Stokey, Nancy L., and Robert E. Lucas, Jr., with Edward C. Prescott (1989) *Recursive Methods in Economic Dynamics*; Cambridge, MA: Harvard University Press.

Sutter, Daniel (2000) "The Transition from Authoritarian Rule: A Game Theoretic Approach," *Journal of Theoretical Politics*, 12, 67–89.

Tarrow, Sidney (1991) "Aiming at a Moving Target: Social Science and the Recent Rebellions in Eastern Europe," *PS: Political Science and Politics*, 24, 12–20.

Tarrow, Sidney (1998) *Power in Movement: Social Movements and Contentious Politics*, 2nd edition; New York: Cambridge University Press.

Tawney, R. H. (1941) "The Rise of the Gentry, 1558–1640," *Economic History Review*, 11, 1–38.

Therborn, Goran (1977) "The Rule of Capital and the Rise of Democracy," *New Left Review*, 103, 3–41.

Thoenig, Mathias, and Thierry Verdier (2003) "A Theory of Defensive Skill-Biased Innovation and Globalization," *American Economic Review*, 93, 709–28.

Thompson, Edward P. (1963) *The Making of the English Working Class*; New York: Pantheon Books.

Thompson, Edward P. (1975) *Whigs and Hunters: The Origin of the Black Act*; New York: Pantheon Books.

Thompson, Leonard (1995) *A History of South Africa*; New Haven: Yale University Press.

Ticchi, Davide, and Andrea Vindigni (2003a) "On Wars and Political Development. The Role of International Conflicts in the Democratization of the West," Unpublished. Department of Politics, Princeton University.

Ticchi, Davide, and Andrea Vindigni (2003b) "Democracies and Armies," Unpublished. Department of Politics, Princeton University.

Tilly, Charles (1990) *Coercion, Capital, and European States, A.D. 990–1990*; Cambridge: Basil Blackwell.

Tilly, Charles (1995) *Popular Contention in Britain, 1758–1834*; Cambridge, MA: Harvard University Press.

Tilly, Charles (2004) *Contention and Democracy in Europe, 1650–2000*; New York: Cambridge University Press.

Tilton, Timothy (1974) "Social Origins of Liberal Democracy: The Swedish Case," *American Political Science Review*, 68, 561–71.

Trefler, Daniel (1995) "The Case of Missing Trade and Other Mysteries," *American Economic Review*, 85, 1029–46.

Trudeau, Robert (1993) *Guatemalan Politics: The Popular Struggle for Democracy*; Boulder: Lynne Rienner.

Tullock, Gordon (1971) "The Paradox of Revolution," *Public Choice*, 11, 89–99.

Turnbull, C. M. (1989) *A History of Singapore, 1819–1988*; Oxford: Oxford University Press.

Verner, Andrew M. (1990) *The Crisis of Russian Autocracy: Nicholas II and The 1905 Revolution*; Princeton: Princeton University Press.

Verney, Douglas (1957) *Parliamentary Reform in Sweden, 1866–1921*; Oxford: Clarendon Press.

Waisman, Carlos H. (1999) "Argentina: Capitalism and Democracy," in Larry Diamond, Jonathan Hartlyn, and Juan J. Linz (eds.). *Democracy in Developing Countries: Latin America*, 2nd edition; Boulder: Lynne Rienner Publishers.

Wallerstein, Michael (1999) "Wage Setting Institutions and Pay Inequality in Advanced Industrial Societies," *American Journal of Political Science*, 43, 649–80.

Wantchekon, Leonard (1999) "Strategic Voting in Conditions of Political Instability: The 1994 Elections in El Salvador," *Comparative Political Studies*, 32, 810–34.

Weingast, Barry R. (1997) "The Political Foundations of Democracy and the Rule of Law," *American Political Science Review*, 91, 245–63.

Weingast, Barry R. (1998) "Political Stability and Civil War: Institutions, Commitment, and American Democracy," in Robert Bates, Avner Greif, Margaret Levi, Jean-Laurent Rosenthal, and Barry R. Weingast (eds.). *Analytic Narratives*; Princeton: Princeton University Press.

Williams, Robert G. (1986) *Export Agriculture and the Crisis in Central America*; Chapel Hill: University of North Carolina Press.

Williams, Robert G. (1994) *States and Social Evolution: Coffee and the Rise of National Governments in Central America*; Chapel Hill: University of North Carolina Press.

Williamson, D. C. (1998) *Bismarck and Germany, 1862–1892*, 2nd edition; New York: Longman.

Williamson, Jeffrey G. (1985) *Did British Capitalism Breed Inequality?* Boston: Allen and Unwin.

Williamson, Jeffrey G. (1999) "Real Wages, Inequality and Globalization in Latin America before 1940," *Revista de Historia Economica*, 17, 101–42.

Williamson, John (1993) "Democracy and the Washington Consensus," *World Development*, 21, 1329–36.

Williamson, Oliver E. (1985) *The Economic Institutions of Capitalism: Firms, Markets, Relational Contracting*; New York: Free Press.

Wintrobe, Ronald (1998) *The Political Economy of Dictatorship*; New York: Cambridge University Press.

Wittman, Donald (1983) "Candidate Motivation: A Synthesis of Alternative Theories," *American Political Science Review*, 77, 142–57.

Wood, Elizabeth J. (2000) *Forging Democracy from Below: Contested Transitions in Oligarchic Societies*; New York: Cambridge University Press.

Wood, Gordon (1969) *Creation of the American Republic 1776–1787*; Chapel Hill: University of North Carolina Press.

Woodside, David (1976) *Community and Revolution in Modern Vietnam*; Boston: Houghton Mifflin.

Wright, Randall D. (1996) "Taxes, Redistribution, and Growth," *Journal of Public Economics*, 62, 327–38.

Yashar, Deborah J. (1997) *Demanding Democracy: Reform and Reaction in Costa Rica and Guatemala, 1870s–1950s*; Stanford: Stanford University Press.

Zeldin, Theodore (1958) *The Political System of Napoleon III*; New York: St. Martin's Press.

Index